The Letters of Chan Master
Dahui Pujue

The Letters of Chan
Master Dahui Pujue

Translated by

JEFFREY L. BROUGHTON WITH
ELISE YOKO WATANABE

OXFORD

UNIVERSITY PRESS

OXFORD
UNIVERSITY PRESS

Oxford University Press is a department of the University of Oxford. It furthers
the University's objective of excellence in research, scholarship, and education
by publishing worldwide. Oxford is a registered trade mark of Oxford University
Press in the UK and certain other countries.

Published in the United States of America by Oxford University Press
198 Madison Avenue, New York, NY 10016, United States of America.

CIP data is on file at the Library of Congress
ISBN 978-0-19-066416-9

1 3 5 7 9 8 6 4 2
Printed by Sheridan Books, Inc., United States of America

For Wm. Theodore de Bary

因舉佛氏之學與吾儒有甚相似處。如云。有物先天地。無形本寂寥。
能為萬象主。不逐四時凋。又曰。樸[撲]落非它物。縱橫不是塵。山河
及大地。全露法王身。又曰。若人識得心。大地無寸土。看他是甚麼
樣見識。今區區小儒。怎生出得他手。宜其為他揮下也。此是法眼禪
師下一派宗旨如此。今之禪家皆破其說。以為有理路。落窠臼。有礙
正當知見。今之禪家多是麻三斤。乾屎橛之說。謂之不落窠臼。不墮
理路。妙喜之說。便是如此。然又有翻轉不如此說時。

*The learning of the Buddhists—what similarities does it have with our
Confucian school? For example [some Buddhists and Confucians say things
like]: "There is a thing that precedes heaven and earth, formless and from the
outset quiescent, capable of being the host of the myriad images, not chasing
after the fading of the four seasons." Also: "Scattered about, but not something
else; across and athwart, but not mundane sense objects: the mountains, rivers,
and great earth completely reveal the body of the dharma king." Also: "If one
has come to know one's own mind, the great earth has not an inch of land."
Let's look at just what sort of level of understanding this is! Today trifling and
trivial little Confucians [who espouse this sort of thing]—how could they achieve
success? It is fitting that they be dismissed by others! This is the core axiom of
the Fayan lineage of Chan [which emphasized that Chan and the scriptural
Buddhist teachings are identical]—but all of those in today's Chan school assail
this doctrine, considering it to be [dropping into] rationality or falling into stereotyped formulas, holding that it impedes a correct level of understanding. Most of
those in today's Chan school natter on about* three pounds of linen thread or
dried turd. *They call this "not falling into stereotyped formulas" and "not
dropping into rationality." The doctrine of Chan Master Dahui is exactly like
this—however, there are times when he turns around and doesn't talk like this.*

—From *Master Zhu's Classified Sayings* (朱子語類 126.43)
of the Southern Song Confucian Zhu Xi (朱熹; 1130–1200)

—Chinese Text Project, http://ctext.org/zhuzi-yulei/ens?searchu=
%E4%BB%8A%E4%B9%8B%E7%A6%AA%E5%AE%B6

Contents

Abbreviations

Araki

Araki Kengo 荒木見悟, trans. *Daie sho* 大慧書. Zen no goroku 禅の語録 17. Tokyo: Chikuma shobō, 1969.

This modern Japanese translation of a Five-Mountains (Gozan 五山) reprint edition of *Letters of Dahui* has light annotation and in some cases summaries of sections. The section divisions do not coincide with those of Mujaku. It is stored in the Ochanomizu Library in Tokyo.

Cases of Song and Yuan Confucians

Huang Zongxi 黃宗羲 and Quan Zuwang 全祖望, eds. *Song Yuan xue'an* 宋元學案. 4 vols. Beijing: Zhonghua shuju, 1989.

Song Yuan xue'an 宋元學案 (*Cases of Song and Yuan Confucians*) is a Qing-period compilation consisting of brief biographies, philosophies, literary works, and school affiliations of eighty-seven Confucians (*ru* 儒) from the Song and Yuan dynasties. In the notes the first number refers to the *juan* 卷 number; the numbers within parentheses are the volume (1–4) number and page number. Example: 26 (2.997).

CBETA

Chinese Buddhist Electronic Text Association. http://www.cbeta.org.

Gozanban

Shiina Kōyū 椎名宏雄, ed. *Gozanban Chūgoku zenseki sōkan* 五山版中国禅籍叢刊 10: *Shibun sekitoku* 詩文尺牘. Kyoto: Rinsen shoten, 2013.

The text used for this translation is the *Dahui Pujue chanshi shu/Daie Fukaku zenji sho* 大慧普覺禪師書 on pp. 603–652, a photographic reproduction of a Five-Mountains reprint edition. It is stored in the Tanimura Bunko of Kyoto University (京都大学図書館谷村文庫).

Hōgo

Ishii Shūdō 石井修道, trans. *Zen goroku* 禅語録. Daijō butten Chūgoku Nihon hen 大乗仏典中国日本篇 12. Tokyo: Chūō kōron sha, 1992.

Annotated modern Japanese translation of *Dharma Talks of Chan Master Dahui Pujue* (*Dahui Pujue chanshi fayu* 大慧普覺禪師法語) found in fascicles 19–24 of the *Taishō* edition of *Sayings Record of Chan Master Dahui Pujue* (*Dahui Pujue chanshi yulu* 大慧普覺禪師語錄).

Hucker

Hucker, Charles O. *A Dictionary of Official Titles in Imperial China*. Stanford, CA: Stanford University Press, 1985.

English renderings for official titles derive from this standard reference work.

Hyesim

Taehan pulgyo Chogye chong kyoyukwŏn pulhak yŏnguso kyojae p'yŏnch'an wiwŏnhoe 大漢佛教曹溪宗教育院佛學研究所教材編纂委員會, ed. *Sajip sagi* 四集私記. Seoul: Chogye chong ch'ulp'ansa, 2008.

The *Sajip sagi* 四集私記 (*Private Notes on the* Fourfold *Collection*) consists of nine commentaries on the *Fourfold Collection*, a compilation of four Chan texts used in Korean seminaries since at least the eighteenth century: two on *Sŏjang* 書狀 (*Letters of Dahui*); two on *Tosŏ* 都序 (Zongmi's *Chan Prolegomenon*); two on *Chŏryo* 節要 (Chinul's *Excerpts*); and three on *Sŏnyo* 禪要 (Gaofeng's *Essentials of Chan*). The commentary in Chinese on *Letters of Dahui* by Chin'gak Hyesim (真覺慧諶; 1178–1234), the *Sŏjang ki* 書狀記 (*Notes on the* Letters), is pp. 18–115. The format is a schematic of each letter followed by glosses of words and phrases. Hyesim, the principal disciple of Pojo Chinul (普照知訥; 1158–1210), stresses *hwadu* (*huatou* 話頭) practice.

Korean Anonymous

Taehan pulgyo Chogye chong kyoyukwŏn pulhak yŏnguso kyojae p'yŏnch'an wiwŏnhoe 大漢佛教曹溪宗教育院佛學研究所教材編纂委員會, ed. *Sajip sagi* 四集私記. Seoul: Chogye chong ch'ulp'ansa, 2008.

For a description of the *Sajip sagi* 四集私記 (*Private Notes on the Fourfold Collection*), see Hyesim. The *Sŏjang chŏknan ki* 書狀摘難記 (*Notes on Plucking out Difficulties from the* Letters) in Chinese by an anonymous commentator is pp. 120–155. The format is glosses of words and phrases.

Lü and Wu

Lü Youxiang 呂有祥 and Wu Longsheng 吳隆升, eds. *Dahui shu* 大慧书. Zhongguo chanzong dianji congkan 中国禅宗典籍丛刊. Zhengzhou: Zhongzhou guji chubanshe, 2008.

A lightly annotated edition of *Letters of Dahui*.

Mujaku

Mujaku Dōchū 無著道忠. Daie Fukaku zenji sho *kōrōju* 大慧普覺禪師書栲栳珠. Kyoto: Zenbunka kenkyūjo, 1997.

The Daie Fukaku zenji sho *kōrōju* 大慧普覺禪師書栲栳珠 (Letters of Chan Master Dahui Pujue: *Pearl in the Wicker-Basket*; 1723), a commentary in Chinese on *Letters of Dahui* by the Rinzai scholar-monk Mujaku Dōchū (1653–1744), is a masterful elucidation of the *Letters*. This volume contains a reproduction of the manuscript in Mujaku's own hand. *Pearl in the Wicker-Basket* contains a variety of information on all aspects of the text: paraphrases that expand on terse original lines; excellent philological work; the tracking down of most sources; tracing themes across letters; the listing of "old" and "mistaken" interpretations, and so forth. The format is words and phrases (each marked by a triangle), followed by Mujaku's comments. In the following translation the dating of most letters, the section divisions within the sixty-two letters, and the brief headings at the beginning of each section division within each letter derive from Mujaku.

Song History

Ershisi shi 二十四史. 20 vols. Vols. 14–16, *Song shi* 宋史, edited by Tuo Tuo 脫脫, et al. Beijing: Zhonghua shuju, 1997.

In the notes the first number refers to the *juan* 卷 number; the numbers within parentheses are the volume (14–16) number and page number. Example: 382 (16.2999).

T

Takakusu Junjirō 高楠順次郎 and Watanabe Kaigyoku 渡邊海旭, eds. *Taishō shinshū daizōkyō* 大正新脩大藏經. 100 vols. Tokyo: Taishō issaikyō kankōkai, 1924–1934.

Takagi

Takagi Ryūen 高木龍淵, ed. *Zōkan bōchū* Daie Fukaku zenji sho 增冠傍注 大慧普覺禪師書. Kyoto: Baiyō shoin, Meiji 36/1903.

The *Zōkan bōchū* Daie Fukaku zenji sho 增冠傍注大慧普覺禪師書 (Letters of Chan Master Dahui Pujue *with Commentary at the Top of the Page and the Sides of Lines*) is an edition of *Letters of Dahui* with commentary by the Rinzai master Takagi Genseki (高木元碩; 1842–1918), who eventually became head of Tenryū-ji (天龍寺管長) in Kyoto. The commentary is of two types: words and phrases in small font inserted at the sides of lines in the text to facilitate reading and longer background notes at the top of the page.

ZGK

Yoshizawa Katsuhiro 芳澤勝弘, ed. *Shoroku zokugo kai* 諸録俗語解. Kyoto: Zen bunka kenkyūjo, 1999.

Shoroku zokugo kai 諸録俗語解 (*Explanations of Colloquial Words in Zen Records*) is a compilation of glossaries of difficult words and phrases in nineteen Chan texts by Kyoto Rinzai scholar-monks dating to sometime after 1804. The third glossary (pp. 49–81) is on *Letters of Dahui*.

Introduction

Epistolary Chan

Epistolary literature has long been a key element of the culture of the West. One has only to think of Seneca's *Moral Letters to Lucilius* on Stoic philosophy or the epistles of the New Testament. In China, epistolary literature has never assumed such centrality. Letters have no significant role in the Confucian canon.[1] However, the Chan school of Buddhism did produce important letter collections. Within the vast corpus of Chan literature, one such collection stands out: *Letters of Chan Master Dahui Pujue* (*Dahui Pujue chanshi shu* 大慧普覺禪師書; hereinafter *Letters of Dahui*), long known in Japan as the most renowned of the "letters of the three great masters."[2] Beyond such well-known collections, the sayings records (*yulu* 語錄) of numerous Chan masters include a selection of letters.

No other set of Chan letters has attained anywhere near the prominence and influence of *Letters of Dahui*, which has been prized for centuries throughout East Asia. It has served as a practice manual, molding the practice program of many Southern Song, Yuan, and Ming dynasty Linji Chan masters; of Koryŏ Sŏn; and of Hakuin's Zen of the Edo period. Thus,

---

1. Antje Richter, ed., *A History of Chinese Letters and Epistolary Culture* (Leiden: Brill, 2015), 1: "One reason for the relative neglect of epistolary matters in China seems to be that letters do not play a significant role in the Confucian canon, in contrast to the epistles in the New Testament, whose cultural significance lead [*sic*] to a sustained scholarly interest in this medium of written communication."

2. The "letters of the three great masters" (*san daishi sekitoku* 三大師尺牘) are: *Letters of Dahui; Letter Collection of Chan Master Nan of Mt. Huanglong* (*Huanglong shan Nan chanshi shuchi ji* 黃龍山南禪師書尺集); and *Letters of Preceptor Lingyuan* (*Lingyuan heshang biyu* 靈源和尚筆語). *Gozanban*, 551–652, contains Gozan editions of these three collections and discusses them at 677–684.

a complete English translation is of importance for the study of East Asian Chan as a whole.[3] The following translation of *Letters of Dahui* employs the best Japanese and Korean commentaries. These Japanese and Korean commentarial traditions are a direct reflection of the key role of this epistolary collection in Korean Sŏn and Japanese Rinzai Zen.

Letters of Dahui is a compilation of sixty-two letters of the Southern Song Linji Chan teacher Dahui Zonggao (大慧宗杲; 1089–1163). Fifty-nine letters are addressed to forty individuals of the scholar-official class (*shidafu* 士大夫), the elite class in Chinese society, "those who were, were entitled to be, or had been officials in government service,"[4] including one woman of this class. There are also two letters to Linji Chan masters at the end of the collection, both of which consist of advice on how to navigate a teaching career. These sixty-two letters, of course, could represent only a fraction of Dahui's epistolary output over his teaching career. In only three cases is Dahui's letter preceded by some portion of the scholar-official's question letter; however, context is not a problem as quite often Dahui supplies passages from a now non-extant question letter. Each letter can be taken as a free-standing, self-contained "dharma talk."

These sixty letters to lay persons are fascinating as documents directed at specific individuals inhabiting distinctive niches, relatively high or low, in the social-political landscape of Song-dynasty China and possessing discrete levels of development or "ripening" on the Buddhist path. When we view the letters in this light, the personality of the recipient and Dahui's response to that particular personality holds the foreground. But we must at the same time remain aware that Dahui in many cases regarded letters as a means to reach students beyond the recipient—that they were not always crafted for the recipient alone, but for a wider audience of the recipient's friends and peers. Dahui assumed at least some of his letters would be copied, circulated, and studied as "dharma talks," explicating his style of Chan practice. As he says in letter #46.4, "Please exchange these letters and have a read—that would be splendid!" (See also #24.14.) Many

---

3. J. C. Cleary, *Swampland Flowers: The Letters and Lectures of Zen Master Ta Hui* (Boston: Shambhala, 1977), has translations of portions of selected Dahui letters from the Ming dynasty compendium *Zhiyue lu* (指月錄; 1602). There are almost no annotations. Also Miriam L. Levering, "Ch'an Enlightenment for Laymen: Ta-hui and the New Religious Culture of the Sung" (PhD diss., Harvard University, 1978), has translations of excerpts from *Letters of Dahui*.

4. Hucker, 429.

of the originals in Dahui's hand came to be regarded as "private treasures" (see section #63) and mounted as hanging scrolls, and several letter sheets have survived as such in Japanese collections.

Letters of Dahui, because it presents Chan practice in the quotidian context of human interaction between highly individualized actors, is a vivid and evocative text, not a dry Chan treatise. As a counterexample, we have the Yuan-dynasty compilation *Chan Collection on Breaking Through the Sensation of Uncertainty* (*Chanzong jueyi ji* 禪宗決疑集), a Chan text very similar in substance.[5] Both are presentations of Dahui's style of "doing *gongfu*" (*zuo gongfu* 做工夫), that is, engaging in Buddhist practice or cultivation. (The literal meaning of *gongfu* is "expenditure of energy and time in working," but in the West the term has acquired the meaning "martial arts," probably due to some sort of misunderstanding or mistranslation.) Although these two texts share the entire Dahui vocabulary on *gongfu* and propound essentially the same *gongfu* approach, stylistically they are poles apart.

Letters of Dahui is highly personalized and nonlinear—we are almost in Dahui's room overhearing him praise, encourage, berate, deflate pretensions, and occasionally crack jokes or make puns in a face-to-face encounter with a lay disciple (he sometimes ends a letter with "Ha! Ha!"). The *Chan Collection on Breaking Through the Sensation of Uncertainty*, on the other hand, is a schematic tractate in rigidly sequential format, laying out a formal schema for Dahui's style of *gongfu* under twenty-one balanced and somewhat stilted rubrics. It addresses "students" (i.e., Chan monks) in the abstract, not named laypeople of varying social rank with a range of understandable and human spiritual obstacles, as in the case of *Letters of Dahui*. Indeed, a large part of the appeal of the *Letters of Dahui* can be credited to the tactful, humorous, and forceful personality of Dahui that emerges, amounting to an unintentional but vivid self-portrait.

A Brief Biography of Dahui

The following introduction centers on the book—*Letters of Dahui*—not the man Dahui, whose life incurred drastic ups and downs due to his association with certain members of the scholar-official class in the context of the politics of the imperial center. (Also, this introduction does not take into

---

5. The *Chanzong jueyi ji* is by Duanyun Zhiche (斷雲智徹; 1310–?), who was in the Dahui line. This text assumes a monastic context, not a lay one like *Letters of Dahui*.

full account the vast stock of material in Dahui's enormous sayings record and compilations.) He experienced both the top—abbotship of the premier Chan establishment of the day—and the bottom—exile to the deep South (the only more treacherous site of exile was Hainan Island). His exile was due to his association with members of the "hawk party" at court, which was in favor of retaking the North from the Jin/Jurchen instead of pursuing an appeasement strategy. There are already several excellent treatments of Dahui's biography in English and Japanese.[6] Nevertheless, it is helpful to start with a very brief outline of Dahui's life.[7]

The name Dahui (大慧) was given him in his late years by an emperor; Zonggao (宗杲) was his taboo-name, the name not to be used by his disciples. (Some scholars refer to him as Zonggao, others as Dahui.) He also used the names Tanhui (曇晦), Miaoxi (妙喜), and Yunmen (雲門). "Chan Master Pujue" (普覺禪師) was a posthumous title bestowed by an emperor. He was born in Xuanzhou (宣州) in Anhui to the Xi (奚) family, but his family's background and his early life are a bit of a blank—we do know that he did not get a full classical education.[8] He left home at sixteen, receiving the name Zonggao and taking the full precepts the following year. At nineteen he went on pilgrimage in Ezhou (鄂州) and in Hubei trained in Caodong Chan under Dongshan Daowei (洞山道微). Also he practiced for three years with Zhantang Wenzhun (湛堂文準) of Mt. Baofeng (寶峰山)

6. See, for instance, Levering, "Ch'an Enlightenment for Laymen," 18–62; Miriam Levering, "Dahui Zonggao (1089–1163): The Image Created by His Stories about Himself and by His Teaching Style," in Zen Masters, ed. Steven Heine and Dale S. Wright (Oxford: Oxford University Press, 2010), 91–116; Morten Schlütter, How Zen Became Zen: The Dispute over Enlightenment and the Formation of Chan Buddhism in Song Dynasty China (Honolulu: University of Hawai'i Press, 2008), 105–107; Steven Heine, Like Cats and Dogs: Contesting the Mu Kōan in Zen Buddhism (Oxford: Oxford University Press, 2014), 49 (a "Dahui Timeline"); Ishii Shūdō , "Daiei Fukaku zenji nenpu no kenkyū," Parts 1, 2, and 3, Komazawa daigaku bukkyō gakubu kenkyū kiyō 37 (1979): 110–143; 38 (1980): 97–133; 40 (1982): 129–175 (a kakikudashi rendering of the Chronological Biography with annotations); and Ishii Shūdō, "Daie goroku no kiso teki kenkyū (ge): Daie den kenkyū no saikentō," Komazawa daigaku bukkyō gakubu kenkyū kiyō 33 (1975): 151–171 (a "reexamination" of Dahui's biography).

7. The framework for this outline is based on Gozanban, 681–682.

8. Levering, "Dahui Zonggao (1089–1163): The Image Created by His Stories about Himself and by His Teaching Style," 94: "Dahui was not a fully educated literatus, although he received a literary education through the age of thirteen. In his extant discourse records Dahui tells his listeners and readers virtually nothing about his secular background.... His family does not appear to have been a prominent one. Neither Dahui himself nor his Annalistic Biography [Nianpu] tells us anything about family or recent ancestors who served in government positions. I have searched the extant lists of exam graduates in gazetteers for his unusual surname, Xi, in his family's home region and found only one name. That name could not have fit Dahui's family."

in Hongzhou (洪州) in Jiangxi. Wenzhun was in the Huanglong (黃龍) wing of Linji Chan. At Wenzhun's urging, he went to practice with Juefan Huihong (覺範慧洪), who was also in the Huanglong wing, and visited the layman Zhang Shangying (張商英; 1043–1122).[9] Huihong is the compiler of the *Record of Clear Talks in the Forest* (*Linjianlu* 林間錄), which embraces the identity of Chan and the scriptural teachings of Buddhism in the manner of Guifeng Zongmi and Yongming Yanshou, and is often associated in modern scholarship with "lettered Chan" (*wenzi chan* 文字禪).[10]

The retired official and Buddhist layman Zhang Shangying had a profound influence on Dahui, recommending that he practice under Yuanwu Keqin (圓悟克勤; 1063–1135). In Xuanhe 6/1124, Dahui did practice under Keqin of Tianning Monastery (天寧寺) in the eastern capital Kaifeng (Henan) and became one of his successors. Keqin was in the Yangqi (楊岐) wing of Linji Chan. Note the shift from the Huanglong wing of Linji Chan to the Yangqi wing. Generalizations about the difference between these two are a shaky endeavor—but perhaps we could say that Huanglong showed more of an affinity for literary erudition, poetry, and the Zongmi-Yanshou stress on the identity of Chan and the teachings; and Yangqi showed more of an affinity for the "old standards" (*guze* 古則) and Linji's stick-and-shout style. Dahui had a broad background in various strains of Chan and was able to exhibit this breadth and flexibility later on in his career (see letter #48).

Fleeing the military disturbances of the Tungusic Jurchen (Jin) army, Dahui entered Yunju Hermitage (雲居庵) on Mt. Yunju in Jiangxi. In Shaoxing 4/1134, he moved to Yangyu Hermitage (洋嶼庵) in Fuzhou (Fujian). In Shaoxing 8/1138, he was invited by the court through the agency of Grand Councilor Zhang Jun (張浚; see letter #23) to take up the abbotship of Jingshan (徑山), that is, Nengren Xingsheng Wanshou Chan Monastery (能仁興聖萬壽禪寺) on Mt. Jing. This was the foremost of the

---

9. For Juefan Huihong, see George Albert Keyworth III, "Transmitting the Lamp of Learning in Classical Chan Buddhism: Juefan Huihong (1071–1128) and Literary Chan" (PhD diss., University of California, Los Angeles, 2001), 209–387. For Zhang Shangying, see Miriam Levering, "Dahui Zonggao and Zhang Shangying: The Importance of a Scholar in the Education of a Song Chan Master," *Journal of Song-Yuan Studies* 30 (2000): 115–139.

10. See Jeffrey Lyle Broughton, *Zongmi on Chan* (New York: Columbia University Press, 2009); and Albert Welter, *Yongming Yanshou's Conception of Chan in the* Zongjing lu: *A Special Transmission within the Scriptures* (Oxford: Oxford University Press, 2011).

five official "Five-Mountains" Chan monasteries. At Jingshan he became known for a revival of Linji Chan, drawing 1,700 Chan monks.

Shaoxing 11/1141 marks a break in his life—the following roughly sixteen years were years of exile in the South. A few of the letters at the end of Volume One of *Letters of Dahui* and most of the letters of Volume Two date from this exile period. In Shaoxing 11/1141, because of his connection to Zhang Jiucheng (張九成), his name was dropped from the monastic registry, and he was exiled to Hengzhou (衡州) in Hunan, where he spent ten years (from age fifty-three to sixty-three). He was subsequently banished to Meizhou (梅州) in Guangdong (from age sixty-three to sixty-eight). In other words, he spent his fifties and sixties far removed from the great monastic establishments of the metropolitan Lin'an/Hangzhou area. In Shaoxing 26/1156, he was restored to monastic status. The following year he had close contact with Hongzhi Zhengjue (宏智正覺; 1091–1157), the most prominent figure of the revived Song-dynasty Caodong tradition.[11] In Shaoxing 28/1158, at the age of seventy for the second time he took up the abbotship of Jingshan, and, in Longxing 1/1163, at the age of seventy-five, he died at Mingyue Hall (明月堂) on Jingshan, leaving behind the following verse for his disciples:

> Birth is just *in that way.*
> Death is just *in that way.*
> Having a verse or not having a verse,
> What's the big deal![12]

Ninety-four dharma successors are listed.[13]

The Editor-in-Chief of Letters of Dahui: *Huang Wenchang*

Three of Dahui's dharma successors were involved in the compiling and editing of *Letters of Dahui*: the two Chan monks Xuefeng Huiran

---

11. On Dahui and Hongzhi, see Schlütter, *How Zen Became Zen*, 132–137. See also Christopher Byrne, "Poetics of Silence: Hongzhi Zhengjue (1091–1157) and the Practice of Poetry in Song Dynasty Chan *Yulu*" (PhD diss., McGill University, 2015). Byrne points out (p. 80) that silence (*mo* 默) is Hongzhi's favorite word.

12. *Dahui Pujue chanshi nianpu* 大慧普覺禪師年譜: 生也只恁麼。死也只恁麼。有偈與無偈。是甚麼熱大。(CBETA, J01, no. A042, p. 806, c19–20).

13. According to *Xu chuandeng lu* 續傳燈錄, T2077.51.685b5–c24.

(雪峯慧然) and Lingyin Daoyin (靈隱道印), and the scholar-official Huang Wenchang (黃文昌; 1128–1165).[14] The Japanese Edo-period Rinzai scholar-monk Mujaku Dōchū (1653–1744), in his commentary on *Letters of Dahui*, delineates their respective roles. Dahui's two Chan monks amassed as much of Dahui's correspondence as they could lay their hands on, copied out these materials, and sorted them; the lay disciple Huang pruned and distilled this mass of material, creating a cohesive text of manageable size:

> Huiran for twenty years served Master Dahui. In gathering and recording materials he lost nothing. Daoyin arranged these materials in an orderly manner. Huang Wenchang *selected the gist for a reedited collection*, and thus the term *reedited* [appears after his name]. What Huiran recorded and Daoyin edited was extensive, but what Wenchang reedited was an abbreviation.[15]

We can surmise that Huang carefully picked out a relatively small number of letters from the mass assembled by the two monks, deleted much of the standard epistolary format (though some amount remains), removed passages deemed to be too obscure for readers outside of the immediate orbit of Dahui and the recipients, and worked to enhance literary elegance. And Huang was certainly possessed of the proper credentials for this editorial task. A precocious student of the classical tradition in his student years, by his twenties he was a litterateur of great ability. His literary talent, combined with a devotion to Dahui-style Chan practice, made him the ideal editor for *Letters of Dahui*, which is not the only Dahui text he

14. For the few non-Chan sources that mention Huang, see Chang Bide, Wang Deyi, Cheng Yuanmin, and Hou Junde, eds., *Songren zhuanji ziliao suoyin* (Taipei: Dingwen shuju, 1980), 4:2885–2886. The information on Huang comes from this entry.

15. Mujaku, 35: 忠曰蓋慧然二十年侍師隨得采錄無遺失道印編次者條理黃文昌採其肝要重編集故曰重編也其慧然之所錄道印之所編廣矣文昌之重編畧矣. Mujaku, 34, cites Xuefeng Huiran 雪峯慧然 in a list of ninety-four successors of Dahui in *Xu chuandeng lu* 續傳燈錄 (T2077.51.685c7); he also quotes the *Dahui Pujue chanshi pushuo* 大慧普覺禪師普說: "Attendant Huiran followed Dahui for the longest time. For more than twenty years he was at the master's side, enduring a great many hardships" [然侍者隨老漢最久二十餘年在身邊喫辛苦極多] (CBETA, M059, no. 1540, p. 807, b10–11). Lingyin Daoyin 靈隱道印 is also listed as one of Dahui's ninety-four successors in *Xu chuandeng lu* 續傳燈錄 (T2077.51.685b17). Mujaku, 35, cites Huang Wenchang 黃文昌 in a list of seventy-five successors of Dahui in *Jiatai pudenglu zong mulu* 嘉泰普燈錄總目錄 (CBETA, X79, no. 1558, p. 283, b30 // Z 2B:10, p. 15, c9 // R137, p. 30, a9).

edited: he is also listed as the editor of *Dharma Talks of Chan Master Dahui Pujue* (*Dahui Pujue chanshi fayu* 大慧普覺禪師法語).[16]

Huang (Layman Jingzhi 淨智 or Layman "Pure Wisdom"), a native of Jiangxi, passed the Metropolitan-Graduate examination in Shaoxing 18/ 1148 (at the very young age of twenty-one) and eventually, through the rec- ommendation of Zhang Jun (張浚; see letter #23), became a compiler in the Bureau of Military Affairs (*shumi yuan* 樞密院). Note that Zhang Jun was instrumental in Dahui's pre-exile court appointment to the abbacy of Jingshan in Shaoxing 8/1138. Huang died at the age of thirty-eight. Early in his career he became friends with one of the greatest of all Southern Song poets, Yang Wanli (楊萬里; 1127–1206). Yang, who in his own words was obsessed with literature, particularly poetry, for his whole life, met Huang when they both held lowly posts in Jiangxi, and Yang's collected works, the *Sincerity Studio Collection* (*Chengzhai ji* 誠齋集), contains an essay of reminiscences of Huang entitled "Lament for Huang Shiyong" (*Huang Shiyong aici* 黃世永哀辭):

Shiyong, personal name Wenchang, was a man of Nanfeng [in Jiangxi]. The three generations from his paternal grandfather to Shiyong all passed the Metropolitan-Graduate examination, but Shiyong passed the examination at the earliest age—he was just twenty-one years old! At the beginning, he was in charge of records [i.e., the Recorder handling the flow of documents in and out] for Gan district [in Jiangxi]. At the time, I was [in my first official post as] prefectural Administrator of Revenue. After my going back and forth visiting Shiyong for about a year, the two of us became col- leagues for three years. From our very first meeting we became friends. As for Shiyong's loftiness and erudition—I was unable to reach his limits. His learning took "not being embarrassed by leaks in the roof" as its ideal [i.e., he could examine his own flaws without losing face]. In the literary arts, there was nothing beyond his capa- bilities, nothing beyond his artistry.[17]

---

16. Komazawa daigaku toshokan, ed., *Shinsan zenseki mokuroku* (Tokyo: Komazawa daigaku toshokan, 1962), 289, under *Dharma Talks*, states "reedited by Huang Wenchang" (*Huang Wenchang chongbian* 黃文昌重編). The same is the case with *Hōgo*, 95 and 339 (a modern Japanese translation of the *Dharma Talks* included as fascicles 19–24 of the *Taishō* edition of *Sayings Record of Chan Master Dahui Pujue* [T no. 1998A]).

17. 永名文昌。南豐人。自其祖至世永三世策進士第。而世永策進時。年最少。蓋生二十 有一也。初主贛縣簿。予時為州戶掾。予之來去後於世永者一年。而為寮者三年。一

Coming from someone of Yang's literary talent, this is high praise indeed. Evidence of how tirelessly Huang Wenchang worked for the publication of Dahui's sayings is found in Huang's postface to *Letters of Dahui* (section #63 of Volume Two):

> Chan Master Dahui spoke dharma for over forty years, and his words fill all-under-heaven. Habitually, he did not allow followers to record his words, but Chan monks privately wrote them down and transmitted them. In time they became books. In his late years, because many people made ardent requests of him, he allowed them to circulate in the world. Even so, in his assembly there were earlier and later followers; and there were differences in the details and omissions of what his students saw and heard. Also, each of the dharma talks obtained by talented and virtuous members of the scholar-official class was stored away as a private treasure, and there is no way to examine all of them. The quantity gathered here is not at all exhaustive. Please wait until I have collected more and compiled a follow-up volume!

The recipients of the first sixty letters were all members of the elite class of scholar-officials. Their ranks run the gamut, from an exalted Grand Councilor and Vice Ministers of various ministries at the imperial center to lowly District Magistrates and instructors in local Confucian academies. Dahui did not concern himself only with powerful and prominent lay students of Chan. He also instructed people who passed their lives in relative obscurity. Perhaps his project was to "seed" the scholar-official class with his sort of Chan.

Why did Huang include so many letters to lay figures and so few to Chan monks in his edition of *Letters of Dahui*? Surely Dahui, like other

---

見即定交。世永之高遠深博者。予不能竟也。其學以不愧屋漏為宗。於文無所不能。無所不工。(*Chengzhai ji* 誠齋集, 45.23–25; Chinese Text Project, http://ctext.org/wiki.pl?if=gb&res=176604). Yang Wanli, like his friend Huang Wenchang, had a connection to the recipient of letter #23 in *Letters of Dahui*, the illustrious Zhang Jun (張浚). At the time Zhang was in exile in Yongzhou, his cultivation slogan (from the *Great Learning*) was "rectify mind—make mind sincere" (*zhengxin chengyi* 正心誠意). Yang Wanli repeatedly sought a meeting with Zhang to no avail. Yang sent Zhang letters and was finally granted a meeting. He was profoundly impressed by the grand old man, so impressed he took Zhang as his mentor and resolved to apply himself to Zhang's slogan. Yang even named his studio "Sincerity Studio" (*chengzhai*) after Zhang's slogan and took *chengzhai* as a sobriquet. See J. D. Schmidt, *Yang Wan-li* (Boston: Twayne Publishers, 1976), 17–19.

Chan masters of his era, wrote letters to Chan people, Chan monk disciples, Chan venerables, and so forth, and presumably a significant number of these would have been available to Huang in the mass of letters he
inherited from Dahui's two monks. Other Song Chan letter collections,
such as *Letter Collection of Chan Master Nan of Mt. Huanglong* (*Huanglong
shan Nan chanshi shuchi ji* 黃龍山南禪師書尺集) and *Letters of Preceptor
Lingyuan* (*Lingyuan heshang biyu* 靈源和尚筆語), do not show the same
heavy tilt toward letters to lay people.[18]

It may have been that Huang was interested in featuring a particular facet of Dahui's teaching style, one which in the West has come to be
known by the Japanese coinage *kanna Zen* (看話禅), the Chan of "constantly keeping an eye on a *huatou* (話頭)." A *huatou* is a pivotal phrase
(*ju* 句) from a Chan dialogue or other source.[19] Maybe Huang's controlling idea of *huatou* practice led him, editorially, to focus almost exclusively
on compelling letters that promoted that style of practice—letters which
turned out to be largely addressed to lay people. The preponderance of
letters to lay people in the *Letters of Dahui* does not in and of itself suggest
that Dahui taught *huatou* practice only to lay people, and another style of
practice to monks. Interestingly, Huang's other editorial project involving Dahui, *Dharma Talks of Chan Master Dahui Pujue*, does have a higher
proportion of Chan monks.[20] Nevertheless, just as in the case of *Letters
of Dahui*, in *Dharma Talks huatou* practice again dominates as a practice
taught to lay people, *but never appears in Dahui's words directed at Chan
monks.*[21] But even this is not conclusive evidence that Dahui reserved *huatou* practice for lay people.

---

18. See n. 2. The Huanglong Huinan (黃龍慧南; 1002–1069) collection contains fifty-four
letters, most addressed to Chan masters, Chan head seats, venerables, and so forth. Only
three are addressed to a friend and two to Confucian scholars. Of the thirty-three names
that appear in the letter collection of Lingyuan Weiqing (靈源惟清;?–1117), twenty-four are
Chan monastics (called "Chan Person," "Preceptor," and so forth) and only nine are scholar-
officials/Buddhist laymen. The Huanglong Huinan collection states that it was "edited by
the Mt. Yao monk Shousu" (*Yaoshan seng Shousu bian* 堯山僧守素偏[編]). *Gozanban*, 553,
678, and 680.

19. The specific *huatou*s mentioned in this introduction and the following translation have
been italicized, put in bold font, and often provided with the Chinese original—for instance,
***wu** 無 (no)* and ***dried turd** (ganshijue 乾屎橛)*.

20. *Dharma Talks* contains seven dharma talks to "Chan persons" (*chanren* 禪人); one to a
non-Chan Buddhist monk (a "lecture master"); and thirty-two to lay people.

21. There is also a set of twenty-five dharma talks (*fayu* 法語) appended to an edition of the
General Sermons of Chan Master Dahui Pujue (*Dahui Pujue chanshi pushuo* 大慧普覺禪師普說;
CBETA, M059, no. 1540, p. 961, a3–p. 976, b14). This set consists of twenty-two dharma talks

Any argument that Dahui intended *huatou* practice exclusively for lay people is not an open-and-shut case—we do have two sources, the *General Sermons of Chan Master Dahui Pujue* and *Chronological Biography of Chan Master Dahui Pujue* (*Dahui Pujue chanshi nianpu* 大慧普覺禪師年譜; under Shaoxing 4/1134), that record Dahui teaching *huatou* practice to a Chan monk. The former states:

> Later Dahui was in residence at Yangyu Hermitage [in Fujian]. From the fifth day of the third month until the twenty-first day of the third month [of Shaoxing 4/1134], in succession he produced thirteen people [who obtained his dharma]. Also, he accepted an old preceptor of eighty-four years of age, who was called "Venerable Dabei." Dahui asked him: "The one who is not a companion of the myriad dharmas—**what person is that?**" Dabei said: "I can't call it up!" Dahui also asked: "The one who can't call it up—**what person is that?** Answer quickly! Answer quickly!" Dabei suddenly awoke. Sweat flowed down his back—from the very outset it had all been a matter of his not having confidence in awakening. Suddenly, all-at-once he awakened. *I, Dahui, from this point onward implemented huatous and very often spoke of them for people.*[22]

Dahui's encounter with the monk Dabei Xian, and letter #1 of *Dahui's Letters*, a reply to the layman Vice Minister Ceng Tianyou, both date to 1134: These appear to be the earliest evidence we can identify of Dahui's employing the *huatou* method with either monks or lay people, though in neither case is it yet his favorite **wu** 無 *huatou*. And whether Dahui gave *huatous*

---

for lay people and three for "Chan people." Once again, none of the three to Chan people mentions *huatou* practice.

22. *Dahui Pujue chanshi pushuo* 大慧普覺禪師普說: 後來住洋嶼庵從三月初五至三月二十一連打發十三人又接得箇八十四歲老和尚喚作大悲長老問他不與萬法為侶者是甚麼人云喚不起又問喚不起者是甚麼人速道速道他豁然省淶背汗流元初盡是不信悟底忽然一時悟山僧從此話頭方行每與人說 (CBETA, M059, no. 1540, p. 885, b18–p. 886, a2). The *Chronological Biography of Chan Master Dahui Pujue* under Shaoxing 4/1134 says: "Also, the Venerable Dabei Xian, who was eighty-four years of age, along with the assembly entered the Master's room. The Master asked: 'The one who is not a companion of the myriad dharmas—**what person is that?**' Xian said: 'I can't dredge it up!' The Master said: '"The one who can't dredge it up—**what person is that?** Answer quickly! Answer quickly!' Xian was about to respond when the Master struck him with the stick. Xian suddenly had a great awakening" [又大悲閑長老年八十有四隨眾入室師問不與萬法為侶是什麼人閑曰扶不起師曰扶不起是什麼人速道速道閑擬對師便打忽然大悟] (CBETA, J01, no. A042, p. 799, b21–24). Nothing is known of Xian.

to other monks after Dabei Xian is unknown. Nevertheless, as Ishii Shūdō states, 1134 is the inaugural year in which Dahui "brings *huatou*-practice Chan to maturity."[23]

Dating of the Letters

Free-standing editions of *Letters of Dahui* are divided into two fascicles, which in this translation are called Volume One and Volume Two. (The edition included in *Sayings Record of Chan Master Dahui Pujue* is divided into six fascicles.) The commentator Mujaku Dōchū dates about forty of the total of sixty-two letters in the collection by reference to the *Chronological Biography of Chan Master Dahui Pujue*. When there is more than one letter to the same scholar-official, I have assumed that the letter(s) following the first letter dates from around the same time as the first.

Relying for the most part upon Mujaku's dating work, we can make the following observations. Of the twenty-seven letters in Volume One, two letters, #13 and #22, cannot be dated; of the remainder, all are pre-exile letters except letter #23 from the Meizhou-exile period and letters #25–#27 from the Hengzhou-exile period. Of the thirty-five letters in Volume Two, two letters, #60–#61, cannot be dated; of the remainder, letters #28–#50 are all Hengzhou-exile letters; letters #51–#59 are post-exile letters; and the last letter, #62, is from the Meizhou-exile period. Two post-exile letters, #58–#59 (and perhaps #57), date from Dahui's restoration to the abbotship of the premier Five-Mountains monastery Jingshan at the end of his life. In other words, most of Volume One is pre-exile material, most of Volume Two exile and post-exile material. Huang Wenchang seems to have made an editorial decision to select letters dating from all phases of the life of the Master, showing the entire consistent arc of his long teaching career.

Confucianism and the Chan Gongfu of Dahui

Of the thirty-nine scholar-officials represented in *Letters of Dahui*, a total of seventeen have biographical entries in the *Song History*, indicating a

---

23. Ishii Shūdō, trans., *Zen goroku*, Daijō butten Chūgoku Nihon hen 12 (Tokyo: Chuō kōron sha, 1992), 514, in a brief synopsis of the *Chronological Biography* under the year Shaoxing 4/ 1134 states: "Dahui goes from Jiangxi province to Fuzhou. Begins his attack on the perverse Chan of silence-as-illumination, and brings *kanna* Zen to maturity" [大慧、江西省より福州へ行き、默照邪禪の攻擊を開始し、看話禅を大成する。].

certain level of political importance.[24] Eight of the thirty-nine have entries in the *Cases of Song and Yuan Confucians* (*Song Yuan xue'an* 宋元學案), a Qing-period compilation consisting of brief biographies, philosophies, literary works, and school affiliations of eighty-seven Confucians from the Song and Yuan dynasties, indicating their importance in the history of Neo-Confucianism.[25] These very high percentages show that among Dahui's students were some of the cream of the intellectual elite of Song China. Clearly, these gentlemen saw no conceptual contradiction between Chan and the Confucianism they imbibed as young people and lived out in their daily lives, often in very demanding positions in the imperial bureaucracy. As Koichi Shinohara has said, they "did not conceive of their Ch'an studies as something that implied rejecting Confucianism."[26] A perfect example is Lü Juren (呂居仁; ca. 1083–1145; letters #29 and #31–#32), who attained the "presented-scholar" degree and became a "Secretariat Drafter," a post involving the handling of central government documents. Lü was a poet and prolific writer on typical Confucian themes, with works to his credit such as: *Exegesis of the Spring and Autumn Annals, Admonishing Childish Ignorance,* and *Record of the Source.* He appears in the *Cases of Song and*

---

24. The seventeen are: Vice Minister Ceng Tianyou (letter #1); Participant in Determining Governmental Matters Li Hanlao (letter #7); Administrator of the Bureau of Military Affairs Fu Jishen (letter #10); Vice Minister Chen Jiren (letter #14); Auxiliary Academician of the Hall for Treasuring Culture Liu Yanxiu (letter #19); Controller-general Liu Yanchong (letter #20); Grand Councilor Zhang Deyuan (letter #23); Palace Writer Zhu Yanzhang (letter #25); Secretariat Drafter Lü Juren (letter #29); Principal Graduate Zhu Shengxi (letter #33); Participant in Determining Governmental Matters Li Taifa (letter #36); Vice Minister Xiang Bogong (letter #43); Vice Minister Zhang Zishao (letter #48); Administrator of the Bureau of Military Affairs Lou Zhao (letter #51); Defender-in-Chief Cao Gongxian (letter #53); Secretariat Drafter Principal Graduate Zhang Anguo (letter #58); and Grand Councilor Tang Jinzhi (letter #59).

25. The eight are: Vice Minister Ceng Tianyou (letter #1); Controller-General Liu Yanchong (letter #20); Grand Councilor Zhang Deyuan (letter #23); Secretariat Drafter Lü Juren (letter #29); Principal Graduate Zhu Shengxi (letter #33); Participant in Determining Governmental Matters Li Taifa (letter #36); Vice Minister Zhang Zishao (letter #48); and Secretariat Drafter Principal Graduate Zhang Anguo (letter #58).

26. Koichi Shinohara, "Ta-hui's Instructions to Tseng K'ai: Buddhist 'Freedom' in the Neo-Confucian Context," in *Meeting of Minds*, ed. Irene Bloom and Joshua A. Fogel (New York: Columbia University Press, 1997), 187 (Tseng K'ai = Vice Minister Ceng Tianyou of letter #1). Shinohara's perceptive article argues: "It is tempting to speculate that Tseng K'ai's spiritual cultivation under Ch'an master Yüan-wu and Ta-hui's letters to him might have served as a helpful preparation for his difficult career as a Confucian statesman in the turbulent years that followed. The exercise of political 'freedom' in the face of anticipated difficulties, a well-attested Confucian tradition, might in the case of Tseng K'ai also have been supported by the spiritual 'freedom' that he cultivated under Ch'an masters Yüan-wu and Ta-hui" (185).

Yuan Confucians, indicating stature in the Neo-Confucian firmament.[27] *But he also was an enthusiastic* huatou *practitioner under Dahui—his hua-tous were* **wu 無** *and* **dried turd.**"[28]

In fact, Dahui-style *huatou* practice was tailor-made to be continuously carried out right in the midst of daily action, and this would include, of course, Confucian moral action within the various contexts of family life, official bureaucratic duties, imperial court politics, political exile, and so forth. Dahui's practice was designed for all situations of daily life: those of "stillness" (for instance, periods of sitting practice on the bamboo chair or sitting cushion—see letters #1.6 and #4.2), and those of "noisiness" (the hubbub of one's official duties in, say, the Bureau of Military Affairs or the Chief Transport Office). In letter #34.6, a reply to a scholar-official who scored at the very top of the list in the rigorous official examinations, Dahui gives the following advice:

Please quickly apply energy. Don't break off even for a little bit. At all times, whether in the midst of walking, standing, sitting, or lying down, keep your eye on [**wu 無**]. In situations where you are read-ing classics, philosophers, histories, and collections, where you are

---

27. Lü's Confucian side is encapsulated in sayings recorded in his entry in the *Cases of Song and Yuan Confucians* (2.1234 and 1242): "Learning should take the *Classic of Filial Piety*, the *Analects*, the *Mean*, the *Great Learning*, and the *Mencius* as the basis—carefully taste them and examine them in detail.... Lü Juren said: 'The two words *forbearance* and *shame* are the motto of the ancients. Students should think closely about this and make effort" [學問當以孝經論語中庸大學孟子爲本熟味詳究.... 呂居仁謂忍詬二字古之格言學者可以詳思而致力].

28. The *Golden Medicinal Decoction of the Buddhadharma* (*Fofa jintang bian* 佛法金湯編; 1327), which covers the biographies and sayings of 398 external protectors of Buddhism and lay Buddhist believers—including emperors, officials, and famous Confucians—from the time of the Buddha down to the late Yuan dynasty, says: "Lü Benzhong, secondary name Juren, early in the Shaoxing era [1131–1162] was granted the 'presented-scholar' degree and appointed Secretariat Drafter. He habitually pursued poetry with utmost thoroughness. He became immersed in Chan and fell ill.... Benzhong sent letters to Dahui asking for a sum-mary of Chan. Dahui's answer letter [letter #29.1–3] in abbreviated form said: 'The thousands upon thousands of instances of uncertainty are just the *single uncertainty*. When [single uncertainty] about the *huatou* is smashed, the thousands upon thousands of instances of uncertainty are smashed at the very same time.... If you intently ask questions of other people about the words of the buddhas, about the words of the patriarchs, and about the words of the old monks of all the regions, then in endless aeons you'll never attain awaken-ing!' Benzhong naturally had an awakening" [呂本中: 本中. 字居仁. 紹興初賜進士第。除中書舍人。平生因詩以窮。耽禪而病。.... 本中嘗致書問大慧禪要。慧答書。略曰。千疑萬疑只是一疑。話頭上疑破。則千疑萬疑一時破。若一向問人。佛語又如何。祖語又如何。諸方老宿語又如何。永劫無有悟時也。本中自是有省。] (CBETA, X87, no. 1628, p. 433, c5–12 // Z 2B:21, p. 481, b8–15 // R148, p. 961, b8–15).

cultivating [the Confucian constant virtues of] benevolence, righteousness, ritual, wisdom, and faith, where you are following ritual in serving elders and superiors, where you are exhorting students, where you are eating your meals, keep pressing hard [with **wu** 無]! Suddenly you'll "lose your hemp sack"! What more is there to say?

And in letter #11.4, a reply to a scholar-official who worked in the Bureau of Military Affairs, Dahui states that his style of practice leads not only to "gaining energy" for the attainment of Buddhist awakening but also to a more effective and effortless wielding of political power as well. It makes a Confucian scholar-official a better and more effective Confucian scholar-official, a more effective man of politics:

I definitely look forward to this: a penetrating great awakening, a brightness in your heart, like ten-thousand suns and moons, the worlds of the ten directions in a single moment becoming bright, without the slightest other thought—for the first time you will be joined to the ultimate. In fact, you are capable of this. It will not be in just the arena of samsara that you will gain energy! On another day, when you once again wield political power, you'll make the emperor surpass the legendary sage-kings Yao and Shun—it will be like pointing to something right in the palm of your hand.

Dahui's Diagnosis of Scholar-Officials' Stumbling Block in the Study of Chan

Dahui's analyzes the main problem of the scholar-official class in the study of Chan thus: They are accustomed to relying on their intellectual sharpness and knowledge, earned through grueling years of study of classical texts and the highly demanding examination system; but such sharpness, the one honed tool in their tool kit, is counterproductive on the Chan path. A certain kind of "dullness" is the one tool they need:

Letter #14.1: The reason most of today's members of the scholar-official class are incapable of comprehending *this matter* and decisively attaining release is simply because their disposition is too intellectually sharp and their knowledge excessive. As soon as they see the Chan master open his mouth and begin to move his tongue, they immediately come to a snap understanding. Therefore, if any-thing, this is inferior to the dull-witted person who, free of a lot of perverse knowledge and perverse awareness, in a headlong fashion without expectations dashes against each skillful method and each gesture, each word and each phrase [i.e., each *upāya* of the teacher].

***

Letter #35.9: But today's scholar-officials are often impatient in their desire to understand Chan. They ruminate about the sutra teach-ings and the sayings of the patriarchal masters, wanting to be able to explain them with clear understanding. Little do they imagine that the state of clear understanding, on the contrary, is a matter of *not* clearly understanding. . . . As for my making members of the scholar-official class be dull-witted, this is my reasoning. Taking a "first" in the "dull-wittedness examination" is no bad thing! The only thing to be feared is the turning in of a blank answer paper. Ha! Ha!

***

Letter #42.1: Scholar-officials, in studying this Way, contrary [to common assumption], *must* rely on dull-wittedness [as a means] to gain entrance to awakening. But, if they get fixated on their dull-wittedness and say, "I haven't a chance in hell," then they'll be in the clutches of the Māra of dull-wittedness!

Perverse Chan According to Dahui

Dahui speaks a lot of the "party of perverse teachers" (*xie shi bei* 邪師輩), "perverse Chan," "perverse poison," "perverse understandings," and so forth—he thought there was a considerable amount of perversity float-ing around in the Chan of the day. He even composed a treatise on the topic, which appears to have been lost. It is described, however, in the *Chronological Biography of Chan Master Dahui Pujue*, in the entry for Shaoxing 4/1134 when Dahui was forty-six: "At the time [perverse] Chan followers put aside wonderful awakening as superfluous and made stu-dents tire themselves out over stillness-silence: for this reason he com-posed a *Disquisition on Distinguishing Perverse and Correct*, to attack these and thereby save students from the fraud of the moment."[29] Dahui also

---

29. 時宗徒撥置妙悟使學者困於寂默因著辨正邪說而攻之以救一時之弊 (CBETA, J01, no. A042, p. 799, a28–30).

insistently addressed warnings to his students against these dangers of perverse Chan in *Letters of Dahui*. For instance, letter #35.6 says:

> Having no confidence in the existence of an entrance to awakening, they [i.e., the perverse teachers] consider awakening a deception; they consider awakening "starting second" at a game of chess; they consider awakening as *upāya*-speech; they consider awakening a term to lure beings along. People like this cheat others and cheat themselves, mislead others and mislead themselves. You must be careful!

"Making students tire themselves out over stillness-silence" (*jimo* 寂默) refers to the well-known catchphrase "silence-as-illumination" (*mozhao* 默照), one of a pair of Chan illnesses/defects that comes in for particularly sustained criticism by Dahui. The other half of the pair is *guandai* (管帶), which is best left untranslated for the moment. This pair, "silence-as-illumination" and *guandai*, is quoted in *General Sermons of Chan Master Dahui Pujue* (*Dahui Pujue chanshi pushuo* 大慧普覺禪師普說) as the perverse teachers' own in-house terminology. Dahui's own term for "silence-as-illumination" is "quelling delusive thought" (*wanghuai* 忘懷 and *wangqing* 忘情); his own term for *guandai* is "[effortfully] concentrating mind" (*zhuoyi* 著意). Two passages in *General Sermons of Chan Master Dahui Pujue* use these terms. The first runs:

> Members of the scholar-official class, in studying the Way, don't get beyond two wrong branches at a fork in the road. One is "[effortfully] quelling delusive thought"; the other is "concentrating mind." "[Effortfully] concentrating mind" is what the hogwash teachers call *guandai*. "Quelling delusive thought" is what the hogwash teachers call "silence-as-illumination." If the two illnesses, *guandai* and "silence-as-illumination," are not eliminated, one will never be capable of escaping samsara.[30]

---

30. 士大夫學道不出二種歧路一曰忘懷一曰著意所謂著意者杜撰長老喚作管帶是也忘懷者杜撰長老喚作默照是也管帶默照二種病不除則不能出生死 (CBETA, M059, no. 1540, p. 961, b17–19).

Now let us attend to this term *guandai* (管帶), one of the terms in *Letters of Dahui* most resistant to a reasonably satisfactory rendering. Mujaku Dōchū, in his classic Zen glossary *Notes on Kudzu Verbiage* (*Kattōgo sen* 葛藤語箋) defines *guandai* as follows: "The *guan* means 'bring under control'; the *dai* is like 'securing something to the body by a belt.' The term *guandai* means '[effortfully] concentrating mind nonstop.' "[31] From this we can settle on a workable rendering of *guandai*: to continuously "engird mind"—"to keep the mind secured, as with a girdle," so to speak. The second passage in the *General Sermons* runs:

> At the present time, not only Chan monks, but members of the scholar-official class who are clever and bright and erudite and learned in books, collectively have two types of illness. If they aren't given to "[effortfully] concentrating mind," they are given to "[effortfully] quelling delusive thought." By "quelling delusive thought" they fall into the "ghost-cave of Black Mountain." In the canonical teachings, this is called "torpor." "Concentrating mind" only gets you the fluttering-about of thoughts. One thought continues into another, and, before the earlier thought has stopped, a later thought continues. In the teachings, it's called "restlessness."[32]

Thus, we can formulate the following equations: (1) what the perverse teachers call "silence-as-illumination" (*mozhao* 默照) = Dahui's term "[effortfully] quelling delusive thought" = falling into the "ghost-cave of Black Mountain" = "torpor" (Sanskrit *styāna*), which is usually rendered into Chinese with "dark sinking" (*hunshen* 昏沈); and (2) what the perverse teachers call "engirding mind" (*guandai* 管帶) = Dahui's term "[effortfully] concentrating mind" = "restlessness" (Sanskrit *auddhatya*) as a result, which is usually rendered into Chinese with "excitedness" (*diaoju* 掉舉). For Dahui, the plausible-sounding "silence-as-illumination" and

---

31. Yanagida Seizan, ed., *Zenrin shōki sen Kattōgo sen Zenrin kushū benbyō*, 2 vols., Zengaku sōsho 9 (Kyoto: Chūbun shuppansha, 1979), 2.19: 忠曰管者意領也帶者如帶物不離身也管帶著意不忘也.

32. 今時不但禪和子。便是士大夫聰明靈利博極群書底人。箇箇有兩般病。若不著意。便是忘懷。忘懷則墮在黑山下鬼窟裏。教中謂之昏沈。著意則心識紛飛。一念續一念。前念未止後念相續。教中謂之掉舉。(T47.1998A.884c17–21).

"engirding mind" are nothing but the maladies "torpor" and "restlessness" in disguise. *Huatou* practice is the antidote to all of it, as we see in letter #12.2:

> When sitting, permit neither torpor nor restlessness. Torpor and restlessness are things that the earlier noble ones severely warned against. When you are doing stillness-sitting, the moment you become aware of the appearance of these two illnesses, merely lift to awareness the *huatou* of "dog has no buddha-nature." Without exerting any effort to push these two illnesses away, they will immediately settle down in compliance.

How much stress should be placed upon the practice of sitting? Dahui holds that sitting has its place on the Chan path but must not be valued in and of itself as an ultimate. The perverse teachers take awakening as an *upāya* and sitting as the ultimate—hence their insistence on the primacy of sitting—but Dahui says "in investigating the ultimate principle take awakening as the standard" (letters #58.6 and #59.1) and says sitting is an *upāya*, to be used when needed, as in letter #15.4:

> When it is time to deal with things, just deal with them. When you feel the need to do stillness-sitting, just do stillness-sitting. When sitting, you must not grasp at sitting as an ultimate. At the present time, of the party of perverse teachers, most take "silence-as-illumination" stillness-sitting as an ultimate dharma, misleading younger students. I don't fear making enemies of them. I vigorously scold them in order to repay the kindness of the buddhas, and to rescue beings from the con-men of this end-time of the dharma.

Here are a few brief passages from Dahui texts that explicitly link "engirding mind" and "silence-as-illumination" with excessive sitting:

Preceptor Yantou said: When previously I was on pilgrimage I probed Chan with the honored monks of one or two places. All they did was have students day-and-night "engird mind," sit until they produced callouses on the rump and until the water in their mouths was drained dry; first they would face Dīpaṃkara Buddha, and, from the black-lacquer darkness in their bellies, they would say: "I keep my Chan sitting safe!"[33]

***

The old barbarian Bodhidharma for nine years suffered defeat [i.e., his nine years of sitting facing a wall were a defeat]—what a pity that he was mistaken all that time! The result has been that the followers of "silence-as-illumination" do sitting for years on end.[34]

***

They fervently close the eyes and assume the appearance of death. They call it "stillness-sitting," "mind-contemplation," and "silence-as-illumination." In turn they take this perverse view and use it to lead ignorant mediocrities, saying: "If you can attain stillness [in sitting] for one day, that's one day's *gongfu*."[35]

As might be expected, Dahui's polemic on perverse Chan was passed down to later generations of his line. For instance, Yanxi Guangwen (偃溪 廣聞; 1189–1263), who was in the Yangqi-Dahui branch of Linji Chan, in the following Dharma-convocation talk is clearly perpetuating Dahui on perverse "silence-as-illumination":

Spoken at a Dharma convocation: "'*Utter silence*—unexcelled awakening is gotten from this. *Clear understanding*—a smack on the golden pheasant, and one sees the light.' Chan disciples! Both of these are senile!"[36]

---

33. *Zheng fayan zang* 正法眼藏: 是我向前行脚時。參著一兩處尊宿。只教日夜管帶。坐得骨臀生胝。口裏水漉漉地。初向然燈佛。肚裏黑漆漆地道。我坐禪守取。(CBETA, X67, no. 1309, p. 558, a9–11 // Z 2:23, p. 2, d15–17 // R118, p. 4, b15–17). Yantou's (嚴頭) dates are 828–887.

34. *Dahui Pujue chanshi yulu* 大慧普覺禪師語錄 (*Sayings Record of Chan Master Dahui Pujue When He Was for a Second Time Abbot of Nengren Chan Monastery on Mt. Jing/Dahui Pujue chanshi zai zhu jingshan nengren chanyuan yulu* 大慧普覺禪師再住徑山能仁禪院語錄): 老胡九年話墮。可惜當時放過。致令默照之徒。鬼窟長年打坐。(T1998A.47.836b3–4).

35. *Dahui Pujue chanshi yulu* 大慧普覺禪師語錄 (*Dharma Talks of Chan Master Dahui Pujue/Dahui Pujue chanshi fayu* 大慧普覺禪師法語): 一向閉眉合眼。做死模樣。謂之靜坐觀心默照。更以此邪見。誘引無識庸流曰。靜得一日。便是一日工夫。(T1998A.47.895b14–16).

36. *Yanxi Guangwen chanshi yulu* 偃溪廣聞禪師語錄: 上堂。默默。無上菩提從此得。了了。金雞一拍扶桑曉。衲僧門下。二俱漏逗。(CBETA, X69, no. 1368, p. 732, a10–11 // Z 2:26, p. 134, a4–5 // R121, p. 267, a4–5).

Dahui's Huatou *Practice: An Inheritance from His Teacher(s)?*

Huatou (話頭)[37] practice is the core of *Letters of Dahui*. Did Dahui invent *huatou* practice or were there antecedents within his lineage that were passed down to him? Modern scholars have not been able to settle on a consensus. Ishii Shūdō states: "*Huatou* practice came to be established via criticism of silence-as-illumination Chan. In particular, as to the final stage of the evolutionary process [in the development of *huatou* practice], its entanglement with the inheritance of the practice style of Wuzu Fayan [i.e., the teacher of Dahui's teacher] is probably an important issue"; Ogawa Takashi goes further, suggesting that a *huatou* developmental line can be traced from Wuzu Fayan's proto-*huatou* of the "tasteless" **acrid bun-filling of iron (*tie suan xian* 鐵酸餡)** to Yuanwu Keqin's "unchewable" **iron rod (*tie juezi* 鐵橛子)** and on to Dahui's **wu** 無.[38] However, Morten Schlütter speaks of Dahui's "creation of kanhua Chan, which Dahui saw as an answer to, and cure for, silent illumination."[39] Miriam Levering argues that Dahui did indeed "invent" *huatou* practice and that an additional target, beyond the silence-as-illumination of Caodong Chan, was the popularity of the Pure Land practice of *nianfo/nembutsu*, invocation

---

37. I have left the word *huatou* untranslated (as I have done with *gongfu* 工夫). The definition of *huatou* in Yunqi Zhuhong's (雲棲袾宏; 1535–1615) *Correcting-Errors Collection* (*Zheng e ji* 正訛集) is probably the best we have: "In all of these dialogues [i.e., old standards/cases] there is a *single phrase of vital importance, and that is the huatou*" [總其問答中緊要一句。則為話頭。] (CBETA, J33, no. B277, p. 78, c27–28).

38. Ishii Shūdō, "*Daie Sōkō to sono deshitachi (roku)*," *Indogaku bukkyōgaku kenkyū* 23, no. 1 (1974): 338–339: さらに黙照禅批判を通して看話禅が確立されていったことである。特に最後の形成過程は五祖法演の宗風の継承ともからんで重要な問題であろう。Ogawa Takashi, *Zen no goroku dōdoku*, Zen no goroku 20 (Tokyo: Chikuma shobō, 2016), 77–94. Furthermore, Ishii holds that a prime target of Dahui's silence-as-illumination criticism was the Caodong teacher Zhenxie Qingliao (真歇清了; 1088–1151). See Ishii Shūdō, "*Daie Sōkō to sono deshitachi (hachi)*," *Indogaku bukkyōgaku kenkyū* 25, no. 1 (1977): 257–261.

39. Schlütter, *How Zen Became Zen*, 105: "In this chapter, I will discuss Dahui's famous attacks on silent illumination and his equally famous creation of kanhua Chan, which Dahui saw as an answer to, and cure for, silent illumination.... Since Dahui never named those he had in mind outright when he criticized silent illumination, there has been no scholarly consensus regarding who exactly Dahui was attacking. In the next chapter, I shall therefore discuss in detail evidence showing that the new Caodong tradition was indeed the direct target of silent illumination attacks by Dahui and other Linji masters."

or chanting of the name of the Buddha Amitābha, within the scholar-official class.[40]

I think there is reasonably strong evidence that Dahui did inherit at least the basic ingredients for *huatou* practice. Two letters (question letter #QL 1.4 and Dahui's answer #1.3) would suggest that what Dahui's teacher Yuanwu Keqin taught Vice Minister Ceng was *huatou* practice, with the two *huatous* **Mt. Sumeru** and **put it down**. In addition, the *Arsenal of the Chan School of Chan Master Dahui Pujue* (*Dahui Pujue chanshi zongmen wuku* 大慧普覺禪師宗門武庫), a Chan miscellany or set of "brush notes" (*biji* 筆記) of Dahui's anecdotes and utterances edited by his disciple Daoqian (道謙; d.u.), has the following story about a female lay successor of Yuanwu:

> District Mistress[41] Fan had the name Way-Person "Calmness-and-Long Life." In Chengdu [Sichuan] she practiced with [my teacher] Foguo [Yuanwu]. Foguo had her keep an eye on: ***not mind, not buddha, not [sentient] being—what is it?*** "You must not make comments. You must not talk. Keep on keeping an eye on it. Even without entrance into awakening, you will become aware of your nestling into awakening." She then asked Foguo: "Beyond this what *upāya* does the Preceptor have that will make me understand?" Foguo said: "There is this *upāya*: '***not mind, not buddha, not [sentient] being.***'" "Calmness-and-Long Life" at this point had an awakening and said: "So near at hand from the very start!"[42]

---

40. Miriam L. Levering, "The *Huatou* Revolution, Pure Land Practices, and Dahui's Chan Discourse on the Moment of Death," *Frontiers of History in China* 8.3 (2013): 342: "Scholars have argued that Dahui's invention of *huatou* practice was primarily related to internal Chan rivalries for elite patrons. I argue that Dahui's motive was also connected to a rivalry with Pure Land Buddhism over the making of appeals to lay followers among scholar-officials. Dahui was aware and tried to communicate the usefulness of *huatou* in addressing the elite laity's doubts about birth and death, and in particular their anxieties about facing the decisive moment of death."

41. Hucker, 241: "a title of nobility (*chüeh*) or honor granted to women. . . . in Sung to wives of Chief Secretaries (*shu-tzu*) in the household of the Heir Apparent."

42. 范縣君號寂壽道人。在城都參佛果。果教渠看不是心不是佛不是物是什麼。不得下語。不得開口。看來看去。無入頭便覺悽惶。乃問佛果云。此外有何方便令某甲會去。果云。有箇方便。不是心不是佛不是物。壽於此有省。乃云。元來得恁麼近。(T1998B.47.951a23–28).

This story is repeated in other sources, including *Five Lamps Meet at the Source* (1252)[43] and *Sayings Record of Chan Master Tianru Weize*, where the Yuan-dynasty master Weize raises the story of District Mistress Fan as a standard and makes a comment:

> [Tianru Weize in a talk] again raised the story of the good woman of Chengdu District Mistress Fan's practicing with Preceptor Yuanwu of Zhaojue Monastery. Yuanwu made her keep an eye on: **not mind, not buddha, not [sentient] being—what is it?** District Mistress for a long time didn't awaken. She cried and told Yuanwu: "This *huatou* is a little long and difficult to practice with. What *upāya* does the Preceptor have that will make me understand easily?" Yuanwu said: "Just keep an eye on: **What is it?**" District Mistress from this point onward had a slight awakening and saved on the expenditure of energy. In no time, she actually had an awakening and said: "So near at hand from the very start!" The Master [Tianru Weize] said: "District Magistrate expended painful effort at *gongfu*—she didn't know it was so near at hand from the very start."[44]

At the very least this concretely suggests that some kind of *huatou* practice was already extant in Yuanwu's teaching for Dahui to inherit. Perhaps Dahui's genius was to take an ancillary teaching device from his teacher(s) and to magnify it into a central weapon in the "arsenal of the Chan school."

Dahui's Huatou-*Practice Vocabulary*

In *Letters of Dahui*, Dahui never gives *huatou* practice an explicit name. He simply refers to it as "doing *gongfu* in this way."[45] The following is an

---

43. *Wu deng hui yuan* 五燈會元 (CBETA, X80, no. 1565, p. 412, a11–15 // Z 2B:11, p. 385, d9–13 // R138, p. 770, b9–13).

44. *Tianru Weize chanshi yulu* 天如惟則禪師語錄: 復舉成都善女人范縣君曾參昭覺圓悟和上。令看不是心不是佛不是物是箇甚麼。縣君久而不悟。乃號哭而告圓悟曰。話頭稍長難於參究。和上有何方便使我易會。圓悟曰但看是箇甚麼。縣君自此稍覺省力。未幾果有開悟。乃曰。元來恁麼近那。師云。縣君費盡苦工夫。不知元來恁麼近。(CBETA, X70, no. 1403, p. 777, b13–19 // Z 2:27, p. 425, d14–p. 426, a2 // R122, p. 850, b14–p. 851, a2).

45. The phrase *ruci zuo gongfu* (如此做工夫) appears in letters #1.7, 2.3, 5.1 (three times); 10.5, 24.2, 24.6, 25.7, 40.2, 45.2, and 49.3. The phrase *renme zuo gongfu* (恁麼做工夫) appears in letter #18.3 (two times) and 37.3.

attempt to describe "doing *gongfu* in this way" as accurately as possible in the vocabulary of *Letters of Dahui*. In *Letters of Dahui* (and in *Dharma Talks of Chan Master Dahui Pujue* as well) Dahui employs a grammatical structure of verb + *huatou*, though sometimes only the verbs appear and the *huatou* itself or the word *huatou* is implicit. When the *huatou* itself or the word *huatou* is implied but unstated, it is all too easy to miss the thrust of the passage—to catch the drift and supply the *huatou* or the word *huatou* the reader or translator has to be sensitive to and alerted by the presence of the typical vocabulary Dahui habitually uses when talking *huatou*-practice talk.

Dahui's *huatou*-practice talk employs three verbs to express the operation the student is to perform upon the *huatou*: "rally" to awareness (*tisi* 提撕), "lift up" or "raise up" to awareness (*ju* 舉), and "keep an eye on" (*kan* 看).[46] The first two cluster around the idea of "rousing up, gathering up, arousing, rallying, calling forth, mustering up, or summoning up in the mind." The third is a bit different: "keeping an eye on," "carefully watching over," "keeping guard over," "looking after," and so forth.[47] These verbs are the nucleus of *huatou*-practice talk—when they appear, the reader should be alerted that Dahui is talking about *huatou* practice.

As to the direct object of these verbs, the *huatou* word or phrase itself, the *Letters of Dahui* mentions in passing quite a few. However, two stand out: ***wu*** 無, the all-purpose negative ("to be without or lack object," "there is no object"); and ***dried turd*** (***ganshijue*** 乾屎橛; literally, "dried shit in the shape of a short wooden peg," but sometimes misunderstood as "shit-scraping spatula"). These two *huatou*s have been plucked from dialogues in Chan records.[48] While the ***wu*** 無 *huatou* appears in both pre-exile letters

---

46. When he is warning against "letting go of" or "discarding" the *huatou*, Dahui uses *fangshe* 放捨/*fangque* 放却 and *qi* 棄.

47. ZGK, 6.15: "The term *kan* 看 has the meaning *carefully watch over, keep guard*. As in *look after* a sick person, *keep watch* over a gate, etc." [看は気をつけて見ている 、番をしている意なり。看病、看門などにて知べし。].

48. *Zhaozhou heshang yulu* 趙州和尚語錄: "Question: 'Does even a dog have buddha-nature?' The Master said: '*No* [*wu* 無].' The student said: 'From the buddhas above to the ants below all have buddha-nature. Why not a dog?' The Master said: 'Because *he* has an innate karma-consciousness!' " [問狗子還有佛性也無師云無學云上至諸佛下至蝗子皆有佛性狗子為什麼無師云為伊有業識性在。] (CBETA, J24, no. B137, p. 361, b26–28). *Yunmen Kuangzhen chanshi guanglu* 雲門匡真禪師廣錄: "Question: 'What is Śākyamuni's body like?' The Master said: '*Dried turd.*' " [問如何是釋迦身。師云。乾屎橛。] (T1988.47.550b15). These

and letters dating to Dahui's exile period, the **dried turd** *huatou* only begins to appear in those letters dating to the first period of exile in Hengzhou. Perhaps it was during that period that Dahui came up with this Yunmen *huatou*. (In *Dharma Talks of Chan Master Dahui Pujue*, there is a post-exile talk given to a lay person that employs a different Yunmen *huatou*: **exposed** [*lu* 露]).[49]

Huatou talk frequently uses adverbs like "constantly" or "always" (*shishi* 時時; *chang* 常)—it is repeatedly said that the practitioner lifts the *huatou* to awareness or keeps an eye on the *huatou* "twenty-four hours a day" (*xiang er shi shi zhong* 向十二時中) and "in all four postures" (*si weiyi nei* 四威儀內), that is, walking, standing, sitting, and lying down. One does it "in the midst of everyday activities while responding to conditions" (*riyong ying yuan* 日用應緣). One does it when in "stillness" (*jing* 靜), for instance, at times of Chan sitting or stillness-sitting, and in the midst of "noisiness" (*nao* 鬧), when one is immersed in the hubbub of everyday activities. It is the "only" thing one is to be concerned with—"just" lifting the *huatou* to awareness.[50]

The *Letters of Dahui* (#20.2) says that the **wu** 無 *huatou* is "like a single snowflake atop a red-hot stove." In an instruction to his assembly found in his sayings record Dahui calls this single snowflake a "speck of coolness."[51] This snowflake image also appears in a quatrain in the verse

---

two passages appear as "standards" (*ze* 則) in collections such as the *Wumen guan* 無門關 (standards #1 and #21).

49. *Dharma Talks of Chan Master Dahui Pujue*: "Right here keep your eye on the *huatou*: 'A monk asked Yunmen: "When one kills one's father and mother, one confesses before the buddhas. But when one kills the buddhas and patriarchs, where does one confess?" Yunmen said: "Exposed!" ' If you have resolute willpower, just keep your eye on the word **exposed** [*lu* 露]. Shift the mind that reflects on and discriminates defilement matters onto the word **exposed**. Walking or sitting, rally this word **exposed** to awareness" [*Dahui Pujue chanshi yulu* 大慧普覺禪師語錄: 只就這裏看箇話頭。僧問雲門。殺父殺母向佛前懺悔。殺佛殺祖時却向甚處懺悔。雲門云露。若有決定志。但只看箇露字。把思量分別塵勞中事底心。移在露字上。行行坐坐。以此露字提撕。] (T1998A.47.912a17–21). The Yunmen reference is *Yunmen Kuangzhen chanshi guanglu*, T1988.47.547b28–c1.

50. This is expressed with *zhi* 只, *zhiguan* 只管, *dan* 但, and *danzhi* 但只.

51. *Dahui Pujue chanshi yulu* 大慧普覺禪師語錄 (*Sayings Record of Dahui Pujue at Yangyu Hermitage in Fuzhou/Dahui Pujue chanshi zhu fuzhou yangyu an yulu* 大慧普覺禪師住福州洋嶼菴語錄): "Instruction to the Assembly: '*Mind is buddha*—don't engage in false seeking;/ *Neither mind nor buddha*—desist from inquiring./ On the flame of the red-hot stove a snowflake alights;/ A speck of coolness eliminates hot worries" [示眾。即心即佛莫妄求。非心非佛休別討。紅爐焰上雪華飛。一點清涼除熱惱。] (T1998A.47.844b19–20).

section of his sayings record, entitled "Sending off Monastic Inspector Chao":

> The bottom of the pail of black-lacquer ignorance falls out, and the great earth is expansive;
> The body-mind continuum in samsara is severed, and the emerald-green pool is translucent.
> Just take a single snowflake [*wu* 無] that has landed on the red-hot stove,
> And loose it in the world as a flaming torch that illumines the night.[52]

Dahui on Sitting Practice in the Context of Huatou *Practice*

Where does this leave cross-legged sitting in Dahui's overall scheme of practice?[53] Did Dahui himself practice much cross-legged sitting? Did he regularly advocate sitting to his students? The answer is: while he never absolutized sitting, he did absolutize "the smashing of the mind of samsara" (*shengsi xin po* 生死心破)—i.e., liberation from the rebirth cycle. As Mujaku Dōchū's commentary on *Letters of Dahui* says, "Dahui considers the smashing of the mind of samsara to be the most important thing. This is not necessarily bound up with Zen sitting."[54] Dahui "usually" prescribed sitting for students, though this depended upon the student in question: "It's not that I *don't* usually teach people to do *gongfu* by engaging in sitting in a still place. Sitting is simply one instance of providing medicine in accordance with their illnesses. In fact, my [practice of sitting] has nothing to do with that sort of ['engirding-mind' or 'stopping-to-rest'] formulation" (letter #3.3). He was very critical indeed of the unremitting emphasis placed on sitting by some of the perverse teachers, warning (letter #58.4) against

---

52. *Dahui Pujue chanshi yulu* 大慧普覺禪師語錄 (*Verses of Chan Master Dahui Pujue/Dahui Pujue chanshi jisong* 大慧普覺禪師偈頌): 送超僧鑑: 桶底脫時大地闊 。 命根斷處碧潭清 。 好將一點紅爐雪 。 散作人間照夜燈 。 (T1998A.47.858a29–b2).

53. In *Letters of Dahui* usually *stillness-sitting* (*jingzuo* 靜坐), but occasionally *Chan sitting* (*zuochan* 坐禪) or just *sitting* (*zuo* 坐).

54. Mujaku, 175: 忠曰以生死心破爲肝要不必拘坐禪也.

having an attachment to sitting and taking it as the "ultimate dharma," while discarding awakening as a mere *upāya*:

> Some consider Chan to be lapsing into silence, doing cross-legged sitting in the "ghost-cave of Black Mountain," closing the eyes, calling it the "*state of being* [before the appearance of] Bhīṣma-garjita-svara Buddha" [i.e., the name of the very first buddha to appear in this world] or "your face before your father and mother conceived you," and calling it "silence as constant illumination." This type of party doesn't seek sublime awakening. They take awakening as falling into the secondary grade. They take awakening as duping and intimidating people. They take awakening as something provisionally established [as an *upāya*]. Since they have never had an awakening, they don't believe that awakening exists.

He himself did sitting at need—he says he sometimes woke up in the middle of the night with insomnia and promptly knocked out a sitting session.[55] *Huatou* practice, on the other hand, is a constant, an invariable element, in the *Letters'* version of *gongfu*:

> Letter #30.6: In the four postures of daily activities just always make yourself "composed"—whether in a quiet situation or a noisy situation, always rally **dried turd** [*ganshijue* 乾屎橛] to awareness. The days and months will pass, and "the water buffalo will become more practiced."

***

> Letter #35.8: In the midst of the topsy-turvy discrimination of daily activities, just keep your eye on the word **wu** 無. Don't pay any heed to whether you have awakened or not awakened, whether you have achieved penetration or not.

---

55. *Dahui Pujue chanshi pushuo* 大慧普覺禪師普說: "There are times when I am asleep at night and wake up. I immediately get up and sit. Having sat for some time—no thought at all. I say to myself: 'Realm of the buddhas!' But that's all—you mustn't take sitting as the ultimate standard. Sitting isn't the state of letting go of body and life" [有時夜裏睡纔覺便起來坐坐既久都無所思自謂諸佛境界只這是然不要把為極則不是放身命處] (CBETA, M059, no. 1540, p. 849, b9–11). Dahui means that sitting isn't the same as smashing the mind of samsara.

What Not to Do in Huatou *Practice*

In *Letters of Dahui*, Dahui provides three sets of prohibitions concerning *huatou* practice—things that one must not do (letters #10.5, #14.8, and #58.2). The first and last sets, which have overlap, run:

> You must not produce an understanding [of **wu** 無 as the *wu* of the polarity] *there is* [*you* 有]/*there is not* [*wu* 無].
>
> You must not produce an understanding [of **wu** 無] based on reasoning.
>
> You must not, during the operation of the mind sense-organ, engage in reflection and conjecture [concerning **wu** 無].
>
> You must not, during [actions such as] raising eyebrows or winking eyes, allow the mind of calculation to stop on a single point [such as **wu** 無].
>
> You must not make a "lifestyle" out of the word [**wu** 無].
>
> Also, you must not remain confined to the tiny hidden-away closet of *nothing-to-do*.
>
> You must not, while raising [**wu** 無], understand and "own" it.
>
> You must not quote texts as proof [of **wu** 無].

***

> Coming [at **wu** 無] from the left is not correct; coming [at **wu** 無] from the right is not correct.
>
> Also, you must not have your mind wait for awakening.
>
> Also, you must not, while raising [**wu** 無], understand and "own" it.
>
> Also, you must not concoct a "sublime" understanding [of **wu** 無].
>
> Also, you must not haggle over whether [**wu** 無 is the *wu* of the polarity] *there is* [*you* 有]/*there is not* [*wu* 無].
>
> Also, you must not conjecture that [**wu** 無] is the *wu* 無 of *true non-existence* [*zhen wu* 真無].
>
> Also, you must not sit in the tiny hidden-away closet of *nothing-to-do*.
>
> Also, you must not understand [**wu** 無 in the mode of "Chan suddenness" that is] like a spark from two stones or a lightning bolt.

Obviously, these lists of injunctions could go on *ad infinitum*. Any approach to—or escape from—the *huatou* a practitioner might dream up would be forbidden.

Recurring Motifs in Huatou *Practice*

Nine themes suffuse discussions of *huatou* practice in *Letters of Dahui*. The following is a brief encapsulation:

Theme 1: *You have to do it on your own.* The practitioner or student cannot get awakening from anybody else. It must be accomplished on one's own. *Letters of Dahui* speaks often of self-confidence, awakening on one's own, and so forth:

> Letter #31.2: The buddhas and patriarchs have not a single teaching to give to people. All that is necessary is for the person on duty to have confidence on his own, give assent on his own, see on his own, awaken on his own. If you just latch onto what other people [like the buddhas and patriarchs] have to say [and don't bother to see on your own], I fear [it will be taken that the buddhas and patriarchs] have deceived people.

***

> Letter #14.5: The hilt of this sword lies only in the hand of the person on duty. You can't have someone else do it for you. You must do it yourself. If you stake your life on it, you'll be ready to set about doing it. If you're not yet capable of staking your life on it, just keep pressing hard at the point where the uncertainty is not yet smashed [i.e., go on rallying the *huatou* to awareness]. Suddenly you'll be ready to stake your life on one throw—done!

Theme 2: *You must generate a singular sensation of uncertainty.* The term "uncertainty" (*yi* 疑) refers to the sensations of hesitation, vacillation, wavering, misgiving, having qualms about something, apprehension—even dread and angst—that develop within the round of daily activities. In "doing *gongfu* in this way" the practitioner is to merge, to amalgamate, all these myriad instances of uncertainty and apprehension into one big sensation of uncertainty and apprehension about the *huatou*, and *only* about the *huatou*. This merger of all the little uncertainties into a monolithic, massive uncertainty does not allow for the production of any new tiny, discrete uncertainties. Once this featureless "*huatou*-uncertainty" mass is smashed to smithereens, one is liberated:

> Letter #29.1: The thousands upon thousands of instances of uncertainty are just the "single uncertainty." When [the single] uncertainty

about the *huatou* is smashed, the thousands upon thousands of instances of uncertainty are smashed at the very same time. If [the single uncertainty about] the *huatou* isn't smashed, then upon [and only upon the *huatou*] keep pressing hard with it [exclusively]. If you discard the *huatou*, and produce uncertainty about some other example of the written word, or produce uncertainty about the sutra teachings, or produce uncertainty about the cases of the ancients [i.e., various Chan stories], or produce uncertainty within the troublesome defilements of daily activities, it will all be of the coterie of the Evil One Māra.

***

Letter #30.6: In the four postures of daily activities just always make yourself "composed"—whether in a quiet situation or a noisy situation, always rally **dried turd [*ganshijue* 乾屎橛]** to awareness. The days and months will pass, and "the water buffalo will become more practiced." You absolutely must not separately produce uncertainty about anything outside [the *huatou*]. When uncertainty about **dried turd [*ganshijue* 乾屎橛]** is smashed, instances of uncertainty as numerous as the sand grains of the Ganges River will all be smashed at the same time.

Theme 3: *You must assume a stance of "composure."* The mental attitude required in general for *huatou* practice is composure. *Letters of Dahui*, alluding to a passage from the *Analects* of Confucius ("The gentleman is level and composed; the small man is full of worries"), stipulates that twenty-four hours a day the student is to "make himself composed" (*fangjiao tang-tang de* 放教蕩蕩地). The *huatou* practitioner is to be calm, quiet, leisurely, composed, and unhurried:

Letter #20.2: If you want to make suffering and joy indistinguishable, simply do not "rouse yourself to engird mind" or "employ your mind to quell delusive thought." Twenty-four hours a day make yourself "composed." If suddenly habit-energy from past births arises, don't apply mental exertion to hold it in check. Merely, in the state where the habit-energy arises, keep your eye on the *huatou*: "Does even a dog have buddha-nature? *No* [*wu* 無]." At just that moment [*wu* 無] will be "like a single snowflake atop a red-hot stove."

Theme 4: *You must be neither "tense" nor "slack."* Letters of Dahui sets up a polarity of "being tense/in a rush" and "being slack."[56] Being in a rush leads to the fluttering or restlessness of the perverse teaching or defect called "engirding mind"; being slack leads to the torpor or dark sinking of the perverse teaching or defect called "silence-as-illumination":

> Letter #52.4: In your *gongfu* you shouldn't be in a rush [i.e., when raising the **wu** 無 *huatou* to awareness]. If you're in a rush [in raising the *huatou* to awareness], then you will be restlessly moving. You shouldn't be slack either. If you're slack [in raising the *huatou* to awareness], you will be gloomy and dark [i.e., in torpor]. [The teachings of the perverse teachers] "quelling delusive thought" [i.e., "silence-as-illumination"] and "[effortfully] concentrating mind" [i.e., "engirding mind"] are both mistakes.

***

> Letter #37.3: Just make yourself exist on your own. However, you must not be too tense and must not be too slack. Just do *gongfu* in this way, saving on the endless expenditure of mental energy.

Theme 5: *Saving on the expenditure of [gongfu] energy is gaining [awakening] energy.* The expression "saving energy" (*sheng li* 省力) is central to the praxis program of *Letters of Dahui*. Dahui is quite fond of the slogan "saving on the expenditure of energy *is* gaining energy, and gaining energy *is* saving on the expenditure of energy." Mujaku's commentary on *Letters of Dahui* makes the point that the word *energy* (*li* 力) refers to two different things—"saving energy" refers to *gongfu* energy and "gaining energy" refers to awakening energy.[57] Furthermore, according to Mujaku, there are two types of saving on the expenditure of energy.[58] The first pertains to beginners: by abandoning efforts to understand the Way via intellectual understanding—which is a useless waste of energy—one can save that energy for use in the "reverse-illumination" of one's own mind. The second pertains to seasoned practitioners: as with the ripening of a

---

56. Expressed as *ji* 急/*huan* 緩 or *jin* 緊/*huan* 緩. The term *ji* 急 means "be in a rush; be in a hurry; be restless or fidgety to do something; be agitated by the desire to get something done; be impatient." The term *jin* 緊 ("tense") is used as a synonym. The term *huan* 緩 means "loose; slack; lenient; relaxed; with the tension relieved."

57. See Volume One, n. 185.

58. See Volume One, n. 61.

persimmon, as the ripened area increases (= gaining awakening energy), its unripened area decreases (= saving on the expenditure of *gongfu* energy). Spontaneously, the expenditure of *gongfu* energy diminishes.

Theme 6: *You will eventually notice that the* huatou *has become "tasteless."* At an advanced stage, the student will begin to notice that *huatou* practice has entered a phase wherein the *huatou* no longer has any "taste" or "flavor" (*mei ziwei* 沒滋味/*wu ziwei* 無滋味). *Letters of Dahui* gives assurance that this is a "good *state of being*" (*hao de xiaoxi* 好底消息), a good time, a good place—that this is just the time to apply even more effort:

> Letter #35.5: When you are lifting the *huatou* to awareness, there is definitely no need to perform a lot of tricky maneuvers. While walking, standing, sitting, or lying down, just don't allow interruption. While experiencing joy, anger, sorrow, or happiness, don't produce discrimination. Over and over again lift [the *huatou*] to awareness, over and over again keep your eye on [the *huatou*]. When you notice the *huatou* has no logic, no taste, that your mind is "hot and stuffy," it's the state wherein you, the person on duty, relinquishes his life. Keep this in mind! Upon encountering this realm [of no logic and no taste], don't become fainthearted. This sort of realm is the *state of being* of becoming a buddha or patriarch.

Dahui's "Instructions to the Assembly" appended to the very end of his compendium *Correct Dharma-Eye Depository* (*Zheng fayan zang* 正法眼藏)[59] tells us that getting some "taste" from anything—the sayings of

---

59. Some translations of this title break up the four characters as *zhengfa-yan-zang*, taking *zhengfa* as an equivalent of Sanskrit *saddharma*: *Depository of the Eye of the True Dharma*. I have instead divided the title as *zheng-fayan-zang*: *Correct Dharma-Eye Depository*, i.e., *Depository of the Dharma-Eye that Distinguishes Correctness from Perversity*. In other words, the *correct* modifies *eye*, not *dharma*. The latter interpretation is supported by Dahui's very first comment in the collection and by an explanation of the title in a preface (note underlined portions). Dahui's first comment: "If you don't have a handhold for thoroughly realizing transcendence and possessing the correct eye that is beyond ordinary feelings, then you will not avoid making calculations of gain and loss.... I have just taken these [examples of] thorough realization of transcendence to make people capable of loosening adhesive bondage and coming into possession of the correct eye" [苟非徹證向上巴鼻。具出常情正眼。未免作得失論量。..... 但取徹證向上巴鼻。堪與人解黏去縛具正眼而已。] (CBETA, X67, no. 1309, p. 557, b8–c8 // Z 2:23, p. 2, b2–c8 // R118, p. 3, b2–p. 4, a8). The preface by the Ming-dynasty Caodong master Zhanran Yuancheng (湛然圓澄; 1561–1626) says: "The title *Zheng fayan zang* is difficult to elucidate. Permit me to clarify it with a simile. It is like the pure eye that sees clearly the myriad images, taking them in endlessly and using them inexhaustibly. Therefore, it is called a 'depository.' The depository is the broadest sort of container. In

the ancients, sutra quotations, Chan cases, Chan dialogues, the silence of sitting, the multiplicity of actions of daily life, and so forth—indicates that one has made it into a "stereotyped formula" or "conventional usage" (*kejiu* 窠臼) and taken up a comfortable residence therein.[60] When you don't sit inside any such "nest," you are in the state of "no taste."

Theme 7: *You must keep pressing hard with the* huatou *no matter what.* A common exhortation in *Letters of Dahui* is "keep pressing hard."[61] At the place where the "*huatou*-uncertainty" mass is not yet smashed, one must go right up to the edge of the precipice—and over!

> Letter #14.5: If you stake your life on it, you'll be ready to set about doing it. If you're not yet capable of staking your life on it, just keep pressing hard at the point where the uncertainty is not yet smashed [i.e.,

---

it the perverse and the correct are mixed together. The Jing and Wei Rivers are difficult to distinguish. When you arrive at the perverse, you can snatch up the correct. The correct is the opposite of the perverse. Therefore, it is like the mouth of a spring when it cannot get through because mud and sand have obstructed it. If the dharma eye is not correct, perverse views emerge one after the other. Remove the mud and sand, and the mouth of the stream gets through. Eliminate perverse views, and the dharma eye is correct. If one is not a perfect person, how will he choose?" [正法眼藏者。難言也。請以喻明。譬如淨眼洞見森羅。取之無窮。用之無盡。故名曰藏。夫藏者。含藏最廣。邪正相襍。涇渭難辯。甚至邪能奪正。正反為邪。故似泉眼不通泥沙立壅。法眼不正邪見層出。剔抉泥沙而泉眼通。剪除邪見而法眼正。自非至人其何擇焉。] (CBETA, X67, no. 1309, p. 556, a5–9 // Z 2:23, p. 1, a2–6 // R118, p. 1, a2–6).

60. *Zheng fayan zang* 正法眼藏: "You people spend your entire lives in the Chan monasteries seeking for *this matter* without ever getting it. It doesn't lie in words! Among you there are many with white hair and yellowed teeth who sit inside stereotyped formulas, never able to stick your heads out for your whole life. You know nothing of your mistake. Getting some taste from the sayings of the ancients is taking their sublime sayings as a stereotyped formula. Getting some taste from the chanted sounds and meanings of the sutras is taking the sutras as a stereotyped formula.... Getting some taste from daily activities and actions is taking your raising of your eyebrows, your blinking, and your lifting of the *huatou* to awareness as a stereotyped formula" [你諸人一生在叢林參尋此事無所得者。不在言也。其間多有頭白齒黃坐在窠臼裏一生出頭不得。都不知非。向古人言句上得些滋味者。以奇言妙句為窠臼。於經教中聲名句義上得滋味者。以經教為窠臼。.... 於日用動轉施為處得滋味者。以揚眉瞬目舉覺提撕為窠臼。] (CBETA, X67, no. 1309, p. 630, a7–17 // Z 2:23, p. 74, d11–p. 75, a3 // R118, p. 148, b11–p. 149, a3).

61. The phrase *ya jiangqu* 崖将去/*si ya* 廝崖 means "keep pushing away at; keep pressing hard; go on running down; go on tracking down," and so forth. There is an orthographical question about *ya* 崖. Iriya Yoshitaka and Koga Hidehiko, *Zengo jiten* (Kyoto: Shibunkaku shuppan, 1991), 57, glosses *ya* 崖 thus: "Same as *ai* 捱. Also written as *ai* 挨. The meaning is 'vigorously keep pressing hard; go on running down'" [捱と同じ。挨と書くこともある。ぐいぐいと押しまくる、追いつめてゆく。]. Mujaku, 50, glosses *ya jiang qu* 崖將去 thus: "A colloquialism: 'go on pursuing to the ultimate'—an incisive examination of principle is like going right up to the edge of a precipice" [俗語窮將去也編辟究理趣如到崖邊也].

go on rallying the *huatou* to awareness]. Suddenly you'll be ready to stake your life on one throw—done!

Theme 8: *You must "break through" or "pass through" the* huatou. This breaking through or passing through[62] leads to a state wherein you don't have to ask anything of anybody—you know for yourself:

> Letter #29.3: Also, if your mind is agitated, just lift to awareness the *huatou* of "dog has no buddha-nature" [i.e., *wu* 無]. The words of the buddhas, the words of the patriarchs, the words of the old monks of all the regions have myriad differences; but, if you can break through this word *wu* 無, you'll break through all of them at the very same time, without having to ask anyone anything. If you intently ask questions of other people about the words of the buddhas, about the words of the patriarchs, and about the words of the old monks of all the regions, then in endless aeons you'll never attain awakening!

Theme 9: *You must smash to smithereens the mind of samsara.* The smashing of the mind of samsara (*shengsi xin po* 生死心破) is the *sine qua non* of practice in *Letters of Dahui*. Sometimes *Letters of Dahui* phrases this theme as the smashing of uncertainty about the *huatou*:

> Letter #12.1: If you want true stillness, what's necessary is the smashing of the mind of samsara. Even without doing *gongfu*—if the mind of samsara is smashed—stillness will come of its own accord. The stillness *upāya* [i.e., the practice of sitting] spoken of by the earlier noble ones is solely for *this* [i.e., the smashing of the mind of samsara]. It's just that, during this "latter time" [i.e., after the complete nirvana of the Buddha], the party of perverse teachers doesn't understand the former noble ones' [exhortations to sit] were *upāya* talk.
>
> ***
>
> Letter #30.5: When the sensation of uncertainty is not smashed, birth-death goes on and on and on. If the sensation of uncertainty is smashed, then the mind of samsara [lit., "birth-death"] is cut off.

---

62. The variants are: *touqu* 透取/*toude* 透得/*tou* 透/*touguo* 透過.

If the mind of samsara is cut off, then both buddha-view and dharma-view disappear. If even buddha-view and dharma-view disappear, could there possibly be further production of the sentient-beings-view and defilements-view?

Dahui's Collection Correct Dharma-Eye Depository *and* Letters of Dahui

The *Correct Dharma-Eye Depository* (*Zheng fayan zang* 正法眼藏) describes itself as "a collection with attached comments."[63] It is a collection of old standards (*guze* 古則) with Dahui's comments. The old-standards portion consists of 661 excerpts from numerous Chan records, the most-cited genre being "Instructions to the Assembly" (*shizhong* 示眾). Twenty percent of the snippets are followed by Dahui's comments (*zhuoyu* 著語), which begin with "Miaoxi says." The final portion is "Miaoxi's Instruction to the Assembly." Here is one of the more than 600 excerpts:

> Preceptor Langya Jue instructed the assembly: "Advancing forwards is death; retreating backwards is dying. If you neither advance nor retreat, you fall into the village of *nothing-to-do*. Why so? Though the capital Chang'an is a merry place, it's not one to stay in very long."

> Miaoxi says:
> The cuckoo's sad call spits out a flow of blood—that's useless.
> Better to hold one's tongue and pass what remains of the days of
>   spring.[64]

Dahui's comment is a heptasyllabic couplet—allusive and imagistic in the manner of the mainstream poetry tradition. Various forms of poetry suffuse the Chan records. Throughout Dahui's sayings record we find

---

63. Immediately after the title appears the line: "Chan Master Jingshan Dahui Zonggao collects and attaches comments" [徑山大慧禪師宗杲集并著語] (CBETA, X67, no. 1309, p. 557, a21 // Z 2:23, p. 2, a9 // R118, p. 3, a9]).

64. *Zheng fayan zang* 正法眼藏: 琅邪覺和尚示眾曰。進前即死。退後即亡。不進不退落 在無事之鄉。何故如此。長安雖樂。不是久居。妙喜曰。啼得血流無用處。不如緘口過 殘春。(CBETA, X67, no. 1309, p. 578, a23–b1 // Z 2:23, p. 23, a14–16 // R118, p. 45, a14–16). Langya Huijue (瑯琊慧覺; d.u.) was a Song Linji master, a successor of Fenyang Shanzhao (汾陽善昭; 947–1024). The mouth of the cuckoo is red, and its call is a metaphor for sadness and regret.

hundreds of poems, though few appear in *Letters of Dahui* and *Dharma Talks*.

The *Chronological Biography of Chan Master Dahui Pujue* describes the conditions surrounding the genesis of this collection of old standards and how its title was chosen:

> Shaoxing 17/1147, when the Master was fifty-nine: Attendants requested the Master to come up with a title to a compendium of master-student dialogues and ancient and modern sayings. The Master said: "I am dwelling in exile in Hengyang because of an offense. My door is closed to visitors, and I am engaging in self-examination concerning my errors. There is nothing else to do. During this interval, there are Chan monks requesting instruction, but there is nothing I can do about giving answers to them." The Chan monks Chongmi and Huiran immediately began to copy out the materials. The days and months gradually lengthened, and they produced a huge text. They brought it and begged for a name. With this title, they desired to inform those of later times and ensure that the depository of the correct dharma-eye of the buddhas and patriarchs would never die out. The Master glanced at it and said: "*Correct Dharma-Eye Depository.*"[65]

Thus, the *Correct Dharma-Eye Depository* was compiled sometime around 1147 (perhaps the immediately preceding few years), when Dahui was in exile in Hengzhou in Hunan. At this time Dahui was also writing letters on *huatou* practice and related matters to a number of scholar-officials, and some dating from this time are included in Volume Two of *Letters of Dahui*.[66] The *Letters of Dahui* and the *Correct Dharma-Eye Depository* may presuppose different methods of Chan practice, and may have been intended for different audiences; but for Dahui they were both exemplars of his "outreach" program from the forced seclusion of his Hengzhou base of exile, when he was restricted in his movements and in his ability to receive visitors. As T. Griffith Foulk has said, the *huatou*-practice

---

65. *Dahui Pujue chanshi nianpu* 大慧普覺禪師年譜: 十七年丁卯師五十九歲侍者以師與衲子問答古今語句請名按題篇首云余因罪居衡陽杜門循省外無所用心間有衲子請益不得已與之酬酢禪者沖密慧然隨手抄錄日月浸久成一巨軸持來乞名其題欲昭示後來使佛祖正法眼藏不滅余因目之曰正法眼藏] (CBETA, J01, no. A042, p. 802, c23–29). This passage also appears in Dahui's first comment in the *Correct Dharma-Eye Depository* (CBETA, X67, no. 1309, p. 557, c2–8 // Z 2:23, p. 2, c2–8 // R118, p. 4, a2–8).

66. Examples are: letters #37, 38, 44, 45, 47, and 49, all of which date to 1145–1147.

style "wherever and whenever it has flourished in the Ch'an, Sŏn, and Zen traditions, has always coexisted with the older and more widely accepted practice of comments on koan [*gong'an*] literature."[67]

Mujaku Dōchū's Commentary Pearl in the Wicker-Basket

Three commentaries have been extremely useful in reading and translating *Letters of Dahui*, one by an Edo-period Japanese Rinzai Zen monk and two by Korean Sŏn monks. (For all three, see *Abbreviations*.) Of course, no commentary (including this translation, which is certainly a "commentary") escapes errors in understanding its root text, but these Korean and Japanese commentaries at least give us the "insider" take on *Letters of Dahui* since the thirteenth century. And they probably perpetuate the Song-Yuan Chinese understanding of the text—no Chinese commentary has come down to us. We could disdain the insider take, but that would not be prudent. Besides, it is fascinating to listen in on the insider talk—what they considered the focal points of the text, what they found puzzling when reading it, and so forth. It is comforting for a modern reader to know that they too struggled with certain hard-to-understand passages and occasionally failed in the quest.

The most helpful commentary has been Letters of Chan Master Dahui Pujue: *Pearl in the Wicker-Basket* (Daie Fukaku zenji sho *kōrōju* 大慧普覺禪師書栲栳珠), a manuscript commentary in Chinese on *Letters of Dahui* by the Rinzai scholar-monk Mujaku Dōchū (1653–1744). The manuscript is in Mujaku's own hand. He studied *Letters of Dahui* for virtually his entire adult life.[68] Urs App gives a summary of his tireless engagement with this Chan text:

This is the Chan textual commentary on which Mujaku worked the longest. Historical, geographical, philosophical, doctrinal,

---

67. T. Griffith Foulk, "The Form and Function of Koan Literature: A Historical Overview," in *The Kōan: Texts and Contexts in Zen Buddhism*, ed. Steven Heine and Dale S. Wright (New York: Oxford University Press, 2000), 16.

68. At age twenty-four (Enpō 4/1676), Mujaku was at Bairyū-ji (梅龍寺), a Rinzai temple in Mino (Gifu prefecture), training under a Preceptor Katsudō (活堂和尚). Katsudō at the time was lecturing on *Letters of Dahui*. Later the whole assembly asked the young Mujaku to lecture on *Letters of Dahui*, and he did so. This was the beginning of a deep connection to the text. At age sixty (Shōtoku 2/1712 4th month 1st day), he began work on a ten-fascicle

grammatical, and lexical information is provided with equally metic-
ulous care. This is certainly one of the most elaborate, precise, and
learned commentaries ever written on a Chan text. The wealth of
references to and quotes from other Chan texts, Buddhist scriptures and commentaries, local gazetteers, dynastic histories, etc., is
astonishing.[69]

Pearl in the Wicker-Basket contains paraphrases that expand on terse
original lines, excellent philological work (occasionally, of course, super-
seded by modern scholarship), the tracking down of most sources, the
tracing of themes across letters, the listing of "old" and "mistaken" interpretations, and so forth. The format is words and phrases from *Letters of
Dahui* (each marked by a triangle), followed by Mujaku's comments. In the
following translation, the section divisions within the sixty-two letters, the
brief summaries at the beginning of each section, and the dating of most
letters derive from Mujaku's *Pearl in the Wicker-Basket*. *Pearl in the Wicker-
Basket* on occasion is certainly wrong in its interpretations, but overall it is
a welcome guide for anyone trying to work through such a difficult text as
Letters of Dahui.

The title *Pearl in the Wicker-Basket* is intriguing. Mujaku was given to
capping his Chan commentaries, glossaries, and so forth with delightfully
metaphorical titles.[70] Perhaps this one comes from an anecdote found in
Arsenal of the Chan School of Chan Master Dahui Pujue: "Dongsi at that
very moment just demanded a single pearl, and Yangshan immediately

commentary on *Letters of Dahui* entitled *Pearl in the Wicker-Basket*. At age seventy-one (Kyōhō
8/1723 5th month 27th day), he completed the fifteen-fascicle version of this commentary.
This tracing of Mujaku's involvement with *Letters of Dahui* is based on Iida Rigyō, *Gakushō
Mujaku Dōchū* (Kyoto: Zen bunka kenkyūjo, 1986), 58–59, 152, and 201.

69. Urs App, "Chan/Zen's Greatest Encyclopaedist: Mujaku Dōchū (無著道忠) (1653–
1744)," *Cahiers d'Extrême-Asie* 3 (1987): 171. On Mujaku, also see John Jorgensen, "Zen
Scholarship: Mujaku Dōchū and His Contemporaries," *Zen bunka kenkyūjo kiyō* 27 (2006): 1–
6; John Jorgensen, "Mujaku Dōchū (1653–1744) and Seventeenth-Century Chinese Buddhist
Scholarship," *East Asian History* 32/33 (2008): 25–56; and Yanagida Seizan, "Mujaku Dōchū
no gakumon," *Zengaku kenkyū* 55 (February 1966): 14–55.

70. Another example is: Sayings Record of Preceptor Xutang: *Tilling with an Ox-Plow* (Kidō
goroku *rikō* 虛堂語錄犁耕). Xutang Zhiyu's (虛堂智愚; 1185–1269) sobriquet was "the old
man who has given up tilling" (Xigengsou 息耕叟). This commentary, a trove of Chan lore, is
even more massive than *Pearl in the Wicker-Basket*. See Mujaku Dōchū, Kidōroku *rikō* (Kyoto:
Zen bunka kenkyūjo, 1990).

overturned a single wicker-basket."[71] The pearl is the wish-fulfilling gem (*cintāmaṇi*), contained in the wicker-basket of mind. When the basket is overturned (in the manner of the overturning of the storehouse consciousness or *ālayavijñāna*), the pearl (the mirrorlike wisdom or *ādarśajñāna)* spills out. The pearl of the mind rests within *Letters of Dahui*; in reading it (i.e., "turning" it, as in reading a sutra), the pearl spills out.[72]

Two Korean Commentaries: Hyesim and "Korean Anonymous"

The commentary in Chinese on *Letters of Dahui* by Chin'gak Hyesim (真覺慧諶; 1178–1234), *Notes on the* Letters (*Sŏjang ki* 書狀記), consists of a schematic of each letter followed by exegeses of words and phrases. Hyesim, a fervent practitioner, was the principal disciple of Pojo Chinul (普照知訥; 1158–1210) and became the second teacher of the Sŏn Cultivation Community (*Susŏnsa* 修禪社) established by Chinul. It is noteworthy that Hyesim and some of his students in Baoqing 2/1226 at the Sŏn Cultivation Community compiled the *Collection of Prose and Verse Comments of the Chan Gate* (*Sŏnmun yŏmsong chip* 禪門拈頌集).[73] Using the Chan the transmission records and sayings records as their basis, they selected 1125 "old standards" (*koch'ik* 古則) and to these attached prose and verse comments, sayings from Chan records, and so forth.[74] Hyesim had a strong

---

71. 東寺當時只索一顆珠。仰山當下傾出一栲栳。(T1998B.47.946b11–22). Also, a preface to the *Liandeng hui yao* (聯燈會要) says: "I have heard that 'Dongsi just demanded a single bright pearl, and Yangshan immediately overturned a single wicker-basket.' When I now gaze upon this piece of writing, it spills out all the treasures of heaven and earth. Why stop at overturning a single wicker-basket!" [余聞。東寺只索一顆明珠。仰山當下傾一栲栳。今觀此書。盡泄天地之寶。又何止傾一栲栳也。] (CBETA, X79, no. 1557, p. 11, b3–5 // Z 2B:9, p. 218, b13–15 // R136, p. 435, b13–15).

72. To a far lesser extent I have also used another Japanese commentary: Zen Master Daie Fukaku's Letters *with Commentary at the Top of the Page and the Sides of Lines* (*Zōkan bōchū Daie Fukaku zenji sho* 增冠傍注大慧普覺禪師書), an edition of *Letters of Dahui* with commentary by the Rinzai master Takagi Genseki (高木元碩; 1842–1918), who eventually became head of Tenryū-ji in Kyoto. Takagi was a Meiji man who traveled in both China and Korea. His commentary is of two types: words and phrases in small font inserted at the sides of lines in the root text to facilitate reading and longer background notes at the top of the page. This commentary is occasionally useful for supplying a smooth reading via its insertions at the sides of lines.

73. Contained in Han'guk pulgyo chŏnsŏ p'yŏnch'an wiwŏnhoe, *Han'guk pulgyo chŏnsŏ*, 5.1–5.925.

74. This collection, which is rich in sayings not preserved in other texts, shows a close relationship to the Song master Xinwen Tanben (心聞曇賁) of the Huanglong wing of Linji

affinity for *hwadu* (*huatou*) practice as well as for the Zongmi-Yanshou emphasis on the identity of Chan and the canonical teachings.

Notes on Plucking out Difficulties from the Letters (*Sŏjang chŏknan ki* 書狀摘難記) in Chinese by an anonymous Korean commentator (referred to in the following translation as "Korean Anonymous") is a matter-of-fact exegesis of words and phrases in *Letters of Dahui*. This work is briefer than Hyesim's commentary. We do not know the identity of this commentator, though he seems to have emerged from the same matrix as Hyesim. "Korean Anonymous" supplies a succinct summary of the contents of *Letters of Dahui*:

> The main idea of the *Letters* is distinguishing perverse and correct, and probing the *hwadu* [i.e., *huatou*]. The "silence-as-illumination" [of the perverse teachers] is not the only perversity [for Dahui]. The ten illnesses of the *hwadu* **no/mu** 無, all mental reflection, discrimination, and calculation, the generation of uncertainty about texts, the generation of uncertainty about the sutra teachings—all of it is perverse. The correct approach is merely to rally the single ball of uncertainty to awareness.[75]

This tidy encapsulation of *Letters of Dahui* hits the bullseye—these are indeed the two main themes.

Influence of Letters of Dahui *in China*

Ishii Shūdō, a foremost specialist in Dahui studies, holds that "the *huatou*-practice Chan that Dahui brought to maturity spread explosively and

---

Chan—it quotes Xinwen, about whom little is known, more than one-hundred times. Shiina Kōyū, "*Zenmon nenju shū no shiryō kachi,*" *Indogaku bukkyōgaku kenkyū* 101 (2002): 54–55. Xinwen compiled an extract of Yanshou's enormous *Record of the Mind Mirror* (*Zongjinglu* 宗鏡錄), and, in 1213, thirteen years before the compilation of the *Collection of Prose and Verse Comments of the Chan Gate*, Hyesim did a reprint of the Song edition of this *Record of the Mind Mirror* extract for the Sŏn Cultivation Community. For a translation of the first fascicle of the *Zongjing lu*, see Welter, *Yongming Yanshou's Conception of Chan in the* Zongjing lu, 223–275.

75. Korean Anonymous, 120: 大意辨邪正參話句非但默照爲邪無字十種病及一切思量分別計較文字上起疑經教上起疑皆爲邪單單提撕一箇疑團爲正也. For the illnesses, see the section "What Not to Do in *Huatou* Practice." Pojo Chinul increased eight illnesses to ten.

was decisive in determining the nature of subsequent Linji Chan."[76] It would seem that the *huatou* method expounded in *Letters of Dahui* (and in Dahui's *Dharma Talks*) quite soon after Dahui's time became deeply entrenched among Linji Chan monks. The renowned Neo-Confucian figure Zhu Xi (朱熹; 1130–1200), who died less than forty years after Dahui, made the striking remark that *in his time* the most oft-heard tags of the Chan school were the *huatous* **three pounds of linen thread** and **dried turd**.[77]

The names of Song, Yuan, and Ming masters who propagated Dahui's *huatou*-practice style is quite long. Three prominent names are Mengshan Deyi (蒙山德異; 1231–?), Gaofeng Yuanmiao (高峰原妙; 1238–1295) and his student Zhongfeng Mingben (中峰明本; 1263–1323), but a host of others could be listed. Yunqi Zhuhong's (雲棲袾宏; 1535–1615) anthology of sayings from a wide range of Chan records running from the Tang dynasty to the late Ming, the *Whip for Spurring Students Onward through the Chan Barrier Checkpoints* (*Changuan cejin* 禪關策進), has many sayings that are suffused with Dahui's *huatou* practice, indicating just how deeply this style had penetrated into Linji Chan monastic circles during the Southern Song, Yuan, and Ming dynasties.[78] Ishii's assessment is clearly not an overstatement.

Influence of Letters of Dahui *in Korea*

In the case of Korea, Dahui's *huatou* practice has been utterly dominant. It all begins with Pojo Chinul (1158–1210), who gravitated to the *Platform Sutra*, the *Chan Letter* and *Chan Prolegomenon* of Guifeng Zongmi, and the *Sayings Record of Chan Master Dahui Pujue* (which includes *Letters of Dahui* and *Dharma Talks*).[79] In fact, one of his awakenings is said to have come

---

76. Ishii expresses this view of "*kanna Zen* 看話禅" in his chapter on Song-Dynasty Chan in Tanaka Ryōshō, ed., *Zengaku kenkyū nyūmon*, 2d ed. (Tokyo: Daitō shuppansha, 2006), 147–148: 大慧の大成した看話禅は、爆発的に広まり、その後の臨済禅の性格を決定ずけた。For a convenient list of Ishii's numerous Dahui articles, see Juhn Young Ahn, "Malady of Meditation: A Prolegomenon to the Study of Illness and Zen" (PhD diss., University of California, Berkeley, 2007), 356–357.

77. See the epigraph to this book.

78. For a translation with the Chinese text, see Jeffrey L. Broughton and Elise Yoko Watanabe, trans., *The* Chan Whip *Anthology: A Companion to Zen Practice* (Oxford: Oxford University Press, 2015).

79. For a biography of Chinul, see Robert E. Buswell Jr., *The Korean Approach to Zen: The Collected Works of Chinul* (Honolulu: University of Hawaii Press, 1983), 17–36. For translations of the Zongmi works, see Broughton, *Zongmi on Chan*, 69–179.

from reading *Sayings Record of Chan Master Dahui Pujue.* Chinul never traveled to China but did absorb the Chan works of Guifeng Zongmi and Dahui Zonggao in both letter and spirit. Chinul's magnum opus of 1209, *Excerpts from the Separately Circulated Record of the Dharma Collection with Inserted Personal Notes* (*Pŏpchip pyŏrhaeng nok chŏryo pyŏngip sagi* 法集別行錄節要并入私記) is a guidebook designed by Chinul for the practitioners gathered around him.[80] This work, which was to have such a momentous influence on the overall outlook of Korean Buddhism, rests essentially on two foundation stones: blocks of quotations from Zongmi's *Chan Letter* (with the order rearranged) and, toward the end, quotations from *Sayings Record of Chan Master Dahui Pujue.* (There are, of course, other sources quoted.) Three of the Dahui quotations are from *Letters of Dahui,* one from his *General Sermons,* and three from his *Dharma Talks.*[81] A focus is Dahui's *huatou* practice, which becomes emblematic of Korean Sŏn. In Chinul's schema the all-at-once awakening is awakening to Guifeng Zongmi's *Knowing* (*zhi* 知), the intrinsically pure True Mind; the step-by-step practice is Dahui's *huatou* practice. The *Excerpts* is a creative hybrid of these two. Chinul's preface says:

> Also, I fear that meditators who are not yet capable of quelling delusive thought [i.e., Dahui's term] and being empty and bright, [after all-at-once awakening to Knowing,] will stagnate on the theoretical expression [of Knowing]; and, therefore, toward the end of this text I provide excerpts from sayings on the "direct-and-quick" method by the *original-allotment* master [Dahui Zonggao]. This is essentially to enable practitioners to eliminate any illnesses that may arise connected to Knowing and come to realize the living road of escape from self.[82]

---

80. For the text, see Pojo sasang yŏn'guwon, ed., *Pojo chŏnsŏ* (Seoul: Puril ch'ulp'ansa, 1989), 103–165. For an English translation, see Buswell, *The Collected Works of Chinul,* 262–374; and Robert E. Buswell, Jr., trans., *Numinous Awareness Is Never Dark: The Korean Buddhist Master Chinul's* Excerpts *on Zen Practice,* Korean Classics Library: Philosophy and Religion (Honolulu: University of Hawaiʻi Press), 2016.

81. They are in the order of Chinul's *Excerpts: General Sermons* (T1998A.47.879b8–9); *Dharma Talks* (T1998A.47.907b1–16); *Letters of Dahui* letter #19.6 (T1998A.47.925b28–c6); *Dharma Talks* (T1998A.47.891a22–27); *Letters of Dahui* letter #3.2–4 (T1998A.47.918a21–b25); *Letters of Dahui* letter #10.5 (T1998A.47.921c2–15); and *Dharma Talks* (T1998A.47.891b27–c2).

82. Pojo sasang yŏn'guwon, ed., *Pojo chŏnsŏ,* 103: 又恐觀行者未能忘懷虛朗滯於義理故末後略引本分宗師徑截門言句要令滌除知見之病知有出身活路爾.

Chinul's main disciple Chin'gak Hyesim was a particularly fervent advocate of Dahui's style of practice. His commentary *Notes on the* Letters stresses "practicing the *hwadu*" (*ch'amgu* 參句) at virtually every turn—we might say Hyesim took Chinul's emphasis on Dahui's *huatou* method and amplified it.

After the era of Chinul and his disciples, we have T'aego Pou (太古普愚; 1301–1382), who was deeply immersed in Dahui-style *huatou* practice. He spent 1346–1348 in Yuan-dynasty China, inheriting the dharma of the Linji master Shiwu Qinggong (石屋清珙; 1272–1352), a practitioner of Dahui's *huatou wu* 無.[83] The "Instructions to the Assembly" in *Preceptor T'aego's Sayings Record* (*T'aego hwasang ŏrok* 太古和尚語錄) stresses the uninterrupted *huatou* practice of *Letters of Dahui*:

> As soon as you lift this word *mu* 無 to awareness, the faces of the buddhas of the three times are thrown up. You people! Do you affirm it? If you haven't yet affirmed it, right under this great uncertainty, jettison body-mind, as if it were the moment you fell off a ten-thousand-foot precipice. Have no calculating and no haggling—like a man who has undergone the great death. Toss off any thought of what it is like and only raise this word *mu* 無 to awareness. Twenty-four hours a day in all four postures just make this *hwadu* into your body-mind continuum in the midst of samsara. Never darkening and constantly examining, rally the *hwadu* to awareness and keep it in front of your eyes.... If you exert real effort like this, you will arrive at the state of saving on energy, and this *is* the state of gaining energy. The *hwadu* will naturally ripen and become unified, body-mind will suddenly be empty, congealed, and immobile, with the mind having no place to go to. *Here* it's just the person on duty. If the person on duty rouses up any other thought, he is definitely deluded by his shadow.... If you can't break through, then throw yourself into it without reservation. All that is necessary is that the *hwadu* be continuous—without interruption. It doesn't matter whether there is uncertainty or no uncertainty, taste or no

---

83. A quatrain by Shiwu Qinggong in *Shiwu Qinggong chanshi yulu* 石屋清珙禪師語錄 runs: "Practicing until you break through Zhaozhou's word *wu* 無;/ The golden latch to the mystery gate opens up completely;/ At the third watch beneath the moon the clay ox roars;/ Clear and transparent in the eight directions: the sun over the sea—red" [參得趙州無字透。玄關金鎖盡開通。三更月下泥牛吼。八面玲瓏海日紅。] (CBETA, X70, no. 1399, p. 674, b10–11 // Z 2:27, p. 324, d1–2 // R122, p. 648, b1–2).

taste: beneath this great uncertainty, rally the *hwadu* to awareness, never allow it to darken. Keep on pressing hard.[84]

Of the nine themes of *Letters of Dahui* listed above, this T'aego talk exhibits six: you must do it on your own, the stress on uncertainty, saving on the expenditure of energy is gaining energy, taste versus no taste, keep pressing hard, and breaking through or passing through **wu** 無. T'aego was indeed a very faithful expositor of Dahuiʾs style of *huatou* practice.

Guide to Sŏn (*Sŏn'ga kwigam* 禪家龜鑑) by Chʾŏnghŏ Hyujŏng (清虛休靜; 1520–1604) was published in Korea in Wanli 7/1579.[85] For his handbook, Hyujŏng selected sayings and lines from fifty sutras, treatises, and Chan records, adding commentary and short verses; his disciples edited it. A major section of the *Guide to Sŏn* deals with Dahuiʾs *huatou* practice. Here is a snippet:

> In the main, students must practice the living phrase [i.e., engage in *hwadu* practice] and must not practice the lifeless phrase. If you come to realization vis-à-vis a living phrase, you are capable of being a teacher of the buddhas and patriarchs. If you come to realization vis-à-vis a lifeless phrase, you won't even be able to save yourself. From here onward I will focus the presentation on the living phrase [i.e., the *hwadu*] in order for [the reader] to achieve access to awakening.
>
> You want to see Linji?
>
> You have to be an iron man!

---

84. John Jorgensen, trans., *Seon Dialogues*, Collected Works of Korean Buddhism 8 (Seoul: Jogye Order of Korean Buddhism, 2012), 338–342: 才舉箇無字。三世諸佛面目。掀翻出來。儞等諸人。還肯也無。若未肯信。於此大疑之下。放下身心。如墮萬仞崖下時相似。無計較沒商量。如大死人相似。放捨如何若何之念。單單提箇無字。於十二時中四威儀內。只與話頭爲命根。常常不昧。時時檢察。提撕話頭。帖在眼前。.... 若如此其實用功。則便到省力處。此是得力處也。話頭自然純熟。打成一片。身心忽空。凝然不動。心無所之。這裏只是箇當人。當人若起他念。則決定被影子惑矣。.... 若透不得。則更着精彩。只要話頭。聯綿不斷。不論有疑無疑。有味無味。即此大疑之下。提撕話頭。單單不昧。捱來捱去。Jorgenson provides a translation.

85. Hyujŏng is usually known as Sŏsan taesa (西山大師), "Great Master Sŏsan." His compilation *Sŏn'ga kwigam* 禪家龜鑑 is: CBETA, X63, no. 1255, p. 737, b6–p. 746, a10 // Z 2:17, p. 456, a1–p. 464, c6 // R112, p. 911, a1–p. 928, a6. The term *kwigam* 龜鑑 (*tortoise and mirror*) refers to divination instruments and thus lessons to be learned. According to Robert E. Buswell Jr. and Donald S. Lopez Jr., *The Princeton Dictionary of Buddhism* (Princeton: Princeton University Press, 2014), 841, "the text was originally written in literary Chinese, but was first published in a 1569 Korean vernacular *(ŏnhae)* edition." The Chinese edition attained some popularity in China and Japan.

Comment: There are two methods to *hwadu* [practice]: phrase
and meaning. Practicing the phrase [as thing-in-itself] is the living
phrase of the "direct-and-quick" method [of Sŏn], because it is free
of mental conceptualization, verbalization, and the seizing [of char-
acteristics]. Practicing for meaning is the lifeless phrase of the per-
fect-and-sudden method [of the teachings], because it is entrenched
in rationality, verbalization, intellectual understanding, and the cog-
nition of characteristics.[86]

Lastly, since the 1700s, the *Fourfold Collection* (*Sajip* 四集) has been at
the heart of the Korean monastic curriculum.[87] The *Sajip* consists of: *Letters
of Dahui* (*Sŏjang* 書狀); Guifeng Zongmi's *Chan Prolegomenon* (*Tosŏ* 都序);
Gaofeng Yuanmiao's *Essentials of Chan* (*Sŏnyo* 禪要); and Chinul's *Excerpts*
(*Chŏryo* 節要). Since Gaofeng's *Essentials of Chan* is also a faithful exposi-
tion of Dahui's *huatou* practice, we can readily grasp the central position of
Dahui's style in Korean Sŏn.

Influence of Letters of Dahui *in Japan*

Gozan Zen, the Rinzai Zen of the "Five-Mountains" monasteries of Kyoto
and Kamakura during the period running from before 1300 to around
1500, was the hub of elite Japanese culture of the era. Of the major Gozan
Zen monks, one of the most famous was Gidō Shūshin (義堂周信; 1325–
1388). The most important source for Gidō's life is his autobiography, the
Abbreviated Collection on Empty Flower's Daily Practice (*Kūge nichiyō kufū
ryakushū* 空華日用工夫略集).[88] Evidence of his literary talents in Chinese
surfaced at a very young age—the entry for Genkō 2/1332, when Gidō was

---

86. *Sŏn'ga kwigam* 禪家龜鑑: 大抵學者須參活句莫參死句。活句下薦得堪與佛祖爲師。
死句下薦得自救不了。此下特擧活句使自悟入。　要見臨濟。須是鐵漢。評曰。話頭有
句意二門。參句者徑截門活句也。沒心路沒語路無摸撈故也。參意者圓頓門死句也。有
理路有語路有聞解思相故也。(CBETA, X63, no. 1255, p. 738, b23–c5 // Z 2:17, p. 457, a17–b5
// R112, p. 913, a17–b5). John Jorgensen, trans., *Hyujeong: Selected Works*, Collected Works of
Korean Buddhism 3 (Seoul: Jogye Order of Korean Buddhism, 2012), 72–73. Paraphrasing
General Sermons of Chan Master Dahui Pujue (*Dahui Pujue chanshi pushuo* 大慧普覺禪師
普說): 夫參學者。須參活句。莫參死句。活句下薦得。永劫不忘。死句下薦得。自救不
了。(T1998A.47.870b4–6).

87. Buswell and Lopez, *The Princeton Dictionary of Buddhism*, 738–739.

88. Kageki Hideo, trans., *Kunchū Kūge nichiyō kufū ryakushū: Chūsei zensō no seikatsu to
bungaku* (Kyoto: Shibunkaku, 1982) is an annotated *kakikudashibun* treatment without the
original Chinese text.

eight years old, reads: "One day, among various books in the family library,
I found a one-volume *Record of Linji*. I was delighted and read it. It was as
if I had learned it in a past birth. My parents considered this astonishing
and came to think I had some innate genius."[89] (In fact, within Rinzai
Zen, the *Record of Linji* was to remain in the background until 1654, with
the arrival in Nagasaki of the Chinese Linji master Yinyuan Longqi, who
singled out the *Record of Linji* and who probably served as a stimulus for
its popularity from that time onward.[90]) Entries in Gidō's autobiography
strongly suggest that Gidō in his maturity focused his Zen textual atten-
tions on *Letters of Dahui* and other Dahui works, the *Blue Cliff Collection*,
and two sutras strongly associated with Zen and favored by Dahui: the
Śūraṃgama and the *Perfect Awakening*.[91] Gidō frequently lectured on these
texts and was considered an expert. His preferences highlight the importance of *Letters of Dahui* in the Gozan Zen milieu. Several elegant editions
of the *Letters of Dahui* were printed in Gozan monasteries—in fact, this
translation is based on one of these editions.

Much later, in the Edo period, Hakuin Ekaku (白隱慧鶴; 1685–1769)
was a dedicated champion of the Zen practice described in *Letters of
Dahui*. Even the vocabulary of his polemics directed against Bankei Zen,
Ōbaku Zen, and Sōtō Zen derive from Dahui's critique of perverse Chan
teachers. *Letters of Dahui* was one of Hakuin's favorite texts, and he used
it for his very first lecture meeting at his home temple Shōin-ji, and,
in 1739, at the age of fifty-four, he held a month-long lecture meeting
on *Letters of Dahui*, with more than thirty people in attendance, at the
residence of his lay disciple Akiyama Hashitomo.[92] Hakuin's *Precious
Blossoms from a Thicket of Thorns* (*Keisō dokuzui* 荊叢毒蘂) contains a
piece delivered on that occasion.[93]

89. Kageki, trans., *Kunchū Kūge nichiyō kufū ryakushū*, 4.

90. Helen Baroni, *Ōbaku Zen: The Emergence of the Third Sect of Zen in Tokugawa Japan* (Honolulu: University of Hawaiʻi Press, 2000), 86.

91. For *Letters of Dahui* and other Dahui works in the autobiography, see Kageki, trans., *Kunchū Kūge nichiyō kufū ryakushū*, 135, 220, 240, 276–278, 122, 69, 365, and 367. These two sutras are prominent in *Letters of Dahui*.

92. Norman Waddell, *Poison Blossoms from a Thicket of Thorn* (Berkeley, CA: Counterpoint, 2014), 132.

93. The piece, entitled *Eye-Opening Ceremony for Śākyamuni* (*Shaka tengan* 釋迦點眼), is found in Hakuin oshō zenshū hensan kai, ed., *Hakuin oshō zenshū*, Vol. 2 (Tokyo: Ryūginsha, 1967), 2.14–16. For a translation, see Waddell, *Poison Blossoms from a Thicket of Thorn*, 132–135.

Hakuin's *General Sermon Spreading out the Banquet Mat for the* Xigeng Sayings Record (Sokkōroku *kaien fusetsu* 息耕録開筵普説) is a presentation of his basic Zen program. Xigengsou (息耕叟), "the old man who has given up tilling," is a sobriquet of the Southern Song Linji master Xutang Zhiyu (虚堂智愚; 1185–1269). In this formal Zen work in Chinese we find *Letters of Dahui* right at the heart of that program:

> If you really want to "void" the mind of arising-extinguishing [i.e., what Dahui calls "the smashing of the mind of samsara"], practice the difficult-to-pass-through *huatou* that is like iron ore that has been refined. Suddenly, when you lose the body-mind continuum in samsara, the matter will be finished.... Dahui [*Letters of Dahui* #5.2] says: "In recent times Māra has been strong and the dharma weak. Countless are those who [erroneously] consider the ultimate to be 'by means of [*samādhi* subduing] the *deep-and-still* [consciousness] to enter into fusion with the *deep-and-still* [thusness].'" Dahui also says [*Letters of Dahui* #53.4]: "In recent years there has been a type of perverse Chan. They close their eyes, shut their mouths and fall into silence, and produce false thought—they call this 'the inconceivable matter.' They also call it 'the matter before the appearance of Bhīṣma-garjita-svara Buddha' [i.e., the very first buddha to appear in this world] or 'the matter of the aeon of nothingness before the world begins.' The minute anyone opens his mouth, they call it 'falling into the present.' They also call it 'the fundamental matter.' They take awakening as a nonessential like branches and leaves. From the time they [i.e., the perverse teachers] take their first step they are greatly mistaken." Today also this sort of Māra clique is numerous.... If one goes on practicing in a pure way, and is able one time to smash this "old nest," suddenly the great, perfect mirror wisdom appears.... At first one must practice the dog's-buddha-nature *watō* [i.e., the *mu* 無 *huatou*]. The one who piles up months and years affixed to [*mu* 無] without budging will necessarily attain the state of "gaining energy" [i.e., Dahui's term].[94]

---

94. Hakuin oshō zenshū hensan kai, ed., *Hakuin oshō zenshū*, 2.49–50 and 73: 真實欲空却生滅心。參箇渾剛打就底難透話頭。忽然和命根失時。始了畢。.... 妙喜曰。近世魔彊法弱。以湛入合湛。爲究竟者。不可勝數。又云。近年以來有一種邪禪。以閉目藏

From the Five-Mountains period to the present, *Letters of Dahui* has never lost its core position in Rinzai Zen and Rinzai-oriented scholarship.[95]

Three Hanging Scrolls

The Tokyo National Museum has in its collection two hanging scrolls of fragments from two letters in Dahui's hand (neither contained in *Letters of Dahui*).[96] One letter dates to Dahui's exile in Meizhou (Guangdong) and is to his lay disciple Deng Jing (鄧靖), also known as Layman "No-Characteristics" (*Wuxiang jushi* 無相居士). The other dates to Dahui's last years, when he was once again abbot of the illustrious Jingshan Monastery. The recipient was the abbot of Yanjiao Monastery (演教寺) in Huzhou (湖州) in Zhejiang, not too far from Jingshan. The dominant impression one gets from the calligraphy of both these fragments is self-assurance, even nonchalance. That is perhaps the underlying tone of *Letters of Dahui*. *Letters of Dahui*, of course, also shows an irrepressible sense of humor and little tolerance for pretentiousness (for examples, see letters #19 and #57). Dahui seems to have maintained his assurance and nonchalance both in remote exile when he was cut off from most direct contact with students and friends, and also during the time he was right at the center of things as abbot of the most prestigious Chan monastery in the land.

睛兮盧都地作妄想。謂之不思議事。亦謂之威音那畔空劫以前事。纔開口便喚作落今時。亦謂之根本上事。以悟爲枝葉邊事。蓋渠初發步時便大錯了。今時亦者般魔黨不爲少。.... 若人真參純工去。得一回打破者簡舊寨。乍見大圓鏡智。.... 先須參狗子佛性話。重歲月不踩跟者。必有得力之處。Norman Waddell, *The Essential Teachings of Zen Master Hakuin* (Boston: Shambhala, 1994), 68–69 and 101 has a translation.

95. As for the centrality of *Letters of Dahui* in postwar Rinzai-oriented scholarship, in the 1960s a group of scholars in the field of "Zen studies" (*Zengaku* 禅学) centered around Iriya Yoshitaka and Yanagida Seizan created a series of annotated translations of key Chinese Chan books, originally projected to be twenty volumes. The ultimate result was *Zen no goroku* 禅の語録, 17 vols. (Tokyo: Chikuma shobō, 1969–1976). *Letters of Dahui* was selected as the seventeenth volume and Araki Kengo, a specialist in Song and Ming thought, was designated as the translator. This is the standard translation into modern Japanese and has been consulted extensively in the making of this English translation. (This series was reissued in twenty volumes by Chikuma shobō in 2016.) There is also a modern Japanese translation by a Rinzai Zen layman that is aimed at a general audience: Fujimoto Osamu, *Mu no michi: Daie Zenji no hōgo* (Tokyo: Shunjūsha, 1991).

96. Tokyo National Museum TB-1173 and TB-1172. The former is a National Treasure, the latter an Important Cultural Property. http://www.emuseum.jp/result?s_lang=en&mode=simple&itemCount=8&d_lang=en&word=dahui.

Perhaps Dahui's most creative period was his period of exile—when he produced many letters on *huatou* practice and when he oversaw the compilation of his monumental collection of old standards with comments, the *Correct Dharma-Eye Depository*. The cover art of this book, a painting in the Metropolitan Museum of Art entitled "Chan Master Riding a Donkey," is meant to allude to Dahui's lengthy exile period in his fifties and sixties, since in Chinese painting the donkey rider is an icon of exile, reclusion, and the provinces (in Dahui's case Hunan and Guangdong as opposed to the center, Jingshan and the nearby Southern Song capital Lin'an/ Hangzhou).[97] This painting is by an unidentified artist active in the early thirteenth century, and the inscribed couplet is in the hand of the Linji Chan master Wuzhun Shifan (無準師範; 1177–1249), who, like Dahui, served as abbot of Jingshan. The inscription reads:

> Rains come, mountains dark;
> Taking a donkey for a horse.
>   Written by the Jingshan monk Shifan[98]

We may conclude with the Southern Song Linji Chan master Xutang Zhiyu's (虛堂智愚) encomium to Dahui:

Chan Master Dahui: Ahead of him no Śākyamuni—behind him no Bodhidharma. He cursed the rain and the wind—he was just arrogant. [Those sunk in] the black lacquer [of ignorance] and [Chan masters who carried] a bamboo clapper—he casually whacked both of them. Whether a buddha or a Māra—face-to-face he spat on them. Due to these things Heaven deigned to confer his ill fate: during his seventeen-year exile in Hengyang and Meiyang he had to

---

97. Unidentified artist. Hanging scroll, ink on paper. Image: 64.1 x 33 cm. Bequest of John M. Crawford Jr., 1988 (1989.363.24). For a discussion of this painting, see Wen C. Fong, *Beyond Representation: Chinese Painting and Calligraphy 8th–14th Century* (New York: Metropolitan Museum of Art and Yale University Press, 1992), 349–352. On the Donkey-rider theme, see Peter C. Sturman, "The Donkey Rider as Icon: Li Cheng and Early Chinese Landscape Painting," *Artibus Asiae* 55, no. 1/2 (1995): 43–97.

98. 雨來山暗。認驢作馬。徑山僧師範書。The phrase "taking a donkey for a horse" appears in a comment on an old standard in the *Xutang heshang yulu* 虛堂和尚語錄 (T2000.47.991b27–29), the sayings record of Xutang Zhiyu (虛堂智愚; 1185–1269). Mujaku Dōchū, Kidōroku *rikō* 虛堂錄犂耕, 146 (an enormous commentary on the *Sayings Record of Preceptor Xutang*) suggests that donkey = *upāya*/conventional truth, and horse = *paramārtha*/ ultimate truth.

bear hunger and want. Some mistakenly thought he was ten-thousand miles away ensconced in exile; but, when his life was returned to him, they realized their mistake. From the very outset he had never made amends for any transgressions. This blind, bald-headed fellow managed to acquire the enmity of everyone. Among gods and humans he was one without a second. Attaboy![99]

---

99. *Xutang heshang yulu* 虛堂和尚語錄: 大慧禪師: 前無釋迦 。 後無達磨 。 罵雨罵風 。 祇要做大 。 黑漆竹篦 。 胡打亂打 。 是佛是魔 。 劈面便唾 。 因茲天降其咎 。 衡陽梅陽 。 十七年吞飢忍餓 。 將謂萬里生還知非 。 元來一星子 。 不曾改過 。 者般瞎禿得人憎 。 天上人間無兩箇 。 咄 。 (T2000.47.1032a25–b1).

Letters of Chan Master Dahui Pujue *Volume One*

RECORDED BY CHAN TRAINEE HUIRAN

REEDITED BY LAYMAN
PURE-WISDOM (HUANG WENCHANG)

[*Commentary: Mujaku says, "Most of these letters are replies to laymen. This is because ordained Chan monks have utterly given themselves up to the dharma and hence are always in the assembly, practicing in the daytime and visiting the master's room in the evenings. Laymen, however, serve in office and are entangled in mundane matters, and so are unable to make frequents visits to the master for face-to-face consultation. They can only write letters asking about the Way. This is the reason why this collection is mostly replies to laymen."[1] Korean Anonymous says, "The main idea of the Letters is distinguishing perverse and correct, and practicing the huatou."[2] Mujaku says, "Huiran for twenty years served Master Dahui. In gathering and recording materials he lost nothing. Daoyin arranged these materials in an orderly manner. Huang Wenchang selected the gist for a reedited collection, and thus the term reedited (appears with his name). What Huiran recorded and Daoyin edited was extensive, but what Wenchang reedited was an abbreviation."[3]*]

---

1. Mujaku, 31: 凡此書荅居家者多蓋出家人爲法捨身故常在其會下朝參暮扣焉如居家則身仕官而世相牽纏故不能累謁面參但可書翰問道而已是故荅居家者多矣.

2. Korean Anonymous, 120: 大意辨邪正參話句.

3. Mujaku, 35: 忠曰蓋慧然二十年侍師隨得采錄無遺失道印編次者條理黃文昌採其肝要重編集故曰重編也其慧然之所錄道印之所編廣矣文昌之重編畧矣. Mujaku, 34, cites Xuefeng Huiran 雪峯慧然 in a list of ninety-four successors of Dahui in *Xu chuandeng lu* 續傳燈錄

1. In Reply to Vice Minister Ceng (Tianyou)
(Question Letter Attached)
[Ceng's Question Letter]

[*Commentary:* Mujaku says, "Ceng Kai was living a leisurely life for more than ten years, and this letter is from that period. Thus, Vice Minister *is a form of address using his old official title."*[4] Hyesim says, "The main purport of this question letter is Ceng's presentation of his own feelings and a respectful request for an encapsulation of the dharma."[5] *Presumably dates to around the same time as Dahui's first reply letter below, Shaoxing 4/1134.*]

[QL 1.1: *Relates Ceng's reverence for Dahui*[6]]

Some time ago, when I was in Changsha in Hunan, I received a letter from your teacher, old Master Yuanwu. He praised you by saying that, even though you were a follower who came to him a little late in the day,[7] your attainment was singularly magnificent. [Because of Yuanwu's letter[8]] I've thought about you repeatedly—now going on eight years. I've always regretted that I have never been able to hear in person even the merest bit [of your discourses]— I've only been able eagerly to admire you [from a distance].[9]

(T2077.51.685c7); he also quotes the *Dahui Pujue chanshi pushuo* 大慧普覺禪師普說: "Attendant Huiran followed Dahui for the longest time. For more than twenty years he was at the master's side, enduring a great many hardships" [然侍者隨老漢最久二十餘年在身邊喫辛苦極多] (CBETA, M059, no. 1540, p. 807, b10–11). Lingyin Daoyin 靈隱道印 is also listed as one of Dahui's ninety-four successors in *Xu chuandeng lu* 續傳燈錄 (T2077.51.685b17). Mujaku, 35, cites Huang Wenchang 黃文昌 in a list of seventy-five successors of Dahui in *Jiatai pudeng lu zong mulu* 嘉泰普燈錄總目錄 (CBETA, X79, no. 1558, p. 283, b30 // Z 2B:10, p. 15, c9 // R137, p. 30, a9).

4. Mujaku, 36: 忠曰曾開居聞十餘年蓋作此書在此際則侍郎稱舊官也.

5. Hyesim, 19: 此來狀大旨呈似己情敬請法要也. For entries for Ceng Kai 曾開 (*zi* 字 Tianyou 天游), see *Song History*, 382 (16.2999) and *Cases of Song and Yuan Confucians*, 26 (2.997). Hucker, 427: "Vice Minister [*shilang* 侍郎] is the 2nd executive post in each of the standard Six Ministries (*liu bu* 六部) of the central government."

6. Mujaku, 37: 第一段敘瞻仰. In the following translation, the section divisions within the sixty-two letters, and the brief headings at the beginning of each section division within each letter, derive from Mujaku.

7. Dahui came to Yuanwu in Xuanhe 宣和 7/1125, when Dahui was thirty-seven and Yuanwu already sixty-two.

8. Mujaku, 37, glosses *nian zhi* 念之 thus: "Because of Yuanwu's letter he thought about Dahui" [依圓悟書而念大慧也].

9. Mujaku, 38, glosses *wei qie jing yang* 惟切景仰 thus: "Since I have not been able to hear in person your discourses due to being far away, I've only been able eagerly to admire you from a distance" [既不得親聞言論身在衰境但得心切慕向仰望而已].

[QL 1.2: *Constitutes a summary of Ceng's whole letter*[10]]

In my youthful years, I produced the aspiration for awakening, did hands-on investigation with teachers, and knocked on their doors concerning *this matter*. After entry into adulthood in my twentieth year, because of demands of family and an official career, my application of *gongfu*[11] was no longer undiluted. I have followed this same old routine down to the present. I've gotten old and still have not heard your teachings firsthand. Of this I am continually ashamed.

[QL 1.3: *Develops the topic of Ceng's aspiration for awakening mentioned in the above summary*[12]]

However, my resolve and aspiration by no means come from a superficial level of understanding. I think that, if I don't awaken, that's the end of it; but, if I do awaken, [I must not accept a low level of understanding as sufficient[13]]—I must directly plumb the personal realization of the ancients, that is, the stage of the great stopping-to-rest. Though this mind of mine has never shrunk back and yielded for even a moment, I am aware that my *gongfu*, in the final analysis, has not been uniformly pure. One might say that my intentions are great, but my strength is minuscule.

[QL 1.4: *Develops the topic of Ceng's hands-on investigation with teachers mentioned in the above summary*[14]]

In the past I took pains to beseech old master Yuanwu, and he instructed me with his *Dharma Talks* in six sections.[15] At the beginning of one talk

---

10. Mujaku, 39: 第二段是一篇大綱.

11. Mujaku, 40, glosses *gongfu* 工夫 thus: "The term *gongfu* originally meant *craftsman* or *artisan*; here it means *laboring with mental power; contemplating* on that matter" [忠曰工夫本言匠者今累勞心力思惟那事].

12. Mujaku, 40: 第三段衍上綱中發心.

13. Mujaku, 41, glosses *bu wu ze yi . . . zhi di* 不悟則已乃至之地 thus: "If I awaken, I must not accept a low level of understanding as sufficient. I must directly plumb the awakening of the ancients" [苟悟則不可得小知見以此爲足矣直須徹到古人悟處也].

14. Mujaku, 41: 第四段衍綱中參礼知識.

15. This refers to the *Yuanwu xin yao* 圓悟心要, which contains two dharma talks addressed to Edict Attendant Ceng (示曾待制). See CBETA, X69, no. 1357, p. 475, b21–c12 // Z 2:25, p. 372, a16–b13 // R120, p. 743, a16–b13; and CBETA, X69, no. 1357, p. 498, b11–c2 // Z 2:25, p. 395, a7–b4 // R120, p. 789, a7–b4. Mujaku, 41, claims that the *Yuanwu xin yao* contains

Yuanwu directly shows *this matter*.[16] At the end of another talk Yuanwu raises the stories of two [old] standards,[17] Yunmen's **Mt. Sumeru** and Zhaozhou's ***put it down***, and says: "Do dull-witted *gongfu* and constantly lift [the *huatou*] to awareness, and after a while you will surely have an experience of awakening."[18] Such was his grandmotherly kindness; but I was so lacking in sharpness, and so stuck, that nothing could be done.

[QL 1.5: *Develops the topic of Ceng's family and official career mentioned in the above summary*[19]]

Fortunately, now my private family obligations are all at an end. I have leisure and no other pressing matters.[20] Right now is precisely the time I

---

only four of the six sections and that two have been lost [圓悟心要但載四段如次引其二段逸矣].

16. In the *Yuanwu xin yao*, the second dharma talk to Ceng begins with: "Chan is not mental thought. The Way cuts off meritorious service. If you take mental thought to practice Chan, it is like drilling ice in pursuit of fire or making a hole in the ground to seek out the heavens. It will just increase the trouble to your spirit" [禪非意想。道絕功勳。若以意想參禪。如鑽冰求火堀地覓天。只益勞神。] (CBETA, X69, no. 1357, p. 498, b12–13 // Z 2:25, p. 395, a8–9 // R120, p. 789, a8–9).

17. Mujaku, 42, glosses *liang ze* 兩則 thus: "We take the sayings of the buddhas and patriarchs as norms, and so we speak of [*old*] *standards*" [忠云以佛祖語爲法則故言則也].

18. In the *Yuanwu xin yao*, the first dharma talk to Ceng ends with: "'The Venerable Yanyang asked Zhaozhou: "What about when you don't bring even a single thing?" Zhaozhou said: "**Put it down!**" The Venerable said: "I didn't bring a single thing, so I don't know what to put down." Zhaozhou said: "*Keep your eye on* whether you've ***put it down***."'... 'A monk asked Yunmen: "When you don't produce even a single thought, is there still a mistake?" Yunmen said: "**Mt. Sumeru**."' [Yuanwu's comment:] This also is the *brief-and-to-the-point* [*path*] *of direct severing. Nothing-to-do*, empty mind, quieted thoughts—do dull-witted *gongfu* and just try to lift [the *huatou*]. After a while you will naturally have an experience of awakening" [嚴陽尊者問趙州。一物不將來時如何。州云放下著。者云。一物不將來。未審放下箇什麼。州云看你放不下。嚴陽遂大悟。.... 僧問雲門。不起一念還有過也無。門云須彌山。此又直截省要也。無事虛心靜慮。且下鈍工夫只管舉看。久之當自有入處。] (CBETA, X69, no. 1357, p. 475, c4–12 // Z 2:25, p. 372, b5–13 // R120, p. 743, b5–13). Yuanwu's *brief-and-to-the-point* [*path*] *of direct severing* (*zhijie shengyao* 直截省要) here may be equal to Dahui's *strategic point of the path of direct severing* (*zhijie jing chuyao* 直截徑要處) in letter #2.2 and Dahui's *taking the direct-and-quick path to comprehension* (*jingjie lihui* 徑截理會) in letter #10.5, both of which refer to *huatou* practice. Yuanwu's usage of the vocabulary *direct severing* and *lift* would suggest that what Yuanwu taught Vice Minister Ceng was *huatou* practice, giving Ceng the two *huatous* **Mt. Sumeru** and ***put it down***.

19. Mujaku, 43: 第五段衍綱中弱冠婚官.

20. Mujaku, 43, glosses *xian ju wu ta shi* 閑居無他事 thus: "I am retired from office and have no public duties" [忠曰休官隱退無公務事也].

should go to great pains to whip myself onward in order to fulfill my very first ambition. My only regret is that I have not yet been able to receive your personal instruction.

[QL 1.6: *Develops the topic of Ceng's ignorance of Dahui's teachings and his request for instruction mentioned in the above summary*[21]]

The blunder that is my whole life I have already presented in its entirety. You will surely be able to see through this mind, and I hope you will give me the benefit of your admonitions. How should I do *gongfu* in the midst of daily activities? I pray that I will not wade through any byways[22] but on the straight-cut will intersect with the *original ground!*

[QL 1.7: *Concluding remarks*[23]]

In my speaking like this I have made more than a few blunders. I have sent only sincerity—I have kept nothing concealed from you. I close with the deepest obeisance.

[*1. Dahui's Reply Letter*]

[*Commentary:* Mujaku says, "The main idea of this letter is to show that karmic obstacles are like an illusion.... The illness of the Vice Minister lies in recognizing karmic obstacles as real things and thus generating fears.... This letter dates to Shaoxing 4/1134 when the Master was forty-six. At the time, he was at Yunmen Hermitage at Yangyu in Quanzhou in Fujian."[24] *Pre-exile letter. The subsequent five letters are presumably around the same time as this letter, Shaoxing 4/1134.*]

---

21. Mujaku, 43: 第六段衍綱中未有所聞而請指示也.

22. Mujaku, 44, glosses *bu she ta tu* 不涉他塗 thus: "I hope I will not take any of the many roads of *upāyas*, but directly mesh with the *original allotment*" [某甲願不涉方便多途欲直契當本分也].

23. Mujaku, 44: 第七段結語.

24. Mujaku, 45: 此書大意示業障如幻.... 侍郎之病在認業障爲實物自生怖畏處.... 此書紹興四年甲寅師四十六歲而作時在洋嶼.

[1.1: *Indicates approval for Ceng's question letter*[25]]

Your letter informs me that, from a young age until you became an official, you made a hands-on investigation of Chan with great masters. In
middle age[26] your mind was constrained by the examinations, family, and
official duties. Also, that you were hobbled by bad awareness and bad
habit-energy from past lives and that you were incapable of doing pure
gongfu. Feeling that this was a great fault and brooding over the fact that
among the various illusions of this impermanent world there is not a
single thing that one can take joy in, you have zeroed your mind in the
desire to investigate *this one great matter.* That is extremely pleasing to this
ailing monk's mind.[27]

[1.2: *Admiration for Ceng's wisdom, cultivated in previous lives, that dreads even a small fault*[28]]

Thus, after you became a member of the scholar-official class, you received
a salary from on high and were able to make a living. The examination system, family concerns, and official position are unavoidable in this world
and do not constitute any fault on your part. You've even turned your
"small fault" into a "great dread": How could you have become so consci-
entious, had you not served true teachers, and experienced deep perfum-
ing with the seeds of *prajñā,* across beginningless aeons?

[1.3: *Clarifies that Ceng's "fault" is in essence illusionary and smashes his dread*[29]]

As for your so-called great fault, even sages and worthies can't avoid these
things.[30] If you merely realize that these "faults" are unreal illusions and

---

25. Mujaku, 45: 第一段舉問書替許.

26. Mujaku, 45: "*zhongjian* 中間 means the middle between youth and old age" [忠曰中間者自幼年至老年之中間也].

27. Mujaku, 47, glosses *bing seng* 病僧 thus: "Because Dahui at just that time was ill, he speaks of himself in that way" [蓋大慧適有病故自稱而已].

28. Mujaku, 47: 第二段讚歎宿智怖小罪.

29. Mujaku, 49: 此段明罪性虛幻破怖.

30. Mujaku, 49, glosses 聖賢亦不能免 thus: "Lay bodhisattvas all have family concerns and official position. The three worthies and ten sages all have the residual habit-energy of the defilements" [在家菩薩皆有婚官三賢十聖皆有煩惱餘習不能免也].

not ultimately real dharmas, if you can turn your mind toward the gate of *this*, taking the wisdom-water of *prajñā* to wash away the filth of defilement, making yourself spontaneously refreshed, in the present moment severing at the single stroke of the sword, no longer producing the mind of continuity [and thereby blocking future "faults"[31]]: this will be enough. There is no need to reflect on [time wasted in] the past or on [what things should be like in] the future.[32] Having said that such "faults" are unreal illusions, "when you created karma" is also an illusion; "when you received the retribution of karma" is also an illusion; "when you awaken" is also an illusion; the past, present, and future are all an illusion. If this very day you realize your mistake,[33] then you'll have taken the illusionary medicine to cure the illusionary illness![34] Once the [illusionary] illness has been cured and the medicine [of illusionary awareness] jettisoned, there will be just the same old person [Ceng] as before. But if there were to be "another Ceng" and "another dharma" [separate from his daily activities],[35] then it would be the evil Māra level of understanding of the outsider Ways. You must take this to heart. Just keep pressing hard[36] like this—even when constantly in the midst of "stillness *über alles*" [i.e., engaging in the practice of sitting]—you

---

31. *Zongjinglu* 宗鏡錄: "As for future faults, cut off the mind of continuity and block future faults. This is called *rescuing*" [未來之罪。斷相續心遮未來故。名之為救。] (T2016.48.766a13).

32. Mujaku, 50, glosses *bu bi si qian nian hou* 不必思前念後 thus: "It is not necessary to reflect upon time wasted in past years or what things should be like in future days" [忠曰不必用思量前年空過後日可如何等事也].

33. Mujaku, 50, glosses *jinri zhi fei* 今日知非 thus: "The following text is a simile. The meaning is: this very day realizing your mistake is like taking a medicine to cure an illness" [下文譬如也言今日知非譬如以藥治病也].

34. Mujaku, 50, glosses *yi huanyao fu zhi huanbing* 以幻藥復治幻病 thus: "Illusionary medicine is an awareness with the potential to cure; illusionary illness is the delusion that is cured. It means that both the awareness and the delusion are illusions" [忠曰幻藥乃能治之知覺幻病乃所治之迷倒謂知覺迷倒皆亦幻].

35. Mujaku, 50, glosses *ruo bie you ren you fa* 若別有人有法 thus: "If the same old Vice Minister Ceng were to change his illusory characteristics to separately realize the *dharmakāya*, if he were to divorce from arising-extinguishing to have some other Way of stillness, then it would be the evil Māra level of understanding of the outsider Ways" [舊時曾侍郎若改其相別證法身若離生滅別有寂滅道則邪魔外道見解也].

36. Mujaku, 50, glosses *ya jiang qu* 崖將去 thus: "A colloquialism: *go on pursuing to the ultimate*—an incisive examination of principle is like going right up to the edge of a precipice" [俗語窮將去也編辟究理趣如到崖邊也]. Iriya Yoshitaka and Koga Hidehiko, *Zengo jiten* (Kyoto: Shibunkaku shuppan, 1991), 57, glosses its entry on *ya* 崖 thus: "Same as *ai* 捱. Also written as *ai* 挨. The meaning is *vigorously keep pressing hard; drive to the wall*" [捱と同じ。挨と書くこともある。ぐいぐいと押しまくる、追いつめてゆく。]. Note that "keep pressing hard" is a key verb in Dahui's *huatou* practice vocabualry.

absolutely must never lose track of the words from the two [old] standards, **Mt. Sumeru** and **put it down**.[37] All you have to do is just keep doing this. There is no need to fear things that have already happened and no need to engage in mental reflection. Mental reflection and fear constitute obstacles to the Way.

[1.4: *Shows the mental work necessary to extinguish habit-energy from past lives*[38]]

Before the buddhas merely generate this great vow: "I vow that this mind of mine will be firm and will never retrogress. Relying on the protection of the buddhas, I will meet a good teacher, at a single word from him forget samsara, realize unexcelled perfect awakening, and perpetuate the wisdom-life[39] of the buddhas, in order to repay my debt of enormous gratitude to the buddhas." If you do it in this way, then, after some time, there is no way you will not awaken. I submit for your inspection [the following from the "Entrance into the *Dharmadhātu* Chapter" of the *Huayan Sutra*[40]]: The youth Sudhana generated the thought of awakening due to Mañjuśrī, step-by-step traveled through the south of India, passed through one hundred and ten cities, and investigated with fifty-three teachers. At the finale [when Sudhana reaches the last three teachers: Maitreya, Mañjuśrī, and Samantabhadra], in the time it took for Maitreya to give a flick of the finger, [Sudhana] all-at-once forgot the dharma teachings he had attained from all the previous teachers. Further, due to Maitreya's teaching, he hoped to be allowed to catch a glimpse of Mañjuśrī. Thereupon Mañjuśrī extended his right hand far off into the distance, over one-hundred ten leagues, and patted Sudhana's head, saying: "Good! Good! Good son! If you separate from the root of confidence, then your mind is weakened and sunk in worry, not possessed of practice, in retreat from zeal, producing a fixation on a single good root,

---

37. The term *words from [old] standards* (*zeyu* 則語) sounds similar to (and is perhaps a precursor of) the term *huatou* (話頭), *pivotal phrase [from an old standard]*, as used in Dahui's mature *huatou* practice vocabualry.

38. Mujaku, 51: 第四段正示滅宿習用心.

39. Mujaku, 52, cites: *Xin fu zhu* 心賦注: "*Wisdom-life* is the inexhaustible thusness-nature of your own mind" [慧命者。即自心無盡真如之性。] (CBETA, X63, no. 1231, p. 99, c23 // Z 2:16, p. 18, d14 // R111, p. 36, b14).

40. T279.10.439b6–c11.

satisfied with a little karmic merit, and incapable of skillfully producing practice and vow. Unprotected by a good teacher, you wind up unable to understand this sort of dharma-nature, this sort of logic, this sort of dharma teaching, this sort of practice, and this sort of realm. Whether all-around knowledge, knowledge of various things, exhaustion of the source, understanding, upward movement, explanation, discrimination, realization, getting something—it is impossible to bring any of them to completion." When Mañjuśrī in this way instructed Sudhana, Sudhana all-at-once[41] completed innumerable dharma teachings, became possessed of the immeasurable great wisdom-light, entered the gate of Samantabhadra, in a single moment saw as many teachers as if the three-thousand great-thousand worlds had been smashed into particles of dust and each dust particle were a teacher. He approached each of them, with respect served them, received their teachings, and attained the non-forgetting mindfulness-wisdom adornment-treasury liberation. He ended up in the buddha lands of the hair-follicles of Samantabhadra. When he walked a single step within a single hair-follicle, he passed over inexpressible, inexpressible buddha lands and innumerable worlds—equal to Samantabhadra, equal to the buddhas, equal to the [buddha] lands, equal to practice, equal to all of the freedoms of liberation, non-dual and undifferentiated." At just such a time,[42] one is able, for the first time, to convert the three poisons into the three assemblages of pure precepts,[43] convert the six consciousnesses into the six supernormal powers, convert the defilements into awakening, and convert ignorance into great wisdom. This one excerpt above just deals with Sudhana's reality at the single moment of the finale. Sudhana, in the time it took for Maitreya to snap his fingers, was able suddenly to let go of the *samādhis* [meditative concentrations] he had realized under all those teachers—how much more so his beginningless unreal habit-energy of bad karma! If the "fault" you previously committed is real, then the sense fields in front of

---

41. Mujaku, 66, glosses *yu yan xia* 於言下 thus: "These three characters are not in the sutra text. This is a common expression of the Zen house" [忠曰此三字非經文禪家常語].

42. Korean Anonymous, 121, glosses *dang nenme shi shi neng xia* 當恁麼時始能下 thus: "These are Dahui's words" [大惠言也].

43. Mujaku, 69, for *wei san ju jingjie* 爲三聚淨戒 cites: *Dasheng yi zhang* 大乘義章: "The three assemblages of pure precepts are: restraint precept; embracing-good-dharmas precept; and embracing-sentient-beings precept" [三聚戒者。謂律儀戒攝善法戒攝眾生戒。] (T1851.44.659a5–6).

you right now are all really existent, down to and including: your official position, affluence and eminence, debts of gratitude, and love—all are real. Since they are real, then hells and heavenly palaces are also real; the defilements and ignorance are also real; the creation of karma is also real; receiving karmic recompense is also real; and the dharma teachings that you realize are also real. If you hold this sort of level of understanding, then, for all time into the future, nobody would ever arrive at the buddha-fruit![44] The buddhas of the three times, the patriarchal masters down through the generations, and the various teaching devices would instead be lies.

[1.5: *Relates that both Ceng's question and Dahui's reply are truly sincere*[45]]

I am informed that, when you sent off your letter, you burned incense while facing the noble ones, bowed to [my residence at Yunmen] Hermitage from afar, and afterwards dispatched it. Your mind of sincerity was fervent to such a degree. Although we are not at an extreme distance from each other, we have not had the opportunity to speak face to face. Letting my mind and my brush hand take their spontaneous course, without being aware of it, I have rambled on like this. Although I have been irksome, it emerges from the utmost sincerity. In not one word of it have I dared to deceive you. If I have deceived you, then it is no more than self-deception.

[1.6: *Quotes Śiva-rāgra Brahman to prove the sincerity of Ceng's words*[46]]

Something else has come to mind: Sudhana met [the forty-ninth teacher] Śiva-rāgra Brahman and was able to hear him sincerely speak of liberation: "The past, present, and future buddhas and bodhisattvas from unexcelled awakening have not retrogressed, are not retrogressing, and will not

---

44. Mujaku, 71, for *wu you ren qu foguo* 無有人趣佛果 cites: *Zhong lun* 中論: "If there were no emptiness, what has not yet been attained would not be attained; and there would be no cutting off of the defilements; and there would be no bringing to an end of suffering" [若無有空者。未得不應得。亦無斷煩惱。亦無苦盡事。] (T1564.30.34b26–c5).

45. Mujaku, 72: 第五段敘問酬俱誠實.

46. Mujaku, 73: 第六段引最寂靜證侍郎誠語.

retrogress. The fact that nothing of what they seek remains unfulfilled all comes from extreme sincerity."[47] You are already a companion of the bamboo chair and the sitting cushion [i.e., the implements for the practice of sitting[48]]: no different from Sudhana when he meets Śiva-rāgra Brahman. Also, in sending a letter to me at Yunmen [Hermitage], after facing the noble ones and bowing [in the direction of Yunmen Hermitage] from afar, you dispatched it, just because you wanted my confidence and acceptance. This shows the intensity of your utmost sincerity.

[1.7: *Concluding remarks*[49]]

Just listen: If you just do *gongfu* in this way,[50] in the future—without a doubt—you will complete unexcelled awakening.

2. *Continued [Second Letter in Reply to Vice Minister Ceng]*

[*Commentary: Mujaku says, "The main intention of this letter is to show that intellectual understanding is an obstacle, and because of it one will not be able to arrive at stopping-to-rest."*[51] *Presumably dates to around the same time as letter #1, Shaoxing 4/1134. Pre-exile letter.*]

[2.1: *Indulges in praise*[52]]

Even though your status is one of affluence and eminence, you have not been warped by affluence and eminence. How could this be so, if you hadn't planted wisdom-seeds of *prajñā* in past births?[53]

---

47. T293.10.807c22–27.

48. Mujaku, 74, glosses *yu zhuyi putuan wei lü* 與竹椅蒲團爲侶 thus: "Both are implements for Zen sitting" [二器皆坐禪之具].

49. Mujaku, 76: 第七段詰語.

50. Note that Dahui has not yet explicitly laid out his own schema of *huatou* practice to Ceng, so it can be inferred that "*gongfu* in this way" refers to his teacher Yuanwu's *huatou* method, which Ceng had already been assigned—and which Dahui himself has inherited.

51. Mujaku, 77: 此書大意示知解爲障故不得到休歇地.

52. Mujaku, 77: 第一段歎縱.

53. Mujaku, 77, glosses *su zhi bore zhong zhi* 凤植般若種智 thus: "In past lives he planted the seeds of *prajñā*" [忠曰宿世植得般若種子也].

[2.2: *Censures intellectual understanding as an obstacle—a synopsis of the whole letter*[54]]

The only thing that worries me is that somewhere along the line you have forgotten this [Mahāyāna] mind-set [of not waiting for awakening].[55] Because you've become blocked by your keen intelligence, you have set up in front of you a mind that has something to obtain [i.e., awakening].[56] You are unable to avail yourself of the ancients' direct-and-quick path of severing [i.e., **Mt. Sumeru** and **put it down**[57]]—to attain a decisive stopping-to-rest at the single stroke of the sword.

[2.3: *Censures running around seeking a* real *dharma*[58]]

This illness [of having something to obtain[59]] is not just that of particularly able and virtuous members of the scholar-official class, for Chan monks of long practice also contract it. Most are unwilling to "take a step back" [i.e., to forego running after intellectual knowledge, and instead to search out where intellectual knowledge arises from[60]] and do *gongfu* in terms of

---

54. Mujaku, 77: 第二段責知解爲障此段一篇大綱.

55. Mujaku, 77, glosses *zhong wang ci yi* 中忘此意 thus: "*Midway* means between those past births when you planted *prajñā* and your present life" [忠曰中間謂夙世往古種般若時與今世之中間也] and cites the *Vimalakīrti Sūtra*: "Pūrṇa! This monk long ago produced the Mahāyāna mind. Midway he forgot this aspiration. How can you lead him with the Hīnayāna teaching?" [富樓那。此比丘久發大乘心。中忘此意。如何以小乘法而教導之。] (T475.14.541a2–4).

56. Mujaku, 77, glosses *you suode xin* 有所得心 thus: "*Having something to obtain* means that Chan practitioners in both movement and stillness want to obtain the dharma and want to obtain awakening. Though this idea of facing towards the Way is to be valued, if one takes this mind and puts it right before one's eyes to do *gongfu*, then this mind simply becomes an obstacle and blocks the direct-and-quick road. This is called *having the mind wait for awakening*" [忠曰有所得心者修禪之人起居動靜欲得法欲得悟也此向道之意雖可貴若以此心安在目前下工夫則其心直成隔礙而障徑截之路所謂以心等悟也].

57. Mujaku, 78, glosses *zhi jie jing yaochu* 直截徑要處 thus: "Means **Mt. Sumeru** and **put it down**" [言須彌山放下著也]. Note that by using "direct-and quick," Dahui is employing *huatou*-practice vocabulary, which Mujaku has understood to apply to Yuanwu's *huatous* **Mt. Sumeru** and **put it down**.

58. Mujaku, 78: 第三段責馳求實法.

59. Mujaku, 78, glosses *ci bing* 此病 thus: "The illness of having something to obtain" [有所得之病也].

60. Mujaku, 79, glosses *tui bu* 退步 thus: "Means not running after intellectual knowledge. If intellectual knowledge arises, instead search out where intellectual knowledge arises from. This is taking a step back. In Vice Minister Ceng's question letter [#1.4] it's called 'dull-witted *gongfu*' [by Yuanwu]" [忠曰言不走知解也若知解生却尋知解起處此即退步者也曾侍郎問書所謂鈍工是也].

saving on expenditure of energy.[61] They just, with their clever intelligence, calculate and engage in mental reflection, rushing around seeking on the outside. Even if they happen to experience—outside of clever intelligence, mental reflection, and calculation—a good teacher's demonstration of the "fodder for the *original-allotment*" [i.e., the stick, the shout, verbal teachings, and so forth[62]], most of them, in the face-to-face encounter with the teacher, end up mistakenly thinking that the ancient worthies of old did have a "real" dharma to give people, such as Zhaozhou's **put it down** and Yunmen's **Mt. Sumeru**. Yantou[63] said: "Expelling things is high, and

---

61. Mujaku, 79, glosses *sheng li* 省力 thus: "*Sheng* 省 doesn't have the meaning *awaken* [where it is read *xing*]. It means *save on/economize on/cut down on labor*. There are two types. People who are more or less unripened ordinarily rely on intellectual understanding and intelligence, in their minds storing up words and phrases and properly arranging principles. This involves a lot of labor, and for this Way it's completely useless, incapable of resisting samsara. When one does true *gongfu*, one directly lets go of the usual intellectual understanding and the proper arranging of phrases from the sutras. One only turns the light backwards and does a reverse-illumination, putting one's hand to passing a judgment on mind. The second is people who are more or less ripened. It means that their *gongfu* is gradually ripening, and pure and impure are mixed together. It's like the following. All-at-once phantasmal thoughts arise one-hundred times, and [the practitioner] lifts [the *huatou*] to awareness also one-hundred times. Now phantasmal thoughts arise ninety times, and for the ten times left over he does not labor over lifting [the *huatou*] to awareness—spontaneously it's a pure oneness. This is saving by ten times on the expenditure of energy in lifting [the *huatou*] to awareness. When phantasmal thoughts arise eighty times, it's saving by twenty times on the expenditure of energy in lifting [the *huatou*] to awareness, and so forth. It's like the ripening of a persimmon. When a little bit of ripenedness is added, a little bit of unripenedness is subtracted. When it's half-ripened, then it remains half unripened. A later letter [#6.5] says: 'You gradually notice that the moment of saving on expenditure of energy [in the *gongfu* of raising the *huatou* to awareness] is none other than the state of gaining energy [for awakening], etc.' It's like saying that the persimmon's lack of greenness is yellow ripenedness" [忠曰省者非省悟義乃省除勞力也此有二種一約未熟人謂尋常依知解聰明胸中蓄積言句安排義理其勞力之多而於此道全無益矣不能抵對生死也如真做工夫時直放下平生知解安排經論言句單單回光返照著手心頭判去如是進修此名省力謂省除知解安排勞力也二約已熟人謂工夫漸熟而純駁?相雜譬如一時內妄念起百回舉覺提撕亦百回者今妄念起九十回則其餘十回不勞舉覺提撕自然純一也是省十回提撕力也妄念八十回則省二十回提撕力等可知譬如柿熟少分熟處加則少分生處減已半熟則生處半殘耳後書曰漸覺省力時便是得力處也此此猶言柿無青處即黃熟處耳].

62. Mujaku, 80, glosses *benfen caoliao* 本分草料 thus: "Undoubtedly, as for the stick, the shout, and verbal teachings, students' *original allotment* has the principle of being able to 'eat' these, and teachers dare to provide them with them the stick, the shout, and verbal teachings. Therefore, they are called 'the fodder for the *original-allotment*,' a comparison to the fodder for horses" [蓋棒喝及言句學人本分有可喫此之道理而師家敢與之以棒喝言句故云本分草料以比馬之本分草料也].

63. For a biographical entry for Yantou Quanhuo 巖頭全奯/豁 (828–887), a successor of Deshan Xuanjian 德山宣鑑, see *Jingde chuandeng lu* 景德傳燈錄, T2076.51.326a9–327a10.

pursuing things is low."[64] He also said: "The essential directive of Chan is that you must be on familiar terms with the *phrase* [i.e., the *huatou*].[65] What is *phrase*? When you are thinking of nothing at all, that's called correct *phrase* [i.e., correct *huatou* practice]. It's also called *residing at the pinnacle*. It's also called *abiding*. It's also called *clear*. It's also called *wide-awake*. It's also called the *in-that-way moment*. By means of that *in-that-way* moment, one uniformly annihilates all affirmation/negation. But as soon as [you become fixated upon] *in that way*, [no longer is it thinking of nothing at all, and so] it's immediately not *in that way*.[66] Any affirmation of the *phrase* or negation of the *phrase* is to be shaved off. [The perfection of *prajñā*] is like a ball of fire—if you touch it, you'll be burned.[67] There is no way to approach."[68]

[2.4: *Intellectual brilliance is an obstruction to one's attaining realization*[69]]

Most members of the scholar-official class these days take mental reflection and calculation as their lair.[70] When they hear *in-that-way* talk[71] [such

---

64. This and the following Yantou quotation are found in the Yantou section of *Liandeng hui yao* 聯燈會要 (CBETA, X79, no. 1557, p. 182, c1-10 // Z 2B:9, p. 389, d4-13 // R136, p. 778, b4-13). Hyesim, 27, glosses *que wu* 却物 (expelling things) as *huo ju* 活句 (*living phrase*) and *zhu wu* 逐物 (pursuing things) as *si ju* 死句 (*lifeless phrase*). Korean Anonymous, 122: "Expelling things is probing the *phrase* without mental reflection; pursuing things is probing the *phrase* with mental reflection" [却物參句不思量逐物參句思量].

65. Hyesim, 27: "The essential directive of Chan is the *huatou*" [大統綱宗即是話句].

66. Mujaku, 83, glosses *cai nenme bian bu nenme* 纔恁麼便不恁麼 thus: "When *in that way*, if you're fixated, then it isn't thinking of nothing at all, and so immediately it's not *in that way*. Also, *in that way* becomes a 'correct' position and not *in that way* a 'biased' position" [恁麼時若住著則不是百不思故直下便不恁麼去又恁麼正位不恁麼偏位].

67. Mujaku, 83, cites: *Da zhidu lun* 大智度論 (T1509.25.139c19–21).

68. Mujaku, 83, glosses *you shenme xiangbang chu* 有甚麼向傍處 thus: "You absolutely must soar up and throw your entire self into the flames—you will see that the flames and your self are one and the same" [直須全身奮飛投入去便見焰身無二無別].

69. Mujaku, 83: 第四段引聰慧爲障人證.

70. Mujaku, 83, glosses *kuzhai* 窟宅 thus: "Means that their constant abode is like the cave of a fox or wolf" [謂常居處如狐狼之穴也].

71. Mujaku, 83, glosses *nenme shuohua* 恁麼說話 thus: "Such talk as 'thinking of nothing at all,' 'any affirmation of the *phrase* or negation of the *phrase* is to be shaved off,' etc." [或百不思或是句亦劄非句亦劄等語話也].

as this], they immediately say: "Doesn't that fall into emptiness?" This is like jumping into the water to preempt the boat's capsizing![72] It's quite pathetic. Recently I went to Jiangxi and met Lü Juren [letters #29, #31–#32]. Juren has been interested in *this matter* for a very long time, but he also has a bad case of this illness [of fearing a fall into emptiness].[73] There can be no mistaking that he is bright. I have asked him: "You are 'fearful of falling into emptiness'; but the subject who notices this fear—is he empty or non-empty? Speak!" He stood still, lost in thought,[74] calculating what to reply. Instantly I gave a shout.[75] To this day he's stumped and doesn't have a clue.[76] This is because he takes the mind of seeking awakening[77] and puts it right in front of him, creating his own obstacle—there's no other reason. You, sir, should make an attempt to "do *gongfu* in this way" [i.e., do *huatou* practice].[78] After many, many days and months spontaneously it will "click."[79]

---

72. Mujaku, 84, glosses *zhou wei fan xian zi tiaoxia shui qu* 舟未翻先自跳下水去: "It's like someone's driving a boat (the practitioner). He fears that this boat will overturn and become a danger (fears emptiness). Before it's even overturned, he first throws himself into the sea (falls into intellectual understanding). Even though the boat's overturning and his throwing himself in are different, his drowning in the sea and losing his life are the same" [譬如乘舡者(修行者)恐此舡翻覆可危(怕空)未翻覆已前先投身於海(落知解)也舡覆自投雖有異其沒海喪身一也].

73. Mujaku, 85, glosses *ci bing* 此病 thus: "The illness of fearing a fall into emptiness" [怕落空之病].

74. Mujaku, 86, glosses *zhu si* 佇思 thus: "As before, he was about to use intellectual understanding to answer, and so he stood still, lost in thought" [依前欲以知解答話故佇思也].

75. Mujaku, 86, glosses *yu yi he* 與一喝 thus: "The shout smashes calculation and logical arranging" [喝破計較按排也].

76. A parallel passage in *Dahui Pujue chanshi yulu* 大慧普覺禪師語錄 (*Dahui Pujue chanshi fayu* 大慧普覺禪師法語) runs as follows: "At ordinary times he just takes mental reflection and conjecture as his lair. As soon as he hears someone speak a *huatou* that is not susceptible to mental reflection, he's stumped and doesn't have a clue. He little imagines that it's precisely this state of not having a clue that is the time you jettison your own life" [蓋平時只以思量卜度為窟宅。乍聞說著不得思量底話。便茫然無討巴鼻處。殊不知。只這無討巴鼻處。便是自家放身命底時節也。] (T1998A.47.908a17–20).

77. Mujaku, 86, glosses *qiu wuzheng zhi xin* 求悟證之心 thus: "The mind that has something to obtain" [有所得心也].

78. Mujaku, 86, glosses *ru ci zuo gongfu* 如此做工夫 thus: "*In this way* refers to the baseline of cutting off intellectual understanding, and 'thinking of nothing at all'" [忠曰如此者指泯絕知解百不思之端的]. For "thinking of nothing at all," see #2.3.

79. Mujaku, 509, glosses *zhuzhuo kezhuo* 築著磕著 thus: "In all matters you will tally with the *original allotment*" [忠曰言事事上物物上契當本分也]. ZGK, 12.39 glosses this expression thus: "Translated as *things come together closely/fit to a T*" [ケッチリカッチリと譯す。].

[2.5: *Smashes having something to obtain*[80]]

If you have your mind assume a posture of waiting for awakening, if you have your mind assume a posture of waiting for stopping-to-rest, even if you practice from right now until the future buddha Maitreya appears, you won't be able to attain awakening, you won't be able to attain stopping-to-rest. You will just add on more and more delusive worrying. Preceptor Pingtian said: "The fact that the spirit light [of *prajñā*[81]] never goes dark is the wonderful Way[82] of ten-thousand ages. In entering this gate one does not preserve intellectual understanding."[83]

[2.6: *Also quotes an ancient worthy's words to cut off intellectual understanding and kudzu-verbiage*[84]]

Also, an ancient worthy said: "*This matter* cannot be sought via having-mind, cannot be gotten via no-mind; cannot be reached via language, and cannot be comprehended via stillness or silence."[85] This is top-of-the-line, bogged-down-in-mud-and-water, "old-grandma [*upāya* or skill-in-means] talk."[86] Often those who practice Chan just memorize such talk—little do they imagine that the reason for it is *upāya*. If it's a person who has grit, when he hears even a little bit of this sort of talk, he immediately takes the precious sword of the Vajra King and with a single blow severs the

---

80. Mujaku, 86: 第五段破有所得.

81. Mujaku, 87, glosses *shenguang bu mei* 神光不昧 thus: "The spirit light of *prajñā* is unfathomable; in both the common person and the noble one it never changes and never goes dark" [忠曰般若靈光神妙不可測在凡在聖常不變而不昧].

82. Mujaku, 87, glosses *wan gu huixian* 萬古徽獻 thus: "*Huixian* is wonderful Way" [忠曰徽獻者妙道也].

83. *Jingde chuandeng lu* 景德傳燈錄 (T2076.51.267a16–21). Pingtian Pu'an 平田普岸 (770–843) was a successor of Baizhang Huaihai.

84. Mujaku, 88: 第六段又引古德語斷知解葛藤.

85. *Baoning Renyong chanshi yulu* 保寧仁勇禪師語錄 (CBETA, X69, no. 1350, p. 279, b19–21 // Z 2:25, p. 175, c7–9 // R120, p. 350, a7–9). Renyong was a Song period master in the Yangqi wing of the Linji lineage.

86. Mujaku, 88, glosses *ru ni ru shui* 入泥入水 thus: "*Mud and water* refers to defiled places. It is a metaphor for *upāya* talk that leads people who are not seated in the *original allotment* 'upward [towards the *great matter*]'" [忠曰泥水者污穢之處比方便言句接人不坐本分向上地].

kudzu-verbiage of these four roads:[87] then the road of samsara is cut off; the road of the common person/noble one is cut off; calculation and mental reflection are cut off; and gain/loss and right/wrong are cut off. The person on duty right now is naked, neat and tidy—there is nothing for him to grasp at. How could he not be elated? How could he not be unimpeded?

[2.7: *Quotes the story of an ancient to prove that* this matter *is never intellectual understanding*[88]]

I submit for your inspection: In olden days Preceptor Guanxi made a face-to-face investigation with Linji.[89] When Linji saw him coming, he immediately got down off his seat and seized him by the collar. Guanxi then said: "I understand! I understand!" Linji knew that he had already penetrated to awakening and immediately pushed him out. He had no further words to give him to haggle over. At just such a moment,[90] how could Guanxi have responded with mental reflection and calculation? We are fortunate in having such a model from the past. The reason why people of today have no appreciation whatsoever for this is none other than mental reflection.[91] If Guanxi right from the beginning had manifested even a bit of the mind that waits for awakening, waits for realization, and waits for stopping-to-rest, it couldn't be said that he immediately awakened when grabbed by the collar. [Even if Linji had] bound [Guanxi] hand and foot [instead of just seizing him by the collar[92]] or [Guanxi] had done a circuit of all-under-heaven, [as long as he had something to obtain in his mind,] he still would not have been able to attain awakening or stopping-to-rest.

---

87. Mujaku, 88, glosses *si lu geteng* 四路葛藤 thus: "The four of having mind; no mind; verbalization; and silence" [有心無心語言寂默之四].

88. Mujaku, 88: 第七段引古人因緣證此事本非知解.

89. *Liandeng hui yao* 聯燈會要 (CBETA, X79, no. 1557, p. 95, c5–7 // Z 2B:9, p. 302, b11–13 // R136, p. 603, b11–13) and *Jingde chuandeng lu* 景德傳燈錄 (T2076.51.294b12–16). Guanxi Zhixian 灌溪志閑 (?–895) was a successor of Linji Yixuan.

90. Mujaku, 89, glosses *nenme shi* 恁麼時 thus: "The moment of being seized by the collar" [驀胸擒住時也].

91. Hyesim, 27, glosses *cu xin* 麤心 thus: "Mental reflection and calculation" [思量計較].

92. Mujaku, 89, glosses *fuque shou jiao* 縛却手脚 thus: "Responds to the line *seized him by the collar*" [應驀胸擒住語也].

[2.8: *Intellectual understanding as delusion*[93]]

Habitual calculation and logical arrangement are delusion. Getting swept up in the flow of samsara[94] also is delusion. Getting "fearful and anxious" [about these things][95] also is delusion. Today's practitioners, not noticing that these are an illness, simply bob up and down in [delusion[96]]. As is said in the teachings: "Following after consciousness, not following after wisdom."[97] By doing this one darkens the *original ground* or *original face*.

[2.9: *Flip over consciousness into wisdom*[98]]

If you can all-at-once put down [delusion[99]], engage in no mental reflection or calculation at all,[100] suddenly lose your footing and "tread on the *nose*" [of that one person of the *original allotment*[101]], then this delusion is suddenly the wonderful wisdom of true emptiness, and there is no further wisdom beyond [the elimination of delusion[102]] to be obtained. If there were something beyond that to be obtained, something else to be realized, it would not be [the wonderful wisdom of true emptiness]. When people

---

93. Mujaku, 89: 第八段爲知解安名安名者所謂識情也.

94. Mujaku, 89, glosses *sui shengsi qianliu* 隨生死遷流 thus: "The samsara of the examinations, marriage, and official career—echoes Ceng's previous letter" [隨科舉婚官之生死也即響于前書].

95. Mujaku, 90, glosses *pabu zhangxing de* 性怕怖憧惺底 thus: "*Fearful and anxious* here is intended to smash Ceng's fear about prior 'faults' in his previous letter" [今怕怖憧惺者因破前書怖先罪也].

96. Mujaku, 90, glosses *lixu* 裏許 thus: "Inside delusion" [識情之裏許也].

97. Mujaku, 90, cites the *Vimalakīrti Sūtra*: "Depend on wisdom; don't depend on consciousness" [依於智。不依識] (T475.14.556, c9).

98. Mujaku, 91: 第九段轉識爲智.

99. Mujaku, 91, glosses *fang de xia* 放得下 thus: "Put down the above delusion" [放下得上之識情也].

100. Mujaku, 91, glosses *bai bu siliang jijiao* 百不思量計較 thus: "Responding to Yantou's saying 'thinking of nothing at all'" [應前巖頭百不思語]. See #2.3.

101. Mujaku, 91, glosses *bikong* 鼻孔 thus: "Here the *kong* character has no significance. The meaning is merely tread on the *nose* of that one person of the *original allotment*" [忠曰今者孔字無意義但是踢著本分那一人鼻頭之義耳].

102. Mujaku, 91, glosses *geng wu bie zhi ke de* 更無別智可得 thus: "Beyond the elimination of delusion there is no further wonderful wisdom. Even so, this is a matter that comes after 'treading on the *nose*'" [忠曰除識情外無別妙智也雖然是踢著鼻孔以後事也].

are deluded, they call the east the west;[103] when they reach awakening, the west *is* the east—there is no separate east.

[2.10: *Discusses the fact that wonderful wisdom does not negate samsara*[104]]

This wonderful wisdom of true emptiness is as all-encompassing as the great sky. Within this great sky, is there any single thing that can obstruct it? Though it's not obstructed by any single thing, it in turn does not obstruct the coming and going of all things in its emptiness. This wonderful wisdom of true emptiness is also like that. The defilements of birth/death and common/noble cannot stick [to true emptiness] in the least. Although they can't stick [to true emptiness], there is no obstruction to the coming and going of birth/death and common/noble within [true emptiness].

[2.11: *Urges confidence*[105]]

When one's confidence gets to this point and one's vision is penetrating, then he is a fellow who has obtained the great freedom, and he exits and enters samsara at will. Then for the first time he will be in a certain amount of conformity with Zhaozhou's **put it down** and Yunmen's **Mt. Sumeru**. If your confidence is insufficient and you haven't **put it down**, then please do shoulder **Mt. Sumeru** and lug it around with you everywhere. If you meet a person with a clear eye, present your level of understanding![106] Ha! Ha![107]

---

103. Mujaku, 91, glosses *ren mi shi huan dong zuo xi* 人迷時喚東作西 thus: "East is a metaphor for true wisdom; west is a metaphor for delusion" [忠曰東喻真智西喻識情].

104. Mujaku, 91: 第十段論妙智不破生死.

105. Mujaku, 92: 第十一段勸信.

106. Mujaku, 92, glosses *jusi* 舉似 thus: "Here *jusi* means raise **Mt. Sumeru** and make a presentation to him—haggle over this *huatou*" [今舉似者拈起須彌山呈人看也比商量此話也].

107. Mujaku, 92, glosses *yi xiao* 一笑 thus: "The single laugh is over the joke about **Mt. Sumeru**. This single laugh pertains to both Vice Minister Ceng and Dahui himself. It means: 'I can laugh and you certainly can too!'" [就擔須彌山之戲謔之詞言一笑也乃此一笑係曾侍郎與我大慧兩人也言我可笑公定可笑也]. It can also mean the laugh of awakening.

3. *Continued [Third Letter in Reply to Vice Minister Ceng]*

[*Commentary: Mujaku says, "The main idea of this letter is that Dahui knows the Vice Minister has been misled by perverse teachers and now wants to smash this perverse understanding, enabling the Vice Minister to cease falling prey to perverse teachers."[108] Presumably dates to around the same time as letter #1, Shaoxing 4/1134. Pre-exile letter.*]

[3.1: *In the desire to smash perverse understanding, Dahui first indicates what correct understanding is*][109]

Old Pang said: "Just **vow to empty the existent. Don't reify the non-existent.**"[110] If you just awaken to these two phrases [i.e., *huatous*], the training of a lifetime will be finished.

[3.2: *Lists perverse understandings*[111]]

At the present time, there is a type of shaven-headed heterodox monk who, even though his own eye is not yet clarified, single-mindedly teaches people to stop-to-rest[112] in the very way the [mythic] *gedan*-beast plays dead.[113] If you practice this sort of stopping-to-rest, by the time a thousand buddhas have appeared in this world, you still won't have been able to stop or take a rest! You will just have made your mind more susceptible to delusive worrying. They also teach people, in the course of encountering

---

108. Mujaku, 93: 此書大意大慧知侍郎爲邪師所謬今破其邪解而令之不隨邪師.

109. Mujaku, 93: 第一段欲破邪解先標正解.

110. *Pang jushi yulu* 龐居士語錄 (CBETA, X69, no. 1336, p. 134, b8–14 // Z 2:25, p. 31, b8–14 // R120, p. 61, b8–14). Korean Anonymous, 123: "The first line negates the eternalist view; the second line negates the annihilationist view" [上句破常見下句破斷見也].

111. Mujaku, 93: 第二段列邪解.

112. Mujaku, 94, glosses *xiuqu xiequ* 休去歇去 thus: "This is producing an inferior level of understanding that is based on maintaining the empty quiescence of quelling delusive thought" [此是守忘懷空寂而生解者]. Korean Anonymous, 123, glosses *xiuqu xiequ* 休去歇去 thus: "It merely maintains the one part of thusness, and so it's called 'excluding all phenomenal characteristics'" [但守真如理一分排却一切事相之謂也].

113. Mujaku, 94, glosses *si gedan de* 死獦狚地 thus: "The term *gedan* 獦狚 is the name of a beast that is like a wolf but red in color.... This beast tricks people by playing dead, and then, when they approach, he catches and devours them" [獦狚獸名似狼而赤.... 此獸欺人詐爲死令人近遂搏而食之].

sense objects, to "engird mind";[114] and to quell delusive thought [in] "silence-as-illumination."[115] "Silence-as-illumination" over and over, "engirding mind" over and over—these just increase delusive worries

---

114. Mujaku, 95, glosses *you jiao ren suiyuan guandai* 又教人隨緣管帶 thus: "The term *sui-yuan* 隨緣 means sense objects. One accepts the forms that are seen, the sounds that are heard, and so forth; one contemplates and is mindful [*anusmṛti*] of audibles, forms, and so forth.... The *Śūraṃgama Sūtra* says: 'Ananda said: "At present the Buddha has asked where mind exists, and so I take mind to investigate and seek for it. The potential to investigate I consider to be mind." The Buddha said: "Tut-tut, Ananda, this is not your mind." Ananda, looking around in fear, left his seat, made the respectful gesture of putting his palms together, stood up, and said to the Buddha: "If this is not my mind, what should I call it?" The Buddha told Ananda: "This is the sense objects in front of you—unreal characteristics and thoughts—they are deluding your true nature. Because from time without beginning down to your present birth you have recognized bandits as sons and lost your original constancy, you have been turning on the wheel of samsara"' [T945.19.108c15–21]. Mujaku says: 'The idea here is the same as this sutra quotation, i.e., calculating that all sounds heard and forms seen are simply the *original person*. In fact, forms seen and sounds heard are delusion, the basis upon which false mind arises. Therefore, this letter [to Vice Minister Ceng] later on [#3.4] says: "This produces an inferior level of understanding that maintains a mirror reflection of [sense objects] in front of you"'" [隨緣者緣境也領納所見色所聞聲等境觀念聞者見者是也.... 楞嚴經曰阿難言如來現今徵心所在而我以心推窮尋逐即能推者我將以心佛言咄阿難此非汝心阿難矍然避座合掌起立白佛此非我心當名何等佛告阿難此是前塵虛妄相想惑汝真性由汝無始至于今生認賊為子失汝元常故受輪轉忠曰今意同此謂計一切聞聲見色底直是本來人也其實見聞底是識情也是妄心生之根本故下文曰教人管帶此是守目前鑑覺而生解者].

115. Mujaku, 95, glosses *wangqing mozhao* 忘情默照 thus: "This is not truly quelling delusive thought. It is merely that crude thoughts of such objective supports as forms, sounds, and so forth, are temporarily subdued and that is called *quelling delusive thought*. This is recognizing delusion as fundamentally correct and grasping it. Therefore, when one emerges from *dhyāna*, the false thoughts flutter up in confusion just as before" [忠曰此非謂真忘情也但其緣色聲等麁念暫伏處名忘情耳此是認識情根本爲是執之故出禪定則妄念紛飛如初也]. ZGK, 52–53.216, cites two other key Dahui passages that discuss perverse teachings in Chan. The first is *Dahui Pujue chanshi pushuo* 大慧普覺禪師普說: "Members of the scholar-official class, in studying the Way, don't get beyond two wrong branches at a fork in the road. One is quelling delusive thought; the other is [effortfully] concentrating mind. Concentrating mind is what the hogwash teachers call *guandai* [engirding mind]. Quelling delusive thought is what the hogwash teachers call *silence-as-illumination*. If the two illnesses, engirding mind and silence-as-illumination, are not eliminated, one will never be capable of escaping samsara" [士大夫學道不出二種歧路一曰忘懷一曰著意所謂著意者杜撰長老喚作管帶是也忘懷者杜撰長老喚作默照是也管帶默照二種病不除則不能出生死] (CBETA, M059, no. 1540, p. 961, b17–19); and *Dahui Pujue chanshi yulu* 大慧普覺禪師語錄: "At the present time not only Chan monks, but members of the scholar-official class who are clever and bright and erudite and learned in books, collectively have two types of illness. If they aren't given to [effortfully] concentrating mind, they're given to quelling delusive thought. By quelling delusive thought they fall into the "ghost-cave of Black Mountain." In the teachings, this is called *torpor*. Concentrating mind leads to the fluttering about of thoughts. One thought continues into another, and, before the earlier thought has stopped, a later thought continues. In the teachings, it's called *restlessness*" [今時不但禪和子。便是士大夫聰明靈利博極群書底人。箇箇有兩般病。若不著意。便是忘懷。忘懷則墮在黑山下鬼窟裏。教中謂之昏沈。著意則心識紛飛。一念續一念。前念未止後念相續。教中謂之掉舉。] (T1998A.47.884c17–21).

interminably. [These perverse teachers] utterly misconstrue the *upāyas*[116] of the patriarchal masters and give people preposterous instruction, making them intently waste their whole lives and end up in old age with nothing to show for it. And *then* they teach people to pay no attention to any matter [mundane or supramundane]![117] [They teach:] "Merely *in that way* stop and keep on stopping over and over so that delusive thoughts do not arise. At the moment [when delusive thoughts no longer arise,[118]] it's not a dark ignorance.[119] It's a [bright and luminous] state of awakening." This sort of [perverse teacher] is a poison that blinds people's vision. This is no trivial matter!

[3.3: *Dahui's "original"* gongfu *is free of any such things as engirding mind or stopping-to-rest*[120]]

Usually when I see this bunch, I don't attend to them with the usual polite formalities. Since they do not have the clear eye, they just quote from books[121] and follow their model in teaching people—but how could these books teach anything? If you put your confidence in this sort [of

---

116. Takagi, 13b, at *fangbian* 方便 inserts: "The teaching of Zen sitting" [坐禪觀法].

117. Mujaku, 96, glosses *shi shi mo guan* 是事莫管 thus: "The term *shi shi* 是事 refers to the *one great matter*. These false teachers dissuade [students] from wonderful awakening, and therefore they instruct like this, saying: 'It's a matter of decisively having *nothing-to-do* and no mind—as soon as you think you are about to awaken, it's already a done deed!'" [是事者一大事也此邪師不要妙悟故如是教示謂直下無事無心是也纔思欲悟明則早是事生也]. However, Hyesim, 31, glosses *shi shi mo guan* 是事莫管 thus: "Refers generally to mundane and supramundane matters" [通指世出世間事]. I believe Mujaku is wrong here. A search of the term *shi shi* 是事 as opposed to *ci shi* 此事 (*this one great matter*) shows that in the *Letters of Dahui shi shi* 是事 is used three times in criticisms of perverse teachers and four times in a polite formula at the end of letters ("Let's temporarily shelve these matters"). It is never used in the weighty Buddhist sense that *ci shi* is used.

118. Takagi, 13b, at *nenme* 恁麼 inserts: "Delusive thoughts no longer arise" [情念不生].

119. Mujaku, 96, glosses *bu shi mingran wuzhi* 不是冥然無知 thus: "These perverse teachers say that, even though you have stopped, reached no mind and no thought, and are stupid like stone, soil, and wood, you still possess an awareness that is bright and luminous" [忠曰此邪師謂雖歇得到無心無念如頑石土木亦能昭昭靈靈具知覺也].

120. Mujaku, 98: 第三段大慧正示元來工夫無幾許管帶休歇等事.

121. Mujaku, 96–97, glosses *jiang cezi shang yu* 將冊子上語 thus: "This means that, because their own eye of the Way lacks clarity, the truth doesn't emerge from their own hearts, and so they just take the words of the buddhas and patriarchs, the written words of the sutras and Chan records, to instruct people. However, because their own eye is dark, they mistake the meaning of those texts, and so mislead people" [言自己道眼不分明故不能自胸襟流出故但以佛祖言句經錄文字教示人然自眼闇故誤取其義故誤前人也].

perverse teacher], you'll never be able to practice Chan. It's not that I *don't* usually teach people to do *gongfu* by engaging in sitting in a still place. Sitting is simply one instance of providing medicine in accordance with their illnesses. In fact, my [practice of sitting] has nothing to do with that sort of ["engirding-mind" or "stopping-to-rest"] formulation.[122] I submit for your inspection: Preceptor Huangbo said, "This Chan lineage of ours, which has been transmitted from ancient times, has never taught people to seek intellectual knowledge. The very phrase *studying the Way* is already an *upāya*-phrase to draw people in. However, the Way can't be studied. If you intend to study the Way, on the contrary, you stray from the Way. The Way that has no orientation is called the Mahāyāna mind. This mind is not inside, outside, or in between.[123] In reality it has no orientation. You absolutely must not produce intellectual understanding—that's just speaking of the Way from your present subjective standard. If your subjective standard were to disappear, your mind would have no orientation. The Way, the heavenly real, has never had a name. People of the world can't get a handle on it from inside their delusive subjective world, and this is why the buddhas pop up and expose *this matter*. Fearing that you won't awaken, they provisionally erect the term 'Way.' You must not produce a level of understanding that maintains what is merely nominally existent."[124]

[3.4: *Renders judgments on the above perverse understandings*[125]]

The blind fellows I previously mentioned give mistaken instruction to people. Every one of them acknowledges fish eyes [i.e., *upāyas*] as the bright jewel[126] and produces an inferior level of understanding that maintains the merely nominally existent:

---

122. Mujaku, 98, glosses *shi wu nenme zhishi ren chu* 實無恁麼指示人處 thus: "*Nenme [in that way]* refers to the above teachings of maintaining emptiness and recognizing it as [luminous] awareness. This line means that my instruction is not like that of the perverse teachers" [恁麼者指上來守空認覺知等也言我指示不如邪師所言也].

123. *Vimalakīrti Sūtra* (T475.14.541b17–18).

124. *Huangbo shan Duanji chanshi chuanxin fa yao* 黃檗山斷際禪師傳心法要 (T2012A.48.382.c4–12).

125. Mujaku, 101: 第四段判上邪解.

126. Mujaku, 101–102, glosses *ren yu mu zuo ming zhu* 認魚目作明珠 thus: "*Fish eye* is a metaphor for *upāya*-language. *Bright jewel* is a metaphor for the real Way. This bright jewel is not involved with verbalization" [魚目比方便語明珠比真實道者箇明珠者非涉言句者也].

[Chan illness no. 1:] Some teach people to "engird mind," and this produces an inferior level of understanding that simply maintains a mirror-like reflection of what is in front of one.

[Chan illness no. 2:] Some teach people to go on forcibly "stopping-to-rest" [= "silence-as-illumination"], and this produces an inferior level of understanding that maintains the empty quiescence of quelling delusive thought.[127]

[Chan illness no. 3: Some teach:] "By means of stopping, to reach a state of non-awareness and non-knowing, wherein one is like earth, wood, tile, and stone; at such a moment, it's not a dark non-knowing [but a bright and luminous state of awakening]." Also, this produces an inferior level of understanding that mistakenly attributes reality to *upāyas*, which are no more than linguistic convention used to loosen bondage.

[Chan illness no. 4:] Some teach people to accept all conditions and do a backwards illumination, [telling them:] "Don't allow the emergence of bad awareness." This produces an inferior level of understanding that mistakenly attributes reality to the delusion of the weather-beaten skull.

[Chan illness no. 5:] Some teach people merely to be bold and unconstrained, to give free rein to the self, [telling them:] "Don't pay any attention whatsoever to the movement of thoughts.[128] Thoughts arise and thoughts disappear, without ever having substantiality. If you grasp them as real, then the mind of samsara will arise." This produces an inferior level of understanding that maintains naturalness as the ultimate dharma.

---

127. Mujaku, 102, glosses *shou wang huai kongji* 守忘懷空寂 thus: "The old interpretation is: Quelling delusive thought is not remembering things in the mind, and maintaining empty quiescence is like the no-mind of earth, wood, tile, and stone. Mujaku says: The empty quiescence of quelling delusive thought is still within the borders of delusion, and one should, in addition, exhaust it. However, here they are grasping and maintaining it as if it were like Yantou's *thinking of nothing at all*—thinking of nothing being this empty quiescence of quelling delusive thought. But the empty quiescence of quelling delusive thought is within the borders of thinking and is not yet the attainment of liberation" [舊解曰忘懷者不記事于胸中也守空寂如土木瓦石之無心也忠曰忘懷空寂者猶是情識邊際可更盡之然今執守之如巖頭言百不思則不思者箇忘懷空寂也忘懷空寂是思之邊際也未得解脫].

128. Mujaku, 103, glosses *mo guan sheng xin dong nian* 莫管生心動念 thus: "In fact to take the movement of thoughts as a calamity is incorrect. And to despise it and want to remove it is also incorrect" [忠曰實以生心動念爲患者非是也又嫌之欲除去亦非是也].

The illnesses laid out above[129] are not the fault of students of the Way. All of them arise solely due to the erroneous instruction of blind masters.

[3.5: *Instruction on the correct* gongfu *method*[130]]

You are already in a neat and tidy state. You maintain a mind of the Way that is firm in the truth [and hence impervious to perverse teachers and teachings[131]]. Don't pay any attention whatsoever to whether or not your

---

129. Mujaku, 104: "If you correlate the above perverse levels of understanding with the four illnesses of the *Perfect Awakening Sutra*, then no. 1 (teaching people to engird mind) is the sutra's performing-[various-actions] illness; no. 2 (stopping-to-rest) is the sutra's extinguishing-[defilements] illness; no. 3 (being like earth, wood, tile, and stone) and no. 4 (don't allow the emergence of bad awareness) are the sutra's stopping-[thoughts] illness; and no. 5 (being bold and unconstrained and giving free rein to the self) is the sutra's giving-free-rein-[to-everything] illness" [忠曰上來邪解配之圓覺經四病則初作病(教人管帶)第二滅病(休去歇去)第三第四止病(第三如土木瓦石第四莫教惡覺覺現前)第五任病(放曠任自在)]. *Da fang-guang yuanjue xiuduoluo liaoyi jing* 大方廣圓覺修多羅了義經: "Good Sons! The wonderful dharma realized by those good teachers should be divorced from the four illnesses. What are the four illnesses? The first is the performing illness. If there is a person who speaks like this: 'I perform various actions in my *original mind*, wanting to seek out perfect awakening,' that perfect awakening is not attained by performing, and so we call this an illness. The second is the giving-free-rein illness. If there is a person who speaks like this: 'At present I am not cutting off samsara and not seeking nirvana; nirvana and samsara have no arising-disappearing; I am giving free rein to everything in compliance with the dharma-nature, wanting to seek out perfect awakening,' that perfect awakening is not something you give free rein to, and so we call this an illness. The third is the cessation illness. If there is a person who speaks like this: 'At present I am desisting from all thoughts in my mind forever to obtain the complete nature, in a still levelness wanting to seek out perfect awakening,' that perfect awakening is not joined to ceasing, and so we call this an illness. The fourth is the extinguishing illness. If there is a person who speaks like this: 'At present I am forever cutting off all defilements—my mind-body is, in the final analysis, empty and without existence—in the midst of unreal sense fields and eternal stillness wanting to seek out perfect awakening,' that perfect awakening is not characterized by stillness, and so we call this an illness. The one who divorces from the four illnesses knows purity. Engaging in this contemplation is called correct contemplation. If you have some other contemplation, it is called perverse contemplation" [善男子。彼善知識所證妙法應離四病。云何四病。一者作病。若復有人作如是言。我於本心作種種行欲求圓覺。彼圓覺性非作得故說名為病。二者任病。若復有人作如是言。我等今者不斷生死不求涅槃。涅槃生死無起滅念。任彼一切隨諸法性欲求圓覺。彼圓覺性非任有故說名為病。三者止病。若復有人作如是言。我今自心永息諸念得一切性。寂然平等欲求圓覺。彼圓覺性非止合故說名為病。四者滅病。若復有人作如是言。我今永斷一切煩惱身心畢竟空無所有。何況根塵虛妄境界一切永寂欲求圓覺。彼圓覺性非寂相故說名為病。離四病者。則知清淨。作是觀者名為正觀。若他觀者名為邪觀。] (T842.17.920b19–c3).

130. Mujaku, 104: 第五段正指示工夫法.

131. Mujaku, 104, glosses *cun yi pian zhenshi ... zhi xin* 存一片真實 ... 之心 thus: "The implicit meaning is that, if you preserve a mind of the Way that is firm in the truth, then, even though there may be all sorts of perverse teachers and perverse teachings, how could they gain entrance? It's like a person with frailties—pathogens gain entrance and thereupon

gongfu is "pure." Don't just, on the basis of sayings of the ancients, intently be like a multi-storied stupa, piling layer upon layer [of intellectual under-standing[132]]. This is expending *gongfu* [energy] to no avail, and it will never end. If you just maintain mind on a single point, there's no way that you won't be able to attain awakening. When the time and conditions arrive, spontaneously it will "click." With a "snort" you will awaken! "When you don't produce even a single thought, is there still a mistake?" "*Mt. Sumeru.*" "What about when you don't bring even a single thing?" "*Put it down!*" If your uncertainty *here* is not yet destroyed, just practice *here*. There is no need for you, in addition, to produce nonessentials.[133]

[3.6: *Concluding remarks*[134]]

If you can have confidence in me [as opposed to those previous per-verse teachers[135]], then just practice *in that way*. Beyond this there is no buddhadharma to be taught to people. If your confidence is insufficient, then do as you please: "Make inquiries of good teachers in the North and in the South: but for every 'fox doubt' that any teacher resolves for you, there will always be another 'fox doubt.'"[136]

---

become illness. Perverse teachers' spotting mistakes is always due to students' not being in the truth and not being firm" [忠曰底理言存真實堅固向道之心則雖有種種邪師種種邪教豈能入耶譬人有虛弱之處邪氣隨入遂成病爲邪師見誤者皆因不實不堅固也].

132. Mujaku, 104, glosses *ru die tazi* 如疊塔子 thus: "Simile for producing layer upon layer of understanding" [忠曰蓋比重重生解會也].

133. Mujaku, 105, glosses *bu bi zi sheng zhiye ye* 不必自生枝葉也 thus: "There are two mean-ings. The first is: If your uncertainty concerning these two standards is not yet smashed, you should just have uncertainty over these two standards and should not, in addition, produce uncertainty concerning remaining basic standards, sutra texts, and so forth. When the ball of uncertainty over these two standards is smashed, then your myriad other cases of uncer-tainty are all simultaneously smashed. Another meaning is: When your uncertainty over these two standards is not yet smashed, merely rally these two standards to awareness. You should not, concerning these two cases, produce such nonessentials as knowledge and intel-lectual understanding. The latter meaning is correct" [有二義言於此兩則疑不破但可疑此兩則更不可於餘本則餘經文等上生疑也此兩則上疑團破則自餘千疑萬疑可皆一時破也又義於此兩則疑不破但提撕此兩則不可兩則上種種知見解會之枝葉也後義是也].

134. Mujaku, 105: 第六段結語.

135. Mujaku, 105, glosses *ruo xinde yunmen* 若信得雲門 thus: "Here he adds the two charac-ters *Yunmen* [i.e., one of Dahui's names] in opposition to the previous perverse teachers" [今加雲門兩字者對前之邪師也].

136. Mujaku, 105, cites *Foguo Yuanwu chanshi biyanlu* 佛果圜悟禪師碧巖錄 (T2003.48.162b8–11). Mujaku, 106, glosses *hu yi* 狐疑 thus: "It means: You ask that teacher and do not under-stand, and a 'fox doubt' is unresolved. You ask this teacher and again don't understand, and

4. Continued [Fourth Letter in Reply to Vice Minister Ceng]

[*Commentary:* Mujaku says, "The main intention of this letter is to show that still-ness and noisiness are a single taste."[137] Presumably dates to around the same time as letter #1, Shaoxing 4/1134. Pre-exile letter.]

[4.1: *Indulges Ceng with praise*[138]]

I have carefully read your letter. I see that during the four postures of walking, standing, sitting, and lying down, not for a moment have you been snatched up by public affairs. In the midst of the [worldly] torrent you're always doing fierce self-reflection, and you have never eased up in the least. As time goes on, your mind of the Way has grown ever more firm. This is deeply gratifying to me.

[4.2: *Shows that stillness and noisiness are a single thusness.*[139]]

However, the troublesome defilements of the world are like the flames of a fire: When will they ever come to an end? Right in the midst of noisiness you must not forget the matter of [the stillness of] the bamboo chair and the sitting cushion. In the past [when you were] keeping your mind in the state of stillness *über alles* [by practicing sitting, it should have been] precisely for the purpose of use in the midst of noisiness.[140] If you haven't gained energy in the midst of noisiness from it, then it's the same thing as not having done *gongfu* in the midst of stillness! I gather [from your letter you suppose] that the karmic conditions in your previous births have been mixed,[141] and so now you lament this karmic

---

so a 'fox doubt' is unresolved. There's no end to it" [忠曰言問彼師而未了故狐疑未決問此師而復未了故狐疑未決終無了期而已].

137. Mujaku, 106: 此書大意示靜鬧一味.

138. Mujaku, 106: 第一段歎縱.

139. Mujaku, 106: 第二段示靜鬧一如.

140. Mujaku, 106, glosses *pingxi liu xin jingsheng chu* 平昔留心靜勝處 thus: "One who loves stillness can't bear noisiness. Stillness/noisiness is a polarity of dharmas in samsara. Therefore, if you can in the midst of "stillness *über alles*" Zen sitting nurture *the matter prior to stillness/noisiness*, then you will be able to use it in the midst of noisiness" [忠曰愛靜者必不任鬧靜鬧是對待生死法故能於靜勝坐禪中養靜鬧以前事則當於鬧中能用得也].

141. Mujaku, 106, glosses *qianyuan boza* 前緣駁雜 thus: "This means: if you calculate it, in previous births you have been half-tied to supramundane karmic conditions and half greedy

retribution.[142] It's only [in this one matter that] I disagree with your assessment. When you activate this thought [that in the midst of the defilements you are incapable of doing pure *gongfu*],[143] then it becomes a blockage to the Way. An ancient worthy said: "When, following along in the flow of samsara, you recognize the [*original*] nature, there is neither joy nor sadness."[144] The *Vimalakīrti Sūtra* says: "It is like the fact that the dry land of a high plain does not produce lotus flowers, but the silt of the low wetlands does produce this flower."[145] The old barbarian [the Buddha] said: "Thusness does not have a fixed self-nature; following along with conditions, it brings to completion all dharmas."[146] [The Buddha] also said: "[The *original nature*], moving in response to conditions, pervades everywhere, but it is always located at this awakening seat."[147] Could all these quotations be deceiving people? If one takes the state of stillness as correct and the state of noisiness as wrong, it becomes a denial of "mundane" characteristics in a search for the "reality" characteristic, a departure from samsara's arising-disappearing in a search to quiet it. When you like stillness and dislike noisiness, it's just right for applying [*gongfu*] energy. Suddenly in noisiness you'll collide with and overturn the stillness-time *state of being*:[148] this energy will

---

for mundane things. Because you've been mixed in this way, in your present birth you are fettered by mundane things and fail to attain a pure practice" [言計之於前世半結出世緣半貪世間事如此駁雜故今世亦爲世事所羈絆不得純一修行也].

142. Hyesim, 32, glosses *ci bao zhi tan* 此報之歎 thus: "lament that your *gongfu* is not pure" [工夫不純之歎].

143. Mujaku, 107, glosses *dong ci nian* 動此念 thus: "You have the thought that in the midst of the defilements you are incapable of doing *gongfu*. Once you activate this thought, it becomes an enormous blockage to advancing on the Way" [念塵勞間不得做工夫事也若此念一動則大爲進道之障礙矣].

144. From a verse of the twenty-second patriarch Manorhita 摩拏羅 in the *Jingde chuandeng lu* 景德傳燈錄 (T2076.51.213c19–214a25).

145. T475.14.549b6–7.

146. *Zongjing lu* 宗鏡錄, T2016.48.458a22–23.

147. *Da fangguang fo huayan jing* 大方廣佛華嚴經, T279.10.30a6–8.

148. Mujaku, 109, glosses *zhuangfan jingshi xiaoxi* 撞翻靜時消息 thus: "As for highly valued, stored up *stillness-time state of being*, at the moment you overturn it in the midst of noisiness, you devote yourself to being beyond stillness/noisiness and become a person with the freedom to exit or enter at will" [所珍藏之靜時消息於閙中打翻時出身於靜閙之外爲出入自在人也].

surpass that of [sitting on] the bamboo chair and sitting cushion by a thousand or ten-thousand times.[149] Please listen: I'm definitely not misleading you here!

[4.3: *Praises raising Old Pang's words to awareness*[150]]

I gather [from your letter] that you've internalized Old Pang's two phrases [i.e., the two *huatous* **vow to empty the existent** and **don't reify the non-existent**] as an admonitory inscription, for all walking, standing, sitting, and lying down. Good! Nothing could be added. [Now,] should you, right at the moment you're in noisiness, generate a loathing for it, you'll just be throwing your own mind into disarray. Should you, right at the moment you're in the midst of activated thoughts [i.e., noisiness], just rally Old Pang's two phrases to awareness, then it will be a dose of [the medical prescription called] "coolness-dispersal" that is taken when one has a fever.

[4.4: *Relates the idea that stillness and noisiness are a single thusness*[151]]

You possess a resolute confidence and are a man of great wisdom. For a long time, you've been doing *gongfu* in the midst of stillness, and so I have dared to say these kinds of things.[152] In the case of other people it would not be suitable. If I spoke in this way to a highly conceited person whose karmic consciousness is in a state of disorder, it would only be adding to his carrying-pole load of bad karma.

---

149. Mujaku, 109, cites: *Shaoshi liu men* 少室六門: "If one obtains his understanding from events, his vital energy will be robust. Those who see dharma from the medium of events, never lose mindfulness anywhere. In the case of those whose understanding is from the medium of the written word, their vital energy is weak" [若從事上得解者。氣力壯。從事中見法者。即處處不失念。從文字解者。氣力弱。] (T2009.48.370b8–10).

150. Mujaku, 109: 第三段讚提撕老龐語.

151. Mujaku, 110: 第四段敘示靜鬧一如之意.

152. Mujaku, 110, glosses *fang gan shuo zhei ban hua* 方敢說這般話 thus: "*These kinds of things* refers to the above line 'should you, right at the moment you're in noisiness, generate a loathing for it, you'll just be throwing your own mind into disarray'" [這般話者指上若正鬧時生厭惡則乃是自擾其心耳之語].

[4.5: *Raises a connection with a previous letter*[153]]

The various Chan illnesses I described in a previous letter—did you manage to understand them in detail?

5. *Continued [Fifth Letter in Reply to Vice Minister Ceng]*

[*Commentary: Mujaku says, "The main idea is Dahui's rejoicing at Ceng's understanding of the* upāya-*words of the ancients."*[154] *Presumably dates to around the same time as letter #1, Shaoxing 4/1134. Pre-exile letter.*]

[5.1: *Lauds Ceng*[155]]

I have been informed [by your letter]: "[Bodhidharma's words] 'Without: desist from all objective supports; within: have no panting in the mind. [With a mind like a wall,] you can enter the Way'[156] is but an expression of the gate of *upāyas*. So, entering the Way by means of the gate of *upāyas* is okay. But when one holds on tight to the *upāyas* and does not let them go, then it constitutes an illness." Certainly it is as you say. I read your letter and could not help being happy to point of leaping about.

[5.2: *Relates in detail that Ceng is in concord with Dahui's idea*[157]]

At present, all over the place, the "black-lacquer-bucket faction" [of perverse teachers] just holds on tight to *upāyas* and does not let them go. They instruct people in a "real" dharma and thereby render blind quite a few people. Therefore, I have composed a *Disquisition on Distinguishing Perverse and Correct*[158] in order to rescue them. In recent times Māra has

---

153. Mujaku, 111: 第五段舉前書結.

154. Mujaku, 111: 大意隨喜解古人方便語.

155. Mujaku, 111: 第一段讚許.

156. *Shaoshi liu men* 少室六門, T2009.48.370a25–26.

157. Mujaku, 112: 第二段具陳同我意.

158. Dahui's chronological biography, the *Dahui Pujue chanshi nianpu* 大慧普覺禪師年譜, in the entry for Shaoxing 4/1134 when Dahui was forty-six, says: "At the time Chan followers put aside wonderful awakening as useless and made students tire themselves out over

been strong and the dharma weak. Countless are those who consider the ultimate to be "by means of [*samādhi* subduing] the *deep-and-still* [consciousness] to enter into fusion with the *deep-and-still* [thusness]."[159] This constitutes holding on tight to *upāyas* and not letting them go. Students who consider these [real] "teachers" are as numerous as grains of hemp and millet. In recent times, with a cohort of Chan monks, I've been emphasizing these very two matters[160]—it's exactly as you've said in your letter, not a single word is mistaken.

[5.3: *Rejoices over assisting Ceng's growth spurt*[161]]

If one doesn't keep his mind inside *prajñā* continuously moment after moment, then he will be incapable of seeing through the various different *upāyas* of the noble ones of the past. You have already caught hold of the hilt of the sword. You already have the hilt in your hand, so why should you worry about [the illness of holding on tight to] *upāyas* and not letting them go and thus not entering the Way? Just do *gongfu* in this way. Read the various lines of the sutras and the sayings records of the Chan ancients—yet again just do this sort of *gongfu*. With *huatous* like **Mt. Sumeru, put it down, dog has no buddha-nature, bamboo clapper,**[162] **in one**

---

stillness-silence, and for this reason he composed a *Disquisition on Distinguishing Perverse and Correct* to attack this and thereby save them from the fraud of the moment" [時宗徒撥置妙悟使學者困於寂默因著辨正邪說而攻之以救一時之弊] (CBETA, J01, no. A042, p. 799, a28–30). Mujaku, 112, comments: "The compilation of the *Disquisition on Distinguishing Perverse and Correct* and the writing of this letter were in the same year [1134]" [按作辨邪正說與作此書同年也].

159. Allusion to *Śūraṃgama Sūtra*, T945.19.155a4–7. A commentary on the *Śūraṃgama Sūtra*, the *Lengyan jing yi shu shi yao chao* 楞嚴經義疏釋要鈔, glosses *zhan ru he zhan* 湛入合湛 thus: "*Zhan ru he zhan*: the first *zhan* [*deep-and-still*] is consciousness; the second *zhan* is the real. It means using *samādhi* to subdue the *zhan* consciousness and make it return to fusion with the principle of thusness-stillness. In this way thusness [falsely] becomes an extreme of consciousness" [湛入合湛者上湛是識下湛是真謂以定伏於湛識合歸真如寂湛之理也斯乃真如是識邊際也。] (CBETA, X11, no. 267, p. 86, a2–3 // Z 1:16, p. 423, d15–16 // R16, p. 846, b15–16).

160. Mujaku, 113, glosses *ju ci liang duan* 舉此兩段 thus: "The first is considering the ultimate to be 'by means of [*samādhi* subduing] the *deep-and-still* [consciousness] to enter into fusion with the *deep-and-still* [thusness]'; the second is 'holding on tight to *upāyas* and not letting them go'" [一者湛入合湛爲究竟者二者守方便不捨者].

161. Mujaku, 113: 第三段隨喜助激.

162. On this *huatou*, see *Dahui Pujue chanshi nianpu* 大慧普覺禪師年譜 (CBETA, J01, no. A042, p. 796, c9–33)); *Dahui Pujue chanshi pushuo* 大慧普覺禪師普說 (CBETA, M059, no. 1540, p. 1004, a10–b4); and *Wumen guan* 無門關, T2005.48.298b14–17.

gulp suck up the water of West River,[163] *cypress tree in the garden*[164]—yet again just do *gongfu* in this way. Don't, in addition [to these *upāyas* for entering the Way], engender some other level of understanding; don't seek out some other logic; and don't concoct some other crafty maneuver. You—in the midst of the torrent—are capable of this sort of constantly raising [the *huatou* to awareness[165]]: if you fail to achieve success in this practice, then it's the buddhadharma that's not efficacious. Keep this in mind!

[5.4: *Shows that dreams and awakening are a single thusness*[166]]

I am informed by your letter that you dreamed during the night that you burned incense and entered my room in an extremely calm and unhurried manner. You absolutely must not understand this as a dream. You must realize that you really entered the room. I submit for your inspection [this *Prajñāpāramitā Sūtra* passage]: "Śāriputra asked Subhūti: 'Is speaking of the six perfections in a dream the same as speaking of them when awake?' Subhūti said: 'This question is profound, and so I cannot explain. Maitreya bodhisattva is in this assembly. Go and ask him.' "[167] Tsk! What a slip-up! Xuedou commented [on this passage with[168]]: "If at that time [Śāriputra] hadn't let it go and right away had given the single stab—'Who names *Maitreya*? And just who *is* Maitreya?'—he would have immediately experienced the ice's melting and the tiles' disintegrating." Tsk! Now Xuedou has slipped up too! Suppose somebody were to ask: "Let's say that Edict Attendant Ceng at night dreamed that he entered Dahui's room—now tell me, is it the same as doing it in the awakened state?" I would immediately say to him: "Who is the room-enterer? Who is the one who witnesses the room-enterer? Who is the one who is doing the dreaming, and who is the

---

163. See *Jingde chuandeng lu* 景德傳燈錄, T2076.51.263b13–17.

164. See *Gu zunsu yulu* 古尊宿語錄 (CBETA, X68, no. 1315, p. 77, b23–c4 // Z 2:23, p. 154, a15–b2 // R118, p. 307, a15–b2).

165. Mujaku, 114, glosses *ti duo* 提掇 thus: "*Tiduo* has the meaning *rallying* [the huatou] *to awareness*" [忠曰提掇即提撕義].

166. Mujaku, 115: 第四段示夢覺一如.

167. *Mohe bore boluomi jing* 摩訶般若波羅蜜經, T223.8.347a1–b9.

168. *Liandeng hui yao* 聯燈會要 (CBETA, X79, no. 1557, p. 17, a17–18 // Z 2B:9, p. 224, a11–12 // R136, p. 447, a11–12). The *Liandeng hui yao* of Huiweng Wuming (晦翁悟明; d.u.), who was in the Dahui line, was completed in 1183. This flame-of-the-lamp record incorporates the whole of Dahui's *Correct Dharma-Eye Depository*. Xuedou's comment appears elsewhere.

one who relates the happenings of the dream? Who is the one who does not understand this as a dream, and who is the one who really enters the room?" Tsk! Once again a major slip-up!

6. *Continued [Sixth Letter in Reply to Vice Minister Ceng]*

[*Commentary:* Mujaku says, "The main idea is that erecting a resolute will necessarily leads to effectiveness."[169] Presumably dates to around the same time as letter #1, Shaoxing 4/1134. Pre-exile letter.]

[6.1: *Proves that, with a mind of sincerity, it is not necessary to have an "upward (towards the great matter)" level of understanding*[170]]

I have carefully read your letter over and over again. It serves to show that you are possessed of a mind as firm as iron and stone, that you have erected a resolute will, and that you are unwilling to do things in a careless or sloppy manner. Just keep on pressing hard *in that way.* On the final day of the twelfth month [at the end of your life] you'll even be able to engage Old King Yama [Judge of the Dead]. Cease all blather[171] of "suddenly opening [Maheśvara's, i.e., the great lord of the universe Śiva's] third eye on the top of the head," "grasping the precious sword of the Vajra King," or "sitting on the top of Vairocana Buddha's head."

[6.2: Gongfu *may ripen only gradually, but it does not lack effectiveness*[172]]

I once said to a dharma friend, a layman:

---

169. Mujaku, 118: 大意說立決定志則必有靈驗.

170. Mujaku, 118: 第一段證明有誠實心不要向上見解.

171. Mujaku, 120: "Although you speak of issues of 'upward [towards the *great matter*]', if you don't erect a resolute will, of what use will it be? But if thought after thought you erect a resolute will, it will be okay if you don't speak of 'upward' matters" [忠曰言口雖説向上事心不立決定志濟甚麼用心心若立決定志則口不說向上事亦可也]. Presumably Ceng had been speaking of such matters.

172. Mujaku, 120: 第二段工夫漸熟不能無靈驗.

Present-day students of the Way just seek quick results,[173] unaware that this is a mistake. Even worse, they say: "*Nothing-to-do*, eliminating sense objects, stillness-sitting, and thoroughly investigating the self are a waste of time—not as good as reading some sutras, doing some recitations of the *nembutsu*, doing a lot of obeisances in front of the buddhas, and confessing the bad actions committed during one's life. We must escape the iron rod in the hand of Old King Yama [Judge of the Dead]!" This is the course of action of an idiot.

Today's Daoists, completely under the sway of phantasmal thought, go about visualizing the solar quintessence and beams of moonlight;[174] ingesting mists and breath [i.e., practicing Daoist breath control].[175] Even if they were capable of keeping their bodily form for a long life without being affected by cold and heat, they wouldn't be able to turn their minds completely towards *prajñā*.

[6.3: *A good karmic connection to prajñā certainly will never be lost*[176]]

A noble one of former times [Baizhang Huaihai] has said clearly: "For example, a fly can alight here and there, but the only place it can't alight is on top of a flame. Sentient beings are also like that. They are capable of alighting on objective supports, but the only objective support they can't alight upon is *prajñā*."[177] When from moment to moment [sentient beings] do not retreat from [the resoluteness experienced when they[178]] first produced the thought of awakening; and they take the consciousness

---

173. Mujaku, 120, glosses *qiu su xiao* 求速效 thus: "They want fast awakening. If you want to obtain quick results, this mind [of wanting] blocks the gate of awakening" [忠曰欲急悟也苟欲速得效驗此心障悟門].

174. Mujaku, 121, glosses *ri jing yue hua* 日精月華 by citing the *Yun ji qi qian* 雲笈七籤, a Song dynasty Daoist compendium in 120 fascicles compiled by Zhang Junfang 張君房.

175. Mujaku, 122, glosses *tun xia fu qi* 吞霞服氣 by citing the *Xu bo wu zhi* 續博物志, a Song dynasty text in 10 fascicles compiled by Li Shi 李石.

176. Mujaku, 123: 第三段善結緣般若決定不失.

177. *Gu zunsu yulu* 古尊宿語錄 (CBETA, X68, no. 1315, p. 7, a7–9 // Z 2:23, p. 83, c18–d2 // R118, p. 166, a18–b2).

178. Mujaku, 123, glosses *gou niannian bu tui chuxin* 苟念念不退初心 thus: "It means: do not retreat from the resoluteness of the time when one first produced the thought of awakening" [言不退屈初發心時之志也].

that makes mundane defilements into objective supports and turn [that consciousness] backwards to engage *prajñā*: even if they don't make a thorough penetration in the present life, at the very end of life they will most definitely not be led along by bad karma and fall into a bad rebirth path. When reborn in the next life, in accordance with the strength of their vow in the present life, they will assuredly have "ready-made" enjoyment within *prajñā*. This is a done deal—there can be no doubt of it.

[6.4: *The real and the unreal are mutually exclusive*[179]]

With matters of the sentient-being realm, if there hasn't been any application of training, from time without beginning habit-energy has had the potential to ripen, and the karmic path has ripened accordingly. [The *Mencius* says: "The superior man deeply aims for it by means of the Way, wanting to get it for himself. Having gotten it for himself, he abides in it firmly. Abiding in it firmly, he depends on it deeply. Depending upon it deeply,] he has naturally seized on it on the left and right, meeting with its source."[180] One must apply oneself to "shelving" [the matters of the sentient-being realm]. As for the supramundane mind that trains in *prajñā*, from time without beginning [some sentient beings] have turned their backs on it. When they unexpectedly hear a good teacher speak frankly, naturally enough they're unable to understand! One must erect a resolute will in order to engage this [supramundane mind of *prajñā*]. Certainly only one of them [i.e., mundane and supramundane] can prevail. If one enters deeply into this state [i.e., the supramundane mind of *prajñā*], then, even if that state [i.e., mundane dharmas in the sentient-being realm] is not eliminated,[181] all the Māra-like teachers of outside Ways will spontaneously crawl away, quashed! In the "unripe state" [supramundane] make oneself do "ripe" [mundane],[182] and in the "ripe

---

179. Mujaku, 124: 第四段真妄對遣.

180. *Mencius, Li lou xia* 離婁下.

181. Mujaku, 125, glosses *ci chu ruo ru ... bi chu yun yun* 此處若入 ... 彼處云云 thus: "The study of *prajñā* is at present the focus of Vice Minister Ceng. Therefore, the study of *prajñā* refers to *this state* and mundane dharmas in the sentient-being realm refers to *that state*" [忠曰學般若今曾侍郎所專也故學般若指此處矣而世間法眾生界指彼處也].

182. Mujaku, 126, glosses *sheng chu fangjiao shu* 生處放教熟 thus: "The 'unripe state' is *prajñā*; the 'ripe state' is the sentient-being realm" [生處是般若熟處是眾生界] and cites

state" [mundane] make oneself do "unripe" [supramundane]. This is the name of the game.[183]

[6.5: *Concludes with showing the efficacy of Dahui's style of* gongfu[184]]

In doing *gongfu* in the midst of daily activities, having caught hold of the hilt of the sword, one gradually becomes aware that an instance of saving on the expenditure of [*gongfu*] energy is none other than the state of gaining [awakening] energy.[185]

7. *In Reply to Participant in Determining Governmental Matters Li (Hanlao) (Question Letter Attached)*
[Li's Question Letter]

[Commentary: Hyesim says, ""The main point of this question letter is Li's presenting his level of understanding and making a solemn request for the dharma."[186] The following letters, Li's two question letters and Dahui's two reply letters, went back and forth in Shaoxing 5/1135. Pre-exile letters.]

Foguo Keqin chanshi xinyao/Yuanwu xinyao 佛果克勤禪師心要/圓悟心要 (CBETA, X69, no. 1357, p. 474, a12–14 // Z 2:25, p. 370, d1–3 // R120, p. 740, b1–3).

183. Mujaku, 126, glosses *zheng wei ci ye* 政爲此也 thus: "*This refers to the above this state*" [忠曰此者指上此處]. Hyesim, 37: "*It's precisely for the sake of this* refers to the above line [*all the Māra-like teachers of outside Ways*] *will spontaneously crawl away, quashed!*" [政爲此之比指上自然竄伏句].

184. Mujaku, 126: 第五段結示效驗.

185. Mujaku, 126, glosses *jian jue shengli ... de li chu ye* 漸覺省力 ... 得力處也 thus: "The *energy of saving on the expenditure of energy* is the energy of rallying [the *huatou*] to awareness in *gongfu*—one will attain a saving of the energy involved in rallying [the *huatou*] to awareness. The *energy of gaining energy* is the getting-awakening energy. [The person drinking water] knows for himself whether it is cold or warm" [忠曰省力之力者工夫提撕力即得省提撕力也得力之力者得悟力也即冷煖自知底也].

186. Hyesim, 38: 此狀大旨呈見重請. For a biographical entry for Li Bing 李邴 (*zi* Hanlao 漢老), see *Song History*, 375 (16.2957–58). Hucker, 517: The official title *can-zheng* 參政 "is a quasi-official abbreviation of *canzhi zhengshi* 參知政事 (*Participant in Determining Governmental Matters*), i.e., a Vice Grand Councilor (*fuxiang* 副相, *shaozai* 少宰)."

[QL 7.1: *Li thanks the Master for stimulation*[187]]

I recently visited your room and had my ignorance triggered by you: suddenly I had an access to awakening. When I turn around and look at the dullness of my nature, the learning and understanding of my whole life is completely steeped in deluded views. I've been seizing this and jettisoning that; and, as if I were wearing a silk garment to walk through bramble bushes, I've gotten myself entangled. Now, with "the single laugh," I've been all at once released [from doubt[188]]. You can imagine how happy and grateful I am. Had you, the great Chan artisan, not taken a winding road to bequeath your compassion upon me, how could it have come to this?

[QL 7.2: *Li relates the state of gaining energy*[189]]

Since I arrived in the city [of Quanzhou[190]], in putting on my clothes and eating, in keeping company with my children and grandchildren, in all matters I am doing just as I was doing before. I have lost any feelings of being caught up [in all these aspects of daily life], and yet I haven't come to consider [this gaining energy] to be special or remarkable in any way.[191] The rest of my habit-energies from past births and obstructions [due to karma from] the distant past has gradually lightened. I dare not forget your exhortation at the time we parted.[192]

---

187. Mujaku, 128: 第一段謝師之激發.

188. Following *Jiatai pudeng lu* 嘉泰普燈錄: "Now, with 'the single laugh,' I've been all at once released from doubt" [今一笑頓釋所疑] (CBETA, X79, no. 1559, p. 432, a22 // Z 2B:10, p. 163, b16 // R137, p. 325, b16).

189. Mujaku, 128: 第二段自敘得力之處.

190. Mujaku, 128, glosses *zi dao cheng zhong* 自到城中 thus: "In the city of Quanzhou [in coastal Fujian]" [忠曰蓋泉州城中也]. Mujaku cites *Dahui Pujue chanshi nianpu* 大慧普覺禪師年譜 (CBETA, J01, no. A042, p. 799, c14–16) and comments: "Thus we know that Participant in Determining Governmental Matters Li in Shaoxing 5/1135 visited Dahui. Dahui at this time was at Yunmen Hermitage in Xiaoxi in Quanzhou. This correspondence went back and forth in Shaoxing 5/1135" [即知李參政紹興五年參大慧大慧此時在泉州小溪雲門庵也此書往復在紹興五年].

191. Mujaku, 129, glosses *bu zuo qite zhi xiang* 不作奇特之想 thus: "In the state of gaining [awakening] energy I don't produce any thought that it's special or remarkable or to be treasured. The meaning is: he's not caught up in knowables" [忠曰亦於得力之處不生奇特寶愛之念也言不滯所知也].

192. Mujaku, 129, glosses *lin bie dingning yun yun* 臨別叮嚀云云 thus: "At the time Participant in Determining Governmental Matters Li returned from Yunmen Hermitage to the city.... this exhortation is [the *Śūraṃgama Sūtra* line] mentioned in Dahui's answer letter: "As to principle, one all-at-once awakens; one rides this awakening, and there is a complete melting

[QL 7.3: *Li begs for serious instruction*[193]]

No matter how much I think back over it, even though I have for the first time managed to enter the gate, I still find that the great dharma is not yet bright. In responding to karmic abilities and leading beings,[194] in my encounters I am not without obstructions. I look forward to your further instruction, enabling me to arrive at the final outcome, so that there is no blemish on your dharma-seat.

[7. Dahui's Reply Letter]

[*Commentary:* Mujaku says, "*The main idea of this letter is: when the sagely embryo is nurtured, spontaneously the great dharma becomes bright, and one responds to karmic abilities of beings without obstruction. . . . This letter dates to Shaoxing 5/1135 when the Master was forty-seven.*"[195] Pre-exile letter.]

[7.1: *Dahui certifies Li's awakening*[196]]

Your letter informs me of the following:

> Since I arrived in the city [of Quanzhou], in putting on my clothes
> and eating, in keeping company with my children and grandchil-
> dren, in all matters I am doing just as I was doing before. I have lost
> any feelings of being caught up [in all these aspects of daily life],
> and yet I haven't come to consider [this gaining energy] to be special
> or remarkable in any way. My habit-energies from past births and
> obstructions [due to karma from] the distant past have gradually
> lightened.

---

away. But phenomena are not all-at-once removed; only by a graduated sequence are they exhausted" [忠曰李參政自雲門菴歸城中時也.... 其叮嚀之語者蓋苔書所謂理則頓悟乘悟併銷事非頓除因次第盡之語也].

193. Mujaku, 130: 第三段乞重誨.

194. Mujaku, 130, glosses *ying ji jie wu* 應機接物 thus: "From these words down to *no blemish on your dharma-seat*, Participant in Determining Governmental Matters Li, in spite of being a layperson, seems to be [talking about] teaching and benefitting beings" [忠曰由此語及下無玷於法席之語李參政雖是俗漢似爲化度利生也].

195. Mujaku, 131: 大意謂聖胎長養則自然大法明白應機無礙.... 此書紹興五年乙卯師四十七歲而作.

196. Mujaku, 131: 第一段證明悟得.

I repeatedly read these words of yours aloud, and I was happy to the point of leaping about. This is precisely evidence of your having studied the buddhadharma. Supposing you were not a *great person* of extraordinary capability who has comprehended all matters in "the single laugh," then you would not be able to understand that our Chan house in fact has an untransmittable purport. Were it not so, you would never, throughout eternity, have been able to destroy your "two-word dharma teaching" of doubt and anger [that you expressed formerly at my attacking the perverse "silence-as-illumination" Chan teachers that you had confidence in].[197] Even if the great sky had become my mouthpiece, and the grasses, trees, tiles, and stones had emitted light-rays of wisdom, helping me to expose the principles [of "silence-as-illumination"[198]], nothing could have been done. I just believe that *this matter* can't be transmitted and can't be learned. You must realize on your own, awaken on your own, affirm on your own, stop-to-rest on your own, and then you will for the first time get to the end of things. You promptly with "the single laugh" extinguished having something to obtain. Beyond that what more is there to say? The Old Golden-faced Master [Śākyamuni] said: "Don't seize upon all the conditioned, unreal things verbalized by sentient beings. Though you don't rely on the path of verbalization, don't be attached to the nonverbal."[199] As your letter said: "I have lost any feelings of being caught up in [all these aspects of daily life], and yet I haven't come to consider [this gaining energy] to be special or remarkable in any way."[200] In a roundabout way this tallies with what the Old Golden-faced Master said. What accords with these words is called buddha word; what departs from these words

---

197. Mujaku, 131, glosses *yi nu er zi famen* 疑努二字法門 thus: "When Participant in Determining Governmental Matters Li heard Dahui scold the perverse teachers of silence-as-illumination, he was in some cases doubtful and in some cases angry. Later, beneath Dahui's words, he had a great awakening and repented of his past doubt and anger. Now, Dahui raises these words" [忠曰李參政聞大慧呵默照邪師或疑或怒後於大慧言下大悟懺悔昔疑努今舉其詞也]. Mujaku cites letter #12.3.

198. Mujaku, 132, glosses *zhu shuo daoli* 助說道理 thus: "Help Dahui's exposing of the principles of silence-as-illumination—speaking with different mouths but the same voice" [助大慧所說破默照道理異口同音說也].

199. *Da fangguang fo huayan jing* 大方廣佛華嚴經, T279.10.129b3–5.

200. Mujaku, 133, glosses *ju wang juzhi ... zhi xiang* 既亡拘滯 ... 之想 thus: "*Lost being caught up* is not seizing the unreal things of verbalization, and *not consider to be special or remarkable* is not being attached to the nonverbal" [忠曰亡拘滯者即是不取言說虛妄事也不作奇特想者即是不著無言說也].

is called the word of Māra, the Evil One. In the past I made a great vow:[201] I would rather substitute this body of mine for that of all sentient beings and undergo sufferings in the hells than ever with my words compromise the buddhadharma [by bending to accommodate] customary etiquette and in the process blinding everyone [i.e., what I am about to say to you is not a case of bending to accommodate your feelings].

[7.2: *Don't seek to ask questions of other people*[202]]

You have already reached an *in-that-way* level of knowing that *this matter* cannot be obtained from someone else. Simply "do just as you were doing before"—beyond that it is not necessary to ask questions about whether the great dharma is bright or not yet bright, whether your responding to karmic abilities is obstructed or not. If you entertain such thoughts, you are not "doing just as you were doing before." I have been informed that, after the summer retreat,[203] you again went out [and did just as you were doing before]. That is extremely pleasing to this ailing monk's mind. If, beyond that, you ceaselessly in a hubbub rush about seeking [to ask such questions], that would not be appropriate.

[7.3: *Urges nurturing of the sagely embryo*[204]]

The other day I saw that you were [at the first bodhisattva stage,] the "joyous,"[205] and so I didn't dare to speak too frankly—I feared that you would

---

201. Mujaku, 133, cites *Dahui Pujue chanshi nianpu* 大慧普覺禪師年譜 (CBETA, J01, no. A042, p. 796, c30–33).

202. Mujaku, 134: 第二段莫求問他人.

203. Mujaku, 134, glosses *guo xia* 過夏 thus: "Participant in Determining Governmental Matters Li, being an official, could not be in the city [of Quanzhou] during the restrictive period of the summer retreat [*ango*]" [忠曰李參政官人不可在城中安居結制]. The term *ango* refers to the intensive training of the summer rain's retreat at Chan monasteries. Li had participated in such a summer intensive at Dahui's Yunmen Hermitage in Yangxu. In India, this was the rainy season retreat of three months when monks stayed in the monasteries and concentrated on study and practice.

204. Mujaku, 134: 第三段勸聖胎長養.

205. Mujaku, 134–135, glosses *huanxi* 歡喜 thus: "The first stage is the path of vision and is called the 'joyous stage.' This is what is meant here" [忠曰初地見道名歡喜地此之謂也]. The first of the ten bodhisattva stages (*daśabhūmi*) is called "joyous" (*pramuditā*) and coincides with the attainment of the path of vision (*darśanamārga*); the remaining nine stages coincide with the attainment of the path of cultivation (*bhāvanamārga*).

fail to get the meaning of my words. Given that you have now stabilized at the "joyous" stage, I dare to express myself. *This matter* truly is not easy—you must feel embarrassed for your shortcomings. Often those of sharp faculties and superior wisdom apprehend [the "joyous stage"] without the expenditure of effort, and so they subsequently produce the thought that [*this matter*] is easy, and hence do not engage in [the subsequent nine stages of] practice.[206] Most of them go on being snatched up by the many sense objects in front of their eyes and are unable to assume the role of autonomous subject. Many days and months pass, but their delusion does not recede. Their Way-strength cannot attain victory over the strength of karma, and Māra gets a suitable opportunity. They are certain to be grabbed up by Māra. Even by life's end they still have not gained any [awakening] energy. A thousand times you must remember my words of the previous day[207] [from the *Śūraṃgama Sūtra*]: "As to principle, one all-at-once awakens; one rides this awakening, and there is a complete melting away. But phenomena are not all-at-once removed; [only] by a graduated sequence are they exhausted."[208] Walking, standing, sitting, and lying down, you absolutely must not forget this quotation.

[7.4: *Answers the question about the great dharma's not yet being bright*[209]]

Beyond this there are various different sayings of the ancients—in no case should you take [these *upāyas*] as "real" [teachings].[210] However, you must not take them as "unreal" either. If you become practiced over a long period of time, spontaneously and secretly you will tally with your own

---

206. Takagi, 22a, at *xiuxing* 修行 inserts: "post-awakening" [悟後].

207. Refers to the line *I dare not forget your exhortation at the time we parted* in Li's question letter #7.2; Mujaku, 135, glosses *qian wan jiqu qianri zhi yu* 千萬記取前日之語 thus: "This is the question letter's *exhortation at the time we parted*. It is the four lines below" [忠曰此即問書所謂臨別叮嚀之語是也下文四句也].

208. *Śūraṃgama Sūtra*: 理則頓悟。乘悟併銷。事非頓除。因次第盡。(T945.19.155a8–9).

209. Mujaku, 136: 第四段荅大法不明之問.

210. Mujaku, 136, glosses *bu ke yi wei shi* 不可以爲實 thus: "As *upāyas* the ancients bequeath a single line or a single saying, and therefore these should not be taken as 'real' teachings. However, the gate of *upāyas* has a variety of sequences of ideas and intentionalities, and, if you do not rely on them, then you have no other clues for entering awakening. Therefore, you also should not consider them to be 'unreal constructs'" [忠曰爲方便垂一句一語故不可爲實法也然方便門頭有種種語脉意地不依之則遂無他入路故亦不可爲虛設矣].

original mind. There is no need separately to seek out something superior and out-of-the-ordinary [like "the great dharma's becoming bright" and your "responding to karmic abilities of beings without obstruction"].[211]

In the past Preceptor Shuilao, when [in the mountains] looking for a wisteria [branch to make into a walking stick], asked Mazu: "What was the patriarchal master Bodhidharma's intention in coming from the West?" Mazu said: "Draw near, and I will tell you." Shuilao then drew near, and Mazu, blocking him at the chest, pushed him down with one shove. Shuilao without thinking got back up and, clapping his hands, gave out "the great laugh." Mazu said: "What principle did you see that you laugh like that?" Shuilao said: "The immeasurable meanings of the thousands upon thousands of dharma teachings— today on the tip of a single hair I understand the source of all of them." Mazu paid him no heed [i.e., did not certify his great awakening].[212]

Xuefeng, knowing that Gushan's karmic conditioning was ripe,[213] one day suddenly seized him by the collar and said: "What is this?" Gushan, his doubts dissolved, awakened. But his mind of awakening immediately disappeared. All he did was, with a slight smile, raise his arms and wave them about.[214] Xuefeng said: "Are you setting up [the concept of] a principle?" Gushan again waved his arms, saying: "Preceptor, you know there's no such thing as principle!" Xuefeng immediately left off.

Chan Master Mengshan Daoming was chasing after Postulant Lu [i.e., the sixth patriarch Huineng].[215] When they got as far as the

---

211. Mujaku, 136, glosses *bie qiu shusheng qite* 別求殊勝奇特 thus: "You should not separately seek out something unusual like the great dharma's becoming bright. In all cases that is incorrect" [忠曰不可別求大法分明之奇特縱求得皆是不是者].

212. Mujaku, 136, glosses *Mazu bian bu guan ta* 馬祖便不管他 thus: "and did not certify his great awakening" [亦不證明他大悟]. See *Jingde chuandeng lu* 景德傳燈錄, T2076.51.262c8–11.

213. *Jingde chuandeng lu* 景德傳燈錄, T2076.51.351a2–16.

214. Mujaku, 136, glosses *yaoye* 搖曳 by citing *Fozu tongji* 佛祖統紀: "Hui'an.... one day showed illness. He sat straight and *raised his arms and waved them about, warning everyone not to be noisy*. At the time of transmigrating he said: 'The Buddha has arrived!' He ordered everyone to recite *nembutsu* and quickly departed. His age was ninety-six" [慧安.... 一日 示疾。端坐以手搖曳。戒眾人勿誼。移時曰佛至矣。令眾念佛倏然脫去。壽九十六。] (T2035.49.282a14–18).

215. *Jingde chuandeng lu* 景德傳燈錄, T2076.51.232a1–18.

Dayu Mountain Range [on the border of Jiangxi and Guangdong, Daoming] snatched at the robe and bowl. Mr. Lu flung them on top of a stone, saying: "This robe is the seal of faith [of the transmission of the dharma, i.e., proof that the master has transmitted the dharma to the disciple]—is it something we should fight over with brute force? If you want it, then take it." Daoming made no move to pick it up and then said: "I am seeking the dharma—it's not for the sake of the robe and bowl. Please, Postulant, instruct me!" Mr. Lu said: "Not thinking of good and not thinking of bad: at just such a moment, what is your *original face*?" Daoming right then had a great awakening. With sweat pouring from his entire body and tears streaming down his face, he bowed and said: "Beyond the speech with a hidden meaning that you just uttered,[216] is there still another meaning?" Mr. Lu said: "What I just spoke for you now has no hidden meaning. If you do a reverse-illumination of your [*original*] *face*, the hidden meaning will be right at your side. If I were to speak of it, then it couldn't be taken as the true hidden meaning.[217]

When the three stories of these three honored monks are compared to your experience of "in 'the single laugh' released from doubt," is it superior or inferior? Please try to judge for yourself.[218] Did your [experience] have any separate unusual principle?[219] If it does have such a separate thing, then it seems that, on the contrary, you didn't achieve release from doubt [in "the single laugh"].

---

216. Mujaku, 138, glosses *mi yu* 密語 thus: "Refers to the line *not thinking of good ... original face?*" [忠曰不思善乃至本來面目之語].

217. *Liu zu dashi fabao tan jing* 六祖大師法寶壇經, T2008.48.349b24–28; *Jingde chuandeng lu* 景德傳燈錄, T2076.51.232a10–14.

218. Mujaku, 139, glosses *qing zi duan kan* 請自斷看 thus: "This is a response ... to the line *spontaneously and secretly tally with your own original mind [#7.4]*" [忠曰應 ... 自然默默契自本心矣之語].

219. Mujaku, 139, glosses *bie you qite daoli me* 別有奇特道理麼 thus: "The meaning is: if these three *gong'ans* are one with what you apprehended, then all the *gong'ans* should naturally be one with it. Therefore, if for a long time you nurture entrance into awakening, then all the different stories will be clarified within your own awakening" [忠曰言此三則公案若與公之得處一般則一切公案自然可一般故久久長養省入處則差別因緣於自悟中當分明也].

[7.5: *Answers the question about having obstruction in leading beings*[220]]

Just worry about becoming a buddha—don't worry about not being able to speak dharma like a buddha. From ancient times people who have attained the Way, once they themselves have enough, take their own surplus[221] to respond to karmic abilities and lead beings. They are like a mirror on a mirror-stand, or a bright pearl in the palm—if a Central Asian barbarian comes, they reflect a Central Asian barbarian; and, if a Han Chinese comes, they reflect a Han Chinese. It's not a matter of [effortfully] concentrating mind. If one were to [effortfully] concentrate mind, there would exist a "real" dharma to give to people.[222]

[7.6: *Connects to the above two sections*[223]]

If you want to have the great dharma be bright, and to respond to karmic abilities without stagnation, "do just as you were doing before."[224] It is not necessary to ask other people questions [about whether your own great dharma is bright or not yet bright].[225] After some time you yourself will nod with understanding.

[7.7: *Summing up: Dahui enjoins Li a second time*[226]]

The words [from the *Śūraṃgama Sūtra*] that I mentioned to you face to face at the time of our parting—please write them as an inscription at the right of your seat. Beyond this there is nothing else to say. Even if there

---

220. Mujaku, 139: 第五段荅應接有礙之問.

221. Mujaku, 140, glosses *tui ji zhi yu* 推己之餘 thus: "The *yu* [*surplus left over*] is the key word. It is like a wealthy family's taking the surplus left over to benefit the poor—it doesn't decrease their foundation" [忠曰餘字眼也如富家以剩餘惠貧不損元本也].

222. Mujaku, 140, glosses *you shi fa yu ren yi* 有實法與人矣 thus: "If there were a 'real' dharma given to people, it would necessarily be a false dharma. Also, the word *real* is a response to the previous *the different sayings* [*of the ancients*]—*in no case should you take them as* real [#7.4]" [忠曰若有實法與人必是妄法也又實字應前差別言句皆不可以爲實].

223. Mujaku, 140: 第六段結上二段.

224. Mujaku, 140, glosses *reng jiu* 仍舊 thus: "You must stop the seeking mind and have *nothing-to-do*. The meaning is: you should nurture" [忠曰須歇求心而無事去也言當長養也].

225. Mujaku, 140, glosses *bu bi wen ren* 不必問人 thus: "The meaning is: even though *this matter* does not preclude asking people questions, it's not something that can be finished by asking questions of people, and so questioning is not necessary" [言此事雖不妨問人然非問人可了畢者故不須問也].

226. Mujaku, 141: 第七段総結再囑.

were something more to say, for you at your stage, it's all idle talk. Too much kudzu-verbiage! Let's temporarily shelve these matters.

8. Continued [Second Letter in Reply to Participant in Determining Governmental Matters Li] (Question Letter Attached)
[Li's Question Letter]

[*Commentary:* Hyesim says, *"The main purport of this letter is for Li to present his enlightenment."*[227] *This question letter and Dahui's reply letter date to Shaoxing 5/1135. Pre-exile letters.*]

[QL 8.1: *Li narrates the personal experience he has gained*[228]]

Recently I received your reply letter with your instruction, and I completely understand its deep purport. My personal experience extends to three things. 1. Events have no "going against me" or "going in my direction"—I respond according to conditions, and no residue [of events] is left in my heart.[229] 2. When habit-energy from my past lives is dense, even without adding on an attempt to eliminate it, all by itself it lightens. 3. The cases of the ancients, about which in the past I was in the dark, once in a while I temporarily can see them. This is not false talk on my part [that is aimed at deceiving you and first deceives myself[230]].

[QL 8.2: *Relates that the previous question did not involve separately seeking out (something superior and out-of-the-ordinary)*][231]

My saying in a previous letter that "the great dharma is not yet bright" was because I was worried about being satisfied with getting a little

---

227. Hyesim, 43: 狀大旨呈見發明.

228. Mujaku, 141: 第一段敘得驗.

229. Mujaku, 141, glosses *bu liu xiong zhong* 不留胸中 thus: "At present towards sense objects that go against me or go in my direction I have no grasping attachments" [今於順逆無所執著也].

230. Mujaku, 141, glosses *fei zi mei zhe* 非自昧者 thus: "*Zi mei* means *false talk*. With false talk aimed at deceiving others, one first deceives oneself" [忠曰自昧謂妄語也妄語欲欺人者先自欺己].

231. Mujaku, 142: 第二段敘前問非別求.

bit[232]—[as Mencius says] one should "extend and strengthen."[233] How could I possibly be separately seeking out a superior [and out-of-the-ordinary] understanding?

[QL 8.3: *Li comprehends that phenomena are not all-at-once removed*[234]]

Purifying and eliminating [the defilements] in the present flow [i.e., step-by-step practice], in principle, is not non-existent. How could I dare not inscribe [the *Śūraṃgama Sūtra* quotation] and wear it [constantly] at my waist-belt?

[8. Dahui's Reply Letter]

[*Commentary:* Mujaku says, "The main idea of this letter is again to show the nurturing of the sagely embryo."[235] This letter dates to Shaoxing 5/1135. Pre-exile letter.]

[8.1: *Dahui sends his regards*[236]]

After receiving your letter, my esteem for you has increased more and more. In recent days, in responding to conditions [in the midst of daily activities], are you bold and unconstrained? Are you free and able to act as you wish? In the four postures [of walking, standing, sitting, and lying down] you aren't overcome by the defilements, are you? Are you able to make the two extremes of waking and sleeping a single thusness?[237] In the state of "doing just as you were doing before," are you free of any feelings of being caught up by things? You're not carrying on in the mindset of

---

232. Mujaku, 142, glosses *de shao wei zu* 得少爲足 thus: "Remaining in the state of awakening without exhausting the inexhaustible dharma teachings" [忠曰留悟處不盡無盡法門也].

233. *Mencius, Gongsun Chou shang* 公孫丑上.

234. Mujaku, 142: 第三段領事非頓除.

235. Mujaku, 142: 大意又示聖胎長養.

236. Mujaku, 142: 第一段問候.

237. Mujaku, 143, glosses *wumei er bian yi ru fou* 寤寐二邊得一如否 by citing *Śūraṃgama Sūtra*, T945.19.151b29–c1.

samsara, are you? "Just exhaust 'common' delusive thought—there is no separate 'noble' understanding."[238]

[8.2: *Encourages the nurturing of the sagely embryo*[239]]

You already with "the single laugh" have opened up the true eye, and the *state of being* [of the common-person realm—misfortune-fortune, sickness-health, and so forth]—has all-at-once disappeared.[240] Gaining [awakening] energy or not gaining [awakening] energy—the person drinking water knows for himself whether it is cold or warm. Thus, in the midst of daily activities, you should rely on the words of the Golden-faced Old Master: "Scrape out the main substance [of greed, anger, and stupidity]; eliminate the auxiliary causes [such as the five forbidden pungent foods]; and go against karma in the present [such as killing, stealing, and licentiousness]."[241] This [gradual practice] is the awakened fellow's true *upāya* in the midst of no *upāya*s, true practice and realization in the midst of no practice and realization, and true seizing and discarding in the midst of no seizing and discarding.[242] An ancient said: "When the skin completely comes off, only the one true fruit/reality remains."[243] Also, "when

238. *Wansong laoren pingchang tiantong jue heshang song gu congrong an lu* 萬松老人評唱天童覺和尚頌古從容庵錄, T2004.48.228c1–2.

239. Mujaku, 143: 第二段勸聖胎長養.

240. Mujaku, 144, glosses *xiaoxi dun wang* 消息頓亡 thus: "The *state of being* of the common-person realm suddenly extinguished.... The *state of being* of humans is birth-death, misfortune-fortune, illness-health, and so forth" [忠曰凡夫境界消息忽滅也.... 忠曰人之消息者生死禍福病健等也].

241. *Śūraṃgama Sūtra*: "What are the three types of gradualness? The first is practice—it eliminates the auxiliary causes. The second is true practice—it scrapes out the main substance. The third is increase-and-advance—it goes against the activated karma" [云何名為三種漸次。一者修習。除其助因。二者真修。剗其正性。三者增進。違其現業。] (T945.19.141b27–29). Hyesim, 43: "The main substance is greed, anger, and stupidity. The supplementary causes are the five forbidden pungent roots [such as leek, scallion, garlic, onion, and ginger]. Karma in the present is killing, stealing, and licentiousness" [正性貪嗔痴助因五辛現業殺盜淫也].

242. Mujaku, 145, glosses *wu qu she zhong* 無取捨中 thus: "*Bodhi* [awakening] should be seized, and the *kleśas* [defilements] should be discarded, but, within true principle, there is no *this matter*. Therefore, we say *no seizing and discarding*" [忠曰菩提可取煩惱可捨然真理中無此事故言無取捨也].

243. Mujaku, 145, cites a saying of Chan Master Lizhou Yaoshan Weiyan 澧州藥山惟儼禪師 (745–828) in *Wu deng hui yuan* 五燈會元 (CBETA, X80, no. 1565, p. 109, a19–b8 // Z 2B:11, p. 82, a10–b5 // R138, p. 163, a10–b5).

the manifold boughs of the sandalwood tree completely come off, there is only true sandalwood."²⁴⁴ This is the highest purport of going against karma in the present, eliminating the supplementary causes, and scraping out the main substance [of the defilements]. Give it a try—think about it.

[8.3: *Conclusion*²⁴⁵]

Talking in this way to one with the standing of a fellow who has awakened to *this matter* is very much like a fan in December.²⁴⁶ But I fear that in the South [where you are²⁴⁷] cold and warmth are still variable,²⁴⁸ and so a fan like this can't be dispensed with.²⁴⁹ Ha! Ha!

9. *In Reply to Supervising Secretary Jiang (Shaoming)*

[*Commentary: Mujaku says, "The main idea of this letter is to urge getting close to a good friend so you can admire his style of virtue."²⁵⁰ This letter dates to Shaoxing 5/1135 when Dahui was forty-seven.²⁵¹ Pre-exile letter.*]

---

244. Mujaku, 145: "I have not yet found the source for this saying" [此語未發所出].

245. Mujaku, 145: 第三段結.

246. Mujaku, 145, glosses *layue shanzi* 臘月扇子 thus: "Useless" [忠曰無用處].

247. Mujaku, 145, glosses *nan di* 南地 thus: "Participant in Determining Governmental Matters Li at the time was in Quannan [in Fujian], and so Dahui says *in the South*" [忠曰李參政時在泉南故言南地].

248. Mujaku, 146, glosses *han xuan bu chang* 寒暄不常 thus: "Dahui fears that Li has not yet attained a pure oneness [in his practice]. Though Participant in Determining Governmental Matters Li himself says "no residue is left in my heart" [i.e., I have no grasping-attachment toward sense objects], Dahui still encourages him in this manner. It can be said that the Master's compassion is very profound" [忠曰恐未得純一無雜也雖李參政自言不留胸中大慧勸勵如此宗師慈悲可謂深重].

249. Mujaku, 146, glosses *ye shao bu de* 也少不得 thus: "On those occasions when you are hot, you can again use this fan. *Cold* is a metaphor for awakening; *warm* is a metaphor for the rising of habit-energies [from past lives]. When you are enjoying coolness on New Year's Eve in Guangnan, even though it's December in the South, you can again use the fan" [忠曰或時暄熱可復用此扇子也寒比覺悟暄比習氣發也廣南除夜納涼則南地雖臘月可復用扇也].

250. Mujaku, 146: 大意勸親近善友可慕其風德.

251. The dating is according to Lü and Wu, 35. Jiang has no biography in *Song History*. Hucker, 133: "Supervising Secretary (*jishizhong* 給事中) refers to "officials normally charged to monitor the flow of documents to and from the throne, to return for revision any documents considered improper in form or substance, to check on the implementation of imperial

[9.1: *Dahui praises and advises Jiang*[252]]

A lifetime of a hundred years' duration—how many can there be? You began as a humble scholar and have served successively in high official positions. You are someone who has received first-class good fortune in the world. You are capable of knowing shame, and you have turned your mind towards the Way, studying the supramundane dharma of gaining release from samsara. Also, you are someone who is in a first-class advantageous position in the world. You must by all means pull yourself together and have a thick hide[253]—you must not accept the directives of others.[254] If on your own you comprehend your "birth year" and "astrological sign" [i.e., your *original allotment*[255]] and make clear to yourself just where you're standing, then in both the mundane and the supramundane you will be a *great person* who has finished.

[9.2: *Taking joy in being close to a good friend*[256]]

I am informed that day after day you are talking about the Way with the Participant in Determining Governmental Matters [i.e., Li Hanlao, aka Li Bing, of letters #7–8]. Splendid! Splendid! This gentleman has stopped the mind that rushes about seeking,[257] and has attained a severing of the path of verbalization and the extinguishing of the state having mental objects. Concerning the various contrasting [*upāya-*]roads [i.e., the thousands of

---

orders, to criticize and propose imperial policies, and sometimes to assist in keeping the Imperial Diary."

252. Mujaku, 147: 第一段贊許勸導.

253. Mujaku, 147, glosses *lengque mianpi* 冷却面皮 thus: "Cut off affect and have an iron face" [忠曰絕人情而鐵面也]. Korean Anonymous, 126, glosses the phrase thus: "It is not merely not accepting the instructions of perverse teachers and directly lifting up the *original allotment*, but also not relying on receiving through transmission" [非但不受邪師指示直擧本分而不假傳受者也].

254. Mujaku, 148, glosses *chapai* 差排 thus: "Means *commands of perverse teachers*" [忠曰言邪師指揮也].

255. Mujaku, 148, glosses *benming yuanchen* 本命元辰 thus: "*Benming* is the year of one's birth; *yuanchen* is the astrological sign of one's birth year. They are to be taken as metaphors for one's own *original allotment*" [忠曰本命自生歲也元辰者生年所司星辰也以喻自己本分矣].

256. Mujaku, 149: 第二段喜親近善友.

257. *Zhenzhou Linji Huizhao chanshi yulu* 鎮州臨濟慧照禪師語錄, T1985.47.497b7–8.

different sayings of the ancients²⁵⁸], he has looked closely at the "foothold" of the ancients, without being ensnared by the sayings used as *upāyas* by the ancients. This is how he [i.e., Li Hanlao] is now—I see this, and that's why I haven't said another word to him. I was afraid it would appear I was taking him for a dimwit. I am waiting for him in the future to want to have a talk with me, and then for the first time we will put our eyebrows together up close and have a discussion. It's not that we've ended it as it stands. If a student of the Way has not yet stopped the mind that rushes around seeking, even if he and I were to put our eyebrows together and have a discussion, [he would still be seeking answers of me and so] of what benefit would it be? That would be no more than "a crazy person running around outside the pale."²⁵⁹ An ancient said: "Getting close to a good person is like walking around in the fog. Although your clothes are never soaking wet, from time to time they do get damp."²⁶⁰ Just talk with Participant in Determining Governmental Matters [Li]. I very much pray you will do so.

[9.3: *One should not make strained interpretations of the old standards*²⁶¹]

You should not take the sayings passed down by the ancients and casually poke and pry into them. For instance, when the Great Teacher Hongzhou Ma encountered Preceptor Huairang, [Huairang] spoke dharma: "For instance, when an ox is drawing a cart and the cart doesn't go, is it right to hit the cart or is it right to hit the ox?"²⁶² Master Ma, upon hearing this, knew immediately what he was driving at. The few lines of this saying— all the masters of the various regions give dharma talks on them that are startling like thunder and bolts of lightning,²⁶³ inexhaustible like clouds

---

258. Takagi, 25b, at *chabie yi lu* 差別異路 inserts: "the thousands of different sayings of the ancients" [古人言句千差萬別].

259. Mujaku, 150: "Even though Dahui is speaking of Li Bing [i.e., Li Hanlao], he is indirectly exposing Supervising Secretary Jiang" [忠曰雖言李邴旁破江給事]. Mujaku, 514, for the source of the simile cites *Preceptor Baozhi's Verses on the Twelve Hours* (*Baozhi heshang shier shi song* 寶誌和尚十二時頌) in *Jingde chuandeng lu* 景德傳燈錄, T2076.51.450a17–b15.

260. *Guishan jingce zhu* 溈山警策註 (CBETA, X63, no. 1239, p. 228, b1 // Z 2:16, p. 146, b10 // R111, p. 291, b10).

261. Mujaku, 150: 第三段不可亂解古則.

262. *Jingde chuandeng lu* 景德傳燈錄, T2076.51.240c23–24.

263. Mujaku, 151, glosses *ru lei ru ting* 如雷如霆 thus: "By their strange and sublime wording they startle people like thunder and bolts of lightning" [忠曰奇言妙句驚人如雷霆].

and rain,[264] but they haven't understood it. It's just preposterous verbiage and strained exegeses of the words. Actually, your smug exegesis [of the old case] at the end of the letter you [i.e., Supervising Secretary Jiang] wrote to [my student] Zhoufeng[265]—when I read it I couldn't help letting loose a huge laugh.[266] You should be listed in the same criminal indictment as [those teachers] who say, "It's *Tathāgata* Chan!" or "It's Patriarchal Chan!"— and exiled to the same locale!

[9.4: *Dahui prohibits the composing of verses*[267]]

I carefully scanned the verse you sent—it was superior to the two verses of a previous day. But from now on you should stop this sort of thing. Making one verse after another—will there ever come a time when there will be an end to it? Imitate Participant in Determining Governmental Matters [Li Hanlao]—how is it that he doesn't compose verses? Why doesn't he compose even a single word? It is just that those who know the rules are cautious. [Li] does occasionally [compose a verse that] reveals a little, and naturally it scratches the place where I itch. As [Li's] verse on an image [of Śākyamuni's] descent from the mountain says, "Wherever he encountered people, he confronted deceptive words head on."[268] This saying could serve as medicinal eyedrops for Chan monks![269] You'll see

---

264. Mujaku, 151, glosses *ru yun ru yu* 如雲如雨 thus: "Their eloquence is inexhaustible, like clouds or a downpour of rain [忠曰辯才無盡如雲如雨澆].

265. Chan Master Zhoufeng Qinglao 舟峯慶老禪師, one of Dahui's ninety-four dharma successors, appears in *Xu chuandeng lu* 續傳燈錄, T2077.51.685c16. Mujaku, 152, glosses *shu wei duzhuan jiezhu* 書尾杜撰解注 thus: "Supervising Secretary Jiang wrote a letter to Zhoufeng. At the end of this letter Supervising Secretary Jiang gave an exegesis of an old-standard story" [江給事作書與舟峰其書尾江給事解注古則因緣也].

266. Mujaku, 153, glosses *bu jue jue dao* 不覺絕倒 thus: "Your exegesis was irrelevant, and so I gave out a great laugh" [忠曰所解注沒交涉故大笑也].

267. Mujaku, 153: 第四段制止作頌.

268. This verse is presumably one that Li Hanlao inscribed on a painting of Śākyamuni's coming out the mountains after six years of asceticism. This pictorial subject, only implied in classical Buddhist texts and Chan transmission records, emerged within Chan during the Song dynasty. See Gregory Levine and Yukio Lippit, *Awakenings: Zen Figure Painting in Medieval Japan* (New York: Japan Society, 2007), 42. The verse appears as the third in a set of four verses in the *Shending Yunwai Ze chanshi yulu* 神鼎雲外澤禪師語錄 (CBETA, J33, no. B280, p. 294, a7–8).

269. Mujaku, 154, glosses *dian yan yao* 點眼藥 thus: "If you put drops of eye-medicine in the eyes, the eyes can see clearly. The words of this verse can open peoples' eye of the Way, and, therefore, it is a metaphor for medicinal eyedrops" [忠曰眼藥點之於眼則得眼目分明也其頌語能開人道眼故比點眼藥也].

for yourself one of these days.[270] There is no need for me to annotate it to death.[271]

[9.5: *Conclusion*[272]]

I've recently gotten the impression that you have undergone a complete change,[273] and are expending a great deal of energy for the sake of *this matter*. Therefore, carried away, I have written this letter at great length.[274]

10. In Reply to Administrator of the Bureau of Military Affairs Fu (Jishen)

[*Commentary: Mujaku says, "The main idea of this letter is the teaching that knowledge is empty-quiescent."*[275] *This letter dates to Shaoxing 8/1138 when Dahui was fifty.*[276] *Pre-exile letter.*]

[10.1: *Dahui allows an elucidation of dharma for Fu*[277]]

Your letter informs me that, since your early years you've been well acquainted with having confidence in this Way, but that in your later years,

---

270. Mujaku, 154, glosses *gong yi ri zi jian yi* 公異日自見矣 thus: "Means that on another day, after awakening, you will see for yourself the sublimity of Li Bing's [i.e., Li Hanlao's] verse" [忠曰言公他日悟後自見李邴頌妙處也].

271. Mujaku, 154, glosses *bu bi shanseng zhupo ye* 不必山僧注破也 thus: "Means that one of these days you will come to understand it on your own and won't wait upon my exegesis of it" [言他日公自解得而不待我注解也].

272. Mujaku, 154: 第五段結.

273. Takagi, 27a, at *gaibian* 改變 inserts: "changed old habit-energy" [改變舊習].

274. Mujaku, 154, glosses *gu zuo ci shu* 故作此書 thus: "Note: These words imply that this letter is not an answer letter. I think the word *answer* in the title is a mistake. Also, the talk at the beginning of the letter is not the talk of an answer letter.... It's not a matter of Supervising Secretary Jiang's presenting a letter consisting of proper questions about the Way.... Therefore, Dahui in a leisurely manner writes this letter urging and encouraging him—it's not an answer letter for Jiang's sake" [忠曰按此語此書非荅書題荅字恐訛書首語亦非荅書之語也....蓋非江給事呈正問道書....故大慧從容作書勸勉非爲之荅書耳].

275. Mujaku, 154: 大意示知解寂滅法門.

276. The dating is according to Lü and Wu, 37. For a biographical entry for Fu Zhirou 富直柔 (*zi* Jishen 季申), see *Song History*, 375 (16.2960–61). Fu was the grandson of the Northern Song Grand Councilor (*zaixiang* 宰相) Fu Bizhi 富弼之. Hucker, 436: "Bureau of Military Affairs [*shumi yuan* 樞密院] was "the paramount central government agency in control of the state's military forces."

277. Mujaku, 156: 第一段許說示.

"blocked by knowledge," you have not had a single experience of awakening and want to come to know *upāya*s for embodying the Way from dawn to dusk. Since I accept your extreme sincerity, I dare not stand by as an outsider. To rely on your confession in order to render a verdict on the case, a little kudzu-verbiage [is called for; i.e., the dharma talk below²⁷⁸].

[10.2: *Dahui censures the "blocked-by-knowledge" viewpoint²⁷⁹*]

The "knowledge" that has "blocked" the Way for you—it's just this very seeking for awakening. What other "knowledge" could there be that serves as a "blockage" for you? In the final analysis, what is it that you are calling "knowledge"? Where does this "knowledge" come from? And who is the one who is being "blocked"? Just this single line of yours [i.e., "in my later years, blocked by knowledge, I have not had a single experience of awakening"²⁸⁰] harbors three upside-down viewpoints: 1. You yourself saying that you are blocked by knowledge [i.e., you yourself have created the knowledge that you yourself are blocked by²⁸¹]. 2. You yourself saying that you are not yet awakened and thus have been satisfied with being a deluded person [i.e., you keep yourself stagnating in non-awakening].²⁸² 3. On top of that, in the midst of delusion you are assuming a posture of waiting for awakening [i.e., you yourself have created the delusion, but you yourself are waiting for awakening²⁸³]. It's just these three upside-down viewpoints that are

---

278. Mujaku, 157, glosses *geteng shaoxu* 葛藤少許 thus: "Means the dharma talk in the text below" [言下文說法也].

279. Mujaku, 157: 第二段責自以知解爲障.

280. Mujaku, 157, glosses *ci yi ju* 此一句 thus: "Refers to the line *in my later years, blocked by knowledge, I have not had a single experience of awakening*" [指晚年爲知解所障未有一悟入處之語].

281. Mujaku, 157, glosses *zi yan wei zhijie yun yun* 自言爲知解云云 thus: "The significance of the word *yourself* is grave. It means: you yourself created the knowledge, but you yourself are blocked by it. How could this not be an upside-down viewpoint? Therefore, Dahui employs the word *yourself*" [忠曰自字意重言汝自造作知解却自被障之豈非顛倒耶故言自].

282. Mujaku, 157, glosses *zi yan wei wu yun yun* 自言未悟云云 thus: "This means: there is no one blocking your awakening. You yourself go on stagnating in non-awakening. You yourself are satisfied with being a deluded person. But you yourself say: 'I am not yet awakened.' How could this not be an upside-down viewpoint? Therefore, Dahui employs the word *yourself*" [忠曰言無人障汝悟者汝自滯留不悟去自甘作迷人却自言我未悟豈非顛倒耶故言自].

283. Mujaku, 157, glosses *geng zai mi zhong yun yun* 更在迷中云云 thus: "Waiting for awakening is delusion. You yourself create delusion, but you yourself wait for awakening. How could this not be an upside-down viewpoint?" [忠曰待悟的即是迷也自造作迷却自待悟豈非顛倒耶].

the basis of samsara. You absolutely must arrive at the state wherein not a single thought arises. The mind of upside-down viewpoints will be severed, and then you will come to know that there is no delusion to be annihilated, no awakening to wait for, and no knowledge to be blocked by. The person drinking water knows for himself whether it is cold or warm. After a long while spontaneously you will not generate this ["blocked-by-knowledge"] way of looking at things. Concerning the mind that has the ability to know *this is "knowledge"*[284]—see whether that can be "blocked"; concerning the mind that has the ability to know *this is "knowledge"*—are there various sorts [of mind, i.e., is there more than one mind]?[285]

[10.3: *But the ancient worthies used knowledge without making it into a blockage*[286]]

Those of great wisdom since ancient times have all taken "knowledge" as their companion. They take "knowledge" as an *upāya*. Making use of that "knowledge" they dispense an evenhanded compassion, and making use of that "knowledge" they perform buddha deeds. They are like the dragon that has attained the habitat of his waters and the tiger that is at home in the mountains [i.e., stabilized in the *original allotment*]. They never take this ["knowledge"[287]] as a source of worry—this is just because they are able to know the *place* from which "knowledge" arises.[288] Once you realize

---

284. Mujaku, 158, glosses *zhi zhijie de xin shang* 知知解底心上 thus: "As the eye can't see the eye or the finger can't point at the finger" [忠曰如眼不見眼如指不指指].

285. Mujaku, 158, glosses *you ru xuduo ban ye wu* 有如許多般也無 thus: "The *Jingde Era Transmission of the Lamp Record* Chan Master Yangshan Ji section says: 'A monk asked: "Aside from this beyond-the-norms, is there any other *upāya* to enable students to attain awakening?" The Master said: "Both *there is another* and *there is not another* will make your mind ill at ease. What place are you from?" The monk replied: "I'm a man of Youzhou." The Master said: "Do you still long for that place?" The monk replied: "I constantly long for it." The Master said: "That place's towers, groves, parks, people, and horses side by side—do your remembrances consist of various kinds?" The monk replied: "When I arrive *here*, I have no point of view at all"' [T2076.51.283c13–18] . . . This idea is identical to the one [in Dahui's words]" [忠曰傳燈錄十一仰山寂禪師章曰僧曰。除此格外。還別有方便令學人得入也無。師曰。別有別無令汝心不安。汝是什麼處人。曰幽州人。師曰。汝還思彼處否。曰常思。師曰。彼處樓臺林苑人馬駢闐。汝返思底還有許多般也無。僧曰。某甲到遮裏一切不見有。. . . 忠曰此意同之].

286. Mujaku, 158: 第三段古德却用知解不爲障.

287. Mujaku, 158, glosses *bu yi ci wei nao* 不以此爲惱 thus: "*This* refers to knowledge" [忠曰此者指知解也].

288. Mujaku, 158, glosses *ta shide zhijie qi chu* 他識得知解起處 thus: "*They* is those of great wisdom since ancient times. The meaning is: they are able to know the *place* from which

the *place* from which it arises, this "knowledge" becomes the site of liberation [i.e., the site of the Buddha's awakening beneath the tree], the *place*
where you escape samsara. Since it is the site of liberation, the *place* where
you escape samsara, then any knowing or understanding *as a thing-in-itself*
is extinguished. Since knowing or understanding is extinguished, the one
who knows "knowledge" cannot but be extinguished. "Awakening," "nirvana," "thusness," "buddha-nature"—they cannot but be extinguished.
Beyond that what can you be "blocked by," and beyond that where will you
seek "awakening"?[289] The old one Śākyamuni said: "Karmas arise from
mind. Therefore, it is said that mind is like an illusion. If you divorce
from these false discriminations, then all the rebirth paths disappear."[290]
A monk asked Preceptor Dazhu: "'What sort of thing is great nirvana?'
Dazhu said: 'Not creating the karma of samsara is great nirvana.' The
monk asked: 'What sort of thing is the karma of samsara?' Dazhu said:
'Seeking great nirvana is the karma of samsara.'"[291] Also, an ancient said:
"If a student of the Way for a single thought-moment calculates ['*this* is]
samsara,' he falls into the Way of Māra. To produce views for even a single thought-moment is to fall into outsider Ways."[292] Also, the *Vimalakīrti*
says: "The Māras take joy in samsara, but bodhisattvas, who are in the
midst of samsara, do not reject it. The followers of outsider Ways take joy
in the various views, but bodhisattvas, who are in the midst of views, are
unmoved by them."[293] These are precisely models of "taking knowledge
as a companion, taking knowledge as an *upāya*, making use of knowledge
to dispense an evenhanded compassion, and making use of knowledge to
perform buddha deeds." It is just because they [i.e., the bodhisattvas] realize that "the three incalculable aeons [of the bodhisattva path]" are empty,
that "samsara and nirvana" have [always] been quiescent.

---

that knowledge arises, and, therefore, they use the knowledge but are not used by the knowledge" [忠曰他者從上大智慧之士也謂能識得起處故能使知解不爲知解所使也].

289. Mujaku, 159, glosses *geng you he wu ke zhang ... wuru* 更有何物可障 ... 悟入 thus:
"*Can be blocked by* and *awakening* both refer to the words of Administrator of the Bureau
of Military Affairs Fu (at the beginning of this letter)—Dahui demolishes them both" [忠
曰言可障言悟入皆舉樞密語(在書首)而折之].

290. *Da fangguang fo huayan jing*, T279.10.235b23–25. The speaker is actually Samantabhadra
Bodhisattva.

291. *Jingde chuandeng lu* 景德傳燈錄, T2076.51.247a16–18.

292. *Huangbo shan Duanji chanshi chuanxin fa yao* 黃檗山斷際禪師傳心法要,
T2012A.48.381b22–23.

293. T475.14.544c8–10.

[10.4: *Fu has violated Dahui's directive to avoid perverse teachings*[294]]

Having not yet reached *this level*,[295] you must not get drawn into the "ghost-cave"[296] by the nonsense preached by perverse teachers. Closing your eyes [in the practice of sitting] will produce phantasmal thoughts.[297] In recent times, as the Way of the patriarchs has declined, this [perverse] crew has been burgeoning. It is truly "one blind person guiding a pack of blind people, leading them by the hand into a pit of fire"[298]—one should have deep pity for them. I hope you will stiffen your backbone [and not follow the teachings of these perverse masters[299]]. Don't exhibit this sort of behavior [i.e., the "silence-as-illumination" of closing the eyes]![300] Those who exhibit

---

294. Mujaku, 162: 第四段逆令避邪說.

295. Mujaku, 162, glosses *ji wei dao zhe ge tiandi* 既未到遮箇田地 thus: "Dahui has seen through his attachment to 'stillness *über alles*.' Therefore, there is this dharma talk, which appears in the next letter" [忠曰大慧看破他著靜勝故有此說法見于次書].

296. Mujaku, 162, cites *Chi xiu Baizhang qinggui* 敕修百丈清規: "Chan Master Fayun Yuantong scolded people for closing their eyes in Zen sitting. He called it 'the ghost-cave of Black Mountain'" [法雲圓通禪師呵人閉目坐禪。謂黑山鬼窟。] (T2025.48.1143a11–12).

297. Two passages from the *Dahui Pujue chanshi yulu* 大慧普覺禪師語錄 (from *Dharma Talks of Dahui* and *Letters of Dahui*) expand on this Dahui theme. The first is: "Intently closing your eyes and producing the appearance of death—they call this 'sitting in stillness, contemplating mind, silence-as-illumination.' Furthermore, they take this perverse view to seduce the ignorant mediocrities, saying: 'If you get stillness for one day, that's one day's *gongfu*.' Painful!" [一向閉眉合眼。做死模樣。謂之靜坐觀心默照。更以此邪見。誘引無識庸流曰。靜得一日。便是一日工夫。苦哉。] (*Dahui Pujue chanshi fayu* 大慧普覺禪師法語; T1998A.47.895b14–17). The second passage is: "Some consider Chan to be lapsing into silence, doing cross-legged sitting in the 'ghost-cave of Black Mountain,' closing the eyes, calling it the '*state of being* [before the appearance of] Bhīṣma-garjita-svara Buddha' [i.e., the name of the very first buddha to appear in this world] or 'your face before your father and mother conceived you,' and calling it 'silence as constant illumination.' This type of party doesn't seek sublime awakening. They take awakening as falling into the secondary grade. They take awakening as duping and intimidating people. They take awakening as something provisionally established [as an *upāya*]. Since they have never had an awakening, they don't believe that awakening exists." [或以無言無說。坐在黑山下鬼窟裏。閉眉合眼。謂之威音王那畔父母未生時消息。亦謂之默而常照。為禪者。如此等輩。不求妙悟。以悟為落在第二頭。以悟為誑謼人。以悟為建立。自既不曾悟。亦不信有悟底。] (*Letters of Dahui* #58.4; T1998A.47.941c2–7).

298. Mujaku, 162, cites *Jingde chuandeng lu* 景德傳燈錄, T2076.51.311a16.

299. Mujaku, 162, glosses *ying zhuo jiliang gu* 硬著脊梁骨 thus: "Means: not follow their teachings" [言不隨他教也].

300. Mujaku, 162, glosses *zhe ban qujiu* 遮般去就 thus: "The silence-as-illumination of closing the eyes" [閉眉合眼底默照也]. For *qujiu* 去就, see *Zhuangzi, Qiushui* 秋水.

this sort of behavior,[301] although they can temporarily restrain this smelly skin bag of a body, they then [go on to] consider this to be the ultimate: but their minds are still swirling about like wild horses.[302] Even if their minds are temporarily "parked," it's like grass with a stone pressing down on it—before you know it it's growing again. Wanting directly to seize unexcelled awakening and arrive at the place of ultimate peace and joy—how unreasonable is that! I also was once misled by this crew.[303] If later I had not encountered a true teacher [i.e., Yuanwu[304]], I probably would have spent my whole life in vain. Every time I reflect on this, I find it completely intolerable. Because of this, I don't stint on oral karma [in exposing false teachers[305]] and try my utmost to save people from this fraud. Right now I am a person [like the ancient Qu Boyu] who still gradually is coming to realize his mistakes.[306]

[10.5: *Dahui shows the exertion of mind in* gongfu[307]]

If you want to take the direct-and-quick path to comprehension, you must obtain the explosive shattering of *this single thought*[308]—then you will bring samsara to an end. That's called "awakening." But you absolutely must not maintain your mind in a state of waiting for this shattering. If you maintain your mind in the state of [waiting for] shattering, then the time of shattering will never come in an eternity of aeons. Just take the mind of false thought and upside-down viewpoints, the mind of reflection and discrimination, the

---

301. Mujaku, 162, glosses *zuo zhe ban qujiu de* 作遮般去就底 thus: "Refers to perverse teachers and perverse students" [忠曰指邪師邪徒也].

302. Mujaku, 163, glosses *xinshi fenfei* 心識紛飛 thus: "Those for whom Zen sitting is the ultimate are often like this" [忠曰坐禪爲究竟者往往如是]. For wild horses, see *Zhuangzi, Xiaoyaoyou* 逍遙遊.

303. Mujaku, 163, glosses *wei ci liu suowu* 爲此流所誤 thus: "Haven't yet verified who this master is" [忠曰未攷其師爲何人].

304. Mujaku, 163, glosses *zhen shanzhishi* 真善知識 thus: "Means Yuanwu" [忠曰謂圓悟也].

305. Mujaku, 164, glosses *bu xi kouye* 不惜口業 thus: "In exposing perverse teachers what oral karma is there?" [忠曰破邪師何口業之有也].

306. Mujaku, 164, glosses *zhi fei* 知非 by citing *Huainanzi, Yi yuan dao xun* 淮南子一原道訓.

307. Mujaku, 164: 第五段示工夫用心.

308. Mujaku, 164, glosses *bo de yi po* 曝地一破 thus: "*Explosive shattering of the single thought is wonderful awakening*" [忠曰念子曝破者妙悟也]. However, Hyesim, 47: "*Single thought is the huatou*" [念子話頭]. It might be both.

mind that loves living and hates death, the mind of knowing-seeing and understanding, the mind that takes joy in stillness and loathes noisiness—and all-at-once lay them aside! Precisely in the state where you have laid them aside, keep an eye on the *huatou*:[309] A monk asked Zhaozhou: "Does even a dog have buddha-nature?" Zhou said: "*Wu* 無."[310] This one word [*wu* 無] is a weapon to dampen down a lot of bad knowing and bad awareness.

> You must not produce an understanding [of *wu* 無 as the *wu* of the polarity] *there is* [*you* 有]/*there is not* [*wu* 無].
> You must not produce an understanding [of *wu* 無] based on reasoning.
> You must not, during the operation of the mind sense-organ, engage in reflection and conjecture [concerning *wu* 無].
> You must not, during [actions such as] raising eyebrows or winking eyes, allow the mind of calculation to stop on a single point [such as *wu* 無].[311]

---

309. Mujaku, 165, glosses *zhi jiu anxia chu yun yun* 只就按下處云云 thus: "*In the state where you have laid them aside* does not mean keeping an eye on the things that are laid aside. Having laid them aside here, you should keep an eye on the *gong'an*. For example, *not thinking of good and not thinking of bad* is what is laid aside. *What is my original face* is the *huatou* you keep an eye on" [忠曰就按下處者非謂看其按下底物按下了於此可看公案也譬如不思善不思惡是按下底也那箇是某本來面目是看話頭底也].

310. Mujaku, 165, cites the Ming-dynasty compendium *Tianyue mingkong ji* 天樂鳴空集 by Bao Zongzhao 鮑宗肇: "Dahui, at the end of his *Zheng fayan zang*, picks up all the 'illnesses' of the age. He knows that the great dharma is declining, and there is no alternative. He teaches people to grasp their ordinary habitual knowledge, make it into a bundle, and throw it at some other world. And after that they are only to probe the single phrase, the tasteless *huatou*. This is the beginning of 'raising the *wu* 無 *huatou*.' It really originated in the Song dynasty" [大慧於正法眼藏之末悉拈時病知大法將頹遂不得已教人把平日所習知解得力處縛作一束拋向他方世界然後唯將一句無義味話頭參究是提無字話頭之始實起於宋也] (CBETA, J20, no. B097, p. 485, c19–22). This seems to be referring to the "Instructions to the Assembly" (*shizhong* 示眾) at the end of *Zheng fayan zang* 正法眼藏 (CBETA, X67, no. 1309, p. 629, c11–p. 633, b22 // Z 2:23, p. 74, c9–p. 78, b14 // R118, p. 148, a9–p. 155, b14).

311. One possible interpretation of *yang mei shun mu* 揚眉瞬目 (*raising eyebrows, winking eyes*) places it in the context of daily activities (*riyong* 日用). For instance, Dahui's *Zheng fayan zang* 正法眼藏: "Getting *taste* from everyday activities, action, and behavior is to make *raising eyebrows, winking eyes*, lifting of something to awareness, pulling up by the ears into a burrow [i.e., a stereotyped or formulaic place of retreat]" [於日用動轉施為處得滋味者。以揚眉瞬目舉覺提撕為窠臼。] (CBETA, X67, no. 1309, p. 630, a16–17 // Z 2:23, p. 75, a2–3 // R118, p. 149, a2–3). Another possible interpretation of *yang mei shun mu* 揚眉瞬目 places it in the context of the Chan master's "unreserved functioning of the buddha-nature" (*quanti zuoyong* 全体作用). For instance, *Yunmen Kuangzhen chanshi guanglu* 雲門匡真禪師廣錄 says: "The Master once said: 'Snapping fingers, chuckling, raising eyebrows, winking eyes, picking up the hammer, holding the flywhisk straight

You must not make a "lifestyle" out of the word [**wu** 無].[312]

Also, you must not remain confined to the tiny hidden-away closet
of *nothing-to-do*.[313]

You must not, while raising [**wu** 無], understand and "own" it.

You must not quote texts as proof [of **wu** 無].[314]

Just twenty-four hours a day, in all four postures [i.e., walking, standing, sitting, and lying down] constantly rally the *huatou* to awareness, constantly lift
the *huatou* to awareness: Does even a dog have buddha-nature? "No [**wu** 無]."
Without leaving your round of daily activities, try to do *gongfu* in this way. In
short order[315] you will understand for yourself.

---

up, or sketching a circle—all of these are fishing tools. Not two words of buddhadharma
have ever been spoken. If spoken, it would have been spraying shit and piss'" [師有時
云。彈指謦欬揚眉瞬目拈槌竪拂。或即圓相。盡是撩鉤搭索。佛法兩字未曾道著。道
著即撒屎撒尿。] (T1998.47.556a24–26). Mujaku, 166, glosses *duogen* 椓根 thus: "*Duogen*
means: the mind of calculation does not stop on a single point" [椓根謂量度意停住一處
也]. ZGK, 58–59.247 glosses *duogen* 椓根 thus: "The basic meaning is: in the final analysis to stop at 'this' place, fixing your feet and not advancing" [畢竟其處に止息し、足を住
めて進まざるを本義とす。].

312. Mujaku, 166, glosses *xiang yulu shang zuo huoji* 向語路上作活計 thus: "From the sayings of the ancients to produce *taste* and fall in love with it" [忠曰古人語句上自出理味自
愛之也].

313. ZGK, 9.30, glosses *wushi jia* 無事甲 thus: "The *jia* 甲 can also be *ge* 閣 or *jia* 夾. In an
old commentary on the *Kuya man lu* 枯崖漫錄 [a collection of Chan anecdotes dated 1263] we
find: 'The *ge* 閣 can be *jia* 甲 or *jia* 夾. All are colloquial language.' In colloquial language,
there are many cases of usage for sound only without being restricted by the meanings of
the characters. A *ge* 閣 is a tiny hidden-away room or closet [奥の小ざしき或いは物おき].
The phrase *wushi jia* 無事甲 should be translated as *useless place* [無用の處]." This exegesis
is confirmed by *Jiatai pudeng lu* 嘉泰普燈錄 (1204): 有宗坐在無事閣裏。(CBETA, X79, no.
1559, p. 441, b24 // Z 2B:10, p. 172, c16 // R137, p. 344, a16).

314. Pojo Chinul's (普照知訥; 1158–1210) magnum opus, *Excerpts from the Separately
Circulated Record of the Dharma Collection with Inserted Personal Notes* (*Pŏpchip
pyŏrhaeng nok chŏryo pyŏngip sagi* 法集別行錄節要並入私記) adds two more illnesses
to this list: "Moguja [Chinul] says: 'This dharma talk [of Dahui] only makes known
eight types of illness. If we examine what he has said from beginning to end, there
are also the two illnesses of making [the **mu** 無 *huatou*] into the *mu* 無 of true *mu*
無 [i.e., true emptiness/*zhen kong* 真空, an emptiness that does not go against wonderful existence/*miao you* 妙有] and holding onto delusion while waiting for awakening. Therefore, altogether there are ten illnesses'" [收牛子曰。此法語。但彰八種
病。若檢前後所說。有真無之無。將迷待悟等二種。故合成十種病也。] (Pojo sasang
yŏn'guwon, ed., *Pojo chŏnsŏ*, 163).

315. Mujaku, 168, glosses *yue shi ri* 月十日 thus: "Means: very quickly achieve success.... a
vernacular expression" [忠曰言太速成功也.... 俗語也].

[10.6: *Mundane affairs do not hinder* gongfu[316]]

Of the official matters of an enormous prefecture, none will constitute a hindrance for you. An ancient said: "*Here* I am the living mind of the patriarchal masters—what thing is there that can detain it?"[317] If one were to separate oneself from the round of daily activities with some other aim in view, that would be separating from waves to seek water, separating from metal utensils to seek metal. The more you seek, the further away it will be.

11. Continued [Second Letter in Reply to Administrator of the Bureau of Military Affairs Fu]

[*Commentary: Hyesim says, "The main purport of this letter is putting forth effort in the midst of noisiness." Mujaku notes: "This letter and the next letter form a back-and-forth exchange, so both date to Shaoxing 8/1138. This can be argued for by the endings of the letters."[318] Pre-exile letters.*]

[11.1: *Dahui rejoices and sends his regards*[319]]

In recent days, I have come to know that you have taken *this matter* into your thoughts and that you are bravely and ferociously practicing zeal— [your *gongfu* has been] a pure oneness without admixture.[320] I could not help being happy to point of leaping about. Throughout the twenty-four hours of the day are you able, amidst the extensive demands of your work, to maintain correspondence [with *this matter*]? Have the two extremes of waking and sleeping attained a single thusness?

---

316. Mujaku, 168: 第六段世務不妨工夫.

317. Mujaku, 169, glosses *wo zhe li shi huo de zushi yi* 我這裡是活底祖師意 thus: "The ancient is Linji. . . . Note: The *Record of Linji* doesn't have this saying" [古人臨濟也. . . . 忠按臨濟錄無此全語]. Mujaku, 169, glosses *juzhi ta* 拘執他 thus: "*Ta* is that one person" [忠曰他者那一人也]. Hyesim, 48: "*Living patriarchal masters* is the living phrase [i.e., the *huatou*]. The *ta* character refers to this" [活底祖師者活句他字指此也].

318. Mujaku, 169: 忠按此書及第三書相繼往復蓋在紹興八年書尾可辯之. Hyesim, 48: 又狀大旨鬧中着力.

319. Mujaku, 169: 第一段隨喜問訊.

320. Mujaku, 169, glosses *zhunyi wu za* 純一無雜 thus: "Here means: your *gongfu* has been one of pure effort" [今言工夫無雜用心也].

[11.2: *Reprimands Fu for liking "stillness* über alles"[321]]

If that's not yet the case, you absolutely must not keep on getting submerged in empty quiescence. An ancient called this the "lifestyle" of the "ghost-home of Black Mountain."[322] [If you do thus, then] for eternal aeons into the future, there will never come a time when you will attain liberation. The other day I received your letter,[323] and I was worried for sure you were already addicted to the *samādhi* of "stillness *über alles*" [i.e., wallowing in the practice of sitting]. When I inquired of Mr. Zhige,[324] I came to know that situation was, in fact, as I expected [i.e., my worries were confirmed]. In general, above-average gentlemen who have experienced worldly affairs have been long stuck inside the contamination of the defilements. When suddenly they are instructed by someone [i.e., a perverse teacher] to do *gongfu* in a state of stillness and silence, unexpectedly they obtain a placidity in their breasts, and they immediately come to mistakenly recognize this as ultimate peace and joy. Little do they imagine that it is like using a stone to press down grass.[325] Though they are temporarily aware of cutting off the *state of being* [of the common-person realm—misfortune-fortune, sickness-health, and so forth], what about the root that remains? How could there ever come to be a time that they realize [true] quietude?

---

321. Mujaku, 169: 第二段斥好靜勝.

322. Mujaku, 170, glosses *heishan xia guijia huoji* 黑山下鬼家活計 thus: "'Black Mountain' is the abode of *kiṃnaras* [celestial musicians at the court of Kubera, the god of wealth]. Now it is called 'ghost-cave,' but that isn't much deviation. Also, it is encircled by two iron mountains and is a dark place where ghosts dwell. It can also be called the 'ghost-cave of Black Mountain.' Thus, it compares perverse Chan's attachment to the taste of itty-bitty Chan to a cave-house" [忠曰黑山緊那羅住處今稱鬼窟不多違又鐵圍兩山間黑闇處鬼住亦可稱黑山鬼窟蓋比邪禪著小禪味爲窟宅矣]. Mujaku also glosses *guijia huoji* 鬼家活計 thus: "Chewing up a small portion of *theory-taste* and coming to love it deeply—this is called 'lifestyle of a ghost-home'" [忠曰嚼出小分理味而深愛著之此謂鬼家活計也].

323. Mujaku, 170, glosses *zuo jie lai hui* 昨接來誨 thus: "The phrase *lai hui* refers to a letter from Mr. Fu to Dahui. Although we don't know exactly what was in this letter, from the drift of the text we can deduce that Fu was wallowing in Zen sitting, and so Dahui says: 'I am worried'" [來誨者自富公寄大慧書也其書雖明不言以文路推之似耽坐禪也故曰私慮也].

324. Unknown.

325. Mujaku, 170, glosses *si shi ya cao* 似石壓草 thus: "Using stillness to suppress noisiness" [忠曰以靜抑鬧也].

[11.3: *Shows true quietude*[326]]

If you want true quietude to manifest, you must, in the midst of blazing arising-extinguishing [i.e., samsara], abruptly—in one bound—jump clear. [If you do that,] without lifting a finger, you will churn long rivers into precious ghee and curds of fresh milk, and change the great earth into yellow gold.[327] At the critical moment, you will be free: to catch and to release, to kill and to give life, to benefit others and to benefit the self. Whatever you undertake, it will never go awry. Noble ones of the past called it the "*dhāraṇī* gate of the inexhaustible treasury," the "play-of-magical-powers gate of the inexhaustible treasury," the "wish-fulfilling liberation gate of the inexhaustible treasury."[328] How is this not the "special competence"[329] of the true *great person?* However, it's not something that can forcibly be created. It's nothing but the *original allotment* of *my mind* that's always been there. I hope you will quickly throw yourself into it without reservation.[330]

[11.4: *Relates in advance the post-awakening realm and urges Fu on*[331]]

I definitely look forward to this: a penetrating great awakening, a brightness in your heart, like ten-thousand suns and moons, the worlds of the ten directions in a single moment becoming bright, without the slightest other thought—for the first time you will be joined to the ultimate. In fact, you are capable of this. It will not be in just the arena of samsara that you will gain energy! On another day, when you once again wield political power, you'll make the emperor surpass the legendary sage-kings Yao and Shun—it will be like pointing to something right in the palm of your hand.[332]

---

326. Mujaku, 170: 第三段示真正寂滅.

327. Mujaku, 171, cites *Zongjing lu* 宗鏡錄, T2016.48.769c27–770a5.

328. For these three, Mujaku, 171–172, cites: *Da fangguang fo huayan jing* 大方廣佛華嚴經, T279.10.107b18–19; T279.10.206c16–18; and T279.10.8b27–28.

329. Mujaku, 172, cites the *Zhou yi* 周易, *Shang xi ci* 上係辭.

330. *Hōgo*, 97 and 341, n. 17, renders *zhuo jingcai* 著精彩 thus: "Throw yourself into it completely/without reservation" [本気に打ち込んで] and comments that Dahui often demanded this.

331. Mujaku, 173: 第四段預敘悟後境界勸勵.

332. *Analects, Ba yi* 八佾.

12. Continued [Third Letter in Reply to Administrator of the Bureau of Military Affairs Fu]

[*Commentary:* Hyesim says, "The main purport of this letter is similar to that of the previous letter."³³³ This letter dates to Shaoxing 8/1138. Pre-exile letter.]

[12.1: *Scolds Fu for acknowledging a link between "stillness über alles" and beginners*³³⁴]

I am informed by your letter that "for a beginner to do a little stillness-sitting *gongfu* is, in itself, a good thing." Your letter also says: "I myself would never dare erroneously evince the stillness-[*über-alles*] viewpoint." [Such words bring to my mind] the words of the Old Golden-faced Master: "It's like a person who first stops up his own ears, then gives out a great shout, wanting other people to not hear it."³³⁵ Truly, you're creating your own problems! If the mind of samsara is not yet smashed,³³⁶ during the twenty-four hours of daily activities you are like "a dead person whose soul lingers on, unaware and unknowing."³³⁷ Furthermore, do you actually have leisure time to waste in pondering stillness/noisiness?³³⁸ In the assembly at the complete nirvana of the Buddha, Broad-Forehead the Butcher laid

---

333. Hyesim, 49: 有狀大旨如前.

334. Mujaku, 175: 第一段呵認著靜勝初機.

335. Mujaku, 175, cites *Śūraṃgama Sūtra*: "Therefore, Ananda, if you continue to kill beings while cultivating *dhyāna*, it's like a person who first stops up his own ears, then gives out a great shout, wanting other people to not hear it. This is called wanting to conceal the obvious" [是故阿難若不斷殺修禪定者。譬如有人自塞其耳。高聲大叫求人不聞。此等名為欲隱彌露。] (945.T19.132a19–21). The commentary *Shoulengyan yi shu zhu jing* 首楞嚴義疏注經 explains: "*Stopping up the ears* is cultivating *dhyāna*. *Great shout* is performing killing. *Wanting other people to not hear it* is making known obvious suffering. How could that not be sad!" [塞耳修禪。高聲行殺。求不聞之道。彰彌露之苦。豈不悲夫] (T1799.39.913b15–16). Mujaku also comments: "This simile is not easy to understand" [忠曰此譬不易解].

336. Mujaku, 175, glosses *shengsi xin wei po* 生死心未破 thus: "Dahui considers the smashing of the mind of samsara to be the most important thing. This is not necessarily bound up with Zen sitting" [忠曰以生死心破爲肝要不必拘坐禪也].

337. Mujaku, 176, cites: *Xuansha Shibei chanshi guanglu* 玄沙師備禪師廣錄 (CBETA, X73, no. 1445, p. 15, b7–12 // Z 2:31, p. 190, b9–14 // R126, p. 379, b9–14).

338. Mujaku, 176, glosses *geng tao shen xian gongfu ... nao ye* 更討甚閑工夫 ... 鬧耶 thus: "The meaning is: from the outset he is but an unaware and unknowing dead fellow. What leisure time is there for discussing his creating a stillness view or not creating a stillness view? It means that stillness view/non-stillness view should only be discussed vis-à-vis

down his butcher's knife and immediately became a buddha.[339] That didn't
come from *gongfu* in the midst of stillness [i.e., stillness-sitting]! And wasn't
he a beginner? When you read this, you'll surely think that it couldn't be
so. You'll have to make the excuse that he [i.e., Broad-Forehead the Butcher]
was the magical creation of an ancient buddha—and that people of the
present don't have this power! If you hold such a viewpoint, then you have
no confidence [that your own mind is endowed with] the excellence [of the
awakened nature that is all-at-once completed in an instant[340]], and you'll be
content with being an inferior person. In this Chan gate of ours it matters
not a whit whether one is a beginner or an expert, whether one has been
practicing for a long time or awakened early on. If you want true stillness,
what's necessary is the smashing of the mind of samsara. Even without
doing *gongfu*—if the mind of samsara is smashed—stillness will come of
its own accord. The stillness *upāya* [i.e., the practice of sitting] spoken of
by the earlier noble ones is solely for *this* [i.e., the smashing of the mind of
samsara].[341] It's just that, during this "latter time" [i.e., after the complete
nirvana of the Buddha], the party of perverse teachers doesn't understand
the former noble ones' [exhortations to sit] were *upāya* talk.[342]

---

living persons. *What useless gongfu* means *what leisure time*. It means that to discuss stillness
view/non-stillness view vis-à-vis this sort of [dead] fellow is truly wearisome and of no benefit whatsoever" [忠曰言元來是冥冥蒙蒙死漢耳何遑論其作靜見不作靜見耶言靜見不靜見
可對生人而論之耳甚閑工夫者猶言何遑也言對此般漢而論靜見不靜見誠勞而無益也].

339. *Da ban niepan jing* 大般涅槃經, T375.12.722b18–22.

340. Mujaku, 177, glosses *bu xin zi shusheng* 不信自殊勝 thus: "You will have no confidence
that your own mind is endowed with the excellence of the awakened nature that is all-at-once
completed in an instant" [忠曰不信自心具剎那頓成之覺性之殊勝也].

341. Mujaku, 177, glosses *xian sheng suoshuo ... zheng wei ci ye* 先聖所說 ... 正爲此也
thus: "The stillness *upāya* is the Zen sitting contemplation practice of stillness. This stillness is an *upāya*. It is not that stillness is the Way itself, and, therefore, *precisely for the sake of
this* refers to the smashing of the mind of samsara" [忠曰寂靜方便者寂靜坐禪觀行也此寂
靜即方便也非寂靜是道故正爲此者此指生死心破也].

342. Mujaku, 177, glosses *zi ci moshi ... yu er* 自此末世 ... 語耳 thus: "In the final analysis,
connects to the former noble ones' being errorless. *Upāya talk* is discussions of Zen sitting.
[The party of perverse teachers] doesn't understand that the [former noble ones] discussed
Zen sitting for the sake of the smashing of the mind of samsara. On the contrary, they grasp
onto Zen sitting in stillness as an ultimate. They are mistaken [忠曰畢竟結先聖無過也方
便語者說坐禪是也不會爲生死心破說坐禪却執坐禪寂靜爲究竟誤了也]. The term *moshi*
末世 is a rendering of Sanskrit *paścimakāla* (*latter time*), which refers to the time after the
Buddha's complete nirvana.

[12.2: *Shows true gongfu*³⁴³]

If you have enough confidence in me,³⁴⁴ in the state of noisiness [i.e., in the state of your ordinary daily activity³⁴⁵] make an attempt to keep your eye on the *huatou* of "dog has no buddha-nature" [i.e., the *huatou* **wu** 無]. Without getting into any discussion of awakening versus non-awakening, just when your mind is in a hubbub,³⁴⁶ merely try to rally [the *huatou*] to awareness, lift [the *huatou*] to awareness. Are you aware of stillness [in noisiness]?³⁴⁷ Are you aware of gaining [awakening] energy? If you are aware of gaining [awakening] energy, you must not let go [of the *huatou*]. When you want to do stillness-sitting,³⁴⁸ simply light a stick of incense and do stillness-sitting. When sitting, permit neither torpor nor restlessness. Torpor and restlessness are things that the earlier noble ones severely warned against. When you are doing stillness-sitting, the moment you become aware of the appearance of these two illnesses, merely lift to awareness the *huatou* of "dog has no buddha-nature." Without exerting any effort to push these two illnesses away, they will immediately settle down in compliance. As the days and months pass, you will become aware that saving on the expenditure of [*gongfu*] energy is none other than

---

343. Mujaku, 177: 第二段示真正工夫.

344. Mujaku, 177, glosses *ruo xinde shanseng ji* 若信得山僧及 thus: "The word *me* reflects back onto the above word *perverse teachers*. The meaning is: if you have confidence in the perverse teachers, then it's over, but, if you have confidence in what I say, then try out [my suggestion] in the text below" [忠曰舉山僧對映上邪師字言信邪師則已若信山僧說則試可如下文].

345. Mujaku, 177, glosses *xiang nao chu* 向鬧處 thus: "This is ordinary [daily activity]. It isn't the word *noisiness* below. At present he is wallowing in 'stillness *über alles*,' and therefore Dahui counters with *in noisiness*" [忠曰是尋常不下之文字也今渠耽靜勝故反言向鬧也].

346. Mujaku, 178, for *raorao* 擾擾 cites: Zhuangzi, *Tiandao pian* 天道篇.

347. Mujaku, 178, glosses *hai jue jing ye wu* 還覺靜也無 thus: "The stillness you get in the state of noisiness is true stillness" [忠曰於鬧處所打得之靜則其靜也].

348. Mujaku, 178, glosses *yao jingzuo shi* 要靜坐時 thus: "Refers to the effort of Zen sitting. *This matter* is neither stillness nor noisiness. Previously Dahui scolded about stillness and scolded his addiction to it as an ultimate. If you see the scolding and give your assent, then you must not do stillness-sitting. But [such a prohibition] also constitutes an obstacle. Therefore, Dahui permits: if you want to do stillness-sitting, do stillness-sitting. His teaching the method of stillness-sitting is a response to karmic abilities" [忠曰示坐禪用心也夫此事非靜又非鬧者呵靜者呵其耽著為究竟若見呵又謂然則不可得靜坐是亦成障礙故且許欲靜坐則為靜坐矣便教坐之法應機者也].

the state of gaining [awakening] energy. Even without doing *gongfu* in the midst of stillness [i.e., even in the absence of stillness-sitting] just *this* [i.e., constantly lifting the *wu* 無 to awareness[349]] is *gongfu*!

[12.3: *Cites Li Bing (i.e., Li Hanlao) and makes an anticipatory remark about Li and Fu's meeting each other*[350]]

As for Participant in Determining Governmental Matters Li [letters #7–#8], when we first met in Quannan [Quanzhou in Fujian] recently, he heard me strongly criticize the perverse Chan of "silence-as-illumination" as blinding people's eyes. At first he didn't care for this and was half doubtful and half angry. But when he unexpectedly heard me recite the *huatou* **cypress tree in the garden**,[351] he suddenly smashed the pail of black lacquer and with "the single laugh" understood everything.[352] He believed [my criticism of perverse Chan was impartial[353]], and I started to speak without reservation. I didn't browbeat him in the least. [He knew that my criticism of "silence-as-illumination" Chan] was not an argument between me and other people. To me he repented [of his past doubt and anger[354]]. This gentleman [i.e., Li Hanlao] right now is there [in Quanzhou]. Please try to ask him whether or not [what I have said, i.e., my criticism of the perverse Chan of "silence-as-illumination"] is correct.

349. Mujaku, 179, glosses *yi bu zhuo zuo jing zhong gongfu* 亦不著做靜中工夫 thus: "Constantly lifting the word *wu* 無 to awareness—*this* is *gongfu*" [常常提撕無字遮箇便是工夫也].

350. Mujaku, 179: 第三段引李郙證且爲相見張本.

351. Araki, 58, reads *hua* 話 as *huatou* 話頭. See *Gu zunsu yulu* 古尊宿語錄 (CBETA, X68, no. 1315, p. 77, b23–c4 // Z 2:23, p. 154, a15–b2 // R118, p. 307, a15–b2).

352. See letter #7.1.

353. Mujaku, 179, glosses *fang xin* 方信 thus: "Participant in Determining Governmental Matters Li believed Dahui's criticism of perverse Chan was impartial" [忠曰李參政信大慧排邪無私曲].

354. Mujaku, 180, glosses *dui shanseng chanhui* 對山僧懺悔 thus: "Li Bing [Li Hanlao] to Dahui repented his past doubt and anger" [忠曰李郙對大惠悔過曾疑怒也].

[12.4: *Points out a good friend to connect with*[355]]

Advanced Seat Daoqian[356] has already gone to Futang [in Fujian].[357] I don't know whether he has already arrived there. This fellow has practiced Chan and experienced more than his share of bitter suffering—indeed, for more than ten years he fell into "dried-up" Chan.[358] In recent years for the first time he has attained the place of peace and joy. When you meet each other, try to ask him what sort of *gongfu* he's doing. "One who has roved about inclines towards sympathy for the traveler."[359] I suspect he will surely express his thoughts with extreme sincerity.

13. [Confidential] Auxiliary Note to Reply to Participant in Determining Governmental Matters Li (Hanlao) [Letters #7–8]

[*Commentary:* Hyesim says, "The main purport of this letter is to rescue Administrator of the Bureau of Military Affairs Fu."[360] Probably dates to Shaoxing 8/1138.]

---

355. Mujaku, 180: 第四段指示善友而結.

356. Mujaku, 180–181, cites a biographical entry in *Liandeng hui yao* 聯燈會要 (CBETA, X79, no. 1557, p. 150, c16–p. 152, c9 // Z 2B:9, p. 357, b9–p. 359, b2 // R136, p. 713, b9–p. 717, b2). Daoqian was a dharma successor of Dahui.

357. Mujaku, 181, glosses Futang 福唐 thus: "This letter was written in Shaoxing 8/1138" [忠曰此書紹興八年作].

358. Mujaku, 181, glosses *yi chang . . . ru ku chan* 亦嘗 . . . 入枯禪 thus: "'Dried-up' Chan is not necessarily limited to silence-as-illumination. Whatever inclines toward 'dried-up-and-dead' Chan is called this. *Enter into* is *fall into*. This also applies to Administrator of the Bureau of Military Affairs Fu" [忠曰枯禪不可必局默照凡偏枯死禪皆可稱之入者陷入亦者亦于富樞密也].

359. This line is often quoted in Chan texts. The *Nanshi Wenxiu chanshi yulu* 南石文琇禪師語錄: "The Master said: 'One who has roved about inclines towards sympathy for the traveler; one who loves his cups cherishes the person who is drunk'" [師云。曾為浪子偏憐客。自愛貪杯惜醉人。] (CBETA, X71, no. 1422, p. 704, a4–5 // Z 2:29, p. 191, d4–5 // R124, p. 382, b4–5).

360. Hyesim, 50: 大旨救取富樞. Mujaku, 182, glosses *bie zhi* 別紙 thus: "To *Letter in Reply to Participant in Determining Governmental Matters Li* [letters #7–8] Dahui in addition composed this 'separate sheet' as an auxiliary attachment. It discusses the matter of Administrator of the Bureau of Military Affairs Fu and is relying on Li to employ an *upāya*—to practice skill-in-means for advancing Fu on the Chan path. Such is the Master's great compassion. Therefore, this word *reply* in the title *Reply to Participant in Determining Governmental Matters Li* relates to the original letters *Reply to Participant in Determining Governmental Matters*. Because this

[13.1: *Raises the point that Mr. Fu is stagnating in perverse Chan*[361]]

When Administrator of the Bureau of Military Affairs Fu [letters #10–12] recently was in Sanqu [in Zhejiang], there was an occasion of his inquiring about the Way by letter. Thereupon, in one instance I knocked out some kudzu-verbiage [i.e., a reply letter] in which I had to "fall in with thieves" [i.e., use *upāya*-language] not a few times.[362] But he is still stagnating in "silence-as-illumination." Surely he has been drawn into the "ghost-cave" by perverse teachers! Now I have received another letter [from Mr. Fu], and once again he is clinging to stillness-sitting as "good." With this sort of obsession, how will he be able to practice "Jingshan Monastery Chan" [i.e., my sort of Chan]? This time, in the reply to his letter, I once again engaged in bit-by-bit kudzu-verbiage, with no stinting on the [bad] oral karma [accrued by talking about *this matter*[363]]. I was severe in rooting out his abuses. But I don't know whether he is willing to "turn his head around and flip over his brain" [i.e., turn away from the perverse and revert to the correct[364]], and in the midst of daily activities keep his eye on the *huatou*. A prior noble one said: "Even if you might break the precepts to the magnitude of Mt. Sumeru, you must not be 'perfumed' by even a single perverse thought from these perverse teachers. If a mustard seed's amount of it is present in your consciousness, it's like oil's getting into flour—you'll never get it out."[365] This gentleman [Mr. Fu] is a case of this!

---

separate sheet is never mentioned in the [original] replies, and because this separate sheet is on account of the letter that Administrator of the Bureau of Military Affairs Fu sent to Dahui, the editor Huang Wenchang made the editorial decision to place it here" [蓋苔李參政別更作此別紙副之言富樞密事託之以方便是即宗師大慈也故此苔李參政之苔字係苔參政本書耳此別紙終不見苔彼語故又此別紙爲富樞密發之書故黃文昌編置此處也].

361. Mujaku, 183: 第一段舉富公滯邪.

362. Mujaku, 183, glosses *luo cao bu shao* 落草不少 thus: "Didn't reside in the jade tower or golden hall—for the sake of this person fell into the gate of secondary meaning [i.e., the 'downward' gate of differentiation, relying on *upāya*]" [忠曰不居玉樓金殿爲此人落第二義門也].

363. Mujaku, 183, glosses *bu xi kouye* 不惜口業 thus: "*This matter* from the outset is inexpressible. Therefore, whoever wags his tongue to speak dharma is creating evil karma" [忠曰此事本無可言說者是故凡動舌說法皆是罪業].

364. Hyesim, 50, glosses *hui tou yun yun* 回頭云云 thus: "Turn away from the perverse and revert to the correct" [回邪返正].

365. Mujaku, 183: "I have not yet determined the source text of this saying" [此語未考所出].

[13.2: *Encourages Li to employ "having matters in common" with Fu*[366]]

If you meet with Mr. Fu, make an attempt to get a look at the kudzu-verbiage that I sent him in reply [i.e., letters #10–12] and thereupon employ an *upāya* to rescue this person. Of the four means of conversion, "having matters in common" is the strongest.[367] Should you undertake to open wide this dharma gate, it will enable him to have confidence and enter. That [i.e., your help from the sidelines] will not only "save my expenditure of energy" by half,[368] it will also enable him to have enough confidence[369] to be willing to leave his old "cave."

14. In Reply to Vice Minister Chen (Jiren)

[*Commentary:* Mujaku says, "This letter dates to Shaoxing 9/1139 when the Master was fifty-one. . . . The main idea of this letter is to explain that dull faculties are not an obstacle to attaining the Way."[370] *Pre-exile letter.*]

---

366. Mujaku, 183: 第二段勸同攝.

367. The four *saṃgrahavastu* (*means of conversion*) of the bodhisattva are: giving; kind words; helpfulness; and *samānārthatā* (*having matters in common*). Mujaku, 183–184, glosses *yi tong-shi she wei zuiqiang* 以同事攝爲最強 thus: "Here the term *having matters in common* has two meanings. The first is: Participant in Determining Governmental Matters is an official, and Administrator of the Bureau of Military Affairs Fu is an official—therefore, we can speak of 'having matters in common.' The second is: Participant in Determining Governmental Matters in the past fell into silence-as-illumination, and Bureau of Military Affairs Fu is currently stagnating in silence-as-illumination—therefore, we can speak of 'having matters in common'" [今言同事有二義一參政仕官人富樞仕官人故言同事二參政昔陷默照富樞今滯默照故言同事矣].

368. Mujaku, 184, glosses *shengde shanseng yi ban li* 省得山僧一半力 thus: "If Dahui as one person expends energy to save this person, and Li Bing [Li Hanlao] from the sidelines helps him, then Dahui's labor will be reduced by half" [忠曰大慧一人出力救此人時李邴自傍助之則省大慧勞力一半者也].

369. Mujaku, 184, glosses *shi qu xinde ji* 使渠信得及 thus: "The meaning is: if I as one person rebuff him, he will still have a little confidence left and may hold onto his first point of view. If you also speak in unison with me in scolding him for his grasping, he will to some extent take a turn for the better and come to have confidence" [忠曰言我一人斥他猶少信可執初見若公亦與我異口同聲呵他所執渠庶幾轉機信入也].

370. Mujaku, 184–185: 此書紹興九年己未師五十一歲而作. . . . 此書大意說鈍根不妨得道. For a biographical entry for Chen Jue 陳桷 (*zi* Jiren 季壬), see *Song History*, 377 (16.2969). Hucker, 414: "Vice Minister [*shaoqing* 少卿] is a common title for 2nd-tier executive officials of central government agencies headed by Chief Ministers (*qing* 卿), e.g., the various Courts (*si* 寺) such as the Court of the Imperial Stud (*taipu si* 太僕寺)."

[14.1: *Contrary to what is expected, Dahui praises Chen's dull faculties*[371]]

Your letter informs me that "you want to give heed to *this great matter*, but your disposition is extremely dull-witted." If that were actually the case, I should have to congratulate you! The reason most of today's members of the scholar-official class are incapable of comprehending *this matter* and decisively attaining release is simply because their disposition is too intellectually sharp and their knowledge excessive. As soon as they see the Chan master open his mouth and begin to move his tongue, they immediately come to a snap understanding. Therefore, if anything, this is inferior to the dull-witted person who, free of a lot of perverse knowledge and perverse awareness, in a headlong fashion without expectations dashes against each skillful method and each gesture, each word and each phrase [i.e., each *upāya* of the teacher].[372] Even if the Great Teacher Bodhidharma were to appear and employ all his hundred magical powers [to appraise the dull-witted person's level of understanding[373]], the reason why Bodhidharma wouldn't be able to make anything of him is precisely because [the dull-witted person] is free of obstruction by rationality. People of sharp faculties, on the contrary, who are obstructed by their sharp faculties, are incapable of: "BANG!—smashed!"[374] Even though they imitate on the basis of cleverness and intellectual prowess, in the matter of self and the *original allotment*, on the contrary, they fail to gain [awakening] energy.

[14.2: *Quotes ancients to prove the above*[375]]

Therefore, Preceptor Nanquan said: "These days there are a lot of Chan teachers who are searching for a stupid, dull-witted person, but they

---

371. Mujaku, 185: 第一段却讃他鈍根.

372. Mujaku, 185, glosses *yi ji yi jing* 一機一境 thus: "The term *yi ji* refers to the teacher's skillful methods, his skillful manipulation of words, his raising the eyebrows and winking, etc., when he is receiving students. The term *yi jing* refers to his picking up the hammer, his holding the flywhisk erect, etc." [忠曰一機者接學者時作略語言三昧揚眉瞬目等一境者拈槌豎拂等].

373. Mujaku, 185, glosses *yongjin bai zhong shentong* 用盡百種神通 thus: "Even if the Great Teacher Bodhidharma were to appear and employ various magical transformations, he wouldn't be able to appraise his level of understanding and render a judgment" [忠曰.... 縱達磨大師出來用種種神變可不能復勘辨彼也].

374. Mujaku, 186, glosses *cui de bian zhe bo de bian po* 啐地便折曝地便破 thus: "Both refer to awakening without wading through karmic effort" [忠曰皆言悟入不涉造作也].

375. Mujaku, 186: 第二段引古證上.

cannot find a single one."³⁷⁶ Preceptor Zhangjing said: "The ultimate principle is inexpressible. People these days have no idea of that, and go to
great lengths to learn other things [i.e., things beyond ultimate principle
such as the written and spoken word, the six perfections and ten-thousand
practices³⁷⁷], taking that to be an achievement. They don't perceive that the
self-nature [that everyone innately possesses] from the outset has never
been a sense object [that you can study or practice], that it's the mirror-
awareness existent in the wonderful, great liberation gate, unstained and
unobstructed. Such a luminosity has never ceased. From former aeons
until the present, it goes without saying, it has undergone no change. It
is like the solar disk that illuminates near and far—even though its light
touches all forms, it does not mingle with any of them. That wondrous
light is not created by reliance on cultivation [i.e., it is perfectly complete
from the outset]. [Common persons] do not understand this, and so they
seize images of the ten-thousand things. It's just as if one rubbed his
[innately clear] eyes and falsely produced [unreal] flowers in the sky, tir-
ing oneself out to no purpose, passing through numerous aeons in vain.
If you can do a reverse-illumination, [you will see that] there is no 'second
person' [i.e., no separate 'you' who becomes 'a buddha'³⁷⁸] and that none of
your actions and behavior detract from reality."³⁷⁹

[14.3: *Shows that mind from the outset is neither sharp nor dull*³⁸⁰]

You yourself say that your faculties are "dull"; so try this sort of reverse-
illumination: the one who has the ability to know dullness—is he, after
all, dull-witted? If you don't turn the light backwards and do a reverse-
illumination, and you merely perpetuate the dull-wittedness, your production of more worry and distress is piling illusion on top of illusion,

---

376. Mujaku, 186, cites: *Gu zunsu yulu* 古尊宿語録 (CBETA, X68, no. 1315, p. 69, c7–8 // Z
2:23, p. 146, b6–7 // R118, p. 291, b6–7).

377. Mujaku, 186, glosses *xi ta shi* 習他事 thus: "*Other* means *beyond ultimate principle*, i.e.,
the sense objects spoken of below. Whatever there is of the written and spoken word, the six
perfections and ten-thousand practices, is all *things beyond ultimate principle*" [忠曰他者至理
之外也即下所謂塵境也凡文字言句六度萬行皆是至理之外事也].

378. Mujaku, 187, glosses *wu di-er ren* 無第二人 thus: "Means: the person in question *is it*.
It's not that there is a separate person becoming a buddha" [忠曰言當人即是也非別有餘人
成佛也].

379. Mujaku, 186, cites: *Jingde chuandeng lu* 景德傳燈録, T2076.51.252b21–29.

380. Mujaku, 188: 第三段示心本非利鈍.

adding more [unreal] flowers in the sky on top of the [unreal] flowers in the sky. Just listen to me: the one who has the ability to know that his disposition is dull is most definitely not dull. Although you must not perpetuate this "dull-wittedness," you also must not discard this "dull-wittedness practice" [i.e., doing a reverse-illumination on dullness].[381] Seizing and discarding, sharpness and dullness, lie in people, not in [the true] mind.[382] This [true] mind, and the buddhas of the three times, are of a single substance: they are non-dual. If they were to be dual, then dharma wouldn't be the same everywhere. Receiving the teaching and transmitting mind are both unreal [i.e., students can't receive this true mind from teachers, and teachers can't transmit it to students].[383] You are seeking the true and real, but going ever more amiss. If you merely come to know that the [true] mind of the single substance and of non-duality definitely does not lie in [discriminations such as] sharp and dull, seizing and discarding, then you will see the moon and forget the finger [pointing at the moon],[384] decisively severing [all discriminations] at the single stroke of the sword. If you further hesitate, thinking about "before" and calculating upon "after," then it's calculating that something "really" exists in the empty fist;[385] vainly "adoring the odd and playing with strangeness" in the midst of the sense organs, sense objects, and dharmas; and falsely imprisoning oneself in the midst of the five aggregates and eighteen elements [which produce sensory experience]. You'll never put an end to it!

---

381. Mujaku, 188, glosses *sui bu de shouzhuo yun yun* 雖不得守著云云 thus: "Just do a reverse-illumination on dullness—this is practice" [只返照鈍底此爲參也].

382. Mujaku, 188, glosses *zai ren bu zai xin* 在人不在心 thus: "*Not lie in mind* means true mind" [不在心者真心也].

383. Mujaku, 189, glosses *shou jiao chuan xin* 受教傳心 thus: "This wonderful mind—students can't receive it from teachers, and teachers can't transmit it to students. It is just the buddhas and the buddha realm" [此箇妙心學者不得受之於師師不得傳之於學者唯佛與佛境界也].

384. Mujaku, 189, cites: *Da fangguang yuanjue xiuduoluo liaoyi jing* 大方廣圓覺修多羅了義經, T842.17.917a27–28.

385. Mujaku, 189, cites *Yongjia zhengdao ge* 永嘉證道歌, T2014.48.396c10–11; he glosses *kong ju zhi shang sheng shi jie* 空拳指上生實解 thus: "Within the fist there is no thing, just as in the nature there is neither sharpness nor dullness. *Producing reality understanding* is calculating that such things as sharpness and dullness exist" [忠曰拳内無物如性中無利鈍也生實解者計有利鈍事也].

[14.4: *Relates that those of sharp faculties easily accept perverse teachings and orders Chen not to worry that his faculties are dull*[386]]

In recent years, there has been a type of perverse teacher who speaks "silence-as-illumination" Chan. They teach people: twenty-four hours a day, pay no attention to any matter [mundane or supramundane],[387] and go on stopping-to-rest. They do not permit students to voice even a sound [i.e., the silence of "silence-as-illumination"[388]]. They fear "falling into the present epoch" [as opposed to "before the aeon of nothingness," i.e., before a single thought arose[389]]. Frequently members of the scholar-official class, who are "used" by their own cleverness and sharp faculties, are apt to detest noisiness. When all of a sudden they are made to do stillness-sitting by the party of perverse teachers, and it seems to them that they are saving on the expenditure of energy,[390] they immediately think they've got it right. They do not seek any further for wonderful awakening—they simply take this silence as the ultimate standard. I don't stint on oral karma [in talking about these false teachers] and try my utmost to save people from this fraud. At present there are some few who are gradually coming to notice their mistake.

[14.5: *Orders correct* gongfu[391]]

I hope that you will just practice at the point where the sensation of uncertainty is not yet smashed—walking, standing, sitting, and lying down,

---

386. Mujaku, 190: 第四段敘利根却受邪教令不患根鈍.

387. Mujaku, 190, glosses *shi shi mo guan* 是事莫管 thus: "*This matter* means the *one great matter*" [忠曰是事者謂一大事]. However, Hyesim, 31, glosses *shi shi mo guan* 是事莫管 differently: "Generally refers to mundane and supramundane matters" [指世出世間事].

388. Mujaku, 190, glosses *bu de zuo sheng* 不得做聲 thus: "This is *silence-as-illumination*" [忠曰是即默照也].

389. Mujaku, 190, glosses *kong luo jinshi* 恐落今時 thus: "As opposed to *before the aeon of nothingness*, speaks of falling into the present epoch. *Before the aeon of nothingness* refers to the time before a single thought arose" [忠曰對空劫以前言落今時也空劫以前指一念未生時].

390. Mujaku, 190, glosses *que jian shengli* 却見省力 thus: This *saving on the expenditure of energy* means *getting stillness*—this is what is described earlier as 'like a stone pressing down on grass.' It is not the *saving on the expenditure of energy* of Dahui's *saving on the expenditure of energy* → *gaining energy*" [忠曰此省力者言且得靜前所謂如石壓草是也非省力得力之省力也].

391. Mujaku, 190: 第五段令下正工夫.

never letting go [of the *huatou*]: A monk asked Zhaozhou whether a dog
has the buddha-nature. Zhou said: "*Wu* 無!" This one word [*wu* 無] is a
sword for smashing the uncertainty-mind of samsara. The hilt of this
sword lies only in the hand of the person on duty. You can't have someone
else do it for you. You must do it yourself. If you stake your life on it, you'll
be ready to set about doing it. If you're not yet capable of staking your life
on it, just keep pressing hard at the point where the uncertainty is not yet
smashed [i.e., go on rallying the *huatou* to awareness[392]]. Suddenly you'll
be ready to stake your life on one throw—done! At just that time, you'll
be confident that stillness-time *is* noisiness-time, that noisiness-time *is*
stillness-time, that talking-time *is* silence-time, that silence-time *is* talking-time.[393] You won't have to ask anyone else about this [i.e., you'll have
confidence in it on your own], and also spontaneously you won't accept the
nonsensical teachings of perverse teachers. I very much pray [you will go
practicing in the above manner[394]].

[14.6: *Quotes the words of Zhenjing*[395]]

Formerly Zhu Shiying by letter asked Preceptor Yun'an Zhenjing:[396]

"The buddhadharma is extremely subtle. In daily activities, how
should I exert mind, how should I engage in personal examination? I hope out of compassion you will instruct me." Zhenjing
replied: "The extreme subtlety of the buddhadharma is its non-
duality. It is just that, if you have not reached its subtlety, then you
are in a state of discrepancy. If you have reached its subtlety, then
you are a person who has awakened to [your own *original*] mind. If

392. Mujaku, 191, glosses *ya jiang qu* 崖將去 thus: "One's personal practice of rallying the
huatou to awareness" [提撕本參也].

393. Mujaku, 191, glosses *jing shi bian shi . . . bian shi yu shi de* 靜時便是 . . . 便是語時底 thus:
"A response to two points in the previous section: *a stillness-sitting that detests noisiness* and *in
silence-as-illumination you must not make a sound*" [忠曰應前段厭惡聞靜坐及默照不得做聲
之二件].

394. Mujaku, 191, glosses *zhi dao* 至禱 thus: "Pray you will go practicing in the above manner" [禱祝如上修去也].

395. Mujaku, 191: 第六段引真淨語.

396. Zhu Shiying 朱世英 (*ming* Xianhan 顯漢) was a late Northern Song official. He was a
student of Zhenjing Kewen (1025–1102), who was in the Huanglong wing of Linji Chan. For
this quotation from Zhu's letter, Mujaku, 192, cites *Linjian lu* 林間錄 (CBETA, X87, no. 1624,
p. 274, a19–b7 // Z 2B:21, p. 322, a11–b5 // R148, p. 643, a11–b5).

you know in accordance with reality that your own mind from the outset has always been a buddha—free in accordance with reality, peaceful and joyful in accordance with reality, liberated in accordance with reality, purified in accordance with reality—it's just a matter of exerting your own mind in the midst of daily activities. As for the unreal magical creations of your own mind, catch hold of them and use them in freedom,[397] without differentiating which is right and which wrong. Making the mind move in a certain direction and engaging in mental reflection are already incorrect. If you don't move the mind in a certain direction, one after the other [the myriad unreal magical creations] are the heavenly real, one after the other a bright subtlety, one after the other like a lotus flower to which water does not cling. Purity of mind surpasses that [lotus flower]. Therefore, from delusion about your own mind there is the becoming of a sentient being, and from awakening to your own mind there is becoming a buddha; sentient beings are buddhas, and buddhas are sentient beings. It is because of delusion and awakening that there is this and that. Most students of the Way at present do not have confidence in their own mind, are not awakened to their own mind. They don't get enjoyment of the bright subtlety of their own mind; they don't get the liberation of peace and joy of their own mind. They falsely hold that outside of this mind there is a 'Chan Way,' falsely erect the special and remarkable, falsely produce seizing and discarding. [Under these circumstances] even if you engage in practice, you will fall into an outside Way or into the extremist annihilationism of 'Chan peace and quiet' found in the Hīnayāna-hearer and private-buddha vehicles."

[14.7: *Sheds light on Yun'an's dharma talk above*[398]]

[Zhenjing in his letter is saying]: "Even if you practice, I fear you will fall into the pit of annihilationism or the pit of eternalism."[399] The one with

---

397. Mujaku, 193, cites *Zhenzhou Linji Huizhao chanshi yulu* 鎮州臨濟慧照禪師語錄, T1985.47.498a9–10.

398. Mujaku, 194: 第七段敷衍上雲菴語説法.

399. Mujaku, 194, cites: *Yongjia zhengdao ge* 永嘉證道歌, T2014.48.396c3.

annihilationist views severs the innate bright nature of one's own mind and single-mindedly grabs onto an emptiness that is outside mind, stagnating in "Chan peace and quiet." The one with eternalist views fails to awaken to the emptiness of all dharmas and grabs onto all the conditioned dharmas of the world, taking them as an ultimate. The party of perverse teachers teaches members of the scholar-official class "to unify mind, to do stillness-sitting, to pay no attention to any matter [mundane or supramundane], and to go on stopping-to-rest." Isn't this nothing other than using [false] mind to put [false] mind to rest, using [false] mind to put a stop to [false] mind, using [false] mind to exert [false] mind?[400] If you practice in this way, how could you not fall into an outside Way or into the extremist annihilationism of "Chan peace and quiet" found in the Hīnayāna-hearer and private-buddha vehicles? How would you be able to reveal your own mind's bright-and-wonderful enjoyment, ultimate peace and joy, purity according to reality, and the wonders of the magical creations of liberation? It is necessary that the person on duty be capable of seeing on his own, awakening on his own; naturally "unturned" by the sayings of the ancients, but able to "turn" the sayings of the ancients. It is like the pure wishing jewel[401] placed in a mire of mud—it will go through thousands of years without being stained. This is because the *original substance* [of the jewel] is innately pure. This [*original*] *mind* is also like this. Only at the very moment of going astray, it [seems to be] deluded by troublesome defilements, but the substance of this [*original*] *mind* can never be deluded. It is like "the lotus flower to which water does not cling." If you can suddenly awaken to the innate buddhahood of this [*original*] *mind*, [it will be apparent that] ultimate freedom, peace and joy in accordance with reality, and various wonderful functionings never come to you from outside—because you have been endowed with them from the outset. The Old Golden-faced Master said: "There is no really-existent dharma called 'unexcelled perfect awakening,' and there is no really-existent dharma spoken by a *tathāgata*."[402] If you determine that things like that [i.e., the

---

400. Mujaku, 194–195, glosses jiang xin xiu xin … yong xin 將心休心 … 用心 thus: "These minds are both called *false mind*. The rester and the stopper are also false mind; the rested and the stopped are also false mind. It is using false mind to exert false mind. How could this be true stopping-to-rest? Also, *rest* and *stop* constitute one set phrase—they should not be read as two separate words" [忠曰此心皆言妄心能休能歇亦是妄心所休所歇亦是妄心是即以妄心用妄心也豈是真休歇耶又休與歇分字造語耳無別義].

401. Mujaku, 195, cites: *Da fangguang yuanjue xiuduoluo liaoyi jing* 大方廣圓覺修多羅了義經, T842.17.914c6–7.

402. Mujaku, 196, cites: *Jingang bore boluomi jing* 金剛般若波羅蜜經, T235.8.749b13–16.

innate endowment of freedom, peace, and joy spoken of above] really exist as substantive entities, you would not be correct—you'll have no other alternative, because of your delusion/awakening and seizing/discarding, but to end up reasoning that some of these things do exist. However, they are no more than *upāya* speech for the sake of those who have not yet arrived at wonderful [awakening]. The reality is that, as substantive entities, none of them exist [i.e., wonderful functionings of freedom, peace, and joy, etc. do not exist].

[14.8: *Again urges correct* gongfu⁴⁰³]

Please just exert your mind in the following way:

> In your daily activities twenty-four hours a day you must not grasp samsara or the Buddha Way as really existent.
> You must not deny samsara or the Buddha Way, reverting to the non-existence of annihilationism. Just keep an eye on [*wu* 無]: Does even a dog have buddha-nature? Zhaozhou said: "*Wu* 無!"
> You should not, during the operation of the mind sense-organ, engage in conjecture [concerning *wu* 無].
> You should not make a "lifestyle" out of the word [*wu* 無].⁴⁰⁴
> Also, you must not, while [the Chan master] is speaking [of *wu* 無], understand and "own" it.⁴⁰⁵
> Also, you must not understand [*wu* 無 in the mode of "Chan suddenness" that is] like a spark from two stones or a lightning bolt. Does even a dog have buddha-nature? *Wu* 無! Just practice *in that way*.⁴⁰⁶

---

403. Mujaku, 196: 第八段再勸正工夫結.

404. Mujaku, 197, glosses *xiang yanyu shang zuo huoji* 向言語上作活計 thus: "Either attaching comments or composing verses. Whoever speaks of rationality is creating a lifestyle on verbalization" [忠曰或著語或作頌凡一切說道理是言語上活計也]. However, Mujaku, 166, glosses *xiang yulu shang zuo huoji* 向語路上作活計 differently: "From the sayings of the ancients to produce *taste* and fall in love with it" [忠曰古人語句上自出理味自愛之也].

405. Mujaku, 197, glosses *xiang kaikou chu chengdang* 向開口處承當 thus: "This refers to the master's speaking. It is like the meaning of letter #10's *while raising* [*wu* 無], *understand and 'own' it*." [忠曰師家開口處也如前十八張向舉起處承當之義].

406. Mujaku, 197, glosses *xiang ji shi huo shan dian guang chu* 向擊石火閃電光處 thus: "Taking the disposition to all-at-once awakening as 'Chan.' Many Chan students have this illness" [忠曰以頓機為禪也禪者多此病].

Also, you must not have your mind wait for awakening or wait
for stopping-to-rest. If you have your mind wait for awakening
or wait for stopping-to-rest, you'll end up having nothing
whatsoever to do with [awakening].

15. *Continued [Second Letter in Reply to Vice Minister Chen]*

[Commentary: Mujaku says, "The main purport of this letter is to show
that engaging mind in 'careful self-monitoring' is counter to the Way."⁴⁰⁷
Presumably dates to around the time of letter #14, Shaoxing 9/1139. Pre-exile
letter.]

[15.1: *Raises Chen's question letter to show the method* of gongfu⁴⁰⁸]

Your letter informs me that, after you received my previous letter the other
day, every time you encountered inescapable [work routines⁴⁰⁹] in the
midst of noisiness, you always "conducted a careful self-monitoring," but
you "did not yet have *gongfu* charged with energy." Just these inescapable
situations were already *gongfu*! If you, on top of that, apply energy towards
"careful self-monitoring," then, on the contrary, you'll end up even more
distant [from awakening].

[15.2: *Quotes ancients to prove that one should not apply energy towards "careful self-monitoring"⁴¹⁰*]

Of old, Old Huayan of Wei superior prefecture [in Hebei] said:
"Buddhadharma lies right in daily activities, right in walking, standing,
sitting, and lying down, right in drinking tea and eating, right in exchang-
ing greetings—right in all conduct and action [e.g., inescapable work
routines]. But the activation of thoughts [i.e., applying energy to "conduct

---

407. Mujaku, 197: 此書大意示擬心點檢違背道.

408. Mujaku, 197: 第一段舉來書示工夫法.

409. Mujaku, 197, glosses *duobi bu de* 躲避不得 thus: "Work routines that cannot be escaped"
[忠曰事務不可得避處也].

410. Mujaku, 198: 第二段引古證不可著力點檢.

careful self-monitoring"] is incorrect."[411] When you are right in your inescapable [work routines], by all means avoid the activation of thoughts, that
is, the production of any notion of "careful self-monitoring." The patriarchal master [Sengcan] said: "Discrimination does not arise, and an empty
brightness spontaneously illuminates."[412] Also, Layman Pang said: "The
matter of daily activities—it's no big deal. It's just my being casually harmonious. Towards all sense objects I exhibit neither seizing nor discarding. [In the face of sense objects] in no case do I turn my back on them.
Vermilion and purple [i.e., marks of high court rank] have nothing to do
with me. Here in the mountains there is not a speck of dust. Supernatural
powers and wonderful functioning—they are drawing water and carrying firewood."[413] Also, the former noble one [Bodhidharma] said: "It is
merely that whatever involves mental discriminations, calculations, and
[the realm of objects] manifested by one's own mind, is all a dream."[414]
Remember [these sayings of the ancients]!

[15.3: *Again instructs Chen to avoid turning (the spotlight of) mind onto "careful self-monitoring"*[415]]

When in the midst of inescapable [work routines], you must never, on top
of that, turn [the spotlight of] mind onto anything. When you don't turn
[the spotlight of] mind onto anything, everything is "ready-made." There's
no need to examine whether you are of sharp faculties or dull faculties—
this matter of sharpness/dullness has absolutely nothing to do with *him*
[i.e., the true person]; this matter of stillness/distraction has absolutely
nothing to do with *him*. At precisely the moment you are in the midst of

---

411. Mujaku, 198, cites *Yun wo ji tan* 雲臥紀譚 (CBETA, X86, no. 1610, p. 672, c12–17 // Z
2B:21, p. 14, c12–17 // R148, p. 28, a12–17). Mujaku, 199, glosses *ju xin dong nian you que bu shi
ye* 舉心動念又却不是也 thus: "The above *all conduct and action* is the *inescapable*. This *but the
activation of thoughts is incorrect* is *applying energy to careful self-monitoring*" [忠曰上所作所爲
即是觸避不得者此舉心動念却不是即著力點檢].

412. Mujaku, 199, cites *Xin xin ming* 信心銘, T2010.48.376c6–7 and 376c28–29. Mujaku,
199, comments: "*Applying energy to careful self-monitoring* is the arising of discrimination.
Therefore, Dahui quotes this saying. Also, *discrimination does not arise* is the activation of
thoughts" [忠曰著力點檢是分別生者也故引此語又分別不生是舉心動念者也].

413. Mujaku, 199, cites *Pang jushi yulu* 龐居士語錄 (CBETA, X69, no. 1336, p. 131, a13–18 // Z
2:25, p. 28, a7–12 // R120, p. 55, a7–12).

414. Mujaku, 200, cites *Shao shi liu men* 少室六門, T2009.48.370b1–3.

415. Mujaku, 201: 第三段重示忌擬心點檢.

inescapable [work routines], suddenly you will "drop the burlap sack"[416] and, without even being aware of it, will clap your hands and give "the great laugh." Remember this! Remember this! As to *this matter*, if you deploy even the slightest amount of *gongfu* to seize realization,[417] it's like someone's "caressing the sky with his hands"[418]—you'll only tire yourself out more and more.

[15.4: *Again raises the instruction spoken of in*
the previous letter[419]]

When it is time to deal with things, just deal with them. When you feel the need to do stillness-sitting, just do stillness-sitting. When sitting, you must not grasp at sitting as an ultimate. At the present time, of the party of perverse teachers, most take "silence-as-illumination" stillness-sitting as an ultimate dharma, misleading younger students. I don't fear making enemies of them. I vigorously scold them in order to repay the kindness of the buddhas, and to rescue beings from the con-men of this end-time of the dharma.

16. In Reply to Edict Attendant Zhao (Daofu)

[*Commentary: Mujaku says, "This letter dates to Shaoxing 9/1139 when the Master was fifty-one.... The main idea of this letter is to esteem Zhao Daofu's faculty of 'little confidence' (as an opportunity for practice)."*[420] *Pre-exile letter.*]

---

416. Mujaku, 201, glosses *da shi budai* 打失布袋 thus: "Same as laying down a heavy load" [忠曰與放下重擔一般也]. Takagi, 38a, at *budai* 布袋 inserts: "Knowledge" [知解]. Budai is a legendary mendicant appropriated by Chan. Numerous paintings show him as a corpulent vagabond carrying a burlap sack (*budai*) on a staff. He passed through villages laughing and playing with children and was considered to be a magical-transformation body of Maitreya.

417. Mujaku, 201, glosses *ci shi ruo yong yi hao mao gongfu yun yun* 此事若用一毫毛工夫云云 thus: "Here it means: *gongfu* is the so-called 'careful self-monitoring.' Losing 'careful self-monitoring' is true *gongfu*" [忠曰今言工夫者所謂點檢也打失點檢底是真工夫也].

418. Mujaku, 201, cites *Śūraṃgama Sūtra*, T945.19.112c29–113a2.

419. Mujaku, 201: 第四段再舉前書所言教示. Mujaku adds: "*Should not grasp at silence-as-illumination stillness-sitting* is for receiving students of dull faculties. It is an exhortation" [所謂不可執靜坐默照也是接鈍根丁寧之意也].

420. Mujaku, 203: 此書紹興九年已未師五十一歲而作.... 此書大意貴趙道夫之少信根. Zhao (*zi* Daofu 道夫) is unknown. Hucker, 475: "Edict Attendant [*daizhi* 待制] is a litterateur apparently assigned to take notes on imperial pronouncements during the Emperor's meetings with officials.... in Song members of the Hanlin Academy (*Hanlin yuan* 翰林院)."

[16.1: *The need to produce resolute confidence*[421]]

Your letter informs me of the whole story in detail. [Your letter quotes what] the Buddha said: "All that has mind can become a buddha."[422] This mind is not the mind of mundane worries and phantasmal thought. It refers to the mind of producing the unexcelled, great awakening [i.e., the *bodhicitta* or *aspiration to awakening*]. If there is this [aspiration-to-awakening] mind, then there is no being that will not become a buddha. Of members of the scholar-official class studying the Way, most create obstacles for themselves, the reason being that they do not have resolute confidence [in the aspiration for awakening]. The Buddha also said: "Confidence is the source of the Way, the mother of karmic merit. It nourishes all good dharmas and cuts off the snare of doubt, allowing one to exit the 'desire-flood'[423] and showing one the unexcelled path to nirvana."[424] Also: "Confidence can increase the quality of wisdom; confidence can assure that one arrives at the *tathāgata* stage."[425]

[16.2: *Urges a penetrating awakening in the present birth*[426]]

Your letter informs me that, with your dull faculties, you have not yet been able to achieve a penetrating awakening, but you still want to plant buddha-seeds in the mind-field [so that they will ripen in a future birth]. Although these words come easily to you, nevertheless, they have profound repercussions. "Just possess the willing mind, and it certainly won't deceive you."[427] Present-day members of the scholar-official class studying the Way often, in instances where they should be slack, on the contrary, are in a rush; in instances where they should be in a rush, on the contrary, they are

---

421. Mujaku, 203: 第一段要發信決定.

422. Mujaku, 203, cites: *Da ban niepan jing* 大般涅槃經, T375.12.769a17–22.

423. The *four floods* (*catur-ogha* = *si baoliu* 四瀑流) are: desire (*yu* 欲); existence (*you* 有); views (*jian* 見); and ignorance (*wuming* 無明).

424. Mujaku, 204, cites *Da fangguang fo huayan jing* 大方廣佛華嚴經, T279.10.72b18–20.

425. Mujaku, 204, cites *Da fangguang fo huayan jing* 大方廣佛華嚴經, T279.10.72b23–24.

426. Mujaku, 205: 第二段勸今生徹悟.

427. Mujaku, 205, cites *Guishan jingce* 溈山警策. See *Guishan jingce ju shi ji* 溈山警策句釋記 (CBETA, X63, no. 1240, p. 253, a12–16 // Z 2:16, p. 171, b9–13 // R111, p. 341, b9–13). Mujaku, 205, glosses *dan ban kenxin bi bu xiang zuan* 但辦肯心必不相賺 thus: "*Willing mind is willing to plant buddha-seeds. Manage the willing mind* relates to the student; *not deceive you* relates to the teacher" [忠曰肯心者自肯種佛種也辦肯心係學者不相賺係師家].

slack.[428] Layman Pang said: "One day, when a viper has gotten into your underpants [and you should be in a rush to get it out], try to [be slack and] ask the master: 'What season is it?'"[429] Concerning matters from yesterday, there are already today those who can't remember them. Once you're reborn in a future birth, you can't possibly remember [what you vowed in a previous birth]. If you decisively want to break through in this life, don't doubt the buddhas, don't doubt the patriarchs, don't doubt birth, don't doubt death. You must have resolute confidence and possess resolute aspiration [for awakening]—moment after moment be like someone trying to put out a fire on his head. If you keep pressing hard like this—even if you're not yet awakened—then, for the first time, you can be said to be of "dull faculties." [However,] if you in the present are saying of yourself that your faculties are dull, that you are unable in the present birth to achieve an awakening, that you want to plant buddha-seeds in order to make a karmic connection [in a future birth]—that is wanting to arrive without doing any walking. It doesn't make any sense!

[16.3: *Saving on the expenditure of energy is gaining energy*[430]]

I am always telling those who have confidence in this Way: gradually you will become aware that the state of saving on the expenditure of [gongfu] energy in the midst of the twenty-four hours of daily activities is none other than the state of gaining [awakening] energy in the study of the Buddha [Way]. [Only you can know] your own gaining of [awakening] energy—other people can't know, and you can't take it out and have other people take a look. Therefore, Postulant Lu [i.e., the sixth patriarch Huineng] said to Advanced Seat Daoming: "If you reverse-illumine your

---

428. Mujaku, 205, glosses *jin shi . . . huan chu que ji yun yun* 今時 . . . 緩處却急云云 thus: "*At places where they should be in rush, on the contrary, they are slack* corresponds exactly to Edict Attendant Zhao's illness. In the present birth he ought to be focused on penetrating awakening, but, on the contrary, he says he is 'planting buddha-seeds in the mind-field,' expecting things in future births" [忠曰急處却放緩是正當趙待制之病今生宜悟徹而却云且種佛種子於心田期當當來世].

429. Mujaku, 205, comments: "This saying is not contained in the *Pang jushi lu*, or in the Layman Pang sections of the *Chuandeng, Hui yuan, Zongmen tong yao*, etc." [忠曰此語龐居士錄傳燈會元宗門統要等龐居士章不載]. Lü and Wu, 51–52, states that this quotation appears in *Tang shi ji shi* 唐詩紀事, 49, a Song compilation of famous pieces by Tang poets compiled by Ji Yougong 計有功 (active in the Shaoxing era).

430. Mujaku, 207: 第三段辨省力即得力.

own *original face*, you'll notice that the secret meaning is right there."[431] Exactly so! The "secret meaning" is none other than the state of gaining [awakening] energy in the midst of daily activities: the state of gaining [awakening] energy is none other than the state of saving on the expenditure of [*gongfu*] energy.

[16.4: *Discard mundane matters and probe the* huatou[432]]

Worldly defilements—you pick up one and dispose of another—they're never-ending. [You say to yourself that] the reason why in the midst of the four postures [of walking, standing, sitting, and lying down] you have never discarded them is because from beginningless time you have had a "deep" karmic connection with them, because from beginningless time you have had a "shallow" karmic connection with *prajñā*-wisdom. When all of a sudden you hear the discourse of a good teacher, you think: "This is one of those difficult-to-understand deals!" [But let's say,] if from beginningless time your karmic connection to the defilements had been "shallow," and karmic connection to *prajñā* "deep": What would be difficult for you to understand? All you have to do is in the "deep" state make yourself do "shallow," and in the "shallow" state make yourself do "deep"; in the "unripe" state just make yourself do "ripe," and in the "ripe" state just make yourself do "unripe." As soon as you notice that you are reflecting upon defilement-matters [such as "deep"/"shallow"], without applying energy to shove them away, merely—while in the state of reflecting—do a smooth-flowing "pivot" to the *huatou*.[433] You will save on the expenditure of limitless [*gongfu*] energy and also gain limitless [awakening] energy.[434] Please just keep pressing hard like this. Never maintain your mind in a state of waiting for awakening—and then suddenly you will spontaneously go on waking up.

---

431. *Jingde chuandeng lu* 景德傳燈錄, T2076.51.232a1–18.

432. Mujaku, 208: 第四段放捨世事參究話頭.

433. Perhaps this is something like the Japanese *sumō* technique called *utchari* (うっちゃり): making a last-minute backward pivot at the edge of the ring and throwing one's opponent out. For an excellent example, see 2016 May Grand Sumo Tournament, 15th Day, Hakuhō v. Kakuryū.

434. Mujaku, 209, glosses *sheng wuxian li yi de wuxian li* 省無限力亦得無限力 thus: "The first *energy* is *gongfu* energy; the second *energy* is getting-awakening energy. Thus, the two *energy* words have different meanings" [忠曰上力者工夫力下力者得悟力故上下力字意別].

[16.5: *Urges questioning of a dharma friend*[435]]

I imagine that you are meeting the Participant in Determining Governmental Matters [Li Hanlao; letters #7–8 and #13] on a day-to-day basis. Other than the board game of chess, have you been discussing these sorts of things with him? If you're merely playing chess and haven't talked about these sorts of things—"right when the black and white stones are not yet divided up, overturn the board and scatter the stones"—question him! Seek out "that single chess move" [i.e., the *Aah!* of awakening]![436] If you can't seek it out, you really will be a fellow of dull faculties! Let's temporarily shelve these matters.[437]

17. In Reply to Administrator for Public Order Xu (Shouyuan)

[*Commentary:* Mujaku says, "This letter dates to Shaoxing 10/1140 when the Master was fifty-two.... The main idea of this letter is the need to possess the energy of great confidence."[438] Pre-exile letter.]

[17.1: *Quotes ancient sayings ordering the erection of the mind of confidence*[439]]

The Old Golden-faced Master said: "Confidence is the source of the Way, the mother of karmic merit. It nourishes all good dharmas."[440] Also: "Confidence can increase the virtue of wisdom; confidence can assure that one arrives at the *tathāgata* stage."[441] If you are about to go

---

435. Mujaku, 209: 第五段勸問著道友.

436. Mujaku, 209, glosses *na yi zhuo* 那一著 thus: "'That single chess move' of *Aah!*" 团下一著子也].

437. Mujaku, 209, glosses *gu zhi shi shi* 姑置是事 thus: "If you are truly a dull-witted one, there is nothing I can do. Let's shelf these matters and not discuss them" [若真箇鈍則我無可奈之何且置不論之也].

438. Mujaku, 210: 此書紹興十年庚申師五十二歲而作…. 此書大意要具大信力. Xu has no biography in *Song History*. Hucker, 451 and 449: "*Sili* 司理 is a common quasi-official reference to an Administrator for Public Order (*sikou canjun* 司寇參軍, *sili canjun* 司理參軍) on the staff of a prefecture (*fu* 府, *zhou* 州)…. a petty official on the staffs of many Prefects (*zhifu* 知府, *zhizhou* 知州), responsible for supervising police activities at the prefectural seat."

439. Mujaku, 210: 第一段引古語令立信心.

440. Mujaku, 204, cites: *Da fangguang fo huayan jing* 大方廣佛華嚴經, T279.10.72b18–20.

441. Mujaku, 204, cites: *Da fangguang fo huayan jing* 大方廣佛華嚴經, T290.10.72b23–24.

a thousand miles, it begins with one step. The tenth-stage bodhisattva has severed the obstructions and realized the dharma teachings. At the beginning, he enters from the ten confidences [i.e., the first ten of the fifty-two stages of bodhisattva practice] and only afterwards ascends to the "dharma-cloud" stage [i.e., the tenth bodhisattva stage] and the completion of perfect awakening. The first stage [of the ten bodhisattva stages] is the "joyous" stage because, due to confidence, he produces joy. If you decisively make your backbone erect and want to be a fellow who spans both the mundane and supramundane—you must be of pure cast-iron—then things will go well. If you are half bright and half dark—half confidence and half lacking in confidence—most certainly things won't go well.

[17.2: *One must awaken on one's own*[442]]

This matter is not part of ordinary human conventions and cannot be handed over as a transmission. It is necessary that you comprehend on your own, and only then will there be a hastening "upward [towards the *great matter*]." If you seize upon the verbal arguments of other people, for endless aeons there will never come a time when it stops.

[17.3: *One must divorce from the realm of desires*[443]]

Thousands and ten-thousands of times during the twenty-four hours of the day, don't allow yourself to waste time [on anything other than the following]: day by day, in your daily venue of activities, you're "complete and radiant" and not the least different from Śākyamuni and Bodhidharma.[444] If from the outset the person on duty does not see with penetration, does not break through, and wholeheartedly jumps into sense objects such as sounds and forms, then, the more he seeks a way out from the inside [of sense objects such as sounds and forms], the more he will have no relationship [to awakening].

---

442. Mujaku, 212: 第二段要自悟.

443. Mujaku, 212: 第三段要離欲境.

444. Mujaku, 212, cites: *Zhenzhou Linji Huizhao chanshi yulu* 鎮州臨濟慧照禪師語錄, T1985.47.497b12–14.

[17.4: *There is no harm in your producing the aspiration for awakening late*[445]]

This matter is not something that only goes well after long practice with teachers and after touring Chan monasteries. At the present time, there are many in the Chan monasteries whose hair has gone white and teeth have turned yellow—without their having been able to comprehend. Also, there are many who, upon first entering a Chan monastery, due to one "poke" [i.e., a word, a gesture, etc., from the teacher] immediately "flip"— they immediately understand everything. Producing the aspiration for awakening may have "earlier" and "later," but the time of awakening has no "earlier" and "later."[446]

[17.5: *Dahui quotes ancients who had the aspiration for awakening late but awakened early, once again emphasizing erecting the mind of resolute confidence*[447]]

Of old, Commandant Li Wenhe[448] practiced with Shimen Cizhao.[449] At a single phrase from Cizhao, Li understood and "owned" it. He coincided with the myriad things, composed a verse and presented it to Cizhao:

---

445. Mujaku, 212: 第四段不妨汝發心遲晚.

446. Mujaku, 213, glosses *wu shi wu xianhou* 悟時無先後 thus: "*Producing the aspiration for awakening has earlier and later* means there are some who produced the aspiration for awakening ten or twenty years before, and there are those who produced the aspiration for awakening yesterday or today—therefore, there is *before* and *after*. *The time of awakening does not have earlier and later* means: it's not the case that one produces the aspiration early and so should awaken early; it's not the case that one produces the aspiration late and so should awaken late. There are those who produce the aspiration late and awaken early; there are those who produce the aspiration early but awaken late. It can't be a fixed given, and so it is said *the time of awakening does not have earlier and later*" [忠曰發心有先後者謂有自十年二十年已前發心者有昨日今日發心者故有前後也悟時無前後者謂非早發心故可早悟非遲發心故可晚悟矣有晚發心早悟者有早發心却晚悟者不可一定故言悟時無先後也].

447. Mujaku, 213: 第五段引古人發心晚而早悟者再立決定信心.

448. This is Li Zunxu 李遵勗 (988–1038), compiler of the *Tiansheng guangdeng lu* 天聖廣燈錄. See Albert Welter, *Yongming Yanshou's Conception of Chan in the* Zongjing lu: *A Special Transmission within the Scriptures* (Oxford: Oxford University Press, 2011), 210–211. Mujaku, 213, cites: *Jiatai pudeng lu* 嘉泰普燈錄 (CBETA, X79, no. 1559, p. 423, c23–p. 424, a1 // Z 2B:10, p. 155, a12–14 // R137, p. 309, a12–14).

449. Mujaku, 214, cites *Tiansheng guangdeng lu* 天聖廣燈錄 (CBETA, X78, no. 1553, p. 499, a12–b17 // Z 2B:8, p. 376, c15–p. 377, a8 // R135, p. 752, a15–p. 753, a8). Cizhao's dates are 965–1032.

To study the Way you must be a man of iron;
Set about making effort in mind, and you will immediately
    understand.
Directly seize unexcelled awakening;
Pay no attention whatsoever to affirmation/negation.[450]

All you have to do is: at this very moment keep pressing hard—don't stop until you die. You must not think in terms of "before" and "after," and you must not produce worry and distress. Worry and distress block the Way. I very much pray [you will go practicing in the above manner].

18. Continued [Second Letter in Reply to Administrator for Public Order Xu]

[*Commentary: Mujaku says, "This letter hereby hands down the dharma-name Limpid."*[451] *Presumably dates to around the same time as letter #17, Shaoxing 10/1140. Pre-exile letter.*]

[18.1: *Because Xu has confidence and aspiration, Dahui permits the bestowing of a dharma-name*[452]]

You possess correct confidence and have established correct aspiration— these are the foundation for becoming a buddha or patriarch. I hereby confer upon you the Way-name "Zhanran" [*Limpid*].

[18.2: *Explains the meaning of this Way-name*[453]]

When you are *Limpid* like undisturbed water, an empty brightness spontaneously illumines all—without expending any energy that wearies your mind.[454] Mundane and supramundane dharmas are not separated from *Limpid*—[the mundane and the supramundane interpenetrate so

---

450. Mujaku, 214, cites *Liandeng hui yao*, 聯燈會要 (CBETA, X79, no. 1557, p. 115, c24–p. 116, a4 // Z 2B:9, p. 322, c6–10 // R136, p. 644, a6–10).

451. Mujaku, 216: 此書因說湛然號垂化.

452. Mujaku, 216: 第一段爲有信願許授法號.

453. Mujaku, 216: 第二段解道號之義.

454. Mujaku, 216, cites: *Xin xin ming* 信心銘, T2010.48.376c29.

completely that] there isn't the slightest overspill.[455] Just take this *Limpid* seal and "seal" all places, and there will be neither right nor non-right— one after the other liberation, one after the other a bright marvelousness,[456] one after the other reality. When functioning, all will be *Limpid*, and, when not functioning, all will be *Limpid*. The patriarchal master [Bodhidharma] said: "It is merely that whatever involves mental discriminations, calculations, and [the realm of objects] manifested by one's own mind, is all a dream."[457] If mind and consciousness are calmed, and there is not a single pulse of thought, it is called perfect awakening. Awakening being perfect, then, twenty-four hours a day, in the midst of daily activities, seeing forms, hearing sounds, smelling smellables, perceiving tastables, coming into contact with touchables, perceiving dharmas, walking, standing, sitting, or lying down, speaking or being silent, acting or being still: all is *Limpid*. And spontaneously you won't concoct upside-down viewpoints— whether there are thoughts or there are no thoughts: all is purity. Having obtained purity, when in action, you reveal the function of *Limpid*; when not in action, you revert to the substance of *Limpid*. Although substance and function are different, *Limpid* is oneness. It is like cutting up sandalwood—every sliver is still sandalwood.[458]

[18.3: *Orders Xu to discard the perverse and incline to the correct*[459]]

At the present time, there is a type of fellow [i.e., teachers of perverse Chan] who talks hogwash. They themselves don't have a stable footing,[460] yet they just teach people: "unify mind in stillness-sitting." While sitting [students] are taught not to voice even a sound. This faction can only be called "truly pathetic." Please just "do *gongfu* in this way" [i.e., practice my style of Chan].

---

455. Mujaku, 216, glosses *wu jianhao toulou* 無纖毫透漏 thus: "The completely mundane supramundane, and the completely supramundane mundane—therefore there isn't the slightest leakage" [忠曰全世間之出世間全出世間之世間故無少許透漏也].

456. Mujaku, 216, cites: *Śūraṃgama Sūtra*, T945.19.120a2–4.

457. Mujaku, 200, cites: *Shao shi liu men* 少室六門, T2009.48.370b1–3.

458. Mujaku, 217, cites *Xin fu zhu* 心賦注 (CBETA, X63, no. 1231, p. 88, c23 // Z 2:16, p. 7, d14 // R111, p. 14, b14).

459. Mujaku, 217: 第三段令捨邪就正.

460. Mujaku, 217, glosses *jin shi you.... gong yi* 今時有.... 公矣 thus: "Dahui fears that *Limpid*, who is like undisturbed water, will be inundated with silence-as-illumination Chan. Therefore, he makes this criticism" [忠曰恐湛然不動瀁默照故有此斥破].

Although I have instructed you like this [i.e., given you verbal instruction in *gongfu*], I truly couldn't avoid it; if you were to suppose that "doing *gongfu* in this way" is a really existent thing, it would contaminate you.

[18.4: *With a flip Dahui directly discusses the essence of mind and snatches away the name* Limpid[461]]

This mind has no real substance. How could it be forcibly arrested and stabilized?[462] Should you decide to arrest it, in what place do you intend to put it? There's no place to put it—[in the essence of mind] there is no "four seasons or eight holidays," no "past or present," no "common or noble," no "gain or loss," no "stillness or confusion," no "birth or death." There is no name *Limpid*.[463] There is no substance *Limpid*. There is no function *Limpid*. There is no [Dahui] in this way saying *Limpid* and no [Administrator for Public Order Xu] in this way perceiving my saying *Limpid*. If you see with this sort of penetration, it won't have been a waste for me to have created this name for you, and it won't be a waste for you to have received this name. What about it? What about it? [Can you see with this sort of penetration]?[464]

19. In Reply to Auxiliary Academician of the Hall for Treasuring Culture Liu (Yanxiu)

[*Commentary:* Mujaku says, "This letter dates to Shaoxing 9/1139 when the Master was fifty-one. The main idea of this letter is that Liu Yanxiu, after having had an experience of awakening to the dog huatou, should go on to develop it. Therefore, Dahui tells him to nurture the sagely embryo. Thus, this letter is an 'upward (towards the great matter)' dharma talk. Its true intention is Dahui's

---

461. Mujaku, 217: 第四段一轉直論心體奪湛然號.

462. Mujaku, 217, glosses *ruhe yingshou she de zhu* 如何硬收攝得住 thus: "Dahui criticizes the stabilization of the above perverse teachings and spontaneously snatches away the above talk about '*Limpid*, who is like undisturbed water'" [忠曰破上邪教住著自奪上湛然不動說].

463. Mujaku, 218, glosses *wu zhanran zhi ming* 無湛然之名 thus: "This essence of mind from the outset has no name. How could it have the name *Limpid*?" [忠曰此心體本無名字豈有名湛然者耶].

464. Mujaku, 218, glosses *ruhe ruhe* 如何如何 thus: "Means: can you see with penetration? What about it? What about it?" [忠曰言可見得徹去耶如何如何也].

ordering the refining of what [Yanxiu's younger brother] Yanchong [letter #20–21] has developed."[465] *Pre-exile letter.*]

[19.1: *Explains that mind and sense objects are a single thusness*[466]]

In the past few days it has been hot and humid. Are you enjoying your leisure time,[467] unconstrained and untroubled by mental exertion, not thwarted [in your practice] by the evil Māras? During the four postures of your daily activities, are you a single thusness with the *huatou* "dog has no buddha-nature" [i.e., the **wu** 無 *huatou*]? Are you capable of making no discrimination between the two extremes of movement and stillness? Are the states of dreaming and being awake joined? Are principle and phenomena fused? Are mind and its sense objects both one thusness? As Old Pang said:

> Mind is thusness, and sense objects are also thusness;
> They are neither real nor unreal.
> Pay no heed to existence;
> Don't get arrested by non-existence.
> Don't recognize the noble one or the worthy as "correct"—
> An ordinary person who's finished with the matter.[468]

If you're really an ordinary person who has finished with the matter—Śākyamuni and Bodhidharma, what lumps of clay! The three vehicles [i.e., hearer, private buddha, and bodhisattva vehicles] and twelve divisions of the teachings—what meaningless bubbling sounds from a boiling pot!

---

465. Mujaku, 219: 此書紹興九年己未師五十一歲而作.... 此書大意劉彥修於狗子話有悟處之後發之故諭之以聖胎長養故此書向上說法也其正意爲令諫弟彥沖所發也. For a biographical entry for Liu Ziyu 劉子羽 (zi Yanxiu 彥修), see *Song History*, 370 (16.2932–33). Hucker, 370: "Hall for Treasuring Culture [baowen ge 寶文閣] was from 1067 a palace building served by members of the Institute of Academicians (xueshi yuan 學士院)." Araki, 90, mentions that he was one of Zhu Xi's 朱熹 teachers during Zhu Xi's youth. See the epigraph of this book, where Zhu Xi evinces some knowledge of Dahui's style of Chan.

466. Mujaku, 219: 第一段說心境一如.

467. Mujaku, 219, cites *Analects, Shu er* 述而: "During the Master's leisure time he was relaxed and enjoyed himself" [子之燕居申申如也夭夭如也].

468. Mujaku, 220, cites *Pang jushi yulu* 龐居士語錄 (CBETA, X69, no. 1336, p. 134, a21–23 // Z 2:25, p. 31, a15–17 // R120, p. 61, a15–17)).

[19.2: *Shows the method for nurturing the sagely embryo*[469]]

Within *this gate* you have self-confidence and freedom from doubt—these are not trifling matters. [Now] you must in the "unripe" state make yourself do "ripe," and in the "ripe" state make yourself do "unripe"; and then you will begin to be in correspondence with *this matter* to some extent. Oftentimes members of the scholar-official class, in the midst of [encountering sense objects] that are not in accordance with [their wishes], catch a glimpse of the ground [of the Way-mind]; but, in the midst of [sense objects] that accord [with their wishes], lose [the Way-mind]. I must impress this upon you. When you are in the midst of sense objects that are in accordance with your wishes, you must constantly keep in mind the times when they don't go according to your wishes. Don't forget for a moment! "Just get the root—don't worry about the branches."[470] Just know about how to become a buddha [i.e., the root]—don't worry that you're not able to speak as a buddha [i.e., the branches].[471] As for "this single chess move," getting [awakening] is easy but maintaining it [i.e., nurturing the sagely embryo/practice] is difficult.[472] Don't ever neglect this! You must make both the head [i.e., achieving a thorough penetration/awakening] and the tail [i.e., nurturing the sagely embryo/practice] correct.[473] [As the *Mencius* says,] "Extend and strengthen"[474]—only afterwards push forward from the surplus of your own [awakening] to reach all beings.

---

469. Mujaku, 221: 第二段示長養聖胎法.

470. Mujaku, 222, cites *Yongjia zhengdao ge* 永嘉證道歌, T2014.48.396a19–21.

471. Mujaku, 222, glosses *mo chou fo bu jie yu* 莫愁佛不解語 thus: "Has two meanings: not understanding the words of the different stories of the ancients and also not understanding how you yourself should speak dharma in receiving others" [不解古人差別因緣之語又不解自家接人言語二義].

472. Mujaku, 222, glosses *de yi shou nan* 得易守難 thus: "Getting awakening is easy, but nurturing it is extremely difficult" [忠曰得悟則易長養極難].

473. Mujaku, 222, glosses *xu jiao tou zheng wei zheng* 須教頭正尾正 thus: "*Head and tail* is like saying *beginning and end*. Generally, though people achieve a one-time thorough penetration (*head correct*), afterwards they do not nurture the sagely embryo and thus necessarily lose what they have gained (*tail not correct*). Therefore, after a thorough penetration, one must add nurturing—then *both the head and tail will be correct*" [忠曰頭尾猶言始終也凡人一回雖透徹如頭正而後後不長養聖胎則必打失所得如尾不正故透徹之後須加長養乃頭亦正尾亦正也]. Hyesim, 57: "*Head and tail* is awakening and practice" [頭尾悟修].

474. *Mencius, Gongsun Chou shang* 公孫丑上.

[19.3: *Relates that Yanxiu's younger brother Yanchong has been misled by perverse teachers and orders Yanxiu to rescue him*[475]]

What you've apprehended is already free of being stuck in any "single corner" [and so perverse teachings have no way in].[476] I take it that, in the midst of daily activities, you're not involved in [such perverse teachings as] "rouse yourself to engird mind"[477] and "in a dried-up mind quell delusive thought."[478] In recent years[479] the Chan Way and the buddhadharma have weakened dreadfully. There is a kind of old monk who talks hogwash, and utterly has no awakening of his own: "His karmic consciousness is boundless—he has no basis to rely upon."[480] With no true "skill" for coping with students [and their individual karmic capacities], he teaches them all to be like him: [sitting in cross-legged posture,] eyes tightly shut in a "black-lacquer [ignorance]" sort of way. This he calls "silence as constant illumination." [Your younger brother] Yanchong [letters #20–21] has been misled by this bunch. I find this very troubling, very troubling! I wouldn't be having this talk with you if you yourself hadn't awakened to [the *huatou* **wu** 無 of] "dog has no buddha-nature." By all means let's drop the mask [of social convention between us[481]] and unstintingly come up with strategies to rescue this person [i.e., Liu Yanchong[482]]—I appeal to you.

---

475. Mujaku, 222: 第三段述舍弟彥沖被邪師謬而令救度之.

476. *Analects, Shu er* 述而: "If I raise one corner and the student doesn't come back with the other three corners, I do not repeat." Mujaku, 222 glosses *ji bu zhi zai yi yu* 既不滯在一隅 thus: "Meaning of *one corner* or *one extreme*. What you've apprehended has no orientation, and, therefore, perverse teachings cannot gain entrance" [忠曰一隅一邊之義謂所得無方所故邪教不入也].

477. Mujaku, 222, glosses *qi xin guandai* 起心管帶 thus: "Engirding mind against visibles, audibles, and perception. This is the calumny of 'increasing'" [忠曰管帶見聞覺知底是也此乃增益之謗].

478. Mujaku, 222, glosses *ku xin wang huai* 枯心忘懷 thus: "Maintaining an empty quiescence. This is the calumny of 'decreasing.' Dahui wants to speak of Yanchong, so first he speaks of his brother Ziyu" [忠曰守空寂也此乃損減之謗已上欲言彥沖先說子羽].

479. Mujaku, 222, glosses *jin nian yilai* 近年已來 thus: "From here on the talk enters into the matter of Yanchong" [忠曰已下說入彥沖事].

480. Mujaku, 222, cites *Jingde chuandeng lu* 景德傳燈錄, T2076.51.283a19–20.

481. Mujaku, 223, glosses *jiangxia mianpi* 將下面皮 as: "*Jiangxia* has the meaning *drop the mask*. Means: set aside human conventions and reveal truth" [將下者脫面具之義言捨人情露真實也].

482. Mujaku, 223, glosses *zhe ge ren* 遮箇人 thus: "Liu Yanchong" [劉彥沖也].

[19.4: *Broadly speaks of* upāyas *for rescuing him* (*Liu Yanchong*)[483]]

Nevertheless, there is one matter that you must be aware of. This gentleman [your brother Yanchong] has dwelled in purity and remained indifferent to worldly desires over many years. He is fixated on the idea that this [purity and indifference[484]] is something quite unusual. If you desire to rescue him, you should utilize "having matters in common"[485] with him, please him, and relieve him of doubts. I hope he will have sufficient confidence [in your words] to be willing to undergo a change. This is as the *Vimalakīrti* says: "First use desires as a fishhook for angling and later make them enter buddha-wisdom."[486] The Old Golden-faced Master said: "Contemplate the succession of dharmas, discriminate dharmas with wisdom; judge right and wrong, don't transgress the dharma-seal; one after the other erect the limitless practice-gates,[487] and make sentient beings sever all doubts."[488] This was to create a standard for the sake of beings, a model for ten-thousand generations. Furthermore, this gentleman's [exacting] personality[489] is quite different from yours. In being reborn in a heaven [because of good karma, Yanchong] is certainly ahead of [the ancient poet] Xie Lingyun; but in becoming a buddha, he is certainly behind Lingyun.[490] This gentleman

---

483. Mujaku, 223: 第四段廣說救他方便.

484. Mujaku, 224, glosses *zhi ci wei qite* 執此爲奇特 thus: "*This* refers to purity and indifference" [忠曰此者指清淨澹薄].

485. The four *saṃgrahavastu* (*means of conversion*) of the bodhisattva are: giving, kind words, helpfulness, and *samānārthatā* (*having matters in common*).

486. Mujaku, 224, cites *Vimalakīrti Sūtra*, T475.14.550b6–7.

487. Mujaku, 224, glosses *wubian xingmen* 無邊行門 thus: "The intention behind Dahui's quoting the sutra focuses on these four characters [*limitless practice gates*]" [忠曰大慧引經意專在此四字].

488. Mujaku, 22, cites *Da fangguang fo huayan jing* 大方廣佛華嚴經, T279.10.97a16–19.

489. On Yanchong's extreme adherence to funeral observances (such as not going out for seventeen years), Mujaku, 225, cites *Song History*, 434 (16.3276).

490. Korean Anonymous, 132: "Yanchong does not reach up to Yanxiu. Meng Yi was Xie Lingyun's [385–433] younger brother. In serving the buddhas Meng Yi was of a pure diligence, and his observance of the precepts was strict. Because he did not yet have confidence in his *original allotment* and just followed external forms in his practice he was to be born into a heaven. Lingyun had confidence in his *original allotment* and practiced the living phrase that is outside the norms [i.e., the *huatou*]. Therefore, becoming a buddha was easy for him" [沖不及彥秀也孟顗謝靈運之弟也事佛精勤而戒行嚴切未信本分而但隨相行故生天上也靈運信其本分而參格外活句故成佛易也]. Dahui is comparing Yanxiu to Xie Lingyun and Yanchong to Meng Yi.

most definitely cannot be drawn in with the lure of *prajñā*.[491] He should be drawn in according to what he is fond of [i.e., purity and indifference to worldly desires].[492] If over a prolonged period of time you "polish" him, I think he will of himself come to know the faults [of the perverse Chan of "silence-as-illumination"[493]]. Whether he will suddenly be willing to jettison [this perverse Chan] can't be known in advance. If he is willing to undergo a change [from the perverse to the correct[494]], then he's a fellow who possesses strength. You must take a step back and allow him "to get ahead of you"[495]—then things will begin to go well.

[19.5: *The fifth, sixth, and seventh sections below are criticism of what the brother Yanchong says in his letter, but this fifth section generally indulges in praise*[496]]

Recently the Chan monk Wei[497] returned, and he had made a copy of a letter he [Yanchong] had written in reply to [one of my other lay students] Old Man Zhang Ziyan.[498] I rejoiced when I gave it a reading, sighing in admiration and delight for several days—it's truly a fine piece of writing; furthermore, it's just like an examination essay on the meaning of the classics! So at the foot of it I had to add the [standard closure of such an essay by way of] comment: "respectfully answered."[499] I don't know whether your evaluation [will coincide with mine].

---

491. Mujaku, 225, glosses *bu keyi zhihui she* 不可以智慧攝 thus: "Yanchong's karma is beautiful, but his karmic connection to *prajñā* is weak. What he is fond of is only pure and disinterested conduct" [彥沖雖行業美而般若緣薄矣但所好者清淨澹泊行履耳].

492. Mujaku, 225, glosses *sui suohao* 隨所好 thus: "What Yanchong is fond of is purity and indifference" [忠曰彥沖所好清淨澹薄也].

493. Mujaku, 225, glosses *zi zhi fei* 自知非 thus: "Can come to know the faults of the perverse Chan of silence-as-illumination" [忠曰可知默照邪禪之非也].

494. Mujaku, 226, glosses *zhuan tou lai* 轉頭來 thus: "Change from the perverse and revert to the correct" [忠曰改邪而歸正也].

495. Mujaku, 226, cites *Foguo Yuanwu chanshi biyan lu* 佛果圜悟禪師碧巖錄, T2003.48.200a23.

496. Mujaku, 226: 第五段已下五六七段批判彥沖書語今第五段総歎縱.

497. Mujaku, 226–227, reports he is not found as a Dahui disciple in the transmission records.

498. Mujaku, 227, glosses *ciyan Laozi* 紫巖老子 thus: "Zhang Deyuan, the son of Commandery Grand Mistress of the State of Qin" [秦國夫人之子張德遠也]. See letter #23.

499. Mujaku, 227, glosses *xia ge jindui* 下箇謹對 thus: "A phrase written by the candidate at the end of his examination paper" [忠曰凡答策問文之尾必書謹對兩字].

[19.6: *Discusses the misguidedness of the perverse teachers*[500]]

Of old:

> Bodhidharma said to the second patriarch [Huike]: "You [should] merely, without: desist from all objective supports; within: have no panting in the mind. With a mind like a wall, you can enter the Way." The second patriarch elucidated this-and-that about mind and nature and thus didn't coincide [with the Way]. One day he suddenly awoke to the essential teaching that Bodhidharma had showed him and promptly said to Bodhidharma: "This time I, your disciple, have for the first time 'desisted from all objective supports.'" Bodhidharma knew that he had already awakened and did not further examine him closely. He just said: "You're not going on to the extreme of annihilationism, are you?" [Huike] said: "No." Bodhidharma said: "How is it for you—[try and say]!" [Huike] said: "It's a clear and constant *Knowing*, and so words cannot reach it." Bodhidharma said: "This is the essence of mind transmitted by the buddhas and patriarchs from ancient times. You have now apprehended—have no further doubts."[501]

Yanchong [in his letter to Ciyan] says: "At night [the false thoughts of] dreaming and during the daytime thoughts [of sense objects]—for ten years [i.e., since I began paying attention to *this matter*[502]] I haven't been able to completely subdue them.[503] Sometimes I practice sitting, still and silent, and intently empty my mind, making thoughts free of objective supports and having nothing to rely upon in phenomena. I become quite aware of a feeling of a relaxed calm."[504] Reading up to this point, I let

---

500. Mujaku, 228: 第六段論邪師教壞.

501. This exchange is found in the *Jingde chuandeng lu* 景德傳燈錄 as a quotation from an unknown work referred to as the *Separate Record* (*Bieji*), T2076.51.219c27–220a2.

502. Mujaku, 228, glosses *shi nian zhi jian* 十年之間 thus: "*Ten years* is the number of years since he began paying attention to *this matter*" [忠曰十年者自留意此事已來年數也].

503. Mujaku, 228, glosses *wei neng quan ke* 未能全克 thus: "*Subdue* is subdue the self. In Chan terminology, it is *Way power conquers karma power*" [忠曰克者克己也若約禪語則道力勝業力之謂也]; cites *Analects, Yan Yuan* 顏淵.

504. Mujaku, 228, glosses *po jue qing'an* 頗覺輕安 thus: "Means: the false thoughts that in the past I couldn't conquer arrive at this relaxed calm. Little does Yanchong imagine that

out a laugh unawares.[505] Why? His "thoughts having been freed of objective supports"—how is this not Bodhidharma's "within: no panting in the mind"? His "having nothing to rely upon in phenomena"—how is this not Bodhidharma's "without: desist from all objective supports"? The second patriarch in the beginning did not understand the *upāya* Bodhidharma was teaching. He mistakenly thought that "without: desist from all objective supports" and "within: have no panting in the mind" [were the "true" Way and thus became implicated in] "elucidating this-and-that" about mind and nature or Way and principle, and the quoting of texts as proof.[506] He was seeking authentication by a teacher. Therefore, Bodhidharma one after the other rejected [Huike's presentations]. [Huike] had no avenue left for exerting his mind; and then, for the first time, he took a step back and reflected: "The words 'your mind will be like a wall' are not Bodhidharma's 'real' teaching!" Suddenly, at "wall," he all-at-once "desisted from objective supports." He immediately saw the moon and forgot the finger,[507] and said: "Clear and constant *Knowing*, and so words cannot reach it." Those [*upāya*-]words [like "your mind will be a wall"] had been a *state of being* deployed by Bodhidharma as the occasion required—they were not the "real" dharma for the second patriarch [i.e., the "real" dharma was his experience of clear and constant *Knowing* in his gut].[508] The bunch of old monks who talk hogwash, having never themselves attained realization, one after the other [seize on the words of the ancients and seek somehow to] knead them together.[509] Although [these perverse teachers]

---

taking stillness to stop noisiness is like using a stone to press down grass" [忠曰言昔所不能勝妄念到此輕安也殊不知以靜止鬧如石壓草也].

505. Mujaku, 228, glosses *bu jue shi xiao* 不覺失笑 thus: "Yanchong's words by chance are the same as Bodhidharma's words to Huike" [忠曰彥沖語偶同達磨語于二祖].

506. Mujaku, 228, glosses *jiang wei wai xi zhu yuan yun yun* 將謂外息諸緣云云 thus: "The second patriarch in the beginning took Bodhidharma's teachings *without: desist from all objective supports; within: have no panting in the mind; with a mind like a wall*. . . . as the 'true' Way and, entrenched in elucidating this-and-that about mind and nature, presented his level of understanding to Bodhidharma" [忠曰二祖初以外息諸緣內心無喘心如牆壁處爲真道而坐在于此說心說性呈見解矣].

507. *Da fangguang yuanjue xiuduoluo liaoyi jing* 大方廣圓覺修多羅了義經, T842.17.917a27–28.

508. Mujaku, 229, glosses *yi fei er zu shi fa* 亦非二祖實法 thus: "Means: it's not what the second patriarch had in his gut—that is 'clear and constant *Knowing*'" [忠曰言非二祖肚裏者有了了常知者如是言也]. Takagi, 45b, at *yi fei er zu shi fa* 亦非二祖實法 inserts: "What the second patriarch apprehended is inexpressible" [二祖所得不可言說也].

509. Mujaku, 229, glosses *zhuxuan niehe* 逐旋捏合 thus: "The term *zhuxuan* is *one after the other*; the term *niehe* is *seize on the words of the ancients and seek to combine them*" [忠曰逐旋次第也捏合取古語索合也].

teach people to stop, their own heart-fires remain ablaze, never flagging day or night. They are like commoners who are in arrears on their bian-nual taxes [i.e., the perverse teachers are "in arrears" on their own "stop-ping"]![510] Yanchong [outwardly] doesn't show very much turmoil—it's just that inside him the poison [of the perverse teachers] has gone deep. All he's doing is the confusion-runaround between external extremes,[511] talk-ing about "movement and stillness," talking about "speech and silence," talking about "getting and losing."

[19.7: *Discusses erroneous interpretations of the sayings of ancient sages*[512]]

On top of that he quotes the *Zhou Changes* and Buddhist texts, forcibly combining things that can't be arranged and reconciled! Truly this is "increasing *avidyā* [ignorance] for the sake of other useless matters."[513] In particular, he hasn't reflected on the single legal case [*gong'an*] of sam-sara—he's never rendered a legal judgment on this case.[514] So, on the final day of the twelfth month [at the end of his life], how will he settle the matter? Just before the light of your eyes is about to go out, it won't do to say to Old Man Yama [Judge of the Dead]: "May I wait a little bit until I have clarified my spirit and settled my thoughts, and then I will come to have an audience with you?" At that very moment, the ability to dis-cuss [the *Changes* and Buddhist texts] with unobstructed ease will be of no use. A "mind like wood or stone" [such as Yanchong has been trying to cultivate] will also be of no use.[515] [When standing before Yama] you

---

510. Mujaku, 229, glosses *ru qian er shui baixing* 如欠二稅百姓 thus: "The two taxes, the annual tribute of wheat and the annual tribute of rice" [忠曰二稅麥年貢米年貢也]. Araki, 91, says it is the grain taxes to be paid in the spring and summer.

511. Mujaku, 230, glosses *wai bian luan zou* 外邊亂走 thus: "In speaking of *stillness*, speaking of *silence*, and speaking of *getting*, Yanchong truly can be said to be confusing inner reality and external extremes. His speaking of *movement*, speaking of *speech*, and speaking of *losing*, needless to say, is the external-extreme confusion" [忠曰說靜說默說得彥沖正謂是內實外邊乱做也其說動說語說失不待言之外邊亂做也].

512. Mujaku, 230: 第七段論謬解古聖語.

513. Mujaku, 230, cites *Zimen jingxun* 緇門警訓, T2023.48.1091a12–16.

514. Mujaku, 230, glosses *wei ceng jie jue* 未曾結絕 thus: "According to the forms of law to render a judgment on this case. Means: the urgent matter right in front of the eyes" [準律令格式判斷了此結公案也言目前急事].

515. Mujaku, 231, glosses *xin ru mu shi* 心如木石 thus: "Response to Yanchong's statement above that runs: 'Sometimes I do cross-legged sitting, still and silent'" [忠曰應前節端坐靜然].

must be a person whose mind of samsara is smashed. If your mind of samsara is smashed, what further need is there to talk about "clarifying the spirit and settling the thoughts"?[516] What further need is there to talk about "unrestrained ease"?[517] What further need is there to talk about Buddhist and non-Buddhist texts?[518] One comprehension will be all comprehensions, one awakening all awakenings, one realization all realizations. It is like cutting a bundle of silk threads—with one cut all-at-once severed. Realizing limitless teachings is also the same way—[you will all-at-once realize them] without any "one after the other." You [Yanxiu] have already awakened to the *huatou* of "dog has no buddha-nature" [i.e., the *huatou* **wu 無**], but can you do anything like this yet [i.e., like "one realization is all realizations"]?[519] If you can't do anything like this yet, you must directly reach the *in-that-way level*. If you've already reached the *in-that-way level*, you should, by means of these [limitless] teachings, produce the mind of great compassion, and, in the midst of sense objects that go against your wishes and those that are in accordance with your wishes, conform to [such defiled places as] mud and water [i.e., implement *upāyas* in the world], not begrudge your life, not stint on [bad] oral karma, and save all sentient beings in order to repay the kindness of the buddhas. This is the activity of the *great person*. If you don't become like this [i.e., do not attain the freedom of "one realization is all realizations"], it's all been for nought. Yanchong [in his letter] quotes Confucius's citing the line in the *Book of Changes* "the Way repeatedly moves,"[520] harmonizes that with the line in the Buddhist sutra "you should produce an unfixed thought,"[521] and declares them identical; he also quotes the *Changes'* phrase "still and immobile,"[522] that is, no different from soil and trees—this is even more ludicrous. I say to him: "If you don't want to summon upon yourself the karma of [the

---

516. Mujaku, 231, glosses *cheng shen ding lü* 澄神定慮 thus: "Response to the above 'making the mind like wood or stone'" [應上心如木石].

517. Mujaku, 231, glosses *zongheng fangtang* 縱橫放蕩 thus: "Response to the above 'with unobstructed ease'" [應上縱橫無礙].

518. Mujaku, 231, glosses *neidian waidian* 內典外典 thus: "Response to the above 'Zhou Changes and Buddhist texts'" [應上周易內典].

519. Mujaku, 231, glosses *hai de ruci ye wei* 還得如此也未 thus: "*Like this* refers to the above realm of 'one realization is all realizations,' etc." [忠曰如此指上來一了一切了等境界].

520. *Zhou Changes* 周易, *Xia xici* 下繫辭.

521. *Jingang bore boluomi jing* 金剛般若波羅蜜經, T235.8.749c22–23.

522. *Zhou Changes* 周易, *Shang xici* 上繫辭.

five crimes of] uninterrupted [punishment in the Avīci Hell], don't slander the true dharma teachings of the *tathāgatas*."[523] Therefore, the sutra says: "You should not produce a thought fixed in forms, and you should not produce a thought fixed in sounds, smellables, tastables, touchables, and dharmas."[524] This means that this wonderful mind of great quiescence cannot be seen via forms or sought through sounds. The sutra phrase "should be unfixed" means this mind has no real substance. The sutra phrase "produce a thought" means this mind "is not positioned apart from the real—wherever it's positioned is the real."[525] The line in the *Changes* "the Way repeatedly moves" cited by Confucius is not talking about this [Buddhist line "should produce an unfixed thought"]. "Repeatedly" in the *Changes* means "again and again"; "move" means "change." Good or bad fortune, calamity and disaster arise from this "movement." The purport of "repeatedly moves" is: returns to the constancy [of the still and immobile], but nevertheless conforms to the Way [of change]. How could you put that together with [the Buddhist line] "should produce an unfixed thought" and make them into a single lump? It's not merely that Yanchong doesn't know the Buddha's meaning, he doesn't even know Confucius's meaning! You [Yanxiu, on the other hand,] come and go in Confucius's teaching as if playing in a garden, and you have also deeply entered the inner chambers of our Buddhist teaching. This sort of hogwash I've scribbled—has it hit the mark?

[19.8: *Quotes an ancient to scold Yanchong*[526]]

Therefore, Guifeng [Zongmi] said: "Primal, penetrating, harmonious, and correct are the virtues of the *qian* trigram [of the *Zhou Changes*]. They begin from the single breath [of primeval chaos]. Eternality, joy, self, and purity are the virtues of the buddhas. They are rooted in the one mind. Focusing on the single breath [of primeval chaos], one becomes supple. Cultivating the one mind one completes the Way."[527] This old master harmonized

---

523. Mujaku, 234, cites *Yongjia zhengdao ge* 永嘉證道歌, T2014.48.396b27–28.

524. Mujaku, 234, cites *Jingang bore boluomi jing* 金剛般若波羅蜜經, T235.8.749c21–22.

525. Mujaku, 235, cites *Zhao lun* 肇論, T1858.45.153a4.

526. Mujaku, 238: 第八段引古結斥.

527. Mujaku, 238, cites *Da fangguang yuanjue xiuduoluo liaoyi jing lueshu* 大方廣圓覺修多羅了義經略疏, T1795.39.524a16–18.

[the two teachings] in this way. Right from the beginning with these two teachings, he doesn't play favorites and has no dissatisfaction with either. But Yanchong's holding that the sutra line "should produce an unfixed thought" and the line in the *Changes* "repeatedly moves" are identical in purport is unacceptable. If we rely on Yanchong's premise, then Confucius and the Old One Śākyamuni would have to shorten their skirts and buy straw sandals. Why is that? One [i.e., Confucius] "repeatedly moves," and the other [i.e., Śākyamuni] is "not fixed anywhere," [and so they both must wear shortened skirts and buy straw sandals to accommodate their incessant running around].[528] I suspect if you've read up to here, you're certainly falling on the floor laughing!

20. *In Reply to Controller-General Liu (Yanchong)*

[*Commentary: Mujaku says, "This letter dates to Shaoxing 9/1139 when Dahui was fifty-one." Hyesim says, "The main purport of this letter is existence and non-existence are a single thusness."*[529] *Pre-exile letter.*]

[20.1: *Censures perverse* gongfu[530]]

Your elder brother Auxiliary Academician [Liu Yanxiu; letter #19] right from the beginning has had no business with [such perverse teachings as] "engirding mind" and "quelling delusive thought," and with the hand

---

528. Mujaku, 240, glosses *mai caoxie* 買草鞋 thus: "Means: If we rely on Yanchong's meaning, Confucius 'repeatedly moves' and so runs around, and Śākyamuni is 'not fixed anywhere' and so runs around. Thus, these two must shorten their skirts and buy straw sandals to run around" [忠曰言依彥沖義則孔子亦屢遷故奔走釋迦亦無所住故奔走然則此二人須著短衣而買草鞋便于奔走故].

529. Mujaku, 242: 此書紹興九年師五十一歲而作. Hyesim, 60: 答彥沖狀大旨有無一如. For entries for Liu Zihui 劉子翬 (*zi* 彥沖), see *Song History*, 434 (16.3276) and *Cases of Song and Yuan Confucians*, 43 (2.1394 and 1399–1401). Hucker, 555: "Controller-general [*tongpan* 通判] was in early Song decades a central government official delegated to serve as resident overseer of the work of a Prefect (*zhizhou* 知州), with the right to submit memorials concerning prefectual affairs without the knowledge of the Prefect; no document issued by the Prefect was considered valid without being countersigned by the Controller-general. . . . After the earliest decades, the appointment became regularized as a Vice Prefect but remained a duty assignment rather than a regular post (*guan* 官)." Araki, 96: Along with his elder brother Yanxiu, Yanchong was one of Zhu Xi's 朱熹 teachers during Zhu Xi's youth. See the epigraph of this book.

530. Mujaku, 242: 第一段責邪工夫.

of confidence he's ["washed his face and] gotten hold of his *nose*" [i.e., his *original face*].[531] Although he cannot yet completely tell the difference between perverse and correct teachers from all over, his foundation is solid, and the perverse poisons [of false teachers]—including "quelling delusive thought" and "engirding mind"—cannot encroach upon him. If [like you[532]] one intently practices "quelling delusive thought" and "engirding mind," but doesn't smash the mind of samsara, the Māra of the five aggregates[533] will gain the advantage. You haven't yet avoided dividing empty space into dualistic states—when in the "stillness" state you experience immeasurable pleasure, and when in "noisiness" state you experience immeasurable suffering.

[20.2: *Exert mind and gain benefit*[534]]

If you want to make suffering and joy indistinguishable, simply do not "rouse yourself to engird mind" or "employ your mind to quell delusive thought." Twenty-four hours a day make yourself "composed" [like the Confucian *Analects'* description of the gentleman].[535] If suddenly habit-energy from past births arises, don't apply mental exertion to hold it in check. Merely, in the state where the habit-energy arises, keep your eye on the *huatou*: "Does even a dog have buddha-nature? *No* [*wu* 無]." At just that moment [*wu* 無] will be "like a single snowflake atop a red-hot stove."[536] If you are one with a

---

531. *Dahui Pujue chanshi yulu* 大慧普覺禪師語錄 (*Dahui Pujue chanshi fayu* 大慧普覺禪師法語): "In the midst of unreal illusion one can keep an eye on the [*wu* 無] *huatou* of Zhaozhou's dog's not having buddha-nature. Suddenly he will 'wash his face and get hold of his *nose*'" [於幻妄中能看箇趙州狗子無佛性話。忽然洗面摸著鼻孔。] (T 1998A.47.908c6–8). Ishii, 382, n. 441, glosses *nose* as *original face* (本来の面目). Mujaku, 242, glosses *mozhe bikong* 摸著鼻孔 thus: "Means: great awakening" [忠曰言大悟也].

532. Takagi, 48b, at *ruo yixiang* 若一向 inserts: "Like you" [如公].

533. The *skandhamāra*, one of the four forms of the demon Māra. The other three are: the Māra of the defilements; the Māra of death; and the divinity Māra (*devaputramāra*). The last attacked the Buddha on the night of the awakening.

534. Mujaku, 244: 第二段用心得益.

535. *Analects, Shu er* 述而: "The gentleman is level and composed; the small man is full of worries" [君子坦蕩蕩、小人長戚戚。].

536. Mujaku, 245, cites *Liandeng hui yao* 聯燈會要 (CBETA, X79, no. 1557, p. 165, c5–9 // Z 2B:9, p. 372, a11–15 // R136, p. 743, a11–15) for the simile. *Dahui Pujue chanshi yulu* 大慧普覺禪師語錄 (*Dahui Pujue chanshi zhu fuzhou yangyu an yulu* 大慧普覺禪師住福州洋嶼菴語錄): "Instruction to the Assembly: *Mind is buddha*—don't engage in false seeking;/ *Neither mind nor buddha*—desist from inquiring;/ On the flame of the red-hot stove

discerning eye and deft hand who leaps over in one bound, you will under-stand the Way of Niutou Lanrong:[537]

> At the time of unmistakeable exertion of mind, unmistakeably there is no-mind/no mind-exertion. If you talk circuitously, you'll be tired out by names and characteristics; but if you engage in "straight talk" [that cuts off names and characteristics], it will not be strenuous or onerous. No-mind/no mind unmistakeably engages in exertion, but constant exertion [of mind] is unmistakeably [constant] no[-mind/no mind]. Still, speaking of "no-mind/no mind" right now is no dif-ferent from "having mind."[538]

These are not words that deceive people.

[20.3: *Quotes an ancient to smash attachment to a life of holy renunciation* (brahmacarya)[539]]

Of old:

> [The twenty-first patriarch of Chan] Vasubandhu always only ever ate one meal a day and never lay down. Twenty-four hours a day he did obeisance to the buddhas. Pure and free of cravings, he was a refuge for the many. The twentieth patriarch Jayata, think-ing of saving [Vasubandhu], asked [Vasubandhu's] followers: "This Vasubandhu practices austerities [*dhutaṅga*] and is able to carry out *brahmacarya* [i.e., a life of holy renunciation]. [But with this sort of practice of purity] how can one expect to attain the Way of the buddhas?" Vasubandhu's followers said: "Our master's zeal is such—how could he not attain it?" Jayata said: "Your master is

---

a snowflake alights; / A speck of coolness eliminates hot worries" [示眾。即心即佛莫妄求。非心非佛休別討。紅爐焰上雪華飛。一點清涼除熱惱。] (T1998A.47.844b19–20). The *huatou* **wu** 無 is a "speck of coolness."

537. Mujaku, 245, glosses *Lanrong* 懶融 by citing *Jingde chuandeng lu* 景德傳燈錄, T2076.51.226c24–227a6, and commenting: "The quotation of Lanrong's words here is because Dahui wants to show the single-taste Way of stillness and noisiness" [忠曰今引懶融語者要示靜閙一味道].

538. Mujaku, 24, cites *Jingde chuandeng lu* 景德傳燈錄, T2076.51.226c25–227c8.

539. Mujaku, 246: 第三段引古人破執梵行者.

distant from the Way. Carrying out painful practices over count-less aeons—all of it is the root of falsity." The disciples could not overcome their anger—the facial color of all of them changed, and in stern voices they said to Jayata: "Honored one! How much vir-tuous conduct have you accumulated that you disparage our mas-ter?" Jayata said: "I don't seek the Way, but neither am I of an upside-down viewpoint.[540] I do not do obeisance to the buddhas, but neither do I slight them.[541] I do not do prolonged sitting, but neither am I lazy. I don't eat one meal a day, but I don't eat mul-tiple times. I haven't experienced having enough, but neither am I avaricious. When the mind has nothing that it wishes for, that is called the Way." Vasubandhu, upon hearing this, produced the wisdom free of the outflows [i.e., attained release from samsara].[542]

And so it is said that [Vasubandhu] "first by means of *samādhi* [medi-tative concentration] shook a firm tree" [i.e., with his initial cultiva-tion of austerities], and "afterwards by means of wisdom uprooted it" [i.e., with his later exposure to Jayata's dharma talk and consequent awakening].[543]

[20.4: *In the light of the above two quotations Dahui renders a judgment on Yanchong's perverse views*[544]]

The bunch of old monks who talk hogwash have you practicing stillness-sitting, and have you wait on becoming a buddha. How could this not

---

540. Mujaku, 248, glosses *wo bu qiu dao yun yun* 我不求道云云 thus: "Means: my seeking of the Way is not the equal of that of Vasubandhu, but neither is my upside-down viewpoint the equal of that of a common-person follower of an outside Way" [忠曰言我求道不如偏行亦顛倒不如凡夫外道].

541. Mujaku, 248, glosses *bu qingman* 不輕慢 thus: "My doing obeisance to the buddhas is not the equal of the frequent obeisances to the buddhas of a practitioner of austerities, but neither do I slight the buddhas" [忠曰言我不如頭陀數數禮佛亦不慢佛].

542. Mujaku, 246, cites *Jingde chuandeng lu* 景德傳燈錄, T2076.51.213a17–28.

543. Mujaku, 248, glosses *suowei xian yi dingdong yun yun* 所謂先以定動云云 by citing *Da ban niepan jing* 大般涅槃經, T375.12.793c26–28; and comments: "Vasubandhu's at the beginning cultivating austerities such as one meal a day, not lying down, etc., is *first by means of samādhi shook* [the firm tree]. Afterwards hearing Jayata's dharma talk and awakening is *by means of wisdom uprooted it*" [忠曰婆修盤頭初修一食不臥等先以定動也後聞闍夜多説法悟是以智拔也].

544. Mujaku, 248: 第四段對上二緣判結邪見.

be the "root of falsity" [spoken of by Jayata]? Also, you say that the still-ness state is errorless and the noisiness state erroneous. How is this not destroying mundane characteristics in a search for a "reality" character-istic? If you practice like this, how will you be able to coincide with the saying of [Niutou] Lanrong [in #20.2]: "Speaking of 'no-mind/no mind' right now is no different from 'having mind.'" Would you please try seri-ously reflecting on this? Vasubandhu at the beginning also mistakenly thought that by doing prolonged sitting without lying down he could become a buddha. As soon as this was highlighted by Jayata, Vasubandhu immediately achieved a realization and produced the wisdom free of the outflows. Truly, this is a case of a good horse's galloping at the mere shadow of the whip. The crazed distraction of sentient beings is an ill-ness. The buddhas by means of a medicine, the perfection of stillness, cure it. When the illness is eliminated but the medicine remains, it's a case of an even more extreme illness. Picking one up [i.e., stillness] and letting one go [i.e., crazed distraction]—when will there ever be an end to it?

[20.5: *Says the world is impermanent and orders Yanchong to hurry along*[545]]

When birth-and-death [mortality] arrives, the two extremes of stillness and noisiness won't be of the least bit of use! Don't tell me that there are many cases in which the noisiness-state is an error, but few cases in which the stillness-state is an error. This is not as good as binding "few" and "many," "gain" and "loss," "stillness" and "noisiness" into a single bundle and dispatching them once and for all out of this world. Then, right in the midst of daily activities, in the state of "neither many nor few, neither still nor noisy, neither gain nor loss," contrive to rally to aware-ness [the *huatou*]: **What the hell is it?** The world is impermanent and speedy, and a century goes by in a snap of the fingers. Furthermore, do you have such leisure time [that you can afford to expend] *gongfu* [energy on] paying attention to "gain," paying attention to "loss," paying atten-tion to "stillness," paying attention to "noisiness," paying attention to "many," paying attention to "few," paying attention to "quelling delusive thought," paying attention to "engirding mind"?

---

545. Mujaku, 249: 第五段說世無常令急切趣向.

[20.6: *Quotes the words of an ancient to prove that* this matter
is not a stillness-like quelling of delusive thought[546]]

Preceptor Shitou said: "Respectfully inform the person who is probing the
mystery: don't vainly pass time."[547] *This single phrase* [i.e., the *huatou* **What
the hell is it?**]—"even when your eyes are open, it's right there; even when
your eyes are closed, it's right there";[548] even when you are "quelling delusive thought," it's right there; even when you are "engirding mind," it's
right there; even during "crazed distraction," it's right there; even during
"stillness," it's right there. This is my way of managing this sort of thing. I
suspect the bunch of old monks who talk hogwash have a different way of
managing things. Pshaw! Let's temporarily shelve these matters.

21. Continued [Second Letter in Reply to Controller-General Liu Yanchong]

[*Commentary:* Hyesim says, "The purport of the second letter in reply is practicing the *huatou in the midst of noisiness."*[549] *Presumably dates to around the
same time as letter #20, Shaoxing 9/1139. Pre-exile letter.*]

[21.1: *Argues that stillness*-über-alles gongfu
is of no benefit[550]]

Over long years you have been doing stillness-*über-alles gongfu*. By the way,
when you open your eyes and respond to things, is your mind-ground
peaceful and carefree?[551] If you haven't yet gained a peaceful and carefree mind-ground, then this stillness-*über-alles gongfu* hasn't gained you
any [awakening] energy. If you've gone through a very long time without

---

546. Mujaku, 249–250: 第六段引古語證結此事非靜然忘懷.

547. Mujaku, 250, cites *Jingde chuandeng lu* 景德傳燈錄, T2076.51.459b7–21.

548. Mujaku, 250, cites *Foguo Yuanwu chanshi biyan lu* 佛果圜悟禪師碧巖錄, T2003.48.150c27.

549. Hyesim, 62: 答又狀旨鬧中參話.

550. Mujaku, 251: 第一段論靜勝無益.

551. Mujaku, 251, glosses *bu shi yu kai yan . . . anxian fou* 不識於開眼 . . . 安閑否 thus: "Dahui
knows that stillness-silence is of no benefit. In his desire to reject this, Dahui first subtly
interrogates him about whether the stillness-silence method is effective or not" [忠曰大慧知
靜默無益欲爲斥之先微詰他有効驗也否].

gaining [awakening] energy, you should seek out the direct-and-quick path to gaining [awakening] energy[552]—then, for the first time, you will not be failing to live up to the considerable amount of *gongfu* you have done in the past.[553] The stillness-*über-alles gongfu* you've been doing in the past has only been for the sake of managing the noisiness aspect. But right at the moment of noisiness your mind is still disturbed by noisiness—this is no different from not having done the stillness-*über-alles gongfu* at all in the past!

[21.2: *Shows the "ready-made" enjoyment that has neither gain nor loss*[554]]

This principle is very near at hand.[555] Even when far off, it's not beyond your vision. Open your eyes—it immediately pokes you [in the eye]; close your eyes, and it is still not lacking in the least. Open your mouth, and it immediately becomes speech; close your mouth, and it's still "ready-made." Just as you are about to produce the thought "I understand and 'own' [*this principle*], it's already given you the slip by 108,000 miles. Just when there is no mental exertion on your part, *this*, most of all, is saving on the expenditure of [*gongfu*] energy. Today most of those who study this Way want to expend energy in seeking. To the extent that they seek it, they lose it; to the extent that they move towards it, it recedes. Furthermore, they fall into the road of intellectual understanding, of gain and loss, saying "there are

---

552. Mujaku, 251, glosses *ruo xujiu wei de li ... chu* 若許久猶未得力 ... 處 thus: "He has already gone through twenty years doing 'quelling-delusive-thought' *gongfu* without gaining energy—thus he knows that this sort of *gongfu* actually is of no benefit. Thus, he should set it aside and seek out the *gongfu* of the direct-and-quick path to gaining energy" [忠曰已積二十年作忘懷工夫猶無得力即如此工夫實無益也然則捨之別求徑截得力工夫可也].

553. Mujaku, 251, glosses *fang shi bu gu fu ... fu ye* 方始不孤負 ... 夫也 thus: "If, over long years the painful practices of your *gongfu* were just for the sake of gaining energy, but you didn't gain energy, then you're turning your back on the intention behind those many years of *gongfu*. If you follow Dahui's instruction on the direct-and-quick path and do gain energy, then, for the first time, you are not turning your back on the basic intention behind those many years of *gongfu*. Please give up holding onto the theories of the perverse teachers and take a look at the state of finally gaining energy" [忠曰積年工夫苦行但爲得力而無得力則背多年工夫意者也若隨大慧徑截指示有得力則始不背多年工夫本意者也言請不執著邪師說而看畢竟得力處也].

554. Mujaku, 252: 第二段示現成受用無得失.

555. Korean Anonymous, 133: "*This principle* refers to the *original allotment* in the midst of daily activities, the realm of the ordinary" [遮箇道理指日用本分平常境也].

many cases in which the noisiness state is a loss, but few cases in which the stillness state is a loss."

[21.3: *Again argues that stillness-silence is of no benefit and urges the* gongfu *of the direct-and-quick path*[556]]

You've been dwelling in the state of stillness *über alles* for more than twenty years. As an experiment—please try to make a presentation of a little bit of that [twenty-years'-worth of awakening] energy that you've gained. If [for twenty years] you've made "[sitting] like a wooden post"[557] into the gaining of [awakening] energy in the midst of stillness, then why, whenever you are in the noisiness state, do you lose [that energy]? Right now, should you want to be able to save on the expenditure of [*gongfu*] energy and have stillness/noisiness be one thusness, merely break through Zhaozhou's *wu* 無! If you can suddenly break through, then you will understand that stillness and noisiness do not obstruct each other. [In this method of raising the *wu* 無 *huatou* to awareness] neither expend energy "propping up [*wu* 無]" nor entertain the notion "there is no propping up [of *wu* 無]."[558]

22. *In Reply to Grand Mistress of the State of Qin*

[*Commentary: (Commandery Grand Mistress) Ji Fazhen was a dharma successor of Dahui. She was the mother of Grand Councilor Zhang Deyuan (Zhang Jun) of letter #23. Her title was an honorific designation granted to mothers and grandmothers of various high-ranking officials.*[559] *Mujaku dates this letter*

---

556. Mujaku, 253: 第三段重論靜默無益勸徑截工夫.

557. Mujaku, 253, glosses *zhuangzhuang de de* 椿椿地底 thus: "The fact that the *gongfu* of stillness-silence and engirding mind lacks free functioning is compared to a wooden post" [忠曰靜默管帶工夫無自在之用喻椿也].

558. Mujaku, 253–254, glosses *yi bu zhuo yong li zhicheng* 亦不著用力支撐 thus: "Should highlight the *non-exertion and non-entertaining*—layer upon layer Dahui shows the method of rallying the *wu* 無 *huatou* to awareness" [忠曰可點不著不作重示提撕無話法也].

559. Hucker, 203: "Commandery Grand Mistress [*jun tai furen* 郡太夫人] is an honorific designation granted to mothers and grandmothers of various high-ranking officials." Mujaku, 254, cites *Jiatai pudeng lu* 嘉泰普燈錄, which lists her as a successor of Dahui: "Commandery Grand Mistress of the State of Qin, Fazhen of the Ji family, was a widow. She declined extravagance, always had vegetarian meals, and practiced the conditioned dharma [i.e., sutra chanting, making offerings, etc.]. Thereupon Dahui dispatched the

to Shaoxing 25/1155, the year the Grand Mistress died.[560] *Araki, however, dates it to "probably about the time Dahui was fifty-one" (Shaoxing 9/1139).*[561] *This letter cannot be decisively dated.*]

[22.1: *Dahui rejoices in her awakening and seals her realization*[562]]

[My disciple,] the Chan monk Daoqian, has returned, and I appreciate the words in the letter you sent as well as the verses you wrote out. At the beginning, I even entertained serious doubt [about your awakening]. After I made a careful inquiry of Daoqian, I came to realize that you were not deceiving yourself. [Your letter states:] "A matter not understood from countless aeons back cleared up before my eyes. It's not something that one gets from other people. For the first time, I came to know that the

---

Chan monk Daoqian to make inquiries of her son, the Duke of Wei [Zhang Deyuan/ Zhang Jun]. The Duke of Wei asked him to stay. Daoqian guided with the Way of the Chan patriarchs. Fazhen one day asked Daoqian: 'How does Preceptor Jingshan [Dahui] teach people?' Daoqian answered: 'The Preceptor only teaches people to keep an eye on such *huatous* as: *dog has no buddha-nature* [*wu* 無] and *bamboo clapper.* But then you must not attach comments. You must not engage in mental reflection. You must not, while raising [the *huatou*], comprehend. You must not, while [the Chan master] is speaking [of the *huatou*], understand and "own" it. 'Does even a dog have buddha-nature? *Wu* 無!' He just *in that way* teaches people to keep an eye on [*wu* 無]. Thereupon Fazhen came to have firm confidence. During the night, she rose to do sitting and probed the aforementioned *huatou*. She passed through without stagnation. Daoqian said goodbye and returned [to Dahui]. Fazhen personally wrote out a summary on entering the Way;/ It's composed several verses that she presented to Dahui. The last ran: 'All day long I read the sutras;/ It's like an encounter with someone I've long known./ Don't say there frequently are obstructions;/ One lifting [of *wu* 無 to awareness] makes it new!'" [秦國夫人計氏法真: 自寡處。屏去紛華。常蔬食。習有為法。因大慧遣謙禪者致問其子魏公。魏公留。謙以祖道誘之。真一日問謙。徑山和尚尋常如何為人。謙曰。和尚只教人看狗子無佛性及竹篦子話。只是不得下語。不得思量。不得向舉起處會。不得向開口處承當。狗子還有佛性也無。無。只恁麼教人看。真遂諦信。於中夜起坐。以前話究之。洞然無滯。謙辭歸。真親書入道粟略。作數偈呈慧。其後曰。終日看經文。如逢舊識人。莫言頻有礙。一舉一回新。] (CBETA, X79, no. 1559, p. 405, c9–17 // Z 2B:10, p. 137, a9–17 // R137, p. 273, a9–17).

560. Mujaku, 255, cites *Dahui Pujue chanshi nianpu* 大慧普覺禪師年譜: "Shaoxing 26/1156 when the Master was sixty-eight: On the twenty-first day of the first month the Master left Meiyang.... At the time, Grand Councilor Zhang Deyuan was residing in Changsha. His mother Grand Mistress of the State of Qin inquired of the Master about the Way" [二十六年丙子師六十八歲正月二十一日離梅陽.... 時丞相和國張公德遠居長沙其母秦國夫人間道於師] (CBETA, J01, no. A042, p. 804, a27–b16). Mujaku subsequently revises Shaoxing 26/1156 to Shaoxing 25/1155, the year of the Grand Mistress's death.

561. Araki, 100.

562. Mujaku, 255: 第一段隨喜所悟印證.

pleasures of dharma joy and *dhyāna* delight[563] are things to which mundane pleasures cannot compare." I was happy for you, State Mistress, over many days. [So much so that] I forgot about eating and sleeping.

[22.2: *Dahui instructs her not to stagnate in "upward (towards the* great matter*)"*[564]]

[Your letter also states:] "My son [Zhang Deyuan of letter #23] became Grand Councilor, and I became Mistress of State, but that's not enough to be held in high esteem." On the rubbish heap [of phantasmal thought and the defilements] you've recovered the priceless treasure [i.e., the buddha-nature].[565] For a hundred aeons, a thousand births, its enjoyment is inexhaustible. So, for the first time, you've got "true" esteem: however, you absolutely must not grasp this ["true"] esteem. If you grasp it, you will fall into "venerating esteem,"[566] and won't produce compassion, wisdom, and pity for sentient beings. Please remember this!

23. *In Reply to Grand Councilor Zhang (Deyuan) [Zhang Jun]*

[*Commentary: Mujaku says, "The main idea of this letter is instruction to Zhang about exerting mind while he is living in exile."*[567] *In Shaoxing 16/1146 Zhang submitted a policy statement to the ruler advocating armed resistance to the Jin (Jurchen) in the north. This greatly angered the powerful Qin Hui 秦檜 (1090–1155), who advocated peace with the Jin at virtually any price, and he ordered the Censors and Remonstrators to discuss Zhang's case. In Shaoxing 20/1150 Zhang was shifted to exile in Yongzhou (Changsha in Hunan). In Shaoxing 25/1155 his*

---

563. Mujaku, 256, cites: *Lotus Sutra*, T262.9.27c28–29.

564. Mujaku, 256: 第二段示莫滯向上.

565. Mujaku, 256, glosses *wujia baozhu* 無價寶珠 thus: "*Rubbish heap* is compared to phantasmal thought and the defilements; *priceless treasure* is compared to the buddha-nature" [忠曰糞塪堆比妄想煩惱宝珠比佛性].

566. Mujaku, 256, glosses *duo zai zun gui zhong* 墮在尊貴中 thus: "Here means grasping the state of 'upward (towards the *great matter*)' and of the non-arising buddha as 'correct.' This is a falling" [今者執向上無生佛處爲是此爲墮].

567. Mujaku, 259: 此書大意示謫居用心. For entries for Zhang Jun 張浚 (*zi* Deyuan德遠), see *Song History*, 361 (16.2880–84) and *Cases of Song and Yuan Confucians*, 44 (2.1414–18). Hucker, 126, describes Grand Councilor (*chengxiang* 丞相) in general terms: "A title of great significance in Chinese history, normally indicating the most esteemed and influential

mother (letter #22) died. He returned to Sichuan, but in Shaoxing 26/1156 by imperial order he was commanded to take up residence again in Yongzhou. In that year Emperor Gaozong retired, and Emperor Xiaozong assumed the throne. Zhang was restored, and in Longxing 1/1163 he was enfeoffed as the "Duke of Wei." Mujaku says, "This letter was composed when Dahui was still in exile in Meizhou (Shaoxing 21/1151 to the first month of Shaoxing 26/1156)."[568]]

[23.1: *Dahui sends his regards*[569]]

I send my respects. You are spending "leisure time"[570] in a Buddhist monastery, passing your days together with those superior monks of the monastery,[571] playing in the sea of the Vairocana Buddha treasury, carrying out buddha-deeds as appropriate. You have little illness and few worries. In your daily life, you have good fortune in many matters.

[23.2: *Dahui expresses condolences over Zhang's living in exile and gives instruction on mental exertion in daily activities*[572]]

It's been so with all the sages of the past.[573] [As in the *Huayan Sutra*,] "moment after moment you are in the extinction-of-all-dharmas *samādhi*,

---

member(s) of the officialdom, who was leader of and spokesman for the officialdom vis-à-vis the ruler and at the same time the principal agent for implementing the ruler's wishes in all spheres, civil and military." The following summary of Zhang's career (useful because of the nature of Dahui's letter to him) is based the *Song History* entry for Zhang Jun. Mujaku, 257–258, provides a transcription of the relevant portions.

568. Mujaku, 263: 蓋此書大慧猶在梅州時作.

569. Mujaku, 260: 第一段問候.

570. Mujaku, 260, glosses *yanju* 燕居 thus: "Zhang Jun was living in exile in Yongzhou, and so Dahui says 'leisure time'" [忠曰張浚謫居永州故言燕居也]. *Analects, Shu er* 述而: "During the Master's leisure time he was relaxed and enjoyed himself" [子之燕居申申如也夭夭如也].

571. Mujaku, 260, glosses *yu bi shangren* 與彼上人 thus: "The important monks of that monastery" [忠曰言其寺主僧] and cites *Vimalakīrti Sūtra*, T475.14.544a26–28.

572. Mujaku, 261: 第二段弔謫居示日用用心.

573. Mujaku, 261, glosses *cong shang zhusheng … ran* 從上諸聖 … 然 thus: "Dahui's all of a sudden leading off with these words means that the matter of the Grand Councilor's being exiled must be avoided as a taboo matter. Therefore, Dahui cannot speak openly of it. He says that many of the sages and worthies of the past who maintained the Way and did not pander to the world met exile and punishment. Therefore, Dahui says 'it has been so with all' in order to console him" [忠曰俄然成此語者言丞相被謫事可諱也故不得露言之耳言古之聖賢亦守道不阿世而遭謫罰人多矣故言莫不皆然蓋慰諭之者也].

never retrogressing on the bodhisattva path, never abandoning the task of the bodhisattva, never abandoning the mind of great compassion, cultivating the perfections without taking a break, contemplating all the buddha lands, with no wearying whatsoever. You never discard the vow to convey sentient beings [to the other shore of nirvana]; you never cut off the task of turning the dharma wheel; you never abandon the work of teaching sentient beings. All your superior vows attain completion; you come to know the differentiations between all the worlds, enter into the buddha lineage, and reach the other shore of nirvana."[574] These are ordinary family matters that the *great person* enjoys during all four postures [of walking, standing, sitting, and lying down]. You, great layman, in *this* [i.e., maintaining the Way in the midst of exile] are tirelessly zealous; and yours truly, in *this*, is also [like you] a "Puzhou man" [i.e., a "bandit"].[575] I don't know if you would allow an outsider [like me] to stick his hand in [your business].[576]

[23.3: *Shows how to exert mind while living in exile*[577]]

I hear that since your arrival in Changsha,[578] you've been—[like Vimalakīrti] at Vaiśālī—silent, and have deeply entered into non-duality.

---

574. Mujaku, 261, cites *Da fangguang fo huayan jing* 大方廣佛華嚴經, T279.10.231c27–232a25.

575. Mujaku, 263–264, glosses *Miaoxi yu ci yi zuo puzhou ren* 妙喜於此亦作普州人 thus: "This letter was composed when Dahui was still in exile in Meizhou, and, therefore, the word *this* refers to protecting the Way when encountering exile, without being submissive. This is the great mind of the bodhisattva, and Layman Zhang has already been able to carry this out. Dahui also is protecting the Way when encountering exile, and, therefore, the two are the same within. They are both men of the Way.... *The Puzhou man sends off the bandit* is topolect: the two are the same within, etc. It means that all Puzhou men are bandits and, therefore, the sender and the sent are equally bandits" [蓋此書大慧猶在梅州時作故有此言謂守道遭謫而不屈是菩薩大心而居士已能行之大慧亦守道遭謫故兼身在內可同道人也.... 普州人送賊方語曰兼身在內此此謂普州人皆是賊故送者被送者並是賊也]. This line is perhaps an allusion to the fact that Qin Hui, Zhang's opponent at court, called Zhang a "a national traitor/bandit" and wanted him executed (*Song History*, 361 [16.2882]: 秦檜 .... 反謂淩爲國賊、必欲殺之。).

576. Mujaku, 264, glosses *bu zhi hai xu wairen cha shou fou* 不識還許外人插手否 thus: "As for the phrase *stick his hand in*, most Puzhou men coming from Puzhou are bandits who 'stick their hands in' other people's things. Zhang Jun practiced it energetically. Dahui is also a person in exile and wants to be a bandit of the same type. However, he doesn't know whether the Zhang Jun will permit Dahui to be a bandit of the same type. In the final analysis, the meaning is: may we travel together as companions?" [忠曰插手語自普州来普州人多賊插手於他物也言公力行之大慧亦謫居人欲作同類賊然不知公許大慧作同類賊也否畢竟許同行同伴也否之義也].

577. Mujaku, 264: 第三段示謫居用心.

578. Presumably refers to his exile to Yongzhou (Changsha in Hunan) in Shaoxing 20/1150.

This [entrance into exile/non-duality] is not outside of your allotment—because dharma is *in that way*. I hope you, layman, will enjoy [the bud-dhadharma] *in that way*. If you do so, the Māras and followers of outside Ways will certainly become good divinities who protect the dharma.[579] Your various residual divergent views are all [unreal] sense fields mani-fested by your own mind—they have nothing to do with anyone else. I don't know whether you are able to take them as such. How about it?

24. *In Reply to Judicial Commissioner Zhang (Yangshu)*

[*Commentary: Mujaku says, "This letter dates to Shaoxing 10/1140 when the Master was fifty-two." Hyesim says, "The purport of this letter is just to urge the Aah! of awakening."*[580] *Pre-exile letter.*]

[24.1: *Praises Zhang's ordinary conduct*[581]]

Your actions and behavior, Old Layman, are darkly fused with the Way, but you've not yet been able to attain the moment of letting out the *Aah!* [of awakening]. If, in responding to conditions in daily life, you don't lose the steps you have hitherto made, even if you haven't yet attained the moment when you let out an *Aah!*, on the final day of the twelfth month [at the end of your life] Old One Yama [Judge of the Dead] will still have to cup his hands on his chest in obeisance and surrender.[582] How much

---

579. Mujaku, 264–265, glosses *ze zhu mo waidao* 則諸魔外道 thus: "*The Māras.... *means: if you are in the extinction-of-all-dharmas *samādhi*, never retrogressing on the bodhisattva path, etc., then those of the bad party at court who in past days slandered you and wished you harm will all come to respect you, becoming good divinities who will protect you" [諸魔云云者言若入一切法滅盡三昧不退菩薩道等則昔日詆公欲害公朝廷惡輩皆却可愛敬公爲護公身善神也].

580. Mujaku, 265: 此書紹興十年庚申師五十二歲而作. Hyesim, 65: 答張提刑狀旨但勸团地一下. Zhang Yangshu has no biography in *Song History*. Hucker, 405 and 497: "*Tixing* 提刑 is a variant or abbreviation of *tidian xingyu gongshi* 提點刑獄公事 (Judicial Commissioner).... responsible for supervising the judicial and penal operations of Prefectures (*zhou* 州) and Districts (*xian* 縣), and joined with Fiscal Commissioners in awarding merit ratings (*kao* 考) to all officials serving in subsidiary units of territorial administration."

581. Mujaku, 266: 第一段賛平居行履.

582. Mujaku, 266, glosses *gong shou gui jiang* 拱手歸降 thus: "When birth-and-death arrives, your Way-power will conquer your karmic power, and, therefore, King Yama won't be able to do anything to you" [忠曰生死到來時道力能勝業力故閻羅王不得奈他何也].

more so if, for a single moment, you have gotten in correspondence [with *this matter*]?

[24.2: *Dahui shows his method of* gongfu[583]]

Although it's not a case of "as soon as my eyes lighted on [that man, the Way in him was apparent],"[584] when I contemplate your conduct, in things big and small you are judicious—there is nothing that is excessive and nothing that does not measure up. This is precisely the state of fusion with the Way. Once you've arrived *here*, there is no need to produce any notion of "defilements," nor is there a need to produce any notion of "buddhadharma." "Buddhadharma" and "defilements" are both matters of no concern. However, you also must not produce a notion of "matters of no concern." Merely turn the radiance backwards and do a reverse-illumination: The one who produces the notion of *in that way*—what place does he come from? At the time of action and behavior[585]—what form does he take? Once you know [the form that he takes in daily] action, do as you wish—nothing won't be dealt with, nothing will be left over. At just that *in-that-way* time, to whose protective power could he be indebted? If you do *gongfu* in this way over days and month, as with someone training in archery, you'll naturally hit the bullseye.

[24.3: *Demonstrates that karmic consciousness has the characteristic of a shifting flow*[586]]

Sentient beings are of an upside-down viewpoint—they "lose themselves and pursue things."[587] Absorbed in a few flavors of the [five] desires [i.e., forms, sounds, smells, tastes, and touchables[588]], they are pleased to receive immeasurable suffering. Day by day, before they even open their eyes,

---

583. Mujaku, 267: 第二段示工夫之法.

584. Mujaku, 267, cites *Zhuangzi, Tian Zifang* 田子方.

585. Takagi, 53a, at *suozuo suowei* 所作所爲 inserts: "Daily activities" [日用].

586. Mujaku, 268: 第三段顯示業識遷流相.

587. Mujaku, 268, cites *Foguo Yuanwu chanshi biyan lu* 佛果圜悟禪師碧巖錄, T2003.48.182b19–21.

588. Mujaku, 268, glosses *shao yu wei* 少欲味 thus: "A few flavors of the desires—the flavors of the five desires" [忠曰少許欲味也五欲之味也].

before they get out of bed, when they are only half-awake, their minds flutter about, scattered dissolutely in accordance with phantasmal thought.
Even before the doing of good and bad actions has become manifest, from
the time before they've even gotten out of bed, within their minds the
heavens [resulting from good action] and the hells [resulting from bad
action] are "ready-made." When they reach the point at which [good and
bad manifest actions] are about to go into effect, there has already been a
fall into the eighth [consciousness, i.e., the storehouse consciousness[589]].
Didn't the Buddha say:

> All sense faculties are manifestations of self-mind. As for the store-
> house consciousness, the vessel-world and the organ-body, they are
> constructed and projected by your own false thought. They are like
> the flow of a river, like seeds, like a lamp, like the wind, like the
> clouds—from moment to moment they change. Moving impetu-
> ously like a monkey, taking joy in impure places like a fly, thirsting
> after things but never satisfied, like a wind-driven fire—the cause
> is beginningless false habit-energy from past births that is like a
> windlass drawing water from a well.[590]

When you see through this, it's called the "wisdom of neither 'persons'
nor 'self.'"

[24.4: *Shows exertion of mind to gain benefit*[591]]

The heavens and hells aren't in another place—they are merely in the
mind of the person on duty when he is half-awake, before he has gotten
out of bed. They definitely don't come from the outside. [When good and
bad thoughts] are about to arise but have not yet arisen,[592] when you are
about to wake up but have not yet woken up, you absolutely must look back
[i.e., do a reverse-illumination]. When you are looking back, you must not

---

589. *Gozanban* is missing *shi* 識, but *Dahui Pujue chanshi pushuo* 大慧普覺禪師普說 has this
line as: 及待發時已落在第八識佛不云乎 (CBETA, M059, no. 1540, p. 963, b5–6). Mujaku,
269, glosses *yi luo zai di-ba* 已落在第八 thus: "Means it is already too late" [言太遲了也].

590. Mujaku, 269, cites *Laṅkāvatāra Sūtra*, T670.16.487c24–28.

591. Mujaku, 271: 第四段示用心得益.

592. Mujaku, 271, glosses *fa wei fa* 發未發 thus: "When good and bad thoughts are about to
arise but have not yet arisen" [忠曰善惡之念欲發而未發].

employ energy in striving to do so. If you do strive to do so, then you will expend [useless] energy. Didn't the [third] patriarch [Sengcan] say: "If you try to cease agitation and revert to cessation, cessation will entail even more agitation."[593] As soon as you become aware of your gradually saving on the expenditure of [*gongfu*] energy in the midst of the troublesome defilements of daily activities, that is none other than the state wherein you, the person on duty, gain [awakening] energy;[594] that is the state wherein the person on duty becomes a buddha or patriarch; that is the state wherein the person on duty changes the hells into heavens; that is the state wherein the person on duty [returns] to the stable seat [of his own home]; that is the state wherein the person on duty escapes samsara; that is the state wherein the person on duty "makes the emperor the superior of [the legendary monarchs] Yao and Shun"; that is the state wherein "the person on duty raises the exhausted populace from impoverishment"; and that is the state wherein "the person on duty shelters his sons and grandsons."

[24.5: *Once more a "warning whip" (i.e., a saying of Yongjia) orders Zhang to jettison both good and non-good*[595]]

When you get to *here*, even speaking about buddhas, speaking about patriarchs, speaking about mind, speaking about the [true] nature, speaking about mystery, speaking about the miraculous, speaking about principle, speaking about phenomena, speaking about good, and speaking about bad are matters of external extremes—these sorts of matters still belong to the external. How much worse, in the midst of the troublesome defilements, to *do* things that the former noble ones scolded us about! Even committing good actions is not permitted—so how could the commission of non-good actions be permitted? If you have sufficient confidence in these statements, you will realize that Yongjia's saying "walking is Chan, sitting is Chan; throughout speech and silence, movement and stillness, the

---

593. Mujaku, 272, cites *Xin xin ming* 信心銘, T2010.48.376b26–27.

594. Mujaku, 272, glosses *bian shi dangren de li zhi chu* 便是當人得力之處 thus: "Dahui usually likes to say this. Although common persons attain saving on the expenditure of energy, they don't value it highly and protect it. Because it's an easy matter, they thereupon let it go and lose it. Because the Master has pity for them, he often speaks of it" [忠曰大慧尋常好說之者凡人雖得省力不珍護之爲容易事故遂放失師爲憐之每每說之].

595. Mujaku, 272: 第五段重警策令捨法非法. "Warning whip" (*jingce* 警策) is a literary term for a pithy text of few words that is concise and to the point.

substance is calm and at rest"[596] is not a falsehood. Please rely on this in going through experience—be changeless from beginning to end. Then, even if you don't achieve a penetrating realization of your very own *original ground,* even if you don't gain a clear vision of your very own *original face,* the "unripe" state will already be "ripe," and the "ripe" state will already be "unripe." Be sure to remember this!

[24.6: *Encourages wonderful awakening*[597]]

As soon as you become aware of the state of saving on expenditure of [*gongfu*] energy, that is none other than the state of gaining [awakening] energy. I always speak these words to those who have entered into *this* [i.e., entered the Way[598]]. Having frequently heard this said to them, most people neglect it and are unwilling to take up it as a fact. Layman, as an experiment try doing *gongfu* in this way![599] In just ten or so days, you'll spontaneously be able to perceive [where you fall on the spectrum of] saving on expenditure of [*gongfu*] energy, not saving on expenditure of [*gongfu*] energy; gaining [awakening] energy, not gaining [awakening] energy. The person drinking water knows for himself whether it is cold or warm. It can't be articulated to people; it can't be presented to people. A former worthy said: "Realization can't be shown to people; as for principle, if you don't realize it, you won't understand."[600] Those of self-realization, self-apprehension, self-confidence, and self-awakening [in order to clear their own way] shove aside examples of those who have in the past realized, have in the past apprehended, have already attained confidence, and have already attained awakening; and only then do they wordlessly align with [those realizers of the past]. Those who have not yet realized, not yet apprehended, not yet

---

596. Mujaku, 272, cites *Yongjia zhengdao ge* 永嘉證道歌, T2014.48.396a10–11; and comments: "Looking at these words one should realize that Chan is not the defilements and also is not the buddhadharma" [忠曰看此等語可知禪非是塵勞又非是佛法也].

597. Mujaku, 273: 第六段勸激妙悟.

598. Mujaku, 273, glosses *ge zhong ren* 箇中人 thus: "Those who have entered the Way" [忠曰入道中人也].

599. Mujaku, 274, glosses *jushi shi ruci zuo gongfu kan* 居士試如此做工夫看 thus: "*Like this* refers to the above text: 'when good and bad thoughts are about to arise but have not yet arisen, when you are about to wake up but have not yet woken up, you absolutely must do a *backwards-look-illumination*'" [忠曰如此者指上文發未發覺未覺時切須照顧].

600. Mujaku, 274, cites *Jingde chuandeng lu* 景德傳燈錄, T2076.51.459c7–8.

attained confidence, and not yet awakened: not only do they lack confidence in themselves—they also lack confidence that there are other people who have attained access to this sort of realm. Old Layman, you have a natural endowment that places you close to the Way, and so, in fact, there is no need for you to change your actions and behavior. Compared to other people, out of 10,000 parts, you've already understood 9,999. Your only lack is "the single snort":[601] and then you're done!

[24.7: *Shows that mental reflection is not the Way*[602]]

When members of the scholar-official class study the Way, most don't really comprehend. Unless there is oral discussion and mental reflection, they are blank, with "nowhere to put their hands and feet."[603] They don't believe that the state of not having anywhere to put your hands and feet is precisely the *good state*. They single-mindedly want to engage in mental reflection until they succeed in obtaining something, to pursue oral discussion until they achieve understanding. Little do they imagine that they've made a mistake. The Buddha said: "The *tathāgata* explains all sorts of matters with all his metaphors, but there is no metaphor capable of explaining this dharma. Why? Because [this dharma] cuts off the road of comprehension and is inconceivable."[604] Have confidence in the certainty that mental reflection and discrimination block the Way!

[24.8: *The Way in and of itself cuts off mental reflection*[605]]

If you attain the "severing of the times 'before' and 'after,' "[606] then the road of knowledge will be spontaneously cut off. If you attain the cutting-off of the road of knowledge, even if you speak of all sorts of things, they will all be this dharma [spoken of in the above *Huayan Sutra* quotation[607]]. Once

---

601. Mujaku, 274, glosses *pen de* 噴地 thus: *"With a 'snort' is Aah!"* [猶言囮地].

602. Mujaku, 274: 第七段示思量非道.

603. Mujaku, 275, cites *Analects, Zilu* 子路.

604. Mujaku, 275, cites *Da fangguang fo huayan jing*, T279.10.277b20–23.

605. Mujaku, 275: 第八段示道體絕思量.

606. Mujaku, 275, cites *Vimalakīrti Sūtra*, T475.14.540a6.

607. Mujaku, 275, glosses *shuo zhongzhong shi jie ci fa ye* 說種種事皆此法也 thus: "The above *Huayan* passage" [忠曰上華嚴說].

this dharma has become bright, then this state of brightness is the inconceivable realm of great liberation. This very realm itself is also inconceivable. Since this realm is inconceivable, all the metaphors [of the *tathāgata*] are also inconceivable. All the various sorts of matters [explained by the *tathāgata* with his metaphors] are also inconceivable. This very inconceivability is also inconceivable—even these words are unfixed! This very unfixedness is also inconceivable—if you go around in circles trying to pinpoint it in that way, whether matters or dharma or metaphors or sense objects [of daily activities⁶⁰⁸], it's like a circle with no beginning, no starting place, no ending place—it's all the inconceivable dharma. Therefore, it is said: "When the bodhisattva dwells in inconceivability, therein anything can be conceived. When you have entered into this state of the inconceivable, thought and non-thought are both calmed."⁶⁰⁹

[24.9: *Shows that if Zhang exhausts dharma-defilement, he can realize the Way and produce autonomous functioning⁶¹⁰*]

However, you must not abide in the state of calmness. If you abide in the state of calmness, then you will be possessed by "measuring with the *dharmadhātu*" [i.e., using ultimate reality as a measuring stick]. In the teachings, this is called "dharma-defilement" [i.e., producing all sorts of views about the buddhadharma⁶¹¹]. Once you have extinguished "measuring with the *dharmadhātu*" and all-at-once washed away any sort of idea of "remarkable and outstanding," then, for the first time, keep an eye on [a *huatou*] such as: **cypress tree in the garden; three pounds of linen thread; dried turd; dog has no buddha-nature** [i.e., **wu** 無]; **in one gulp suck up the water of West River;** and **East Mountain walks on water.** If you can suddenly break through the one phrase [i.e., the *huatou*], then, for the first time, it can be called the "immeasurable transference of the *dharmadhātu*."⁶¹² If you see things as they truly are, practice *in that way*, and function *in that way*, then

608. Takagi, 56a, at *jingjie* 境界 inserts "Daily activities" [日用].

609. Mujaku, 276, cites *Da fangguang fo huayan jing* 大方廣佛華嚴經, T279.10.165a7-9.

610. Mujaku, 276: 第九段示盡法塵則能契道起自在用.

611. Mujaku, 277, glosses *fa chen fannao* 法塵煩惱 thus: "Means dharma views or dharma delusions—producing all sorts of views about the buddhadharma" [忠曰謂法見法惑也於佛法上生種種見也].

612. Mujaku, 278, cites *Śūraṃgama Sūtra*, T945.19.142c4-5.

you will be able to manifest the land of the Treasure King on the tip of a single hair, sit inside a minute atom, turn the great dharma wheel, bring to completion all sorts of dharmas, destroy all sorts of dharmas—all will arise from "I." For instance, the strongman extends his arms without the assistance of another person's strength, and the lion roams about without seeking a companion. Even if all sorts of outstanding and miraculous realms manifest themselves before you, your mind will be unperturbed; even if all sorts of realms of bad karma manifest themselves before you, your mind will not be fearful. During the four postures of daily activities, in responding to conditions, you will be bold and unconstrained, trusting the *original nature* to engage in free and easy wandering.

[24.10: *Bears a distant connection to the above passage about heavens and hells*[613]]

Having reached *this level*, for the first time it can be said that there are no heavens and there are no hells. Yongjia said: "If there are no people [i.e., sentient beings], there are no buddhas. The great thousand worlds, as numberless as the grains of sand of the Ganges, are like foam on the sea. All the noble ones and worthies are like the flash of a bolt of lightning."[614] If this old one [Yongjia] had not arrived at *this level* [in which "measuring with the *dharmadhātu*" is extinguished], how could he have spoken this way?[615]

[24.11: *Continues the above text's criticism of the nihilistic viewpoint*[616]]

There are a great many people who misunderstand this saying. If they haven't penetrated to the source, they won't avoid relying on those words ["there are no people and there are no buddhas"] to produce [a nihilistic]

---

613. Mujaku, 279: 第十段承上文遙結 … 天堂地獄之語.

614. Mujaku, 279, cites *Yongjia zhengdao ge* 永嘉證道歌, T2014.48.396c23–24.

615. Mujaku, 279, glosses *ruo bu dao zhege … lai* 若不到遮箇 … 來 thus: "If Yongjia had spoken like this without having arrived at the *level* in which measuring with the *dharmadhātu* is extinguished, it would merely have been the annihilationist view of the outsider Ways" [忠曰永嘉若不到法界量滅田地而如此說則但是外道空見也].

616. Mujaku, 279: 第十一段承上文斥撥無見.

understanding.[617] Thereupon they will say that everything is non-existent, negate cause-and-effect, consider all the teachings spoken by the buddhas and patriarchs to be "false"—and call them [i.e., the buddhas and patriarchs] deluders of people. If this illness [i.e., the illness of the perverse view of an annihilationist emptiness] is not eliminated, then, lacking discrimination and rules, they will incur calamities. The Buddha said: "In the floating mind of falsity there are many clever 'views.' "[618] If they don't grasp "existence," then they grasp "non-existence." If they don't grasp these two, then they have surmising and conjecturing about "both existence and non-existence." Even if they notice this illness [of "both existence and non-existence"], they will surely fall into attachment to "neither existent nor non-existent."

[24.12: *Discriminates between the four alternatives of the outside Ways and the four alternatives of the buddhadharma*[619]]

Therefore, the former noble ones earnestly exhort us—they make us divorce from the four alternatives [listed below];[620] make us cut off the hundred negations; make us instantly sever [the four alternatives] at the single stroke of the sword; make us no longer mindful of "before" and "after"; and make us sever the crowns of the heads of the thousand noble ones. The four alternatives are: "exist," "not exist," "neither exist nor not-exist," and "both exist and not-exist." If you manage to break through these four alternatives, upon hearing it said that all dharmas are "really existent," though "I too follow along with that" and say that they "exist," nevertheless it's not a case of being blocked by this "really exists" [i.e., the

---

617. Mujaku, 279, glosses *bu mian yi yu sheng jie* 不免依語生解 thus: "Won't avoid relying on the word-traces 'there are no people and there are no buddhas' to produce a nihilistic understanding" [忠曰依無人無佛言迹生撥無之解].

618. Mujaku, 281, cites *Da fangguang yuanjue xiuduoluo liaoyi jing* 大方廣圓覺修多羅了義經, T842.17.916a2–3.

619. Mujaku, 281: 第十二段辨外道四句佛法四句.

620. The Sanskrit is *catuṣkoṭi*. Robert E. Buswell Jr. and Donald S. Lopez Jr., *The Princeton Dictionary of Buddhism* (Princeton: Princeton University Press, 2014), 172: "A dialectical form of argumentation used in Buddhist philosophy to categorize sets of specific propositions.... In the sūtra literature, the *catuṣkoṭi* is employed to categorize the speculative philosophical propositions of non-Buddhists (*tīrthika*) in a list of fourteen 'indeterminate' or 'unanswered' (*avyākrita*) questions to which the Buddha refused to respond."

extreme of eternalism]. Upon hearing it said that all dharmas are really "non-existent," though "I too follow along with that" and say that they "do not exist," nevertheless it's not the empty-headed "non-existence" of the world [i.e., the extreme of annihilationism]. Upon hearing it said that all dharmas are "both existent and non-existent," though "I too follow along with that" and say that they "both exist and not exist," nevertheless it's not joke-talk [*prapañca*]. Upon hearing it said that all dharmas are "neither existent nor non-existent," though "I too follow along with that" and say that they are "neither existent nor non-existent," nevertheless it's not a contradiction. As Vimalakīrti says: "[If, Subhūti, you were to see no 'buddha,' hear no 'dharma'; and if you were then to take the six heretical teachers as your teachers; and, if because of them, you were to leave home; and if,] what the six teachers of the outside Ways have fallen into, you too were to follow along with and fall into: [then you would be worthy of my food offering]."[621]

[24.13: *Scolds members of the scholar-official class for shallow confidence*[622]]

Most scholar-officials studying the Way are unwilling to empty out their minds and listen to the instruction of the good teacher. As soon as the good teacher opens his mouth, he [i.e., the scholar-official], before even a word is uttered, "suddenly understands." But when you make him cough it up completely [i.e., make him present his level of understanding,[623] it's clear] he has "suddenly misunderstood"! What he understood just before uttering a word was also stagnation in verbalization. There is also another type [of scholar-official]. He is earnestly proud of his intellect and talks in terms of "reason." [He says:] "Of the various worldly arts, there are none that I don't understand. There is only this one matter of Chan that I have not yet understood." At each official posting he invites a number of hogwash-talking old monks to a banquet. When the meal is over, he has them [i.e., the monks] throw off restraint and freely speak their minds. Then, in his discriminative consciousness, he commits to memory this hogwash of a sermon. He later appraises [the level of understanding of other] people

---

621. Mujaku, 283, cites *Vimalakīrti Sūtra*, T475.14.540b29–c4.

622. Mujaku, 283: 第十三段呵士大夫輕信.

623. Mujaku, 283, glosses *jiao qu tulu jin* 教渠吐露盡 thus: "*Cough it up completely* means *make him present his level of understanding*" [教吐露者教呈其見解也].

with a line [from this hogwash sermon] here and a line there, calling it
"repartee [i.e., question-and-answer] Chan."[624] "If in the end I have one
more line and you have nothing to say, then I have won!" When he runs
into a fellow with the clear eye of reality, he doesn't recognize him. Even
if he does recognize him, he lacks resolute confidence. He is not ready to
"stabilize" like a four-legged chair firmly attached to the ground.[625] Even if
he comes to some sort of comprehension through a master, he will rely on
his old ways [acquired from the hogwash-talking old monks[626]] to demand
[from the teacher] the "seal of approval." When he comes upon a teacher
who, towards sense objects that go against his wishes and those that are
in accordance with his wishes, displays the *original-allotment* tongs [for
forging steel], he is intimidated and dares not approach. This sort is to be
labeled "pathetic."

[24.14: *Dahui relates his intention behind composing the letter*[627]]

Old Layman, you in your younger years passed the "presented-scholar"
examination and rose in the world. Whatever official post you are in, you
respond to the times in performing beneficial deeds. Your [morals and]
literary compositions,[628] as well as your accomplishments, surpass that of
others, but you have never bragged. You are single-minded: you want only
to take a step back and really understand *this great matter* of origination-
by-dependence. Moved by this extreme sincerity, I have inconsiderately
gone on and on like this. It's not you alone[629] that I want to inform about

---

624. Mujaku, 284, glosses *si chan* 厮禪 thus: "Repartee Chan. Means question-and-answer
Chan" [相禪也言問答也].

625. Mujaku, 284–285, glosses *si leng ta de* 四楞塌地 thus: "Like spreading the four corners
of a seat so that they are firmly stabilized on the ground. It is a simile for letting go of one's
previous cleverness and cutting off all intellectual understanding" [忠曰如敷坐具四角帖帖
著地也譬於放下從來自己聰明都絕知解也].

626. Mujaku, 285, glosses *yi jiu* 依舊 thus: "Like what he acquired from the hogwash-talking
old monks" [忠曰如杜撰長老所也].

627. Mujaku, 285: 第十四段述造書之意.

628. Mujaku, 285, glosses 文章事業 thus: "This *wenzhang* is not limited to the *wenzhang* of
writing on paper with a brush. Whatever virtue and righteousness is revealed to the outside
world is called *wenzhang*. It is the *wenzhang* of 'morals-and-*wenzhang*'" [忠曰此文章不局著
紙筆之文章凡德義顯於外此云文章所謂道德文章之文章也].

629. Mujaku, 286, glosses *fei du yao jushi yun yun* 非獨要居士云云 thus: "Means: I didn't
compose this letter for you alone. I wanted to reach a type of being with karmic abilities like

these sorts of illnesses. I also want to encourage beginning bodhisattvas in the accumulation of the equipment [i.e., karmic merit and knowledge] for entering the Way.

25. *In Reply to Palace Writer Zhu (Yanzhang)*

[*Commentary: Mujaku says, "This letter is dated to Shaoxing 13/1143 when the master was fifty-five." Hyesim says, "The purport of the Zhu letter is to awaken to emptiness and practice the* huatou.*"*[630] *Hengzhou-exile letter.*]

[25.1: *The severing of "before" and "after" is the method for stopping mind*[631]]

I have heard that you have shut your gate [in seclusion] and are doing "wall-contemplation" [i.e., the practice of sitting].[632] This is good medicine for stopping the mind. If beyond that you "bore into old paper" [i.e., blindly read old books in your attachment to the written word],[633] you will surely bring up roots and shoots of samsara that have been in your storehouse consciousness from time without beginning, create impediments for good roots, and create impediments that block the Way—of this there is no doubt. If you can stop mind, then stop it for a little while[634]—past events, whether good or bad, whether they went against you or for you: don't reflect on any of them. As for present events [i.e., daily activities],

---

yours—that is why I composed this long letter" [忠曰言作此書非獨爲公也欲爲如公一類機故作此長書也].

630. Mujaku, 288: 此書紹興十三年癸亥師五十五歲而作. Hyesim, 67: 注狀旨達空參話. For a biographical entry for Zhu Zao 注藻 (*zi* Yanzhang 彦章), see *Song History*, 445 (16.3340–41). Hucker, 345 and 223: "*Neihan* 內翰, lit., inner (i.e., palace) writing brush (wielders): Palace Writers.... unofficial reference to members of the Hanlin Academy (翰林院).... a loosely organized group of litterateurs who did drafting and editing work in the preparation of the more ceremonious imperial pronouncements and the compilation of imperially sponsored historical and other works."

631. Mujaku, 288: 第一段示前後際斷是息心法.

632. Mujaku, 288, glosses *biguan* 壁觀 thus: "Because at this time Zhu had been demoted and was in Yongzhou [Changsha in Hunan]. Zhu at the time was sixty-five; he died at the age of seventy-six" [忠曰蓋此時公落職在永州公時年六十五後七十六卒].

633. Mujaku, 288, glosses *geng zuan guzhi* 更鑽故紙 thus: "Means: be attached to the written word" [忠曰言著文字]; and cites: *Jingde chuandeng lu* 景德傳燈錄, T2076.51.268a10–19.

634. Mujaku, 289, glosses *de xi xin qie xi xin* 得息心且息心 thus: "Means: if you can stop it, then stop it for a little while. If you can't stop mind, you need not consider it a peril" [忠曰言得息則且息若不得息心亦不必患之].

if you can skip any of them, then skip them.[635] Sever [the ten-thousand things] at the single stroke of the sword—you must not hesitate! As for future events, naturally they won't be a continuation [of past and present compulsions]. The old one Śākyamuni said: "The mind does not falsely seize past dharmas, does not covet matters of the future, and is not fixed in [dharmas of] of the present—comprehending that the three times are all empty and still."[636]

[25.2: *Shows the* gongfu *method of rallying the* huatou *to awareness*[637]]

Just keep your eye on: "A monk asked Zhaozhou: 'Does even a dog have buddha-nature?' Zhou said: '*Wu* 無.'" Please just switch the mind of useless mental reflection backwards onto the word **wu** 無; and, as an experiment, just try to mentally reflect [on **wu** 無]. Suddenly, in a state immune to mental reflection, you'll attain the smashing of *this single thought*[638]—this is none other that the state wherein you will comprehend [the empty calmness[639] of] the three times [of past, present, and future]. At the time [that *the single thought is smashed and you*] comprehend, arranging [words and phrases in literary compositions] is impermissible; making calculations about [what is skillful and what is clumsy in literary matters] is impermissible; and quoting [classical texts] as authorities is impermissible.[640] Why? The state of [smashing *the*

---

635. Mujaku, 289, glosses *de sheng bian sheng* 得省便省 thus: "Means: Having closed the gate to do wall-contemplation, if you can omit mundane events, then omit them for a little while. If you can't omit them, you need not consider it a peril" [言杜門壁觀若得省世事且省之若亦省不得不必患之].

636. Mujaku, 289, cites: *Da fangguang fo huayan jing* 大方廣佛華嚴經, T279.10.156b24–26.

637. Mujaku, 289: 第二段示提撕工夫法.

638. Hyesim, 67: "The *single thought* is the *huatou*" [一念話頭]. Takagi, 59b, at *zhe yi nian* 遮一念 inserts: "The false mind of samsara" [生死妄心也].

639. Mujaku, 289, glosses *liaoda san shi* 了達三世 thus: "Comprehend the empty calmness of the three times. *Here* there is no such thing as the three times" [忠曰了達三世空寂也者裡都無三世事].

640. Mujaku, 289–290, glosses *liaoda shi anpai bu de* 了達時安排不得 thus: "*At the time the single thought is smashed and you comprehend* is the state of gaining [awakening] energy.... *anpai jijiao yinzheng* means: the scholar's habitual pursuits always involve the composition of literary works. This includes: arranging words and phrases in literary compositions; making calculations about skillful and clumsy in literary matters; and quoting classical texts as authorities" [忠曰念破了達時即是得力處也.... 忠曰安排計較引證者學士平生事業皆是著文章時事謂安排文字計較巧拙引證典].

single thought and] comprehending is incompatible with "arranging," incompatible with "calculating," incompatible with "textual citation." No matter how much you quote texts, calculate, and arrange, it will have nothing to do with comprehension. Just make yourself "composed"[641] and don't reflect on "good and bad" at all. Don't engage in [such perverse Chan teachings as] "[effortfully] concentrating mind" and "quelling delusive thought."[642] When you do "concentrating mind," there is floating [upon sense objects, i.e., restlessness[643]]; when you "quell delusive thought," there is torpor. If you do neither "concentrating mind" nor "quelling delusive thought," then "good and bad" will no longer be "good and bad"—if you comprehend *in this way*, where could the Māra of birth-and-death possibly attach to you?[644]

[25.3: *The "warning whip" (of a saying of Xuefeng Zhenjue) points out impermanence*[645]]

Your name "Zhu Yanzhang" fills all-under-heaven. What you've gotten all your life by arranging, what you've gotten by calculating, what you've gotten by quoting texts is literary accomplishment, fame, and official position. In your later years, you've [experienced karmic recompense in which,] due to prior causes, there have been corresponding results—which one of [those results] is the "real thing"? Having composed limitless elegant turns of the literary language—what single line of it has enabled you to gain [*gongfu*] energy? How much of a difference is there between someone whose fame is conspicuous and someone who hides the light of his virtue? How much of a difference is there between you, when your official position had reached [the exalted level of] that of the "great Two Drafting Groups,"[646] and you, when you were at the

---

641. *Analects, Shu er* 述而: "The gentleman is level and composed; the small man is full of worries" [君子坦蕩蕩、小人長戚戚。].

642. Mujaku, 290, glosses *wanghuai* 忘懷 thus: "This *quelling delusive thought* is not necessarily the *quelling delusive thought* of the perverse Chan of *quelling delusive thought* and *engirding mind* spoken of in the above text" [忠曰此忘懷非必前文所謂忘懷管帶邪禪之忘懷也]. Mujaku's reading seems to be mistaken.

643. Mujaku, 290, glosses *liutang* 流蕩 thus: "The mind floats upon sense objects. It is called *restlessness*" [忠曰心流蕩境上也謂掉舉也].

644. Mujaku, 290, cites: *Zhenzhou Linji Huizhao chanshi yulu* 鎮州臨濟慧照禪師語錄, T1985.47.499a22–23.

645. Mujaku, 290: 第三段警策示無常.

646. The term *liang zhi* 兩制 refers to the Two Drafting Groups on duty in the Administration Chamber, where Grand Councilors presided over the central government. One group

[lowly] student stage of a "Cultivated Talent?"[647] Right now you are already approaching seventy years of age. No matter how much talent you have had—what do you want to accomplish now? On the final day of the twelfth month [at the end of your life] how will you settle the matter? The killer-demon of impermanence[648] doesn't stop for even a moment. Xuefeng Zhenjue said:

> "Time goes swiftly—in an instant:
> The floating world—how can one live in it for any length of time?
> I came down from the [Flying-Monkey] Mountains [in Fujian-
>   Jiangxi][649] at almost thirty-two years of age;
> Since entering Min [i.e., returning to Fuzhou], it's already been
>   more than four decades.
> Other people's mistakes—I have no time to go on and on about
>   them;
> My own errors—I must step-by-step get rid of them.
> This for the sake of informing the red and purple-clothed officials
>   who fill that court:
> 'King Yama [Judge of the Dead]—I don't fear the [exalted badge of
>   the] golden bag at your belt!' "[650]

An ancient earnestly exhorted us in this way—for the sake of what?

[25.4: *Judges the relative weight of karmic obstacles for poor and rich people*[651]]

The ignorant, mediocre people of the world, pressed by hunger and cold, in their daily activities have no leeway to think about anything else. If they

---

consisted of Hanlin Academicians of the Institute of Academicians, collectively called Inner Drafters (*neizhi* 内制); the other consisted of nominal members of the Secretariat, collectively called Outer Drafters (*waizhi* 外制). The collective designation of both groups was Drafters. Hucker, 309.

647. The term *xiuzai* 秀才 is the unofficial designation of all candidates in a Metropolitan Examination in the civil service recruitment examination sequence. Hucker, 248.

648. Mujaku, 292, cites: *Zhenzhou Linji Huizhao chanshi yulu* 鎮州臨濟慧照禪師語錄, T1985.47.497b16.

649. Mujaku, 293, glosses *chu ling* 出嶺 thus: "The Flying-Monkey Range across Fujian and Jiangxi" [忠曰飛猿嶺在福建江西兩處].

650. *Xuefeng Yicun chanshi yulu* 雪峰義存禪師語錄 (CBETA, X69, no. 1333, p. 84, b20–23 // Z 2:24, p. 485, d2–5 // R119, p. 970, b2–5).

651. Mujaku, 295: 第四段判貧貴人業障輕重.

can just keep their bodies a little warm and feel no hunger in their bellies, that's the end of it. [Because they notice] only these two matters, they are incapable of being vexed by the Māra of birth-and-death. When you compare them to those who have received wealth and status, the weight [of vexation by Māra] is utterly unequal. In the case of those who have received wealth and status, their bodies are always warm and their bellies full. They have not been pressed by hunger and cold, but, on the contrary, they do have a lot of [problems] that cannot be given form in words. Therefore, they are always in the net of the Māra of birth-and-death, with no way to escape. The exception is those who from past births [have practiced in order to get future karmic fruits and thus] possess the "body of a Daoist immortal"—they can see right through and realize.

[25.5: *Encouragement*[652]]

A former noble one said: "The sudden arising [of phantasmal thought] is illness; not continuing [such thoughts] is medicine. Don't fear the arising of thoughts; just fear slowness of awakening."[653] "Buddha" means "awakening." Because he was constantly awakened, he is called the "Greatly Awakened One." He is also called "King of Awakening." Moreover, [buddhas] are all created from common persons. "In the past he was a man—how could we not do what he did?"[654]

[25.6: *Uses the realization of impermanence as an encouragement*[655]]

The lifetime span of a century—how much time can you have left? Moment after moment you must act as if you are putting out a fire on your head. [In this impermanent world,] in doing good deeds, one still fears that [one will die] before they come to completion.[656] How much more so is this the case, when every moment you are utterly unawakened in the midst of the

---

652. Mujaku, 296: 第五段激勵.

653. Mujaku, 296, glosses *xiansheng yun* 先聖云 thus: "I haven't yet identified this former noble one" [忠曰先聖未考]; and cites *Zongjing lu* 宗鏡錄, T2016.48.638a18–19.

654. Mujaku, 296, cites *Zongjing lu* 宗鏡錄, T2016.48.839a12–14.

655. Mujaku, 296: 第六段證無常以勸勉.

656. Mujaku, 297, glosses *zuo hao shi yun yun* 做好事云云 thus: "Means: in this impermanent world, in doing good deeds, one still fears that one will die before they come to completion" [言無常世間作善事猶恐其事未成就而死去].

defilements? Dreadful! Horrible! Recently from Lü Juren [letters #29, #31–#32] I received a letter at the beginning of the fourth month. It informed me of the death of Ceng Shuxia.[657] Juren said: "[The killer-demon of impermanence] has once again removed one after another of those with whom I have had friendly contact. It's simply unnerving [that I am aging, and *this matter* is not yet finished.]"[658]

[25.7: *Dahui consoles him over producing the aspiration for awakening in his late years*[659]]

Recently he [i.e., Lü Juren] has been heartfelt [in his *gongfu*] for the sake of *this matter*. You too regret that your sudden turn [to *this matter*] has been a little late. Some time ago I wrote him a return letter that said: "Just make the single thought of finally realizing your mistake into your standard—pay no heed to whether 'late' or 'early.' The single thought of realizing your mistake is the basis of becoming a buddha or patriarch, the sharp tool for destroying Māra's net, the road for escaping samsara." I hope that you too will just do *gongfu in this way*.

[25.8: *Discusses proof of the efficacy of* gongfu[660]]

When the *gongfu* you are doing gradually ripens, then, in your daily activities, twenty-four hours a day, you will become aware that you are saving on expenditure of [*gongfu*] energy. When you become aware that you are saving on expenditure of [*gongfu*] energy, you must not become slack. Concerning the state of saving on expenditure of [*gongfu*] energy, just keep pressing hard. Keep pressing hard, over and over. When you are no longer conscious of the existence of this state of saving on expenditure of [*gongfu*] energy, you are not extremely far from awakening.[661] Just keep an eye on

---

657. Mujaku, 297, mentions that Ceng Shuxia 曾叔夏 and Liu Yanli 劉彥禮 do not have biographical entries in *Song History*.

658. Mujaku, 297, glosses *zhi shi ke wei* 直是可畏 thus: "It's not that this Dahui follower fears death. Means: he is aging and, in progressing towards this Way, *this matter* is not yet finished. Therefore, he fears death" [忠曰非徒畏死也謂年老方趣向此道而其事未了故直畏死去也].

659. Mujaku, 297: 第七段慰諭晚年發心.

660. Mujaku, 297: 第八段論工夫效驗.

661. Mujaku, 298, glosses *bu zheng duo ye* 不爭多也 thus: "These are not words of complete approval. Means: not extremely far from awakening; gradually approaching awakening" [忠曰不全許語也言與悟底不太遠也漸近于悟也].

the word *wu* 無. Don't pay any attention to whether you have awakened or not. I very much pray [you will go on practicing in the above manner].

26. Continued [Second Letter in Reply to Palace Writer Zhu]

[*Commentary:* Hyesim says, "The purport of this letter is to urge Zhu's practice of Mr. Man-in-charge."[662] *Presumably dates to around the same time as letter #25, Shaoxing 13/1143. Hengzhou-exile letter.*]

[26.1: *Dahui urges him to continue with the good progress he's made*[663]]

I have been informed that you have shut your gate and cut off contact, omitted all mundane matters, and are from dawn to dusk only rallying to awareness the *huatou* I showed you [i.e., the *wu* 無 *huatou*[664]]. Very good! Very good! Having in the past devoted effort to this mind [of rallying the *huatou* to awareness],[665] you should "take awakening as your standard."[666] If you are cringing and cowering, if you are thinking that your character is mean and of low ability, and beyond this you are seeking for a clue to awakening, then truly you've become someone who is in the Containing-the-Origin Hall [i.e., the Tang-dynasty palace hall in the capital Chang'an], but asks where the capital Chang'an is located!

[26.2: *Points out* Mr. Man-in-charge[667]]

Just when you are rallying [the *huatou*] to awareness—who is doing it? And the knower who knows that his character is mean and of low ability— who is that? I don't evade oral karma, speaking clearly without holding

---

662. Hyesim, 68: 又狀旨勸參主人公.

663. Mujaku, 298: 第一段隨善勸勵.

664. Mujaku, 298, glosses *suoju huatou* 所舉話頭 thus: "The *wu* 無 *huatou*" [無話也].

665. Mujaku, 298, glosses *ji bian ci xin* 既辨此心 thus: "Means: you have been inattentive to mundane matters and rallied the *huatou* to awareness" [忠曰言辨闊略世事提撕話頭之意也].

666. Mujaku, 298, cites *Guishan jingce zhu* 溈山警策註 (CBETA, X63, no. 1239, p. 230, c8 // Z 2:16, p. 148, d5 // R111, p. 296, b5).

667. Mujaku, 299: 第二段揭示主人公.

anything back for your sake. There's just one Zhu Yanzhang—there aren't two separate ones. There being only one Zhu Yanzhang—beyond him, from where would come the one who rallies [the *huatou*] to awareness, the one who knows that his character is mean and of low ability, the one who seeks for a place to get a clue to awakening? You should know that all of them are shadows of [*Mr. Man-in-charge*] Zhu Yanzhang.[668] They have no relationship whatsoever to *him*—Zhu Yanzhang [i.e., the true *Mr. Man-in-charge*].[669] If it's the true Zhu Yanzhang, his character certainly isn't mean and of low ability, and he certainly isn't seeking for a place to get a clue to awakening. If you can just have sufficient confidence in your very own *Mr. Man-in-charge*, there will be no need to fabricate a lot of anxieties[670] concerning this whole assortment [of Zhu Yanzhang*s*].

[26.3: *Quotes the story of an ancient*[671]]

"In the past there was a monk[672] who asked Yangshan: 'The all-at-once awakening of Chan—in the final analysis, what *upāyas* are there for entering therein?'[673] Yangshan said: 'This idea is extremely difficult. If you are a person of the highest faculties and highest wisdom among the followers of the Chan patriarchal lineage, hearing but once you have a thousand awakenings and obtain the great *dhāraṇī* [i.e., the true principle]. A person with this sort of faculties is very rare. There are, however, people whose faculties are slight and wisdom inferior. Therefore, an ancient worthy

---

668. Mujaku, 300, glosses *jie shi Zhu Yanzhang yingzi* 皆是注彥章影子 thus: "*All* refers to the fact that the one who rallies the *huatou* to awareness, the one who realizes that his character is mean and of low ability, and the one who seeks for a place to get a clue to awakening are all reflections of *Mr. Man-in-charge*" [忠曰皆者指提撕底知陋劣底求入頭底盡是主人公之影子].

669. Mujaku, 300, glosses *bu gan ta Zhu Yanzhang* 不干他注彥章 thus: "The true *Mr. Man-in-charge* isn't the one rallying the *huatou* to awareness, isn't the one realizing that his character is mean and of low ability, and isn't the one seeking for a place to get a clue to awakening" [忠曰真主人公不提撕不知陋劣不求入頭也].

670. ZGK, 66.282, glosses *xiaode* 消得 thus: "In vernacular language *no need to speak of* or *no need to do a fabrication*" [俗語に不消說不消一捏].

671. Mujaku, 300: 第三段引古人因緣.

672. Mujaku, 300, cites *Jingde chuandeng lu* 景德傳燈錄, T2076.51.283c9–19; and *Wu deng hui yuan* 五燈會元 (CBETA, X80, no. 1565, p. 190, c7–17 // Z 2B:11, p. 163, c13–d5 // R138, p. 326, a13–b5).

673. Mujaku, 300, glosses *ru men* 入門 thus: "Means: What *upāyas* are there for entering?" [忠曰言有何方便入做也].

said: "If you don't do Chan sitting to quiet thoughts, when you reach *here*, you will be utterly befuddled." '[674] The monk said: 'Beyond these [two] patterns,[675] is there any other *upāya* to enable students to enter awakening?' Yangshan said: 'Whether there is or isn't another, it won't make your mind calm down. Right now I ask you—where are you from?' [The monk] said: 'I'm from Youzhou [in northern Hebei].' Yangshan said: 'Do you still feel nostalgic for that place?' [The monk] said: 'I'm always nostalgic for it.' Yangshan said: 'The towers and hunting parks of that place—people and horses fill up the place. When you recollect it [i.e., do a reverse-illumination], does what you are nostalgic for have a lot of categories?'[676] [The monk] said: 'When I reach *here*, I don't see the existence of anything at all.' Yangshan said: 'Your understanding still lies in a sense object [i.e., you are still perceiving the absence of "anything at all"].[677] Your "confidence rank" is correct, but your "*man-[in-charge]* rank" is not.' "[678]

[26.4: *Explains the confidence rank and* man-(in-charge) *rank*[679]]

Because I have a case of grandmotherly kindness, I must attach a commentary [to the above]. [The one at] the "*man-[in-charge]* rank" is Zhu Yanzhang. [The one at] the "confidence rank" is the knower who knows that his character is mean and of low ability, the seeker who seeks for a place to get a clue to awakening. When you are correctly rallying the *huatou*

674. Mujaku, 300, cites *Jingde chuandeng lu* 景德傳燈錄, T2076.51.440c20–441b7.

675. Mujaku, 301, glosses *chu ci ge wai* 除此格外 thus: "Beyond *hearing but once and having a thousand awakenings* and *Zen sitting and quieting thoughts*" [忠曰一聞千悟與安禪靜慮之外也].

676. Mujaku, 301, glosses *fansi si de* 返思思底 thus: "He makes this monk's mind respond to the thousands of differentiations and makes him view them, but he makes his responding and viewing mind do a reverse-illumination on it: actually, it is formless and lacks those thousands of differentiations" [忠曰令此僧心應千差萬別令観之却以其應底観底心令返照之實無形段實無千差萬別也].

677. Mujaku, 301, glosses *ru jie you zai jing* 汝解猶在境 thus: "Because the principle of emptiness is still in front of him, it says *sense object*" [空理在目前故云境也].

678. Mujaku, 302, glosses *xinwei ji shi renwei ji bu shi* 信位即是人位即不是 thus: "*Mr. Man-in-charge* who holds the stick stands out—that is the *man-[in-charge]* rank. Seeing that *Mr. Man-in-charge* who holds the stick stands out—that is the *sense-object rank* or *confidence rank*" [拄杖子主人公突出是人位也見得拄杖子主人公突出是人位者境位也信位也].

679. Mujaku, 303: 第四段解信位人位.

to awareness, do a reverse reflection upon the one who is rallying [the *hua-tou*]—sure enough, it's [*Mr. Man-in-charge*] Zhu Yanzhang, isn't it? When you reach *here*, there won't be even a hair's difference between [the *man-in-charge* rank and the confidence rank].[680] If you're shilly-shallying, you are being misled by the shadows [of *Mr. Man-in-charge* Zhu Yanzhang].[681] Quickly—go at it with heart and soul! You must not be neglectful! You must not be neglectful!

[26.5: *Repeats the previous letter's (#25.1) instruction about stopping mind*[682]]

Do you remember what I wrote in an earlier letter? "If you can stop mind, then stop it for a little while—past events, whether good or bad, whether they went against you or for you, don't reflect on any of them. As for present events [i.e., daily activities], if you can skip any of them, then skip them. Sever [the ten-thousand things[683]] at the single stroke of the sword— you must not hesitate! As for future events, naturally they won't be a continuation [of past and present compulsions]." I don't know what you took away from reading these lines. This is the most important point for saving on expenditure of energy in doing *gongfu*. I very much pray [you will go on practicing in the above manner].

27. Continued [Third Letter in Reply to Palace Writer Zhu]

[*Commentary:* Hyesim says, "The purport of this letter is recognizing illusion and practicing the huatou."[684] *Presumably dates to around the same time as letter #25, Shaoxing 13/1143. Hengzhou-exile letter.*]

---

680. Mujaku, 303, glosses *jian bu rong fa* 間不容髮 thus: "The *confidence rank* flips over into the state of the *man-[in-charge] rank*. It's 'a spark from two stones' or 'the flash of a lightning bolt'" [忠曰信位轉爲人位處擊石火閃電光也].

681. Mujaku, 304, glosses *bei yingzi huo* 被影子惑 thus: "If you shilly-shally, you cannot reach the *man-[in-charge] rank*. The shadows are the *confidence rank*. They are shadows of the *original allotment*" [忠曰若佇思停機不可及人位也影子信位也本分光影也].

682. Mujaku, 304: 第五段再述前書息心指示.

683. Takagi, 62a, at *yi dao liang duan* 一刀兩段 inserts: "Ten-thousand things" [萬事].

684. Hyesim, 69: 狀旨知幻參句.

[27.1: *Dahui offers condolences for Zhu's deceased son*[685]]

I have been informed that your fifth heir did not recover from his illness. The feeling between father and son—the affectionate habit-energy of a thousand births and a hundred aeons are absorbed in it. I suspect that in your present state of mind there's nothing worthwhile. In the world of the five impurities[686] there are all sorts of illusions and not a single real thing. If you, when walking, standing, sitting, and lying down, constantly contemplate this, after many days and months, [the sadness of feeling that nothing is worthwhile[687]] will gradually wear off.

[27.2: *Dahui enables Zhu to sever the source of grief*[688]]

And, just when you are in grief [over losing your son], carefully ponder and inquire: from what place does [this grief] arise? If you can't pursue it to [the source] from which it arises, then the grief of the present moment—from what place could it have come? Right at the time of your grief—is it existent or non-existent? Is it unreal or real? When you over and over again pursue [these questions] to the limit, your mind will have nowhere to go to.[689] If you want to reflect upon [your son's death], just reflect.[690] If you want to cry, just cry. You'll cry again and again, you'll reflect again and again. When you become able to brush away a lot of the affection habit-energies within the storehouse consciousness, in the manner of ice spontaneously reverting to water, you will revert to *my original* [*face*]—there will be no "grief," no "reflection," no "sorrow," and no "joy."[691]

---

685. Mujaku, 304: 第一段弔慰亡子.

686. Mujaku, 304, cites *Lotus Sutra*: "Śāriputra! The buddhas emerge in the evil world of the five impurities [kaṣāya]: aeons impurity; defilements impurity; sentient-beings impurity; views impurity; and life-spans impurity" [舍利弗。諸佛出於五濁惡世，所謂劫濁、煩惱濁、眾生濁、見濁、命濁。] (T262.9.7b23–24).

687. Mujaku, 304, glosses *jianjian xiaomo* 漸漸銷磨 thus: "The sadness of feeling that nothing is worthwhile will gradually wear off" [忠曰無有是處之愁可銷磨也].

688. Mujaku, 304: 第二段令斷憂惱根源.

689. *Hōgo*, 142, renders *xin wu suozhi* 心無所之 thus: "Objects of mind will go missing..." [心の対象が消えて....].

690. Mujaku, 305, glosses *yao siliang dan yun yun* 要思量但云云 thus: "This is the *just be composed* spoken of previously [in #25.2]" [忠曰此是前所謂放教蕩蕩地之義也].

691. Mujaku, 305, glosses *hai wo ge benlai wu fannao ... de qu er* 還我箇本來無煩惱 ... 底去耳 thus: "*There is no grief*, etc. *is* the gaining of [*gongfu*] energy" [忠曰無煩惱等底即是得力底也.

[27.3: *Follow heavenly principle and be consoled*[692]]

[An ancient said:] "Consorting with the mundane *is* the supramundane with nothing left over."[693] The mundane dharma is the buddhadharma; the buddhadharma is the mundane dharma. Father and son, by their nature received from heaven, are one. If the son passes away, and the father neither grieves nor reflects; if the father passes away, and the son neither grieves nor reflects: How on earth could that be possible? If one forcibly suppresses [his grief] and, even at the time he should cry, doesn't dare to cry; and, even at the time he should reflect; doesn't dare to reflect: this utterly defies heavenly principle and denies the heaven-granted nature. It's nothing but raising one's voice to stop the echo,[694] sprinkling on oil to save oneself from fire.

[27.4: *Shows that in the* true nature *there is no grief*[695]]

Right when you are grieving, grief is not something separate [from the buddha-nature—it's the functioning of the buddha-nature].[696] You must not entertain any notion of a separate-[from-the-buddha-nature] extreme. Yongjia said: "The true nature of *avidyā* [ignorance] *is* the buddha-nature; the empty bodies of magical creation *are* the dharma body."[697] These are true words, not deceiving words or lies. When you've become able to see things *in that way*, even if you need to "reflect" and even if you need to "grieve," ["reflection" and "grief"] won't be apprehendable. Doing this contemplation [i.e., that grieving is not something separate from the buddha-nature][698] is called "correct contemplation." Doing the other contemplation

---

692. Mujaku, 305: 第三段順天理而慰諭.

693. Mujaku, 305, cites *Gu zunsu yulu* 古尊宿語錄 (CBETA, X68, no. 1315, p. 264, a15–17 // Z 2:23, p. 341, b3–5 // R118, p. 681, b3–5). The ancient is the Linji master Yunfeng Wenyue 雲峰文悅 (998–1062).

694. Mujaku, 306, cites *Da fangguang yuanjue xiuduoluo liaoyi jing lueshu* 大方廣圓覺修多羅了義經略疏, T1795.39.556c1.

695. Mujaku, 306: 第四段示實性中無煩惱.

696. Mujaku, 306–307, glosses *cong bu shi waishi* 總不是外事 thus: "Sorrow and suffering, viewed by the true eye, are in reality functionings of the buddha-nature. At the time of delusion [the buddha-nature] changes into ignorance, sighs of distress, and suffering" [忠曰憂悲苦惱正眼觀來實是佛性之作用也迷時變作無明愁歎苦惱也].

697. Mujaku, 307, cites *Yongjia zhengdao ge* 永嘉證道歌, T2014.48.395c10.

698. Mujaku, 307, glosses *zuo shi guan* 作是觀 thus: "The contemplation that 'the true nature of ignorance *is* the buddha-nature'" [忠曰無明實性即佛性之觀也].

[i.e., that grieving is separate from the buddha-nature][699] is called "perverse contemplation."[700] If you've not yet differentiated perverse and correct, it's just the right time to apply energy [to your *huatou* practice]. This is my take on it. I would never say this to "a person of no wisdom."[701]

Letters of Chan Master Dahui Pujue

Volume One Ends

---

699. Mujaku, 307, glosses *ta guan* 他觀 thus: "The contemplation of 'seeking the buddha-nature outside ignorance and destroying the illusory body in a search for a separate dharma body'" [忠曰無明外求佛性壞幻身別覓法身之觀也].

700. Mujaku, 307, cites *Da fangguang yuanjue xiuduoluo liaoyi jing* 大方廣圓覺修多羅了義經, T842.17.920c2–3.

701. Mujaku, 307, cites *Lotus Sutra*, T262.9.16a9–10.

Letters of Chan Master
Dahui Pujue *Volume Two*

RECORDED BY CHAN TRAINEE HUIRAN

28. *In Reply to Chief Transport Commissioner Xia*

[*Commentary: Mujaku says, "This letter is dated to Shaoxing 13/1143 when the master was fifty-five."[1] Hyesim says, "The purport of the letter in reply to Chief Transport Commissioner Xia is Dahui's allowing that their (Ways) silently agree."[2] Hengzhou-exile letter.*]

[28.1: *Dahui raises the letter from Xia and indulges him in the fact that they coincide in the Way[3]*]

I have been informed [by your letter]: "If we coincide in the Way,[4] then throughout heaven and earth we are on common ground. If our inclinations differ, even if we meet face to face, there will be a gap like that between the ancient states of Chu and Yue." These are honest words! *This* is the wonderful [Way] that can't be transmitted! It occurs to you to

---

1. Mujaku, 308: 此書紹興十三癸亥師五十五歲而作.

2. Hyesim, 69: 答夏運使狀旨許他默契. Xia has no biography in *Song History*. Hucker, 599 and 543: *Chief Transport Commissioner* (*yunshi* 運使) is an "abbreviation of *du caoyun shi* 都漕運使.... Chief Transport Office [*du caoyun si* 都漕運司] ... managed the transport of tax grains to the dynastic capital, supervising local Transport Offices (*caoyun si* 漕運司).

3. Mujaku, 308: 第一段舉來書縱道契.

4. Mujaku, 308, glosses *dao qi* 道契 thus: "The meaning is not *coincide with this Way*. Means: Chief Transport Commissioner Xia's Way and Dahui's Way are identical in view and attainment. Therefore, it says *coincide in the Way*" [忠曰非契當此道之義也謂夏運使道與大慧道同見同得故言道契也].

write a letter to me, and, even before you've taken up the brush and swept away the dust on the paper, I've already with both hands handed over [the wonderful Way that can't be transmitted[5]]. Also, why wait for the "firm patience" [of the fifty-two stages of bodhisattva practice] or the "ultimate" [buddha fruit[6]]—or wait until another day [when we can meet[7]]? As for this Way-principle, only realizers wordlessly coincide with it; it's difficult to speak of it with run-of-the-mill types.

[28.2: *Praises Xia's not being turned by sense objects*[8]]

[Your post in] Yanping [in Fujian] is a fine locale in the Min Mountain Range. If you are able to control your own defilements and not get turned by "gate-pivots"[9] that go against you or go in your direction,[10] then you are the person of great liberation. This person is capable of turning every single "gate-pivot." In his daily activities, he is lively like a fish waving its tail, and nothing can bind or impede him. If you decisively understand and "own" things *in that way*, spontaneously there will not be even a minute hair that constitutes an obstruction for the "I" [i.e., for you, Chief Transport Commissioner Xia].

---

5. Mujaku, 309, glosses: *yi liang shou fenfu le* 已兩手分付了 thus: "Before you have composed the letter to me, I've already with both hands handed over the wonderful Way that can't be transmitted. There's nothing else left to bequeath" [於未作寄吾書已前大慧早兩手分付不傳妙了無復遺餘也].

6. Mujaku, 310, glosses *jiujing* 究竟 thus: "Ultimate rank is the buddha fruit" [忠曰究竟位佛果也].

7. Mujaku, 310, glosses *yi si ta ri ye* 以俟他日耶 thus: "Note: In Chief Transport Commissioner Xia's letter perhaps there was something about meeting each other on another day, and so Dahui has this answer" [按蓋夏運使書中或有俟他日相見等語故有此答也].

8. Mujaku, 310: 第二段讚他不被境轉.

9. For the term *guanliezi* 關捩/棙子 (literally *barrier-gate pivot/latch*), Komazawa daigaku nai zengaku daijiten hensanjo, ed., *Shinban Zengaku daijiten* (Tokyo: Taishūkan shoten, 1985), 191, gives two meanings: (1) "key-and-lock or machine that makes one go upward to freedom" and (2) "tricks/dodges/mechanisms by which one is manipulated" (自身があやつられるからくり). The example for the latter is this very line in *Letters of Dahui*. One can "turn" gate-pivots or "be turned" by them.

10. Mujaku, 310, glosses *ni shun* 逆順 thus: "Although the *ni* character [*go against you*] is present, here the idea focuses on the *shun* [*go in your direction*], because Xia is in the beautiful scenery of the Min Range" [忠曰雖帶逆字今意專在順處閩嶺佳山水之間故]. Dahui is saying that the main danger for Xia is being "turned" by the "gate-pivot" of the scenic beauty of the mountains in which he currently resides.

[28.3: *Sayings of the ancients tied to the previous section*[11]]

An ancient had a saying: "The buddhas speak all the dharma teachings in order to convey all minds [to the other shore of nirvana]. I lack all mind, so what need have I of all the dharma teachings?"[12] Also, Lanrong said:

> At the time of unmistakeable exertion of mind, unmistakeably there is no-mind/no mind-exertion. If you talk circuitously, you'll be tired out by names and characteristics; but if you engage in "straight talk" [that cuts off names and characteristics], it will not be strenuous or onerous. No-mind/no mind unmistakeably engages in exertion, but constant exertion [of mind] is unmistakeably [constant] no[-mind/no mind]. Still, speaking of "no-mind/no mind" right now is no different from "having mind."[13]

It's not just Lanrong who is like this [i.e., who responds to things with no-mind[14]]. You and I are both *in this*.[15] The matter *in this* is impossible to take out and show people. This is precisely what I spoke of before [#28.1]—"wordlessly coinciding."

29. *In Reply to Secretariat Drafter Lü (Juren)*

[*Commentary: Mujaku says, "This letter is dated to Shaoxing 13/1143 when the master was fifty-five."*[16] *Hyesim says, "The purport of the letter in reply*

---

11. Mujaku, 311: 第三段引古語結前.

12. Mujaku, 311, cites Guifeng Zongmi's *Chan Prolegomenon* (*Chanyuan zhuquanji duxu* 禪源諸詮集都序), T2015.48.411b8–10. The ancient is the sixth patriarch Huineng.

13. Quoted in letter #20.2.

14. Mujaku, 312, glosses *Lanrong rushi* 懶融如是 thus: "*Like this* refers to responding to things with no-mind" [忠曰如是者無心應物處].

15. The term *qizhong* 其中 refers to both the Chan ultimate thing (such as *gezhong* 箇中 [*in this*] or *geli* 箇裏 [*in this*]) and *Analects, Weizheng* 爲政: ["When your words give few occasions for blame and your actions few occasions for repentance, then emolument lies *in this*" [祿在其中矣].

16. Mujaku, 313: 此書紹興十三年癸亥師五十五歲而作.

to Lü is: just practice the living phrase (i.e., the huatou)."[17] Hengzhou-exile letter.]

[29.1: *Dahui rejects having many instances of uncertainty*[18]]

The thousands upon thousands of instances of uncertainty[19] are just the "single uncertainty." When [the single] uncertainty about the *huatou* is smashed, the thousands upon thousands of instances of uncertainty are smashed at the very same time. If [the single uncertainty about] the *huatou* isn't smashed, then upon [and only upon the *huatou*[20]] keep pressing hard with it [exclusively].[21] If you discard the *huatou*, and produce uncertainty about some other example of the written word, or produce uncertainty about the sutra teachings, or produce uncertainty about the cases of the ancients [i.e., various Chan stories],[22] or produce uncertainty within the troublesome defilements of daily activities, it will all be of the coterie of the Evil One Māra.

[29.2: *Dahui shows his method of* gongfu[23]]

You must not, while raising [the *huatou*], understand and "own" it. Also, you must not engage in reflection and conjecture. Just concentrate mind

---

17. Hyesim, 70: 答呂狀旨但參活句. For entries for Lü Benzhong 呂本中 (zi Juren 居仁), see *Song History*, 376 (16.2965) and *Cases of Song and Yuan Confucians*, 36 (2.1231 and 1233–42). Hucker, 417 and 193–194: "*Sheren* 舍人 is an abbreviation of *zhongshu sheren* 中書舍人.... Drafter in the Secretariat (*zhongshu sheng* 中書省) or Secretariat Drafter, principally a handler of central government documents."

18. Mujaku, 313: 第一段斥多疑.

19. Mujaku, 313, glosses *qian yi wan yi* 千疑萬疑 thus: "Because the *source* is not yet clarified, all sorts of uncertainties arise. Because the letter from Lü Juren inquired about his uncertainty and apprehension concerning the sayings of the buddhas and patriarchs and the sayings of the old monks of all the regions, Dahui all at once lines them up and orders Lü to focus his uncertainty on the *huatou* of his personal practice" [忠曰根源未明故種種疑起耳蓋呂居仁來書問佛祖語句諸方老宿語可疑者故大慧一時列下但令疑本參話].

20. Mujaku, 313, glosses *jiu shangmian* 就上面 thus: "On top of the *huatou*" [忠曰話頭之上也]. Hyesim, 71: "*Shangmian* is the top of the *huatou*" [上面話頭上面].

21. However, Mujaku, 313, glosses *yu zhi si ya* 與之厮崖 thus: "*Zhi* refers to the *huatou*" [忠曰之指話頭].

22. Mujaku, 313, glosses *guren gong'an shang* 古人公案上 thus: "*Gong'ans* outside your personal practice. To look at the various Chan stories—with the exception of the time after your uncertainty is smashed" [忠曰本參外公案也除疑破後看差別因緣也].

23. Mujaku, 313: 第二段示工夫法.

upon reflecting on the state that cannot be reflected upon. Your mind will
have nowhere to go—"the mouse will enter the ox's horn" [i.e., all tricky
maneuvers will be severed[24]], and then you will be "felled" [like a giant tree;
i.e., you will emit the *Aah!*[25]].

[29.3: *Shows that you and you alone should keep an eye on the* huatou[26]]

Also, if your mind is agitated, just lift to awareness the *huatou* of "dog has
no buddha-nature" [i.e., **wu** 無]. The words of the buddhas, the words of the
patriarchs, the words of the old monks of all the regions have myriad differences; but, if you can break through this word **wu** 無, you'll break through
all of them at the very same time, without having to ask anyone anything. If
you intently ask questions of other people[27] about the words of the buddhas,
about the words of the patriarchs, and about the words of the old monks of
all the regions, then in endless aeons you'll never attain awakening!

30. In Reply to Director Lü (Longli)

[*Commentary: Mujaku says, "This letter dates to Shaoxing 13/1143 when the
Master was fifty-five.... As for the main intention of this letter, its speaking
of the matter of Lü Juren (letters #29, #31–#32) is its true intention, and its
speaking of the matter of Lü Longli, Juren's younger brother, is not its true
intention."*[28] *Takagi says, "This letter speaks of lifting the* **dried turd** *huatou
to awareness in order to smash the myriad instances of uncertainty and quotes
the* Nirvana Sutra *in support of smashing the arising-extinguishing mind."*[29]
Hengzhou-exile letter.]

---

24. Mujaku, 313, glosses *laoshu ru niujiao* 老鼠入牛角 thus: "Tricky maneuvers will be severed" [忠曰伎倆絕也].

25. Mujaku, 313, glosses *bian jian daoduan* 便見倒断 thus: "*Daoduan* is like felling a great
tree—means the time of *Aah!*, the single sound emitted upon great awakening" [倒断者如
截倒大木謂団地一聲大悟時節也].

26. Mujaku, 314: 第三段示自家可看取.

27. Mujaku, 314, glosses *ruo yixiang wen ren yun yun* 若一向問人云云 thus: "Because, in the
letter to Dahui, Lü asked about ancient and contemporary sayings" [忠曰蓋來書問古今語來].

28. Mujaku, 314–315: 此書紹興十三年癸亥師五十五歲而作.... 又曰此書大意以言呂居仁
事爲本意其言呂郎中事者非正意也.

29. Takagi, 2.2b: 此章舉乾屎橛破万疑引證涅槃經破生滅心. Lü Longli has no biography
in *Song History*. Hucker, 301: "*Director* [*langzhong* 郎中] of a Section or Bureau in a Ministry
(*bu* 部) or in some agency of comparable status."

[30.1: *Uses encouragement of (of Longli's older brother) Juren as a pretext*[30]]

Twice from your elder brother [Lü] Juren [*letters #29, #31–#32*] I have received letters,[31] and he's been extremely busy for the sake of *this matter*. And he very well should be in a panic—he's already sixty, and his engagement with official life has ended. Why would he wait any further?[32] If he doesn't get into a panic *ahead of time*, on the final day of the twelfth month [at the end of his life] how will he be able to handle things skillfully? I hear that recently you've also been busy [for the sake of *this matter*]. The only thing is, this being in a panic is just the *state of being* on the final day of the twelfth month. "[A monk asked Yunmen:] 'What sort of thing is a buddha?' [Yunmen said:] '**Dried turd**' [*ganshijue* 乾屎橛]." If one doesn't break through *here*, then it will be "more of the same" on the final day of the twelfth month![33]

[30.2: *Censures Lü Longli for devoting himself to knowing others but not knowing himself—in reality Dahui is censuring Lü Juren*[34]]

Bookworms spend their whole lives boring into old paper [i.e., devote their lives to reading books[35]]—they want to be informed concerning these [learned] matters.[36] They broadly peruse a ton of books and engage in

---

30. Mujaku, 315: 第一段託居仁勸勉. Mujaku adds: "If you look at the matter just in terms of this section, Juren serves as a pretext to encourage Longli. If you look at it in terms of the main idea of the letter as a whole, Juren's being in a panic is the main idea" [忠曰若但約此一段則託居仁而勸隆禮也若約一篇大意則居仁著忙爲大意].

31. Mujaku, 315, glosses *lingxiong Juren liang de shu* 令兄居仁兩得書 thus: "Dahui twice got letters from the elder brother Juren. These seven characters are the axle of the whole letter" [忠曰大慧兩回得令兄居仁書也此七字一篇機軸也].

32. Mujaku, 315, glosses *geng dai ruhe* 更待如何 thus: "What further matter could he be waiting for? Waiting for something beyond death that doesn't exist?" [忠曰更可待何事待死之外事不可有也].

33. Mujaku, 315, glosses *zhe li bu tou yun yun* 遮裡不透云云 thus: "Means: if you don't break through the **dried-turd** huatou, then the *busy* state in your heart will be the same at the time birth-and-death arrives" [言若不透乾屎橛話則胸中之忙與生死到來時可同也].

34. Mujaku, 315: 第二段責但務知他家而不知自家底裡責呂居仁.

35. Mujaku, 316, glosses *zuan guzhi* 鑽故紙 thus: "Devote oneself to reading books" [忠曰務閲書藉也].

36. Mujaku, 316, glosses *shi shi yao zhi* 是事要知 thus: "The matter of *this matter* is not the matter of the *one great matter*. It's just the stories and histories of ancient and modern

high-falutin' talk and far-flung discussions. "And what about Confucius?"
"And what about Mencius?" "And what about Zhuangzi?" "And what about
the *Zhou Changes*?" "What about political order and upheaval in the past
and present?" They are pursued relentlessly by these words and phrases—
until they are topsy-turvy. When they hear someone raise a single word
from the philosophers of the ancient hundred schools, they immediately
recite on and on from innumerable volumes and consider it an embar-
rassment if there is even a single matter that they don't know about. But
when it comes to asking them about their own *original allotment*[37] there
isn't a single one of them that knows anything! This could be called "to
the end of one's days counting the treasure of others, but never having
even a half-cent oneself."[38] In vain they do one "go-around" [from birth
to death[39]] in this world. When freed [in death] from their "outflows-in-
a-shell" [i.e., form body[40]], they don't know whether they will ascend to a
heaven or enter a hell. Following the power of their karma they flow into
various rebirth paths—they don't know [which one they will end up in],
and yet, if it concerns matters of other people [i.e., the people in classical
texts and the histories[41]], whether minute or great matters, there are none
they don't know about!

[30.3: *Discusses the fact that the scholarly bent is a wash-out— in reality Dahui is talking about Lü Juren*[42]]

In the case of scholar-officials, those who have read many books have much
avidyā [ignorance]. Those who have read few books have little *avidyā*. Those

---

times. Means: all forms of learning" [忠曰是事之事非一大事之事但是古今故事來歷言一切學術也].

37. Mujaku, 317, glosses *zijia wu li shi* 自家屋裏事 thus: "The matter of: where do I myself come from at birth and at death where do I myself go?" [忠曰自己生何處來死向何處之事].

38. Mujaku, 317, cites *Da fangguang fo huayan jing* 大方廣佛華嚴經, T278.9.429a3–5.

39. Mujaku, 317, glosses *kong lai ... yi zao* 空來 ... 一遭 thus: "Doing one go-around from birth to death" [忠曰自生到死如繞之一遭也].

40. ZGK, 68.287, glosses *kelouzi* 殼漏子 thus: "Here it is a metaphor for the form body" [今は色身に喻うるなり。].

41. Mujaku, 317, glosses *bieren jia li shi* 別人家裏事 thus: "In opposition to *self* Dahui says *other people*. It is Confucius, Mencius, Zhuangzi, the *Zhou Changes*, etc., and matters having to do with kings and marquises of the Zhou, Qin, Han, Wei, etc." [忠曰對自己言別人即孔子孟子莊子周易等周秦漢魏等王侯事也].

42. Mujaku, 317: 第三段論學趣不可底裡言呂居仁.

who have attained small official posts have small grasping of self/other. Those who have attained big official posts, have big grasping of self/other— the say of themselves: "I am smart and quick-witted." But when they confront success or failure even as minute as the autumn down of birds,[43] their smarts and quick-wittedness are nowhere to be seen. Of the books that they have read throughout their lives, not one word is of any use. That's because from the time they learned to write their first character they have been making a mistake—all they wanted was to score wealth and status.[44]

[30.4: *Dahui summons him to wake up and confers a* huatou[45]]

Those who do score wealth and status—how many can there really be? Be willing to turn your head and brain towards investigating what is right under your own feet. The "I" who scores this wealth and status—what place does this "I" come from? And the one who right now is receiving the wealth and status—on a later day [when he dies] what place does he go to? Having realized that you don't know where he comes from, and you don't know where he goes to, you immediately become aware that your mind is stupefied. Just when [you realize that your own mind] is stupefied—and that this has nothing to do with anyone else—right *here* just keep an eye on the *huatou*: "A monk asked Yunmen: 'What sort of thing is a buddha?' Yunmen said: '**Dried turd**' [**ganshijue** 乾屎橛]." Just lift this *huatou* [**dried turd**] to awareness.

[30.5: *Rejects calculation*[46]]

Suddenly when you run out of tricky maneuvers, you will awaken. By all means avoid investigating the written word in order to cite quotations and

---

43. Mujaku, 317–318, glosses *ji hu lin qiuhao lihai* 及乎臨秋毫利害 thus: "This *success or failure* doesn't mean ordinary success or failure. Dahui is talking about the imperial government's suffering defeat as 'success/failure'" [忠曰此利害者非謂尋常利害也天下政之成敗言利害也].

44. Mujaku, 318, glosses *zhi yu qu fugui er* 只欲取富貴耳 thus: "That's because, from the time they first set their aspirations on scholarship, they have not been reflecting on clarifying heavenly principle, implementing good government throughout all-under-heaven, assisting the sovereign and ruling the people, but have just calculated about scholarship and coveted official position in order to obtain wealth and status" [忠曰自初心學問時不思量明天理行天下政佐君治民但計學問而貪官祿得富貴故也].

45. Mujaku, 318: 第四段喚醒授話.

46. Mujaku, 319: 第五段斥計較.

haphazardly making surmises and exegeses. Even if your exegesis attains perfect clarity and your discourse settles the matter, it's all the "lifestyle" of a "ghost-home [in Black Mountain]."⁴⁷ When the sensation of uncertainty is not smashed, birth-death goes on and on and on. If the sensation of uncertainty is smashed, then the mind of samsara [lit., "birth-death"] is cut off. If the mind of samsara is cut off, then both buddha-view and dharma-view disappear. If even buddha-view and dharma-view disappear, could there possibly be further production of the sentient-beings-view and the defilements-view?

[30.6: *Dahui shows his method of* gongfu⁴⁸]

Just shift the stupefied mind over to engagement with the *huatou dried turd* [*ganshijue* 乾屎橛]. The mind that fears samsara, the mind of stupefaction, the mind of reflection and discrimination, and the mind that affects smart-ness naturally won't operate. When you become aware that this mind is not operating, don't fear [that you are] falling into [the extreme view of an annihilationist] emptiness.⁴⁹ Suddenly, where [your stupefied mind and the *huatou* are] engaging, you will cut off *states of being*—and everyday life will come to be filled with unsurpassed rejoicing and joy. Having attained the cutting off of *states of being*, you won't be hindered any more by the production of buddha-view, dharma-view, sentient-beings view, reflection, discrimination, the affecting of "smartness," and talk about reason. In the four postures of daily activities just always make yourself "composed"⁵⁰— whether in a quiet situation or a noisy situation, always rally *dried turd* [*ganshijue* 乾屎橛] to awareness. The days and months will pass, and "the

---

47. Mujaku, 170, glosses *heishan xia guijia huoji* 黑山下鬼家活計 thus: " 'Black Mountain' is the abode of *kiṃnaras* [celestial musicians at the court of Kubera, the god of wealth]. Now it is called 'ghost-cave,' but there's not much difference. Also, it is encircled by two iron mountains and is a dark place where ghosts dwell. It can also be called the 'ghost-cave of Black Mountain.' This is comparable to perverse Chan's taking the taste of itty-bitty Chan for its cave-house" [忠曰黑山緊那羅住處今稱鬼窟不多違又鐵圍兩山間黑闇處鬼住亦可稱黑山鬼窟蓋比邪禪著小禪味爲窟宅矣]. Mujaku also glosses *guijia huoji* 鬼家活計 thus: "Chewing up a small portion of *theory-taste* and coming to love it deeply—this is called 'life-style' of a 'ghost-home'" [忠曰嚼出小分理味而深愛著之此謂鬼家活計也].

48. Mujaku, 320: 示工夫法.

49. Mujaku, 320, glosses *mo pa luo kong* 莫怕落空 thus: "Falling into emptiness still involves a mental object. If truly this mental object is cut off, there's no emptiness to be fallen into" [忠曰落空猶是心行若真箇心行絕無有可落之空].

50. *Analects, Shu er* 述而: "The gentleman is level and composed; the small man is full of worries" [君子坦蕩蕩、小人長戚戚。].

water buffalo will become more practiced." You absolutely must not separately produce uncertainty about anything outside [the *huatou*[51]]. When uncertainty about **dried turd** [*ganshijue* 乾屎橛] is smashed, instances of uncertainty as numerous as the sand grains of the Ganges River will all be smashed at the same time.

[30.7: *At the beginning raises Lü Juren's letter*[52]]

Even before this I have written to Juren in this way. Recently Zhao Jingming[53] brought me another letter [from Juren]. In that letter Juren for a second time inquired:

> I wonder if, apart from this [i.e., rallying **dried turd** (*ganshijue* 乾屎橛) to awareness], there is any other method of doing *gongfu*? Also, [when engaged in daily activities] like raising one's arms, moving one's feet, putting on clothes, and eating meals, how should one carry out one's personal practice? Is it just a matter of keeping an eye on the *huatou* or is there some other method of personal practice? Also, the *one great matter* about which I have been uncertain and apprehensive for my whole life even now has not been resolved, that is: is there annihilation after death or not [i.e., is there karma and rebirth or not]? How can I come to a definitive understanding of this? Also, there's no need for you to quote what the sutras and treatises say and no need to refer to the cases of the ancients.[54] I rely only on what is right in front of

---

51. Mujaku, 320, glosses *di-yi bu de xiang waimian . . . ye* 第一不得向外面 . . . 也 thus: "*Outside* means outside your personal practice of the *huatou* **dried turd**. Speaking like this to Longli is not Dahui's basic intention. His basic intention lies in the next talk that enters into the matter of Lü Juren" [忠曰外面者本參乾屎橛話外也又曰向隆禮如是言非本意其本意在次說入呂居仁事].

52. Mujaku, 320: 第七段初舉呂居仁書.

53. Mujaku, 320, glosses *Zhao Jingming* 趙景明 thus: "Have not yet identified him. The letter that Zhao Jingming brought from Juren is another letter sent to Dahui after the "thousands upon thousands of sensations of uncertainty" answer letter [#29]. The words in it are seen in the text below" [未考忠曰趙景明所持來書即千疑萬疑答書後更又寄來也其中語見于下文].

54. Mujaku, 323, glosses *bu yao yin jinglun* 不要引經論 thus: "Juren's idea is: if you say that the theory of the flow of samsara to later lives is standard in holy writ—that sutra says this, and this treatise says that—and therefore I must have confidence in it; or the *gong'ans* of the ancients haggle like this—and therefore I must have confidence in it, then I am unable to have confidence in these things. I merely have to have clear instruction based on sound reasons right before my eyes before I can have confidence" [忠曰居仁意謂若言後世流轉

my eyes: please give me direct and clear instruction for rendering a verdict on whether annihilationism or non-annihilationism is actually the case.

When I contemplate this sort of talk from Juren, it's inferior to a fellow in a three-family village with few worldly responsibilities, who dies without a lot of rubbish[55] and at death achieves a quick liberation [i.e., awakening].

[30.8: *Dahui relates his first answer letter*[56]]

I said point-blank to him [#29.1–2]:

The thousands upon thousands of instances of uncertainty are just the "single uncertainty." When [the single] uncertainty about the *huatou* is smashed, the thousands upon thousands of instances of uncertainty are smashed at the very same time. If [the single uncertainty about] the *huatou* isn't smashed, then upon [and only upon the *huatou*] keep pressing hard with it [exclusively]. If you discard the *huatou*, and produce uncertainty about some other example of the written word, or produce uncertainty about the sutra teachings, or produce uncertainty about the cases of the ancients [i.e., various Chan stories], or produce uncertainty within the troublesome defilements of daily activities, it will all be of the coterie of the Evil One Māra. You must not, while raising [the *huatou*], understand and "own" it. Also, you must not engage in reflection and conjecture. Just concentrate mind upon reflecting on the state that cannot be reflected upon. Your mind will have nowhere to go—"the mouse will enter the ox's horn" [i.e., all tricky maneuvers will be severed], and then you will be "felled" [like a giant tree, i.e., you will emit the *Aah!*].

I've gone and written it down like this in an easy-to-understand form. But now once more he's blathering away with inquiries. I wonder where his

---

之說是聖言量彼經如是說此論如是談故須信之又古人公案如是商量故須信之則我不得信之但可據目前歷然道理分明指示方得信而已].

55. Hyesim, 73: "*Rubbish* is reflection and discrimination" [糞壤者思量分別].

56. Mujaku, 323: 第八段述第一答書.

considerable smartness and knowledge have gone to! Doesn't he believe what I said [in #30.3]: "Of the books that they have read throughout their lives, upon arrival *here*, not one word is of any use."

[30.9: *General introduction to the sections below*[57]]

But now I have no alternative but once again for his sake to let loose a little "badmouthing."[58] If I just let it go [at the "thousands upon thousands of instances of uncertainty" passage of letter #29.1[59]], then it will seem that, having been asked the question [about annihilation] by him, I wasn't able to come up with an answer. [For this reason,] when this letter arrives, immediately send it to him and have him give it a reading.

[30.10: *Shows that the many instances of uncertainty are the* single uncertainty[60]]

Juren himself says he's sixty years of age, but *"this matter* hasn't yet been resolved." Ask him: what you don't yet understand—could it be that "raising one's arms, moving one's feet, putting on clothes, and eating meals [during your daily activities]" is what you don't yet understand? If it is "raising one's arms, moving one's feet, putting on clothes, and eating meals," how will you come to an understanding of that? Little does he imagine that, the one who wants to know definitely whether or not there is annihilation after death is the very one who [after death] will be eating the iron stick in front of the Old One Yama [Judge of the Dead], King of the Hells! If this [single] uncertainty [about the *huatou*] is not smashed,[61] then he will flow on through samsara, and it will never come to an end. Say

---

57. Mujaku, 324: 第九段総論起下段.

58. Mujaku, 324, glosses *fang xie e qi xi* 放些惡氣息 thus: "Means: words and phrases." [謂言句也]. ZGK, 70.291, cites *Dahui Pujue chanshi yulu* 大慧普覺禪師語錄 (*Dahui Pujue chanshi pushuo*大慧普覺禪師普說): "If it's a Chan practitioner right now, approach in the blink of an eye. Do a 'circle.' Shout a shout or give a clap of the hands. Leave with a snap of the sleeves. Let loose this kind of 'badmouthing'" [若是如今禪和家。便近前彈指。打箇圓相。喝一喝拍一拍。拂袖便行。放出這般惡氣息。] (T1998A.47.879a23–25).

59. Mujaku, 324, glosses *ruo zhi ninme xiu qu* 若只恁麼休去 thus: "Means: the 'thousands upon thousands of instances of uncertainty' letter and that's all" [忠曰言千疑萬疑答書而已].

60. Mujaku, 324: 第十段示多疑一疑.

61. Mujaku, 325, glosses *ci yi bu po* 此疑不破 thus: "This is the uncertainty of 'the thousands upon thousands of instances of uncertainty are just the single uncertainty.' It is the

to Juren: "The thousands upon thousands of instances of uncertainty are just the 'single uncertainty.' If [the single] uncertainty about the *huatou* is smashed, the uncertainty about whether or not there is annihilation after death will instantly melt like ice, disintegrate like a shattered pot."

[30.11: *Arguing about annihilationism and non-annihilationism*[62]]

Beyond that he has ordered me to give him direct and clear instruction with a judgment on whether or not there is annihilation [after death], but this sort of knowledge is no different from [the extremes of annihilationism and eternalism of] of the outside Ways. His whole life of composing works with a lot of elegant turns of the literary language[63]—what purpose has that served? In the past all over the place he has loosed this sort of [literary] "bad breath" to "perfume" people. I cannot just leave it at that—I shall let loose a little badmouthing to perfume him! He has ordered me not to quote the sutra teachings and the cases of the ancients [i.e., Chan stories], but to rely only on what is right in front of the eyes—directly and clearly to instruct him on whether there is annihilation after death. Of old Chan Master Zhidao asked the sixth patriarch:[64]

> "Your student since leaving home has been reading the *Nirvana Sutra* for more than ten years. I don't yet understand its main idea. Will the master please instruct me?" The patriarch said: "What part do you not yet understand?" Zhidao replied: "'All conditioned things are impermanent; these are arising-disintegrating dharmas. Once arising-disintegrating has disintegrated, stillness is joyful.'[65] Concerning this I am perplexed." The patriarch said: "What sort

---

generating of the [single] uncertainty in one's personal practice" [忠曰千疑萬疑只是一疑之疑也乃是於本參生疑也].

62. Mujaku, 326: 第十一段辯斷滅不斷滅.

63. Mujaku, 326, glosses *zuo xuduo zhi hu zhe ye* 做許多之乎者也 (*zhi, hu, zhe,* and *ye* are "empty words" or "particles" in the literary language) thus: "Lü Juren composed the *Exegesis of the Spring and Autumn Annals* in ten fascicles, *Admonishing Childish Ignorance* in three fascicles, and *Record of the Source* in five fascicles. See his biography in *Song History*" [忠曰呂居仁作春秋解十卷童蒙訓三卷師友淵源錄五卷見本傳].

64. For the following lengthy quotation, Mujaku, 326, cites *Jingde chuandeng lu* 景德傳燈錄, T2076.51.239b23–240a8.

65. Mujaku, 326, cites *Da ban niepan jing* 大般涅槃經, T7.1.204c23–24.

of doubt do you entertain?" Zhidao said: "All sentient beings have two bodies, the form body and the dharma body. (*This is the same thing Juren is saying.*) The form body is impermanent—arising and disintegrating. The dharma body is permanent—neither knowing nor aware. The *Nirvana Sutra* says: 'Once arising-disintegrating has disintegrated, stillness is joyful.'[66] I don't know which body is in stillness and which experiences joy. If it's the form body, when the form body disintegrates, the four elements [i.e., earth, water, fire, and wind] disperse—the entirety of suffering. Suffering can't be called joy. If it's the dharma body, the stillness [of the dharma body] is identical to [insentient things such as] grass, trees, tiles, and stones. How would it experience joy? Also, the dharma-nature is the substance that is arising-disintegrating, and the five aggregates are the functioning of that arising-disintegrating. A unitary [eternal] substance has a fivefold functioning, and so arising-disintegrating is eternal. Arising is the production of function from substance; disintegrating is the reversion of function to substance. If [death and] rebirth is allowed, then for the sentient-being class [the wheel of repeated births and deaths] cannot be severed. If [death and] rebirth isn't allowed, then [sentient-beings] are eternally in stillness and identical to insentient things. In that case, all dharmas are locked in by nirvana and can't even arise. What joy could exist?" (*Zhidao and Juren stand charged with the same crime.*)

When the sixth patriarch arrived *here*, he was unable to employ the ways of doing things of Linji and Deshan [i.e., Deshan's stick and Linji's shout], and so he had to let loose a little bad breath back at him:

"You are a son of Śākya—why do you practice the perverse views of annihilationism and eternalism of the outside Ways, and say this and that about the dharma of the highest vehicle? According to your understanding, beyond the form body there is a separate dharma body, and one seeks for a stillness separate from arising-disintegrating. Also, conjecturing that nirvana is eternal and joyful, you say that there is a body that experiences [joy]. That is a miserly grasping onto samsara, being engrossed in mundane joy. You must now

66. *Da ban niepan jing* 大般涅槃經, T374.12.451a1.

come to know: Because all deluded people recognize the coming together of the five aggregates as a self-body characteristic, discriminate all dharmas and consider them to be external-object characteristics, love life and hate death, flow along moment after moment, not realizing that [both the death you hate and the life you love[67]] are dream illusions and unreal imputations, being turned on the wheel for naught, turning eternal and joyful nirvana over into a suffering characteristic, all day long rushing about seeking—the Buddha, having compassion for these beings, shows them the true joy of nirvana. Not even for a moment is [nirvana] characterized by *arising;* not even for a moment is it characterized by *disintegrating.* Beyond that there is no arising-disintegrating that can disintegrate (*Juren, please focus your eyes here*)—this is the appearance of stillness. At just the time of its appearance there is no reflecting upon *appearance,* and that is called *eternal joy.* This joy has neither experiencer [i.e., the five-aggregates body experiencing worldly joy[68]] nor non-experiencer [i.e., the non-awareness of insentient things[69]] (*this is obvious*). How could there be a named thing that is unitary in substance and fivefold in function? How much less could one further say that nirvana "locks in" all dharmas and makes them eternally non-arising? This slanders the buddhas and destroys the dharma (*Juren, you are doing some of this*). Hear my verses (*spread apart and not in order*):

Unexcelled, great nirvana is perfectly bright and constantly
   still and illuminating.
Ordinary, stupid people mistakenly consider it to be death—
   outside Ways grasp it as annihilation.
The people who pursue the two inferior vehicles view it as no
   further action [on the part of body and mind].
These all belong to deluded calculation—the root of the sixty-
   two wrong views.

---

67. Mujaku, 332, glosses *menghuan xujia* 夢幻虛假 thus: "Both the death you hate and the life you love are dream illusions and unreal imputations" [忠曰所惡死所好生皆是夢幻虛假也].

68. Mujaku, 333, glosses *ci le wuyou shouzhe* 此樂無有受者 thus: "It's not the five-aggregates body experiencing worldly joy" [忠曰非如五蘊和合身受世樂也].

69. Mujaku, 333, glosses *yi wuyou bushouzhe* 亦無有不受者 thus: "It's not the non-awareness of insentient things" [忠曰非如土木瓦石無知無覺].

To falsely erect terms of unreal imputation [like *death,
    annihilation,* and *non-action*[70]]—how could this be truth? (*If
    Juren wants to see truth, all he has to do is look at this single line
    [and see that it applies to his* annihilated/not annihilated*].*)

Only the *person* who surpasses the norm (*Juren has not
    yet seen this* person) comprehends neither seizing nor
    discarding [of annihilation/eternality]. (*Juren has had this
    doubt for thirty years.*)

[That *person* who surpasses the norm] knows that the five-
    aggregates and any self within the aggregates (*Juren
    perhaps seeks to exit from here but lacks a method*),

Externally manifested forms and images (*don't "eye" the
    flowers [as real]*), and sound characteristics one after the
    other (*they swindle and kill people*)

Are all equally like a dream or an illusion (*half-saved*)—thus
    not producing views of *common persons/noble ones.*

There is no production of the interpretation *nirvana* (*Juren
    has also not seen this* person)—the two extremes and three
    times having been severed.

Even though constantly functioning in response to various
    levels of faculties, there is no production of a concept of
    functioning.

There is discrimination of all dharmas but not the
    production of the concept of *discriminating.*

The fire at the end of an aeon burns everything to the sea,
    and the winds blow the mountains so that they collide
    with each other.

Yet it is the joy of true, eternal stillness—thus is nirvana
    characterized.

I am now forcing myself to speak in this way to make you
    discard perverse views. (*It's only Juren who is unwilling to
    discard them.*)

Don't have a literal understanding (*Juren—keep that in mind!*)
    and maybe you will understand a small part of this. (*Juren
    doesn't even enjoy the use of this small part!*)

Having heard the verse, Zhidao suddenly had a great awakening.
    (*[The story of Zhidao has been] not a little kudzu-verbiage!*)

---

70. Mujaku, 334, glosses *wang li xu jiaming* 妄立虛假名 thus: "*Death, annihilation,* and *non-
action* are all terms of unreal imputation" [忠曰云死云斷云無作皆假名也].

Just this single "mess" of a story is a finger that directly and clearly points for Juren. If Juren, upon seeing this, says that it is still the discourse of the sutras and treatises and still refers to the cases of the ancients—if he still has this sort of viewpoint—after death he will fall into a hell like a shooting arrow!

31. *[Second Letter] in Reply to Secretariat Drafter Lü (Juren)*

[*Commentary: Hyesim says, "The purport of this letter in reply to Lü Juren is making deluded thought non-operational and practicing the huatou."*[71] *Presumably dates to around the time of letter #30, Shaoxing 13/1143.*[72] *Hengzhou-exile letter.*]

[31.1: *Shows the exertion of mind in* gongfu[73]]

I hear [from your question letter] that "in daily activities I haven't let up on doing *gongfu*; my *gongfu* has ripened and I've bumped into a 'gate-pivot' [i.e., I've had an awakening]."[74] Now that you've mentioned "*gongfu*": rotate the mind that reflects on mundane defilements onto **dried turd [*ganshijue* 乾屎橛]** and make deluded consciousness non-operational like that of a human figure sculpted from clay or wood. When you notice that you're completely "in the dark," and there isn't any basis you can grasp—that is a *good state of being*: don't fear [that this is] falling into [the extreme view of an annihilationist] emptiness. Also, don't think about whether you're going to attain awakening "early" or "late." If you are maintaining that sort of mind, you've fallen into perverse Ways. The Buddha said: "This dharma is not something that can be understood through reflection and

71. Hyesim, 76: 答呂居仁狀旨忘情參話.

72. Lü and Wu, 97, states that this letter was composed when Dahui was roughly fifty-five (Shaoxing 13/1143).

73. Mujaku, 340: 第一段示工夫用心.

74. There is a question concerning where the material from Juren's question letter ends. Mujaku, 340, glosses *cheng riyong bu chuo zuo gongfu* 承日用不輟做工夫 thus: "The words of the question letter end here [*haven't let up on doing* gongfu].... Some say that up to *bumped into a gate-pivot* is the words of the question letter. This interpretation achieves the meaning of 'waiting for awakening,' and so it is wrong" [忠曰問書語止此.... 或曰至關捩子矣問書語此義成等悟義故非也]. Here I believe Mujaku is wrong and the anonymous commentator(s) are correct. I have punctuated accordingly.

discrimination."[75] When there is understanding [through reflection and discrimination], then calamity arises. The one who realizes that understanding cannot be gotten through reflection and discrimination—*who* is that? It's just *this* Lü Juren.[76] You must not turn your head [around looking for some other person].

[31.2: *Shows the functioning of* Mr. Man-in-charge[77]]

Prior to this in a letter in reply to your younger brother Longli [letter #30[78]] I said everything that needs to be said about "Chan illness."[79] The buddhas and patriarchs have not a single teaching to give to people. All that is necessary is for the person on duty to have confidence on his own, give assent on his own, see on his own, awaken on his own. If you just latch onto what other people [like the buddhas and patriarchs] have to say [and don't bother to see on your own], I fear [it will be taken that the buddhas and patriarchs] have deceived people. *This matter* definitely is free of characteristics of verbal expression, free of characteristics of mind and its objective supports, free of characteristics of the written word.[80] The knower who knows that [*this matter*] is free of all characteristics is just Lü Juren. The doubter who doubts whether "I, Lü Juren," will be annihilated after death is also just Lü Juren. The seeker who seeks "direct and clear instruction" [on annihilationism/non-annihilationism] is also just Lü Juren. In the twenty-four hours of daily activities—sometimes angry, sometimes happy, sometimes engaged in reflection, sometimes engaged in discrimination, sometimes immersed in torpor, sometimes immersed in restlessness—all of them are just Lü Juren. Just this Lü Juren can effect outstanding magical creations, can together with the buddhas and patriarchs roam in the

---

75. Mujaku, 341, cites *Lotus Sutra*, T262.9.7a20–21; and comments: "If you say *when is the time of awakening*, then it's discrimination and phantasmal thought. Therefore, Dahui's quotes buddha word" [忠曰若謂何時是悟時則是分別妄想故爲引佛語].

76. Mujaku, 341, glosses *zhi shi ge Lü Juren* 只是箇呂居仁 thus: "This is relying on shadows to show *Mr. Man-in-charge*" [忠曰此是依影子示主人公也].

77. Mujaku, 341: 第二段示主人公作用.

78. Mujaku, 341, glosses *da Longli shu* 答隆禮書 thus: "This is the previous letter that distinguishes annihilation and non-annihilation" [忠曰即前書辨斷滅不斷滅者也].

79. Mujaku, 341, glosses *chan bing* 禪病 thus: "In fact, Dahui condemned Juren's perverse doubts. Here Dahui tactfully refers to it as 'Chan illness'" [忠曰實罵斥居仁邪疑今婉詞云說禪病而已].

80. Mujaku, 341, cites *Dasheng qixin lun* 大乘起信論, T1666.32.576a10–13.

radiant sea of stillness and great liberation and complete both mundane and supramundane matters. It's just that Lü Juren's confidence doesn't extend to [having confidence in the true Lü Juren].[81] If your confidence can extend to that, please rely on these "footnotes" of mine to enter [the meditative concentration of the "just-one-Lü-Juren"] *samādhi*.[82] Suddenly, when you arise from this *samādhi*, you'll lose "the nose you were born with"[83]—that will be a "penetrating through and through" [i.e., awakening].

32. Continued [Third Letter in Reply to Secretariat Drafter Lü Juren]

[*Commentary: Korean Anonymous says, "Do not produce reflection—merely keep your eye on the* huatou.*"*[84] *Presumably dates to around the time of letter #30, Shaoxing 13/1143. Hengzhou-exile letter.*]

[32.1: *Shows exertion of mind*[85]]

Your younger brother Ziyu[86] stopped in at my place along his way and gave me a letter from you. Upon reading it, you can imagine how gratified I was. [Your letter states that "this world] is impermanent and speedy, and a century of time is like a flash of lightning—the time of karmic recompense surely arrives." [The *huatou*] **dried turd [*ganshijue* 乾屎橛]**—how are you doing in bringing it to awareness? When [this *huatou*] has no basis, no taste, and there's boredom in your belly, that's none other than the *good state of being*.[87] You absolutely must not, while raising [**dried turd**], understand and "own" it. Also, you must not remain confined to the tiny

---

81. Mujaku, 342, glosses *zhi shi Lü Juren xin bu ji* 只是呂居仁信不及 thus: "From the outset the towering and imposing Lü Juren has only been acquainted with false thought and upside-down views; and so he does not have confidence in the true Lü Juren" [忠曰本是巍巍堂堂呂居仁但是認妄想顛倒故不信真箇呂居仁而已].

82. Hyesim, 76: "Enter this *samādhi*: it's just one Juren" [入是三昧只是一箇居仁是].

83. Hyesim, 76: "*Nose you were born with* is mental objects" [孃生云云識心行].

84. Korean Anonymous, 139: 莫作思量但看話頭.

85. Mujaku, 342: 第一段示用心.

86. Mujaku, 342, glosses *Ziyu* 子育 thus: "Has no biography in *Song History*. In Benzhong's [i.e., Juren's] biography his name is not mentioned" [宋史無傳呂本中傳不言名].

87. *Letters of Dahui* #54.4: "The time when you become aware of squirming in your belly and distress in your mind is precisely the *good time*." [只覺得肚裏悶。心頭煩惱時。正是

hidden-away closet of *nothing-to-do.*[88] You shouldn't allow a situation in which there is [**dried turd**] when you are lifting it to awareness, and no [**dried turd**] when you're not lifting it to awareness [i.e., the *huatou* **dried turd** should be there all the time]. Just rotate the mind that reflects on mundane defilements onto **dried turd.**[89] Mental reflections go on and on—nothing can be done about that. When your tricky maneuvers are suddenly exhausted, you will spontaneously awaken. You must not have your mind wait for awakening. If you have your mind wait for awakening, then in endless aeons you won't be able to attain awakening.

[32.2: *Supporting the growth of deep confidence*[90]]

Prior to this in a letter in reply to your younger brother Longli [letter #30] I said everything that needs to be said about the painful illness of bookworms. I hear that you have simply placed that letter at the right of your seat [so you can constantly refer to it as a primer]. If you do *gongfu* in the way expressed in this [letter], even if you don't attain a penetrating awakening, you will be able to differentiate the perverse from the correct, you will not be blocked by perverse Māra teachers, and your planting of *prajñā*-seeds will be very deep. Even if you don't attain realization in this life, in the future you will be reborn as a human being, and you will have "ready-made" enjoyment. Without the expenditure of [*gongfu*] energy and without being snatched up by bad karma, at the time of the termination of your life you'll be able to "flip over" your karma. How much more so if, for a single moment, you get in correspondence [with *this matter*]? Day by day by day you must not reflect on any other matter. Just reflect upon **dried turd** [*ganshijue* 乾屎橛]. Don't ask about when you will awaken. I very much pray [you will go practicing in the above manner].

好底時節。]; and *Dahui Pujue chanshi pushuo* 大慧普覺禪師普說: "The time of squirming in your belly—that's the *good place*" [肚裏悶時正是好處] (CBETA, M059, no. 1540, p. 967, b3). Therefore: *good state of being* [*hao de xiaoxi* 好底消息] = *good time* [*hao de shijie* 好底時節] = *good place* [*hao chu* 好處].

88. See the note for the same prohibition in letter #10.5.

89. Mujaku, 342–343, glosses *hui zai ganshijue shang* 回在乾屎橛上 thus: "Originally Lu Juren's personal practice was *dog has no buddha-nature* [*wu* 無]. With the further mention of **dried turd**, it seems he has changed his personal practice" [忠曰本呂居仁本參狗子無佛性也又言乾屎橛似改本參也].

90. Mujaku, 343: 第二段成褫深信.

[32.3: *Post-awakening realm*[91]]

As for the time of awakening, the timetable is indeterminate.[92] [Awakening] won't be stunning to a lot of people [i.e., it's an event of your own mind];[93] you are forthwith peaceful and quiet. Naturally you're not uncertain and apprehensive about the buddhas, not uncertain and apprehensive about the patriarchs,[94] not uncertain and apprehensive about birth, not uncertain and apprehensive about death. If you can reach the stage of "no-uncertainty," then you're at the buddha stage. At the buddha stage, from the outset, there is no uncertainty. There is neither awakening nor delusion, neither birth nor death, neither existence nor non-existence, neither nirvana nor *prajñā*, neither buddhas nor sentient beings. And there is no [Dahui] who speaks *thus*. There is no [Lü Juren who] accepts these words [of Dahui]. There is no [Lü Juren who] doesn't accept [these words of Dahui]. There is no [Lü Juren who] knows that he is not accepting [these words of Dahui]. There is no speaking *thus* [on Dahui's part that] is not accepted. Juren! Have complete confidence in *thus*. Toward the buddhas just *thus*. Toward the patriarchs just *thus*. Toward awakening just *thus*. Toward delusion just *thus*. Toward uncertainty just *thus*. Toward birth just *thus*. Toward death just *thus*. Toward the troublesome defilements in the midst of everyday activities just *thus*. Toward annihilation or non-annihilation after death just *thus*. Toward holding an official position at court just *thus*. Toward spending a leave of absence in the stillness [of a Daoist temple in the mountains] just *thus*. Toward dwelling [in the illustrious Five-Mountains monastery] on Mt. Jing surrounded by a 1,700-strong

---

91. Mujaku, 343: 第三段悟後境界.

92. Mujaku, 343, glosses *wu shi yi wu shijie yun yun* 悟時亦無時節云云 thus: "If there is *gongfu* with confidence in the teachings of the teacher, then, when the time/karmic conditions arrive, spontaneously it's 'built.' Also, this time is indeterminate. If contemplation is clear and confidence power robust, in five to seven days it will be efficacious. If contemplation is not clear and confidence power weak, it will take perhaps ten to twenty years, up to five to ten lifetimes, etc." [忠曰信師教工夫則時節因緣到來自然築著又其時節無定若觀察明了信力強盛則五日七日亦有靈驗矣若觀察不明了信力軟弱則或十年二十年乃至五生十生等也].

93. Mujaku, 343, glosses *yi bu jing qun dong zhong* 亦不驚羣動衆 thus: "Means: awakening has no timetable and isn't an event that is stunning to people. Because it is self-mind awakening to self-mind, it's just forthwith peaceful and quiet" [言悟亦無時節亦非驚人事以自心悟自心故只是即時怙怙地而已].

94. Mujaku, 344, glosses *bu yi fo bu yi zu* 不疑佛不疑祖 thus: "The numerous occurrences of the word *yi* [*uncertainty*] comes from Lü Juren's 'thousands upon thousands of instances of uncertainty' [in letter #29.1]" [忠曰言多疑字亦是自呂居仁作千疑萬疑來].

monastic community just *thus*. Toward exile in provincial Hengzhou just *thus*.[95] Juren! Do you have sufficient confidence? Toward sufficient confidence just *thus*. Toward lack of sufficient confidence just *thus*. In the end, how? *Thus* and *thus*. Toward *thus* just *thus*![96]

33. *In Reply to Principal Graduate Zhu (Shengxi)*

[*Commentary: Mujaku says, "This letter dates to Shaoxing 14/1144 when the Master was fifty-six."*[97] *Hyesim says, "The main purport of the letter in reply to Zhu is just to encourage the Aah! of awakening."*[98] *Hengzhou-exile letter.*]

[33.1: *Dahui sighs over Zhu's deep confidence*[99]]

From a young age, you've earned a place for yourself in the world.[100] You came in first on the list of passers [of the final civil-service examination that

---

95. Mujaku, 345, glosses *zhu Jingshan zhi zai Hengzhou* 住徑山至在衡州 thus: "With these two events Dahui is speaking of matters connected to himself. Note: according to the *Dahui Chronological Biography*, on the twenty-fourth day of the seventh month of Shaoxing 7/1137, at the age of forty-nine, he entered the monastery at Jingshan [outside Lin'an/Hangzhou in Zhejiang]. Also, in Shaoxing 11/1141, at age fifty-three, he was exiled to Hengzhou [in Hunan]. Also, in Shaoxing 28/1158, at age seventy, for a second time he took up residence at Jingshan" [忠曰此二事大慧言自己事按大慧年譜紹興七年丁巳師四十九歲七月二十四日入院徑山又紹興十一年辛酉曰師五十三歲責衡州又紹興二十八年戊寅曰師七十歲再住徑山].

96. Mujaku, 346, glosses *rushi yi zhi rushi* 如是亦只如是 thus: "All the instances of *thus* above mean: 'Return the horses to the sunny side of Mt. Hua and let the cattle loose in the pastures of Taolin'" [忠曰上諸如是者歸馬于華山之陽放牛于桃林之野]. The allusion is from *Book of Documents, Wucheng* 武成: the war has ceased, and there is no further need for soldiers.

97. Mujaku, 348: 此書紹興十四年甲子師五十六歲而作.

98. Hyesim, 78: 答注狀大旨但勸囝地一下. For entries for Zhu Yingchen 注應辰 (*zi* Shengxi 聖錫), see *Song History*, 387 (16.3025–27), and *Cases of Song and Yuan Confucians*, 46 (2.1451–57). Hucker, 187: "*Principal Graduate* [*zhuangyuan* 狀元], designation of the candidate who stood first on the list of passers of the final examination in the civil service recruitment examination sequence. In Song the top 3 passers were sometimes all called Principal Graduates.... The designation was highly coveted and esteemed, and it usually led to a prestigious initial appointment and subsequent career in the civil service."

99. Mujaku, 348: 第一段嘆深信.

100. Mujaku, 348, glosses *miao nian* 妙年 thus: "Zhu Shengxi at five could read books and at ten could compose poetry. At eighteen he came in first in the Metropolitan-Graduate examinations" [忠曰注聖錫五歲知讀書十歲能詩十八進士第一人]. The "Metropolitan Graduate" was the most esteemed "doctoral" examination degree.

got you the most esteemed "doctoral" degree]. You haven't allowed yourself to
be caged by wealth and status—if you hadn't [taken up the vow to cut off the
limitless defilements] a hundred aeons and a thousand births ago, and been
supported by the strength of this vow,[101] how could you be capable of carrying out this [sort of astonishing conduct]? Also, you are sincere towards *this
one great matter*, moment after moment never retrogressing—you possess
resolute confidence and resolute willpower. How could a shallow fellow be
capable of such things?

[33.2: (*Dahui rejects Zhu's quoting the essay* In Defense of the Dharma) *showing that Confucianism and Buddhism are in agreement*[102]]

Old Gautama said: "Only *this one matter* is truth. The other two [vehi-
cles] are not true [i.e., are *upāyas* or skill-in-means]."[103] Please apply
the whip—you mustn't be neglectful: *mundane matters* are just *this* [*one
matter*]! [Your letter paraphrased Zhang Shangying's essay *In Defense of
the Dharma*:] "Didn't the former sage [Confucius] say: 'Hearing the Way
in the morning, in the evening I can die satisfied.' I wonder what Way
is the one he heard."[104] Having gotten to this point, how can you permit

---

101. Mujaku, 348, glosses *yuanli suo chi* 願力所持 thus: "A hundred aeons and a thousand
births ago you were able to vow: 'the defilements are inexhaustible—I vow to cut them off.'
Because you are supported by the strength of this vow, in the present birth you are not
deluded by wealth and status and the sense objects of the five desires. If it were not so, how
could you be capable of carrying out this sort of astonishing conduct?" [忠曰言自百劫千生
已前可誓煩惱無盡誓願斷爲其願力所持故今生亦不被富貴五欲境惑亂也不然豈能致如是
奇異行跡哉].

102. Mujaku, 348: 第二段示儒佛一致.

103. Mujaku, 348, cites *Lotus Sutra*, T262.9.8a21. Araki, 147, makes the observation that "the
original idea in the *Lotus Sutra* is that only the one vehicle is real and the other two vehicles—
hearer vehicle and independent-buddha vehicle—are *upāyas*, but here Dahui is conflating
this one matter with Zen awakening."

104. Mujaku, 349, cites *Analects*, *Li ren pian* 里仁篇 and says that this passage from Zhu's
letter is similar to the opening lines of Zhang Shangying's (張商英; 1043–1122) essay
In Defense of the Dharma (*Hufa lun* 護法論: "Confucius said: 'Hearing the Way in the
morning, in the evening I can die satisfied.' Did he take benevolence, righteousness,
loyalty, and faith as the Way? If he did, then Confucius assuredly had benevolence, righteousness, loyalty, and faith. Did he take long life and not growing old as the Way? If he
did, that's why he said 'in the evening I can die satisfied.' In actuality, what Way was he
seeking to hear? How could it not be the Way of the compassionate Buddha's knowing
mind, seeing the nature, and achieving unexcelled *bodhi*?" [孔子曰。朝聞道夕死可矣。
以仁義忠信為道耶。則孔子固有仁義忠信矣。以長生久視為道耶。則曰夕死。可矣。

yourself to blink in hesitation like this?[105] You shouldn't continue on and quote [Zhang's essay where it says] "my Way has a single principle that runs through it. [How could it not be the Way of the compassionate Buddha?]"[106] What you must have is confidence on your own and awakening on your own. Talk, in the end, constitutes no basis to rely upon.[107]

[33.3: *Censures Zhu for empty chat that does not involve seeking awakening*[108]]

Once you see on your own, awaken on your own, and attain sufficient confidence on your own, even without talking and propounding various aspects of things, you'll be unobstructed. Just fear being one of those people who talk[109] and propound various aspects of things, but don't see and haven't awakened. Old Gautama pointed them out as "highly presumptuous people."[110] They are also called "people who slander wisdom."[111] They are also called "people of the great lie." They are also called "people who cut off the wisdom-life of the buddhas." Even if a thousand buddhas were to appear in the world, [these people] wouldn't offer to confess their transgressions! But once you've broken through the dog-has-no-buddha-nature *huatou* [*wu* 無[112]], this sort of talk [i.e., *upāya*-talk

---

是果求聞何道哉。豈非大覺慈尊識心見性無上菩提之道也。] (T2114.52.638a14–17). For Zhang, see Miriam Levering, "Dahui Zonggao and Zhang Shangying: The Importance of a Scholar in the Education of a Song Chan Master," *Journal of Song-Yuan Studies* 30 (2000): 115–139.

105. Mujaku, 349, glosses *qi rong zha yan* 豈容眨眼 thus: "Means: you should take a direct look. When deluded consciousness is cut off, without mincing matters it's the Way" [忠曰言可直下看也情識絕則直下是道也].

106. Mujaku, 349, cites *Analects, Li ren pian* 里仁篇.

107. Mujaku, 349, glosses *wu pingju* 無憑據 thus: "Taking phrases to prove phrases in the end is no basis to rely upon" [忠曰以辭證辭終無據者也].

108. Mujaku, 349: 第三段責空談不求悟者.

109. Iriya Yoshitaka and Koga Hidehiko, *Zengo jiten* (Kyoto: Shibunkaku shuppan, 1991), 181, gives ~*si* ~似 as a verb suffix that shows the direction toward which the action of the verb is directed. However, Mujaku, 350, mistakenly glosses *shuode si* 說得似 thus: "Resembles *prajñā*" [相似般若也].

110. Mujaku, 350, cites *Lotus Sutra*, T262.9.7a7–11.

111. Mujaku, 350, cites *Xin fu zhu* 心賦注 (CBETA, X63, no. 1231, p. 108, c6–9 // Z 2:16, p. 27, c13–16 // R111, p. 54, a13–16).

112. Mujaku, 351, glosses *gouzi wu foxing hua* 狗子無佛性話 thus: "Because this was Principle Graduate Zhu's personal practice from the outset" [忠曰蓋注狀元本參也].

such as "slandering wisdom," "cutting off the wisdom-life of the buddhas," etc.,] will constitute "lies";[113] at the present moment [when you
have not yet broken through *wu* 無] you shouldn't understand them as
"lies."

[33.4: *Praises Lü Juren's drive*[114]]

Recently, from Lü Juren [letters #29, #31–#32], I received two letters in
succession. Both letters said: "During the summer I have constantly kept
your letter in reply to my younger brother Longli [letter #30] at the right of
my seat [as instruction], taking attaining awakening as my standard."[115] I
have also heard that [Lü Juren] copied [this letter in reply to Lü Longli] and
presented it to you. In recent generations honored "dukes and marquises"
like him are as rare as the flowers of the *udumbara* tree[116]—they appear
only once [in a thousand years].

[33.5: *Relates the perfect fusion and freedom of post-awakening*[117]]

Some time ago, [when you came to visit me] on the mountain [in the envi-
rons of Hengzhou, Hunan],[118] for your sake I frequently spoke this type of
talk [i.e., "slandering wisdom," "cutting off the wisdom-life of the buddhas,"
etc.]. I watched the fleeting movements of the pupils of your eyes—you'd
understood ninety percent and only lacked the *Aah!* [i.e., the sound emitted
upon awakening]. Once you've let out an *Aah!*, Confucianism is Buddhism,

---

113. Mujaku, 351, glosses *que cheng wangyu* 却成妄語 thus: "In the post-awakening realm, there
are no transgressions that can be confessed, no wisdom-life that can be cut off, no *prajñā* that
can be slandered. Therefore, talk of slandering *prajñā*, cutting off wisdom-life, etc., should all
be considered 'lies.' Before awakening, one should not speak of them as 'lies'" [忠曰悟後境
界無罪可懺悔無慧命可斷無般若可謗故謗般若斷慧命等語皆可爲妄語也若又未悟以前不
可言妄語也].

114. Mujaku, 351: 第四段讚居仁勸發.

115. Mujaku, 351, glosses *yi de wei qi* 以得爲期 thus: "Meaning: taking awakening as my standard" [忠曰以悟爲則之義也].

116. Mujaku, 351, cites *Lotus Sutra*, T262.9.7a15–16.

117. Mujaku, 351: 第五段述悟後圓融自在.

118. Mujaku, 351, glosses *shantou* 山頭 thus: "*Mountain* means Mt. Huayao or Mt. Yi" [忠曰山
頭謂花藥山或謂伊山也] and cites *Dahui Pujue chanshi nianpu* 大慧普覺禪師年譜 (CBETA,
J01, no. A042, p. 802, a22–26).

Buddhism is Confucianism, monks are laymen, laymen are monks, ordinary people are sages, sages are ordinary people, I am you, you are I, heaven is earth, earth is heaven, waves are water, water is waves. Stirring butter, butter-fat, and cream into a single taste; and melting wine carafes, platters, hairpins, and bracelets into a single metal[119] lie within *me*, not within other people. Reaching *this level* [of great awakening, all dharmas turn[120]] according to *my command*: "I am the dharma king who has freedom in the midst of the dharmas."[121] How could gain/loss and affirmation/negation be a hindrance? It's not that one forces things—it's because the principle of things is *thus*.

[33.6: *Cites Layman Vimalakīrti to arouse and encourage Zhu*[122]]

As for *this realm*, how can anyone, with the exception of "Old Vimalakīrti" [i.e., Zhang Zishao of letter #48], have complete confidence in it? Even if one has confidence [in the existence of this realm], how can he get it into the palm of his hand and make it his own? [Though you haven't yet seen this realm,] you already have complete confidence [that there is such a realm].[123] You've already had a peek at it.[124] You already are capable of discriminating between perverse and correct. The only thing you haven't been able to do is get it into the palm of your hand and make it your own. At the time you can get it into the palm of your hand and make it your own, you will make no distinctions such as old/young[125] and will not

---

119. Mujaku, 352, cites Guifeng Zongmi's *Chan Prolegomenon* (*Chanyuan zhuquanji duxu* 禪源諸詮集都序), T2015.48.398b27–c2. This is Pei Xiu's preface.

120. Mujaku, 353, glosses *dedao zhe ge tiandi* 得到遮箇田地 thus: "For the person who arrives at this realm of great awakening, all dharmas turn *according to my mind*, and therefore it is said *according to my command*" [忠曰到此大悟境界之人一切萬法皆隨我意專故言由我指揮].

121. Mujaku, 353, cites *Lotus Sutra*, T262.9.15b6–7.

122. Mujaku, 353: 第六段又引無垢激勸.

123. Mujaku, 353, glosses *yi xinde ji* 已信得及 thus: "Even though Principal Graduate Zhu has not yet seen this thing, in advance he has confidence that there is this thing" [忠曰注狀元雖未見其物先信有其物也].

124. Mujaku, 353, glosses *yi qu dejian* 已覷得見 thus: "Principal Graduate Zhu is like someone who opens the box and sees the thing inside" [忠曰注狀元如開箱見其物也].

125. Mujaku, 353, glosses *bu fen lao shao* 不分老少 thus: "Principal Graduate Zhu is still young, and so it says *make no distinctions such as old/young*" [忠曰注狀元年猶少故云不分老少].

be immersed in such distinctions as smart/stupid.[126] It's like the direct handing over of the rank of the god Brahmā to a mediocrity—there is no sequence of stages.[127] Yongjia said: "In one leap you will directly enter the *tathāgata* stage."[128] Just listen to me—I'm definitely not deceiving you!

34. *Continued [Second Letter in Reply to Principal Graduate Zhu]*

[*Commentary: Mujaku says, "This letter ... takes three sections (#34.2–4) as one big section that is a general discussion of the purport of the non-duality of the Way and study."[129] Hyesim says, "The main purport of this letter is encouraging Zhu to do a 'flip' (a transformation-of-the-basis)."[130] Presumably dates to around the time of letter #33, Shaoxing 14/1144. Hengzhou-exile letter.*]

[34.1: *Answers Zhu's question and gives general encouragement*[131]]

In my daily activities, I've stopped all entanglements[132]—things are just *thus*. Don't trouble yourself worrying about me. What littlest thing do you find lacking in your situation? In the world, it can be said that everything is suf-ficient. If you can, within *this gate*, do a "flip,"[133] and then there will be no

---

126. Mujaku, 353, glosses *bu zai zhi yu* 不在知愚 thus: "Principal Graduate Zhu is incompa-rably smart, and so it says *be immersed in such distinctions as smart/stupid*" [忠曰注狀元聰明無比故云不在知愚].

127. Mujaku, 353, cites *Xin huayan jing lun* 新華嚴經論, T1739.36.729a4–8.

128. Mujaku, 353, cites *Yongjia zhengdao ge* 永嘉證道歌, T2014.48.396a18–19.

129. Mujaku, 354: 此書 ... 以此三段作大段一段看總論道學無二之旨.

130. Hyesim, 79: 答又狀大旨但勸翻身一擲.

131. Mujaku, 354: 第一段答問候総勸.

132. Mujaku, 354, glosses *mou wan yuan xiu ba* 某萬緣休罷 thus: "Dahui refers to himself with the pronoun *mou*. Principal Graduate Zhu asks a question about Dahui's place of exile. Because his thoughts are not free, Dahui says: 'I've stopped all entanglements—my daily activities are just *thus*" [忠曰某大慧自稱蓋注狀元問候言謫居境界想不自在故大慧答云我日用萬緣休罷而只如此耳].

133. The *fan shen yi zhi* 翻身一擲 refers to the *transformation-of-the-basis* (*āśraya-parāvṛtti* = *zhuan yi* 轉依) of the Yogācāra school.

stopping you from "coiling 100,000 strings of cash around your waist and mounting a crane to fly over to become a Prefect in Yangzhou."[134]

[34.2: *Cites a Way-attainer who "flipped" the sense objects and obtained freedom*[135]]

Of old, Yang Wengong, that is, Yang Danian,[136] at thirty years of age[137] visited Chan Master Guanghui Lian[138] and rid himself of the thing blocking up his chest.[139] After that, whether at court or in retirement at his ancestral locale, he was always of an unchangeable integrity, unswayed by honor and rank, not in thrall to wealth and status. That said, he was not of a mind to make light of honor and rank, wealth and status. As for the Way's existing in [such an attitude], it's because the principle of things is *thus*. Zhaozhou said: "People are controlled by the twenty-four hours of the day—I control the twenty-four hours of the day."[140] This saying of this old master is not about forcing things—again, it's because the principle of things is *thus*.

[34.3: *Correctly relates the oneness of the Way*[141]]

Strictly speaking, "study" [i.e., cultivation] and "the Way" [i.e., realization of the Way] are one.[142] But at present, ["Way-Study" (i.e., Neo-Confucian)]

---

134. From the *Stories of Yin Yun* (*Yin Yun xiaoshuo* 殷芸小説) by Yin Yun 殷芸 of the Liang dynasty.

135. Mujaku, 355: 第二段引得道者轉境自在證.

136. This is Yang Yi 楊億 (974–1020), editor of the *Jingde chuandeng lu* 景德傳燈錄. See Albert Welter, *Yongming Yanshou's Conception of Chan in the* Zongjing lu: *A Special Transmission within the Scriptures* (Oxford: Oxford University Press, 2011), 210–211.

137. Mujaku, 356, glosses *sanshi sui* 三十歲 thus: "As for Dahui's highlighting Danian's age of thirty, because Principal Graduate Zhu is also in the prime of life, it proves those in the prime of life are capable of attaining the Way" [忠曰特舉大年三十歲者注狀元盛年故證盛年人亦可得道也]. Zhu was about twenty-seven to thirty years of age.

138. Mujaku, 356, glosses *jian Guanghui Lian Gong* 見廣慧璉公 thus: "Guanghui Yuanlian [951–1036] succeeded Shoushan Shengnian; Yang Yi succeeded Guanghui Yuanlian" [廣慧(元)璉嗣首山(省)念楊億嗣廣慧璉].

139. Mujaku, 357, glosses *chuqu ai ying zhi wu* 除去礙膺之物 thus: "Means ball of uncertainty" [言疑團也].

140. Mujaku, 357, cites *Gu zunsu yulu* 古尊宿語錄 (CBETA, X68, no. 1315, p. 78, a7–8 // Z 2:23, p. 154, c11–12 // R118, p. 308, a11–12).

141. Mujaku, 357: 第三段正述道一.

142. Mujaku, 357, glosses *wei xue wei dao yi ye* 爲學爲道一也 thus: "Here Dahui is talking about the *Daoxue* [Way Study, referred to in Western scholarship as 'Neo-Confucianism'] of

scholars frequently consider [the cultivation of the five constant virtues] "benevolence, righteousness [*yi* 義], ritual, wisdom, and faith" to constitute "Study"; and consider such categories as "investigating things," "loyalty and reciprocity," and "unity pervades all" to constitute the "Way." This [binary division by Way-Study scholars] is just like a riddle; or a group of blind persons' groping an elephant, where each one goes about describing a different clue! Didn't Śākyamuni say: "Relying on thinking to calculate the realm of perfect awakening of the *tathāgatas* is like using the glow of fireflies to incinerate Mt. Sumeru."[143] When you approach the juncture of life/death and calamity/good fortune,[144] [Principal Graduate Zhu, you will find] you will have gained no [awakening] energy at all—it will be due to this [reliance on thinking and calculating]. [The Han-dynasty philosopher] Yangzi said: "*Study* is that by which one cultivates the *nature*."[145] [What Yangzi calls] the *nature* is the *Way*—the Golden-faced Old Master said: "The *nature* becomes the unexcelled *Way*."[146] Guifeng [Zongmi] said: "Doing things in accordance with *yi* 義 is called awakened mind; doing things not in accordance with *yi* 義 is called frenzied mind. Frenzied mind is based in deluded thoughts—on the verge of death one is led along by karma. Awakening is not based in deluded thoughts—on the verge of death one can 'flip over' karma. The word *yi* 義 here is *yi* as in 'rational principle,'[147] not *yi* as in the righteousness of [the constant Confucian virtues to be cultivated] 'benevolence and righteousness.' "[148] But when we take a look at this Guifeng saying right now, this old master Guifeng hasn't shirked dividing space into two poles. Benevolence is the benevolence of

the Confucian school" [忠曰今述儒家之道學也]. It appears that Zhu's question letter probably discussed *Daoxue* concerns in some detail.

143. Mujaku, 360, cites *Da fangguang yuanjue xiuduoluo liaoyi jing* 大方廣圓覺修多羅了義經, T842.17.915c23–26.

144. Mujaku, 360, glosses *lin shengsi huofu* 臨生死禍福 thus: "Principal Graduate Zhu is not similar to Yang Danian in gaining [awakening] energy" [注狀元不似楊大年得力者爲是也].

145. Mujaku, 360, glosses *Yangzi yun*. . . . *yi xing ye* 楊子云. . . . 亦性也 thus: "Yangzi also divided study-cultivation into two" [忠曰楊子亦以學修與性分爲二者也] and cites: *Yangzi fayan yi* 楊子法言一, *Xuexing pian* 學行篇. Yangzi is the Han-dynasty philosopher Yang Xiong (54 B.C. to A.D. 18).

146. Mujaku, 361, cites *Śūraṃgama Sūtra*, T945.19.131b5–7.

147. Mujaku, 362, glosses *yili zhi yi* 義理之義 thus: "Guifeng's meaning is that the *yi* of rational principle is the Way. . . . Guifeng also takes the Way and study as two" [忠曰圭峯意義理之義道也. . . . 此圭峯亦以道與學爲二也].

148. Mujaku, 361, cites *Jingde chuandeng lu* 景德傳燈錄, T2076.51.308b6–13.

the [*original*] *nature* [i.e., *true nature* or *dharma-nature*]. Righteousness [*yi* 義] is the righteousness of the [*original*] *nature*.[149] Ritual is the ritual of the [*original*] *nature*. Wisdom is the wisdom of the [*original*] *nature*. Faith is the faith of the [*original*] *nature*. The *yi* 義 of rational principle is also the [*original*] *nature*.[150] Doing things not in accordance with *yi* 義 is going against this [*original*] *nature*. Doing things in accordance with *yi* 義 is going along with this [*original*] *nature*. Thus, "going along with" and "going against" lie only within people—they do not lie within the [*original*] *nature*. Benevolence, righteousness, ritual, wisdom, and faith lie within the [*original*] *nature*, not within people. Some people are worthies and some idiots, but in the [*original*] *nature* there is neither. If benevolence, righteousness, ritual, wisdom, and faith were to lie only within worthies and not within idiots, then the Way of the sages would involve sorting out—seizing [worthies] and jettisoning [idiots]. It would be as though, when heaven causes rain, it selects the place to rain down. Therefore, I said that benevolence, righteousness, ritual, wisdom, and faith lie within the [*original*] *nature*, not within people; worthiness and idiocy, going along with and going against, lie within people, not within the [*original*] *nature*. Yangzi spoke of "cultivating the *nature*," but the [*original*] *nature* cannot be cultivated. It's just a matter of going along with [the *original nature*] or going against [the *original nature*]; worthiness or idiocy.[151] This is Guifeng's saying "awakened mind [i.e., going along with the *original nature*] and frenzied mind [i.e., going against the *original nature*]." This is Zhaozhou's saying "controlling the twenty-four hours [i.e., going along with the *original nature*] and being controlled by the twenty-four hours [i.e., going against the *original nature*]." Once you understand the [*original-*]*nature-produced* state of benevolence, righteousness, ritual, wisdom, and faith [i.e., understand that the five arise in dependence upon the *original nature*/*dharma-nature*], then "investigation of things," "loyalty and reciprocity," and "unity pervades all things" are also within this [i.e., within the *original nature*]. Dharma Master Zhao said:

---

149. Mujaku, 362, glosses *yi nai xing zhi yi* 義乃性之義 thus: "The line below 'the *yi* of rational principle is also the nature' takes Guifeng's saying 'the word *yi* 義 here is the *yi* of rational principle' and Dahui's saying '*yi* 義 is the *yi* of the [*original*] *nature*' to be in agreement" [下義理之義亦性也者以圭峰云義理之義與大慧云義乃性之義爲一致也].

150. Mujaku, 362, glosses *yili zhi yi yi xing ye* 義理之義亦性也 thus: "The meaning is: rational principle and the [*original*] *nature* are a single thing" [忠曰意謂理與性一物也].

151. Mujaku, 363, glosses *yi shunbei xianyu er yi* 亦順背賢愚而已 thus: "Meaning: cultivating and not cultivating lie in people, not in the nature" [忠曰言修與不修者在人而不在性也].

"The potential to be heaven and to be human—how could heaven and humans have that potential? [I.e., the *original nature* has it.]"[152] Therefore, I said: "*Study* and the *Way* [i.e., cultivation and realization] are one."

[34.4: *Shows the principle of responding according to conditions*[153]]

Strictly speaking, the sages set up teachings without seeking fame or bragging about their own merit[154]—just as spring dispenses flowers and trees. As for the fact that [flowers and trees] are endowed with this [*original*] *nature*, when the time and the conditions arrive, each and every one, without being aware of each other, follows its *fundamental nature*—big, small, straight, round, long, short, some blue-green, some yellow, some red, some green, some foul-smelling, some fragrant—simultaneously coming forth. It's not that spring itself can cause big, small, straight, round, long, short, blue-green, yellow, red, green, foul-smelling, and fragrant. These are all a matter of the *innate nature*—encountering conditions, they simply issue forth. Baizhang said: "If you want to understand the meaning of *buddha-nature*, you should contemplate time and origination-by-dependence. When the time arrives, this principle automatically manifests."[155] Also, Master Huairang said to Master Mazu: "Your studying the teaching of the mind-ground is like planting seeds [i.e., causes]. My speaking the essence of dharma is like the rain and dew [i.e., conditions]. When your conditions come together, you will see the Way."[156] Therefore, I said that the sages set up teachings without seeking fame or bragging about their own merit— they do it just to enable students to *see the nature* and complete the Way. "Old Vimalakīrti" [i.e., Zhang Zishao of letter #48] said:[157] "Since the Way

152. Mujaku, 364, cites *Zhao lun* 肇論, T1858.45.158c1–4.

153. Mujaku, 365: 第四段示因緣感遇理.

154. Mujaku, 365, glosses *bu qiu ming bu fa gong* 不求名不伐功 thus: "They just want students to rely on the teachings to open up the innate nature and, in a response to conditions, attain a seeing of the nature" [只欲學者依教開發本有性因緣感遇得見性矣].

155. Mujaku, 366, cites *Liandeng hui yao* 聯燈會要 (CBETA, X79, no. 1557, p. 64, a16–18 // Z 2B:9, p. 270, d13–15 // R136, p. 540, b13–15).

156. Mujaku, 366, cites *Jingde chuandeng lu* 景德傳燈錄, T2076.51.240c29–241a1.

157. Mujaku, 366–367, glosses: *Wugou laozi zhi shi ye* 無垢老子至是也 thus: "This ties in with the words of section 4" [忠曰此結是第四段語].

lies in a single mustard seed, a single mustard seed is weighty; since the Way lies in all-under-heaven, all-under-heaven is weighty."[158]

[34.5: *Dahui arouses and encourages Zhu*[159]]

Even though you have "ascended to the hall" of Vimalakīrti, you have yet to "enter his room."[160] You have seen his façade, but you have yet to see his inner [sanctum]. A hundred years of time lies in just a single instant: you awaken in an instant, and all that I've said above is not the "real" meaning [i.e., in the *original nature* there is no plethora of things such as awakening/distraction, going along with/going against, worthy/idiot, study and Way are one/not one, etc.[161]] However, once you've awakened, taking them as "real" lies in you, and taking them as "not real" lies in you. It's like a bottle gourd floating on the water[162]—even with no one setting it in motion, it's always at ease. When you touch it, it moves; when you press down on it, it turns round and round. It's not forced—it's because the *dharma*[*nature*] is *thus*.

[34.6: *Shows the method of rallying the* huatou *to awareness*[163]]

Concerning Zhaozhou's no-buddha-nature *huatou* [**wu** 無], you, [Principal Graduate Zhu,] are like someone who is arresting a thief and already knows the location of his hideout—you simply haven't caught him yet.[164] Please quickly apply energy. Don't break off even for a little bit. At all times, whether in the midst of walking, standing, sitting, or lying down, keep your

---

158. Mujaku, 367, cites *Luohu yelu* 羅湖野錄 (CBETA, X83, no. 1577, p. 394, b14–22 // Z 2B:15, p. 500, b11–c1 // R142, p. 999, b11–p. 1000, a1). The *Rustic Record of the Luo Lake* is an example of the genre of Chan "brush notes" (*biji* 筆記).

159. Mujaku, 367: 第五段激勸.

160. Mujaku, 367, cites *Analects, Xianjin pian* 先進篇.

161. Mujaku, 367, glosses *jie fei shi yi* 皆非實義 thus: "In the [original] nature there is no plethora of things such as awakening/distraction, going along with/going against, worthy/idiot, study and Way are one/not one, etc." [忠曰性中都無惺悟狂亂順背賢愚學道一不一等幾多事].

162. Mujaku, 368, cites *Foguo Yuanwu chanshi biyan lu* 佛果圜悟禪師碧巖錄, T2003.48.180b8–9.

163. Mujaku, 368: 第六段示提撕法.

164. Mujaku, 368, cites *Śūraṃgama Sūtra*, T945.19.107a8–10.

eye on [*wu* 無]. In situations where you are reading classics, philosophers, histories, and collections,[165] where you are cultivating [the Confucian constant virtues of] benevolence, righteousness, ritual, wisdom, and faith, where you are following ritual in serving elders and superiors, where you are exhorting students, where you are eating your meals, keep pressing hard with [*wu* 無[166]]! Suddenly you'll "lose your hemp sack"![167] What more is there to say?

35. *In Reply to Auxiliary in the Hall [of the Dragon Diagram] Zong*

[*Commentary: Mujaku says, "This letter dates to Shaoxing 14/1144 when the Master was fifty-six."[168] Hyesim says, "The main purport of the letter in reply to Auxiliary in the Hall Zong is cut off thoughts and practice the* huatou.*"[169] Hengzhou-exile letter.*]

[35.1: *Negates erroneous understanding*[170]]

Your letter informs me: "In responding to conditions in my daily wading through the differentiated sense objects I am always in the midst of the buddhadharma." Also: "In the midst of my daily activities, my movements and various demeanors, I use the dog-has-no-buddha-nature *huatou* [*wu* 無]

---

165. Mujaku, 368, glosses *du shu shi* 讀書史 thus: "Reading classics, philosophers, histories, and collections" [忠曰讀經子史集也]. These are the four main categories into which traditional bibliographers divide classical Chinese literature.

166. Mujaku, 369, glosses *xue zhi si ya* 學之厮崖 thus: "The *zhi* refers to the *huatou*" [忠曰之者指話頭也].

167. The meaning of the phrase *lose your hemp sack* is clarified in *Dahui Pujue chanshi pushuo* 大慧普覺禪師普說: "During the twenty-four hours of the day, don't apply your mind at any other place. Just upon the *huatou* continually go to the limit. Suddenly your mind will have nowhere to go to and you will *lose your hemp sack*—this is returning to the stable seat of your own home" [十二時中莫向別處用心只於話頭上窮來窮去驀然心無所之打失布袋便是歸家穩坐處] (CBETA, M059, no. 1540, p. 944, b18–19).

168. Mujaku, 369: 此書紹興十四年甲子師五十六歲而作.

169. Hyesim, 81: 答宗直閣狀大旨絕想參話. Zong has no biography in *Song History*. Hucker, 161: "*Auxiliary in the Hall of the Dragon Diagram* [*zhi longtu ge* 直龍圖閣] was from 1016 a designation used for men assigned to the Hanlin Academy (*Hanlin yuan* 翰林院) without having nominal status as a member, to assist in the drafting of imperial proclamations." *Zhige* 直閣 is an abbreviation.

170. Mujaku, 369: 第一段破謬解.

to brush away the sense fields." If you do that sort of *gongfu*, I'm afraid that, in the end, you won't attain awakening. Please do a *backwards-look-illumination* [i.e., a *reverse-illumination*] at what is right under your feet this very moment. The differentiated sense objects—from what place do they arise?[171] In the midst of your movements and various demeanors,[172] in every turn of your body, how could you possibly use the dog-has-no-buddha-nature *huatou* [*wu* 無] to "brush away the sense fields"?[173] And the knower who knows the "brushing away of the sense fields"—*who* is that?[174] Didn't the Buddha say: "Sentient beings are of an upside-down viewpoint—they are deluded about self and pursue things."[175] Things from the outset lack self-nature—those deluded about self are pursuing "them" on their own and that is all. The sense objects from the outset lack differentiation[176]—those deluded about self are differentiating "them" and that is all. You say that, though you daily wade through the differentiated sense objects, you are in the midst of the buddhadharma. If you're in the midst of the buddhadharma, then it's not the differentiated sense objects; if you're in the midst of the differentiated sense objects, then it's not the buddhadharma. Picking up one and releasing the other—when will there ever be an end of it? Broad-Forehead the Butcher, at the nirvana assembly, threw down his butcher-knife and at once became a buddha.[177] *He didn't do a lot of blathering!*

---

171. Mujaku, 369, glosses *chabie zhi chu qi* 差別至處起 thus: "This is the method of doing a *backwards-look-illumination*. All external sense objects arise from the discriminations of the mind of the unreal" [忠曰此照顧之法也夫惟外境悉由妄心分別生].

172. Mujaku, 369, cites *Mencius, Jin xin xia* 盡心下.

173. Mujaku, 369, glosses *ruhe yi gouzi zhi pochu qingchen* 如何以狗子至破除情塵 thus: "It's a rebuke. From the outset, the sense-fields thing and the brush-away thing have never existed" [忠曰詰責也本不可有情塵事破除事].

174. Mujaku, 370, glosses *neng zhi pochu zhi ashei* 能知破除至阿誰 thus: "This is a shadow of *Mr. Man-in-charge*" [此即主人公之影子].

175. Mujaku, 370, cites *Foguo Yuanwu chanshi biyan lu* 佛果圜悟禪師碧巖錄, T2003.48.182b20–21; and *Śūraṃgama Sūtra*, T945.19.111c25–26.

176. Mujaku, 370, glosses *jingjie ben wu chabie* 境界本無差別 thus: "Dahui negates the question letter's words *differentiated sense objects*. From the outset, they are the one true *dharmadhātu*. Ignorance deludes self and suddenly thoughts arise—self and other are differentiated" [忠曰破問書差別境界語本是一真法界無明迷己忽然念起自他分矣].

177. *Da ban niepan jing* 大般涅槃經, T375.12.722b18–22. Mujaku, 370, glosses *guang'e tu'er yun yun* 廣額屠兒云云 thus: "This analogy means: Broad-Forehead had a great faculty of confidence and, at a single word, immediately had sufficient confidence to become a buddha. How could that be like Auxiliary in the Hall Zong, who spits out a lot of words like 'in the midst of the buddhadharma,' 'brush away sense fields,' etc.? Therefore, Auxiliary in the Hall Zong should merely cease his various understandings and at once become a buddha"

[35.2: *Shows the exertion of mind in* gongfu[178]]

When you are responding to conditions in the midst of your daily activities and you become aware that you are wading through differentiated sense objects, merely, in the very state of differentiation, lift to awareness the dog-has-no-buddha-nature *huatou* [*wu* 無]. There's no need to produce any notion of "brushing away." There's no need to produce any notion of "sense fields." There's no need to produce any notion of "differentiation." There's no need to produce any notion of "buddhadharma." Just keep your eye on the dog-has-no-buddha-nature *huatou* [*wu* 無]. Just lift the word *wu* 無 to awareness. And there's no need to harbor any sort of waiting for awakening.

[35.3: *Shows that if your exertion of mind is mistaken, everything becomes differentiated*[179]]

If you harbor any sort of waiting for awakening, then "sense objects" will become a differentiation, the "buddhadharma" will become a differentiation, "sense fields" will become a differentiation, the "dog-has-no-buddha-nature *huatou*" will become a differentiation, interruptions in [lifting the *huatou*] will become a differentiation, no interruptions [in lifting the *huatou*] will become a differentiation, "being misled by the sense fields so your body-mind is not at peace and joyful" will become a differentiation, and "a knower who knows a lot of differentiations" will become a differentiation! If you want to get rid of this illness [of differentiation[180]], just keep your eye on the word *wu* 無. Just keep your eye on it. Broad-Forehead the Butcher threw down his butcher knife and said: "I am one buddha among a thousand buddhas!" Is this story fact or fabrication?[181] If you haggle over

---

[忠曰此喻合者謂廣額有大信根不說一言一句直下信得及成佛豈如宗直閣吐幾多在佛法中破除情塵等語哉故宗直閣亦但可休種種知解而立地成佛也].

178. Mujaku, 370: 第二段示工夫用心.

179. Mujaku, 371: 第三段用心誤則一切成差別.

180. Mujaku, 371, glosses *ci bing* 此病 thus: "The illness of differentiation" [忠曰差別之病也].

181. Mujaku, 371, glosses *shi shi shi xu* 是實是虛 thus: "If Auxiliary in the Hall Zong immediately had confidence, he too could say 'I am one buddha among a thousand buddhas!' However, he is given to verbalization about principle and in his mind preserves differentiations. Therefore, towards Broad-Forehead's saying 'I am one buddha among a thousand buddhas!' he is doubtful whether it is fabrication or fact. With this sort of doubt, he has again fallen into differentiation" [忠曰宗直閣若復直下信得及則亦可千佛一數然但是口說理心存差別故於廣額言千佛一數亦或疑虛乎實乎若如此疑惑即又落差別了也].

whether it is fact or fabrication, then you've entered right into the realm of differentiation. That would not be as good as severing at the single stroke of the sword. You must not think about "before" and "after." If you think about "before" and "after," then it's once again differentiation!

[35.4: *Quotes the saying of an ancient to render a judgment on Zong's mistaken understanding of "brushing away sense fields"*[182]]

Xuansha said:[183]

As for *this matter*, one cannot limit it—the road of thought doesn't reach it. It's not dependent upon being adorned [by the six perfections and myriad practices[184]]; from the outset it is true stillness. In the midst of daily activities such as speaking or laughing there is clarity everywhere—there isn't the slightest thing lacking. People of the present time, unaware of this principle, falsely wade through [effortful] performance [of cultivation] and wade through sense objects,[185] grasping everywhere, and bound to one thing after another. Even if they are aware that sense objects are disordered and names and characteristics are unreal, they immediately decide to focus mind and restrain thoughts, to re-absorb phenomenal characteristics into emptiness, to close the eyes [in cross-legged sitting]. Whenever thoughts arise, one after another they "brush them away"—as soon as a subtle thought arises, they immediately suppress it. This sort of level of understanding is an outside Way that falls into nihilism. They are like a dead person whose soul lingers

---

182. Mujaku, 371: 第四段引古語判結他破除情塵謬解.

183. Mujaku, 371, cites: *Xuansha Shibei chanshi guanglu* 玄沙師備禪師廣錄: 限約不得。心思絕路。不因莊嚴。本來真靜。動用語笑。隨處明了。更無欠少。今時人不悟箇中道理。妄自涉事涉塵。處處染著。頭頭繁絆。縱悟。則塵境紛紜。名相不實。便擬凝斂念。攝事歸空。閉目藏睛。終有念起。旋旋破除。細相纔生。即便過捺。如此見解。即是落空亡底外道。魂不散底死人。溟溟漠漠。無覺無知。塞耳偷鈴。徒自欺誑。(CBETA, X73, no. 1445, p. 15, b6–12 // Z 2:31, p. 190, b8–14 // R126, p. 379, b8–14). Xuansha's dates are 835–908.

184. Mujaku, 372, glosses *bu yin zhuangyan* 不因莊嚴 thus: "Adorn it with the external six perfections and myriad practices" [忠曰以外六度萬行莊嚴他].

185. Mujaku, 372, glosses *wang zi she shi she chen* 妄自涉事涉塵 thus: "*Shih* means doing effortful performance of cultivation; *chen* means to do a cultivation that involves unreal characteristics" [忠曰事謂作有爲造作修行塵謂作有相對待修行也].

on. Dark and silent, they lack awareness and knowing. They steal a
bell [and run off with it—when it makes a sound, fearing that others
will hear,] they cover their ears.[186] Such self-deception is all in vain!

Your letter's talking about ["brushing away the sense fields," and so
forth] is exactly the illness that Xuansha excoriated. The perverse teachers of "silence-as-illumination" are a pit for burying people. You must be
careful!

[35.5: *Dahui again shows his method of* gongfu[187]]

When you are lifting the *huatou* to awareness, there is definitely no
need to perform a lot of tricky maneuvers. While walking, standing,
sitting, or lying down, just don't allow interruption. While experiencing joy, anger, sorrow, or happiness,[188] don't produce discrimination.
Over and over again lift [the *huatou*] to awareness, over and over again
keep your eye on [the *huatou*]. When you notice the *huatou* has no
logic, no taste, that your mind is "hot and stuffy," it's the state wherein
you, the person on duty, relinquishes his life. Keep this in mind! Upon
encountering this realm [of no logic and no taste], don't become faint-
hearted. This sort of realm is the *state of being* of becoming a buddha
or patriarch.

[35.6: *Orders Zong to avoid perverse teachers*[189]]

But the present-day party of perverse teachers of "silence-as-illumination"
just takes sinking into silence as the "ultimate standard"—they call this
"the matter [prior to the appearance of] Bhīṣma-garjita-svara Buddha" [i.e.,
the very first buddha to appear in this world], or they call it "the matter of

---

186. Mujaku, 373, cites *Huainanzi* 淮南子十六, *Shuo shan xun* 說山訓. Mujaku, 374, comments: "The idea is: perverse people forcibly press the *original nature* into no-knowing and
no-awareness, but, when the *original nature* increases, they can't stop its active functioning.
How could following your perverse view produce no-knowing and no-awareness? It's like
covering your own ears—though you don't hear, the sound of the bell never stops" [忠曰今
意謂邪人以本性強抑爲無知無覺而本性長時不息動用豈隨汝邪見爲無知無覺耶譬如自耳
自掩之雖爲不聽而鈴音常不止鳴也].

187. Mujaku, 374: 第五段重示工夫法.

188. Mujaku, 374, cites the *Doctrine of the Mean* (*Zhongyong* 中庸).

189. Mujaku, 375: 第六段令避邪師.

the aeon of nothingness before the world begins."[190] Having no confidence in the existence of an entrance to awakening, they consider awakening a deception; they consider awakening "starting second" at a game of chess; they consider awakening as *upāya*-speech; they consider awakening a term to lure beings along. People like this cheat others and cheat themselves, mislead others and mislead themselves. You must be careful!

[35.7: *In advance showing the realm of getting awakening*[191]]

In the midst of the four postures of daily activities, as you are "wading through differentiated sense objects,"[192] you will become aware that an instance of saving on the expenditure of [*gongfu*] energy is none other than the state of gaining [awakening] energy. And the state of gaining [awakening] energy is the maximization of saving on expenditure of [*gongfu*] energy.[193] If you resort to even a hairsbreadth of willpower to prop up [the *huatou*], that will certainly be a perverse dharma, not the buddhadharma![194] Merely have a mind of long-term tenacity and keep pressing hard with the dog-has-no-buddha-nature *huatou* [**wu** 無]. Keep pressing hard—your mind will have nowhere to go. Suddenly it will be like awakening from sleep, like a lotus flower opening up, like the clouds' splitting open and the sun's appearing. When you arrive at the

---

190. Caodong teachers did use such slogans. *Hongzhi chanshi guanglu* (宏智禪師廣錄): "Before the aeon of nothingness and Bhīṣma-garjita-svara Buddha there was another heaven and earth [lit., a 'Jug Heaven,' a world produced inside a jug by an immortal]" [空劫威音前。別有一壺天。] (T2001.48.43c23-24). Also, see "pure ultimate light-comprehension" (*jingji guang tongda* 淨極光通達; letter #53.4, p. 284) at T2001.48.66a7.

191. Mujaku, 375: 第七段預示得悟境界.

192. Mujaku, 375, glosses *she chabie jingjie* 涉差別境界 thus: "Dahui raises a line from Zong's letter" [忠曰舉他來書語].

193. Mujaku, 375–376, glosses *de li chu ji sheng li* 得力處極省力 thus: "Without toiling over lifting and rallying [the *huatou*] to awareness, one is naturally 'of a piece' with the Way. It's the 'water-buffalo's exposed on faraway ground'" [忠曰不勞舉覺提撕自然與道一片所謂水牯牛露迥迥地]. A quatrain in *Shixi Xinyue chanshi yulu* 石溪心月禪師語錄 entitled "Snow Ox" (雪牛) runs: "Exposed on faraway ground but you can't pursue it;/ For the moment it's again walking among the weeds in the depths of the village. /Its monochrome skin and hair have been traded in;/ The load it is shouldering must be these sentient beings" [露迥迥地趁不去。時復深村荒草行。一色皮毛都換了。荷擔須是者眾生。] (CBETA, X71, no. 1405, p. 63, c13-15 // Z 2:28, p. 63, b14-16 // R123, p. 125, b14-16).

194. Mujaku, 376, glosses *ding shi xiefa fei fofa ye* 定是邪法非佛法也 thus: "Auxiliary in the Hall Zong wants to take the buddhadharma to *prop up* differentiated sense objects and *brush them away*. Therefore, he shows a perverse dharma" [忠曰宗直閣欲以佛法支撐差別境界破除之故示是邪法也].

in-that-way time, naturally [the buddhadharma and the differentiated sense objects] will become "of a piece."[195]

[35.8: *Warns against getting rid of the various sense objects*[196]]

In the midst of the topsy-turvy discrimination of daily activities, just keep your eye on the word **wu 無**. Don't pay any heed to whether you have awakened or not awakened, whether you have achieved penetration or not. The buddhas of the three times are just people with *nothing-to-do*. The patriarchal masters down through the generations are also just people with *nothing-to-do*. An ancient venerable said: "Just be *in things*—but comprehend *nothing-to-do*. In seeing forms and hearing sounds you mustn't become [blind and] deaf."[197] Another ancient venerable said: "The idiot gets rid of sense objects but doesn't eliminate mind; the wise one eliminates mind but doesn't get rid of sense objects."[198] When you exhibit no-mind in all places, then the various differentiated sense objects spontaneously disappear.

[35.9: *Warns against impetuously advancing (towards clear understanding)*[199]]

But today's scholar-officials[200] are often impatient in their desire to understand Chan. They ruminate about the sutra teachings and the sayings of the patriarchal masters, wanting to be able to explain them with clear

---

195. Mujaku, 376, glosses *ziran cheng yi pian yi* 自然成一片矣 thus: "When you arrive at this, for the first time you are able to make the buddhadharma and differentiated sense objects truly of a piece" [忠曰至此始可佛法與差別境界真箇成一片也].

196. Mujaku, 376: 第八段誡除境多事.

197. Mujaku, 376, cites *Chanlin sengbao zhuan* 禪林僧寶傳 (CBETA, X79, no. 1560, p. 509, c12–p. 510, a13 // Z 2B:10, p. 239, b8–c15 // R137, p. 477, b8–p. 478, a15). The ancient is Longya Judun 龍牙居遁 (835–923).

198. Mujaku, 377, cites *Huangbo shan Duanji chanshi chuanxin fa yao* 黃檗山斷際禪師傳心法要, T2012A.48.382a4–5; as well as *Jianzhong jingguo xu deng lu* 建中靖國續燈錄 (CBETA, X78, no. 1556, p. 715, a1 // Z 2B:9, p. 93, b13 // R136, p. 185, b13). The speaker in the second is Chan Master Baojue of Mt. Huanglong in Hongzhou (洪州黃龍山寶覺禪師; 1025–1100), that is, Huitang Zuxin 晦堂祖心.

199. Mujaku, 377: 第九段誡躁進.

200. Mujaku, 377, glosses *shidafu* 士大夫 thus: "Speaks in general of the scholar-official class, but the intention is to point to Auxiliary in the Hall Zong" [忠曰泛言士大夫意指宗直閣].

understanding. Little do they imagine that the state of clear understanding, on the contrary, is a matter of *not* clearly understanding. If you break through this word **wu 無**, you won't be asking other people whether you clearly understand or don't clearly understand. As for my making members of the scholar-official class be dull-witted, this is my reasoning. Taking a "first" in the "dull-wittedness examination" is no bad thing! The only thing to be feared is the turning in of a blank answer paper.[201] Ha! Ha!

36. *In Reply to Participant in Determining Governmental Matters Li (Taifa)*

[*Commentary: Mujaku says, "Li Taifa was exiled 'beyond the seas' for more than twenty years.... This letter dates to Shaoxing 19/1149 when the Master was sixty-one.... This letter has 'pressing-down" and 'lifting-up,' 'snatching away' and 'giving free rein,' which is not at all easy to see. Dahui's 'lifting-up' and 'giving free rein' has to do with Li Taifa's being of unconfused mind concerning life/death and calamity/good fortune. Obviously, we can see Dahui's 'pressing-down' and 'snatching away' concerning Taifa's saying that he has had an insight into the Huayan dharmadhātu. Because Dahui has not yet met him face to face, Dahui can't know whether he has really apprehended or not. Because Dahui entertains some doubts from a distance, the intention of 'pressing-down' and 'snatching away' lies outside the words (i.e., the reader must read between the lines) and is very difficult to perceive. Students! Don't do a facile reading!"[202] Hengzhou-exile letter.*]

---

201. Mujaku, 378, glosses *tuo bai* 拕白 thus: "Stopping mundane knowledge and talent and being a stupid, dull-witted Han—doing 'step-backwards' [i.e., reverse-illumination] *gongfu*—even though that's a good thing, all one's life maintaining dull-wittedness without achieving realization, wasting one's whole life, cannot be said to be *that one true phrase*. Therefore, fear it" [忠曰歇世智才覺自爲痴鈍漢退步工夫雖是好事然畢世守鈍無契證分一生空過不得言真箇那一句亦不是也故怕之也].

202. Mujaku, 379–380: 忠曰泰發謫於海外二十餘年.... 此書紹興十九年己巳師六十一歲而作.... 忠曰此書有抑揚縱奪太不易看其揚與縱在泰發於生死禍福不亂心矣顯然可見其抑與奪在自言於華嚴法界有見處蓋大慧未覿面故不可知實得乎不實得乎遙疑著故隱然抑奪意在言外太難見學者勿容易看過. For entries for Li Guang 李光 (*zi* Taifa 泰發), see *Song History*, 363 (16.2889–91) and *Cases of Song and Yuan Confucians*, 20 (2.835–836). Hucker, 517: The official title *canzheng* 參政 "is a quasi-official abbreviation of *canzhi zhengshi* 參知政事 (*Participant in Determining Governmental Matters*), i.e., a Vice Grand Councilor (*fuxiang* 副相, *shaozai* 少宰)." As a measure of how deeply Li fell afoul of the Qin Hui 秦檜 capitulationist clique at court, Li's exile included eight years in malarial Qiongzhou 瓊州, that is, Hainan Island. At the time of this letter he was in exile in Hainan, and Dahui was in exile in Hengzhou.

[36.1: *Dahui relates Li's letter and sighs*[203]]

I have been informed by your letter: "The Huayan multi-layered *dharmadhātu*[204] is certainly not false speech [on the part of the Buddha]. Since it isn't false speech, there must necessarily be a handing over [by the teacher], and there must necessarily be an affirming on one's own [by the student]."[205] When I had read this far, I gave out a long sigh.

[36.2: *Dahui wants to praise Taifa, but, prior to that, he deprecates mundane scholar-officials*[206]]

As for scholars-officials, and their usual [classical] learning,[207] on approaching the juncture of life/death and calamity/good fortune, in eighty or ninety percent of cases [they are like crabs that have been dropped into boiling water]—they flail their arms and legs about in a frenzy.[208] When you examine their conduct,[209] they're not as good as a *nothing-to-do* fellow

---

203. Mujaku, 380: 第一段述來語嗟歎.

204. The four ascending *dharmadhātus* of the Huayan school: the *dharmadhātu* of phenomena (*shi fajie* 事法界); the *dharmadhātu* of principle (*li fajie* 理法界); the *dharmadhātu* of the unimpeded interpenetration of phenomena and principle (*lishi wu'ai fajie* 理事無礙法界); and the *dharmadhātu* of the unimpeded interpenetration of phenomena and phenomena (*shishi wu'ai fajie* 事事無礙法界).

205. Mujaku, 381, glosses *ji fei xuyu zhi zi ken chu* 既非慮語至自肯處 thus: "*Handing over* relates to the teacher's part; *affirming on one's own* relates to the student's part. Means: Li's himself saying that he knows that this is definitely not false speech must entail the teacher's handing over of the seal, and it also must entail his own experience of awakening and assent" [忠曰分付係師家分上自肯係學者分上言自言知其決非慮語必可其處有師家者分付印可又必可有自家悟入肯諾處].

206. Mujaku, 381: 第二段欲贊泰發先貶世士大夫.

207. Mujaku, 381, glosses *shidafu pingxi suoxue* 士大夫平昔所學 thus: "Means: what the world's scholar-official class usually studies is all the books of the sages and worthies—the purport of ethics, benevolence, and righteousness" [言世間士大夫平生所學皆是聖賢書道德仁義旨].

208. Mujaku, 382, glosses *shou zu ju lu* 手足俱露 thus: "When they encounter sense objects that go against them, their *original mind* is revealed. It's like the retracted arms and legs of a crab—when the crab falls into boiling water, they expand" [忠曰遇逆境本心露矣譬螃蟹所收手脚及落湯長展也].

209. Mujaku, 382, glosses *kao qi xing shi* 考其行事 thus: "Scholar-officials usually read the books of the sages and worthies, but from the outset it is not to seek the Way. They merely use these to seek to be successful in attaining wealth and status. Therefore, they do not come up to a *nothing-to-do* fellow who is encumbered by little phantasmal thought" [忠曰其者指士大夫士大夫尋常讀聖賢書本非爲求道但以此求富貴利達故却不及省事漢妄想少者]; and cites letter #30.3.

in a three-family village[210]—wealth and high status, poverty and low status cannot throw *his* mind into confusion![211] And so when you compare them, it is often the case that [the learned member of the scholar-official class with his] knowledge is inferior to [the villager with his] stupidity, the high-status [member of the scholar-official class] is inferior to the low-status [villager].[212] Why [is it that the scholar-official "flails his arms and legs about in a frenzy" and the villager does not]?[213] It's because, at that time when the calamity/good fortune of samsara makes an appearance, [the villager] has never had the capacity for artifice.[214]

[36.3: *Dahui sighs over Li's being able to study both the mundane and supramundane and, at the same time, questions what Li has gotten from the study of Buddhism*[215]]

Minister Duke! Your "usual learning" has already been shown in your [righteous] conduct. At the critical juncture of calamity/good fortune[216] you

---

210. ZGK, 73.300, glosses *sheng shih han* 省事漢 thus: "A *nothing-to-do*/no-mind person" [無事無心の人].

211. Mujaku, 382, cites letter #30.7.

212. Mujaku, 382, glosses *zhi bu ru yu yun yun* 智不如愚云云 thus: "*Knowledge* is the learned scholar-official; *stupidity* is the *nothing-to-do* fellow. *High status* is the scholar-official who has an official position; *low status* is the one in a three-family village. Means: scholar-officials who study ethics, benevolence, and righteousness are inferior to the stupid, low-status person who doesn't know anything about matters of Way-Study [i.e., Neo-Confucianism]" [忠曰智學士大夫愚省事漢貴士大夫在官者賤在三家村裏者謂學道德仁義之士大夫却劣於不知道學之事愚賤人也].

213. Mujaku, 382, glosses *he yi gu* 何以故 thus: "It's not a question about the reason why the *nothing-to-do* fellow is superior to the scholar-official. The reason why the *nothing-to-do* fellow is superior to the scholar-official has already been answered above. This is about the line "wealth and high status, poverty and low status cannot throw *his* mind into confusion," etc. This is the reason why the *nothing-to-do* fellow is superior to the scholar-official. The real question here is about the meaning of the line above "flail their arms and legs about in a frenzy" [蓋非問省事漢勝士大夫之故也其省事漢勝士大夫之所由上已說畢所謂富貴貧賤不能汩其心此此是也此即省事漢勝士大夫之故也今正問次上手足俱露之義也].

214. Mujaku, 383, glosses *shengsi huofu xianqian na shi bu rong wei gu ye* 生死禍福現前那時不容僞故也 thus: "Analogous to, at the present moment, Li Taifa's being in exile and yet talking and laughing as if nothing had happened and full of enthusiasm and fervor" [又如今李參政臨謫流談笑慷慨一如平日是也].

215. Mujaku, 383: 第三段歎學得世出世兼審問學佛所得.

216. Mujaku, 383, glosses *lin huofu zhi ji* 臨禍福之際 thus: "When you scolded Qin Hui and faced exile to Qiongzhou on Hainan island, you talked and laughed as if nothing had

have been like metal purified by smelting, emerging even more lustrous. If you have *also definitively*[217] understood that "the Huayan multi-layered *dharmadhātu* is certainly not false speech," then you definitely aren't fabricating a notion of it as some *other thing* [outside your own nature].[218] The [dross] left over [in the smelting process]—the ups and downs, the sense objects sometimes going against you and sometimes going along with you, the things that are sometimes correct and sometimes perverse—these too are not *other things* [i.e., they also are not outside your own nature].[219] I hope you will constantly conduct this sort of contemplation—I too am *in this* [i.e. in the Chan ultimate *this*; in this state of exile; and as in the *Analects* line "when your words give few occasions for blame and your actions few occasions for repentance, then emolument lies *in this*"].[220]

---

happened, and you were full of enthusiasm and fervor. This is like metal purified by smelting" [忠曰詆秦檜謫瓊州時談笑慷慨一如平日是如精金入火者也].

217. Mujaku, 383, glosses *you jueding zhi huayan yun yun* 又決定知華嚴云云 thus: "Below Dahui sighs over Li's study of the supramundane dharma. The *also* means also, in addition to the mundane dharma. Dahui doubts that this is likely and so uses the word *definitively*. He takes a stone acupuncture needle to Li's baseless words" [忠曰已下歎學出世法又者又於世法也大慧疑其容易故却下決定字砭於其浮語矣].

218. Mujaku, 384, glosses *ding bu zuo ta wu xiang yi* 定不作他物想矣 thus: "The three characters *ding bu zuo* also have to do with Dahui's doubts about this. Therefore, putting them down in addition to the two words above [i.e., *you* and *jueding*] necessitates that this *ding bu zuo* bears the meaning *by all means avoid fabricating*. All these words have this intention on Dahui's part. He is faintly 'snatching-away'. The *multi-layered dharmadhātu* from the outset is something inside your very own nature with an innate endowment of myriad qualities. It's not some other thing [outside your own nature]. You've already come to know that *it's not false speech*. I calculate from a distance that you certainly are capable of not fabricating the notion of some other thing [outside your own nature]. If you do fabricate the notion of some other thing, then it's not coming to know the multi-layered *dharmadhātu*—then the assertion *it's not false speech* is [no more than] a boast." [忠曰定不作三字亦大慧疑之故下之上二必有此定不作下切忌作皆有此意隱然奪者也言重重法界者元是自家性中恒沙萬德本來具足底非他物矣公已知非虛語我遙計公定可不作他物想也若作他物想則非知重重法界所謂非虛語者誇言也].

219. Mujaku, 384, glosses *qi yu qi diang ba dao yun yun* 其餘七顛八倒云云 thus: "Li Taifa perhaps said that the true principle of the buddhadharma should not be other things—that, if there are again mundane upside-down viewpoints, etc., such things lie outside of this. Therefore, Dahui warns him that mundane upside-down viewpoints, sense objects going against you and going along with you, correctness and perversity, are all also the myriad qualities within the nature and *are not some other thing*. *Ups and downs*, etc., is a hidden reference to the career path of an official, or administrative functions by rank, or Li's disobeying Qin Hui and consequently encountering exile, or discussions of matters that involve correctness and perversity, etc." [李泰發或謂佛法真理可非他物若復世間顛倒等在此外也故誡之曰世間顛倒逆順正邪亦皆性中萬德而非他物也七顛八倒等暗言仕官途路或據位行政或忤秦檜遭謫流或論事有正邪等也].

220. *Analects*, *Weizheng* 爲政.

[36.4: *Dahui hopes for a meeting on another day to investigate Li's level of understanding*[221]]

Someday we will be in each other's company on a lonely shore.[222] Let us burn incense and form a karmic connection for meeting in a far distant lifetime—to achieve the multi-layered *dharmadhātu* and thereby make *real* this matter.[223] How could such a thing be called a "mending in a small way"?[224]

[36.5: *Dahui, estimating from a distance, rejects any simple-to-understand interpretation of the preceding section*[225]]

I must add a further note. As for this one passage[226] just now [about our meeting in the distant future to achieve the multi-layered *dharmadhātu*]—by

---

221. Mujaku, 384: 第四段期他日勘撿.

222. Mujaku, 384, glosses *yi ri zhi jikuan zhi bin* 異日至寂寞之濱 thus: "At the time Dahui was under exile, and so he spoke these words. Means: I am enrolled in the local census register and controlled by the Hengzhou local officials—I have no freedom of movement. On another day, if I receive a gracious pardon, in some country or another, along a lonely shore, we will be able to meet" [忠曰時大慧被謫故有此言言我編管身不得自由異日若蒙恩赦於何國寂寞濱得相會].

223. Mujaku, 385, glosses *yi shi qi shi* 以實其事 thus: "This word *real* is the 'eye' of the whole letter. Relying on this one word, the intention of the whole letter is exposed. Means: Li today is saying that the multilayered *dharmadhātu* is not false speech on the part of the Buddha. Dahui fears that this big talk may be 'false speech.' He is waiting for a meeting at another time when he can personally apply the tongs for testing [Li's level of understanding]. He will enable Li to achieve this dharma and enable him to make *real* the present false talk" [忠曰此實字一篇眼目依此一字書翰底意剖露矣言李公今日言重重法界非佛之慮語此箇大話恐是慮妄之語且待他時相見時親下勘辨鉗鎚令成就此法可令實於今之妄言也]. Given that this is a letter written from one exile to another, there may also be a political subtext to wishing for a meeting—their exiled status would have to be rescinded by a change at the political center.

224. Mujaku, 385, glosses *qi xiao bu zai* 豈小補哉 thus: "If he enables Li to realize the multi-layered *dharmadhātu*, then it's a 'big mending'" [忠曰若令證入重重法界則是大補]; and cites *Mencius, Jinxin shang* 盡心上: "Mencius said: 'The people under a hegemon look brisk-cheerful. The people under a true king look bright-glistening. If he kills them, they do not bear a grudge; if he benefits them, they do not credit him. The people day by day shift towards the good, without knowing who is making them do so. Where the noble man passes through there is transformation; where he abides there is the divine. It flows upwards and downwards, identical to heaven and earth. How can it be said that he mends it in a small way!'" [孟子曰。霸者之民。驩虞如也。王者之民。皡皡如也。殺之而不怨。利之而不庸。民日遷善而不知爲之者。夫君子所過者化。所存者神。上下與天地同流。豈曰小補之哉。]. This allusion in its entirety appears to have an overtly political weight.

225. Mujaku, 385: 第五段遙量斥淺近解會.

226. Mujaku, 385, glosses *zhe yi laosuo* 遮一絡索 thus: "The one section on the multi-layered *dharmadhātu*" [忠曰重重法界一段也].

all means avoid understanding it as metaphorical talk pointing at things.[227] Ha! Ha![228]

37. *In Reply to Assistant Director of the Court of the Imperial Clan Zeng (Tianyin)*

[*Commentary:* Mujaku says, "This letter dates to Shaoxing 16/1146 when the Master was fifty-eight."[229] Takagi says, "This letter shows that the situation of the great ball of uncertainty/mind-squirming is crucial."[230] Hengzhou-exile letter.]

[37.1: *Dahui rejoices and encourages Zeng*[231]]

Your natural endowment has placed you close to the Way: your body-mind is pure, and there are no other karmic conditions to constitute a blockage. In just this single point who can match you? Also, in the midst of walking, standing, sitting, and lying down, with the pithy formulation[232] [for

---

227. *Zhuangzi, Fuyan pian* 寓言篇: "Nine out of ten of my words are metaphorical—they rely on extraneous things to discuss the matter at hand. 'A father does not act as matchmaker for his son.' The meaning is: the father's praising him is not as good as someone who is not his father doing so. [The use of such metaphors] is not my fault. It is the fault of people [who would not understand me otherwise]" [寓言十九。籍外論之。親父不爲其子媒。親父譽之。不若非其父者也。非吾罪也。人之罪也。]. Perhaps Dahui is saying to Li Taifa: we shall meet in some distant Buddhist future many births from now (figurative) → we shall meet when the Qin Hui clique is no longer in power and our banishment has been rescinded (literal).

228. Mujaku, 386, glosses *yi xiao* 一笑 thus: "This letter in the one matter of the *dharmadhātu* has not a single word of praise and permission [for Li's claim about the *dharmadhātu*]. On the contrary, word after word has the intention of not giving Li permission. Students must examine and savor this laugh!" [如此書於法界一件一無讚許語却一一語有不許意學者須翫味笑].

229. Mujaku, 387: 此書紹興十六年丙寅師五十八歲而作.

230. Takagi, 2.16b: 此章示大疑團心悶之處是緊要. Zeng has no biography in *Song History*. Hucker, 530–531: "*Zongcheng* 宗丞 is an unofficial reference to an Assistant Director (*cheng* 丞) of the Court of the Imperial Clan (*zongren fu* 宗人府). . . . maintained the imperial genealogy, kept records on births, marriages, deaths, and all other matters pertaining to imperial kinsmen."

231. Mujaku, 387: 第一段隨喜勸勉.

232. Another occurrence of this term *sheng yao chu* (省要處) is *Dahui Pujue chanshi yulu* 大慧普覺禪師語錄 (*Dahui Pujue chanshi fayu* 大慧普覺禪師法語): "Instruction to Chan Person Miaodao: Great Master Dingguang, Miaodao, asked Dahui: 'This mind and this nature—what about delusion and awakening, going towards and turning your back? I beg you to give me instruction in the pithy formulation [for *gongfu*].' Dahui for a long time didn't answer. Miaodao asked again. Dahui laughed and said: 'When it comes to discussion of the pithy

gongfu] that I showed you: constantly rally [the *huatou*] to awareness. Lay off saying, "for a single thought-moment I got in correspondence, and everything is on track." Even if you haven't yet awakened in this birth, just keep pressing hard *in this way* until you arrive at the final day of the twelfth month [at the end of your life]—the Old One Yama [Judge of the Dead] will back off by a thousand miles. Why? Because thought after thought you will be within *prajñā*, with no thought that differs from *prajñā*, with no interruption.

[37.2: *Encourages by quoting the efficaciousness of the inferior Daoist method of* gongfu *and asking how much more efficacious is the superior Chan* huatou-*practice method*[233]]

For example, the Daoist school uses [what we call] "false mind" to "maintain thought."[234] As the days and months go on and on, even they are able to bring their achievement to completion, and they are no longer under the sway of the elements earth, water, fire, and wind. How much more so when the entirety of thoughts is stabilized within *prajñā* [as in our Chan method of *gongfu*]? On the final day of the twelfth month [at the end of your life] how could you not be able to "flip over" your karma?

[37.3: *Shows the method of* gongfu[235]]

Most people right now study the Way with a mind that has something to apprehend—this is an honest-to-goodness case of real "false thought" within "non-false thought"! Just make yourself exist on your own. However,

---

formulation, I can't offer instruction to people. If I could offer instruction, it wouldn't be pithy'" [示妙道禪人: 定光大師妙道問雲門。此心此性迷悟向背如何。乞省要處指示。雲門良久不答。妙道再問。雲門笑曰。若論省要處。則不可指示於人。若可指示。則不省要矣。] (T1998A.47.914b10–14).

233. Mujaku, 387: 第二段引劣況勝勸激.

234. The *Heavenly Recluse* (*Tianyinzi* 天隱子) is a Tang Daoist text by an unknown compiler. It is divided into eight chapters. The sixth chapter, "Maintaining Thought" (*cun xiang* 存想), states: "*Maintaining* means maintaining the spirit of 'I.' *Thought* means thinking of the body of 'I.' Close the eyes, and you will then see the eyes of self. Take in mind, and you will then see the mind of self. Mind and eyes are both inseparable from the body of 'I.' Do no harm to the spirit of 'I,' and then you will have a step-by-step way to *maintaining thought*" [存謂存我之神。想謂想我身。閉目即見自己之目。收心即見自己之心。心與目皆不離我身。不傷我身則存想之漸也。].

235. Mujaku, 387: 第三段示工夫法.

you must not be too tense and must not be too slack. Just do *gongfu* in this way, saving on the endless expenditure of mental energy.

[37.4: *Dahui allows that Zeng's level of understanding is correct*[236]]

In your case, the "unripe" state is already "ripe," and the "ripe" state is already "unripe." Twenty-four hours a day naturally you never fall into "in a dried-up mind quelling delusive thought" or "engirding mind."[237] Although you have not yet passed through to awakening, the Evil-Māra followers of outside Ways [i.e., perverse teachers] already are incapable of taking advantage of you.[238] You are even able to [make an outward show of] a joint "hand" and joint "eye" with these Evil-Māra followers of outside Ways.[239] You [make them retreat from their evil views and] perfect the true dharma,[240] but you don't fall into their number. You are the only person qualified to pull this off.[241] In the case of the other [students of mine], it's not just that they are not as capable in practice as you, it's also that they haven't attained the level of confidence [necessary for temporarily sharing the views of the perverse teachers without falling into their number[242]].

---

236. Mujaku, 388: 第四段許見處正.

237. Mujaku, 388, glosses *ku xin wang huai zhi guan dai* 枯心忘懷至管帶 thus: "Naturally you won't come under the sway of the theories of the perverse teachers" [忠曰自然不隨邪師之說也].

238. Mujaku, 388, glosses *bu neng si qi bian* 不能伺其便 thus: "They can't take the perverse Chan of 'quelling delusive thought' and 'engirding mind' to delude this person!" [忠曰不得以忘懷管帶之邪禪惑亂此人].

239. Mujaku, 388, glosses *gong yi shou tong yi yan* 共一手同一眼 thus: "Means: "It's not only that Zeng doesn't fall into the perverse teachings—he puts out a single hand to save the party of false views. Therefore, outwardly he shows a commonality of hand and eye, but he actually does not share a commonality with them. Because that one hand and that one eye are not in common with the perverse teachers, it is said that he doesn't fall into their number" [忠曰言非但不墮邪教却出隻手救邪見輩故外示同其手眼實不共同也那一手那一眼不共同邪師故言不墮其數矣].

240. Mujaku, 388, glosses *chengjiu bi shi er bu duo qi shu* 成就彼事而不墮其數 thus: "*Perfect* means make them retreat from their evil views and perfect the true dharma" [成就者令彼回惡見而成就正法也].

241. Mujaku, 388, glosses *yu ci* 語此 thus: "*This* refers to [making an outward show of] a joint 'hand' and joint 'eye' without falling into their number" [忠曰此者指共一手同一眼而不墮其數].

242. Mujaku, 388, glosses *wei bi xin deji ye* 未必心得及也 thus: "Means: they are incapable of the confidence necessary to temporarily share the views [of the perverse teachers] without falling into their number" [忠曰言不可得信暫同其見不墮其數之道理也].

[37.5: *Shows the method of rallying the* huatou *to awareness*[243]]

Just keep your eye on the *huatou*. Keep on keeping your eye on the *huatou*. When you become aware that the *huatou* has no basis, that the *huatou* has no taste, that your mind is squirming, then it's just the right time for applying energy—absolutely avoid leaving it to the course of events.[244] Just this squirming state is the state of becoming a buddha or a patriarch, the state of severing the [reproachful] tongues of the people of all-under-heaven.[245] You must not be neglectful! You must not be neglectful!

38. In Reply to Instructor Wang (Dashou)

[*Commentary: This letter probably dates to around Shaoxing 17/1147 when Dahui was fifty-nine.*[246] *Hyesim says, "The main purport of the letter in reply to Instructor Wang is to cut off the consciousnesses and practice the* huatou*."*[247] *Hengzhou-exile letter.*]

[38.1: *Shows the* gongfu *solution*[248]]

I am ignorant of what sort of *gongfu* you have been doing in your daily activities since we parted. If you've been getting tastiness from [discussions of such topics as] "principle and nature," or getting tastiness from the sutra teachings, or getting tastiness from the sayings of the Chan patriarchal masters, or getting tastiness from sense objects you see and hear, or getting tastiness from raising your feet and progressing by steps, or getting tastiness by the functioning of your intellect, you've accomplished nothing whatsoever. If you want decisively to stop-to-rest, pay no heed at

---

243. Mujaku, 388: 第五段示提撕法.

244. Mujaku, 388, glosses *qieji sui ta qu* 切忌隨他去 thus: "*It* refers to the mind of 'your mind is squirming'" [忠曰他者指心頭悶之心也].

245. Mujaku, 388, glosses *zuoduan tianxia ren shetou chu* 坐斷天下人舌頭處 thus: "The people of all-under-heaven cannot question him reproachfully" [忠曰天下人不得撿責詰難於彼也].

246. The dating is according to Araki, 166.

247. Hyesim, 84: 答王教授狀大旨絕識參話. Wang has no biography in *Song History*. Hucker, 142: "*Instructor* [*jiaoshou* 教授] is a title with many uses, most commonly for the heads of Confucian Schools (*ruxue* 儒學) at the Prefecture (*zhou* 州, *fu* 府) level; always low-ranking or unranked."

248. Mujaku, 389: 第一段示工夫去就.

all to all the states where you have usually gotten tastiness.[249] Rather, as an experiment, try to concentrate mind on the ungraspable state, the tasteless state. When you can't concentrate your mind, can't grasp, and gradually become aware that there is no sword hilt to grip, and that rationality and the eight consciousnesses[250] have become inoperative like earth, wood, tile, and stone, don't fear [that this is] falling into [the extreme view of an annihilationist] emptiness. This is the state wherein you, the person on duty, relinquishes his life. You must not be neglectful! You must not be neglectful!

[38.2: *Rejects mundane knowledge and cleverness in argument*[251]]

Most people of cleverness and sharpness are blocked by their cleverness [and sharpness]. And so their eye of the Way doesn't open up. No matter where they go, they are "stopped up." Sentient beings, from beginningless time, are under the sway of the eight consciousnesses, drifting about in samsara, incapable of existing on their own. If you really want to escape samsara and become a happy fellow, you must, at the single stroke of the sword, sever the passageways of the eight consciousnesses, and then you will have some small increment of correspondence [with *this matter*]. Therefore, Yongjia said: "As for inflicting damage on the buddhadharma, and extinguishing karmic merit: There are no cases that do not arise from these eight consciousnesses."[252] How could Yongjia have been lying to people?

[38.3: *Scolds about surmising and conjecturing*[253]]

A little while back I received your letter. All sorts of inclinations in that letter are [Chan] illnesses that I have railed at in the past. Realize that

---

249. Mujaku, 389, glosses *mo guan ta* 莫管他 thus: "You shouldn't consider them good things, and you shouldn't consider them bad things" [忠曰亦不可爲好事亦不可爲惡事也].

250. Mujaku, 389, glosses *xin yi shi* 心意識 thus: "In order: the eighth consciousness [storehouse consciousness], seventh [defiled mind], and six sensory consciousnesses [*vijñānas*]" [忠曰如次八七六識也].

251. Mujaku, 389: 第二段斥世智辯聰.

252. Mujaku, 389, cites *Yongjia zhengdao ge* 永嘉證道歌, T2014.48.396b1–2.

253. Mujaku, 389: 第三段呵愽量卜度.

these sorts of Chan illnesses are rolling around in the back of your head. Now, at the baseless state, the ungraspable state, the tasteless state, as an experiment try to do *gongfu*: a monk asked Zhaozhou: "Does even a dog have buddha-nature?" Zhou said: "**Wu 無.**" The usual clever person, as soon as he hears this standard raised, immediately understands it using the eight consciousnesses, makes surmises and quotes proof texts—he wants the master's handing over [of the "seal"].[254] Little does he imagine that [**wu 無**] doesn't allow quoting of proof texts, doesn't allow surmising, doesn't allow using the eight consciousnesses to understand. Even though he can quote proof texts, can make surmises, can understand, it's all nothing more than random extreme views produced by defiled consciousness within the weather-beaten skull. [At this rate] on this shore of samsara, he will never gain [awakening] energy!

[38.4: *Quotes someone who realized he was wrong in order to render a judgment on Wang's letter*[255]]

Right now in the broad world, the understanding of those so-called "Chan-master venerables" stops at the *state of being* described in your letter. As for the remaining perverse understandings, they're not worth discussion. Now Head Seat Chongmi[256]—he and I were together in the assembly of Chan Master Ping Purong.[257] We both completely got the gist of Purong's teaching—Chongmi considered it to be [the definitive or absolute teaching of] "peace and joy."[258] However, what he had concocted from Purong's teaching stopped at the *state of being* described in your letter. Only when he for the first time realized that he had been wrong, and had merely

---

254. Mujaku, 390, glosses *fenfu chu* 分付處 thus: "He wants the 'seal' of the master" [忠曰欲師家之印可也].

255. Mujaku, 390: 第四段引知非人判結來書.

256. Mujaku, 390, glosses *Mi shouzuo* 密首座 thus: "Chan Master Chongmi of Mt. Yi in Hengzhou was a successor of Dahui" [忠曰衡州伊山冲密禪師嗣大慧].

257. Purong Daoping (普融道平;?–1127) was a Linji master. Mujaku, 390, cites *Dahui Pujue chanshi nianpu* 大慧普覺禪師年譜: "Xuanhe 4/1122: The Master was thirty-four. . . . he was attached to the assembly of Chan Master Purong Ping of Xianping" [宣和四年壬寅: 師三十四歲. . . . 依咸平普融平禪師法席] (CBETA, J01, no. A042, p. 796, b8–13).

258. Mujaku, 390, glosses *jin de Purong yaoling* 盡得普融要領 thus: "Means: in getting what Purong was driving at, the two of us were identical, but I took it as *neyārtha* [provisional teaching], and Chongmi took it as *nītārtha* [definitive or absolute teaching]. This is the difference" [言得其意趣二人相同但我以爲未了密以爲了畢此爲異].

obtained a separate [i.e., provisional] "peace and joy,"[259] did he realize that I [who had told him that his understanding of Purong's teaching was not definitive but provisional] hadn't been deceiving him in the least. Very soon I'll make it a point to have you two meet each other. When you have no affairs to attend to, as an experiment, try to make him spit out the matter. [I don't know] whether you two will hit it off or not.[260]

[38.5: *Encourages stopping exegesis and getting real efficacy*[261]]

"When an eighty-year old enters the imperial examination testing site, truly he's not a child playing games. [If one word on his exam paper is wrong, he's ten-thousand miles from his hometown.]"[262] If birth-and-death [i.e., death] arrives without your having gained [awakening] energy, even if you can speak with the utmost clarity, even if you are capable of coherently reconciling contradictory ideas, even if you can quote proof texts without any discrepancies, it will all have been the "lifestyle" of a "ghost-home"—it won't have had anything at all to do with "I" [i.e., your *original allotment*].[263]

[38.6: *Scolds rendering confused judgments on Chan stories*[264]]

As for the various heterodox understandings [i.e., Chan illnesses] within the Chan gate, verily those who discern dharma watch their step. Most of

---

259. Mujaku, 391, glosses *bie de ge anle chu* 別得箇安樂處 thus: "This is the true state of peace and joy. It was because he had a second contact with Dahui" [忠曰此是真箇安樂之處蓋再遭大慧接得矣].

260. Mujaku, 391, glosses *qide zuoyou yi fou* 契得左右意否 thus: "I don't know whether what Chongmi will say will tally with your karmically-determined abilities or not. If it does indeed tally, then it will be okay" [忠曰未知冲密所言可契合左右機否若合機則可是也].

261. Mujaku, 391: 第五段勸止義解得實效.

262. Mujaku, 391, cites *Liandeng hui yao* 聯燈會要: "When an eighty-year old enters the imperial examination testing site, truly he's not a child [carelessly] playing games. If one word on his exam paper is wrong, he's ten-thousand miles from his hometown" [八十翁翁入場屋。真誠不是小兒戲。一言若差。鄉關萬里。] (CBETA, X79, no. 1557, p. 192, a24–b1 // Z 2B:9, p. 399, b13–14 // R136, p. 797, b13–14).

263. Mujaku, 392, glosses *bu gan wo yi xing shi* 不干我一星事 thus: " 'I' is *that one person* of the *original allotment*" [忠曰我者本分那一人也]. Takagi, 2.18b, inserts: "Means: will not bring even a single trifling benefit to the self" [謂自己分上無一星事之益也].

264. Mujaku, 392: 第六段呵亂判因緣.

those for whom the great dharma is not yet bright[265] often misconstrue [Chan] illnesses as medicine.[266] You must be careful!

39. In Reply to Vice Minister Liu (Jigao)

[*Commentary: Mujaku says, "This letter dates to Shaoxing 18/1148 when the Master was sixty."*[267] *Takagi says, "This letter focuses on the perverse and correct in contemplation."*[268] *Hengzhou-exile letter.*]

[39.1: *Dahui picks up the words of Liu's letter and directly cites them*[269]]

Your letter has informed me: "The final day of the twelfth month has already arrived" [i.e., I have a terminal illness]. That sums it up—if you contemplate like that,[270] then your mind of mundane defilements will naturally vanish. Once the mundane-defilements mind has vanished, then in the coming days, as usual, [you will utter the seasonal salutation that is de rigueur:] "First month of spring—still cold."[271]

---

265. Mujaku, 392, glosses 大法不明 thus: "Those who post-awakening still have obstructions concerning the various Chan stories" [悟後猶於差別因緣有礙也].

266. Mujaku, 393, glosses *yi bing wei yao* 以病爲藥 thus: "Misconstrue the intention of the Chan patriarchs" [忠曰誤認祖意也].

267. Mujaku, 393: 此書紹興十八年戊辰師六十歲而作.

268. Takagi, 2.18b: 此章專示觀念之邪正. Liu has no biography in *Song History*. Hucker, 427: "*Vice Minister* [*shilang* 侍郎] is the 2nd executive post in each of the standard Six Ministries (*liu bu* 六部) of the central government."

269. Mujaku, 393: 第一段拈来語直示.

270. Mujaku, 393, glosses *riyong dang rushi guancha* 日用當如是觀察 thus: "Means: in your daily activities, you just should contemplate: the final day of the twelfth month has already arrived!" [忠曰言日用但合觀念臘月三十日已到].

271. Mujaku, 394, glosses *meng chun you han* 孟春猶寒 thus: "Words of seasonal greetings uttered at the time of the 'two unfoldings of the sitting mat and three bows' [by new arrivals at a Chan monastery]. It is an idiomatic phrase of the Chan monasteries. Therefore, it is spoken on the final day of the twelfth month. The inside story is: having-awakened is identical to not-yet-awakened" [忠曰兩展三禮所唱時令語也叢林熟語故因臘月三十日語言之而已底理言悟了同未悟也]. On the two unfoldings and three bows, see Yifa, *The Origin of Buddhist Monastic Codes in China* (Honolulu: University of Hawai'i Press, 2002), 256, n. 96. Araki, 168, glosses *meng chun you han* 孟春猶寒 thus: "If you pass through the final day of the twelfth month without a hitch, you meet up with early spring and its residual coldness—in the same way, if you smash through the barrier checkpoint of samsara, a life of chipper vitality comes back to you."

[39.2: *Quotes the words of an ancient as proof*[272]]

An ancient worthy [Baizhang] said: "If you want to understand the meaning of *buddha-nature*, you should contemplate time and origination-by-dependence."[273] This "time" is the "time" of the Golden-faced Old Master's appearing in the world to become a buddha, sitting on the thunderbolt seat, vanquishing Māra's army, turning the wheel of dharma, conveying sentient beings to the other shore of nirvana, and entering complete nirvana. This is not different at all from the "time" of the final day of the twelfth month [at the end of your life] that you, Layman Understands-Emptiness,[274] speak of in your letter. To arrive *here*, just contemplate in this way: ["The final day of the twelfth month has already arrived."] "This contemplation is called 'correct contemplation'; any contemplation that differs from this is called 'perverse contemplation.' "[275]

[39.3: *Shows the method of* gongfu[276]]

When you haven't yet differentiated perverse [contemplation] and correct [contemplation], you won't escape being subject to the changes of "time" [as in Baizhang's "time and origination-by-dependence"].[277] If you want not to be under the sway of "time," just all at once let go. In letting go, if you've

---

272. Mujaku, 394: 第二段引古語證成.

273. *Liandeng hui yao* 聯燈會要 (CBETA, X79, no. 1557, p. 64, a16–18 // Z 2B:9, p. 270, d13–15 // R136, p. 540, b13–15). Mujaku, 394, glosses *shijie yinyuan* 時節因緣 thus: "A saying for the final day of the twelfth month demonstrates the phrase *time and origination by dependence*— you should at all times know the meaning of the buddha-nature" [忠曰因臘月三十日語示時節因緣語也乃時時刻刻可識佛性義者也].

274. Mujaku, 395, glosses *Jiekong* 解空 thus: "Liu Jihao is called Layman Understands-Emptiness" [忠曰劉季高號解空居士]; and cites *Dahui Pujue chanshi nianpu* 大慧普覺禪師年譜: "Shaoxing 16/1146: The Master was fifty-eight. Layman Understands-Emptiness, Vice Minister Liu Jihao, copied by hand one section of the *Huayan Sutra* and gave it to the Master as a present" [十六年丙寅: 師五十八歲解空居士侍郎劉公季高手寫華嚴經一部施師受持] (CBETA, J01, no. A042, p. 802, c12–14).

275. Mujaku, 307, cites *Da fangguang yuanjue xiuduoluo liaoyi jing* 大方廣圓覺修多羅了義經, T842.17.920c2–3.

276. Mujaku, 395: 第三段示工夫法.

277. Mujaku, 395, glosses *sui ta shijie qianbian* 隨他時節遷變 thus: "Being controlled by the twenty-four hours of the day. The word *time* is responding to the phrase *time and origination by dependence*" [忠曰被十二時使也時節語應時節因緣語].

gotten to the state wherein there is nothing more you can let go of, don't retain even these words [i.e., "there is nothing more you can let go of"]. As usual, it'll be you, Layman Understands-Emptiness—and no one else![278]

40. Continued [Second Letter in Reply to Vice Minister Liu]

[Commentary: Mujaku says, "This letter is a demonstration in the midst of Vice Minister Liu's illness."[279] It presumably dates to Shaoxing 18/1148 when the Master was sixty. Hengzhou-exile letter.]

[40.1: *Quotes the Buddha to comfort Liu in his illness*[280]]

Our great sage the Buddha was able to empty all [unreal] characteristics, complete the wisdom of the myriad dharmas, but he was not able to extinguish karma already determined [in past births, such as your present illness].[281] How much more so in the case of run-of-the-mill common persons? You, Layman, are already a person within *this*.[282] Presumably you are constantly in this *samādhi* [i.e., the meditative concentration of knowing that karma from past births is unavoidable, and of patience in accepting it].[283]

---

278. Mujaku, 395, glosses *zhi shi Jiekong* 只是解空 thus: "Same idea as the above seasonal greeting *first month of spring—still cold*: having-awakened is identical to not-yet-awakened" [忠曰與上孟春猶寒同意悟了同未悟也].

279. Mujaku, 395: 此書蓋劉公病中所示也.

280. Mujaku, 395: 第一段引佛慰病.

281. Mujaku, 395, glosses *er bu neng ji mie dingye* 而不能即滅定業 thus: "Means: Liu's illness is also karma already determined in past births" [忠曰言病亦是定業也]; and cites *Jingde chuandeng lu* 景德傳燈錄, T2076.51.233b7–c25.

282. Mujaku, 397, glosses *ge zhong ren* 箇中人 thus: "A person with resolute confidence in the Buddha" [忠曰決定信佛人也].

283. Mujaku, 397, glosses *ru shi sanmei* 入是三昧 thus: "Means: the *samādhi* of knowing that karma from past births is unavoidable, and of patience in accepting it" [忠曰謂知定業不可避而忍受之三昧也].

[40.2: *Hands over an ancient standard to enable Liu to do gongfu in the midst of illness*[284]]

In the past, there was a monk who asked an old worthy:[285] " 'The world is hot *in this way*—at what place can I evade it?' The old worthy said: 'Evade it in the charcoal fire beneath the boiling cauldron.'[286] The monk said: 'Well, in the charcoal fire beneath the boiling cauldron, how do I evade it?' The old worthy said: 'There aren't any sufferings that are going to tag along with you!' " I hope that you, Layman, in the midst of the four postures of your daily activities, will do *gongfu* in this way. You must not be neglectful of this old worthy's saying. This is my efficacious medicinal prescription:[287] if this prescription does not tally with you, and you don't hit it off with this approach, then I'm unwilling to bestow upon you an easy transmission. Just boil up a herbal decoction that is for a single moment in correspondence [with this old worthy's saying] and drink it down.[288] There is no need to administer any other decoction. If you should administer any other decoction, it will make you manic. Don't fail to pay close attention to this.

---

284. Mujaku, 397: 第二段授古則令做病中工夫.

285. Mujaku, 397, cites *Jingde chuandeng lu* 景德傳燈錄, T2076.51.364c3–10. The old worthy is Great Master Huixia Liaowu of Mt. Cao in Fuzhou (Jiangxi) 撫州曹山慧霞了悟大師, a Tang dynasty master in the Caodong line.

286. Mujaku, 397, glosses *xiang huotang yun yun* 向鑊湯云云 thus: "Evading it in the midst of the hot defilements of the burning house in the three realms is possible" [忠曰三界火宅熱惱中回避可也].

287. The medicinal prescription (*yao fang* 藥方) as a metaphor for practice goes back to virtually the beginnings of the Chan tradition. From the 680s through the first decade of the 700s a succession of the fifth patriarch Hongren's disciples of the "East Mountain School" (*Dongshan famen* 東山法門) in Qizhou 蘄州 (Hubei) were going northward and taking up residence on Mt. Song and in nearby Luoyang. This stream constitutes the formation of "Metropolitan Chan" (so-called "Northern Chan"). Metropolitan Chan people during this period compiled what might be called "Sengchou 僧稠 apocrypha," works attributed to the much earlier figure Sengchou (480–560), who had visited his master Dhyana Master Buddha at Shaolin Monastery on Mt. Song. We have three examples of this genre on a Dunhuang manuscript (Pelliot Chinese 3559) in a continuum with various Metropolitan texts. One is entitled *Dhyana Master Chou's Medicinal Prescription for Curing the Outflows* (*Chou chanshi yaofang liao youlou* 稠禪師藥方療有漏). For a photographic reproduction, see Yanagida Seizan, *Shoki zenshū shisho no kenkyū* (Kyoto: Hōzōkan, 1967), plate 16; for a transcription, see Yanagida Seizan, "*Denbōhōki* to sono sakusha," *Zengaku kenkyū* 53 (July 1963): 61–62.

288. Mujaku, 397, glosses *yong yi nian xiangying caotang xia* 用一念相應草湯下 thus: "This is the phraseology of medical books. Means: if you're not in correspondence with this *gong'an*, then this illness can't be cured" [醫書之詞也言不相應此公案則此病不可治也]; and cites *Luohu yelu* 羅湖野錄 (CBETA, X83, no. 1577, p. 395, c2–9 // Z 2B:15, p. 501, c5–12 // R142, p. 1002, a5–12).

[40.3: *Shows the merit of the (original) nature*[289]]

As for these herbs that are for a single moment in correspondence [with this old worthy's saying], there's no need to seek them in places other than [the places of daily life]. They are merely right in the midst of your four postures of daily activities—in the bright places as bright as the sun and in the dark places as dark as black lacquer. If you trust your hand to pick up [the herbs] that come [without any process of selection],[290] using the single illumination of the *original ground* [i.e., your *original face*], you won't make any mistakes. [This medicine] is capable of killing people and bringing them back to life. Therefore, the buddhas and patriarchs always employ this medicine, and, entering into the charcoal fire beneath the boiling cauldron, treat the great illness of samsara of suffering sentient beings. They are called "great doctor-kings."[291] I don't yet know whether you, Layman, have sufficient confidence in all this.

[40.4: *Concludes with "upward (towards the* great matter*)"* *and the* original allotment[292]]

If you say: "I on my own have the secret medicinal prescription that isn't transmitted from father to son [i.e., I possess the innate nature that doesn't require cultivation or study[293]], and thus I have no need of your wonderful

---

289. Mujaku, 398: 第三段示性上功德.

290. Mujaku, 398, cites *Yuanwu Foguo chanshi yulu* 圓悟佛果禪師語錄, T1997.47.778c25–26.

291. Mujaku, 399, cites *Vimalakīrti Sūtra*, T475.14.537a26–27.

292. Mujaku, 400: 第四段以向上本分結.

293. Mujaku, 400, glosses *fu zi bu chuan zhi bi fang* 父子不傳之秘方 thus: "The innate nature that doesn't involve cultivation or study is the secret medicinal prescription that isn't transmitted from father to son. It is what the *Laṅkāvatāra Sūtra* calls the *eternally abiding dharma*. Seen with this eye, the meaning is: *evading in the charcoal fire beneath the boiling cauldron* is already the way of applying an antidote and thus falls into the extreme of an effortful exploit" [忠曰本來不涉修得學得本有性是即父子不傳秘方也楞伽經所謂本住法也自此眼觀之則言回避鑊湯爐炭裡早是對治道而落功勳邊也]. The *Laṅkāvatāra Sūtra* passage runs: "The Buddha announced to Mahāmati: 'I, because of the two dharmas, speak like this. What are the two dharmas? The dharma gotten by oneself and the eternally existent dharma are called the two dharmas. Because of these two dharmas, I speak like this. What is the dharma gotten by oneself? If that *tathāgata* has obtained it, I too will obtain it.... What is the eternally abiding dharma? It is the noble path of the ancients, which is like the nature of gold or silver: the *dharmadhātu* is eternally abiding. Whether a *tathāgata* emerges in the world or not, the *dharmadhātu* eternally abides'" [佛告大慧。我因二法故作如是說。云何二法。謂緣自得法。及本住法。是名二法。因此二法故。我如是說。云何緣自得法。若

art of 'evading in the charcoal fire beneath the boiling cauldron,'" then
I look forward to your making a donation of it [to the community]!

41. In Reply to Director Li (Sibiao)

[*Commentary: Mujaku says, "This letter dates to Shaoxing 19/1149 when
the Master was sixty-one."*[294] *Hyesim says, "The main purport of the letter to
Director Li is: before you produce the single thought of 'seeking the direct-and-
quick path,' keep your eye on the* huatou.*"*[295] *Hengzhou-exile letter.*]

[41.1: *Smashing perverse views*[296]]

In the study of this Way by scholar-officials, I don't worry about their not
being clever—I only worry that they are too clever. I don't worry about
their lack of knowledge—I only worry that their knowledge is too much.
Because they are always walking one step out in front of their own consciousness,[297] they blind themselves to the cheerful and self-existent *state
of being* right under their feet. Those who hold a superior grade of perverse
views bundle together seeing, hearing, awareness, and knowledge and consider that to be a "self." They consider the sense fields of direct perception
to be the "dharma gate of the mind-ground." Those who hold an inferior
grade play with karma-consciousness and recognize a "mouth," jabbering
away with their two flapping lips, chatting about the "mystery" and "sublimity" [of the buddhadharma]. Serious cases get to the point of going daft
and composing verses on Chan cases and poems—without sticking to the
rules of poetic composition[298]—saying whatever comes into their heads

---

彼如來所得。我亦得之.... 云何本住法。謂古先聖道。如金銀等性。法界常住。若如來
出世。若不出世。法界常住。] (T670.16.498c21–499a2).

294. Mujaku, 401: 此書紹興十九年己巳師六十一歲而作.

295. Hyesim, 86: 李朗狀大旨向未起求徑要之一念前頭看話句也. Hucker, 301: *"Director
[langzhong 郎中]* of a Section or Bureau in a Ministry (*bu* 部) or in some agency of comparable status."

296. Mujaku, 401: 第一段破邪見解.

297. Mujaku, 401, glosses *xing shi qian yi bu* 行識前一步 thus: "Upon the consciousness they
erect views" [忠曰識上立見解也].

298. Mujaku, 402, glosses *bu le zi shu* 不勒字數 thus: "Means: incorrectly composing verses
on the ancients, prose comments on the ancients, *gāthā*, and *shi* poetry without adhering to
the rules" [謂妄作頌古拈古偈詩不拘法式也]; and cites *Yunwo ji tan* 雲臥紀譚 (CBETA, X86,
no. 1610, p. 675, a9–13 // Z 2B:21, p. 16, d15–p. 17, a1 // R148, p. 32, b15–p. 33, a1). *Chats from
'Crouching in the Clouds' Cottage* is an example of the genre of Chan "brush notes" (*biji* 筆記).

and pointing towards the east and gesticulating towards the west![299] Those who hold the most inferior grade [of perverse views] employ the method of "silence-as-illumination," wordlessness, and [such blather as] "empty! empty! quiescent! quiescent!" to arrive within the "ghost-cave"—all in a search for ultimate peace and joy. As for remaining perverse understandings, they're not worth discussing—you must know of them well enough.

[41.2: *Praises the words in Li's letter*[300]]

Chongmi[301] and the others have returned, and I received the letter you bestowed. When I read it, I was happy beyond words. I will not repeat the conventional formalities found in the exchange of letters. I will only, because of your brave and ferocious ambition in pursuit of the Way, get right to the kudzu-verbiage of your letter.

[41.3: *Argues that the ultimate dharma doesn't have different flavors*[302]]

[You asked about the five houses and seven lineages of Chan, but] Chan has no differences of Deshan and Linji, Fayan and Caodong.[303] It's just that Chan students do not have broad, resolute willpower,[304] and Chan masters do not have a dharma-teaching of "broad fusion" [i.e., they fail to teach the interpenetration of all phenomena/Chan schools]. Hence: [although in the beginning as an *upāya*] there are different entrances for access,[305]

---

299. Mujaku, 402, cites *Zhenzhou Linji Huizhao chanshi yulu* 鎮州臨濟慧照禪師語錄, T1985.47.500b11–12.

300. Mujaku, 402: 第二段贊書言.

301. Mujaku, 390, glosses *Mi shouzuo* 密首座 thus: "Chan Master Chongmi of Mt. Yi in Hengzhou was a successor of Dahui" [忠曰衡州伊山冲密禪師嗣大慧].

302. Mujaku, 403: 第三段論究竟法無異味.

303. Mujaku, 403, glosses *chan wu deshan zhi dong zhi yi* 禪無德山至洞之異 thus: "Li had asked about the five houses and seven lineages of Chan, and therefore there is this answer" [忠曰蓋李公問五家七宗之異來故有此答].

304. Mujaku, 404, glosses *guangda jueding zhi* 廣大決定志 thus: "As for *broad*, because students lack broad willpower, they do a slight investigation of one Chan house, and consider getting that little bit to be enough" [忠曰廣大者學者爲無廣大志少窮一家門庭得少爲足].

305. Mujaku, 404, glosses *suoru chabie* 所入差別 thus: "In the beginning entrance has differences, just as the king's city has twelve gates" [忠曰初入有差別如王城有十二門].

the lodging to which one ultimately returns [i.e., the *original allotment*] certainly has no differences whatsoever.[306]

[41.4: *Shows the* gongfu *method of the direct-and-quick path*[307]]

I am informed by your letter that you want me "to give instruction by letter in the [*gongfu* method of the] direct-and-quick path." With just this single thought "seeking instruction in the direct-and-quick path," you've already stuck your head onto a plate of glue.[308] I mustn't go on and add frost on top of snow![309] Even so, you had a question, and I can't avoid giving an answer. Please take all the sutra teachings, and the Chan *huatous* that you yourself have been keeping your eye on in the past, as well as instructions brought to your attention by other people—the joy you have acquired through their tastiness—and all-at-once fling them down. As before, know nothing of them and understand none of them. Be similar to a three-year-old child—it has consciousness, but it does not yet "understand" anything. Keep your eye on: ***before the production of the single thought of seeking the direct-and-quick path.***[310] Keep on keeping your eye on this. When you become more and more aware of the lack of any basis, and your mind is more and more unsettled, you must not slack off. *Here* is the state where you will sever the heads of a thousand sages! Most students of the Way beat a hasty retreat.

---

306. Mujaku, 404, glosses *jiujing gui su* 究竟歸宿 thus: "The *state of the original allotment* is just one, like the true hall of the imperial compound in the king's city" [忠曰本分田地唯是一如王城帝居正殿].

307. Mujaku, 404: 第四段示徑要工夫法.

308. Mujaku, 404, glosses *ci nao ru jiaopen* 刺腦入膠盆 thus: "Means: before you've generated the single thought of seeking the direct-and-quick path, it's truly the direct-and-quick path. As soon as the single thought of seeking the direct-and-quick path arises, you've already gone down a circuitous path" [言未生求徑要一念已前甚是徑要也纔求徑要一念生早是迂曲了也]; and cites *Foguo Keqin chanshi xinyao* 佛果克勤禪師心要 (CBETA, X69, no. 1357, p. 477, b14–15 // Z 2:25, p. 374, a8–9 // R120, p. 747, a8–9).

309. Mujaku, 404, glosses *bu ke geng xiang xue shang jia shuang* 不可更向雪上加霜 thus: "If, on top of the arising of the thought 'you seek the direct-and-quick path,' Dahui further says he can show the direct-and-quick path, then it's frost on top of snow" [忠曰汝求徑要念生之上大慧更言可示徑要則雪上之霜而已].

310. Note that Dahui is giving Director Li a *huatou* based on Li's own words in his question letter—sometimes Dahui created a *huatou* on the spot rather than using one pulled out of a standard/*gong'an*.

[41.5: *Speaks of what has already been accomplished and firms up his confidence*[311]**]**

If your confidence is sufficient, just keep your eye on: **before the production of the single thought of seeking instruction in the direct-and-quick path.** Keep on keeping your eye on this. If you suddenly wake up from your dream, it won't be a mishap![312] This is the getting-[awakening-] energy *gongfu* that I usually do. Because I know you have resolute willpower, I've become plastered with mud and sodden [i.e., awash in *upāya*-language]—I've taken on this terrible blunder. Beyond this there is nothing I can give you instruction in. If there were something I could give you instruction in, then it wouldn't be a "direct-and-quick path!"

42. In Reply to [Academician of the Hall for] Treasuring Culture Li (Maojia)

[*Commentary:* Mujaku says, "This letter dates to Shaoxing 18/1148 when the Master was sixty."[313] Hyesim says, "The main purport of the letter in reply to Li is: the knower who knows dimwittedness is Mr. Man-in-charge—know in this way and probe the huatou."[314] Hengzhou-exile letter.]

[42.1: *Relates that dimwittedness aids* gongfu[315]]

I have been informed by your letter that, your innate character being of a dimwitted sort, even though you diligently strive[316] to practice cultivation, you've never been able to obtain a method for transcendent awakening.

311. Mujaku, 404: 第五段說已驗做處而固其信.

312. Mujaku, 405, glosses *bu shi cha shi* 不是差事 thus: "Means: if you wake up from the dream and achieve awakening, then it's a very good thing" [言如睡夢之醒而悟去則太是好事].

313. Mujaku, 406: 此書紹興十八年戊辰師六十歲而作. Mujaku glosses *Baowen* 寶文 thus: "Scholar of the Hall for Treasuring Culture" [寶文閣學士也].

314. Hyesim, 87: 答李狀大旨能知鈍者即主人公如是知而參究也. Hucker, 370 and 253: "Hall for Treasuring Culture [*baowen ge* 寶文閣], from 1067 a palace building served by members of the Institute of Academicians (*xueshi yuan* 學士院).... assisted in the drafting and revising of imperial pronouncements and imperially sponsored compilations."

315. Mujaku, 406: 第一段述昏鈍資工夫.

316. Mujaku, 406, cites: *Mao shi* 毛詩, *Gu feng pian*谷風篇.

Some time ago I was in Shuangjing [in Zhejiang], and I replied to a question from Fu Jishen [letter #10]—it was exactly the same as your question. The knower who knows dimwittedness definitely is not dimwitted. Furthermore, what other state are you wishing for, in order to seek out transcendent awakening? Scholar-officials, in studying this Way, contrary [to common assumption], *must* rely on dull-wittedness [as a means] to gain entrance to awakening.[317] But, if they get fixated on their dull-wittedness and say, "I haven't a chance in hell," then they'll be in the clutches of the Māra of dull-wittedness!

[42.2: *Points out* Mr. Man-in-charge[318]]

With those of the usual sort of understanding, in many cases the mind that seeks awakening[319] gets ahead of them and constitutes an obstacle, so that their own true understanding cannot manifest itself. This obstacle is neither something that comes from outside oneself, nor is it something separate from oneself. *Mr. Man-in-charge*, the knower who knows dull-wittedness, is all there is. Therefore, Preceptor Ruiyan,[320] "was usually to be found in his ten-foot-square room, calling out to himself: '*Mr. Man-in-charge!*' He would also respond: 'Yes!' [He then called:] 'Be awake!' He would also respond: 'Yes!' 'In the future don't be hoodwinked by others!' He would also respond: 'Yes! Yes!'" Fortunately, from ancient times there have been models like this.

---

317. Mujaku, 406, glosses *que xu jie hundun ru* 卻須借昏鈍入 thus: "Dimwittedness—how does one rely on it? Means: keeping an eye on the *huatou*: *who is the knower who knows my dimwittedness?* Do this sort of reverse illumination. Keep on keeping your eye on the *huatou*. This is entrance into awakening by dimwittedness" [忠曰昏鈍如何借之謂看能知吾根鈍者是誰如此返照看來看去此即借昏鈍入者也].

318. Mujaku, 406: 第二段揭示主人公.

319. Mujaku, 406, glosses *duo yi qiu zhengwu zhi xin* 多以求證悟之心 thus: "Dahui is making an inference about Director Li's mind. Li thinks: I am diligently seeking awakening, but, because I am innately dimwitted, I will not attain awakening. Little does he imagine that, if he were innately clever and sought awakening, he still wouldn't attain awakening. Why? This has neither cleverness nor dimwittedness. It's just his mind's seeking for awakening that blocks the Way. If he were to stop his mind of seeking, then true understanding would manifest itself" [忠曰大慧推李寶文意彼以謂我勤求證悟性昏鈍故不得證悟也殊不知性聰明而求證悟亦不可得證悟矣其故何也曰是無聰明無昏鈍但求悟故此心障道也若歇得求心則當正知見現前而已].

320. Mujaku, 407, cites *Liandeng hui yao* 聯燈會要 (CBETA, X79, no. 1557, p. 202, b7–24 // Z 2B:9, p. 409, b18–c17 // R136, p. 817, b18–p. 818, a17).

Unreservedly[321] *here* try to rally [the *huatou*] to awareness: **What the hell is it?** This rallyer [of the *huatou*] isn't someone else—he's just this knower who knows dull-wittedness. The knower who knows dull-wittedness also isn't someone else—he's Scholar of the Hall for Treasuring Culture Li's *innate nature* and *birth year* [i.e., your own *original allotment*[322]].

[42.3: *Dahui sweeps away any traces of words and orders Li not to set his mind on lifeless words*[323]]

The preceding words are my giving medicine in response to the illness. I have had no alternative but to point out for you in brief the road to returning to the stable seat of your own home. If you affirm lifeless words and call them your true *innate nature* and *birth year*, then this will be tantamount to endorsing the existence of a "Divine Self,"[324] and there will be less and less of a connection with [your own true *innate nature*]. Therefore, Preceptor Changsha said:

> The reason the person who studies the Way doesn't know the real is because hitherto he has endorsed the existence of a "Divine [Self]" as the basis of the rebirth process for immeasurable aeons. The ignorant mistakenly call [this "Divine Self"] the *original person*.[325]

---

321. Mujaku, 407, glosses *man* 謾 thus: "Don't engage in rational understanding—don't pay any heed to this and that" [不著義理解會不管彼此也].

322. Mujaku, 407, glosses *benming yuanchen* 本命元辰 thus: "One's own birth year—a metaphor for *original allotment*" [自生年星辰也比本分].

323. Mujaku, 407: 第三段掃言語蹤令不認著.

324. Dahui seems to be alluding to the *Śūraṃgama Sūtra* (T945.19.152a14–29): "These people fall into four upside-down viewpoints. One portion is non-eternalism, one portion eternalism. The first of the four is people who view the miraculously bright mind as pervading the worlds of the ten directions, calmly taking it as an ultimate 'Divine Self.' From this they calculate that this 'Self' is an immovable congealed brightness that pervades the ten directions. All sentient beings are born and die within this 'Self Mind.' Thus, we call this 'Self Mind' 'eternalism'" [是人墜入四顛倒見。一分無常一分常論。一者是人觀妙明心遍十方界。湛然以為究竟神我。從是則計我遍十方凝明不動。一切眾生於我心中自生自死。則我心性名之為常。] (T945.19.152a14–29).

325. Mujaku, 408, cites *Jingde chuandeng lu* 景德傳燈錄, T2076.51.274b16–18. The Tang dynasty master Changsha Jingcen 長沙景岑 was a successor of Nanquan Puyuan 南泉普願.

[42.4: *Shows correct* gongfu[326]]

What I said above about relying on dull-wittedness to enter the Way is precisely this.[327] Just keep an eye on the knower who knows this dull-wittedness—when all is said and done, **what the hell is it?**[328] Just keep an eye *here*. There is no need to seek transcendent awakening. Keep on keeping an eye on [the *huatou*]. Suddenly there will be the "great laugh." Beyond this nothing more can be said.

43. In Reply to Vice Minister Xiang (Bogong)

[*Commentary: Mujaku says, "At this time Xiang was Vice Minister of the Ministry of Revenue. . . . This letter dates to Shaoxing 19/1149 when the Master was sixty-one. . . . This letter discusses the single thusness of dream and awakening."*[329] *Hengzhou-exile letter.*]

[43.1: *Briefly discusses the sage's having no dreams*[330]]

One section of your letter asked the question: "After awakening, [for the first time,] are nighttime dreaming and daytime wakefulness one?

---

326. Mujaku, 408: 第四段正示工夫.

327. Mujaku, 408, glosses *jie hundun er ru shi ye* 借昏鈍而入是也 thus: "The knower who knows dimwittedness is 'recognizing spirit.' This is the root of samsara. This is an [unreal] reflection of *Mr. Man-in-charge.* The one who wants to recognize the *true original person* must first know this recognizing spirit, this root of samsara, this reflection of *Mr. Man-in-charge.* Having seen the reflections, he keeps on keeping an eye on the *huatou*, until the time arrives when he suddenly can recognize the *true original person, Mr. Man-in-charge.*" [忠曰能知根鈍者是識神是生死根本是主人公影子欲識真本來人者先須知此識神此生死根本此主人公影子已見影子看來看去一朝時節至忽然可識真本來人主人公而已]. Mujaku puts this line with the preceding section (#42.3). I have moved it to #42.4.

328. Mujaku, 408, glosses *bijing shi ge shenme* 畢竟是箇甚麼 thus: "This is the place that shows true *gongfu*" [忠曰此是正示工夫處].

329. Mujaku, 408–409: 今戶部侍郎也. . . . 此書紹興十九年己巳師六十一歲而作. . . . 忠曰此書論夢覺一如. For a biographical entry for Xiang Ziyin 向子諲 (zi Bogong 伯恭), see *Song History*, 377 (16.2966). Hucker, 427 and 258: "Vice Minister [*shilang* 侍郎] is the 2nd executive post in each of the standard Six Ministries (*liu bu* 六部) of the central government. . . . *Ministry of Revenue* [hu bu 戶部], one of the Six Ministries (*liu bu* 六部) that were the general-administration core of the central government. . . . The Ministry was in general charge of population and land censuses, assessment and collection of taxes, and storage and distribution of government revenues."

330. Mujaku, 409: 第一段畧論聖人無夢.

When one has not yet awakened, are nighttime dreaming and daytime wakefulness one?"[331] The Golden-faced Old Master said: "If you listen to dharma with a mind that grabs onto objective supports, this dharma too becomes an objective support."[332] It is said [in the *Zhuangzi*] that the "perfect person has no dreams";[333] [but this non-existence of dreams] is not the existence [of dreams during the night] and the non-existence [of dreams during the day].[334] It means that "dream" [including both night dreams and the ups-and-downs of daytime] and "non-dream" are the same.[335] When you contemplate it from this point, then in the cases of the Buddha's [night] dream of a golden drum,[336] Emperor Gaozong's [night] dream of [the able minister named] Fu Yue,[337] and Confucius's [night] dream of making offerings to the dead between two pillars[338]— you shouldn't understand them as "dreams," and you shouldn't understand them as "non-dreams."

---

331. Mujaku, 409, glosses *wu yu wei wu meng yu jue yi* 悟與未悟夢與覺一 thus: "Means: after awakening, for the first time, are nighttime dreaming and daytime wakefulness one? When one has not yet wakened, are nighttime dreaming and daytime wakefulness one? Xiang is saying: I am not yet awakened, and nighttime dreaming and daytime wakefulness are not one. I do not know whether Chan Master Dahui, at the beginning, when he was not yet awakened, had already attained the single thusness of nighttime dreaming and daytime wakefulness, or was it only after his great awakening that he attained the single thusness of nighttime dreaming and daytime wakefulness? Or is it that for Chan Master Dahui, at the beginning, when he was not yet awakened, nighttime dreaming and daytime wakefulness were different, and, after he awakened, they were still different? I want to know this, and so I ask the question" [謂悟後始夢與覺一耶未悟時夢與覺一耶之義也言某未悟而夢覺不一未知大慧禪師當初未悟時早得夢覺一如耶或大悟後方得夢覺一如耶又或大慧禪師當初未悟時夢覺別異悟後亦別異耶我欲知之故奉問也].

332. Mujaku, 409, cites *Śūraṃgama Sūtra*, T945.19.111a8–9.

333. Mujaku, 409, cites *Zhuangzi, Tai zongshi pian*太宗師篇.

334. Mujaku, 410, glosses *fei you wu zhi wu* 非有無之無 thus: "The existence of dreams during the night and non-existence of dreams during the day—it's not this sort of *no dreams*" [忠曰夢者夜中所有而日中所無非以如此之無夢].

335. Mujaku, 410, glosses *wei meng yu fei meng yi eryi* 謂夢與非夢一而已 thus: "*Dream* doesn't mean just night dreams—it means that the ups-and-downs of daytime are also dreams" [夢者非謂但夜夢謂日間七顛八倒亦是夢].

336. Mujaku, 410–411, cites *Jin guangming zuisheng wang jing* 金光明最勝王經, T665.16.411a18–413c5. In fact, it is not the Buddha, but Bodhisattva Wonderful Pennant (*Miaochuang pusa* 妙幢菩薩).

337. Mujaku, 411–412, cites *Shi ji* 史記, *Yin benji* 殷本紀.

338. Mujaku, 412, cites *Li ji* 禮記, *Tan gong shang* 檀弓上.

[43.2: *Rejects the common person's division into dream and wakefulness*[339]]

But when you contemplate the world [of the sense fields right before your eyes in your daily activities], it's still like events in a dream.[340] In the teachings [i.e., the *Śūraṃgama Sūtra*] there is a clarification of this. [The events of mundane daily activities and nighttime dreams are all] merely the [single] dream that in its entirety is phantasmal thought.[341] In spite of this sentient beings are of an upside-down viewpoint and take the sense fields right in front of their eyes during daily activities as "real." Little do they imagine that the whole thing [i.e., daily events and nighttime dreams] is a dream—within this [single day-and-night dream[342]] they again produce false discrimination and consider the fluttering about of hallucinations [that are experienced in the nighttime dream[343]] to be the "actual" dream. Little do they imagine that this is truly speaking of a dream inside a dream, an upside-down viewpoint inside an upside-down viewpoint!

[43.3: *In agreement with the Buddha's teachings Dahui extensively explains the meaning of* has no dreams[344]]

Therefore, the Buddha out of great compassion and grandmotherly kindness "enters into all the minute atoms of the provisionally-posited seas in the *dharmadhātu* and, inside atom after atom, gives the dharma teaching that everything is a dream,[345] awakening those numberless sentient beings

---

339. Mujaku, 412: 第二段斥凡夫分夢覺.

340. Mujaku, 412, glosses *que lai naizhi you ru meng zhong shi* 却來乃至猶如夢中事 thus: "*World* is the sense fields right before your eyes in your daily activities" [忠曰世間是日用目前境界者]; and cites *Śūraṃgama Sūtra*, T945.19.131a23–25.

341. Mujaku, 413, glosses *wei meng nai quan wangxiang* 唯夢乃全妄想也 thus: "The events of mundane daily activities and nighttime dreams are all merely the single dream that in its entirety is phantasmal thought" [世間日用事夜間之夢皆唯一場夢而全妄想也].

342. Mujaku, 413, glosses *yu qi zhong yun yun* 於其中云云 thus: "Common persons within this day-and-night dream of the world falsely discriminate it. They also take the nighttime dream as the 'real' dream" [忠曰凡夫於世間日夜夢中虛妄分別之還以夜夢爲實夢也].

343. Mujaku, 413, glosses *xiangxin xinian shenshi fenfei* 想心繫念神識紛飛 thus: "These eight characters describe sentient-beings' nighttime dreams" [忠曰此八字形容眾生夜夢].

344. Mujaku, 413: 第三段約佛說教廣解無夢之義.

345. Takagi, 2.22b, at *meng zizai famen* 夢自在法門 inserts: "Shows that everything is a dream" [示一切皆夢].

fixed in perversity and making them enter into the class of beings fixed in correctness [i.e., bodhisattvas[346]]."[347] This [*Huayan Sutra*] also teaches sentient beings with an upside-down viewpoint to take the "really existent" sense fields right before their eyes as provisionally-posited seas, and makes them awaken to the realization that "dream" and "non-dream" [i.e., the "really existent"] are both illusion[348]—the entirety of "dream" is "reality," the entirety of "reality" is "dream." You can't select one and discard the other. The meaning of the saying "the perfect man has no dreams" is nothing but this.

[43.4: *Relates that a question Dahui had long ago is identical to the question in the present letter*[349]]

The question that appears in your letter is a matter I too had a question about when I was thirty-six.[350] I read it and, without thinking, I got the feeling of scratching an itch. [Just as you put this question to me,] I too put this question to my former master Yuanwu. He just pointed at me, saying: "Cease! Stop this false thought! Stop this false thought!" I [compounded my error by] going on to say: "When I'm not asleep, whatever the Buddha praised, I rely on it and implement it. Whatever the Buddha condemned, I dare not transgress there. Hitherto, I have relied on you, Master, and on whatever odds and ends I have obtained from my performance of *gongfu*: When I am awake, I have obtained enjoyment from all of this. But when I'm in bed and dozing off, half-awake, I'm unable to be *Mr. Man-in-charge*. If I dream I've gotten a treasure of gold, then I'm limitlessly happy within the dream. If I dream

---

346. Hyesim, 89: "Beings fixed in correctness are bodhisattvas" [正定聚菩薩也]. For these categories, Mujaku, 415, cites *Da bore boluomi jing* 大般若波羅蜜多經, T220.6.693a18–20.

347. Mujaku, 414, cites *Da fangguang fo huayan jing* 大方廣佛華嚴經, T279.10.29a5–b3.

348. Mujaku, 415, glosses *ling wu meng yu fei meng xi jie shi huan* 令悟夢與非夢悉皆是幻 thus: "*Non-dream* means the above *really existent*. In sentient beings, it is daily activities that create karma. In sages, it is the direct perception of self-mind. *Are both illusion* means cannot be understood as either existent or non-existent and so said to be "illusion" [*māyā*] [忠曰非夢者言上實有耳在眾生則日用作業在聖人則自心現量也皆幻者不可作有無會故言幻也].

349. Mujaku, 416: 第四段敘昔我疑全同今來疑.

350. Mujaku, 416, glosses *mou sanshiliu sui shi* 某三十六歲時 thus: "In the following year, Xuanhe 7/1125, when the Master was thirty-seven, he connected with Tianning Monastery [in Zhejiang] and for the first time met Yuanwu Keqin" [明年七年乙巳師三十七歲挂搭天寧初見圓悟]. See *Dahui Pujue chanshi nianpu* 大慧普覺禪師年譜 (CBETA, J01, no. A042, p. 796, c8–10).

that I am being menaced by someone with a sword or staff, and I'm at the mercy of negative perceptions, then I'm fearful and terrified within the dream. I reflect: this body of mine is still in good health, and it's only when sleeping that I'm incapable of being *Mr. Man-in-charge*. How much worse will this be when the [four component elements of] earth, water, fire, and wind [of my physical body] are splitting apart in a blaze of suffering—[at death] how could I not be pulled into [further suffering in samsara]?" At that point I was starting to panic! My former master [Yuanwu] also said: "When this huge amount of false thought you are speaking has disappeared, you will have arrived at the state of the constant unity of being awake and being asleep." Upon first hearing [Yuanwu's command to stop engaging in false thought], I didn't yet believe it [was false thought]. Every day I looked at myself—being awake and being asleep were clearly bifurcated. How could I dare to speak Chan with a voice of self-importance? Only if the Buddha's speaking of "the constant unity of being awake and being asleep" was a lie would there be no need to eliminate my illness [of separating being awake and being asleep into two parts]. Buddha-word, in fact, doesn't deceive people, and so I was still of incomplete understanding. Later, when I heard my former master [Yuanwu] raise [the standard] "the place of the emergence of all the buddhas is: *there is a warm breeze from the southeast;/ (the pavilion has a slight coolness)*,"[351] suddenly I rid

---

351. Mujaku, 418, glosses *xun feng zi nan lai* 薰風自南來 thus: "Originally it is a line from a poem by Liu Gongquan" [本是唐柳公權句]. A couplet from a Tang-dynasty linked-verse quatrain precipitated Dahui's awakening under Yuanwu. The *Dahui Pujue chanshi nianpu* 大慧普覺禪師年譜 says: "The Master was thirty-seven.... Chan Master Yuanwu ascended the seat and raised: A monk asked Yunmen: 'What is the place of the emergence of all the buddhas?' Yunmen said: 'East Mountain walks on water.' If it were me, I wouldn't give that answer. If asked 'what is the place of the emergence of all the buddhas,' I would answer: 'There is a warm breeze from the southeast—the pavilion has a slight coolness.' Suddenly Dahui cut off 'before' and 'after'" [師三十七歲....圜悟禪師陞座舉僧問雲門如何是諸佛出身處門云東山水上行若是天寧即不然如何是諸佛出身處薰風自南來殿閣生微涼向這裏忽然前後際斷] (CBETA, J01, no. A042, p. 796, c9–13). Liu Gongquan was a Tang scholar (ninth century) known as an expert in the classics and calligraphy. The quatrain *Linked Verse on a Summer Day* (*Xiari lianju* 夏日聯句) is: "People are all suffering from the blazing heat; /But I love the long summer days./ There is a warm breeze from the southeast; /The pavilion has a slight coolness" [人皆苦炎熱。我愛夏日長。薰風自南來。殿閣生微涼]. The description runs: "On a summer day in Kaicheng 3/838 the emperor Wenzong was composing linked verse with scholars." The first couplet is by the Emperor, the second by Liu. See *Quan Tangshi*, (Beijing: Zhonghua shuju, 1979), 1.4.49.

myself of the thing blocking up my chest.[352] Thereupon I knew that the Golden-faced Old Master's words [in the *Huayan Sutra* quoted above] were truth-words, reality-words, thusness-words; not deceiving words, not lies—that he did not deceive people and was truly the one of great compassion. Even if I were to pulverize my body and lose my life, I could not repay him. The thing blocking up my chest having already been eliminated, I then understood *dreaming time is waking time*[353] *and waking time is dreaming time* as the meaning of the Buddha's saying "the constant unity of being awake and being asleep." Then for the first time I understood that this reasoning cannot be taken out and presented to people, cannot be spoken to people, that it's like a sense object in a dream, which cannot be seized and cannot be discarded. I received your inquiry about whether, for me, there was a difference or not between before I awakened and after I awakened; and, without thinking, I've made a written confession according to the facts. When I read your letter closely, every word was extremely sincere. It wasn't "Chan repartee," nor was it a case of your doing a cross-examination of me. Therefore, I couldn't avoid spitting out the story of the same question I had long ago.

[43.5: *Shows the* gongfu *of dream and wakefulness are one thusness*[354]]

I hope, as an experiment, you will unreservedly rally to awareness Old Layman Pang's words: ***Vow to empty the existent. Don't reify the non-existent.***[355] First forge an understanding that the sense fields right in front of your eyes in daily activities are the dream, and afterwards shift the events in the [nighttime] dreaming onto [the dream] right in front of your eyes[356]—then the Buddha's

---

352. Mujaku, 357, glosses *chuqu ai ying zhi wu* 除去礙膺之物 thus: "Means: the ball of uncertainty" [又曰礙膺者梗胸也言疑團也].

353. Mujaku, 418, glosses *meng shi bianshi wu shi de* 夢時便是寤時底 thus: "*Waking time is* the above *non-dream; non-dream is reality*" [忠曰寤時者上所謂非夢也非夢者實也].

354. Mujaku, 419: 第五段示夢覺一如工夫.

355. *Pang jushi yulu* 龐居士語錄 (CBETA, X69, no. 1336, p. 134, b8–14 // Z 2:25, p. 31, b8–14 // R120, p. 61, b8–14).

356. Korean Anonymous, 145: "'First forge....' is Old Pang's first line; 'shift dreaming....' is Old Pang's second line" [先以目前云云老龐上句却將夢中云云老龐下句].

golden drum, Gaozong's Fu Yue, and Confucius's making offerings to the dead between two pillars will definitely not have been dreams!

44. In Reply to Instructor Chen (Fuxiang)

[*Commentary: Mujaku says, "This letter dates to Shaoxing 15/1145 when the Master was fifty-seven."*[357] *Hyesim says, "The main purport of the letter in reply to Chen is do gongfu without falling into perverse views."*[358] *Hengzhou-exile letter.*]

[44.1: *Laments the flourishing of perverse teachings*[359]]

The decline of this Way has never been as bad as it is today—the discourses on dharma of perverse teachers are as numerous as the seed-clusters of the *akṣa* tree.[360] Each and every one of these teachers claims to have attained the unsurpassed Way. They all chant their perverse teachings, deluding idiotic common persons through the art of sleight of hand.[361]

[44.2: *Smashes the perverse and repays the virtue of the buddhas and patriarchs*[362]]

Therefore, I am always gnashing my teeth over this [deluding of common persons]. Not begrudging my life,[363] I want to support [this Way], want

---

357. Mujaku, 420: 此書紹興十五年乙丑師五十七歲而作.

358. Hyesim, 90: 答陳狀大旨不落邪見而做工也. Chen has no biography in *Song History*. Hucker, 142: "*Instructor* [*jiaoshou* 教授] is a title with many uses, most commonly for the heads of Confucian Schools (*ruxue* 儒學) at the Prefecture (*zhou* 州, *fu* 府) level; always low-ranking or unranked."

359. Mujaku, 420: 第一段悲嘆邪説盛.

360. Mujaku, 420, glosses *echa ju* 惡叉聚 thus: "Numerous" [忠曰多也]; and cites *Śūraṃgama Sūtra*: "The Buddha said to Ananda: 'All sentient beings from beginningless time have all sorts of upside-down viewpoints. Karmic seeds naturally are like clusters of *akṣa* seeds. Practitioners who are incapable of attaining unexcelled awakening—including hearers and independent buddhas—become Outsider-Way Heavenly Māra Kings and their retinue'" [佛告阿難一切眾生。從無始來種種顛倒。業種自然如惡叉聚。諸修行人不能得成無上菩提。乃至別成聲聞緣覺。及成外道諸天魔王及魔眷屬。] (T945.19.108b28–c2). The seeds of this tree (*eleocarpus ganitrus*) form in triplets and fall in clusters. They are used to make mindfulness beads (*nianzhu* 念珠).

361. Mujaku, 421, glosses *huan huo* 幻惑 thus: "As a magician deludes stupid people" [忠曰如幻術惑愚人也].

362. Mujaku, 421: 第二段破邪報佛祖德.

363. Mujaku, 421, cites *Lotus Sutra*, T262.9.36a4–5.

to make [all sentient beings] with their seeds of [*prajñā-*]light³⁶⁴ come to know that there is the *matter of the original allotment* of our Chan house, and I want them to escape falling into the net of perverse views. If, under my watch, just one out of ten-thousand in the sentient-being realm could avoid having his buddha-seeds extinguished, then the Golden-Faced Old Master hasn't sheltered me in vain. As is said [in the sutra:] "With this deep mind serve in numberless buddha-lands. This is called 'repaying the kindness of the buddhas.'"³⁶⁵ However, it's also a fact that I don't know the time [when I'll be able to repay the kindness of the buddhas]—my small strength is insufficient [to rectify the perverse teachings that fill the world].³⁶⁶

[44.3: *Concludes the above*³⁶⁷]

You are already someone who is within *this*, and so it would not do for me not to speak of matters within *this*. It's just that my writing brush has, without my noticing, gotten this far.

45. In Reply to Supervisor Lin (Shaozhan)

[*Commentary:* Mujaku says, "This letter dates to Shaoxing 15/1145 when the Master was fifty-seven."³⁶⁸ Hyesim says, "The main purport of the letter in reply to Lin is: make use of the sutra teachings to elucidate Chan—perform gongfu without falling into any formula."³⁶⁹ Hengzhou-exile letter.]

---

364. Mujaku, 421, glosses *guangming zhongzi* 光明種子 thus: "Means: all sentient beings. *Prajñā* light" [忠曰謂一切衆生也光明般若也].

365. Mujaku, 422, cites *Śūraṃgama Sūtra*, T945.19.119b14–16.

366. Mujaku, 423, glosses *bu zhi shi bu liang li* 不知時不量力 thus: "*Not know time* means: I am in exile, the perverse teachers are at work in the world, and at this time I can't do much. *Do not have strength* means: my small strength is insufficient to rectify the perverse teachings that fill all-under-heaven" [不知時者我配流之身邪師爲世所用是於時不可也不量力者我之少力不足以正滿天下邪説也]. Araki, 182: "At the time Dahui was in exile in Hengzhou 衡州. This reveals that his teaching activities were not going as he had hoped."

367. Mujaku, 423: 第三段結上.

368. Mujaku, 423: 此書紹興十五年乙丑師五十七歲而作.

369. Hyesim, 91: 答林狀大旨借教明宗不落規模而做工. Hucker, 364: Supervisor (of the affairs of . . . agency [*panyuan* 判院]: "signifying that an official holding a regular post was assigned on a temporary or otherwise irregular basis to take charge of an agency, sometimes his own, as a special duty assignment." Mujaku, 423: "Because Lin Shaozhan has no

[45.1: *Replies to the Lin's intention in seeking a dharma-saying from Dahui*[370]]

I am informed by your letter that you are "seeking a single word [of instruction]" from me,[371] so you can do *gongfu* together with people who have confidence in the Way. [As you mention in your letter,] you have already read the *Perfect Awakening Sutra*—in that sutra [there are many excellent words]—why stop at a single word from me?[372] [In the *Perfect Awakening* twelve] great bodhisattvas raise questions concerning their individual doubts, and Śākyamuni takes those doubts into account. He analyzes them clearly one by one, and, for the most part, the bodhisattvas understand. The *huatou* that I previously allocated you is taken from among these. The sutra says:

> At all times—no producing false thought.
> But in the midst of false thoughts—no extinguishing.
> Abiding in the sense objects of false thought—***don't add knowing***
> (*this word [of instruction] precisely!*).[373]
> But in the midst of this non-comprehension—no making the
> distinction: *the real.*[374]

When in the past I was at Yunmen Hermitage [in Quanzhou], I borrowed a verse about this sutra passage:

> The lotus leaf is perfectly round—round like a mirror;
> The water chestnut is perfectly sharp—sharp like an awl.

biographical entry in the *Song History*, we cannot know what *yuan* [Office, Bureau, Court, Academy, Institute, etc.] he supervised" [林少詹無傳不可知判何院].

370. Mujaku, 423: 第一段答求法語意.

371. Mujaku, 423, glosses *qiu yi yu* 求一語 thus: "The phrase *single word* has an indefinite referent—just a nonspecific desire seeking a word of instruction from Dahui" [忠曰一語無定所指但泛欲求大慧指示語也].

372. Mujaku, 423, glosses *jing zhong qi zhi yi yu eryi zai* 經中豈止一語而已哉 thus: "Means: you yourself [in your letter] said that you have read the *Perfect Awakening Sutra*. In this sutra, there are a lot of words—all of them are good clues to awakening. There's no need to wait for a single word from me" [忠曰言公自言看圓覺經其經中有幾多語皆是好箇入處也不待求大慧一語也].

373. Mujaku, 424, glosses *(xiayu) ci yu zui qinqie* (下語)此語最親切 thus: "Of the lines around this, only the principle of this line will clarify things for Supervisor Lin. If he rallies this [i.e., the *huatou* ***don't add knowing***] to awareness, then he can gain [awakening] energy" [前後句中獨此句義理明白林判院若提撕之則可得力]. Here the *huatou* is taken from a sutra.

374. Mujaku, 424, cites *Da fangguang yuanjue xiuduoluo liaoyi jing* 大方廣圓覺修多羅了義經, T842.17.917b9–11.

Wind blows willow catkins—the fuzzy catkins go tumbling;
Rain strikes pear tree blossoms—butterflies take flight.[375]

Just take this verse and place it on top; then take the four lines of the sutra text and align them line by line beneath the verse. The verse becomes the sutra, and the sutra becomes the verse.

[45.2: *Shows the method of* gongfu[376]]

As an experiment, just try to do *gongfu* in this way. Pay no heed to whether you are awakened or not awakened. In your mind desist from being fever-ishly busy,[377] but, at the same time, you must not be easy-going. It's like the method for tuning a stringed instrument: when the tension on the strings hits the right spot, then you can play the tune!

[45.3: *Orders Lin to seek out practice with Chongmi's party*[378]]

When you return, get close to Chongmi's party[379] and "carve and polish"[380] together with them—there will be nothing you won't be able to negotiate in your study of the Way. I very much pray [you will go practicing in the above manner].

46. *In Reply to District Magistrate Huang (Ziyu)*

[*Commentary: The date of this letter is unknown, but it is known that Dahui in Shaoxing 18/1148 at age sixty delivered a Dharma talk to Huang Ziyu.*[381]

---

375. Mujaku, 425, cites *Liandeng hui yao* 聯燈會要 (CBETA, X79, no. 1557, p. 178, c20–p. 180, c3 // Z 2B:9, p. 386, a5–p. 387, d6 // R136, p. 771, a5–p. 774, b6).

376. Mujaku, 426: 第二段示工夫法.

377. Mujaku, 426, glosses *xintou remang* 心頭熱忙 thus: "A mind that wants quick awaken-ing and therefore is in a hurry and super-busy" [今心頭熱忙者欲早悟之心急速而極忙也].

378. Mujaku, 426: 第三段令求同參.

379. For Chongmi, see letters #38.4 and #41.2.

380. Mujaku, 426, cites Mao shi 毛詩, *Weifeng qi'ao pian* 衛風淇澳篇.

381. Mujaku, 427, cites *Dahui Pujue chanshi nianpu* 大慧普覺禪師年譜 (CBETA, J01, no. A042, p. 803, a18–21).

*Hyesim says, "The main purport of the letter in reply to Huang is to stop hasti-
ness in practicing the* huatou.*"*[382] *Hengzhou-exile letter.*]

[46.1: *Points out impermanence and sighs over Huang's turning towards the Way*[383]]

I received your letter. I understand that, on behalf of this *one great matter* of origination by dependence, you are making serious effort: The actions and behavior of the *great person* should be like this. "All is impermanent and fleeting; the matter of samsara is a great one."[384] When you've wasted one day, you've canceled one day's [opportunity for cultivating] good karmic roots. Be fearful! Be fearful!

[46.2: *Discusses the fact that this Way should be studied in the prime years of life*[385]]

You are in the prime of your life.[386] Even though you are of an age when [most people] don't pay attention to good and bad in the creation of karma,[387] [it's wonderful that] you've been able to turn back to *this mind* and train for unexcelled awakening. This is what it means to be a world-class, outstandingly bright fellow. In this world of the five degenerations,[388] what "out-of-the-ordinary thing" could there be that surpasses such a kar-mic opportunity? When you are strong and healthy, quickly changing your orientation [and beginning to study the Way], compared to changing your orientation in old age, brings a million times more energy. I am delighted with you!

---

382. Hyesim, 92: 答黃狀大旨止速參話. Hucker, 158: *District Magistrate* (*zhixian* 知縣) is "the standard designation of the senior local official."

383. Mujaku, 427: 第一段示無常歎向道.

384. Mujaku, 427, cites *Liuzu dashi fabao tan jing* 六祖大師法寶壇經, T2008.48.357b29–c11.

385. Mujaku, 427: 第二段論此道盛年可學.

386. Mujaku, 427, cites *Qian Han shu* 前漢書, *Jia Yi zhuan* 賈誼傳.

387. Mujaku, 427, glosses *bu shi hao e shi* 不識好惡時 thus: "The prime of life is the period when one's physical vigor is flourishing and, in the performance of deeds, one is not cogni-zant of good/bad" [忠曰盛壯時血氣盛而作事不辨善惡也].

388. According to Robert E. Buswell Jr. and Donald S. Lopez Jr., *The Princeton Dictionary of Buddhism* (Princeton: Princeton University Press, 2014), 614, the five *turbidities* (*pañcakaṣāya*) are: degeneration of life span, degeneration of views, degeneration of defilements, degenera-tion of sentient beings, and degeneration of the aeon. During this period, a buddha does not appear in the world.

[46.3: *Warns against seeking a quick awakening*³⁸⁹]

The dharma talks that I have previously written out for you—have you been reading them over from time to time? The thing to keep in mind before anything else is that you must not activate thoughts, must not be feverishly busy, and must not want quick awakening. As soon as you enter-tain these sorts of thoughts, the road will be blocked by these thoughts, and you'll never be able to attain awakening. The patriarchal master said: "When you clutch at it and lose the standard for measuring, you will surely enter the road of perversity. When you let it go naturally, there is no substantive 'going' and 'staying.' "³⁹⁰ This is a case of the patriarchal mas-ter's "spitting out" his mind for the sake of people. Merely, in the state of expending energy in daily activity, don't say: "I need to do [such and such in expectation of awakening³⁹¹]." This gate doesn't allow for expendi-ture of energy.³⁹² I am always delivering this saying to people: "The state of gaining [awakening] energy is the state of saving on expenditure of [*gongfu*] energy; the state of saving on expenditure of [*gongfu*] energy is the state of gaining [awakening] energy." If you produce a single thought of expectation and seek the awakening state, it's no different from sitting in one's own home and asking others, "Where's my house?"

[46.4: *Urges rallying the* huatou *to awareness*³⁹³]

Just take the two words **birth-death** and paste them on the tip of your nose—you must never forget them. Constantly rally the *huatou* [**birth-death**] to awareness. Keep on rallying it to awareness. The "unripe" state will spontaneously become "ripe,"³⁹⁴ and the "ripe" state will spontane-ously become "unripe." I already wrote this saying in a letter to Way-Person

---

389. Mujaku, 428: 第三段誡求急悟.

390. Mujaku, 428, cites *Xin xin ming* 信心銘, T2010.48.376c12–13.

391. Mujaku, 428, glosses 但日用費力云云 thus: "Warns against expending energy in the expectation of awakening" [誡費力望悟].

392. Mujaku, 428, glosses *ci ge men zhong bu rong fei li* 此箇門中不容費力 by citing letter #21.2.

393. Mujaku, 428: 第四段勸提撕.

394. Mujaku, 428, glosses *sheng chu zi shu* 生處自熟 thus: "The 'unripe' *great matter* of origination by dependence gradually 'ripens,' and the 'ripe' world of the five degenerations gradually becomes 'unripe' " [忠曰生大事因緣漸熟熟五濁界事漸生].

"Empty-Characteristics."³⁹⁵ Please exchange these letters and have a read—that would be splendid!

47. In Reply to Instructor Yan (Ziqing)

[*Commentary: This letter dates to Shaoxing 15/1145 when Dahui was fifty-seven.³⁹⁶ Hyesim says, "The main purport of the letter in reply to Yan is, without stagnating in the play of unreal light-and-shadow, attain personal realization of the ground of reality."³⁹⁷ Hengzhou-exile letter.*]

[47.1: *One must not concoct an out-of-the-ordinary understanding³⁹⁸*]

Those who have really reached the stage of "no-uncertainty" are like iron ore that has been refined. For example, even if a thousand sages were to pop up and reveal innumerable superior sense objects, [at the stage of "no-uncertainty"] seeing those objects would be like not seeing them.³⁹⁹ Why would those who are at this [stage of "no-uncertainty"] be concocting any sort of "out-of-the-ordinary" or "superior" rationale?

[47.2: *Quotes a person who attained realization without concocting an out-of-the-ordinary understanding⁴⁰⁰*]

Of old, "when Yaoshan was doing Chan sitting,⁴⁰¹ Shitou asked: 'What are you doing *here*?' Yaoshan said: 'Not doing a single thing.' Shitou said: 'If *in*

---

395. Mujaku, 428, glosses *Kongxiang daoren* 空相道人 thus: "Could this be District Magistrate Huang's mother? Because she was a nun, Dahui calls her 'Way-Person'" [忠曰黃知縣之母乎爲尼故稱道人也]. There is a dharma talk for her in *Dahui Pujue chanshi pushuo* 大慧普覺禪師普說 (CBETA, M059, no. 1540, p. 966, a6–19), where she is referred to as "Way-Person Empty-Characteristics (Pure Perfection)" [示空相道人(淨圓)]. However, *Hōgo*, 383, n. 450: "Way-Person Empty-Characteristics had the taboo name *Pure Perfection* and was the wife of Huang Ziyu."

396. The dating is according to Araki, 190, and Lü and Wu, 126.

397. Hyesim, 92: 答嚴狀大旨不滯光影親證實地. Yan has no biography in *Song History*. Hucker, 142: "*Instructor [jiaoshou* 教授] is a title with many uses, most commonly for the heads of Confucian Schools (*ruxue* 儒學) at the Prefecture (*zhou* 州, *fu* 府) level; always low-ranking or unranked."

398. Mujaku, 429: 第一段要不作奇特會.

399. Mujaku, 429–430, glosses *xian wuliang shusheng jingjie yun yun* 現無量殊勝境界云云 thus: "Innumerable sense objects would not be able to move one about" [無量殊勝境界不可動轉也].

400. Mujaku, 430: 第二段引不作奇特會人證.

401. Mujaku, 430, cites *Jingde chuandeng lu* 景德傳燈錄, T2076.51.311b16–23.

that way, then it's good-for-nothing sitting.' Yaoshan said: 'If it's good-for-nothing sitting, then it's doing something.' Shitou assented to that." Look at those ancients—[never mind innumerable superior sense objects,] even a single good-for-nothing sitting wasn't able to move them at all!⁴⁰²

[47.3: *Points out perverse levels of understanding*⁴⁰³]

Today, most of the gentlemen who study the Way come to a halt at the state of "good-for-nothing sitting." In recent times, in Chan monasteries, this is what the party that "lacks the *nose*" [i.e., lacks the *original face* of the patriarchal masters⁴⁰⁴] is calling "silence-as-illumination." Also, there is a type whose heels have never touched the ground [of the truly real]. They recognize as "real" the [play of unreal] "light-and-shadow"⁴⁰⁵ [i.e., verbiage] coming from a mouth, and go wildly crazy with excitement. Unable to talk ordinary talk, they [love to] concoct [special and sublime] Chan understandings [of everything].⁴⁰⁶ This sort calls karma-consciousness the "innate nature" and "birth year." How could they talk of matters of the *original allotment*?

[47.4: *Quotes Yunmen's teaching on very subtle Chan illnesses*⁴⁰⁷]

Haven't you seen the Great Master Yunmen's saying:⁴⁰⁸

> As long as the light ray [of awakening] hasn't broken through, there are two types of illness. The first: When every place is dark, and

402. Mujaku, 430, glosses *yi ge xianzuo* 一箇閑坐 thus: "Responds to the phrase *innumerable superior sense objects*. Means: *a single* as opposed to *immeasurable* good-for-nothing sittings or as opposed to [*innumerable*] superior sense objects" [忠曰應無量殊勝境界語謂一箇反無量閑坐反殊勝境].

403. Mujaku, 430: 第三段指出邪見解.

404. Mujaku, 430, glosses *wu bikong bei* 無鼻孔輩 thus: "Fellows who have lost the *nose* of the patriarchal masters" [忠曰失却祖師鼻孔漢也].

405. Mujaku, 430, glosses *mentou hukou guangying* 門頭戶口光影 thus: "*Light-and-shadow* is what is below called 'karma-consciousness'" [光影者下所謂業識也]. ZGK, 77.313, glosses *guangying* 光影 thus: "An old commentary says: *light-and-shadow* means *has no real substance*" [古抄に云く光影は、其の實體に非ざるを謂う。].

406. Mujaku, 430, glosses *jin zuo chanhui le* 盡作禪會了 thus: "In every event and every thing they love to concoct special and sublime understandings" [忠曰事事物物愛作奇特玄妙妙解也].

407. Mujaku, 431: 第四段引雲門示微細禪病.

408. Mujaku, 431, cites *Yunmen Kuangzhen chanshi guanglu* 雲門匡真禪師廣錄, T1988. 47.558a20–25.

before you there are "things" [i.e., objects of perception[409]]. The
second: Having passed through the realization that all dharmas
are empty, indistinctly there still seems to be "a something"—this
also is the light ray's not breaking through. Also, concerning the
dharmakāya, there are two types of illness. The first: Having reached
the *dharmakāya*, because dharma-grasping has not been forgotten,
the self-view still remains, and you are sitting at the extreme edge
of the *dharmakāya*. [The second:] Even though you have passed
through the *dharmakāya*, you're not able to let go of it. When you do
a detailed examination—what living, breathing life force is there?
That is also an illness.

Those who at present are studying "the real dharma"[410] take passing through
the *dharmakāya* as the ultimate; but Yunmen, on the contrary, took it as an
illness. They don't know what they should do after having passed through
the *dharmakāya* [i.e., let go of it].[411] At *this* [stage of having let it go], it's like a
person's drinking water—he knows for himself whether it is cold or warm
and doesn't have to ask other people. If he has to ask other people, it's a
fiasco![412] Therefore, I said [in #47.1]: "Those who have really reached the
stage of 'no-uncertainty' are like iron ore that has been refined."

[47.5: *Discusses attaining the Way on one's own
without relying on others*[413]]

It's like when a person eats his fill at a meal—there is no need for him to
ask somebody else: "Am I full or not?" Of old, Huangbo asked Baizhang:

---

409. Mujaku, 432, glosses *mianqian you wu* 面前有物 thus: "*Things* are things you see, hear,
and perceive" [忠曰物是見聞覺知底也].

410. Mujaku, 434, glosses *er jin xue shifa zhe* 而今學實法者 thus: "*Those who at present are
studying 'the real dharma'* refers to the Chan stream during the end time of the dharma, the
party that considers Chan to be names and characteristics and carries out verbal transmis-
sions" [忠曰學實法者如末法禪流以禪爲名相口耳傳授之輩是].

411. Mujaku, 434, glosses *bu zhi touguo fashen le he zuomesheng* 不知透過法身了合作麼生
thus: "Means: Having passed through the *dharmakāya*, in the end, how?" [言透過法身了畢
竟如何].

412. Mujaku, 434, glosses *huoshi ye* 禍事也 thus: "If he asks other people, he hasn't yet
arrived at the stage of 'no-uncertainty'" [忠曰若問別人則爲未到不疑地].

413. Mujaku, 434: 第五段論自得道不求人.

" 'Hitherto, what dharma did the ancients reveal to people?' Baizhang merely righted his sitting posture. Huangbo said: 'What will you transmit to your descendants of later generations?'[414] Baizhang lifted up his robe, stood, and said: 'I mistakenly considered you a *person* [of power, but you talk like this[415]]!' "[416] This is a model for guiding people. Merely keep an eye on your confidence-in-something: has your confidence-in-something *state of being* been severed?[417] If your confidence-in-something *state of being* has been severed, then you naturally won't be taken in by somebody else's sweet-talking discriminations. Linji said: "If you stop the mind that rushes about seeking moment after moment, then you'll be no different from the Old Master Śākyamuni."[418] This is not [empty talk that] deceives people. The seventh-stage bodhisattva, having a mind that seeks buddha-wisdom, is not yet satisfied. Therefore, we call this [seeking buddha-wisdom] "defilement." Truly, there is no place for your "logically arranging"[419]—you must not apply even a bit of "external stuff."[420]

---

414. Mujaku, 435, glosses *houdai ersun zhi shou* 後代兒孫至授 thus: "The dangerous 'upward [towards the *great matter*]'—if you merely do it this way [as Baizhang did], what will you transmit to your descendants of later generations? How can you do without *upāya*?" [忠曰嶮 嶮向上若但如此後代兒孫以何可傳授豈無方便耶也].

415. Mujaku, 435, glosses *ru shi ge ren* 汝是箇人 thus: "I mistakenly considered you a fellow of power, but you talk like this … mm?" [忠曰我將謂汝是一箇有力量底漢然却作如 是語耶也].

416. Mujaku, 434–435, cites *Liandeng hui yao* 聯燈會要 (CBETA, X79, no. 1557, p. 67, b5–6 // Z 2B:9, p. 274, a8–9 // R136, p. 547, a8–9).

417. Mujaku, 435, glosses *zi xin de xiaoxi jue* 自信底消息絕 thus: "*Your confidence-in-something state-of-being has been severed* refers to the place wherein viewpoints have been cast off. If you are uncertain about the [play of unreal] light-and-shadow, *states-of-being* have not yet been severed—you still have the seeking mind" [忠曰消息絕者脫見地處也如疑光影耶未消息絕 也猶有求心也].

418. Mujaku, 435–436, cites *Zhenzhou Linji Huizhao chanshi yulu* 鎮州臨濟慧照禪師語錄, T1985.47.497b7–8.

419. Mujaku, 436, glosses *wu ni anpai chu* 無你安排處 thus: "Seeking buddha-wisdom is still defilement. This stage must not allow for the least seeking mind that arranges things" [忠曰 求佛智猶爲煩惱此地位不可容少分安排求心也].

420. *Shixi Xinyue chanshi yulu* 石溪心月禪師語錄: "In everyone's daily activities one after the other everything is the heavenly real, and one does not make use of 'external stuff' … yes?" [以普人日用現行。一一天真。而不假外料耶。] (CBETA, X71, no. 1405, p. 60, b21–22 // Z 2:28, p. 60, a16–17 // R123, p. 119, a16–17).

[47.6: *Cites Layman Xu's verse about sweeping away all [play of unreal] light-and-shadow*[421]]

Several years ago, there was a Layman Xu[422] who recognized as "real" [the play of unreal "light-and-shadow" verbiage coming from] a mouth and via letter presented his level of understanding: "My everyday activities are empty and spacious, without a single thing that constitutes an opposition. For the first time, I understand that the myriad dharmas of the three realms [i.e., the desire, form, and formless realms] are all from the outset non-existent—truly in joy and happiness I have put down [deluded thought]." Thereupon I showed him a verse:

Don't love purity [i.e., the *empty and spacious* of Xu's letter[423]]—
   purity makes people constricted.
Don't love happiness [i.e., the *joy and happiness* of Xu's letter]—
   happiness makes people manic.
[Respond naturally to things] like water's entrusting to the
   vessel[424]—become square or round, short or long.
Putting down and *not putting down*—please carefully reflect a bit
   further [and see whether you are, in fact, *not putting down*].
The three realms and myriad dharmas—they are not *remote*
   countryside where there is nothing else [i.e., the three realms and
   myriad dharmas are not non-existent].[425]
If the ten-thousand dharmas were merely *like that* [i.e., non-
   existent[426]]—then *this matter* would contravene reason.

---

421. Mujaku, 436: 第六段舉示許居士偈掃盡光影.

422. Mujaku, 436, glosses *Xu jushi* 許居士 thus: "Is this Administrator for Public Order Xu Shouyuan?" [許司理壽源乎]. Letters #17–18 are to this Xu.

423. Mujaku, 436, glosses *jingjie chu* 淨潔處 thus: "This is the above *empty and spacious*" [忠曰即是上空豁豁地者].

424. Mujaku, 436–437, glosses *ru shui zhi ren qi* 如水之任器 thus: "If you naturally respond to things, then purity and impurity, happiness and non-happiness—none of them can go against you" [忠曰自然應物如水之任器則淨不淨快活不快活皆不可背也].

425. Mujaku, 437, glosses *he you xiang* 何有鄉 by citing *Zhuangzi, Xiao yao you* 逍遙遊: "You, Sir, have a large tree and are troubled because it is of no use—why do you not plant it in a tract where there is nothing else, or in a wide and barren wild? There you might saunter idly by its side, or in the enjoyment of untroubled ease sleep beneath it" [今子有大樹患其無用何不樹之於無何有之鄉廣莫之野彷徨乎無爲其側逍遙乎寢臥其下].

426. Mujaku, 437, glosses *ruo zhi bian ninme* 若只便恁麼 thus: "*Like that* refers to the view that the myriad dharmas of the three realms are all from the outset non-existent" [忠曰恁麼者指三界萬法一切元無之見].

This is to inform Layman Xu—his relatives [purity and happiness] are creating a disaster.[427]

Quickly open the sagely eye—no need repeatedly to pray for the avoidance of evil spirits [i.e., just pay no heed to "purity" and "happiness"[428]].

[47.7: *Dahui relates his intention in composing this letter*[429]]

When I got up this morning it was by chance a little cool, and suddenly I remembered the time when you, friend in the Way, for the first time obtained a handhold on awakening. You were still uncertain and apprehensive about whether it was just the [play of unreal] light-and-shadow [of karma-consciousness]. Subsequently, you rallied to awareness your usual uncertainty concerning the case [i.e., the *huatou* **wu** 無]. Then, for the first time, you saw the "blunder" of the old fellow Zhaozhou [in his answer **wu** 無 to the question about whether a dog has buddha-nature]. Without being aware of it, I've let my writing brush go on with this sort of kudzu-verbiage.

48. In Reply to Vice Minister Zhang (Zishao) ["Old Vimalakīrti"]

[*Commentary: Mujaku says, "This letter dates to Shaoxing 19/1149 when the Master was sixty-one."*[430] *Hyesim says, "The main purport of the letter in reply to Zhang is: no stagnating in the 'high' view—teach all beings according to their karmic abilities."*[431] *Hengzhou-exile letter.*]

---

427. Mujaku, 437, glosses *jiaqin zuo huoyang* 家親作禍殃 thus: "Purity and happiness are also not things from without—they are relatives" [忠曰淨潔快活亦是非外物而家親也].

428. Mujaku, 437, glosses *bu xu pin daorang* 不須頻禱禳 thus: "Means: purity and happiness—just pay no heed to them" [言淨潔快活直置不管之].

429. Mujaku, 437: 第七段敍作書之意.

430. Mujaku, 439: 此書紹興十九年己巳師六十一歲而作.

431. Hyesim, 94: 答張狀大旨不滯高見隨機普接. For entries for Zhang Jiucheng 張九成 (*zi* Zishao 子韶), see *Song History*, 374 (16.2950–51) and *Cases of Song and Yuan Confucians*, 40 (2.1301–17). Hucker, 427: "Vice Minister [*shilang* 侍郎] is the 2nd executive post in each of the standard Six Ministries (*liu bu* 六部) of the central government." Huang Zongxi 黃宗羲, at the end of Zhang's entry in the *Cases of Song and Yuan Confucians* (2.1317), attaches a comment: "Zhu Xi said: 'Zhang in the beginning studied in the Guishan school [i.e., the Neo-Confucian school of Yang Shi 楊時, a student of Cheng Yi 程頤 (1033–1107)—later

[48.1: *Discusses the fact that the* Correct Dharma-Eye Depository *does include "roundabout-road" Chan*⁴³²]

You are taking the "sudden" breakthrough that you yourself attained[433] as the ultimate standard of Chan. As soon as you encounter any "wading through logical thinking" and "entering such defiled places as mud and water" for the sake of others [i.e., any participation in the language of *upāya* or skill-in-means], you immediately want to expunge it and extinguish any traces. Upon encountering my compilation entitled *Correct Dharma-Eye Depository*,[434] you immediately said: "Among the successors

---

transmitted to Zhu Xi]. Later Zhang fled Confucianism and reverted to Buddhism. Dahui Zonggao said to him: "You've already attained a handle on awakening. When you begin to teach, you should change the form but not the content. If you speak dharma according to what is appropriate and make different roads converge into one, then you will have no regrets in either the mundane or the supramundane." For this reason, Zhang's writings are all overtly Confucian, but covertly Buddhist. In his separation and reunion, his going out and entering, he strove to stupefy the eyes and ears of the whole world.' Huang Zongxi's note: 'Although Huangpu [i.e., Zhang] did gain energy in the Chan school, nevertheless, he was pure in suffering, and his sincerity was fervent—in what he maintained he never wavered. He never avoided saying he was Chan. If he had changed the form but not the content, then he would have deceived both himself and other people, and he would have lost the 'eye' of even the Chan school'" [宗羲按。朱子言.... 按黃浦雖得力于宗門。然清苦誠篤。所守不移。亦未嘗諱言其非禪也。若改頭換面。便是自欺欺人。并亦失卻宗門眼目也。]. Araki, 193: "Zhang was one of the laymen in whom Dahui placed the most fervent trust. When Zhang fell afoul of the clique of Qin Hui 秦檜 [1090–1155; execrated Song capitulationist] and was exiled, Dahui was also implicated and exiled to Hengzhou. The role that the intellectual tie connecting these two played in the development of the history of Song thought was extremely important."

432. Mujaku, 440: 第一段論正法眼藏收繞路禪.

433. Mujaku, 440, glosses *pie tuo chu* 瞥脫處 thus: "Means: quick-witted. As soon as he sees the master raise a teaching, he already understands and makes a breakthrough" [忠曰謂伶利也纔見師家舉著早會透脫也].

434. The *Zheng fayan zang* 正法眼藏 has the following line after the title: "Chan Master Jingshan Dahui Zonggao Collects and Attaches Comments (徑山大慧禪師　宗杲　集并著語 [CBETA, X67, no. 1309, p. 557, a21 // Z 2:23, p. 2, a9 // R118, p. 3, a9]). The *collection* portion consists of 661 excerpts from a large number of Chan books, the most common genre being "Instructions to the Assembly" (*shizhong* 示眾). Many (but not all) snippets are followed by Dahui's "comments" (*zhuoyu* 著語), which begin with "Miaoxi says" (*Miaoxi yue* 妙喜曰). The final excerpt is "Miaoxi's Instruction to the Assembly" (*Miaoxi shizhong yun* 妙喜示眾云). Mujaku, 440, cites *Dahui Pujue chanshi nianpu* 大慧普覺禪師年譜: "Shaoxing 17/1147, when the Master was fifty-nine: Attendants requested the Master to come up with a title to a compendium of master-student dialogues and ancient and modern sayings. The Master said: "I am dwelling in exile in Hengyang because of an offense. My door is closed to visitors, and I am introspecting for mistakes. I cannot make exertion on the outside. There are Chan monks who want to request instruction, but there is nothing I can do about giving answers to them." The Chan monks Chongmi and Huiran immediately began to copy out the text. The days and months gradually lengthened, and they produced a huge text. They

of Linji there were several masters with the title 'Hermitage Head'[435] who were of the splendidly sharp [all-at-once] karmic capacity—why aren't they included? Those such as National Teacher Zhong [a successor of the sixth patriarch] spoke a 'rational-concept Chan,' misguiding young people, and should definitely have been deleted from your compilation." Your view of the Way is thus proper; but in your dislike for National Teacher Zhong's speaking "old-grandma Chan" [i.e., employing an earnest and kind teaching style that takes a roundabout way or makes detours[436]], you're fixating on the state of purity and loving only "the single chess move, the striking of stones to make a spark, the flash of a lightning bolt" [i.e., the single road of the all-at-once temperament[437]]. Beyond this, you won't countenance even the least rational concept concerning the Way [i.e., won't countenance any "wading through logical thinking" and employing *upāya* language for the sake of others[438]]. This is truly regrettable! Therefore, I will try my level best to advocate [for National Teacher Zhong[439]]. Had not the dharma-nature [attained by National Teacher Zhong] been broad, had not the waves [of his sea of learning] been vast, had not his knowing-seeing in regards to the

---

took it to the Master and begged him to give it a title, desiring clearly to inform those of later times and to ensure that the depository of the correct dharma-eye of the buddhas and patriarchs never dies out. I [Dahui] took a look at it and said: "*Correct Dharma-Eye Depository*" [十七年丁卯師五十九歲侍者以師與衲子問答古今語句請名按題篇首云因罪居衡陽杜門循省外無所用心間有衲子請益不得已與之酬酢禪者沖密慧然隨手抄錄日月浸久成一巨軸持來乞名其題欲昭示後來使佛祖正法眼藏不滅余因目之曰正法眼藏] (CBETA, J01, no. A042, p. 802, c23–29). This passage also appears in Dahui's first comment in the *Zheng fayan zang* (CBETA, X67, no. 1309, p. 557, c2–8 // Z 2:23, p. 2, c2–8 // R118, p. 4, a2–8). The Ming edition of Wanli 44/1616 (*Zokuzōkyō*/CBETA) includes this letter #48, "In Reply to Vice Minister Zhang," at the very beginning of the collection.

435. Mujaku, 440, glosses *Linji xia you shu ge anzhu* 臨濟下有數箇菴主 by citing *Jingde chuandeng lu* 景德傳燈錄: "Chan Master Zhenzhou Linji Yixuan had twenty-two dharma successors.... Hermitage Head Tongfeng.... Hermitage Head Shanyang.... Hermitage Head Huqi.... Hermitage Head Fupen" [鎮州臨濟義玄禪師法嗣二十二人.... 桐峯菴主.... 杉洋菴主.... 虎谿菴主.... 覆盆菴主] (T2076.51.289b10–17).

436. Mujaku, 441, glosses *lao po chan* 老婆禪 thus: "A grandmother's nature is earnest, and so she speaks in a roundabout way. This is called 'old-grandma Chan'" [忠曰老婆性丁寧也故繞路說去言老婆禪也].

437. Mujaku, 441, glosses *ji shi huo shandian guang yi zhuozi* 擊石火閃電光一著子 thus: "The single road of the all-at-once temperament" [忠曰頓機一路也].

438. Mujaku, 441, glosses *bie daoli* 別道理 thus: "The *wading through logical thinking and entering such defiled places as mud and water for the sake of people* spoken of above" [忠曰上所謂涉理路入泥入水爲人底也].

439. Mujaku, 441, glosses *gu mou jin li zhuzhang* 故某盡力主張 thus: "Means: The one who helps National Master Zhong is me, Dahui" [言助援忠國師者我大慧也].

buddhadharma been extinguished, and had not his body-mind continuum
in samsara been severed, then he wouldn't have courageously and reso-
lutely, in such a sure-footed way, have entered such defiled places as mud
and water [i.e., engaged in *upāya* language] for the sake of others.

[48.2: *General discussion of the fact that responses to karmic capacities are each different*[440]]

The karmic capacities of sentient beings are each different. Therefore,
the patriarchs from ancient times established various provisional teaching methods; knowing all the various capacities of sentient beings,
they accorded with those capacities to embrace and transform beings.
Therefore, Chan Master "Big Bug" Cen of Changsha[441] had a saying: "If
I were to raise the Chan teaching in only one direction [i.e., show only
the highest teaching of Chan[442]], the grass in front of the Dharma Hall
would grow a foot deep [i.e., no one would understand, people would
disperse, and so in my empty monastery the grass would grow deep[443]],
and you would have to ask the Prior [to preach the shallow teaching[444]]."[445]
I've gone into the retail trade [i.e., I've hung out my banner and opened
up a shop to sell my wares[446]]—I'm dubbed by people a "Chan master"—
and I have to know all the various karmic capacities of sentient beings in
order to speak dharma. Things like "the single chess move, the striking
of stones to make a spark, the flash of a lightning bolt"—this sort of [all-
at-once] karmic capacity I can, of course, understand and "own." But, if

---

440. Mujaku, 441: 第二段總論應機不同.

441. Mujaku, 442, cites *Jingde chuandeng lu* 景德傳燈錄, T2076.51.273b1–2. Hunan
Changsha Jingcen 湖南長沙景岑 was a Tang master, a successor of Nanquan Puyuan
南泉普願. Yangshan Huiji 仰山慧寂 said he was rowdy like a big bug and so gave him the
nickname "Big Bug Cen" (岑大蟲).

442. Hyesim, 95: "*Raise the Chan teaching* means showing the highest teaching" [舉揚宗教
者示高勝法門]. Korean Anonymous, 148: "*Raise the Chan teaching* means outside-the-norms
Chan" [舉揚宗教格外禪也].

443. Hyesim, 95: "No one would understand, people would disperse, and so in the empty
monastery the grass would grow deep" [無人領會衆皆四散故一寺空虛而草盛也].

444. Hyesim, 95: "Ask the Prior to teach the shallow dharma" [倩人看院者示淺法].

445. Mujaku, 442, cites *Jingde chuandeng lu* 景德傳燈錄, T2076.51.274a10–13.

446. Mujaku, 442, glosses *hanghu li* 行戶裡 thus: "A Chan master's erecting a banner
pole and opening up a shop to teach people is like a merchant's selling wares in his shop"
[宗師建剎竿張門戶爲人之師家猶如市肆買物商賈然].

you employ the wrong [kind of Chan discourse] for the karmic capacity of any given being, then you will "pull his shoots up" [in trying to "help him grow"[447]].

[48.3: *Relates the main idea behind the selection process for the* Correct Dharma-Eye Depository[448]]

Of course I know the single hammer of the "sudden" breakthrough—the quick-tempered fellow who has decisively broken through.[449] [But] because [I'm trying to reach a wide variety of student capacities], in compiling my *Correct Dharma-Eye Depository* I didn't use a [rigid] classification scheme based on Chan lineages—I didn't pay attention to such distinctions as Yunmen, Linji, Caodong, Guishan-Yangshan, and Fayan[450]—I included any and all of those who merely had correct knowing-seeing that could enable people to awaken. When I looked at the two old monks National Teacher Zhong and Dazhu [a successor of Mazu], it was apparent that their Chan is equipped with a multitude of formats. Therefore, I included them in order to save beings of this particular type of karmic capacity [i.e., those whose karmic capacity is geared to step-by-step entrance via rational-concept Chan[451]]. [However,] your letter said that "[National Teacher Zhong] definitely should be deleted." I checked out your idea, and, if the *Correct Dharma-Eye Depository* were to eliminate thoroughly some Chan houses and just include your level of understanding, it would be fine—thus there would be nothing wrong with you yourself compiling a single book that aims at transforming only those of great karmic capacity. There is no need for me to accord with your idea and delete those [rational-concept Chan] masters.

---

447. Mujaku, 443, cites *Mencius, Gongsun Chou shang* 公孫丑上.

448. Mujaku, 443: 第三段述撰集之大意.

449. *Foguo Yuanwu chanshi biyan lu* 佛果圜悟禪師碧巖錄, T2003.48.201b18–19.

450. Hyesim, 95: "The writer of the letter [Zhang] upholds the dharma teachings of the Linji lineage. Dahui didn't use a classification scheme based on Chan schools. He embraced all types of karmic capacities in compiling the collection *Correct Dharma-Eye Depository*" [狀主執臨濟宗眼等法門大慧不分門類隨機普接集正法眼藏].

451. Mujaku, 444, glosses *ci yi lei genqi* 此一類根器 thus: "The karmic capacity that gradually enters via rationality" [忠曰自理致漸入之根器也]. Hyesim, 95: "*Single type of karmic capacity is middle-low capacity*" [一類根器者中下根也].

[48.4: *Smashes the idea that "old-grandma Chan" cuts off the possibility of heirs*[452]]

You say that National Teacher Zhong had no descendants because he spoke an "old-grandma Chan" plastered with mud and "sodden" [i.e., awash in *upāya*-language]. If that's the case, then how about various great old ones [who did not speak "old-grandma Chan"] such as Yantou [successor of Deshan], Muzhou [successor of Huangbo], Niaojiu [successor of Mazu], Wuye of Fenyang [successor of Mazu], Puhua of Zhenzhou [successor of Panshan Baoji, a disciple of Mazu], Advanced Seat Ding [successor of Linji], Yue of Yunfeng [successor of Dayu Shouzhi], and Yu of Fachang [Beichan Zhixian]? Despite the fact that their heirs should fill the land [according to your rationale], today their lineages are silent with no representatives—these gentlemen certainly didn't speak an "old-grandma Chan" plastered with mud and "sodden!"

[48.5: *Dahui makes a turn and smooths thing over*[453]]

Thus, I advocate National Teacher Zhong, and you eliminate him. [Advocacy and elimination] do no harm whatsoever [to the true principle[454]]!

49. In Reply to [Scholar of the Hall of] Clear Stratagems Xu (Zhishan)

[*Commentary: Mujaku says, "This letter dates to Shaoxing 16/1146 when the Master was fifty-eight."*[455] *Hyesim says, "The main purport of the letter in reply to Xu is, in the state where the eight consciousnesses cannot coalesce, practice the huatou."*[456] *Hengzhou-exile letter.*]

---

452. Mujaku, 444: 第四段破老婆禪絕兒孫之義.

453. Mujaku, 444: 第五段轉機蓋覆却.

454. Mujaku, 445, glosses *chu bu xiangfang ye* 初不相妨也 thus: "Advocacy and elimination do no harm whatsoever to the ultimately true principle. The true principle doesn't meddle in advocacy and elimination. Also, advocacy and elimination are functionings of the true principle" [忠曰言主張破除並不害畢竟真理真理不預主張破除也又主張破除是真理作用也].

455. Mujaku, 445: 此書紹興十六年丙寅師五十八歲而作.

456. Hyesim, 96: 答徐狀大旨向心意識湊泊不得處而參話. Xu has no biography in *Song History*. Mujaku, 445, gives Xu's title as *Scholar of the Hall of Clear Stratagems* (*xianmo ge xueshi* 顯謨閣學士), but this official title does not seem to appear in Hucker.

[49.1: *Relates the intention of Xu's letter*[457]]

You have frequently passed on friendly messages to me, and I surmise that it's just[458] that you want to "tame the water buffalo [of the mind of the unreal]" and "squeeze to death this monkey [of false perception[459]]."

[49.2: *Shows that Xu should not put effort into seeking for words and phrases*[460]]

This matter doesn't lie in long experience of Chan monasteries or ample face-to-face investigations with Chan teachers. The only impor-tant thing is—beneath every single word and every single phrase—to directly understand and "own" [*this matter*] and not take any detours. This reality doesn't allow even a hairsbreadth [of words and phrases].[461] Without being able to stop myself, I said "directly"—that's already hav-ing gone a circuitous way. I said "understand and 'own'"—that's already having missed. How much more of a miss is it in the case of "pulling on branches and tendrilled vines" [i.e., kudzu-verbiage], raising quota-tions from the sutra teachings, speaking of "principle and phenomena," out of a desire for the "ultimate!" An ancient worthy [Baozhi] said: "If there is only the slightest [movement of thought], it is defilement."[462] If the water buffalo has not yet been tamed and the monkey is not yet dead, even if you speak rational concepts as numberless as the sands of the Ganges River, it has not the slightest connection at all to "I" [i.e., Mr. Man-in-charge].

---

457. Mujaku, 445: 第一段述來書意.

458. Mujaku, 445–446, glosses *xiang zhi shi yun yun* 想只是云云 thus: "Xu Zhishan has not clearly asked about the Way, but has a number of times sent letters of friendly rapport to Dahui, and, therefore, Dahui surmises that Xu wants to tame the mind of the unreal and attain the true Way" [忠曰蓋徐稚山非明問道來但數數呈書于大慧相親故大慧意計之爲調伏妄心得真道而已].

459. Mujaku, 446, glosses *husunzi* 猢猻子 thus: "Metaphor for false perception" [忠曰比妄識也].

460. Mujaku, 446: 第二段示不可強求言句.

461. Mujaku, 446, glosses *jian bu rong fa* 間不容髮 thus: "Here means: this reality is not a matter of words and phrases" [忠曰今言其實非言句也].

462. Mujaku, 447, cites *Jingde chuandeng lu* 景德傳燈錄, T2076.51.450a17–21. Preceptor Baozhi 寶誌和尚 (418–514) was a thaumaturge absorbed by the Chan tradition.

[49.3: *Shows Xu that he should have confidence in his own mind and not seek to meddle*[463]]

On the other hand, speaking or not speaking are not external matters—[they are both your mind[464]]. Haven't you seen the saying of the old monk of Jiangxi [Mazu Daoyi]: "Speaking is your mind, and not speaking is your mind."[465] If you are determined to directly shoulder the load, to see the buddhas and patriarchs afresh as enemies,[466] then you will get into a little correspondence [with *this matter*]. If for long days and months you do *gongfu* in this way without producing any thought of seeking awakening, the water buffalo will tame itself and the monkey will die of its own accord. Remember this! Remember this!

[49.4: *Dahui confers on Xu his own* huatou—*shows him the method of rallying the* huatou *to awareness*[467]]

Merely, in the state where the ordinary eight consciousnesses cannot coalesce, the state where you can't seize anything, the state where you can't discard anything, keep your eye on the *huatou*: "A monk asked Yunmen: 'What sort of thing is a buddha?' Yunmen said: '**Dried turd [*ganshijue* 乾屎橛].**'" When you are keeping your eye on [this *huatou* **dried turd**], there's no need to use your usual cleverness and sharp intelligence to engage in mental reflection and conjecture. If you engage in mental reflection [on **dried turd**], you'll be 108,000 miles away [from the Way]—yet the Way is not far off![468] Grasping onto non-reflection, non-calculation, and

---

463. Mujaku, 447: 第三段示可信自心不求干也.

464. Mujaku, 447, glosses *ran shuode shuobude* 然說得說不得 thus: "Means: Speaking and not speaking are both your mind" [言說得底說不得底皆是汝心].

465. Mujaku, 447, cites *Mazu Daoyi chanshi guanglu* (*Sijia yulu* 1) 馬祖道一禪師廣錄 (四家語錄卷一) (CBETA, X69, no. 1321, p. 3, a4–6 // Z 2:24, p. 406, b16–18 // R119, p. 811, b16–18).

466. Mujaku, 447, glosses *jian fo jian zu ru sheng yuanjia* 見佛見祖如生冤家 thus: "*Like fresh enemies* has the meaning *not run around seeking on the outside*. *Sheng* is the opposite of *ripe*—it has the meaning *new*. With old enemies, the enmity weakens. With newly formed enemies, the hatred is necessarily deep" [忠曰如生冤家者向外不馳求之義生者熟之對新義也如舊冤則怨害亦可薄也新所結之冤家憎恨之必深矣].

467. Mujaku, 447: 第四段授本參示提撕之法.

468. Mujaku, 448, glosses *wei shi yuan* 未是遠 thus: "The distance from the Way is compared to 108,000 miles. 108,000 miles is still near, and, therefore, it says *not distant*" [忠曰其去道之遠較之於十萬八千里程十萬八千里猶是近故言未是遠也].

not-mental-engagement as "correct" isn't correct either. Tsk! Once more:
What the hell is it? Let's temporarily shelve these matters.

50. *In Reply to Instructor Yang (Yanhou)*

[*Commentary: Mujaku says, "The mention of Changsha at the end of the
letter indicates it was composed during exile in Hengzhou."*[469] *Hyesim says,
"The main purport of the letter in reply to Yang is: grounded in awakening—
maintain one's practice."*[470] *Hengzhou-exile letter.*]

[50.1: *Dahui praises and gives permission to Yang*[471]]

You are of an indomitable nature, but you have an inexplicable gentleness.
At a single word from me you [suddenly broke your self-pride[472]] and came
to an understanding of everything. *This matter* [of the buddhadharma] is
remarkable and outstanding. If it didn't at intervals touch off a certain
number among the indomitable ones, how could the buddhadharma have
continued down to today? Without those like you with the disposition for
prajñā, it couldn't be like this.[473] You're to be congratulated!

[50.2: *Dahui grants Yang a meeting*[474]]

I am informed by your letter that, during the spring and summer of next
year, you want to row the bottomless boat [i.e., make a boat trip to visit
me[475]], blow the holeless flute [to play the non-arising song[476]], make the

---

469. Mujaku, 448: 忠曰見書尾長沙語在衡州作.

470. Hyesim, 96: 答楊狀大旨依悟保任. Hucker, 142: "*Instructor [jiaoshou* 教授] is a title
with many uses, most commonly for the heads of Confucian Schools (*ruxue* 儒學) at the
Prefecture (*zhou* 州, *fu* 府) level; always low-ranking or unranked."

471. Mujaku, 448: 第一段贊許.

472. Mujaku, 448, glosses *zhi yi yan zhi xia yun yun* 致一言之下云云 thus: "At a single word
from me you suddenly broke your self-pride" [於我一言下忽然折我慢也].

473. Mujaku, 448–489, glosses *fei you bore genxing yun yun* 非有般若根性云云 thus: "This
praises the effectiveness attained by Instructor Yang" [忠曰此贊歎所被楊教授之得靈驗也].

474. Mujaku, 449: 第二段許會遇.

475. Mujaku, 449, glosses *zhao wudi chuan* 棹無底船 thus: "Yang's coming by boat" [忠曰蓋
楊公之來船路也]; and cites *Jingde chuandeng lu* 景德傳燈錄, T2076.51.332b12–28.

476. Mujaku, 449, glosses *chui wukong di* 吹無孔笛 thus: "Perform the non-arising
song" [忠曰奏無生曲也]; and cites *Foguo Yuanwu chanshi biyan lu* 佛果圜悟禪師碧巖錄,
T2003.48.178c21.

inexhaustible offering [of a donated meal at my hermitage[477]], talk the non-arising talk[478]—that you want to come to understand the basis that has neither beginning nor end, neither exists nor inexists. I just invite you to come [for a visit to my hermitage] and haggle with me, this faceless fellow. Certainly you won't bungle understanding *this talk* [of the basis that has neither beginning nor end, neither exists nor inexists].

[50.3: *Dahui confers a dharma-name on Yang*[479]]

Also, you require a Way-name. On the spur of the moment I'm about to contaminate *him* [i.e., *that one person* who has always been nameless[480]] by pronouncing the name "Layman *Joyous*." Therefore, the old one Zhenjing said: "The great Way of joyousness is merely right in front of you. If at the crossroads you dither, you'll remain at a standstill."[481] This is the meaning of your dharma-name.

[50.4: *Reveals his feelings about inviting Yang*[482]]

I'm just here in Changsha [in Hengzhou], and planning to stay for a while. If you should happen to get here on a later day, then my hermitage won't be so lonesome.

51. In Reply to Administrator of the Bureau of Military Affairs Lou

[*Commentary: Mujaku says, "This letter dates to Shaoxing 27/1157 when the Master was sixty-nine."*[483] *Korean Anonymous says, "The purport of this letter*

---

477. Mujaku, 449, glosses *shi wujin gong* 施無盡供 thus: "Instructor Yang says he is coming to Dahui's place to set up a vegetarian feast" [蓋楊教授言來設齋也]; and cites *Vimalakīrti Sūtra*, T475.14.552c11–17.

478. Mujaku, 449, cites *Pang jushi yulu* 龐居士語錄 (CBETA, X69, no. 1336, p. 142, a24–b1 // Z 2:25, p. 39, a18–b1 // R120, p. 77, a18–b1).

479. Mujaku, 449: 第三段授道號.

480. Mujaku, 449–450, glosses *tuhu* 塗糊 thus: "Contaminate *him*. Means: *that one person* who has always been nameless. However, right now, by giving *him* a name, Dahui is staining *that one person*" [忠曰污染之也言那一人元無名然今與號是污那一人者也].

481. Mujaku, 450, cites *Gu zunsu yulu* 古尊宿語錄 (CBETA, X68, no. 1315, p. 275, c7–8 // Z 2:23, p. 352, d5–6 // R118, p. 704, b5–6).

482. Mujaku, 450: 第四段露相招之情.

483. Mujaku, 451: 此書紹興二十七年丁丑師六十九歲而作.

to *Administrator of the Bureau of Military Affairs Lou* is: *while confronting sense objects like sounds and forms without falling into sounds and forms, practice the* huatou."484 *Post-exile letter.*]

[51.1: *Inquires about Lou's usual conduct*485]

Since we parted, in the state of responding to conditions in your daily activities, are you still being snatched up by external sense objects or not? Looking at the documents piled up on your desk, are you able to dispose of the official matters in the documents or not? When you encounter people, are you able to be flexible or not? When abiding in the state of stillness— are you free or not of the false thought [that this is "correct"486]? When you are personally investigating *this matter*, are you free of miscellaneous thoughts or not?

[51.2: *Shows that the three times are empty and still*487]

Therefore, the Golden-faced Old Master had a saying: "The mind does not falsely seize past dharmas, does not covet matters of the future, and is not fixed in [dharmas of] of the present—comprehending that the three times are all empty and still."488 Past events, whether good or bad—there is no need to reflect on them. Reflection is an obstruction to the Way. Future events—there is no need to calculate about them. Calculation is wild confusion. When events of the present arrive right in front of you, whether they go against you or go in your direction, there is no need

---

484. Korean Anonymous, 150: 樓樞蜜狀旨當聲色不落聲色而參話. For a biographical entry for Lou Zhao 樓炤 (zi Zhonghui 仲暉), see *Song History*, 380 (16.2985). Hucker, 436: "Bureau of Military Affairs [shumi yuan 樞密院] was "the paramount central government agency in control of the state's military forces."

485. Mujaku, 451: 第一段問平生行履.

486. Mujaku, 451–452, glosses *zhu jijing chu bu wangxiang fou* 住寂靜處不妄想否 thus: "There are two meanings: 1. taking abiding in the state of stillness as 'correct' is false thought; and 2. can you peacefully abide in stillness without chaotic false thought? The first meaning is superior" [忠曰有二義一曰住著寂靜處以此爲是此即是妄想也二曰能安住靜慮中而不紛然妄想也初義爲勝矣].

487. Mujaku, 452: 第二段示三世空寂.

488. Mujaku, 289, cites *Da fangguang fo huayan jing* 大方廣佛華嚴經, T279.10.156b24–26.

to "[effortfully] concentrate mind" on them. "[Effortfully] concentrating mind" will bother your mind.[489] If you just, at the time anything happens, respond according to conditions, you'll be in spontaneous union with this Way-principle.

[51.3: *Relates that it is difficult to transcend sense objects that go in your direction*[490]]

"Sense fields that go against you are easy to deal with; sense fields that go in your direction [such as wealth, status, fame, being in a scenic locale, etc.] are difficult to deal with."[491] For sense objects that go against the will of the "I," all that is needed is the single word "patience"—quiet your mind for a little bit,[492] and the sense object will have passed. As for sense objects that go in your direction—truly there's no way to evade them. [You and those sense fields] are like meeting of a magnet and piece of iron—the two of them, before you know it, fuse into one. If even inanimate things [fuse] like that, how much more so is it the case [between the self and *avidyā/ignorance*]: the self is wholly inside the activated *avidyā* and, [unawares,] is going about making its livelihood.[493] Confronting these sense objects [that go in your direction[494]], if you have no *prajñā*, without being aware and without knowing, you will get drawn by them [i.e., the sense objects] into the net. Once inside [the net], even if you want to look for an escape route, won't it be impossible? Therefore, a former noble one said: "Consorting with the mundane *is* the supramundane with nothing left over."[495] This is the Way-principle here.

---

489. Mujaku, 452, glosses *zhuo yi ze rao* 著意則擾 thus: "This kind is an extreme mistake. It does *not* mean indolently and unrestrainedly paying no attention to any and all matters" [忠曰此般甚諳訛也非謂懶放不管一切事].

490. Mujaku, 452: 第三段敘順境出離難.

491. Mujaku, 452, cites *Rentian baojian* 人天寶鑑 (CBETA, X87, no. 1612, p. 10, c14–18 // Z 2B:21, p. 58, d11–15 // R148, p. 116, b11–15).

492. Mujaku, 453, glosses 定省 thus: here *ding* means *stilling the mind*" [今定者靜心也]. Mujaku cites *Li ji* 禮記, *Qu li shang* 曲禮上.

493. Mujaku, 454, glosses *xianxing wuming quanti zai lixu zuo huoji zhe* 現行無明全身在裏許作活計者 thus: "*Whole body* means this whole body constituting the 'self' that is sunk inside of *avidyā*. It's like a person inside a dwelling making a livelihood" [全身者我此全身沒在無明之裏許如人在屋內作活計也].

494. Mujaku, 454, glosses *dang ci jingjie* 當此境界 thus: "*This* refers to sense objects that go in your direction" [忠曰此者指順境界也].

495. Mujaku, 305, cites *Gu zunsu yulu* 古尊宿語錄 (CBETA, X68, no. 1315, p. 264, a15–17 // Z 2:23, p. 341, b3–5 // R118, p. 681, b3–5). The ancient is the Linji master Yunfeng Wenyue

[51.4: *Smashes a perverse interpretation of [the* upāya-*saying]* "*the mundane is the supramundane*"[496]]

Recently there has been a type of practitioner who misses the point about *upāya*-sayings. Often they misconstrue activated *avidyā* [i.e., the active practicing of mundane lust, anger, and stupidity] as [the meaning of the ancient's *upāya*-saying] "consorting with the mundane [*is* the supramundane with nothing left over]."[497] They take [lines from certain sutras of] the supramundane dharma, [sutras that state that the poisons of *avidyā*—lust, anger, and stupidity—are identical to liberation/the supramundane], forcibly coordinate [these sutra citations], and concoct [a perverse interpretation of the *upāya*-saying] "[Consorting with the mundane *is*] the supramundane with nothing left over."[498] Isn't this pitiable? Only one who early on makes the vow [i.e., the vow "the defilements are inexhaustible—I vow to sever them"] immediately sees through [this wrong interpretation],[499] becomes a "mind-master," and doesn't get drawn in by it.

雲峰文悅 (998–1062). Mujaku, 454, glosses *xiansheng yun rude shijian yun yun* 先聖云入得世間云云 thus: "Dwelling in the midst of mundane sense objects that go in your direction and go against you, if you take *prajñā* to examine them, then you won't be turned by those that go in your direction and those that go against you. If you're not turned by sense objects going in your direction or going against you, then you are a person who, in the midst of such sense objects, directly escapes samsara. This is called 'the supramundane with nothing left over'" [忠曰住世間順逆二境中以智慧覺察之則不爲順逆所轉若不爲順逆所轉則是於順逆境中直離生死者也此名出世無餘也].

496. Mujaku, 454: 第四段破邪解世間即出世間.

497. Mujaku, 454, glosses *ren xianxing wuming yun yun* 認現行無明云云 thus: "They have a mistaken understanding of the ancient's *upāya*-saying 'consorting with the mundane *is* the supramundane with nothing left over.' They recognize practicing the three poisons of *avidyā* as the meaning of 'consorting with the mundane'" [忠曰誤解古人方便語入得世間出世無餘者以行三毒無明認爲入得世間之義].

498. Mujaku, 455, cites three sutras. *Sarvadharmāpravṛttinirdeśa* (諸法無行經): "Greed is nirvana, as are anger and stupidity" [貪欲是涅槃恚癡亦如是] (T650.15.759c13); *Ratnakūṭa* (大寶積經): "If you see a monk whose offenses are heavy, he will not fall into a hell" [若見犯重比丘不墮地獄] (T310.11.652c19); and *Vimalakīrti*: "The goddess said: 'The Buddha for the sake of highly presumptuous people preaches that divorcing from lust, anger, and stupidity is liberation. For those who are not highly presumptuous, the Buddha preaches that lust, anger, and stupidity intrinsically are liberation'" [天曰佛爲增上慢人說離婬怒癡爲解脫耳若無增上慢者佛說婬怒癡性即是解脫] (T475.14.548a16–18).

499. Mujaku, 455, glosses *chu su you shiyuan yun yun* 除夙有誓願云云 thus: "*Vow* means the vow *the defilements are inexhaustible—I vow to sever them. Seeing through* is seeing through the activated three poisons of *avidyā* that can draw the self into the karmic net" [忠曰誓願者謂煩惱無盡誓願斷之誓願也識得破者識破是現行三毒無明能引我入業綱中者也].

[51.5: *Quotes the* Vimalakīrti *to prove the highest principle*[500]]

Therefore, in the *Vimalakīrti Sūtra* there is a saying: "The Buddha for the sake of highly presumptuous people [i.e. those who are not yet fully awakened but claim to be] preaches that divorcing from lust, anger, and stupidity is liberation. For those who are not highly presumptuous, the Buddha preaches that lust, anger, and stupidity are intrinsically liberation."[501] If you can avoid this mistake [of recent practitioners who are not careful about *upaya*], and, in the midst of sense fields that go against you and go in your direction, have no arising or disappearing characteristics, only then can you be free of the label "highly presumptuous person." Only when you're like that can you "consort with the mundane." This is called "a fellow of power."

[51.6: *Dahui cites his own practice as proof, in order to encourage Lou*[502]]

Everything I've said above is something I have personally experienced in the past.[503] Right now in my daily activities I also practice just like this. I hope that you will take advantage of your strength and health to enter this *samādhi* [meditative concentration]. Beyond this, constantly rally to awareness Zhaozhou's word *wu* 無. Over a long period of time you will become well-practiced and suddenly achieve "no-mind." When you smash the pail of black lacquer,[504] that's the state of out-and-out penetration.

52. Continued [Second Letter in Reply to Administrator of the Bureau of Military Affairs Lou]

[*Commentary: Takagi says, "This letter raises the sayings of ancient worthies and at painful spots drills Lou deeply with an awl."[505] Presumably dates to around the time of letter #51, Shaoxing 27/1157. Post-exile letter.*]

---

500. Mujaku, 455: 第五段引淨名證成上理.

501. T475.14.548a16–18.

502. Mujaku, 456: 第六段引證自行勸勉.

503. Mujaku, 456, glosses *pingxi* 平昔 thus: "Means: when I was at the training stage" [忠曰謂學地時也].

504. Mujaku, 456, glosses *zhuangpo qi tong* 撞破漆桶 thus: "Here means the smashing of the ball of uncertainty" [今言疑團之破也].

505. Takagi, 2.33a: 此章擧古德痛處下深錐.

[52.1: *Sustains the idea of Lou's previous letter*[506]]

Concerning *gongfu* in the midst of daily activities, my previous letter already contained quite a bit of kudzu-verbiage. Just leave things as is—"unchanging and unmoving."[507] When things come, respond to them. Spontaneously "things and self will become a single thusness."[508]

[52.2: *Discusses apprehending on your own and knowing on your own*[509]]

An ancient worthy said: "Bold and unconstrained, he gives rein to his 'staying' and 'going'; still and mirror-like, he is awakened to the wellspring. Realization can't be shown to someone else; as for principle, if *you* don't realize it, you won't understand."[510] Realizing on your own and apprehending on your own—you can't pick up realization and present it to somebody else. Only those who have personally attained realization can reveal a little of what is right before the eyes, and then they mutually [nod their heads] in silent alignment.[511]

---

506. Mujaku, 456: 第一段成褸來意.

507. Mujaku, 456, glosses *dan zhi yi jiu bu bian bu dong* 但只依舊不變不動 thus: "The question letter from Lou may have said: 'In dealing with sense objects I am not turned—I'm naturally unchanging and unmoving. I don't know whether that is correct or incorrect.' Because this sort of question came to Dahui, in the text below he says: 'The doubt of Administrator of the Bureau of Military Affairs Lou *is* the questions of the two monks, etc.' These four characters *unchanging and unmoving* are the 'eye' of the whole letter. *Just leave things as is* is Dahui's allowing that what he has said is very good. Lou should be *unchanging and unmoving* as before" [忠曰蓋可來書云某對境不被轉自然不變不動未知是耶不是耶如此間來故下文云樓樞密疑處即是二僧問處此此不變不動四字是一篇眼目也但只依舊者許他所言甚好也可如前來不變不動也].

508. Mujaku, 456, cites *Liandeng hui yao* 聯燈會要 (CBETA, X79, no. 1557, p. 28, a20–22 // Z 2B:9, p. 235, a8–10 // R136, p. 469, a8–10).

509. Mujaku, 456: 第二段論自得自知.

510. Mujaku, 456–457, cites *Jingde chuandeng lu* 景德傳燈錄, T2076.51.459b22–c10. The quotation is from Chengguan's (澄觀; 738–839) *Huang taizi wen xinyao* 答皇太子問心要.

511. Mujaku, 457, glosses *lue lu muqian xiezi* 略露目前些子 thus: "In the case of the self-realization of comrades, by means of a few words a little of the bearing/demeanor of *this matter* is revealed, and the two nod their heads in silent alignment" [忠曰同志之自證得底以少少言句作畧露此事風規則二人默默互點頭也].

[52.3: *Teaches the method of herding the ox*[512]]

I am informed by your letter that "henceforth you will not be deceived by others and will not botch your *gongfu*." You've already got the main idea correctly; you've already caught hold of the hilt of the sword. You're like a good ox-herder who always has the rope in his hands. How could the ox [i.e., mind] then trespass on somebody else's rice paddies? [After the ox is trained, the ox-herder] abruptly releases the rope.[513] Then there's no longer any way to tug on the nostrils of the ox, and the ox meanders around in the open meadow[514] as it pleases. As the old one Ciming said, "Cast things aside in the four directions and cease trying to impede them. Not caught up in the eight directions—you will roam as you wish. Bringing [the mind] back home merely lies in pulling on the rope."[515] If [the ox/mind] is not yet trained to this degree, you should tightly grasp the rope and use *upāyas* to stabilize mind.[516] Once your submersion in *gongfu* has ripened, naturally you will no longer expend mental exertion to dam up [mind; i.e., restrict mind].

[52.4: *Shows straight-ahead* gongfu[517]]

In your *gongfu* you shouldn't be in a rush.[518] If you're in a rush, then you will be restlessly moving. You shouldn't be slack either. If you're slack, you will be gloomy and dark [i.e., in torpor]. [The teachings of the perverse teachers] "quelling delusive thought" [which leads to torpor] and "[effortfully] concentrating mind" [which leads to restlessness] are both mistakes. [*Gongfu*] is like brandishing a sword at the sky[519]—whether it reaches or not is not the issue.

---

512. Mujaku, 457: 第三段教牧牛之法.

513. Mujaku, 457, glosses *mo de fangque suotou* 驀地放却索頭 thus: "After the ox is trained it's like this" [忠曰牛純熟之後如此].

514. Mujaku, 458, cites *Foguo Yuanwu chanshi biyan lu* 佛果圜悟禪師碧巖錄, T2003.48.207b11–12.

515. Mujaku, 458, cites *Gu zunsu yulu* 古尊宿語錄 (CBETA, X68, no. 1315, p. 66, c19–20 // Z 2:23, p. 143, c1–2 // R118, p. 286, a1–2).

516. Mujaku, 458, glosses *shun mo jiang* 順摩将 thus: "Use *upāyas* to stabilize mind" [方便安定心也].

517. Mujaku, 458: 第四段示直前工夫.

518. Mujaku, 458, glosses *gongfu bu ke ji yun yun* 工夫不可急云云 thus: "When rallying to awareness the dog-has-no-buddha-nature *huatou* that I previously conferred on you" [忠曰提撕先所授狗子無佛性話時也].

519. Mujaku, 459, cites *Jingde chuandeng lu* 景德傳燈錄, T2076.51.253b8–20.

[52.5: *Dahui, according to a clause in the law code, winds up his legal case*[520]]

Of old "the honorable master Yanyang asked Zhaozhou:[521] 'What about the time when I don't bring a single thing?' Zhaozhou said: 'Put it down!' Yanyang said: 'Since I didn't bring a single thing, what am I going to put down?' Zhaozhou said: 'If you're not going to put it down, then go on shouldering it!' Yanyang immediately had a great awakening." Also, there was a monk who "asked an old worthy:[522] 'What about when a student can't do anything at all?' The old worthy said: 'I too can't do anything at all.' The monk said: 'The student is at the training stage. Therefore, he can't do anything at all. The preceptor is a great teacher. Why is it that he too can't do anything at all?' The old worthy said: 'If there were anything at all that I could do, then I'd pluck out this *can't-do-anything-at-all* of yours.' The monk immediately had a great awakening." What these two monks awakened to is precisely what you, Administrator Lou, are deluded about [i.e., have not yet awakened to]. What you, Administrator Lou, are doubtful about is precisely what the two monks were asking about.[523] "Dharmas arise from discrimination, and they also extinguish due to discrimination. When you extinguish all discriminated dharmas,[524] in these dharmas there will be no arising and extinguishing."[525]

---

520. Mujaku, 459: 第五段據欵結案.

521. This dialogue appears in Dahui's *Zheng fayan zang* 正法眼藏 (CBETA, X67, no. 1309, p. 560, c6–8 // Z 2:23, p. 5, c6–8 // R118, p. 10, a6–8).

522. Mujaku, 459, cites *Jingde chuandeng lu* 景德傳燈錄, T2076.51.329c16–21. The *can't-do-anything-at-all* answer is that of Shishuang Qingzhu (石霜慶諸; 807–888).

523. Mujaku, 459, glosses *Lou shumi yi chu jishi er seng wen chu* 樓樞密疑處即是二僧問處 thus: "Administrator of the Bureau of Military Affairs Lou entertains a doubt: in dealing with sense objects he is unchanging and unmoving—he doesn't know whether this is correct or incorrect. This is identical to Yanyang's question 'I haven't brought a single thing.... what am I going to put down?' and the monk's asking Shishuang 'what about when a student can't do anything at all?'" [忠曰樓樞密疑對境不變不動未審是耶不是耶之處正同嚴陽問一物既不將來放下箇甚麼僧問石霜云學人奈何不得時如何].

524. Mujaku, 459, glosses *mie zhu fenbie fa* 滅諸分別法 thus: "Administrator of the Bureau of Military Affairs Lou has arrived at the stage of unchanging and unmoving, but he has doubts about whether this is correct or incorrect. This is false discrimination. He must extinguish this discrimination" [忠曰樓樞密到不變不動之地却疑是耶不是耶是妄分別也須滅此分別始得].

525. Mujaku, 459, cites *Jingang sanmei jing* 金剛三昧經, T273.9.372a27–28.

[*52.6: Dahui allows that Lou's apprehending the Way is not far off and encourages him*[526]]

When I carefully examine your letter, the illness is gone, and another medical syndrome [i.e., another Chan illness] should not arise. You are extremely close [to apprehending the Way[527]]—you are even gradually saving on expenditure of [*gongfu*] energy. Please, in the state of saving on expenditure of [*gongfu*] energy, just make yourself "composed."[528] When suddenly there is a smashing like expectorating, a severing like something falling and breaking up, that's the end of it. By all means strive on!

53. *In Reply to Defender-in-Chief Cao (Gongxian)*

[*Commentary: Mujaku say, "This letter dates to Shaoxing 27/1157 when the Master was sixty-nine."*[529] *Hyesim says, "The main purport of the letter in reply to Cao is: in the state your confidence has reached, you will steal a glimpse (of becoming a buddha)."*[530] *Post-exile letter.*]

[*53.1: Dahui relates that he is old but has not abandoned teaching*[531]]

Even though the years roll on,[532] I dare not fail to exhaust my strength in fiercely promoting *this matter* to Chan monks. On some days, after the early morning meal of porridge, the ["enter-the-room"] placard is hung

---

526. Mujaku, 460: 第六段許得道不遠勉勵.

527. Mujaku, 460, glosses *da duan xiang jin* 大段相近 thus: "In the main, Lou has the air of being near to apprehending the Way" [忠曰大抵樣子近于得道也].

528. *Analects, Shu er* 述而: "The gentleman is level and composed; the small man is full of worries" [君子坦蕩蕩、小人長戚戚。].

529. Mujaku, 461: 此書紹興二十七年丁丑師六十九歲而作.

530. Hyesim, 99: 答曹狀大旨向信得及處覷捕也. For a biographical entry for Cao Xun 曹勛 (*zi* Gongxian 公顯), see *Song History*, 379 (16.2981). Hucker, 485: *Defender-in-chief* (*taiwei* 太尉) "is one of the eminent posts in the central government collectively known as the Three Dukes (*san gong*) or the Three Preceptors (*san shi*)."

531. Mujaku, 461: 第一段自叙老不廢化導.

532. Mujaku, 461, glosses *nian yun er wang* 年運而往 thus: "At the time the Master was sixty-nine. According to his *Chronological Biography*, in this year he was dwelling at Mt. Yuwang [Aśoka Monastery in coastal Zhejiang]" [忠曰時師六十九歲按年譜是年住育王].

up,[533] and, like a revolving wheel, one hundred students file through my room. Among them there are those who risk their lives by coming [like fish] to take the bait on the fishhook, and those who are lions that bite people. As for my taking pleasure in this dharma joy and *dhyāna* delight without feeling the least weariness, it is probably because I receive the sympathy of the creator of things.

[53.2: *Sighs over the depth of Cao's confidence in the Way*[534]]

You are blessed with both good fortune and wisdom. Daily you are at the side of the exalted Emperor, and you pay attention to *this great matter* of origination by dependence. Truly this is inconceivable, for as the old one Śākyamuni said: "[Two of the twenty difficulties of human life are:] the difficulty powerful people have in seeing downward; and the difficulty high-status people have in studying the Way."[535] If you hadn't over a hundred aeons and a thousand births served good teachers and deeply planted wisdom-seeds of *prajñā*, how could your confidence have reached this extent? The very extent to which this confidence has reached serves as the basis for your becoming a buddha or patriarch. I hope that, in the state your confidence has reached, you will just steal a glimpse [of becoming a buddha].[536] After a long time you will spontaneously break through.

[53.3: *Discusses the fact that the Way doesn't allow for conceptualization*[537]]

However, the one thing you absolutely must not do is "[effortfully] concentrate mind," logically arrange things, and seek a breakthrough. If you "[effortfully] concentrate mind," you'll be taking a wrong step. The old one

---

533. Mujaku, 461, glosses *bo paizi* 撥牌子 thus: "Hang up the enter-the-room placard" [忠曰撥開入室牌子也].

534. Mujaku, 463: 第二段歎信道之深.

535. Mujaku, 463, cites *Sishi'er zhang jing zhu* 四十二章經註 (CBETA, X37, no. 669, p. 662, b13–15 // Z 1:59, p. 36, b13–15 // R59, p. 71, b13–15) and comments: "Here, of the two difficulties cited, the *difficulty that those with power and high status have in studying the Way* is the crux of the matter" [今引二難中豪貴學道難爲肝要矣].

536. Mujaku, 464, glosses *qu bu* 覷捕 thus: "Grasp it and use it" [把得而用之也].

537. Mujaku, 464: 第三段論道不容思議.

Śākyamuni also said: "The Buddha Way is inconceivable—who could conceive of a buddha?"[538] Also, the Buddha asked Mañjuśrī:[539]

> "Are you in the inconceivable *samādhi?*" Mañjuśrī said: "No, World-honored one. I embody directly the inconceivable—I don't see the existence of any conceiver. Why speak of 'being in' the inconceivable *samādhi?* When I first produced the thought of awakening, I did want to enter this *samādhi.* As for [an effortful attempt at] contemplating it right now, in fact I have no thought of 'entering samādhi.' It's like someone training in archery. After long practice, he becomes skillful. Later, even though he has 'no mind' [that desires to hit the bullseye], because of his long practice, all of the arrows hit the bullseye. I too am like this. At the beginning, I trained in the inconceivable *samādhi,* binding mind to a single objective support. When long practice was completed, and I had no more thought, I was constantly in union with *samādhi.*"

The state of enjoyment of the buddhas and patriarchal masters is not something different from this quotation.

[53.4: *Rejects perverse Chan*[540]]

In recent years in the Chan monasteries there has been a type of perverse Chan. [Its proponents] close their eyes, shut their mouths and fall into silence, and produce false thought—they call this "the inconceivable matter." They also call it "the matter of [before the appearance of] Bhīṣma-garjita-svara Buddha" [i.e., the very first buddha to appear in this world] or "the matter of the aeon of nothingness before the world begins." The minute anyone opens his mouth, they call it "falling into the present." They also speak of "the fundamental matter," also calling it "pure ultimate light-comprehension."[541] They take awakening as falling into the secondary grade; they take awakening as a nonessential, like "branches and leaves." From the time they [i.e., proponents of perverse Chan] take their first step

---

538. Mujaku, 464, cites *Da fangguang fo huayan jing* 大方廣佛華嚴經, T279.10.123c9–17.

539. Mujaku, 464, cites *Da baoji jing* 大寶積經, T310.11.653c17–23.

540. Mujaku, 465: 第四段斥邪禪.

541. Mujaku, 465, cites *Śūraṃgama Sūtra*, T945.19.131a23–25.

they are mistaken, and they're not even aware it's a mistake! They take awakening as something provisionally established [as an *upāya*]. Because they themselves have had no entrance into awakening, they don't believe in the existence of an awakened person. As for this sort, we call them vilifiers of great *prajñā* and severers of the wisdom-life of the buddhas. Even if a thousand buddhas were to appear in the world, [these people] wouldn't offer to confess their transgressions! You have long possessed the eye that can assess people, so you cannot be unaware that these people deck themselves out in the lion skin [of the true dharma], but make the sound of a mere jackal.[542]

[53.5: *Relates his intention to dispatch Fakong on a special errand*[543]]

Even though you and I have not yet met face to face and had a talk, *in this mind* over many years we have silently coincided. Prior to this my answer letters have been extremely inconsistent with proper epistolary form. At present I am dispatching the Chan monk Fakong[544] on a special errand [to deliver this letter] offering my respects. Therefore, [in writing this letter] I haven't had the leisure time to enter into a *samādhi* of deep contemplation. In this way, I just trusted to my writing hand and mind, and, without being aware of it, produced kudzu-verbiage like this. I apologize for my stupidity.

54. *In Reply to Vice Minister Rong (Maoshi)*

[*Commentary: Mujaku says, "This letter dates to Shaoxing 27/1157 when the Master was sixty-nine."*[545] *Hyesim says, "The main purport of the letter in reply to Rong is: Rong in the midst of listening (to dharma) is probing (the* hua-tou*)."*[546] *Post-exile letter.*]

---

542. Mujaku, 466, cites *Zhenzhou Linji Huizhao chanshi yulu* 鎮州臨濟慧照禪師語錄, T1985.47.502b28–29.

543. Mujaku, 466: 第五段敘遣專使意.

544. Mujaku, 466, glosses *Fakong chanren* 法空禪人 thus: "There is no Fakong listed among Dahui's ninety-four dharma successors" [大慧法嗣九十四人而無法空].

545. Mujaku, 467: 此書紹興二十七年丁丑師六十九歲而作.

546. Hyesim, 100: 答榮狀大旨得閩中參究. Hucker, 427: "Vice Minister [*shilang* 侍郎] is the 2nd executive post in each of the standard Six Ministries (*liu bu* 六部) of the central government."

[54.1: *Shows Dahui's method of* gongfu[547]]

According to your letter, you are "keeping mindful and wish to investigate thoroughly *this one great matter* of origination by dependence."
Having in the past devoted effort to *this mind*,[548] it is most important
that you not be in a rush. If you're in a rush, then you'll fall behind even
more. Also, you must not be slack. If you're slack, then you'll become
negligent. It is like the method for tuning a stringed instrument. The
tension on the strings must hit the middle—only then can you play the
tune. Merely, in the state of responding to conditions in daily activities, at all times watch-for-an-opening-to-pounce: this "I," who is able
to resolve right/wrong and crooked/straight for other people, receives
whose favor and ultimately flows from what place? Keep on watching-
for-an-opening-to-pounce—the road of the past "unripe" state will spontaneously "ripen." Once the "unripe" state has "ripened," then the "ripe"
state will become "unripe."

[54.2: *Discusses the "ripe" state of the common person*[549]]

What is the "ripe" state? It is: the five aggregates, six entrances [i.e., sense
organs], twelve loci [i.e., six sense organs and six sense objects], eighteen
sense fields [i.e., the six sense organs, six sense objects, and six sense con-
sciousnesses], the twenty-five types of existence [in the three realms of
desire, form, and formlessness], ignorance, karma-consciousness,[550] the
mind that reflects and calculates—flickering day and night, like a wild
horse that never, even temporarily, stops.[551] This one section [i.e., the "ripe"
state[552]] makes people flow along in samsara, makes people commit bad
actions.

---

547. Mujaku, 467: 第一段示工夫法.

548. Mujaku, 298, glosses *ji bian ci xin* 既辨此心 thus: "Means: you have been inattentive to
mundane matters and have rallied the *huatou* to awareness" [忠曰言辨闊略世事提撕話頭
之意也].

549. Mujaku, 467: 第二段論凡夫熟處.

550. Mujaku, 469, glosses *yeshi* 業識 thus: "The eighth consciousness or *ālaya-vijñāna*"
[第八識也].

551. Mujaku, 469, cites Śūraṃgama Sūtra, T945.19.151c6.

552. Mujaku, 469, glosses *zhe yi laosuo shide ren* 遮一絡索使得人 thus: "The 'ripe' state is the
one section" [忠曰熟處一絡索也].

[54.3: *Relates the post-awakening realm*[553]]

Once this one section [i.e., the "ripe" state] has become "unripe," then awakening, nirvana, thusness, and the buddha-nature immediately become manifest. At the time of their becoming manifest, there can be no reflecting upon their manifestation. Therefore, after the ancient worthy [Preceptor Gaocheng] attained realization and understanding, he could explain the Way:[554] "When [this wondrous true nature[555]] activates the eye organ, it is like a thousand suns—of the ten-thousand images, none are left behind; when [the true nature] activates the ear organ, it is like being in a secluded valley—a big call gets a big echo, a small call a small echo." In these sorts of matters, there is no relying on seeking from another. With no reliance on the power of another, spontaneously in the state of responding to conditions, one is lively like a fish waving its tail.

[54.4: *Confers on Rong his personal practice of wu* 無, *ordering Rong to rally this* huatou *to awareness*[556]]

If you can't yet do this, just pivot this mind that reflects on mundane defilements onto the state unreachable by reflection, and, as an experiment, try to reflect. What is the state unreachable by reflection? A monk asked Zhaozhou whether even a dog has buddha-nature. Zhou said: "**Wu 無**!" This one word [**wu** 無]—no matter what tricky maneuvers you employ, I request that you try to logically arrange this *huatou* or calculate this *huatou*! You may reflect, calculate, and logically arrange, but you won't be able to find a place to put the *huatou*.[557] The time when you become aware of squirming in your belly and distress in your mind is precisely the *good time*. Next, the eighth consciousness [i.e., the storehouse consciousness] stops operating—when you become aware of this, don't let go [of the *huatou*]. Just rally this word **wu 無** awareness. Keep on rallying it to awareness—the

---

553. Mujaku, 469: 第三段敘悟後境界.

554. Mujaku, 469, cites *Chanmen zhu zushi jisong* 禪門諸祖師偈頌 (CBETA, X66, no. 1298, p. 730, c13–p. 731, a14 // Z 2:21, p. 465, b1–c8 // R116, p. 929, b1–p. 930, a8).

555. Mujaku, 469 glosses *ying yan* 應眼 thus: "Means: this wondrous true nature" [言者箇靈妙真性].

556. Mujaku. 470: 第四段授本參令提撕.

557. Mujaku, 470, glosses *dun fang* 頓放 thus: "Here means: there's nowhere you can place it" [今言無處可置也].

"unripe" state will spontaneously "ripen," and the "ripe" state will spontaneously become "unripe."

[54.5: *Raises perverse theories and demolishes them*[558]]

In recent years in the Chan monasteries there have been those who chant
perverse theories and become teaching masters. They say to students:
"Just be concerned only with 'maintaining stillness.'" Though they don't
know what sort of thing this "maintaining" is, and just who it is that's
in this "stillness," nevertheless they say "stillness is the basis." But they
have no confidence in the existence of awakening, saying that awakening
is [a nonessential like] "branches and leaves."[559] And they go on to quote
the dialogue in which a monk asks Yangshan: "'Do people today rely on
awakening?' Yangshan said: 'It's not the case that awakening doesn't
exist. However, [after having awakened, "delusion/awakening" is] falling
to a secondary level.'"[560] You must not tell a dream to an idiot, since he
will immediately understand it as "real"—meaning that [the idiots will
misunderstand the saying] "awakening is falling to a secondary level"
[and take it literally]. Little do they imagine the existence of Guishan's
words warning students—it's intensely painful! He said: "In investigating the ultimate principle take awakening as the standard."[561] [If you dispense with the gate of awakening as these perverse teachers do,] where
are you going to put this Guishan saying?[562] It can't be that Guishan said
this to mislead people of later generations, wanting to make them fall to
a secondary level!

---

558. Mujaku, 471: 第五段舉邪説斥破.

559. Mujaku, 471, glosses *wu de shi zhiye* 悟底是枝葉 thus: "Still silence-as-illumination is
the basis, and, therefore, in opposition to that, they consider awakening to be branches and
leaves" [忠曰靜底默照爲基本故對之以悟底爲枝葉也].

560. Mujaku, 471, cites *Jingde chuandeng lu* 景德傳燈錄, T2076.51.285c20–22 and glosses
thus: "Yangshan's idea is: once you've awakened in and stabilized in the *original allotment*,
and you look at the matter, then from the outset delusion [and awakening] never existed.
Hence, even awakening to the Way is an extreme of a meritorious achievement and thus a
secondary matter" [忠曰仰山意謂悟了安住本分而看則元來不迷故悟道亦是功勲邊而第二
頭也].

561. Mujaku, 473, cites *Guishan jingce zhu* 潙山警策註 (CBETA, X63, no. 1239, p. 230, c8 //
Z 2:16, p. 148, d5 // R111, p. 296, b5).

562. Mujaku, 473, glosses *ci yu you xiang shenchu zhuo* 此語又向甚處著 thus: "Means: having dispensed with the gate of awakening, there's no place to put the saying *take awakening
as the standard*" [忠曰言已掃悟門則以悟爲則之語可無安著處也].

[54.6: *Cites the warning to Defender-in-chief Cao as the model for the next section*[563]]

Audience Attendant Cao [i.e., Defender-in-chief Cao of letter #53[564]] is, like you, also keeping mindful of *this matter.* Fearing that he was being misled by perverse teachers, a while ago—just as in this letter—I blathered on in writing him. This gentleman's intelligence and level of understanding far surpass that of other people. He certainly doesn't misunderstand *upāya*-speech, taking it as "real." It's just that I've not yet had the pleasure of meeting Cao, and I secretly worry about his miscalculating [and so I'd like to warn him and enable him to avoid perverse understandings]. I've heard that you, Old Layman, are his friend in the Way. And so I've wielded my writing brush without being conscious of kudzu-verbiage. When you have leisure time from your official duties, try to visit him and ask to take a look at my letter to him. Then you will know that my expectations for him [just lie in this Way and] do not lie in meeting each other or not meeting each other.[565] He and I have an aspirational rapport. Also, it's not [a case of two of the five improper motivations for] forging a friendship: power and benefit.[566] [In my letter in reply to Cao] I wrote a single sheet, and, when that paper was exhausted, I added another sheet. I didn't have time for embellishments for the sake of outward appearance. This letter is the same way.

[54.7: *Seeing Rong's deep confidence, Dahui speaks up and makes an objection*[567]]

In my previous letter, I relied upon your being a person who has entered into *this*, and therefore I said: "You must never say: 'Having entered old

---

563. Mujaku, 473: 第六段引誡曹閣使爲次段張本.

564. Mujaku, 473, glosses *Cao heshi* 曹閣使 thus: "Defender-in-chief Cao of the previous letter" [忠曰前書曹太尉也].

565. Mujaku, 474, glosses *Miaoxi xiangqi bu zai yan de* 妙喜相期不在眼底 thus: "*Bu zai yan de* is in response to the above line *not yet had the pleasure of meeting Cao.* Means: my expectations for Defender-in-chief Cao merely lie in this Way and do not lie in the meeting each other/not meeting each other of the worldly truth" [不在眼底者應上未目擊語言與曹閣使所期但在此道不在世諦相見不相見].

566. Mujaku, 474, cites the *Guang jue jiao lun* 廣絕交論 of Liu Xiaobiao 劉孝標 of the Liang dynasty. There are five improper types of making friends (*wu jiao* 五交). These are two of them.

567. Mujaku, 475: 第七段見他深信發難發語.

age—what reason could there be [for holding office any longer—I must quickly resign and devote myself solely to the buddhadharma]?' "[568] If you were to do this, then the *good matter* right in front of you would certainly get past you! Though my writing this sort of thing may seem overly blunt, [as in the case of my relationship with Cao,] you and I *also* have a teacher-student rapport,[569] and I've *also* written what I've written without giving it a conscious thought. I am much obliged that you have sufficient confidence in me to take my words and make something of them.

[54.8: *Shows that Rong should, while holding office, complete the buddhadharma*[570]]

If you expand these dharma teachings into the state of responding to conditions in daily activities [i.e., the mundane dharma of engagement in governmental affairs[571]], with the intention of repaying the Emperor, seeking out worthies, and pacifying all-under-heaven, then truly you will not have violated his [i.e., the Emperor's] knowing [you are a talent worthy to be employed[572]]. I hope that, [even though holding office in old age entails all sorts of toil,] you will bear it.[573] If from beginning to end you act just as you

---

568. Mujaku, 475–476, glosses *qie bu ke dao laolao dada yun yun* 切不可道老老大大云云 thus: "The idea of Rong's letter was: I must quickly resign and devote myself solely to study of the buddhadharma—having entered old age, what reason could there be for holding office any longer? Therefore, Dahui warns him: I sincerely warn you not to say that, because of old age, you must take leave from office to focus exclusively on practice of the Buddha Way. Why? The mundane dharma of holding office *is* the buddhadharma. Therefore, if you do as you say, it is taking the mundane and supramundane as two separate dharmas—that's a mistake!" [蓋榮公書意謂須早致仕純一學佛法老大仕官甚無來由故大慧誡之言我懇切誠公謂不可言老大須休官專修佛道何故仕官之世間即是佛法故若如公言以世間出世間爲二法看則是蹉過].

569. Mujaku, 476, glosses *ran yi ji gan xiang tou* 然亦機感相投 thus: "The word *also* is used in reference to Audience Attendant Cao" [忠曰亦於曹閣使].

570. Mujaku, 476: 第八段示可仕官中成佛法也.

571. Mujaku, 476, glosses *riyong ying yuan* 日用應緣 thus: "Responding to conditions in daily activities is the mundane dharma" [忠曰日用應緣世法也]. Takagi, 2.37a, at *riyong ying yuan chu* 日用應緣處 inserts: "To be engaged in governmental affairs" [務政事也].

572. Mujaku, 476, glosses *bu fu qi suozhi* 不負其所知 thus: "*Knowing* refers to the Son of Heaven's knowing that this person is a talent worthy to be employed" [所知者天子知其人賢才舉用也].

573. Mujaku, 476, glosses *zhongzhong kanren* 種種堪忍 thus: "Even though in old age holding office entails toil, for the sake of the Son of Heaven you should bear all sorts of toil" [忠曰老大仕官雖可苦勞而爲天子故當堪忍種種苦勞也].

are doing today, the buddhadharma and the worldly dharma will be fused into oneness. "Sometimes plowing [i.e., studying the buddhadharma], sometimes fighting [i.e., exerting effort in the mundane dharma],"[574] over a long time you will become practiced at killing two birds with one stone. How could you not "coil 100,000 strings of cash around your waist and mount a crane to fly over to [become a Prefect in] Yangzhou"?[575]

55. *Continued [Second Letter in Reply to Vice Minister Rong]*

[*Commentary:* Hyesim says, "The main purport of this second letter is, in confronting sense objects that go against you and go in your direction, gain energy to do gongfu.[576] Presumably dates to around the time of letter #54, Shaoxing 27/1157. Post-exile letter.*

[55.1: *Urges that Rong not retire because of old age*[577]]

Your letter informs me of the censure you have received for "the bell has sounded and the graduated time-markings of the waterclock have run out" [i.e., the criticism you have taken from people for being near the end of life but not resigning from office[578]]. If, in service to the Emperor, you exhaust your sincerity above and bring peace to the common people below, there will naturally be those who "hear the strings of the instrument and praise the tone" [i.e., people who understand you will praise your loyalty and righteousness in not taking leave in spite of having reached old age[579]]. I hope you will firmly endure everything; confronting the sense objects that go against you

---

574. Mujaku, 476, cites the Han Huang 韓滉 biography in the *Jiu Tang shu* 舊唐書; and glosses: "Metaphors for studying the buddhadharma and exerting effort in the mundane dharma" [忠曰比學佛法又勤世法也]. See Liu Xu, et al., comps., *Jiu Tangshu* (Beijing: Zhonghua shuju, 1975), 79 (6.3602).

575. From the *Stories of Yin Yun (Yin Yun xiaoshuo* 殷芸小説) by Yin Yun 殷芸 of the Liang dynasty.

576. Hyesim, 101: 又狀大旨當逆順境得力做工也.

577. Mujaku, 477: 第一段勸不可以老大生退屈.

578. Mujaku, 477, glosses *zhong ming lou jin zhi ji* 鐘鳴漏盡之譏 thus: "The criticism is people of the world's criticizing Vice Minister Rong for being old but not resigning from office" [忠曰譏者世間人譏榮侍郎老而不致仕也].

579. Mujaku, 477, glosses *wen xian shang yin* 聞絃賞音 thus: "If you revere the Emperor and bring peace to the people, people who understand you will praise your loyalty and

or go in your direction—it's just perfect for applying energy!. As is said in the sutra: "With this deep mind serve in numberless buddha-lands. This is called 'repaying the kindness of the country.' "⁵⁸⁰

[55.2: *Urges that Rong should "flip" sense objects that go against him and go in his direction*⁵⁸¹]

As for your usual study of the Way, all you must do is enjoy the sense objects that go against you or go in your direction. When sense objects that go against you or go in your direction appear in front of you and you produce distress, it's exactly the same as never having exerted mind on *this* in the first place. The patriarchal master [the fourth patriarch Daoxin] said: "Sense objects are neither good [i.e., those that go in your direction] nor bad [i.e., those that go against you];⁵⁸² good and bad arise in the mind. If mind doesn't forcibly apply the names ['good' and 'bad'], where would deluded thought arise from? If deluded thought didn't arise, true mind would know everything everywhere."⁵⁸³ If, in the midst of sense objects that go against you or go in your direction, you constantly maintain this contemplation, after a long period of time you will naturally no longer produce distress. Once distress doesn't arise, then you will able to expel Māra and make him into a good spirit that protects the dharma.

[55.3: *Shows that idleness and busyness are one thusness*⁵⁸⁴]

Previously you said: "Having entered old age—what sort of reason could there be [for holding office any longer—I should quickly resign and devote myself solely to the buddhadharma]," and your words still resound in my ears. How could I forget them? [Baizhang said:] "If you want to know the

---

righteousness in not taking leave in spite of having reached old age" [奉君安民則有知音人可賞其忠義至老不休也].

580. Mujaku, 422, cites *Śūraṃgama Sūtra*, T945.19.119b14–16. Dahui has changed *repay kindness of the Buddha* (bao fo en 報佛恩) in the sutra to *repay kindness of the country* (bao guo en 報國恩).

581. Mujaku, 477: 第二段勸可轉逆順境.

582. Mujaku, 477: "*Good* and *bad* are respectively sense objects that go in your direction and sense objects that go against you" [好醜者順逆也].

583. Mujaku, 477, cites *Jingde chuandeng lu* 景德傳燈錄, T2076.51.227b1–3.

584. Mujaku, 478: 第三段示閒忙一如.

meaning of *buddha-nature*, you should contemplate time and origination-by-dependence."[585] Ten-plus years ago you had a time of idleness, but today you have the power of office in your hands, and it's a busy time. You should be mindful of: at the time of idleness, who is idle? At the time of busyness, who is busy?[586] You must have confidence that busyness time has the [buddha-nature] principle of idleness time,[587] and idleness time has the [buddha-nature] principle of busyness time.

[55.4: *Exhorts Rong to have loyalty and confidence and forget the toil*[588]]

Right in the midst of busyness you should take the sovereign's mind as your own mind—you shouldn't forget even for an instant. Police yourself, investigate yourself: How can I repay his kindness? If you constantly hold this thought in mind, then you will certainly advance forward through the hells of the boiling cauldron, charcoal fire, sword-mountain, and sword-forest. How much more so through these minuscule sense objects in front of you that go against you or go in your direction! You will be "in the groove" with this Way. Therefore, without concealing anything, I've spit out all that is in my heart!

56. In Reply to Huang (Jiefu) of the Transit Authorization Bureau

[*Commentary:* Mujaku says, "This letter dates to Shaoxing 27/1157 when the Master was sixty-nine."[589] Korean Anonymous says, "The question letter from

---

585. *Liandeng hui yao* 聯燈會要 (CBETA, X79, no. 1557, p. 64, a16–18 // Z 2B:9, p. 270, d13–15 // R136, p. 540, b13–15).

586. Mujaku, 478, glosses *xian shi shi shei xian zhi shei mang* 閑時是誰閑至誰忙 thus: "This is coming to know the meaning of *buddha-nature*" [忠曰此即可識佛性義者也].

587. Mujaku, 478, glosses *xian shi daoli* 閑時道理 thus: "Way-principle is the buddha-nature. The buddha-nature is no different in idleness and in busyness" [忠曰道理即佛性也佛性於閑於忙無異也].

588. Mujaku, 478: 第四段誠勸忠信忘勞.

589. Mujaku, 479: 此書昭興二十七年丁丑師六十九歲而作. Mujaku notes that Huang Yanjie of the Transit Authorization Bureau 門司黃彥節 is listed as one of the seventy-five dharma successors of Dahui in *Jiatai pudeng lu zong mulu* 嘉泰普燈錄總目錄 (CBETA, X79, no. 1558, p. 283, a8–b4 // Z 2B:10, p. 15, a3–b6 // R137, p. 29, a3–b6).

*Huang of the Transit Authorization Bureau had a lot of kudzu-verbiage, criti-
cizing* tathāgata *Chan/patriarchal Chan."*[590] *Post-exile letter.*]

[56.1: *Praises Huang's "twiddling around" as proper and correct*[591]]

I received your letter together with a lot of kudzu-verbiage.[592] I was
unaware that you could "twiddle around" to this degree. The fact that
your "twiddling around" is lively like a fish waving its tail is precisely
because you're one who has attained self-realization. Gratifying! Very
gratifying!

[56.2: *"Seals" Huang's realization*[593]]

If you just keep on like this, even though there will be people who say of you
that "this official is not grounded in the *original allotment* [of a Confucian
official[594]] and instead talks confusedly [about Chan teachings]," there will
be "others, people of comprehension, who will love it."[595]

[56.3: *Discusses the fact that there is no room for delusive understanding and conjecturing*[596]]

Only those who have awakened will nod their heads [at your Chan *gongfu*].
In the case of the party that [doesn't hear the original voice but just] listens

---

590. Korean Anonymous, 152: 黃門司書所來之狀許多葛藤批判如來祖師二禪也. Huang
has no biography in *Song History*. Hucker, 452–453: The Transit Authorization Bureau
(according to Mujaku, 479: *men si* 門司 = *si men* 司門) was "responsible for monitoring
traffic in and out of the gates of the dynastic capital and through all recognized gateways or
ports of entry into the empire."

591. Mujaku, 479: 第一段贊拈弄諦當.

592. Mujaku, 479, glosses *xuduo geteng* 許多葛藤 thus: "Could be verses on the ancients or
comments on cases, and so below he speaks of *twiddling around*" [忠曰可頌古或拈提類故
下文云拈弄也].

593. Mujaku, 479: 第二段印證.

594. Mujaku, 479, glosses *bu yi benfen* 不依本分 thus: "The *original allotment* of an official"
[忠曰官人本分]. Hyesim, 102: "*Not grounded in the original allotment* is the *original allotment*
of the Confucian school" [不依本分者儒家本分].

595. Mujaku, 479, cites *Jingde chuandeng lu* 景德傳燈錄, T2076.51.450a17–b23.

596. Mujaku, 479: 第三段論他語不容情解卜度.

to its echoes,[597] let's just allow them to drill tortoise shells and break tiles [i.e., engage in the useless conjectures of divination[598]].

[56.4: *Exterminates a return to the "twiddling around" of kudzu-verbiage*[599]]

Still more [twiddling around[600]]: You criticize *tathāgata* Chan/patriarchal Chan—fine, eat my stick! Now tell me: am I praising *him* [i.e. you, Mr. Huang/Huang's *Mr. Man-in-charge*[601]] or punishing *him*? Let's just allow those from all over to be in doubt for another thirty years!

57. *In Reply to District Magistrate Sun*

[*Commentary:* Mujaku says, "This letter dates to Shaoxing 28/1158 when the Master was seventy."[602] Hyesim says, "The main purport of the letter in reply to Sun is: don't slander the true dharma—carefully examine the Chan purport."[603] Post-exile letter—perhaps after Dahui was restored to the Jingshan Monastery abbotship towards the end of his life.]

---

597. Mujaku, 480, glosses *ruo shi ting xiang zhi liu* 若是聽響之流 thus: "Although they may make thousands of conjectures, they can never hit it" [忠曰雖千萬卜度必不可當也]. Hyesim, 102: "Those who listen to the echoes do not hear the original voice. Merely listening to the echoes means people who stagnate in nonessentials like branches and leaves" [聽響者不聞其本聲但聽其響言泥在枝葉人].

598. Hyesim, 102: "*Drill tortoise shells and break tiles* means the dim reflecting [and conjecturing] of divination" [鑽龜打瓦占術暗思量].

599. Mujaku, 480: 第四段剿絶再回葛藤拈弄.

600. Mujaku, 481, glosses *geng pipan zhi hao* 更批判至好 thus: "*Geng* refers to once again twiddling around. Transit Authorization Bureau Huang is doing the criticizing.... The old interpretation is that the above party that listens to the echoes is criticizing *tathāgata* Chan/patriarchal Chan. This interpretation is wrong" [更再拈弄也黃門司批判得也.... 舊解爲上聽響之流批判如來禪祖師禪之義忠曰此義非也]. Araki, 215, translates in accordance with what Mujaku calls the "old interpretation."

601. Mujaku, 481, glosses *qie dao shi shang yi fa yi* 且道是賞伊罰伊 thus: "*Him* is Transit Authorization Bureau Huang" [忠曰伊者黃門司也]. *Him* could also refer to Huang's "true person."

602. Mujaku, 481: 此書紹興二十八年戊寅師七十歲而作. Mujaku states: "Name unknown—I can find no biography" [失名傳不可考].

603. Hyesim, 104: 答孫狀大旨莫謗正法參詳禪旨. Hucker, 158: *District Magistrate (zhixian* 知縣) is "the standard designation of the senior local official."

[57.1: *Sighs in praise—indulges Sun and then snatches away the indulgence*[604]]

I received [your revised edition of the] *Vajraprajñā Sūtra* [i.e., the *Diamond Cutting Sutra*] to which you had added a commentary, and I rejoiced at reading it through one time. Among the members of the scholar-official class of recent times, ones who are as willing as you to take care with Buddhist texts are truly rare. Not apprehending the purport [of Buddhist teachings], they aren't able to have this sort of level of confidence. Not possessing the eye for reading the sutras, they aren't able to spy out the profound meanings in the sutras. You are truly like a "lotus in the midst of fire."[605] I examined it in detail for a lengthy period, but I wasn't able to be free of doubts.

[57.2: *Dahui does a demolition job on Sun's commentary*[606]]

You upbraid the translations of all the sagely masters[607] "for lacking fidelity to the original, throwing the basic truths into disarray, inflating and deleting phraseology, and ignoring the Buddha's intention." You also say: "From the first time I held and chanted [this sutra], I was awakened to the [translation] mistakes. I wanted to seek out a definitive edition and correct the mistakes, but [the various editions] had already been corrupted for a long time and were all duplicates of one another. When I got hold of an edition stored in the state library at the capital, for the first time I had an authoritative text. I also made a study of the metrical treatises on the *Vajraprajñā Sūtra* by Vasubandhu and Asaṅga,[608] and their interpretations were a good fit. At long last all my doubts were resolved.[609] Also, the two masters

---

604. Mujaku, 481: 第一段贊歎縱奪.

605. Mujaku, 482, cites *Vimalakīrti Sūtra*, T475.14.550b4–6.

606. Mujaku, 482: 第二段総破.

607. Mujaku, 482, lists the illustrious translators Kumārajīva, Bodhiruci, Paramārtha, Dharmagupta, Xuanzang, and Yijing.

608. See T1510–1511.

609. Mujaku, 484, glosses *panran wu yi* 泮然無疑 thus: "Means: Reading the treatises of Vasubandhu and Asaṅga made me even more aware of the lack of fidelity in the translation, and reading the edition from the capital library made me even more aware of the translation's inflations and deletions in phrasing—all my doubts were resolved" [忠曰言看天親無著論頌益知翻譯失真又看京師藏本彌覺大句增減而疑泮然而解也].

Changshui[610] and Gushan[611] both relied on the wording but went against
the meaning." When you dared to do this sort of critique, I assume you
certainly must have looked at the Sanskrit text behind the translations done
during the six periods [when the six translators worked], exhaustively investigated the translation errors of all these masters, and only then for the first
time were "all doubts resolved." If, never having had a Sanskrit edition, you
were using only your biased subjective views to peel away the meanings of
the sagely translators, then before we even discuss [the distant matter of]
retribution of cause and effect—slandering the sagely teachings and falling into the interminable hell—I fear that [in the present] knowledgeable
people will see this [i.e., what you were doing] and, just as you pointed out
the mistakes of the various masters, it will boomerang on you![612]

[57.3: *Dahui relates his intention to severely reject Sun*[613]]

An ancient had a saying: "'Though the relationship between friends is
not close, the things they talk about are deep'—this is a way for inviting
a crime."[614] You and I hardly know each other [i.e., our friendship is not a
close one]. You, by means of your sutra commentary, seek my sealing of
your realization. Your wanting to disseminate it for myriad generations
and to plant buddha-seeds in the sentient-being realm—this is a good
action of the first order. And, moreover, you take me as a person in the
midst of *this*, and so by means of our *in-this state of being* I hope for [a
friendship between us] that transcends the form-body. This is why I dare
not go without speaking out.

[57.4: *Quotes an ancient who didn't make false emendations*[615]]

Of old, National Teacher Qingliang [Chengguan of the Tang dynasty]
composed his *Huayan Commentary*. He wanted to correct the errors of

---

610. Mujaku, 484, glosses Changshui 長水 thus: "Changshui Zixuan [?–1038] was a successor of Langya Guangzhao Jue" [長水子璿嗣瑯瑘廣照覺]. He was oriented to the *Śūraṃgama
Sūtra* and followed Zongmi-style "identity of Chan and the teachings."

611. Mujaku, 485, cites Dharma Master Gushan Zhiyuan 孤山智圓法師 in *Fozu tong ji*
佛祖統紀, T2035.49.201b27.

612. Mujaku, 486, cites *Lotus Sutra*, T262.9.58a2–4.

613. Mujaku, 486: 第三段敘斥破之意.

614. Mujaku, 486, cites *Zhanguo ce* 戰國策, *Huainan zi* 淮南子, etc.

615. Mujaku, 487: 第四段引古人不妄改.

the master who did the translation but didn't have in hand the Sanskrit edition—he merely wrote out his findings at the very end of the sutra.[616] For example, in the "Inconceivable Dharma of the Buddhas" chapter [of the *Huayan Sutra*] there is the passage: "All the buddhas have limitless bodies, and their form characteristics are pure. Everywhere they enter into all the rebirth paths without becoming contaminated."[617] Qingliang merely says: "In the first fascicle, third leaf, tenth line of the 'Inconceivable Dharma of the Buddhas' chapter, in the case of *yiqie zhu fo* [i.e., *all the buddhas*], the old translation deletes the character *zhu*."[618] Words beyond this that are dropped in the sutra are all noted at the end of the sutra. Again, Qingliang was a sagely master [of the teachings]—he wasn't incapable of making emendations by inserting and deleting words. His holding back and daring only to write such things at the very end of the sutra is the fear of one who knows dharma. Also, in the sutra there is the phrase *great lapis-lazuli treasure*.[619] Qingliang said: "I think it's probably a transliteration of Indic *vaiḍūrya*, and the old edition is a copyist's mistake."[620] Here again he didn't dare to change it, and once again just made this sort of note at the very end of the sutra.

[57.5: *Rejects the idea that the translations lack fidelity*[621]]

As for the six translation masters in their six periods, it's not the case that they were all scholars of shallow knowledge. At the translation sites, there were those who transliterated words, those who translated the meaning, those who attended to literary polish, those who checked the meanings of the Sanskrit words, those who once again corrected the meanings, and those who collated the Chinese and Sanskrit. But you still think that they

---

616. Mujaku, 488, glosses *dan shu zhi yu jing wei* 但書之于經尾 thus: "The edition in the present canon doesn't have it, because it was deleted in a later generation. It's a pity" [今藏本無之蓋後世刪可惜].

617. Mujaku, 488, cites *Da fangguang fo huayan jing sui shu yan yi chao* 大方廣佛華嚴經隨疏演義鈔, T1736.36.179b1–5.

618. Mujaku, 488, glosses *Qingliang dan yun yun yun* 清涼但云云云 thus: "The *Sui shu yan yi chao* circulating at present does not have this line" [忠曰今流行隨疏演義鈔無此語].

619. Mujaku, 488, cites *Da fangguang fo huayan jing* 大方廣佛華嚴經, T279.10.355b13.

620. Mujaku, 488, glosses *Qingliang yue kong shi yun yun* 清涼曰恐是云云 thus: "The commentary in sixty-six fascicles doesn't have this line" [疏六十六卷無此語].

621. Mujaku, 489: 第五段斥翻譯失真.

made mistakes in translating the sagely [Buddha's] meaning! In spite of
never having had a Sanskrit edition in your hands, you arbitrarily begin
"peeling away." But you want people of later generations to be completely
convinced—isn't that problematic?

[57.6: *Rejects the assertion that Changshui contradicted the meaning*[622]]

For example, you argue that Changshui was fixated on the phrasing and went
against the meaning, but without having a Sanskrit edition as proof, how
could you be so certain he is wrong? Although this gentleman [Changshui]
was a scholar of the teachings, he wasn't the same as other scholars. He made
a hands-on investigation of Chan with Chan Master Langya Guangzhao.[623] At
that time he requested instruction from Langya concerning the meaning of a
passage in the *Śūraṃgama Sūtra* where Pūrṇa asks the Buddha the meaning
of: "If purity is innate, how are the mountains and rivers of the great earth
produced?"[624] Thereupon Langya in a loud voice said: "If purity is innate,
how are the mountains and rivers of the great earth produced?" Changshui
immediately had a great awakening. After that he [assumed the lecture seat,]
opened the front flaps of his robe, and dubbed himself [self-effacingly] a "seat
master" [i.e., the Chan term for a specialist in the teachings[625]]. Undoubtedly,
most seat masters are people who "search through lines of texts and count
the number of characters" [i.e., grasp the written word and are arrested by
unreal characteristics].[626] This is who you have called "fixated on the phrasing and not on the meaning." Changshui was not one of those who lack
insight—he was not one of those who "search through the lines of texts and
count the number of characters."

---

622. Mujaku, 490: 第六段斥長水違義之言.

623. Mujaku, 490, glosses *Langya Guangzhao* 瑯瑯廣照 thus: "Succeeded [the Linji teacher]
Chan Master Fenyang Shanzhao [947–1024]" [嗣汾陽昭禪師].

624. Mujaku, 490, cites, among others, *Wu deng hui yuan* 五燈會元 (CBETA, X80, no. 1565,
p. 251, b23–c1 // Z 2B:11, p. 224, d17–p. 225, a1 // R138, p. 448, b17–p. 449, a1); and for the
Śūraṃgama Sūtra quotation he cites T945.19.120a2–3.

625. Mujaku, 491, glosses *zuozhu* 座主 thus: "The Chan house generally dubs specialists in
the teachings 'seat masters'" [忠曰禪家凡稱教者爲座主].

626. Mujaku, 491, glosses *zuozhu duo shi xun xing shu mo* 座主多是尋行數墨
thus: "Means: most specialists in the teachings grasp the written word and are arrested by
unreal characteristics" [言教者多分執文字拘相]; and cites *Jingde chuandeng lu* 景德傳燈錄,
T2076.51.450a2–3.

[57.7: *Demolishes Sun's deviant interpretation*[627]]

[In the standard edition of the *Vajraprajñā Sūtra* it states that] "*not* by means of the possession of characteristics does one attain perfect awakening."[628] The sutra text is for the most part clear, and this passage is extremely easy to understand. But right from the outset you go way too far in seeking the "out-of-the-ordinary." You want to erect a "different" interpretation and have people follow your lead! [So in your version of the *Vajraprajñā* you drop off the *not*, and to justify this erasure] you quote Asaṅga's treatise [in which Asaṅga has paraphrased—correctly—the same passage from the sutra]:

> It is by means of the *dharmakāya* that one should see a *tathāgata*, because it is not a case of taking the possession of characteristics [to see him]. If that is so, one should not take the possession of characteristics to see a *tathāgata*. 'One should take the possession of characteristics as a cause for obtaining perfect awakening'—in order to disengage from an attachment [to this wrong view], the *Vajraprajñā Sūtra* says: 'Subhūti! What do you think? Should the *tathāgata* take the completion of characteristics to obtain perfect awakening? Subhūti! Do not think like this....' [Asaṅga commentary:] The meaning here clarifies that 'the possession of characteristics' has no essence. Awakening does not take 'the possession of characteristics' as its cause. The reason is that characteristics have the [same] essence as forms [i.e., neither forms nor characteristics have essence]."[629]

This commentary, for the most part, is clear—from the outset you've come to a mistaken view, a mistaken understanding [i.e., you have latched onto Asaṅga's paraphrase of the sutra, "should the *tathāgata* take the completion of characteristics to obtain perfect awakening?" and conveniently ignored the subsequent negation "do *not* think like this"].[630] Now,

---

627. Mujaku, 492: 第七段破孫異解.

628. Mujaku, 492, cites *Jingang bore boluomi jing* 金剛般若波羅蜜經: "The one who sees me by means of forms and seeks me by means of sounds—this person is treading a perverse Way and will be unable to see the *tathāgata*" [若以色見我，以音聲求我，是人行邪道，不能見如來。] (T235.8.752a17–18).

Jingang bore boluomi jing lun 金剛般若波羅蜜經論, T1510b.25.779a29–b7.

630. The commentary's sutra quotation runs: 經言。須菩提。於意云何。如來可以相成就。得阿耨多羅三藐三菩提。須菩提。莫作是念等者。(T1510b.25.779b4–6); the

"forms" are dependently originated characteristics; "characteristics" are the *dharmadhātu* undergoing dependent origination. The Liang dynasty Crown Prince Zhaoming [in his commentary on the *Vajraprajñā Sūtra*] considered that this [sutra's subsequent] line "Do not think like this! A *tathāgata* does not by virtue of the possession of characteristics attain perfect awakening" belonged to the "no-severing no-extinction" section of his thirty-two-part sectioning[631] of the [*Vajraprajñā*] *Sūtra*. This was because he feared that Subhūti's saying "not by virtue of the possession of characteristics" approached the extremist view of severing—Subhūti, even in his mother's womb, knew emptiness-quiescence[632] and had little association with dependently originated characteristics. At the end of Guṇada/Śrīdatta Bodhisattva's treatise [on the *Vajraprajñā Sūtra*], from which you later quote, it says: "If characteristics could be completed, then the time these characteristics extinguish would be called 'severing.' Why? 'Arising'—therefore, 'severing.'" Also, fearing that people wouldn't understand, Guṇada further says: "Why? All dharmas are of a non-arising nature, and therefore far removed from the two extremes of 'severing' and 'eternalism.' Being far removed from the two extremes is the characteristic of the *dharmadhātu*."[633] We can speak of characteristics without speaking of the [dharma] nature because the *dharmadhātu* is the origination by dependence of the [dharma] nature. Because characteristics are the origination by dependence of the *dharmadhātu*, we can speak of characteristics without speaking of the [dharma] nature. This is how Zhaoming of the Liang dynasty could speak of "no-severing no-extinguishing." This ["no-severing no-extinguishing"] section is even clearer. Once again, it's your going way too far in seeking the "out-of-the-ordinary"—all you're doing is forcibly cranking out section

---

stand-alone sutra, *Jingang bore boluomi jing* 金剛般若波羅蜜經, runs: 須菩提。汝若作是念。如來不以具足相故。得阿耨多羅三藐三菩提。須菩提。莫作是念。如來不以具足相故。得阿耨多羅三藐三菩提。(T235.8.752a19–22). Mujaku, 493, comments: "The widely disseminated sutra edition has the *bu* [no/not] character—it's meaning is solid.... District Magistrate Sun in the widely disseminated edition of the sutra erases the first *bu* [no/not] character.... District Magistrate Sun's erasing the first *bu* [no/not] character relies on the idea of Asaṅga's commentary" [流布經有不字者其意固.... 孫知縣於流布經初不字.... 孫知縣削初不字依無著論之意].

631. Mujaku, 497, cites *Jingang bore boluomi zhujie* 金剛般若波羅蜜經註解, T1703.33.228b1–4.

632. Mujaku, 497, cites *Śūraṃgama Sūtra*, T945.19.126b28–c2.

633. *Jingang bore boluomi jing po quzhuo bu huai jiaming lun* 金剛般若波羅蜜經破取著不壞假名論, T1515.25.895b17–c29.

headings in your own commentary! If it's okay to erase words in the *Vajraprajñā Sūtra* as you do, then, wherever you look in the entire Buddhist canon, any word can be erased in accordance with your subjective understanding![634]

[57.8: *Again quotes ancients who didn't make false emendations*[635]]

For example, Han Tuizhi [i.e., the Confucian Han Yu of the Tang] pointed out that in the ["Gong Zhichang" chapter of the] *Analects* of Confucius the character *zhou* should be the [almost identical] character *hua*, saying that an old edition had made a mistake.[636] With Tuizhi's level of erudition making changes [in the original text] would have been okay, but why did he in this way keep the discussion just in his book [*Notes on the* Analects]? Again it's just that those who know dharma are circumspect. Chan Master Guifeng Zongmi[637] wrote the *Great Commentary* and *Great Commentary Notes* on the *Perfect Awakening Sutra*. Zongmi had an experience of realization-awakening with the *Perfect Awakening Sutra*,[638] and only then did he dare to take up his writing brush. In the *Perfect Awakening Sutra*, there is the line "all sentient beings realize [*zheng*] perfect awakening," but Guifeng [in his commentary] changed *realize* [*zheng*] to *possess* [*ju*], saying that the translator had made an error.[639] However, because he hadn't seen a Sanskrit edition, he also in this way kept the discussion just in his commentary, not daring to make a correction to the sutra itself. [Despite Zongmi's learning and modesty,] later on Preceptor Letan Zhenjing[640]

---

634. Mujaku puts this line with the next section (#57.8). I have moved it back to #57.7.

635. Mujaku, 499: 第八段重引古結不可妄改.

636. Mujaku, 500, cites *Han Yu Lunyu bijie* 韓愈論語筆解.

637. For treatments of Zongmi, see Kamata Shigeo, trans., *Zengen shosenshū tojo*, Zen no goroku 9 (Tokyo: Chikuma shobō, 1971); and Jeffrey Lyle Broughton, *Zongmi on Chan* (New York: Columbia University Press, 2009).

638. For the story of Zongmi's stumbling upon the sutra at a dinner at a layman's home, Mujaku, 500, cites *Da fangguang yuanjue xiuduoluo liaoyi jing lueshu* 大方廣圓覺修多羅了義經略疏, T1795.39.523c3-7.

639. Mujaku, 500, cites *Da fangguang yuanjue xiuduoluo liaoyi jing luehshu* 大方廣圓覺修多羅了義經略疏, T1795.39.552c23-25.

640. Mujaku, 501, cites *Jianzhong jingguo xu deng lu* 建中靖國續燈錄 (CBETA, X78, no. 1556, p. 721, b5-7 // Z 2B:9, p. 99, d5-7 // R136, p. 198, b5-7). Zhenjing (1025-1102) was in the Huanglong wing of Linji Chan.

composed his *All Realize Treatise*,[641] and in it he severely scolded Guifeng, calling him a "self-indulgent common person, a fetid-smelling fellow."[642] [The *All Realize Treatise* argues:] If all sentient beings possess perfect awakening but do not realize it, animals will eternally be animals, hungry ghosts will eternally be hungry ghosts—throughout the worlds of the ten directions all would be a [useless] iron hammer-head with no hole [to attach a handle]. There wouldn't be a single person to produce the true [mind] and revert to the origin.[643] There would be no need for common persons to seek liberation. Why? The reason is, if all sentient beings already possessed perfect awakening, there would be no need to seek liberation.

[57.9: *Rejects Sun's sole reliance on the edition stored at the capital*[644]]

You consider the edition stored in the capital to be correct and then take the capital edition as your "authoritative text." If it's an edition stored in the capital, it was brought there from prefectures and superior prefectures of the regions. For example, the two canons [in the East and West Repositories[645]] at Jingshan Monastery both arrived as gifts from the court when it was flourishing, and they too were copies done by sutra copyists in prefectures and superior prefectures of the regions. Ten-thousand mistakes or just one, how will you correctly emend them?

[57.10: *Solves things by letting him take it or leave it*[646]]

If you are free of conceit and scorn for others,[647] you definitely will take my words as of the utmost sincerity, and you won't have to get muddied by what people of the past and present will call your "one great mistake."

---

641. Mujaku, 501, glosses *zhuan Jie zheng lun* 撰皆證論 thus: "Now not extant" [忠曰今不傳].

642. For the criticism, Araki, 225, cites: Dehong Juefan's 德洪覺範 *Shimen wenzi chan* 石門文字禪 (CBETA, J23, no. B135, p. 726, b30–c4).

643. Mujaku, 502, cites *Śūraṃgama Sūtra*, T945.19.147b10–11.

644. Mujaku, 502: 第九段斥獨據京師藏本.

645. Mujaku, 503, glosses *liang zangjing* 兩藏經 thus: "East and West Repositories" [忠曰東西藏也]. Mention of Jingshan Monastery may indicate that this letter dates to Dahui's restoration as abbot there.

646. Mujaku, 503: 第十段任他取捨而去就.

647. Mujaku, 503, glosses *wu ren wo* 無人我 thus: "Internally to have conceit and externally to have scorn for others is *for others and self*" [忠曰內有我慢而外凌蔑他人是爲人我也].

If you graspingly cling on to your own view as correct and positively want to make the emendations [to the *Vajraprajñā Sūtra* text]—and surely have everyone spit upon and curse you—you're free to have the printing blocks cut and have it published! I will just rejoice for you and praise it. You have already specially dispatched someone to bring this sutra [and commentary] to me in order to seek my "seal." Though you and I don't know each other, we are tied together by the dharma. Therefore, without thinking, I've blathered on in contradicting you. I see your extreme sincerity, and so I have spoken even more unreservedly.

[57.11: *Flips to encouraging Sun to awaken to* the great matter *of samsara*[648]]

If you decide you want to pursue to the limit the [twelve divisions of the] teachings and the [three] vehicles and reach the innermost meaning [of the canonical texts], you should seek out a lecture master with a reputable track record, and with singleness of mind make an investigation with him. Go all-out—put your mind to executing a type of teachings-net [that traps sentient beings like fish in a fishing net[649]]. [On the other hand,] if, because impermanence is swift and the matter of samsara great, your *own matter* is not yet clarified, you should seek out a Chan master with experience of the *original allotment* who can smash a person's "cave-lair" in samsara, and with him do intensely painful *gongfu* to the limit. Suddenly you will "smash the pail of black lacquer"—that's the state of breaking through!

[57.12: *Concludes with a warning whip*[650]]

If you just want to supply topics for conversation, you may say: "I've read through a massive number of books and comprehended all of them; I understand Chan and understand the teachings; and I also have carefully checked the places where translation masters and lecture masters of previous generations have not ventured." Flaunting "my" abilities and "my" level of understanding, you can carefully check up on the sages of the three teachings

---

648. Mujaku, 505: 第十一段轉勸醒了生死大事.

649. Mujaku, 505, cites *Foguo Yuanwu chanshi biyan lu* 佛果圜悟禪師碧巖錄, T2003.48.205b8–9.

650. Mujaku, 505: 第十二段警策而結.

[Śākyamuni, Laozi, and Confucius]. And there won't be any need for you to seek somebody's "seal"[651] in order to be allowed to "pass." How about it?

58. In Reply to Secretariat Drafter Principal Graduate Zhang (Anguo)

[*Commentary: Mujaku says, "This letter dates to Shaoxing 29/1159 when the Master was seventy-one."*[652] *Hyesim says, "The main purport of the letter in reply to Zhang is: Zhang should see and hear without falling into seeing and hearing."*[653] *Post-exile letter—after Dahui was restored to the Jingshan Monastery abbotship towards the end of his life.*]

[58.1: *Shows Zhang entering the Way and exerting mind*[654]]

If you definitely want to investigate *this matter* to its very end, just constantly make your mind empty and wide-open.[655] When things come, respond. It's like a person training in archery. [After long practice, he becomes skillful. Later, even though he has "no mind" that desires to hit the bullseye, because of his] long-term [practice, all of the arrows] hit the bullseye. Haven't you seen what Bodhidharma said to the second patriarch: "You [should] merely, without: desist from all objective supports; within: have no panting in the mind. With a mind like a wall, you can enter the Way."[656] At present, as soon as people hear this saying,

---

651. Mujaku, 505, glosses *qiu ren yinke* 求人印可 thus: "Means: no need to seek Dahui's seal" [忠曰言不必求大慧印可也].

652. Mujaku, 507: 此書紹興二十九年己夘師七十一歲而作.

653. Hyesim, 108: 答張狀大旨當見聞不落見聞. For entries for Zhang Xiaoxiang 張孝祥 (*zi* Anguo 安國), see *Song History*, 389 (16.3042) and *Cases of Song and Yuan Confucians*, 41 (2.1340 and 1362). Hucker, 417 and 193–194: "*Sheren* 舍人 is an abbreviation of *zhongshu sheren* 中書舍人.... Drafter in the Secretariat (*zhongshu sheng* 中書省) or Secretariat Drafter, principally a handler of central government documents." Hucker, 187: "*Principal Graduate* [*zhuangyuan* 狀元], designation of the candidate who stood first on the list of passers of the final examination in the civil service recruitment examination sequence. In Song the top 3 passers were sometimes all called Principal Graduates.... The designation was highly coveted and esteemed, and it usually led to a prestigious initial appointment and subsequent career in the civil service."

654. Mujaku, 507: 第一段示入道用心.

655. Mujaku, 507, glosses *xu huahua de* 虛豁豁地 thus: "Have not one thing in your chest—no calculation, false thought, meanings, and understanding" [忠曰胸中無一物無計較妄想義理解會也].

656. *Shaoshi liu men* 少室六門, T2009.48.370a25–26.

they immediately arrange for a stupid sort of state of ignorance—they forcibly engage in a suppression of mind, wanting their mind to be like a wall! As the [sixth] patriarch said: "With that kind of mistake, how could the *upāya* have stood any chance of being understood?"[657] Yantou said: "As soon as [you become fixated upon] *in that way*, [no longer is it thinking of nothing at all, and so] it's immediately not *in that way*. Any affirmation of the phrase or negation of the *phrase* is to be shaved off."[658] This is the model for "without: desist from all objective supports; within: have no panting in the mind." Even if you can't yet do the "snap and smash" of awakening, you won't be flipped about by verbalization. When you're viewing the moon, stop gazing at the finger [pointing at the moon]; when you've returned home, stop asking about the journey.[659]

[58.2: *Dahui confers on Zhang his personal practice of rallying the* huatou *to awareness*[660]]

If deluded consciousness is not yet smashed, then the "heart-fire" will be ablaze. At exactly that sort of moment, just rally to awareness the *huatou* of uncertainty: "A monk asked Zhaozhou, "Does even a dog have buddha-nature?" Zhou said, "**Wu** 無." Just rally and lift [**wu** 無] to awareness:

Coming [at **wu** 無] from the left is not correct; coming [at **wu** 無] from the right is not correct.
Also, you must not have your mind wait for awakening.
Also, you must not, while raising [**wu** 無], understand and "own" it.
Also, you must not concoct a "sublime" understanding [of **wu** 無].
Also, you must not haggle over whether [**wu** 無 is the *wu* of the polarity] *there is* [*you* 有]/*there is not* [*wu* 無].
Also, you must not conjecture that [**wu** 無] is the *wu* 無 of *true non-existence* [*zhen wu* 真無].

---

657. Mujaku, 508, cites *Liu zu dashi fabao tan jing* 六祖大師法寶壇經, T2008.48.356c9–12.

658. Appears in *Liandeng hui yao* 聯燈會要 (CBETA, X79, no. 1557, p. 182, c7–8 // Z 2B:9, p. 389, d10–11 // R136, p. 778, b10–11).

659. Mujaku, 508, cites *Jingde chuandeng lu* 景德傳燈錄, T2076.51.463c10–11; and comments: "*Pointing* and *journey* are metaphors for *upāyas*. After seeing the Way, there is no need to enter into the construction of *upāyas*" [忠曰指程者喻方便也見道之後不用入做方便也].

660. Mujaku, 508: 第二段授本參提撕.

Also, you must not sit in the tiny hidden-away closet of
  nothing-to-do.[661]
Also, you must not understand [**wu** 無 in the mode of "Chan
  suddenness" that is] like a spark from two stones or a lightning bolt.

Even when you reach the point at which there is no exerting of mind and
mind has nowhere to go, don't fear [that this is] falling into [the extreme
view of an annihilationist] emptiness. On the contrary, this is the *good place.*
Suddenly "the mouse will enter the ox's horn" [i.e., all tricky maneuvers will
be severed[662]], and then you will be "felled" [like a giant tree, i.e., you will emit
the *Aah!*].

[58.3: *Discusses whether gaining energy is difficult or easy*[663]]

This matter is neither "difficult" nor "easy." You long ago planted deeply
the seeds of *prajñā*; you served true teachers from time without beginning,
across long aeons; you laid down latent tendencies toward correct knowing and correct insight inside the storehouse consciousness—it's only
because of [these difficulties] that you now [in this birth], upon encountering sense objects in a state of activation, "click" [i.e., in all things coincide
with the *original allotment*[664]]. [This "click" is as easy] as recognizing your
own father and mother in a swarm of ten-thousand people—right at that
very moment you don't have to ask anyone else about it! Spontaneously
the mind of seeking no longer rushes about hither and thither. Yunmen
said:[665] "One should not assert that when one speaks it is [speaking
dharma] and that when one does not speak it isn't [speaking dharma].
One should not assert that when one haggles it is [speaking dharma] and
that when one does not haggle it isn't [speaking dharma]." Also, he himself raised: "Tell me, at the time of no haggling, **what the hell is it?**" Also,
fearing that people would not understand, he again said: "Once more,
what the hell is it?"

---

661. See the note for the same prohibition in letter #10.5.

662. Mujaku, 313, glosses *laoshu ru niujiao* 老鼠入牛角 thus: "Tricky maneuvers are severed"
[忠曰伎倆絕也].

663. Mujaku, 508: 第三段論得力難易.

664. Mujaku, 509, glosses *zhuzhuo kezhuo* 築著磕著 thus: "In all things coincide with the
original allotment" [忠曰言事事上物物上契當本分也].

665. Mujaku, 509–510, cites *Yunmen Kuangzhen chanshi guanglu* 雲門匡真禪師廣錄,
T1988.47.559b5–8.

[58.4: *Smashes perverse teachers*[666]]

In recent years, Chan has had a lot of divergent tendencies:

Some consider getting in one more line at the very end of a question-and-answer exchange to be Chan.[667]

Some consider Chan to be getting into a huddle and debating the stories of the ancients' entering the Way, saying "this is *upāya*, that's real, these words are profound, those words are sublime," sometimes saying a phrase as a stand-in, sometimes making a separate comment.[668]

Some consider Chan to be harmonizing what you see and hear with the [Yogācara] teachings of "the three realms are mind-only" and "the myriad dharmas are consciousness-only."[669]

Some consider Chan to be lapsing into silence, doing cross-legged sitting in the "ghost-cave of Black Mountain," closing the eyes, calling it the *"state of being* [before the appearance of] Bhīṣma-garjita-svara Buddha" [i.e., the name of the very first buddha to appear in this world] or "your face before your father and mother conceived you," and calling it "silence as constant illumination."[670] This type of party doesn't seek sublime awakening. They take awakening as falling into the secondary grade. They take awakening as duping and intimidating people. They take awakening as something provisionally established [as an *upāya*]. Since they have never had an awakening, they don't believe that awakening exists!

---

666. Mujaku, 510: 第四段破邪師.

667. Mujaku, 510, glosses *yi wen yi da yun* yun 一問一答云云 thus: "Oral Chan" [忠曰口頭禪也].

668. Mujaku, 510, glosses *huo yi guren ru dao yinyuan yun* yun 或以古人入道因緣云云 thus: "Mental-calculation Chan" [忠曰計較禪也]. Araki, 230: "In the case of *stand-in words*, when the master makes a comment and, in spite of waiting for the response of the assembly, there is no answer at all forthcoming from the assembly, the master himself comments *in place of* the assembly. In the case of *separate words*, in the face of the haggling words of the other person's dialogue, one *separately* makes a comment using one's own independent level of understanding."

669. Mujaku, 511, glosses *huo yi yan jian er wen yun* yun 或以眼見耳聞云云 thus: "Play-of-unreal-light-and-shadow Chan" [忠曰光影邊禪也].

670. Mujaku, 511, glosses *huo yi wuyan wushuo yun* yun 或以無言無說云云 thus: "Silence-as-illumination Chan.... With the above oral Chan, mental-calculation Chan, play-of-unreal-light-and-shadow Chan, and silence-as-illumination Chan, step-by-step their levels

I constantly speak to Chan monks. Even in the case of the mundane arts and skills, if they have no experience of awakening, they fail to attain sublimity [in the art or skill]. Trying to escape samsara by just employing oral Chan to talk about "stillness" is just like indiscriminately running towards the east when you want to fetch something in the west. The more you seek, the farther away you will be; the more you hurry, the further you will fall behind. This lot we dub "pitiful." Within the teachings they are called people who slander great *prajñā* and cut off the wisdom-life the buddhas. Even if a thousand buddhas were to appear in the world, [these people] wouldn't offer to confess their transgressions! "Just because you have a good karmic cause, doesn't mean that a bad karmic result won't ensue."[671] [In the past I made a great vow:] Even if this body of mine is pulverized into minute atoms, I will never compromise the buddhadharma to accommodate customary etiquette, [and so I dare to say:] if you want to oppose samsara outright, you must smash this pail of black lacquer. Absolutely avoid the scenario of becoming subject to a perverse teacher's *upāya*s and letting him "stamp you with a seal made of winter-melon"[672]—after which you announce: "I understand everything!" This lot is "as numerous as rice grains, hemp, bamboo, or reeds."[673]

[58.5: *Proclaims the idea above about repudiating perversity*[674]]

You are clever and possess a level of understanding that can discriminate, and so you certainly won't be taken in by this sort of evil poison. Even so,

---

of understanding grow deeper, but step-by-step they enter ever more deeply into perversity" [忠曰默照禪也.... 忠曰自上口頭禪計較禪光影禪默照禪漸漸解深而漸漸入邪深矣]. This would make silence-as-illumination Chan the deepest level of understanding and the deepest level of perversity.

671. Mujaku, 513, cites *Jingde chuandeng lu* 景德傳燈錄, T2076.51.444c24–29; and comments: "Here means: although employing the mouth to talk about 'stillness' is mental calculation and logical arrangement, because the buddhadharma is in the mind, it is a good karmic cause. However, relying on this [talking about 'stillness'] to deny wonderful awakening, to cut off the wisdom-life of the buddhas, and to assert that there is no such thing as wonderful awakening, is slandering *prajñā*. Therefore, sinking into slandering dharma and falling into a hell is bringing on a bad karmic result" [忠曰今言以口頭說靜雖是計較安排且以佛法在心頭是善因也然依此撥無妙悟斷絕慧命言無妙悟是謗般若故陷謗法墮獄是招惡果也].

672. Mujaku, 513, cites *Foguo Yuanwu chanshi biyan lu* 佛果圜悟禪師碧巖錄, T2003.48.221c2–3.

673. Mujaku, 513, cites *Lotus Sutra*, T262.9.6a11–13.

674. Mujaku, 514: 第五段伸如上闢邪之意.

I am afraid that, in your fervent desire to achieve quick results you will, without noticing, be contaminated in your encounters with them [i.e., perverse teachers]. Therefore, I've written a certain amount of kudzu-verbiage in this letter. When peered at by a person with the eye of brightness such as yourself—what a *faux pas*!

[58.6: *Again encourages the* gongfu *of rallying the* huatou *to awareness*[675]]

By all means listen to me. Just, in the state of responding to conditions in your daily activities, rally to awareness Zhaozhou's single word **wu** 無. You must not break off. An ancient worthy has a saying: "In investigating the ultimate principle take awakening as the standard."[676] Even if your speech is like a swarm of flowers falling from heaven,[677] if you're not awakened, it's no more than "a crazy person running around outside the pale."[678] Strive on! You must not be neglectful!

59. *In Reply to Grand Councilor Tang (Jinzhi)*

[*Commentary: Mujaku says, "This letter dates to Shaoxing 29/1159 when the Master was seventy-one."*[679] *Hyesim says, "The main purport of the letter in reply to Tang is not stagnating in sense objects that go against you or go in your direction; and practicing the* huatou.*"*[680] *Post-exile letter—after Dahui was restored to the Jingshan Monastery abbotship towards the end of his life.*]

---

675. Mujaku, 514: 第六段重勸工夫提撕.

676. *Guishan jingce zhu* 溈山警策註 (CBETA, X63, no. 1239, p. 230, c8 // Z 2:16, p. 148, d5 // R111, p. 296, b5).

677. Mujaku, 514, cites *Foguo Yuanwu chanshi biyan lu* 佛果圜悟禪師碧巖錄, T2003.48.140b6–7.

678. Mujaku 514, cites *Jingde chuandeng lu* 景德傳燈錄, T2076.51.450a17–b15.

679. Mujaku, 515: 此書紹興二十九年己卯師七十一歲而作.

680. Hyesim, 110: 答湯狀大旨不滯逆順而參句. For a biographical entry for Tang Situi 湯思退 (*zi* Jinzhi 進之), see *Song History*, 371 (16.2938–39). Hucker, 126, describes Grand Councilor (*chengxiang* 丞相) in general terms: "A title of great significance in Chinese history, normally indicating the most esteemed and influential members(s) of the officialdom, who was leader of and spokesman for the officialdom vis-à-vis the ruler and at the same time the principal agent for implementing the ruler's wishes in all spheres, civil and military." Lü and Wu, 157: Tang Situi opposed fighting the Jin, and from beginning to end did not get along with Zhang Jun 張浚 (see letter #23 to Zhang Jun).

[59.1: *Shows mind exertion*[681]]

You, Grand Councilor, have for some time put your mind to *this great mat-ter* of origination by dependence. In the unreality of this *sahā* world [i.e., the domain of Śākyamuni Buddha] where there is always a lack, some-time things go against you and sometimes they go in your direction; but one after the other they are all opportunities for producing the [*mysterious*] *function*.[682] Just constantly make your mind empty and clear and, as occa-sion demands, dispose of those things that should be done in your daily activities.[683] Upon encountering sense objects and conditions, constantly rally the *huatou* to awareness. Don't seek quick results. "In investigating the ultimate principle take awakening as the standard."[684]

[59.2: *Shows the method of* gongfu[685]]

However, you absolutely must not maintain your mind in a state of wait-ing for awakening. If you maintain your mind in a state of waiting for awakening, then the eye of the Way will be blocked by the waiting state of your mind. The more you hurry, the further you will fall behind. Just rally the *huatou* to awareness. Suddenly, in the state of rallying the *huatou* to awareness, the mind of samsara will be cut off—then it will be the state of having returned to the stable seat of your own home.

[59.3: *In advance shows the realm of post-awakening*[686]]

Having reached the *in-that-way* state, you will naturally be able to break through all the various *upāyas* of the ancients, and various heterodox

---

681. Mujaku, 515: 第一段示用心.

682. Mujaku, 515, glosses *fa ji shijie* 發機時節 thus: "The second letter in reply to Vice Minister Chen [letter #15.1] says that 'inescapable situations in the midst of noisiness were already *gongfu!*' That is the idea here. *Produce function* means *produce the mysterious function*" [忠曰前陳少卿第二書所謂鬧中韡避不得處便是工夫了也此此即此義也發機者發得玄機也].

683. Mujaku, 516, cites letter #51.2 as containing the idea here: "When events of the present arrive right in front of you, whether they go against you or go in your direction, there is no need to attach thought to them. Attaching thought to them will bother your mind. If you just, at the time anything happens, respond according to conditions, you'll be in spontaneous union with this Way-principle."

684. *Guishan jingce zhu* 潙山警策註 (CBETA, X63, no. 1239, p. 230, c8 // Z 2:16, p. 148, d5 // R111, p. 296, b5).

685. Mujaku, 516: 第二段示工夫之法.

686. Mujaku, 516: 第三段預示悟後境界.

interpretations on your part will no longer arise. The sutra says: "Cut off
the mind's arising and extinguishing; cut down the dense forest; wash
the contaminations of mind; and untie the graspings of mind."[687] When
in the state of grasping, make your mind mobile. Just at the moment of
being mobile, there will be no principle called "mobility." Naturally everything will be bright, everything revealed. In daily activities, the state of
responding to conditions, whether pure or impure, joyful or angry, going
against you or going in your direction, will be like a pearl rolling about on a
platter—revolving of its own accord without any stimulus. When you
reach *this time*, you can't pick it up and make a presentation to someone
else. It's like a person's drinking water—he knows for himself whether it
is cold or warm.

[59.4: *Dahui smears the perverse teachers*[688]]

National Master Nanyang Zhong had a saying: "Speaking a dharma of
having something to apprehend is making the sound of a jackal."[689] *This
matter* is like a blue sky and bright sun—with one look you can immediately see. The one who can see reality on his own cannot be led astray by
perverse teachers. As I've said to you face to face on previous days: "*This
matter* can't be transmitted. The minute any [of these perverse teachers]
says [they have a secret,] rare and sublime, [to transmit to you], it's a case
of too many people in on the secret [i.e., only one can be in on *this matter*]."
They're scamming you! It would be better to haul these perverse teachers
out in front of you to spit on them!

[59.5: *Argues that good karma with outflows is not the buddhadharma*[690]]

From your student days you've grown into a Grand Councilor. This is the
most honored rank in the mundane dharma. But if you don't awaken
concerning *this matter*, you've come for a rebirth in the southernmost

687. Mujaku, 516, cites *Da fangguang fo huayan jing* 大方廣佛華嚴經, T279.10.339a14–18.

688. Mujaku, 517: 第四段點破邪師.

689. Mujaku, 517, cites *Jingde chuandeng lu* 景德傳燈錄, T2076.51.244b24–26. For jackal,
see *Zhenzhou Linji Huizhao chanshi yulu* 鎮州臨濟慧照禪師語錄, T1985.47.502b28–29.
Nanyang Huizhong (南陽慧忠;?–775) was a successor of the sixth patriarch Huineng.

690. Mujaku, 519: 第五段論有漏善業非佛法

continent of Jambudvīpa [i.e., this world] in vain! When all karmic causes and effects play out, the bad karmic effects are going to be brought to bear upon you and you alone. As said in the teachings: "Generating [karmic causes that bring on] the idiot's 'good fortune' is a calamity that extends for three lifetimes."[691] What is the "calamity that extends for three lifetimes"? In this lifetime—the first—generating [karmic causes that bring on] the idiot's "good fortune" means missing out on seeing the [*original*] *nature*. In the second lifetime, receiving [the pleasant karmic effects of] the idiot's "good fortune" means lacking shame, not doing good things, and intently generating more karma. In the third lifetime, receiving [the karmic effects of] the idiot's "good fortune" will reach an end, but one will still fail to do good things, and, when freed from the "outflows-in-a-shell" [i.e., the form body], one will enter into a hell quick as an arrow. "Rebirth as a human is difficult to obtain, and it is difficult to encounter the buddhadharma; if you don't liberate yourself in the present life, then in just what life will you liberate yourself?"[692]

[59.6: *Tang needs to erect resolute willpower*[693]]

To study this Way, you must have "resolute willpower."[694] If you don't have this resolute willpower, then you'll be like one who does as he's told by a fortune-teller—when you hear him say "east," you will immediately fall in line and run eastward. When you hear him say "west," you will immediately fall in line and run westward. If you have resolute willpower, then you'll stabilize and become the master. Lanrong said: "Suppose there were a single dharma that surpassed nirvana—I say it too would be like a dream

---

691. Mujaku, 520, comments: "I haven't yet found the source" [未檢本說]. There is a couplet in *Hanshanzi shi ji* 寒山子詩集: "The idiot's good fortune is but a temporary support; they bury their heads, doing things that lead to a hell" [常聞國大臣朱紫欝纓祿富貴百千般貪榮不知辱奴馬滿宅舍金銀盈帑屋癡福暫時扶埋頭作地獄忽死萬事休男女當頭哭不知有禍殃前路何疾速家破冷颼颼食無一粒粟凍餓苦悽悽良由不覺觸] (CBETA, J20, no. B103, p. 665, a21–b1). For a translation of the poem, see Robert G. Henricks, *The Poetry of Han-shan* (Albany: State University of New York Press, 1990), 331 (No. 241).

692. *Sixin Wuxin chanshi yulu* 死心悟新禪師語錄 (CBETA, X69, no. 1344, p. 230, c5–6 // Z 2:25, p. 126, b17–18 // R120, p. 251, b17–18).

693. Mujaku, 521: 第六段要立決定志.

694. Mujaku, 521, glosses *xu you jueding zhi* 須有決定志 thus: "Fiercely advancing on the path, taking awakening as your standard, and not being discombulated by other people" [勇猛進道以悟爲則不受人惑也].

or *māya.*⁶⁹⁵ How much more so is this the case with the illusionary, unreal dharmas of the world [which include the perverse teachings of the perverse teachers]⁶⁹⁶—with what sort of frame of mind should you involve yourself with them? I hope you will firm up this "willpower" of yours and take getting [*this matter*] in the palm of your hand to be the meaning of "resolute." Then, even if all the sentient beings on the great earth become Māra kings [i.e., perverse teachers⁶⁹⁷] who want to exasperate you, they will not be able to get the advantage.

[59.7: *Discusses mind* prajñā *and never losing it*⁶⁹⁸]

[When you do *gongfu*] on top of *prajñā*, no *gongfu* is discarded as a waste.⁶⁹⁹ If you maintain mind on top [of *prajñā*], even if you do not awaken in the present life, you have deeply planted seeds, so that, when your life ends, you will not be led along by karma-consciousness to fall into one of the bad rebirth paths. When you exchange your "outflows-in-a-shell" [i.e., form body] and pop up in the next rebirth, you won't have darkened the "I."⁷⁰⁰ Please scrutinize this!

60. In Reply to Judicial Commissioner Fan (Maoshi)

[*Commentary: The date of this letter is unknown.*⁷⁰¹ *Hyesim says, "The main purport of the letter in reply to Fan is, in the state of no-difference-and-no-sameness, practice the* huatou.*"*⁷⁰²]

---

695. Mujaku, 522, cites *Jingde chuandeng lu* 景德傳燈錄, T2076.51.228b22–24. The original is: *Mohe bore boluomi jing* 摩訶般若波羅蜜經, T223.8.276b6–9.

696. Mujaku, 522, glosses *kuang shijian xuhuan* 況世間虛幻 thus: "What is transmitted by the perverse teachers is illusionary and unreal" [被邪師傳授乃虛幻不實發也].

697. Mujaku, 522, glosses *da di youqing jin zuo mowang* 大地有情盡作魔王 thus: "*Māra kings* means perverse teachers" [忠曰魔王謂邪師也].

698. Mujaku, 522: 第七段論存心般若永不失.

699. Mujaku, 523, glosses *bore shang wu xu qi de gongfu* 般若上無虛棄底工夫 thus: "If you do *gongfu* on top of *prajñā*, even for only a short time, the *gongfu* perfumes the storehouse consciousness and is not discarded as a waste" [忠曰言般若上做工夫雖少時工夫熏藏識不虛棄].

700. Mujaku, 524, glosses *mei wo de bu de* 昧我底不得 thus: "Will be able to clearly see the *original person*" [忠曰可明見本來人也].

701. Araki, 235.

702. Hyesim, 110: 答樊狀大旨無同別處參句. Xia has no biography in *Song History*. Hucker, 405 and 497: "*Tixing* 提刑 is a variant or abbreviation of *tidian xingyu gongshi* 提點刑獄公事

[60.1: *Shows that buddha-matters and Chan words are without difference*[703]]

I have been informed by your letter that you "can execute buddha-matters [i.e., the six perfections and ten-thousand practices], but don't understand Chan words [i.e., the 'tasteless' *huatous*]."[704] "Being able to execute" and "not understanding" are neither different nor the same. It's just that the knower who knows he can execute [buddha-matters] *is* [the understander who understands] Chan words. Understanding Chan words but not being able to execute buddha-matters is like sitting in the midst of water and crying out that one is thirsty, or sitting in the midst of bamboo baskets full of food and crying out that one is hungry.[705] What's the difference? You should know that Chan words *are* buddha-matters, and buddha-matters *are* Chan words. Being able to execute and being able to understand exist in people, not in the dharma. If, on top of that, *here* you go on seeking for identity or differentiation, you will be "mistaking an empty fist [used in a game to distract children] for an understanding of the 'real,' adoring the odd and playing with strangeness in the midst of the six sense organs, six sense objects, and dharmas."[706] That's like trying to go forward while stepping backwards. The more you hurry, the further you will fall behind—more and more estranged and distant from it.

[60.2: *Encourages jettisoning false understanding and engaging in "real" gongfu*[707]]

If you want to take the direct-and-quick path to the opening up of your mind-ground, just take "being-able-to-execute" and "not-being-able-to-execute," "understanding" and "not-understanding," "sameness" and

---

(Judicial Commissioner). . . . responsible for supervising the judicial and penal operations of Prefectures (*zhou* 州) and Districts (*xian* 縣), and joined with Fiscal Commissioners in awarding merit ratings (*kao* 考) to all officials serving in subsidiary units of territorial administration."

703. Mujaku, 524: 第一段示佛事禪語無異.

704. Mujaku, 524, glosses *neng xing foshi er bu jie chanyu* 能行佛事而不解禪語 thus: "*Buddha-matters* in Fan's mind means the six perfections and ten-thousand practices. *Chan words* in Fan's mind means the *huatous* that have neither meaning nor taste" [忠曰佛事者樊意謂六度萬行也禪語者樊意謂無義味話頭].

705. Mujaku, 524–25, glosses *ru ren zai shui de zuo jiao ke* 如人在水底坐叫渴 thus: "Executing buddha-matters is like sitting in the midst of water; not understanding Chan words is like crying out that one is thirsty. The meaning of the simile 'food in baskets' is the same" [忠曰云行佛事如在水底坐云不解禪語如叫渴也飯籮之喩義同].

706. Mujaku, 189, cites *Yongjia zheng dao ge* 永嘉證道歌, T2014.48.396c10–11.

707. Mujaku, 525: 第二段勸捨妄解下實工夫.

"non-sameness," "difference" and "non-difference," "being able to mentally reflect like this," "being able to conjecture like that," and sweep them away to the worlds in all the directions. At the place that can't be swept, look at existence/non-existence, sameness/difference. Suddenly thought and ideation will come to an end.[708] At just the moment of *in that way*, there will be no need to ask questions of anyone else.

61. In Reply to Preceptor Shengquan Gui

[*Commentary: Chan Master Longxiang Zhu'an Shigui (1083–1146) was in Dahui's Yangqi wing of Linji Chan. Hyesim says, "The main purport of the letter in reply to Shengquan is: continuously for the sake of your Chan monks directly present them with the original allotment."*[709] *Written sometime before Shigui's death in Shaoxing 16/1146. This letter cannot be dated exactly.*]

[61.1: *Encourages omitting conventional affairs and shouldering teaching the Way*[710]]

Since there are external protectors [i.e., powerful lay patrons] who are never remiss in paying attention to looking after [the affairs of your monastery's storehouse office[711]], it is okay if you yourself put aside "human [logistical] matters" and continuously engage in the performance of "buddha matters" for the sake of the Chan monks under you. Over a long period of time you will spontaneously become outstanding.

[61.2: *Encourages an* original-allotment *approach to guiding people*[712]]

On top of that, the expectation is that in your room [i.e., the "ten-foot square" room of your private quarters within the monastery] you will

---

708. Mujaku, 525, cites the theme of letter #25.2 as identical.

709. Hyesim, 111: 答聖泉狀大旨頻與衲子直似本分. Mujaku, 526, cites a biographical entry for Chan Master Longxiang Zhu'an Shigui 龍翔竹庵士珪禪師 in *Jiatai pudeng lu* 嘉泰普燈錄 (CBETA, X79, no. 1559, p. 389, c11–p. 390, b13 // Z 2B:10, p. 121, a15–d11 // R137, p. 241, a15–p. 242, b11); and also cites a mention of Chan Master Donglin Gui 東林珪禪師 in *Dahui Pujue chanshi nianpu* 大慧普覺禪師年譜 for Dahui's forty-fifth year (CBETA, J01, no. A042, p. 798, c17–19).

710. Mujaku, 527: 勸濁畧世諦荷擔此道.

711. Mujaku, 527, glosses *cun xin xiang zhao* 存心相照 thus: "*Xiang zhao* means looking after the affairs of the storehouse office" [相照者照顧庫司邊事也].

712. Mujaku, 527: 第二段勸本分接人.

examine students meticulously. You mustn't allow sentiment to intrude. You mustn't talk down to them. If you directly present them with the "fodder for the *original allotment*"⁷¹³ and make them awaken and experience on their own, then you'll be the model of an honored monk who embraces students. If you see that they are hesitant and not advancing, and you then send down explanatory words for them, it will not only blind their eyes—it will also result in their losing the means to the very own *original allotment*.

[61.3: *Discusses the fact that our Chan house is not about getting a lot of recruits*⁷¹⁴]

Not getting many people [with potential for the thoroughly enlightened eye⁷¹⁵]—the fact is, this is as it has always been in our Chan school. If you get one *original-allotment* student or even one-half of one, it won't be a betrayal of our usual ideal!

62. In Reply to Elder Gushan Dai

[*Commentary: Gushan Zongdai was a student of Dahui's student Dongchan Siyue. Mujaku says, "The main idea of this letter relates that the model of a teaching master should employ the* original allotment *to guide people.... This letter dates to Shaoxing 24/1154 when the Master was sixty-six."*⁷¹⁶ *Meizhou-exile letter.*]

---

713. Mujaku, 80, glosses *benfen caoliao* 本分草料 thus: "Undoubtedly, as for the stick, the shout, and verbal teachings, students' *original allotment* has the principle of being able to 'eat' these, and teachers dare to provide them with them the stick, the shout, and verbal teachings. Therefore, they are called 'fodder for the *original-allotment*,' a comparison to the fodder for horses" [蓋棒喝及言句學人本分有可喫此之道理而師家敢與之以棒喝言句故云本分草料以比馬之本分草料也].

714. Mujaku, 528: 第三段論吾家得人不在多也.

715. Mujaku, 528, glosses *bu de ren jishi* 不得人即是 thus: "The principle that there can't be many people with the thoroughly enlightened eye" [徹底明眼人無可多理也].

716. Mujaku, 528: 此書大意述宗師體裁可本分接人也....忠曰此書紹興二十四年甲戌師六十六歲作. Mujaku cites *Jiatai pudeng lu* 嘉泰普燈錄 (CBETA, X79, no. 1559, p. 418, b17–19 // Z 2B:10, p. 149, d3–5 // R137, p. 298, b3–5), which gives Chan Master Fuzhou Gushan Zongdai 福州鼓山宗逮禪師 as a successor of Chan Master Donglin Meng'an Siyue 東禪蒙庵思嶽禪師.

[62.1: *Dahui has received the letter with gifts symbolic of the succession*[717]]

A special courier has come, and I have taken delivery of your letter and the incense symbolic [of our dharma succession]. I understand that at Shimen [Cliff Monastery in Fuzhou (Fujian)] you have opened up the dharma, emerged into the world and sung the Way, have not forgotten your roots and so have burned incense for [your teacher and my student] Elder Siyue, and have continued our Yangqi lineage [of Linji Chan].

[62.2: *Shows the method for guiding students who come*[718]]

Since you have already come to understand and "own" *this matter*, you must do things in a lively way from beginning to end. Relying on your "single chess move" of real awakening to live [as an abbot] in peaceful retreat in your ten-foot square room will be as difficult as carrying on your shoulders a hundred-and-twenty-catty load and crossing over a bridge made of a single plank. If your footing slips, you won't be able to preserve your own life—how much less will you be able to "take out the nail, pull out the peg" for students and save those other people!

[62.3: *Extensively cites the ancients as proof*[719]]

An ancient said: "*This matter* is like an eighty-year old's entering the imperial examination testing site. How could he be like a child playing games?"[720] Another ancient [i.e., Chan Master "Big Bug" Cen of Changsha] said: "If I were to raise the Chan teaching in only one direction [i.e., show only the highest teaching of Chan], the grass in front of the Dharma Hall would grow a foot deep [i.e., no one would understand, people would disperse, and so in the empty monastery the grass would grow deep], and you

---

717. Mujaku, 529: 第一段領書信.

718. Mujaku, 530: 第二段示接來學法.

719. Mujaku, 530: 第三段廣引古人證.

720. *Liandeng hui yao* 聯燈會要: "When an eighty-year old enters the imperial examination testing site, truly he's not a child [carelessly] playing games. If one word on his exam paper is wrong, he's ten-thousand miles from his hometown" [八十翁翁入場屋。真誠不是小兒戲。一言若差。鄉關萬里。] (CBETA, X79, no. 1557, p. 192, a24–b1 // Z 2B:9, p. 399, b13–14 // R136, p. 797, b13–14).

would have to ask the Prior [to preach the shallow teaching]."[721] Yantou always said: "Before someone has even opened his mouth, seeing through with a single glance—that's one whose eye is sharp [i.e., a clever fellow who understands before a word is spit out]."[722] National Master Gushan Shenyan said: "[What about] the line of verse about not stepping over to Mt. Shimen."[723] Muzhou said: "An open-and-shut case—I'll excuse you from thirty blows of the stick."[724] Fenyang Wuye said: "Don't engage in phantasmal thought."[725] Whenever Luzu saw a monk entering the gate, he immediately turned around and did cross-legged sitting facing the wall.[726] When working for the sake of others, you should not darken these models, and then you will not lose the Chan purport that has come down to us from ancient times.

[62.4: *Speaks of being equipped with the five conditions*[727]]

Of old Guishan said to Yangshan: "The erection of a dharma pennant and establishment of the Chan purport somewhere[728]—when one is equipped with five conditions, only then can he achieve success."[729] The

---

721. *Jingde chuandeng lu* 景德傳燈錄, T2076.51.274a10–13.

722. Untraced. Mujaku, 531, glosses *yan zhuo shuo de* 眼卓朔地 thus: "One who understands before a word is spit out is a clever fellow" [言向未吐語已前見得即是伶利漢也].

723. Mujaku, 531, cites *Jingde chuandeng lu* 景德傳燈錄, T2076.51.351b22–23; and *Wu deng hui yuan* 五燈會元: "Gushan always said: 'There's another person who doesn't step over to Shimen. There must be a line of verse about not stepping over to Shimen. What about the line of verse about not stepping over to Shimen? I have dwelled there thirty-plus years. Those who came from the five lakes and four seas at the high mountain's peak saw the mountains and played with the waters. But I never saw one person who was sharp and comprehended *this state of being*. At the present is there a person who comprehends? If there is one who comprehends, don't remain concealed among you. If not, it's best you disperse" [鼓山尋常道。更有一人不跨石門。須有不跨石門句。作麼生是不跨石門句。鼓山自住三十餘年。五湖四海來者向高山頂上看山翫水。未見一人快利。通得箇消息。如今還有人通得也未。若通得亦不昧諸兄弟。若無。不如散去。] (CBETA, X80, no. 1565, p. 156, a15–19 // Z 2B:11, p. 129, a9–13 // R138, p. 257, a9–13).

724. Mujaku, 531, cites *Jingde chuandeng lu* 景德傳燈錄, T2076.51.291b17–19.

725. Mujaku, 531, cites *Jingde chuandeng lu* 景德傳燈錄, T2076.51.257a25.

726. Mujaku, 531, cites *Jingde chuandeng lu* 景德傳燈錄, T2076.51.251c28–252a1.

727. Mujaku, 532: 第四段言緣備足.

728. Mujaku, 532, cites *Yongjia zheng dao ge* 永嘉證道歌, T2014.48.396b17–18.

729. Untraced.

five conditions are: the condition of external protectors [i.e., powerful lay patrons]; the condition of lay donors; the condition of Chan students [who come to join and become followers]; the condition of land [for a monastic residence]; and the condition of [a house style of propagating] the Way.[730] I have heard that Censor Zhao Gong[731] is the [external protector] who invited you to take up residence, and [the lay donor] Retired Director of Studies Zheng Gong[732] accompanied you to your installation as abbot. In all-under-heaven these two gentlemen are scholars [of high status]. In this regard, you are for the most part equipped with the five conditions. When Chan students come from the Min region [Fujian], everyone will sigh in admiration over the flourishing state of your dharma-seat [i.e., the condition of having land for a residence], the lay donors committed to you, the scholar-official serving as eternal protector, the absence of Māra blockages in you as abbot [i.e., the condition of a house style of propagating the Way], and Chan students who cluster like clouds. Before your physical strength has begun to decline, you should continuously inspire your Chan monks in *this matter*. When setting about teaching them,[733] you must go at it with heart and soul—you mustn't be careless.

[62.5: *Rejects teachers' falsely bestowing the seal*[734]]

Because in recent years there has been a party of peddlers [i.e., bad students]—everywhere they're studying piles of books, entire shoulder-poles' worth, of "imitation Chan."[735] Frequently teaching masters are careless in dispensing [an easy seal of approval[736] to such students]; with the result

---

730. Mujaku, 532, glosses *dao yuan* 道緣 thus: "Every [teacher's] sayings and actions have a different house style—dangerous precipices, winding roads, and so forth. Thus, students who congregate admire their various house styles, and this is *dao yuan*" [忠曰人人所說所行有別家風嶮峻遠路等也然會下學者慕其各各家風者是道緣也].

731. Mujaku, 532, glosses *Zhao gong* 趙公 thus: "Could not identify" [未可攷].

732. Mujaku, 533, glosses *Zheng gong* 鄭公 thus: "Could not identify" [未可攷].

733. Mujaku, 534, cites *Foguo Yuanwu chanshi biyan lu* 佛果圜悟禪師碧巖錄, T2003.48.180c1–5.

734. Mujaku, 534: 第五段斥宗師妄印可.

735. Mujaku, 534, glosses *yi dui yi dan* 一堆一擔 thus: "They take the sayings of old dead fellows and sutra quotations and record them in their great big books" [忠曰謂以死老漢語經教文字記戴大冊子也]; and cites letter #33.3 as the meaning of *imitation*.

736. Mujaku, 535, glosses *zaoci fangguo* 造次放過 thus: "Means: easily give the seal of approval" [言容易許可也].

that [the students,] having reverentially received this "big talk" as the real thing, then go on in turn to confer such a "seal" upon others—this deceives later people and makes the true Chan mind ever more faint. The [authentic Chan] style of solely transmitting [the mind-seal] and directly pointing [at human mind][737] sweeps the ground free of everything. You must pay close attention!

[62.6: *Discusses the relative importance of property/money and dharma*[738]]

When [my teacher's teacher] the "old-man patriarch" Wuzu[739] was dwelling at Mt. Baiyun [in Shuzhou, Anhui], he once said in a letter in reply to Preceptor Lingyuan:[740] "This summer the villages have harvested no grain, but that doesn't worry me. What does worry me is that, in the entire Monks Hall of several hundred Chan monks, not one of them has broken through the [*wu* 無] *huatou* of a dog's having no buddha-nature.[741] I simply fear that the buddhadharma is on the point of extinction."[742] Please take a look at this example. As for where the teaching master in charge of dharma is to place his mental exertion—how could he attach importance to the amount of money from grain production or the size of the monastery, or be impatient about such detailed affairs as rice and salt?

---

737. Mujaku, 535, cites *Foguo Yuanwu chanshi biyan lu* 佛果圜悟禪師碧巖錄, T2003.48.140a28–b2.

738. Mujaku, 535: 第六段論財法輕重.

739. Wuzu Fayan 五祖法演 (?–1104) was in the Yangqi wing of Linji Chan. Mujaku, 535, glosses *wu zu shi weng* 五祖師翁 thus: "Wuzu Fayan was the teacher of Yuanwu. To Dahui he was grandfather, and so Dahui calls him 'old-man patriarch'" [忠曰五祖演是圜悟之師於大慧爲祖父故以師翁稱]; and cites *Liandeng hui yao* 聯燈會要 (CBETA, X79, no. 1557, p. 135, c24–p. 136, a1 // Z 2B:9, p. 342, c1–2 // R136, p. 684, a1–2).

740. Lingyuan Weiqing 靈源惟清 (?–1117) was in the Huanglong wing of Linji Chan. Mujaku, 535, cites *Jianzhong jingguo xu deng lu* 建中靖國續燈錄 (CBETA, X78, no. 1556, p. 771, a11 // Z 2B:9, p. 149, d6 // R136, p. 298, b6).

741. Araki, 240, translates *hua* 話 as *watō* 話頭 (*huatou*): 一堂数百の禅僧が、ひと夏に一人も狗子無仏性の話頭を理解しないこと. However, Morten Schlütter, *How Zen Became Zen: The Dispute over Enlightenment and the Formation of Chan Buddhism in Song Dynasty China* (Honolulu: University of Hawai'i Press, 2008), 114, renders *hua* 話 as *story*. The difference, of course, is directly relevant to the question of whether Wuzu Fayan taught *huatou* practice.

742. *Rentian baojian* 人天寶鑑 (CBETA, X87, no. 1612, p. 17, b20–24 // Z 2B:21, p. 65, c11–15 // R148, p. 130, a11–15).

[62.7: *Discusses the allotment of tasks*[743]]

Having popped your head into the world and assumed this title "good teacher," you should single-mindedly use the matter of the *original allotment* to guide students coming to you from the four directions. As for all the provisions in the storehouse office, tell the administrators who know cause and effect to divide up the tasks into the various offices. Order them to take charge of these matters and periodically issue a broad summary. There is no need for placing too many monks in these positions. In the case of daily meals, when you always make sure you have leeway with some left over, naturally there will be no wasted effort.

[62.8: *Proves that using the* original allotment *to guide students is beneficial*[744]]

When your Chan monks have arrived inside your room, bring down the sharp edge of the sword blade most severely. Don't do it in a muddled manner. Take, for instance, Chan Master Xuefeng Kong.[745] A while back I was in a group with him at Yunmen Hermitage on Mt. Yunju [in Haihun]. I knew that he, without deceiving himself, was a person in the buddhadharma, and so I fervently presented him with *original-allotment* tongs [for forging metal]. Later, on his own, at another place he awakened. Once the great dharma was bright in him, he was all-at-once able to enjoy the application of the tongs he had received previously from me, and then for the first time he realized that I don't accommodate the buddhadharma to customary etiquette. Last year he sent me his one-volume sayings record.[746] "In moments of haste, he cleaves to the Chan purport of Linji; in moments of suffering setbacks, he cleaves to the Chan purport of Linji."[747] At present I am sending it to the assembly quarters in order to have the party of Chan monks read it. In this connection, I took up the writing brush and wrote a postface for this sayings record, especially exalting it,

---

743. Mujaku, 536: 第七段論事務處分.

744. Mujaku, 537: 第八段證本分接人之有益.

745. Mujaku, 537, cites *Jiatai pudeng lu* 嘉泰普燈錄 (CBETA, X79, no. 1559, p. 353, b12–p. 354, a14 // Z 2B:10, p. 84, d18–p. 85, c14 // R137, p. 168, b18–p. 170, a14).

746. *Xuefeng Huikong chanshi yulu* 雪峰慧空禪師語錄 (CBETA, X69, no. 1346, p. 241, b17 // Z 2:25, p. 137, c10 // R120, p. 274, a10).

747. Playing on *Analects, Li ren pian* 里仁篇.

in order to make it into a model for future dharma talks by *original-allot-ment* Chan monks. Suppose I had in the beginning for his sake [i.e., Chan Master Kong's sake] in a muddled manner spoken [earnest and kind] "old-grandma Chan" [i.e., employed a teaching style that took a roundabout way and made detours]; then, after his eyes had opened, he certainly would have—without a doubt—cursed me!

[62.9: *Gives quotations connected to the above idea*[748]]

Therefore, an ancient said: "I don't attach importance to the virtue of my former teachers; I just attach importance to the fact that my former teachers didn't lay bare everything for me. If they had laid bare everything for me, how could there be today's [awakening]?"[749] In other words, it's this kind of principle [i.e., one must not give it to them on a plate]! Zhaozhou said: "If I were to guide people according to their karmic capacities, then the three vehicles and twelve divisions of the teachings that guided them would actually exist. But *here* I just take the matter of the *original allotment* to guide them. If the student can't be guided, it's because his spirit was dull. It has nothing to do with this old monk."[750] Think about this!

Letters of Chan Master Dahui Pujue

63. *[Postface]*

Chan Master Dahui spoke dharma for over forty years, and his words fill all-under-heaven. Habitually, he did not allow followers to record his words, but Chan monks privately wrote them down and transmitted them. In time they became books. In his late years, because many people made ardent requests of him, he allowed them to circulate in the world. Even

---

748. Mujaku, 538: 第九段引證結上意.

749. Hyesim, 113: "Today's awakening" [今日悟也]. Mujaku, 538, cites *Jingde chuandeng lu* 景德傳燈錄, T2076.51.321b20–322a16. Mujaku, 538, glosses *ruo wei wo shuopo qi you jinri* 若爲我說破豈有今日 thus: "Actually, it's a Xiangyan saying" [忠曰實是香嚴語]; and cites *Liandeng hui yao* 聯燈會要 (CBETA, X79, no. 1557, p. 76, c6–18 // Z 2B:9, p. 283, b12–c6 // R136, p. 565, b12–p. 566, a6).

750. Mujaku, 539, cites *Gu zunsu yulu* 古尊宿語錄 (CBETA, X68, no. 1315, p. 79, a16–19 // Z 2:23, p. 155, d2–5 // R118, p. 310, b2–5).

so, in his assembly there were earlier and later followers; and there were differences in the details and omissions of what his students saw and heard.[751] Also, each of the dharma talks[752] obtained by talented and virtuous members of the scholar-official class was stored away as a private treasure, and there is no way to examine all of them. The quantity gathered here is not at all exhaustive. Please wait until I have collected more and compiled a follow-up volume!

Respectfully Spoken by [Huang] Wenchang

---

751. Mujaku, 539, glosses *jian wen* 見聞 thus: "What his Chan monks saw and heard" [忠曰 衲子之見聞也].

752. Huang Wenchang also edited a version of *Dharma Talks of Chan Master Dahui Pujue (Dahui Pujue chanshi fayu* 大慧普覺禪師法語).

Five-Mountains (Gozan) Edition
Dahui Pujue chanshi shu
大慧普覺禪師書

THE TEXT USED for this translation is the photographic reproduction of a Five-Mountains reprint edition found in Shiina Kōyū 椎名宏雄, ed., *Gozanban Chūgoku zenseki sōkan* 五山版中国禅籍叢刊 10: *Shibun sekitoku* 詩文尺牘 (Kyoto: Rinsen shoten, 2013), 603–652 (text) and 681–683 (bibliographical notes). This elegant edition, which has considerable marginalia, is stored in the Tanimura Bunko of Kyoto University (京都大学図書館谷村文庫). For further details on this and other Five-Mountains editions, see Kawase Kazuma, *Gozanban no kenkyū* (Tokyo: Nihon koshosekishō kyōkai, 1970), 1:411b–412a. Section numbers below derive from Mujaku Dōchū's commentary *Pearl in the Willow Basket* (*Kōrōju* 栲栳珠). Divergences from the edition of *Letters of Dahui* contained in fascicles 25–30 of the *Dahui Pujue chanshi yulu* (大慧普覺禪師語錄; T1998A.47.916b8–943b4), and occasionally from Araki's different Five-Mountains reprint edition, are noted.

大慧普覺禪師書

參學慧然錄

淨智居士黃文昌重編

答曾侍郎 (天游) (問書附)

[*QL* 1.1] 開。頃在長沙。得圜悟老師書。稱公晚歲相從。所得甚是奇偉。念之再三。今八年矣。常恨未獲親聞緒餘。惟切景仰。[*QL* 1.2] 某自幼年發心。參礼知識。扣問此事。弱冠之後。即爲婚官所役。用工夫不純。因循至今。老矣。未有所聞。常自愧歎。[*QL* 1.3] 然而立志發願。實不在淺淺知見之間。以爲不悟則已。悟則須直到古人親證處。方爲大休歇之地。此心雖未嘗一念退屈。自覺工夫終未純一。可謂志願大而力量小也。[*QL* 1.4] 向者痛懇圜悟老師。老師示以法語六段。其初直示此事。後舉雲門趙州放下著。須弥山兩則因緣。令下鈍工。常自舉覺。久久必有入處。老婆心切如此。其奈鈍滯太甚。[*QL* 1.5] 今幸私家塵緣都畢。閑居無佗事。政在痛自鞭策。以償初志。第恨未得親炙教誨耳。[*QL* 1.6] 一生敗闕。己一一呈似。必能洞照此心。望委曲提警。日用當如何做工夫。庶幾不涉佗塗。徑與本地相契也。[*QL* 1.7] 如此說話。敗闕亦不少。但方投誠。自難隱逃。良可憨也。至扣。

[1.1] 承敘。及自幼年至仕官。參礼諸大宗匠。中間爲科舉婚官所役。又爲惡覺惡習所勝。未能純一做工夫。以此爲大罪。又能痛念無常世間種種虛幻無一可樂。專心欲究此一段大事因緣。甚愜病僧意。[1.2] 然既爲士人仰禄爲生。科舉婚官世間所不能免者。亦非公之罪也。以小罪而生大怖懼。非無始曠大劫來。承事真善知識。熏習般若種智之深。焉能如此。[1.3] 而公所謂大罪者。聖賢亦不能免。但知虛幻非究竟法。能回心此箇門中。以般若智水。滌除垢染之穢。清淨自居。從脚下去一刀兩段。更不起相續心。足矣。不必思前念後也。既曰虛幻。則作時亦幻。受時亦幻。知覺時亦幻。迷倒時亦幻。過去現在未來皆悉是幻。今日知非。則以幻藥復治幻病。病瘥藥除。依前只是舊時人。若別有人有法。則是邪魔外道見解也。公深思之。但如此崖將去。時時於靜勝中。切不得忘了須弥山放下著兩則語。但從脚下著實做將去。己過者不須怖畏。亦不必思量。思量怖畏。即障道矣。[1.4] 但於諸佛前。發大誓願。願此心堅固。永不退失。仗諸佛加被。遇善知識。一言之下。頓亡生死。悟證無上正等菩提。續佛慧命。以報諸佛莫大之恩。若如此。則久久無有不悟之理。不見。善財童子從文殊發心。

漸次南行。過一百一十城。參五十三善知識。末後於彌勒一彈指頃。頓亡前來諸善知識所得法門。復依彌勒教。思欲奉覲文殊。於是文殊。遙伸右手。過一百一十由旬。按善財頂曰。善哉善哉善男子。若離信根。心劣憂悔。功行不具。退失精勤。於一善根。心生住著。於少功德。便以爲足。不能善巧發起行願。不爲善知識之所攝護。乃至不能了知如是法性。如是理趣。如是法門。如是所行。如是境界。若周遍知。若種種知。若盡源底。若解了。若趣入。若解說。若分別。若證知。若獲得。皆悉不能。文殊如是宣示善財。善財於言下。成就阿僧祇法門。具足無量大智光明。入普賢門。於一念中。悉見三千大千世界微塵數諸善知識。悉皆親近。恭敬承事。受行其教。得不忘念智莊嚴藏解脫。以至入普賢毛孔刹。於一毛孔。行一步。過不可說不可說佛刹。微塵數世界。與普賢等。諸佛等。刹等。行等。及解脫自在悉皆同等。無二無別。當恁麼時。始能回三毒爲三聚淨戒。回六識爲六神通。回煩惱爲菩提。回無明爲大智。如上遮一絡索。只在當人末後一念真實而已。善財於彌勒彈指之間。尚能頓亡諸善知識所證三昧。況無始虛偽惡業習氣耶。若以前所作底罪爲實。則現今目前境界。皆爲實有。乃至官職富貴恩愛。悉皆是實。既是實。則地獄天堂亦實。煩惱無明亦實。作業者亦實。受報者亦實。所證底法門亦實。若作遮般見解。則盡未來際。更無有人趣佛乘矣。三世諸佛。諸代祖師。種種方便。翻爲妄語矣。[1.5] 承公發書時。焚香對諸聖。及遙礼菴中。而後遣。公誠心至切如此。相去雖不甚遠。未得面言。信意信手。不覺忉怛如許。雖若繁絮。亦出誠至之心。不敢以一言一字相欺。苟欺公。則是自欺耳。[1.6] 又記得。善財見最寂靜婆羅門。得誠語解脫。過去現在未來諸佛菩薩。於阿耨菩提。無已退。無現退。無當退。凡有所求。莫不成滿。皆由誠至所及也。公既與竹椅蒲團爲侶。不異善財見最寂靜婆羅門。又發雲門書。對諸聖。遙礼而後遣。只要雲門信許。此誠至之劇也。[1.7] 但相聽。只如此做工夫。將來於阿耨菩提。成滿無疑矣。

又。

[2.1] 公處身富貴。而不爲富貴所折困。非夙植般若種智。焉能如是。[2.2] 但恐中忘此意。爲利根聰明所障。以有所得心在前頓放故。不能於古人直截徑要處。一刀兩段。直下休歇。[2.3] 此病非獨賢士大夫。久參衲子亦然。多不肯退步就省力處做工夫。只以聰明意識。計較思量。向外馳求。乍聞知識向聰明意識思量計較外。示以本分草料。多是當面蹉過。將謂從上古德有實法與人。如趙州放下著。雲門須彌山之類。是也。巖頭曰。却物爲上。逐物爲下。又曰。大統綱宗。要須識句。甚麼是句。百不思時喚作正句。亦云居頂。亦云得住。亦云歷歷。亦云惺惺。亦云恁麼時。將恁麼時。等

破一切是非。纔恁麼。便不恁麼。是句亦剗。非句亦剗。如一團火相似。觸著便燒。有甚麼向傍處。[2.4] 今時士大夫多以思量計較爲窟宅。聞恁麼說話。便道莫落空否。喻似舟未翻。先自跳下水去。此深可憐愍。近至江西。見呂居仁。居仁留心此段因緣甚久。亦深有此病。渠豈不是聰明。某嘗問之曰。公怕落空。能知怕者。是空耶。是不空耶。試道看。渠佇思。欲計較祗對。當時便與一喝。至今茫然討巴鼻不著。此蓋以求悟證之心在前頓放。自作障難。非干別事。公試如此做工夫。日久月深。自然築著磕著。[2.5] 若欲將心待悟。將心待休歇。從腳下參到彌勒下生。亦不能得悟。亦不能得休歇。轉加迷悶耳。平田和尚曰。神光不昧。萬古徽猷。入此門來。莫存知解。[2.6] 又古德曰。此事不可以有心求。不可以無心得。不可以語言造。不可以寂默通。此是第一等。入泥入水。老婆說話。往往參禪人。只恁麼念過。殊不子細看是甚道理。若是箇有筋骨底。聊聞舉著。直下將金剛王寶劍。一截截斷此四路葛藤。則生死路頭亦斷。凡聖路頭亦斷。計較思量亦斷。得失是非亦斷。當人腳跟下。淨倮倮赤灑灑。沒可把。豈不快哉。豈不暢哉。[2.7] 不見。昔日灌谿和尚。初參臨濟。濟見來。便下繩牀。驀胷擒住。灌谿便云。領領。濟知其已徹。即便推出。更無言句與之商量。當恁麼時。灌谿如何思量計較祗對得。古來幸有如此牓樣。如今人總不將爲事。只爲麁心。灌谿當初。若有一點待悟待證。待休歇底心在前時。莫道被擒住便悟。便是縛却手脚。遍四天下挖一遭。也不能得悟。也不能得休歇。[2.8] 尋常計較安排底是識情。隨生死遷流底亦是識情。怕怖憧惶底亦是識情。而今參學之人。不知是病。只管在裏許。頭出頭沒。教中所謂。隨識而行。不隨智。以故昧却本地風光。本來面目。[2.9] 若或一時放得下。百不思量計較。忽然失脚。蹋著鼻孔。即此識情便是真空妙智。更無別智可得。若別有所得。別有所證。則又却不是也。如人迷時喚東作西。及至悟時。即西便是東。無別有東。[2.10] 此真空妙智。與太虛空齊壽。只遮太虛空中。還有一物礙得佗否。雖不受一物礙。而不妨諸物於空中往來。此真空妙智亦然。生死凡聖垢染。著一點不得。雖著不得。而不礙生死凡聖於中往來。[2.11] 如此信得及。見得徹。方是箇出生入死。得大自在底漢。始與趙州放下著。雲門須彌山。有少分相應。若信不及。放不下。却請擔取一座須彌山。到處行脚。遇明眼人。分明舉似。一笑。

又。

[3.1] 老龐云。但願空諸所有。切勿實諸所無。只了得遮兩句。一生參學事畢。[3.2] 今時有一種剃頭外道。自眼不明。只管教人死獝狙地。休去歇去。若如此休歇。到千佛出世。也休歇不得。轉使心頭迷悶耳。又教人隨緣管帶。忘情默照。照來照去。帶來帶去。轉加迷

悶。無有了期。殊失祖師方便。錯指示人。教人一向虛生浪死。更
教人是事莫管。但只恁麼歇去歇得來。情念不生。到恁麼時。不是
宜¹然無知。直是惺惺歷歷。遮般底。更是毒害。瞎却人眼。不是小
事。[3.3] 雲門尋常見此輩。不把做人看待。彼既自眼不明。只管將冊
子上語。依樣教人。遮箇作麼生教得。若信著遮般底。永劫參不得。
雲門尋常不是不教人坐禪向靜處做工夫。此是應病與藥。實無恁麼指
示人處。不見。黃檗和尚云。我此禪宗。從上相承以來。不曾教人求
知求解。只云學道。早是接引之詞。然道亦不可學。情存學道。却成
迷道。道無方所。名大乘心。此心不在內外中間。實無方所。第一不
得作知解。只是說汝而今情量處爲道。情量若盡。心無方所。此道天
真。本無名字。只爲世人不識。迷在情中。所以諸佛出來說破此事。
恐你不了。權立道名。不可守名而生解也。[3.4] 前來所說瞎眼漢。錯
指示人。皆是認魚目作明殊。守名而生解者。教人管帶。此是守目前
鑑覺而生解者。教人硬休去歇去。此是守忘懷空寂而生解者。歇到無
覺無知。如土木瓦石相似。當恁麼時。不是冥然無知。又是錯認方便
解縛語而生解者。教人隨緣照顧。莫教惡覺現前。遮箇又是認著軀殼
情識而生解者。教人但放曠任其自在。莫管生心動念。念起念滅。本
無實體。若執爲實。則生死心生矣。遮箇又是守自然體。爲究竟法而
生解者。如上諸病。非干學道人事。皆由瞎眼宗師錯指示耳。[3.5] 公
既清淨自居。存一片真實堅固向道之心。莫管工夫純一不純一。但
莫於古人言句上。只管如疊塔子相似。一層了又一層。枉用工夫。
無有了期。但只存心於一處。無有不得底。時節因緣到來。自然築
著磕著。嚗地省去耳。不起一念還有過也無。云須彌山。一物不將
來時如何。云放下著。遮裏疑不破。只在遮裏參。更不必自生枝葉
也。[3.6] 若信得雲門及。但恁麼參。別無佛法指似²人。若信不及。一
任江北江南問王老。一狐疑了一狐疑。

又。

[4.1] 細讀來書。乃知四威儀中。無時間斷。不爲公冗所奪。於急流
中。常自猛省。殊不放逸。道心愈久愈堅固。深愜鄙懷。[4.2] 然世
間塵勞。如火熾然。何時是了。正在鬧中。不得忘却竹椅蒲團上事。
平昔留心靜勝處。正要鬧中用。若鬧中不得力。却似不曾在靜中做工
夫一般。承有前緣駁雜。今受此報之歎。獨不敢聞命。若動此念。
則障道矣。古德云。隨流認得性。無喜亦無憂。淨名云。譬如高原
陸地不生蓮花。卑濕淤泥乃生此花。老胡云。真如不守自性。隨緣
成就一切事法。又云。隨緣赴感靡不周。而常處此菩提座。豈欺人

---

1. Translation follows T and Araki = 冥.

2. T = 示.

哉。若以靜處爲是。鬧處爲非。則是壞世間相而求實相。離生滅而
求寂滅。好靜惡鬧時。正好著力。驀然鬧裏撞翻靜時消息。其力能
勝竹椅蒲團上千萬億倍。但相聽。決不相誤。[4.3] 又承以老龐兩句。
爲行住坐臥之銘箴。善不可加。若正鬧時生厭惡。則乃是自擾其心
耳。若動念時。只以老龐兩句提撕。便是熱時一服清涼散也。[4.4] 公
具決定信。是大智慧人。久做靜中工夫。方敢說這般話。於佗人分
上。則不可。若向業識茫茫增上慢人前。如此說。乃是添佗惡業擔
子。[4.5] 禪門種種病痛。已具前書。不識曾子細理會否。

又。

[5.1] 承諭。外息諸緣。內心無喘。可以入道。是方便門。借方便門。以
入道則可。守方便而不捨。則爲病。誠如來語。山野讀之。不勝歡喜
踊躍之至。[5.2] 今諸方漆桶輩。只爲守方便而不捨。以實法指示人。
以故瞎人眼不少。所以山野作辨邪正說。以救之。近世魔強法弱。以
湛入合湛爲究竟者。不可勝數。守方便不捨。爲宗師者。如麻似粟。
山野近嘗與衲子輩。舉此兩段。正如來書所說。不差一字。[5.3] 非左
右留心般若中。念念不間斷。則不能洞曉從上諸聖諸異方便也。公
已捉著欛柄矣。既得欛柄在手。何慮不捨方便門而入道耶。但只如此
做工夫。看經教并古人語錄種種差別言句。亦只如此做工夫。如須彌
山。放下著。狗子無佛性話。竹篦子話。一口吸盡西江水話。庭前栢
樹子話。亦只如此做工夫。更不得別生異解。別求道理。別作伎倆
也。公能向急流中時時自如此提掇。道業若不成就。則佛法無靈驗
矣。記取記取。[5.4] 承夜夢焚香。入山僧之室。甚從容。切不得作夢
會。須知是真入室。不見。舍利弗問須菩提。夢中說六波羅蜜。與覺
時同別。須菩提云。此義幽深。吾不能說。此會有彌勒大士。汝往
彼問。咄漏逗不少。雪竇云。當時若不放過。隨後與一剳。誰名彌
勒。誰是彌勒者。便見氷銷瓦解。咄雪竇亦漏逗不少。或有人問。只
如曾待制夜夢入雲門之室。且道與覺時同別。雲門即向佗道。誰是
入室者。誰是爲入室者。誰是作夢者。誰是說夢者。誰是不作夢會
者。誰是真入室者。咄亦漏逗不少。

又。

[6.1] 來書細讀數過。足見辦鐵石心。立決定志。不肯草草。但只如此
崖。到臘月三十日。亦能與闔家老子廝抵。更休說豁開頂門眼。握
金剛王寶劒。坐毗盧頂上也。[6.2] 某嘗謂方外道友曰。今時學道之
士。只求速效。不知錯了也。却謂無事省緣。靜坐體究爲空過時光。
不如看幾卷經。念幾聲佛。佛前多礼幾拜。懺悔平生所作底罪過。要

免閭家老子手中鐵棒。此是愚人所爲。而今道家者流。全以妄想心。想日精月華。吞霞服氣。尚能留形住世。不被寒暑所逼。況迴此心此念。全在般若中耶。[6.3] 先聖明明有言。喻如太末蟲處處能泊。唯不能泊於火燄之上。衆生亦尔。處處能緣。唯不能緣於般若之上。苟念念不退初心。把自家心識緣世間塵勞底。回來抵在般若上。雖今生打未徹。臨命終時。定不爲惡業所牽。流落惡道。來生出頭。隨我今生願力。定在般若中現成受用。此是決定底事。無可疑者。[6.4] 衆生界中事。不著學。無始時來習得熟。路頭亦熟。自然取之左右。逢其原。須著撥置。出世間學般若心。無始時來背違。乍聞知識說著。自然理會不得。須著立決定志。與之作頭抵。決不兩立。此處若入得深。彼處不著排遣。諸魔外道。自然竄伏矣。生處放教熟。熟處放教生。政爲此也。[6.5] 日用做工夫處。捉著欛柄。漸覺省力時。便是得力處也。

答李參政(漢老) (問書附)

[QL 7.1] 邴近扣籌室。伏蒙激發蒙滯。忽有省入。顧惟根識暗鈍。平生學解。盡落情見。一取一捨。如衣壞絮行草棘中。適自纏繞。今一笑頓釋。欣幸可量。非大宗匠委曲垂慈。何以致此。[QL 7.2] 自到城中。著衣喫飯。抱子弄孫。色色仍舊。既亡拘滯之情。亦不作奇特之想。其餘凤習舊障。亦稍輕微。臨別叮嚀之語。不敢忘也。[QL 7.3] 重念。始得入門。而大法未明。應機接物。觸事未能無礙。更望有以提誨。使卒有所至。庶無玷於法席矣。

[7.1] 示諭。自到城中。著衣喫飯。抱子弄孫。色色仍舊。既亡拘滯之情。亦不作奇特之想。宿習舊障。亦稍輕微。三復斯語。歡喜踊躍。此乃學佛之驗也。儻非過量大人。於一笑中。百了千當。則不能知吾家果有不傳之妙。若不尔者。疑怒二字法門。盡未來際。終不能壞。使太虛空爲雲門口。草木瓦石皆放光明。助說道理。亦不奈何。方信此段因緣。不可傳。不可學。須是自證自悟自肯自休。方始徹頭。公今一笑頓亡所得。夫復何言。黃面老子曰。不取衆生所言說一切有爲虛妄事。雖復不依言語道。亦復不著無言說。來書所說。既亡拘滯之情。亦不作奇特之想。暗與黃面老子所言契合。即是說者。名爲佛說。離是說者。即波旬說。山野平昔有大誓願。寧以此身代一切衆生。受地獄苦。終不以此口將佛法以爲人情。瞎一切人眼。[7.2] 公既到恁麼田地。自知此事不從人得。但且仍舊。更不須問大法明未明。應機礙不礙。若作是念。則不仍舊矣。承過夏後。方可復出。甚愜病僧意。若更熱荒馳求不歇。則不相當也。[7.3] 前日見公歡

喜之甚。以故不敢說破。恐傷言語。今歡喜既定。方敢指出。此事極
不容易。須生慚愧始得。往往利根上智者。得之不費力。遂生容易
心。便不修行。多被目前境界奪將去。作主宰不得。日久月深。迷而
不返。道力不能勝業力。魔得其便。定爲魔所攝持。臨命終時。亦不
得力。千萬記取前日之語。理則頓悟。乘悟併銷。事非頓除。因次第
盡。行住坐臥。切不可忘了。[7.4] 其餘古人種種差別言句。皆不可以
爲實。然亦不可以爲虛。久久純熟。自然默默契自本心矣。不必別求
殊勝奇特也。昔水潦和尚。於採藤處。問馬祖。如何是祖師西來意。
祖云。近前來。向你道。水潦纔近前。馬祖攔胸一踢踢倒。水潦不
覺起來。拍手呵呵大笑。祖曰。汝見箇甚麼道理便笑。水潦曰。百千
法門。無量妙義。今日於一毛頭上。盡底識得根源去。馬祖便不管
佗。雪峯知皷山緣熟。一日忽然驀胸擒住曰。是甚麼。皷山釋然了
悟。了心便亡。唯微笑。舉手搖曳而已。雪峯曰。子作道理耶。皷山
復搖手曰。和尚。何道理之有。雪峯便休去。蒙山道明禪師。趁盧行
者。至大庾嶺。奪衣鉢。盧公擲於石上曰。此衣表信。可力爭耶。任
公將去。明舉之不動。乃曰。我求法。非爲衣鉢也。願行者開示。盧
公曰。不思善。不思惡。正當恁麼時。那箇是上座本來面目。明當時
大悟。通身汗流。泣淚作礼曰。上來密語密意外。還更有意旨否。盧
公曰。我今爲汝說者。即非密意。汝若返照自己面目。密却在汝邊。
我若說得。即不密也。以三尊宿三段因緣。較公於一笑中釋然。優劣
何如。請自斷看。還更別有奇特道理麼。若更別有。則却似不曾釋然
也。[7.5] 但知作佛。莫愁佛不解語。古來得道之士。自己既充足。推
己之餘。應機接物。如明鏡當臺。明珠在掌。胡來胡現。漢來漢現。
非著意也。若著意。則有實法與人矣。[7.6] 公欲大法明。應機無滯。
但且仍舊。不必問人。久久自點頭矣。[7.7] 臨行面稟之語。請書於座
右。此外別無說。縱有說。於公分上。盡成剩語矣。葛藤太多。姑置
是事。

又。

[QL 8.1] 邴比蒙　誨　答。　備　悉深旨。邴自有驗者三。一事無逆
順。隨緣即應。不留智中。二宿習濃厚。不加排遣。自尔輕微。三
古人公案。舊所茫然。時復瞥地。此非自昧者。[QL 8.2] 前書大法
未明之語。蓋恐得少爲足。當擴而充之。豈別求勝解耶。[QL 8.3]
淨除現流。理則不無。敢不銘佩。

[8.1] 信後益增瞻仰。不識日來隨緣放曠。如意自在否。四威儀中。
不爲塵勞所勝否。寤寐二邊。得一如否。於仍舊處。無走作否。於生
死心。不相續否。但盡凡情。別無聖解。[8.2] 公既一笑。豁開正眼。

消息頓亡。得力不得力。如人飲水冷煖自知矣。然日用之間。當依黃
面老子所言。刳其正性。除其助因。違其現業。此乃了事漢。無方便
中真方便。無修證中真修證。無取捨中真取捨也。古德云。皮膚脫落
盡。唯一真實在。又如栴檀繁柯脫落盡。唯真栴檀在。斯違現業。除
助因。刳正性之極致也。公試思之。**[8.3]** 如此說話。於了事漢分上。
大似一柄臘月扇子。恐南地寒暄不常。也少不得。一笑。

答江給事 (少明)

[9.1] 人生一世。百年光陰。能有幾許。公白屋起家。歷盡清要。此是
世間第一等受福底人。能知慚愧。回心向道。學出世間脫生死法。又
是世間第一等討便宜底人。須是急著手腳。冷却面皮。不得受人差
排。自家理會本命元辰。教去處分明。便是世間出世間一箇了事底大
丈夫也。**[9.2]** 承連日去與參政道話。甚善甚善。此公歇得馳求心。
得言語道斷。心行處滅。差別異路。覰見古人腳手。不被古人方便文
字所羅籠。山僧見渠如此。所以更不曾與之說一字。恐鈍置佗。直候
渠將來自要與山僧說話。方始共渠眉毛廝結理會在。不只恁麼便休。
學道人。若馳求心不歇。縱與之眉毛廝結理會。何益之有。正是癡
狂外邊走耳。古人云。親近善者。如霧露中行。雖不濕衣。時時有
潤。但頻與參政說話。至禱至禱。**[9.3]** 不可將古人垂示言教。胡亂穿
鑿。如馬大師遇讓和尚。說法云。譬牛駕車。車若不行。打車即是。
打牛即是。馬師聞之。言下知歸。遮幾句兒言語。諸方多少說法。如
雷如霆如雲如雨底。理會不得。錯下名言。隨語生解。見與舟峯書尾
杜撰解注。山僧讀之不覺絕倒。可與說如來禪祖師禪底。一狀領過。
一道行遣也。**[9.4]** 來頌子細看過。却勝得前日兩頌。自此可已之。
頌來頌去。有甚了期。如參政相似。渠豈是不會做頌。何故都無一
字。乃識法者懼耳。間或露一毛頭。自然抓著山僧痒處。如出山相頌
云。到處逢人驀面欺之語。可與叢林作點眼藥。公異日自見矣。不必
山僧注破也。**[9.5]** 某近見公頓然改變。爲此事甚力。故作此書不覺縷
縷。

答富樞密 (季申)

[10.1] 示諭。蚤歲知信向此道。晚年爲知解所障。未有一悟入
處。欲知日夕體道方便。既荷至誠。不敢自外。據欵結案。葛
藤少許。**[10.2]** 只遮求悟入底。便是障道知解了也。更別有甚麼知解
爲公作障。畢竟喚甚麼作知解。知解從何而至。被障者復是阿誰。
只此一句。顛倒有三。自言爲知解所障是一。自言未悟甘作迷人
是一。更在迷中將心待悟是一。只遮三顛倒。便是生死根本。直須

一念不生顛倒心絕。方知無迷可破。無悟可待。無知解可障。如人
飲水冷煖自知。久久自然不作遮般見解也。但就能知知解底心上。
看還障得也無。能知知解底心上。還有如許多般也無。[10.3] 從上
大智慧之士。莫不皆以知解爲儔侶。以知解爲方便。於知解上行平
等慈。於知解上作諸佛事。如龍得水。似虎靠山。終不以此爲惱。
只爲佗識得知解起處。既識得起處。即此知解便是解脫之場。便是
出生死處。既是解脫之場。出生死處。則知底解底當體寂滅。知
底解底既寂滅。能知知解者。不可不寂滅。菩提涅槃真如佛性。不
可不寂滅。更有何物可障。更向何處求悟入。釋迦老子曰。諸業
從心生。故說心如幻。若離此分別。則滅諸有趣。僧問大珠和尚。
如何是大涅槃。珠云。不造生死業。是大涅槃。僧云。如何是生死
業。珠云。求大涅槃。是生死業。又古德云。學道人一念計生死。
即落魔道。一念起諸見。即落外道。又淨名云。衆魔者樂生死。菩
薩於生死而不捨。外道者樂諸見。菩薩於諸見而不動。此乃是以知
解爲儔侶。以知解爲方便。於知解上行平等慈。於知解上作諸佛事
底樣子也。只爲佗了達三祇劫空。生死涅槃俱寂靜故。[10.4] 既未
到遮箇田地。切不可被邪師輩胡說乱道。引入鬼窟裏。閉眉合眼
作妄想。迩來祖道衰微。此流如麻似粟。真是一盲引衆盲。相牽
入火坑。深可憐愍。願公硬著脊梁骨。莫作遮般去就。作遮般去
就底。雖暫拘得箇臭皮袋子住。便以爲究竟。而心識紛飛。猶如
野馬。縱然心識暫停。如石壓草。不覺又生。欲直取無上菩提。
到究竟安樂處。不亦難乎。某亦嘗爲此流所誤。後來若不遇真善
知識。幾致空過一生。每每思量。直是凥耐。以故不惜口業。力
救此弊。今稍有知非者。[10.5] 若要徑截理會。須得遮一念子爆地
一破。方了得生死。方名悟入。然切不可存心待破。若存心在破
處。則永劫無有破時。但將妄想顛倒底心。思量分別底心。好生
惡死底心。知見解會底心。欣靜厭鬧底心。一時按下。只就按下
處。看箇話頭。僧問趙州。狗子還有佛性也無。州云無。此一字
子。乃是摧許多惡知惡覺底器仗也。不得作有無會。不得作道理
會。不得向意根下思量卜度。不得向揚眉瞬目處探根。不得向語路
上作活計。不得颺在無事甲裏。不得向舉起處承當。不得向文字中
引證。但向十二時中。四威儀內。時時提撕。時時舉覺。狗子還有
佛性也無。云無。不離日用。試如此做工夫看。月十日。便自見得
也。[10.6] 一郡千里之事。都不相妨。古人云。我遮裏是活底祖師
意。有甚麼物能拘執佗。若離日用。無³有趣向。則是離波求水。離
器求金。求之愈遠矣。

又。

[II.I] 竊知日來以此大事因緣爲念。勇猛精進純一無雜。不勝喜躍。能二六時中。熾然作爲之際。必得相應也未。寤寐二邊得一如也未。[II.2] 如未。切不可一向沈空趣寂。古人喚作黑山下鬼家活計。盡未來際。無有透脫之期。昨接來誨。私慮左右必已耽著靜勝三昧。及⁴詢直閣公。乃知果如所料。大凡涉世有餘之士。久膠於塵勞中。忽然得人指令。向靜默處做工夫。乍得胷中無事。便認著以爲究竟安樂。殊不知。似石壓草。雖暫覺絕消息。奈何根株猶在。寧有證徹寂滅之期。[II.3] 要得真正寂滅現前。必須於熾然生滅之中。驀地一跳跳出。不動一絲毫。便攪長河爲酥酪。變大地作黃金。臨機縱奪殺活自由。利佗自利。無施不可。先聖喚作無盡藏陀羅尼門。無盡藏神通游戲門。無盡藏如意解脫門。豈非真大丈夫之能事也。然亦非使然。皆吾心之常分耳。願左右快著精彩。[II.4] 決期於此。廓徹大悟。胷中皎然。如百千日月。十方世界一念明了。無一絲毫頭異想。始得與究竟相應。果能如是。豈獨於生死路上得力。異日再秉鈞軸。致君於堯舜之上。如指諸掌耳。

又。

[12.1] 示諭。初機得少靜坐工夫亦自佳。又云。不敢妄作靜見。黃面老子所謂。譬如有人自塞其耳。高聲大叫。求人不聞。真是自作障難耳。若生死心未破。日用二六時中。冥冥蒙蒙地。如魂不散底死人一般。更討甚閑工夫。理會靜理會鬧耶。涅槃會上廣額屠兒。放下屠刀便成佛。豈是做靜中工夫來。渠豈不是初機。左右見此。定以爲不然。須差排渠作古佛示現。今人無此力量。若如是見。乃不信自殊勝。甘爲下劣人也。我此門中。不論初機晚學。亦不問久參先達。若要真箇靜。須是生死心破。不著做工夫。生死心破。則自靜也。先聖所說寂靜方便。正爲此也。自是末世邪師輩。不會先聖方便語耳。[12.2] 左右若信得山僧及。試向鬧處看狗子無佛性話。未說悟不悟。正當方寸擾擾時。謾提撕舉覺看。還覺靜也無。還覺得力也無。若覺得力。便不須放捨。要靜坐時。但燒一炷香。靜坐。坐時。不得令昏沈。亦不得掉舉。昏沈掉舉。先聖所訶。靜坐時。纔覺此兩種病現前。但只舉狗子無佛性話。兩種病不著用力排遣。當下怗怗地矣。日久月深。纔覺省力。便是得力處也。亦不著做靜中工夫。只遮便是工夫也。[12.3] 李參政。頃在泉南初相見時。見山僧力排默

---

4. Araki = 乃.

照邪禪瞎人眼。渠初不平。疑怒相半。驀聞山僧頌庭前栢樹子話。忽然打破桼桶。於一笑中。千了百當。方信山僧開口見膽。無秋毫相欺。亦不是爭人我。便對山僧懺悔。此公現在彼。請試問之。還是也無。[12.4] 道謙上座。已往福唐。不識已到彼否。此子參禪喫辛苦更多。亦嘗十餘年入枯禪。近年始得箇安樂處。相見時。試問渠。如何做工夫。曾爲浪子。偏憐客。想必至誠吐露也。

答李參政別紙 (漢老)

[13.1] 富樞密[5]頃在三衢時。嘗有書來問道。因而打葛藤一上。落草不少。尚爾滯在默照處。定是遭邪師引入鬼窟裏無疑。今又得書。復執靜坐爲佳。其滯泥如此。如何參得徑山禪。今次答渠書。又復縷縷葛藤。不惜口業。痛與剗除。又不知肯回頭轉腦。於日用中看話頭否。先聖云。寧可破戒如須彌山。不可被邪師熏一邪念。如芥子許。在情識中。如油入麪。永不可出。此公是也。[13.2] 如與之相見。試取答渠底葛藤一觀。因而作箇方便。救取此人。四攝法中。以同事攝爲最強。左右當大啟此法門。令其信入。不唯省得山僧一半力。亦使渠信得及。肯離舊窟也。

答陳少卿 (季任)

[14.1] 承諭。欲留意此段大事因緣。爲根性極鈍。若果如此。當爲左右賀也。今時士大夫。多於此事。不能百了千當。直下透脫者。只爲根性太利。知見太多。見宗師纔開口動舌。早一時會了也。以故返不如鈍根者無許多惡知惡覺。驀地於一機一境上。一言一句下撞發。便是達磨大師出頭來。用盡百種神通。也奈何佗不得。只爲佗無道理可障。利根者返被利根所障。不能得啐地便折。嚗地便破。假饒於聰明知解上學得。於自己本分事上。轉不得力。[14.2] 所以南泉和尚云。近日禪師太多。覓箇癡鈍人不可得。章敬和尚曰。至理亡言。時人不悉。強習佗事。以爲功能。不知自性元非塵境。是箇微妙大解脫門所有鑑覺。不染不礙。如是光明。未曾休廢。曩劫至今。固無變易。猶如日輪遠近斯照。雖及衆色。不與一切和合。靈燭妙明。非假鍛鍊。爲不了故。取於物象。但如捍目妄起空花。徒自疲勞。枉經劫數。若能返照。無第二人。舉措施爲。不虧實相。[14.3] 左右自言根鈍。試如此返照看。能知鈍者。還鈍也無。若不回光返照。只守鈍根。更生煩惱。乃是向幻妄上。重增幻妄。空花上。更添空花

---

5. Supplied from T.

也。但相聽。能知根性鈍者。決定不鈍。雖不得守著遮箇鈍底。然亦不得捨却遮箇鈍底參。取捨利鈍。在人不在心。此心與三世諸佛。一體無二。若有二。則法不平等矣。受教傳心。但爲虛妄。求真覓實。轉見參差。但知得一體無二之心。決定不在利鈍取捨之間。則便當見月亡指。直下一刀兩段。若更遲疑。思前筭後。則乃是空拳指上。生實解。根境法中。虛捏怪。於陰界中。妄自囚執。無有了時。[14.4] 近年以來。有一種邪師。說默照禪。教人十二時中。是事莫管。休去歇去。不得做聲。恐落今時。往往士大夫。爲聰明利根所使者。多是厭惡閙處。乍被邪師輩指令靜坐。却見省力。便以爲是。更不求妙悟。只以默然爲極則。某不惜口業。力救此弊。今稍有知非者。[14.5] 願公只向疑情不破處參。行住坐臥。不得放捨。僧問趙州。狗子還有佛性也無。州云。無。遮一字子。便是箇破生死疑心底刀子也。遮刀子欛柄。只在當人手中。教別人下手不得。須是自家下手始得。若捨得性命。方肯自下手。若捨性命不得。且只管在疑不破處崖將去。驀然自肯捨命一下。便了。那時方信靜時便是閙時底。閙時便是靜時底。語時便是默時底。默時便是語時底。不著問人。亦自然不受邪師胡說亂道也。至禱至禱。[14.6] 昔朱世英嘗以書。問雲菴真淨和尚云。佛法至妙。日用如何用心。如何體究。望慈悲指示。真淨曰。佛法至妙無二。但未至於妙。則互有長短。苟至於妙。則悟心之人。如實知自心究竟本來成佛。如實自在。如實安樂。如實解脫。如實清淨。而日用唯用自心。自心變化。把得便用。莫問是之與非。擬心思量。早不是也。不擬心。一一天真。一一明妙。一一如蓮花不著水。心清淨超於彼。所以迷自心故。作衆生。悟自心故。成佛。而衆生即佛。佛即衆生。由迷悟故。有彼此也。如今學道人。多不信自心。不悟自心。不得自心明妙受用。不得自心安樂解脫。心外妄有禪道。妄立奇特。妄生取捨。縱修行。落外道二乘禪寂斷見境界。[14.7] 所謂修行恐落斷常坑。其斷見者。斷滅却自心本妙明性。一向心外著空。滯禪寂。常見者。不悟一切法空。執著世間諸有爲法。以爲究竟也。邪師輩。教士大夫。攝心靜坐。事事莫管休去歇去。豈不是將心休心。將心歇心。將心用心。若如此修行。如何不落外道二乘禪寂斷見境界。如何顯得自心明妙受用。究竟安樂。如實清淨。解脫變化之妙。須是當人自見得。自悟得。自然不被古人言句轉。而能轉得古人言句。如清淨摩尼寶珠。置泥潦之中。經百千歲。亦不能染污。以本體自清淨故。此心亦然。正迷時。爲塵勞所惑。而此心體。本不曾惑。所謂如蓮花不著水也。忽若悟得此心本來成佛。究竟自在。如實安樂。種種妙用。亦不從外來。爲本自具足故。黃面老子曰。無有定法名阿耨多羅三藐三菩提。亦無有定法如來可說。若確定本體實有恁麼事。又却不是也。事不獲已。因迷悟取捨故。說道理有若干。爲未至於妙者。方便語耳。其實本體。亦無若干。[14.8] 請公只恁麼用心。日用二六時中。不得執生死佛道是有。不得撥生死佛道歸無。但只看。狗子還有佛性也無。趙州云。無。切不可向意根下卜度。不可向言語上作活計。又不得向開口處承當。又不得向擊石火閃電光處會。狗子還有佛性也無。無。但只如此參。亦不得將心待悟。待休歇。若將心待悟。待休歇。則轉没交涉矣。

又。

[15.1] 示諭。自得山野向來書之後。每遇鬧中譁避不得處。常自點檢。而未有著力工夫。只遮譁避不得處。便是工夫了也。若更著力點檢。則又却遠矣。[15.2] 昔魏府老華嚴云。佛法在日用處。行住坐臥處。喫茶喫飯處。語言相問處。所作所爲處。舉心動念。又却不是也。正當譁避不得處。切忌起心動念。作點檢想。祖師云。分別不生。虛明自照。又龐居士云。日用事無別。唯吾自偶諧。頭頭非取捨。處處勿張乖。朱紫誰爲號。丘山絕點埃。神通并妙用。運水及般柴。又先聖云。但有心分別計較。自心見量者。悉皆是夢。切記取。[15.3] 譁避不得時。不得更擬心。不擬心時。一切現成。亦不用理會利。亦不用理會鈍。總不干佗利鈍之事。亦不干佗靜乱之事。正當譁避不得時。忽然打失布袋。不覺拊掌大笑矣。記取記取。此事若用一毫毛工夫取證。則如人以手撮摩虛空。只益自勞耳。[15.4] 應接時。但應接。要得靜坐。但靜坐。坐時不得執著坐底。爲究竟。今時邪師輩。多以默照靜坐。爲究竟法。疑誤後昆。山野不怕結怨。力詆之。以報佛恩。救末法之弊也。

答趙待制 (道夫)

[16.1] 示諭。一一備悉。佛言。有心者。皆得作佛。此心非世間塵勞妄想心。謂發無上大菩提心。若有是心。無不成佛者。士大夫學道。多自作障難。爲無決定信故也。佛又言。信爲道元。功德母。長養一切諸善法。斷除疑網。出愛流。開示涅槃無上道。又云。信能增長智功德。信能必到如來地。[16.2] 示諭。鈍根未能悟徹。且種佛種子於心田。此語雖淺近。然亦深遠。但辦肯心。必不相賺。今時學道之士。往往緩處却急。急處却放緩。龐公云。一朝蛇入布裩襠。試問宗師甚時節。昨日事。今日尚有記不得者。況隔陰事。豈容無忘失耶。決欲今生打教徹。不疑佛。不疑祖。不疑生。不疑死。須有決定信。具決定志。念念如救頭然。如此做將去。打未徹時。方始可說根鈍耳。若當下便自謂我根鈍。不能今生打得徹。且種佛種結緣。乃是不行欲到。無有是處。[16.3] 某每爲信此道者說。漸覺得日

用二六時中省力處。便是學佛得力處也。自家得力處。佗人知不得。亦拈出與人看不得。盧行者謂道明上座曰。汝若返照自己本來面目。密意盡在汝邊。是也。密意者。便是日用得力處也。得力處。便是省力處也。[16.4] 世間塵勞事。拈一放一。無窮無盡。四威儀內。未嘗相捨。爲無始時來。與之結得緣深故也。般若智慧。無始時來。與之結得緣淺故也。乍聞知識說著。覺得一似難會。若是無始時來。塵勞緣淺。般若緣深者。有甚難會處。但深處放教淺。淺處放教深。生處放教熟。熟處放教生。纔覺思量塵勞事時。不用著力排遣。只就思量處。輕輕撥轉話頭。省無限力。亦得無限力。請公只如此崖將去。莫存心等悟。忽地自悟去。[16.5] 參政公想日日相會。除圍碁外。還曾與說著遮般事否。若只圍碁。不曾說著遮般事。只就黑白未分處。掀了盤。撒了子。却問佗。索取那一著。若索不得。是真箇鈍根漢。姑置是事。

答許司理 (壽源)

[17.1] 黃面老子曰。信爲道元。功德母。長養一切諸善法。又云。信能增長智功德。信能必到如來地。欲行千里。一步爲初。十地菩薩。斷障證法門。初從十信而入。然後登法雲地。而成正覺。初歡喜地。因信而生歡喜故也。若決定豎起脊梁骨。要做世出世間沒量漢。須是箇生鐵鑄就底方了得。若半明半暗。半信半不信。決定了不得。[17.2] 此事無人情。不可傳授。須是自家省發。始有趣向分。若取佗人口頭辦。永劫無有歇時。[17.3] 千萬十二時中。莫令空過。逐日起來應用處。圓陀陀地。與釋迦達磨。無少異。自是當人見不徹。透不過。全身跳在聲色裏。却向裏許求出頭。轉沒交涉矣。[17.4] 此事亦不在久參知識。遍歷叢林。而後了得。而今有多少在叢林。頭白齒黃。了不得底。又有多少乍入叢林。一撥便轉。千了百當底。發心有先後。悟時無先後。[17.5] 昔李文和都尉。參石門慈照。一句下承當。便千了百當。嘗有偈。呈慈照云。學道須是鐵漢。著手心頭便判。直取無上菩提。一切是非莫管。但從脚下崖將去。死便休。不要念後思前。亦不要生煩惱。煩惱則障道也。祝祝。

又。

[18.1] 左右具正信。立正志。此乃成佛作祖基本也。山野因以湛然名公道號。[18.2] 如水之湛然不動。則虛明自照。不勞心力。世間出世間法。不離湛然。無纖毫透漏。只以此印。於一切處印定。無是無不是。一一解脫。一一明妙。一一實頭。用時亦湛然。不用時亦湛然。

祖師云。但有心分別計較自心見量者。悉皆是夢。若心識寂滅。無一
動念處。是名正覺。覺既正。則於日用二六時中。見色聞聲。齅⁶香了
味。覺觸知法。行住坐臥。語默動靜。無不湛然。亦自不作顛倒想。
有想無想。悉皆清淨。既得清淨。動時顯湛然之用。不動時歸湛然之
體。體用雖殊。而湛然則一也。如析栴檀。片片皆栴檀。[18.3] 今時有
一種杜撰漢。自己腳跟下不實。只管教人攝心靜坐。坐教絕氣息。此
輩名爲真可憐愍。請公只恁麼做工夫。山野雖然如此指示公。真不得
已耳。若實有恁麼做工夫底事。即是污染公矣。[18.4] 此心無有實體。
如何硬收攝得住。擬收攝向甚處安著。既無安著處。則無時無節。無
古無今。無凡無聖。無得無失。無靜無亂。無生無死。亦無湛然之
名。亦無湛然之體。亦無湛然之用。亦無恁麼說湛然者。亦無恁麼受
湛然說者。若如是見得徹去。徑山亦不虛作此號。左右亦不虛受此
號。如何如何。

答劉寶學 (彥脩)

[19.1] 即日烝溽。不審燕處悠然。放曠自如。無諸魔撓否。日用四威
儀內。與狗子無佛性話一如否。於動靜二邊。能不分別否。夢與覺合
否。理與事會否。心與境皆如否。老龐云。心如境亦如。無實亦無
虛。有亦不管。無亦不拘。不是聖賢。了事凡夫。若真箇作得箇了
事凡夫。釋迦達磨。是甚麼泥團土塊。三乘十二分教。是甚麼熱盌
鳴聲。[19.2] 公既於此箇門中。自信不疑。不是小事。要須生處放教
熟。熟處放教生。始與此事少分相應耳。往往士大夫。多於不意中。
得箇瞥地處。却於如意中。打失了。不可不使公知。在如意中。須
時時以不如意中時節在念。切不可暫忘也。但得本莫愁末。但知作
佛。莫愁佛不解語。遮一著子。得易守難。切不可忽。須教頭正尾
正。擴而充之。然後推己之餘。以及物。[19.3] 左右所得。既不滯在
一隅。想於日用中。不著起心管帶。枯心忘懷也。近年已來。禪道佛
法。衰弊之甚。有般杜撰長老。根本自無所悟。業識茫茫。無本可
據。無實頭伎倆收攝學者。教一切人。如渠相似。黑漆漆地。緊閉
却眼。喚作默而常照。彥沖被此輩教壞了。苦哉苦哉。遮箇話。若
不是左右悟得狗子無佛性。徑山亦無說處。千萬捋下面皮。痛與手
段。救取遮箇人。至禱至禱。[19.4] 然有一事。亦不可不知。此公清
淨自居。世味澹薄。積有年矣。定執此爲奇特。若欲救之。當與之同
事。令其歡喜。心不生疑。庶幾信得及。肯轉頭來。淨名所謂。先以
欲鉤牽。後令入佛智。是也。黃面老子云。觀法先後。以智分別。

---

6. T = 嗅.

是非審定。不違法印。次第建立無邊行門。令諸衆生断一切疑。此乃爲物作則。萬世楷模也。況此公根性。與左右迴不同。生天定在靈運前。成佛定在靈運後者也。此公決定不可以智慧攝。當隨所好攝。以日月磨之。恐自知非。忽然肯捨亦不可定。若肯轉頭來。却是箇有力量底漢。左右亦須退步。讓渠出一頭始得。[19.5] 比暐禪歸。錄得渠答紫巖老子一書。山僧隨喜讀一遍。讚歎歡喜累日。直是好一段文章。又似一篇大義。末後與之下箇謹對。不識左右以謂如何。[19.6] 昔達磨謂二祖曰。汝但外息諸縁。內心無喘。心如牆壁。可以入道。二祖種種說心說性。俱不契。一日忽然省得達磨所示要門。遽白達磨曰。弟子此回始息諸縁也。達磨知其已悟。更不窮詰。只曰莫成断滅去否。曰無。達磨曰。子作麼生。曰了了常知故。言之不可及。達磨曰。此乃從上諸佛諸祖。所傳心體。汝今既得。更勿疑也。彥冲云。夜夢晝思。十年之間。未能全克。或端坐靜默。一空其心。使慮無所縁。事無所託。頗覺輕安。讀至此不覺失笑。何故。既慮無所縁。豈非達磨所謂內心無喘乎。事無所託。豈非達磨所謂外息諸縁乎。二祖初不識達磨所示方便。將謂外息諸縁。內心無喘。可以說心說性。說道說理。引文字證據。欲求印可。所以達磨一一列下。無處用心。方始退步。思量心如牆壁之語。非達磨實法。忽然於牆壁上。頓息諸縁。即時見月亡指。便道。了了常知。故言之不可及。此語亦是臨時被達磨拶出底消息。亦非二祖實法也。杜撰長老輩。既自無所證。便逐旋揑合。雖教他人歇。渠自心火熠熠。晝夜不停。如欠[7]二稅百姓相似。彥冲却無許多勞攘。只是中得毒深。只管外邊乱走。說動說靜。說語說默。說得說失。[19.7] 更引周易內典。硬差排和會。真是爲佗閑事。長無明。殊不思量一段生死公案。未曾結絕。臘月三十日。作麼生折合去。不可眼光欲落未落時。且向閻家老子。道待我澄神定慮少時。却去相見得麼。當此之時。縱橫無礙之說。亦使不著。心如木石。亦使不著。須是當人生死心破始得。若得生死心破。更說甚麼澄神定慮。更說甚麼縱橫放蕩。更說甚麼內典外典。一了一切了。一悟一切悟。一證一切證。如斬一結絲。一斬一時断。證無邊法門亦然。更無次第。左右既悟狗子無佛性話。還得如此也未。若未得如此。直須到恁麼田地始得。若已到恁麼田地。當以此法門。興起大悲心。於逆順境中。和泥合水。不惜身命。不怕口業。拯拔一切。以報佛恩。方是大丈夫所爲。若不如是。無有是處。彥冲引孔子稱易之爲道也屢遷。和會佛書中應無所住而生其心。爲一貫。又引寂然不動。與土木無殊。此尤可笑也。向渠道。欲得不招無間業。莫謗如來正法輪。故經云。不應住色生心。不應住聲香味觸法

7. T = 缺.

生心。謂此廣大寂滅妙心。不可以色見聲求。應無所住。謂此心無實體也。而生其心。謂此心非離真而立處。立處即真也。孔子稱易之爲道也屢遷。非謂此也。屢者荐也。遷者革也。吉凶悔吝。生乎動。屢遷之旨。返常合道也。如何與應無所住而生其心。合得成一塊。彥冲非但不識佛意。亦不識孔子意。左右於孔子之教。出没如游園觀。又於吾教。深入閫域。山野如此杜撰。還是也無。[19.8] 故圭峯云。元亨利貞。乾之德也。始於一氣。常樂我淨。佛之德也。本乎一心。專一氣而致柔。修一心而成道。此老如此和會。始於儒釋二教。無偏枯。無遺恨。彥冲以應無所住而生其心。與易之屢遷。大旨同貫。未敢相許。若依彥冲差排。則孔夫子與釋迦老子。殺著買草鞋始得。何故。一人屢遷。一人無所住。想讀至此。必絕倒也。

答劉通判 (彥冲)

[20.1] 令兄寶學公。初未嘗知管帶忘懷之事。信手摸著鼻孔。雖未盡識得諸方邪正。而基本堅實。邪毒不能侵。忘懷管帶在其中矣。若一向忘懷管帶。生死心不破。陰魔得其便。未免把虛空膈8截作兩處。處靜時受無量樂。處鬧時受無量苦。[20.2] 要得苦樂均平。但莫起心管帶。將心忘懷。十二時中。放教蕩蕩地。忽爾舊習瞥起。亦不著用心按捺。只就瞥起處。看箇話頭。狗子還有佛性也無。無。正恁麼時。如紅爐上一點雪相似。眼辦手親者。一遉遉得。方知懶融道。恰恰用心時。恰恰無心用。曲談名相勞。直說無繁重。無心恰恰用。常用恰恰無。今說無心處。不與有心殊。不是誑人語。[20.3] 昔婆修盤頭。常一食不臥。六時禮佛。清淨無欲。爲衆所歸。二十祖闍夜多。將欲度之。問其徒曰。此徧行頭陀。能修梵行。可得佛道乎。其徒曰。我師精進如此。何故不可。闍夜多曰。汝師與道遠矣。設苦行歷於塵劫。皆虛妄之本也。其徒不憤9。皆作色厲聲。謂闍夜多曰。尊者蘊何德行。而譏我師。闍夜多曰。我不求道。亦不顛倒。我不禮佛。亦不輕慢。我不長坐。亦不懈怠。我不一食。亦不雜食。我不知足。亦不貪欲。心無所希。名之曰道。婆修聞已。發無漏智。所謂先以定動。後以智拔也。[20.4] 杜撰長老輩。教左右靜坐等作佛。豈非虛妄之本乎。又言靜處無失。鬧處有失。豈非壞世間相。而求實相乎。若如此修行。如何契得嬾融所謂。今說無心處。不與有心殊。請公於此。諦當思量看。婆修初亦將謂長坐不臥。可以成佛。纔被闍夜多點破。便於言下知歸。發無漏智。真是良馬見鞭影而行也。衆生狂亂

8. T and Araki = 隔.

9. Translation follows T 不憤 = 不勝憤 and Araki 不憤 = 不勝其憤.

是病。佛以寂靜波羅蜜藥治之。病去藥存。其病愈甚。拈一放一。何時是了。[20.5] 生死到來。靜鬧兩邊。都用一點不得。莫道鬧處失者多。靜處失者少。不如少與多。得與失。靜與鬧。縛作一束。送放佗方世界。却好就日用非多非少。非靜非鬧。非得非失處。略提撕看是箇甚麼。無常迅速。百歲光陰。一彈指頃便過也。更有甚麼閑工夫。理會得。理會失。理會靜。理會鬧。理會多。理會少。理會忘懷。理會管帶。[20.6] 石頭和尚云。謹白參玄人。光陰莫虛度。遮一句子。開眼也著。合眼也著。忘懷也著。管帶也著。狂亂也著。寂靜也著。此是徑山如此差排。想杜撰長老輩。別有差排處也。咄且置是事。

又。

[21.1] 左右做靜勝工夫。積有年矣。不識於開眼應物處。得心地安閑否。若未得安閑。是靜勝工夫。未得力也。若許久借[10]未得力。當求箇徑截得力處。方始不孤負[11]平昔許多工夫也。平昔做靜勝工夫。只爲要支遣箇鬧底。正鬧時。却被鬧底聒擾自家方寸。却似平昔不曾做靜勝工夫一般耳。[21.2] 遮箇道理。只爲太近。遠不出自家眼睛裏。開眼便刺著。合眼處亦不欠[12]少。開口便道著。合口處亦自現成。擬欲起心動念承當。渠早已蹉過十萬八千了也。直是無你用心處。遮箇最是省力。而今學此道者。多是要用力求。求之轉失。向之愈背。那堪墮在得失解路上。謂鬧處失者多。靜處失者少。[21.3] 左右在靜勝處住了二十餘年。試將些子得力底來看則箇。若將椿椿地底。做靜中得力處。何故却向鬧處失却。而今要得省力靜鬧一如。但只透取趙州無字。忽然透得。方知靜鬧兩不相妨。亦不著用力支撐。亦不作無支撐解矣。

答泰國太夫人

[22.1] 謙禪歸。領所賜教。并親書數頌。初亦甚疑之。及詢謙子細。方知不自欺。曠劫未明之事。豁尔現前。不從人得。始知法喜禪悅之樂。非世間之樂可比。山野爲國太。歡喜累日。寢食俱忘。[22.2] 兒子作宰相。身作國夫人。未足爲貴。糞埽[13]堆頭。收得無價之寶。百劫千生。受用不盡。方始爲真貴耳。然切不得執著此貴。若執著。則墮在尊貴中。不復興悲起智。憐愍有情耳。記取記取。

---

10. Translation follows T and Araki = 猶.

11. T = 辜負.

12. T = 缺.

13. T and Araki = 掃.

答張丞相 (德遠)

[23.1] 恭惟。燕居阿練若。與彼上人。同會一處。娛戲毗盧藏海。隨宜作佛事。少病少惱。鈞候動止萬福。[23.2] 從上諸聖。莫不皆然。所謂¹⁴於念念中。入一切法滅盡三昧。不退菩薩道。不捨菩薩事。不捨大慈悲心。修習波羅蜜。未嘗休息。觀察一切佛國土。無有厭倦。不捨度衆生願。不斷轉法輪事。不廢教化衆生業。乃至所有勝願。皆得圓滿。了知一切國土差別。入佛種性。到於彼岸。此大丈夫四威儀中。受用家事耳。大居士。於此力行無倦。而妙喜於此。亦作普州人。又不識還許外人插手否。[23.3] 聞到長沙。即杜口毗耶。深入不二。此亦非分外。法如是故。願居士如是受用。則諸魔外道。定來作護法善神也。其餘種種差別異旨。皆自心現量境界。亦非佗物也。不識居士以爲何如。

答張提刑 (暘叔)

[24.1] 老居士所作所爲。冥與道合。但未能得団地一下耳。若日用應緣。不失故步。雖未得団地一下。臘月三十日。闔家老子。亦須拱手歸降。況一念相應耶。[24.2] 妙喜老漢。雖未目擊。觀其行事。小大折中。無過不及。只此便是道所合處。到遮裏。不用作塵勞想。亦不用作佛法想。佛法塵勞。都是外事。然亦不得作外事想。但回光返照。作如是想者。從甚麼處得來。所作所爲時。有何形段。所作既辦。隨我心意。無不周旋。無有少剩。正¹⁵恁麼時。承誰恩力。如此做工夫。日久月深。如人學射。自然中的矣。[24.3] 衆生顛倒。迷己逐物。耽少欲味。甘心受無量苦。逐日未開眼時。未下牀時。半惺半覺時。心識已紛飛。隨妄想流蕩矣。作善作惡。雖未發露。未下牀時。天堂地獄。在方寸中。已一時成就矣。及待發時。已落在第八。佛不云乎。一切諸根。自心現。器身等藏。自妄想相。施設顯示。如河流。如種子。如燈。如風。如雲。刹那展轉壞。躁動如猿猴。樂不淨處如飛蠅。無猒足如風火。無始虛偽習氣因。如汲水輪等事。於此識得破。便喚作無人無我智¹⁶。[24.4] 天堂地獄。不在別處。只在當人半惺半覺。未下牀時方寸中。並不從外來。發未發。覺未覺時。切須照顧。照顧時。亦不得與之用力爭。爭著則費力矣。祖不云乎。止動歸止。止更彌動。

---

14. T = 以.

15. T and Araki = 正當.

16. T = 知.

纔覺日用塵勞中。漸漸省力時。便是當人得力之處。便是當人成佛作祖之處。便是當人變地獄作天堂之處。便是當人穩坐之處。便是當人出生死之處。便是當人致君於堯舜之上之處。便是當人起疲氓於凋瘵之際之處。便是當人覆蔭子孫之處。[24.5] 到遮裏。說佛。說祖。說心。說性。說玄。說妙。說理。說事。說好。說惡。亦是外邊事。如是等事。尚屬外矣。況更作塵勞中先聖所訶之事耶。作好事尚不肯。豈肯作不好事耶。若信得此說及。永嘉所謂。行亦禪。坐亦禪。語默動靜。體安然。不是虛語。請依此行履。始終不變易。則雖未徹證自己本地風光。雖未明見自己本來面目。生處已熟。熟處已生矣。切切記取。[24.6] 纔覺省力處。便是得力處也。妙喜老漢。每與箇中人說此話。往往見說得頻了。多忽之。不肯將爲事。居士試如此做工夫看。只十餘日。便自見得省力。不省力。得力。不得力矣。如人飲水冷煖自知。說與人不得。呈似人不得。先德云。語證則不可示人。說理則非證不了。自證自得自信自悟處。除曾證曾得已信已悟者。方默默相契。未證未得未信未悟者。不唯自不信。亦不信佗人有如此境界。老居士天資近道。現定所作所爲。不著更易。以佗人較之。萬分中。已省得九千九百九十九分。只欠噴地一發便了。[24.7] 士大夫學道。多不著實理會。除却口議心思。便茫然無所措手足。不信無措手足處。正是好處。只管心裏要思量得到。口裏要說得分曉。殊不知。錯了也。佛言。如來以一切譬喻。說種種事。無有譬喻能說此法。何以故。心智路絕。不思議故。信知。思量分別障道必矣。[24.8] 若得前後際斷。心智路自絕矣。若得心智路絕。說種種事。皆此法也。此法既明。即此明處。便是不思議大解脫境界。只此境界。亦不可思議。境界既不可思議。一切譬喻。亦不可思議。種種事亦不可思議。只遮不可思議底。亦不可思議。此語亦無著處。只遮無著處底。亦不可思議。如是展轉窮詰。若事若法若譬喻若境界。如環之無端。無起處。無盡處。皆不可思議之法也。所以云。菩薩住是不思議。於中思議不可盡。入此不可思議處。思與非思。皆寂滅。[24.9] 然亦不得住在寂滅處。若住在寂滅處。則被法界量之所管攝。教中謂之法塵煩惱。滅却法界量。種種殊勝。一時蕩盡了。方始好看庭前栢樹子。麻三斤。乾屎橛。狗子無佛性。一口吸盡西江水。東山水上行之類。忽然一句下透得。方始謂之法界無量回向。如實而見。如實而行。如實而用。便能於一毛端。現寶王刹。坐微塵裏。轉大法輪。成就種種法。破壞種種法。一切由我。如壯士展臂。不借佗力。師子游行。不求伴侶。種種勝妙境界現前。心不驚異。種種惡業境界現前。心不怕怖。日用四威儀中。隨緣放曠。任性逍遙。[24.10] 到得遮箇田地。方可說無天堂無地獄等事。永嘉云。亦無人亦無佛。大千沙界海中漚。一切聖賢如電拂。此老若不到遮箇田地。如何說得出來。[24.11] 此語錯會者甚多。苟未徹根源。不

免依語生解。便道一切皆無。撥無因果。將諸佛諸祖所說言教。盡以
爲虛。謂之誆惑人。此病不除。乃莽莽蕩蕩。招殃禍者也。佛言。虛
妄浮心。多諸巧見。若不著有。便著無。若不著此二種。便[17]於有無
之間。傳[18]量卜度。縱識得此病。定在非有非無處著到。[24.12] 故先
聖苦口叮嚀。令離四句。絕百非。直下一刀兩段。更不念後思前。
坐斷千聖頂頸。四句者。乃有。無。非有非無。亦有亦無。是也。
若透得此四句了。見說一切諸法實有。我亦隨順與之說有。且不被
此實有所礙。見說一切諸法實無。我亦隨順與之說無。且非世間虛
豁之無。見說一切諸法亦有亦無。我亦隨順。與之說亦有亦無。且
非戲論。見說一切諸法非有非無。我亦隨順。與之說非有非無。且
非相違。淨名云。外道六師所墮。汝亦隨墮。是也。[24.13] 士大夫學
道。多不肯虛却心。聽善知識指示。善知識纔開口。渠已在言前。一
時領會了也。及至教渠吐露盡。一時錯會。正好在言前領略底。又却
滯在言語上。又有一種。一向作聰明說道理。世間種種事藝。我無不
會者。只有禪一般。我未會在。當官處呼幾枚杜撰長老來。與一頓
飯喫却了。教渠恣意乱說。便將心意識。記取遮杜撰說底。却去勘
人一句來一句去。謂之厮禪。末後我多一句。你無語時。便是我得
便宜了也。及至撞著箇真實明眼漢。又却不識。縱然識得。又無決
定信。不肯四楞塌地放下。就師家理會。依舊要求印可。及至師家
於逆順境中。示以本分鉗鎚。又却怕懼不敢親近。此等名爲可憐愍
者。[24.14] 老居士妙年登高第起家。所在之處。隨時作利益事。文章
事業。皆過人。而未嘗自矜。一心一意。只要退步著實。理會此段大
事因緣。見其至誠。不覺忉怛如許。非獨要居士識得遮般病痛。亦作
勸發初心菩薩。入道之資粮也。

答汪內翰 (彥章)

[25.1] 承杜門壁觀。此息心良藥也。若更鑽故紙。定引起藏識中無始時
來生死根苗。作善根難。作障道難。無疑。得息心。且息心已。過去
底事。或善或惡。或逆或順。都莫思量。現在事。得省便省。一刀兩
段。不要遲疑。未來事。自然不相續矣。釋迦老子云。心不妄取過去
法。亦不貪著未來事。不於現在有所住。了達三世悉空寂。[25.2] 但
看。僧問趙州。狗子還有佛性也無。州云。無。請只把閑思量底心。
回在無字上。試思量看。忽然向思量不及處。得遮一念破。便是了達
三世處也。了達時。安排不得。計較不得。引證不得。何以故。了達

處。不容安排。不容計較。不容引證。縱然引證得。計較得。安排
得。與了達底了。沒交涉。但放教蕩蕩地。善惡都莫思量。亦莫著
意。亦莫忘懷。著意則流蕩。忘懷則昏沈。不著意。不忘懷。善不是
善。惡不是惡。若如此了達。生死魔。何處摸搽。[25.3] 一箇汪彥章。
聲名滿天下。平生安排得。計較得。引證得底。是文章。是名譽。
是官職。晚年收因結果處。那箇是實。做了無限之乎者也。那一句得
力。名譽既彰。與匿德藏光者。相去幾何。官職已做到大兩制。與作
秀才時。相去多少。而今已近七十歲。儘公伎倆。待要如何。臘月三
十日。作麼生折合去。無常殺鬼。念念不停。雪峰真覺云。光陰倏忽
暫須臾。浮世那能得久居。出嶺年登三十二。入閩早是四旬餘。佗
非不用頻頻舉。已[19]過還須旋旋除。爲報滿城朱紫道。閻王不怕佩金
魚。古人苦口叮嚀。爲甚麼事。[25.4] 世間愚庸之人。飢寒所迫。日用
無佗念。只得身上稍煖。肚裏不飢。便了。只是遮兩事。生死魔却不
能爲惱。以受富貴者較之。輕重大不等。受富貴底。身上既常煖。肚
裏又常飽。既不被遮兩事所迫。又却多一件不可說底無狀。以故常在
生死魔網中。無由出離。除宿有靈骨。方見得徹。識得破。[25.5] 先聖
云。瞥起是病。不續是藥。不怕念起。唯恐覺遲。佛者覺也。爲其常
覺故。謂之大覺。亦謂之覺王。然皆從凡夫中做得出來。彼既丈夫。
我寧不尔。[25.6] 百年光景。能得幾時。念念如救頭然。做好事。尚
恐做不辦。況念念在塵勞中。而不覺也。可畏可畏。近收呂居仁四月
初書。報曾叔夏劉彥禮死。居仁云。交游中。時復抽了一兩人。直是
可畏。[25.7] 渠迩來爲此事甚切。亦以瞥地回頭稍遲爲恨。比已作書答
之云。只以末後知非底一念爲正。不問遲速也。知非底一念。便是成
佛作祖底基本。破魔網底利器。出生死底路頭也。願公亦只如此做工
夫。[25.8] 做得工夫漸熟。則日用二六時中。便覺省力矣。覺得省力
時。不要放緩。只就省力處崖將去。崖來崖去。和遮省力處。亦不知
有時。不爭多也。但只看箇無字[20]。莫管得不得。至禱至禱。

又。

[26.1] 伏承杜門息交。世事一切闊略。唯朝夕以某向所舉話頭提
撕。甚善。甚善。既辦此心。當以悟爲則。若自生退屈。謂根性陋
劣。更求入頭處。正是含元殿裏。問長安在甚處尔。[26.2] 正提撕時。
是阿誰。能知根性陋劣底。又是阿誰。求入頭處底。又是阿誰。妙喜
不避口業。分明爲居士說破。只是箇汪彥章。更無兩箇。只有一箇汪

19. Translation follows T and Araki = 已.

20. T = 字.

彥章。更那裏得箇提撕底。知根性陋劣底。求入頭處底來。當知皆是汪彥章影子。並不干佗汪彥章事。若是真箇汪彥章。根性必不陋劣。必不求入頭處。但只信得自家主人公及。並不消得許多勞攘。[26.3] 昔有僧問仰山。禪宗頓悟。畢竟入門的意如何。山曰。此意極難。若是祖宗門下。上根上智。一聞千悟。得大總持。此根人難得。其有根微智劣。所以古德道。若不安禪靜慮。到遮裏。總須茫然。僧曰。除此格外。還別有方便。令學人得入也無。山曰。別有別無。令汝心不安。我今問汝。汝是甚處人。曰。幽州人。山曰。汝還思彼處否。曰。常思。山曰。彼處樓臺林苑。人馬駢闐。汝返思。思底還有許多般也無。曰。某甲到遮裏。一切不見有。山曰。汝解猶在境。信位即是。人位即不是。[26.4] 妙喜已是老婆心切。須著更下箇注腳。人位即是汪彥章。信位即是知根性陋劣。求入頭處底。若於正提撕話頭時。返思能提撕底。還是汪彥章否。到遮裏。間不容髮。若佇思停機。則被影子惑矣。請快著精彩。不可忽。不可忽。[26.5] 記得前書中嘗寫去。得息心。且息心已。過去底事。或善或惡。或逆或順。都莫理會。現在事。得省便省。一刀兩段。不要遲疑。未來事。自然不相續矣。不識曾如此覷捕否。遮箇便是第一省力做工夫處也。至禱至禱。

又。

[27.1] 伏承第五令嗣。以疾不起。父子之情。千生百劫。恩愛習氣之所流注。想當此境界。無有是處。五濁世中。種種虛幻。無一真實。請行住坐臥。常作是觀。則日久月深。漸漸消磨矣。[27.2] 然正煩惱時。子細揣摩窮詰。從甚麼處起。若窮起處不得。現今煩惱底。却從甚麼處得來。正煩惱時。是有是無。是虛是實。窮來窮去。心無所之。要思量。但思量。要哭。但哭。哭來哭去。思量來思量去。抖擻得藏識中許多恩愛習氣盡時。自然如冰²¹歸水。還我箇本來。無煩惱。無思量。無憂無喜底去耳。[27.3] 入得世間。出世無餘。世間法則佛法。佛法則世間法也。父子天性一而已。若子喪。而父不煩惱。不思量。如父喪而子不煩惱。不思量。還得也無。若硬止遏。哭時又不敢哭。思量時。又不敢思量。是特欲逆天理。滅天性。揚聲止響。潑油救火耳。[27.4] 正當煩惱時。總不是外事。且不得作外邊想。永嘉云。無明實性即佛性。幻化空身即法身。是真語實語。不誑不妄等語。怎麼見得了。要思量。要煩惱。亦不可得。作是觀者。名爲正觀。若佗觀者。名爲邪觀。邪正未分。正好著力。此是妙喜決定義。無智人前莫說。

---

21. T = 水.

大慧普覺禪師書上

大慧普覺禪師書下
參學慧然錄

答夏運使

[**28.1**] 示諭。道契則霄壤共處。趣異則覿面楚越。誠哉是言。即此乃不傳之妙。左右發意欲作妙喜書。未操觚拂紙。已兩手分付了也。又何待堅忍究竟。以俟佗日耶。此箇道理。唯證者方默默相契。難與俗子言。[**28.2**] 延平乃閩嶺佳處。左右能自調伏。不爲逆順關捩²²子所轉。便是大解脫人。此人能轉一切關捩²³子。日用活鱍鱍地。拘牽惹絆佗不得。苟若直下便恁麼承當。自然無一毫毛於我作障。[**28.3**] 古德有言。佛說一切法。爲度一切心。我無一切心。何用一切法。又嬾²⁴融云。恰恰用心時。恰恰無心用。曲談名相勞。直說無繁重。無心恰恰用。常用恰恰無。今說無心處。不與有心殊。非特嬾²⁵融如是。妙喜與左右亦在其中。其中事難拈出似人。前所謂默默相契。是也。

答呂舍人 (居仁)

[**29.1**] 千疑萬疑。只是一疑。話頭上疑破。則千疑萬疑一時破。話頭不破。則且就上面與之廝崖。若棄了話頭。却去別文字上起疑。經教上起疑。古人公案上起疑。日用塵勞中起疑。皆是邪魔眷屬。[**29.2**] 第一不得向舉起處承當。又不得思量卜度。但著意就不可思量處思量。心無所之。老鼠入牛角。便見倒斷也。[**29.3**] 又方寸若鬧。但只舉狗子無佛性話。佛語祖語諸方老宿語。千差萬別。若透得箇無字。一時透過。不著問人。若一向問人佛語又如何。祖語又如何。諸方老宿語又如何。永劫無有悟時也。

---

22. T = 棕.

23. T = 棕.

24. T = 懶.

25. T = 懶.

答呂郎中 (隆礼)

[30.1] 令兄居仁。兩得書。爲此事甚忙。然亦當著忙。年已六十。從官又做了。更待如何。若不早著忙。臘月三十日。如何打疊得辦。聞左右迩來亦忙。只遮著忙底。便是臘月三十日消息也。如何是佛。乾屎橛。遮裏不透。與臘月三十日何異。[30.2] 揩大家一生鑽故紙。是事要知。博覽群書。高談闊論。孔子又如何。孟子又如何。莊子又如何。周易又如何。古今治亂又如何。被遮些言語使得來。七顛八倒。諸子百家。纔聞人舉著一字。便成卷念將去。以一事不知爲恥。及乎問著佗自家屋裏事。並無一人知者。可謂終日數佗寶。自無半錢分。空來世上打一遭。脫却遮殻漏子。上天堂也不知。入地獄也不知。隨其業力流入諸趣。並不知。若是別人家裏事。細大無有不知者。[30.3] 士大夫。讀得書多底。無明多。讀得書少底。無明少。做得官小底。人我小。做得官大底。人我大。自道我聰明靈利。及乎臨秋毫利害。聰明也不見。靈利也不見。平生所讀底書。一字也使不著。蓋從上大人丘乙已²⁶時。便錯了也。只欲取富貴耳。[30.4] 取得富貴底。又能有幾人。肯回頭轉腦。向自己脚跟下推窮。我遮取富貴底。從何處來。即今受富貴底。異日却向何處去。既不知來處。又不知去處。便覺心頭迷悶。正迷悶時。亦非佗物。只就遮裏看箇話頭。僧問雲門。如何是佛。門云。乾屎橛。但舉此話。[30.5] 忽然伎倆盡時。便悟也。切忌尋文字引證。胡乱博²⁷量注²⁸解。縱然注²⁹解得分明。說得有下落。盡是鬼家活計。疑情不破。生死交加。疑情若破。則生死心絕矣。生死心絕。則佛見法見亡矣。佛見法見尚亡。況復更起衆生煩惱見耶。[30.6] 但將迷悶底心。移來乾屎橛上。一抵抵住。怖生死底心。迷悶底心。思量分別底心。作聰明底心。自然不行也。覺得不行時。莫怕落空。忽然向抵住處絕消息。不勝慶快平生。得消息絕了。起佛見法見衆生見。思量分別。作聰明。說道理。都不相妨。日用四威儀中。但常放教蕩蕩地。靜處鬧處。常以乾屎橛提撕。日往月來。水牯牛自純熟矣。第一不得向外面別起疑也。乾屎橛上疑破。則恒河沙數疑一時破矣。[30.7] 前此亦嘗如此寫與居仁。比趙景明來得書。書中再來問云。不知離此別有下二³⁰夫處也無。又如舉手動足著衣喫飯。當如何體究。爲復只看話頭。爲復別有體究。又平生一大疑事。至今未

---

26. T = 己.
27. Translation follows T = 搏.
28. T = 註.
29. T = 註.
30. Translation follows T and Araki = 工.

了。只如死後斷滅不斷滅。如何決定見得。又不要引經論所說。不要
指古人公案。只據目前。直截分明。指示剖判斷滅不斷滅實處。觀渠
如此說話。返不如三家村裏省事漢。却無如許多糞壤死也。死得瞥
脫。[30.8] 分明向佗道。千疑萬疑。只是一疑。話頭上疑破。則千疑
萬疑一時破。話頭不破。則且就話頭上與之廝崖。若棄了話頭。却
去別文字上起疑。經教上起疑。古人公案上起疑。日用塵勞中起疑。
皆是邪魔眷屬。又不得向舉起處承當。又不得思量卜度。但只著意
就不可思量處思量。心無所之。老鼠入牛角。便見倒斷也。寫得如此
分曉了。又却更來忉忉怛怛地問。不知許多聰明知見。向甚處去也。
不信道平生讀底書。到遮裏一字也使不著。[30.9] 而今不得已。更爲
佗放些惡氣息。若只恁麼休去。却是妙喜被渠問了。更答不得也。
此書繳到。便送與渠一看。[30.10] 居仁自言。行年六十歲。此事未
了。問渠。未了底。爲復是舉手動足著衣喫飯底未了。若是舉手動足
著衣喫飯底。又要如何了。佗殊不知。只遮欲了知決定見得死後斷滅
不斷滅底。便是閻家老子面前喫鐵棒底。此疑不破。流浪生死。未有
了期。向渠道。千疑萬疑。只是一疑。話頭若破。死後斷滅不斷滅之
疑。當下冰銷瓦解矣。[30.11] 更教直截分明。指示剖判斷滅不斷滅。
如此見識。與外道何異。平生做許多之乎者也。要作何用。渠既許多
遠地。放遮般惡氣息來熏人。妙喜不可只恁麼休去。亦放些惡氣息。
却去熏佗則箇。渠教不要引經教及古人公案。只據目前。直截分明指
示斷滅不斷滅實處。昔志道禪師問六祖。學人自出家覽涅槃經近十餘
載。未明大意。願師垂誨。祖曰。汝何處未了。對曰。諸行無常。
是生滅法。生滅滅已。寂滅爲樂。於此疑惑。祖曰。汝作麼生疑。
對曰。一切眾生。皆有二身。謂色身法身也(此乃居仁同道)。色身無
常。有生有滅。法身有常。無知無覺。經云。生滅滅已。寂滅爲樂
者。未審是何身寂滅。何身受樂。若色身者。色身滅時。四大分散。
全是苦。苦不可言樂。若法身。寂滅即同草木瓦石。誰當受樂。又法
性是生滅之體。五蘊是生滅之用。一體五用。生滅是常。生則從體起
用。滅則攝用歸體。若聽更生。即有情之類。不斷不滅。若不聽更
生。即永歸寂滅。同於無情之物。如是則一切諸法。被涅槃之所禁
伏。尚不得生。何樂之有(可與居仁一狀領過)。祖師到遮裏。不能臨
濟德山用事。遂放些氣息還佗云。汝是釋子。何習外道斷常邪見。
而議最上乘法。據汝所解。即色身外。別有法身。離生滅。求於寂
滅。又推涅槃常樂。言有身受者。斯乃執吝生死。耽著世樂。汝今當
知。佛爲一切迷人。認五蘊和合爲自體相。分別一切法。爲外塵相。
好生惡死。念念遷流。不知夢幻虛假。枉受輪迴。以常樂涅槃。翻
爲苦相。終日馳求。佛愍此故。乃示涅槃真樂。剎那無有生相。剎
那無有滅相。更無生滅可滅(到此請著眼睛)。是則寂滅現前。當現前
時。亦無現前之量。乃謂常樂。此樂無有受者。亦無有不受者(猶較

些子)。豈有一體五用之名。何況更言涅槃禁伏諸法。令永不生。此
乃謗佛毀法(居仁亦有一分子)。聽吾偈曰(分疎不下)。無上大涅槃。圓
明常寂照。凡愚謂之死。外道執爲斷。諸求二乘人。目以爲無作。盡
屬情所計。六十二見本。妄立虛假名。何爲真實義(居仁要見實處但看
此一句子)。唯有過量人(未見其人)。通達無取捨(居仁更疑三十年)。
以知五蘊法。及以蘊中我(居仁在裏許求出無門)。外現眾色像(莫眼
花)。一一音聲相(賺殺人)。平等如夢幻(救得一半)。不起凡聖見。不作
涅槃解(亦未見其人)。二邊三際斷。常應諸根用。而不起用想。分別
一切法。不起分別想。劫火燒海底。風鼓山相擊。真常寂滅樂。涅槃
相如是。吾今強言說。令汝捨邪見(只是居仁不肯捨)。汝勿隨言解(居
仁記取³¹)。許汝知少分(只遮少分也不消得³²)。志道聞偈。忽然大悟(葛
藤不少)。只遮一絡索。便是直截分明。指示居仁底指頭子也。居仁見
此。若道猶是經論所說。尚指古人公案。若尚作如此見。入地獄如箭
射。

答呂舍 人(居仁)

[31.1] 承日用不輟做工夫。工夫熟。則撞發關捩³³子矣。所謂工夫者。思
量世間塵勞底心。回在乾屎橛上。令情識不行。如土木偶人相似。覺
得昏怛没巴鼻可把捉時。便是好消息也。莫怕落空。亦莫思前算後。
幾時得悟。若存此心。便落邪道。佛云。是法非思量分別之所能解。
解³⁴著即禍生。知得思量分別不能解者是誰。只是簡呂居仁。更不得回
頭轉腦也。[31.2] 前此答隆禮書。說盡禪病矣。諸佛諸祖。並無一法與
人。只要當人自信自肯自見自悟耳。若只取佗人口頭說底。恐誤人。
此事決定離言說相。離心緣相。離文字相。能知離諸相者。亦只是呂
居仁。疑佗死後斷滅不斷滅。亦只是呂居仁。求直截指示者。亦只是
呂居仁。日用二六時中。或瞋或喜或思量或分別或昏沈或掉舉。皆只
是呂居仁。只遮呂居仁。能作種種奇特變化。能與諸佛諸祖同。游
寂滅大解脫光明海中。成就世間出世間事。只是呂居仁信不及耳。
若信得及。請依此注³⁵脚。入是三昧。忽然從三昧起。失却孃生鼻孔。
便是徹頭也。

---

31. T = 此.

32. Araki = 息.

33. T = 棙.

34. T = – 解.

35. T = 註.

又。

[32.1] 令弟子育經由。出所賜教。讀之喜慰可知。無常迅速。百歲光陰。如電閃。便是收因結果底時節到來也。乾屎橛如何覺得。没巴鼻。無滋味。肚裏悶時。便是好底消息也。第一不得向舉起處承當。又不得颺在無事甲裏。不可舉時便有。不舉時便無也。但將思量世間塵勞底心。回在乾屎橛上。思量來思量去。無處奈何。伎倆忽然盡。便自悟也。不得將心等悟。若將心等悟。永劫不能得悟也。[32.2] 前此答隆禮書。說盡揩大家病痛矣。承只置在座右。若依此做工夫。雖未悟徹。亦能分別邪正。不爲邪魔所障。亦種得般若種子深。縱今生不了。來生出頭。現成受用。亦不費力。亦不被惡業奪將去。臨命終時。亦能轉業。況一念相應耶。逐日千萬不要思量別事。但只思量乾屎橛。莫問幾時悟。至禱至禱。[32.3] 悟時亦無時節。亦不驚羣動衆。即時怗怗地。自然不疑佛。不疑祖。不疑生。不疑死。得到不疑之地。便是佛地也。佛地上本無疑。無悟無迷。無生無死。無有無無。無涅槃。無般若。無佛無衆生。亦無恁麼說者。此語亦不受。亦無不受者。亦無知不受者。亦無恁麼說不受者。居仁如是信得及。佛亦只如是。祖亦只如是。悟亦只如是。迷亦只如是。疑亦只如是。生亦只如是。死亦只如是。日用塵勞中亦只如是。死後斷滅不斷滅亦只如是。在朝廷作從官亦只如是。宮觀在靜處亦只如是。住徑山一千七百衆圍遶亦只如是。編管在衡州亦只如是。居仁還信得及麼。信得及亦只如是。信不及亦只如是。畢竟如何。如是如是。如是亦只如是。

答汪狀元 (聖錫)

[33.1] 左右妙年自立。便在一切人頂頸上。不爲富貴所籠羅。非百劫千生願力所持。焉能致是。又能切切於此一大事。念念不退轉。有決定信。具決定志。此豈淺丈夫所能。[33.2] 老瞿曇云。唯此一事實。餘二則非真。請著鞭不可忽。世間事只遮是。先聖豈不云乎。朝聞道夕死可矣。不知。聞底是何道。到遮裏。豈容眨眼。不可更引吾道一以貫之去也。須自信自悟。說得底終是無憑據。[33.3] 自見得。自悟得。自信得及了。說不得。形容不出。却不妨。只怕說得似。形容得似。却不見。却不悟者。老瞿曇指爲增上慢人。亦謂之謗般若人。亦謂之大妄語人。亦謂之斷佛慧命人。千佛出世。不通懺悔。若透得狗子無佛性話。遮般說話。却成妄語矣。而今不可便作妄語會。[33.4] 呂居仁比連收兩書。書中皆云。夏中答隆禮書。常置座右。以得爲期。又聞。嘗錄呈左右。近世貴公子。似渠者。如優曇鉢花時一現耳。[33.5] 頃在山頭。每與公說遮般話。見公眼目定動。領覽得九分九

鼇[36]。只欠団地一下尔。若得団地一下了。儒即釋。釋即儒。僧即俗。俗即僧。凡即聖。聖即凡。我即你。你即我。天即地。地即天。波即水。水即波。酥酪醍醐。攪成一味。鉼[37]盤釵釧。鎔成一金。在我。不在人。得到遮箇田地。由我指揮。所謂我爲法王。於法自在。得失是非。焉有罣礙。不是強爲。法如是故也。[33.6] 此箇境界。除無垢老子。佗人如何信得及。縱信得及。如何得入手。左右已信得及。已覷得見。已能分別是邪是正。但未得入手耳。得入手時。不[38]分老少。不在智愚。如將梵位直授凡庸。更無階級次第。永嘉所謂。一超直入如來地。是也。但相聽。決不相誤。

又。

[34.1] 某萬緣休罷。日用只如此。無煩軼念。左右分上。欠少箇甚麼。在世界上。可謂千足萬足。苟能於此箇門中。翻身一擲。何止腰纏十萬貫。騎鶴上揚州而已哉。[34.2] 昔楊文公大年。三十歲見廣慧璉公。除去礙膺之物。自是已後。在朝廷。居田里。始終一節。不爲功名所移。不爲富貴所奪。亦非有意輕功名富貴。道之所在。法如是故也。趙州云。諸人被十二時使。老僧使得十二時。此老此說。非是強爲。亦法如是故也。[34.3] 大率爲學爲道。一也。而今學者。往往以仁義禮智信爲學。以格物忠恕一以貫之之類爲道。只管如愽[39]謎子相似。又如眾盲摸象。各說異端。釋不云乎。以思惟心。測度如來圓覺境界。如取螢火燒須彌山。臨生死禍福之際。都不得力。蓋由此也。楊子云。學者所以修性。性即道也。黃面老子云。性成無上道。圭峯云。作有義事。是惺悟心。作無義事。是狂亂心。狂亂由情念。臨終被業牽。惺悟不由情。臨終能轉業。所謂義者是義理之義。非仁義之義。而今看來。遮老子亦未免析虛空爲兩處。仁乃性之仁。義乃性之義。禮乃性之禮。智乃性之智。信乃性之信。義理之義亦性也。作無義事。即背此性。作有義事。即順此性。然順背在人。不在性也。仁義禮智信。在性不在人也。人有賢愚。性即無也。若仁義禮智信。在賢而不在愚。則聖人之道。有揀擇取捨矣。如天降雨。擇地而下矣。所以云。仁義禮智信在性。而不在人也。賢愚順背。在人而不在性也。楊子所謂修性。性亦不可修。亦順背賢愚而已。圭峯所謂。惺悟狂亂。是也。趙州所謂。使得十二時。被十二時使。是也。若識得

---

36. Araki = 厘.

37. Translation follows Araki = 鈃.

38. T = 一.

39. Translation follows T = 摶.

仁義禮智信之性起處。則格物忠恕一以貫之。在其中矣。肇法師云。能天能人者。豈天人之所能哉。所以云。爲學爲道。一也。**[34.4]** 大率聖人設教。不求名。不伐功。如春行花木。具此性者。時節因緣到來。各各不相知。隨其根性。大小方圓長短。或青或黃。或紅或綠。或臭或香。同時發作。非春能大能小。能方能圓。能長能短。能青能黃。能紅能綠。能臭能香。此皆本有之性。遇緣而發耳。百丈云。欲識佛性義。當觀時節因緣。時節若至。其理自彰。又讓師謂馬師曰。汝學心地法門。如下種子。我說法要。譬彼天澤。汝緣合故。當見其道。所以云。聖人設教。不求名。不伐功。只令學者見性成道而已。無垢老子云。道在一芥。則一芥重。道在天下。則天下重。是也。**[34.5]** 左右嘗升無垢之堂。而未入其室。見其表。而未見其裏。百歲光陰。只在一剎那間。剎那間悟去。如上所說者。皆非實義。然既悟了。以爲實亦在我。以爲非實亦在我。如水上葫蘆。無人動著。常蕩蕩地。觸著便動。捺著便轉轆轆地。非是強爲。亦法如是故也。**[34.6]** 趙州狗子無佛性話。左右如人捕賊。已知窩盤處。但未捉著耳。請快著精彩。不得有少間斷。時時向行住坐臥處看。讀書史處。修仁義礼智信處。侍奉尊長處。提誨學者處。喫粥喫飯處。與之厮崖。忽然打失布袋。夫復何言。

答宗直閣

[35.1] 示諭。應緣日涉差別境界。未嘗不在佛法中。又於日用動容之間。以狗子無佛性話。破除情塵。若作如是工夫。恐卒未得悟入。請於脚跟下照顧。差別境界。從甚麼處起。動容周旋之間。如何以狗子無佛性話。破除情塵。能知破除情塵者。又是阿誰。佛不云乎。眾生顛倒。迷己逐物。物本無自性。迷己者自逐之耳。境界本無差別。迷己者自差別耳。既日涉差別境界。又在佛法中。既在佛法中。則非差別境界。既在差別境界中。則非佛法矣。拈一放一。有甚了期。廣額屠兒。在涅槃會上。放下屠刀。立地便成佛。豈有許多忉忉怛怛來。**[35.2]** 日用應緣處。纔覺涉差別境界時。但只就差別處。舉狗子無佛性話。不用作破除想。不用作情塵想。不用作差別想。不用作佛法想。但只看狗子無佛性話。但只舉箇無字。亦不用存心等悟。**[35.3]** 若存心等悟。則境界也差別。佛法也差別。情塵也差別。狗子無佛性話也差別。間斷處也差別。無間斷處也差別。遭情塵惑亂身心不安樂處也差別。能知許多差別底亦差別。若要除此病。但只看箇無字。但只看。廣額屠兒放下屠刀。云我是千佛一數。是實是虛。若作虛實商量。又打入差別境界上去也。不如一刀兩段。不得念後思前。念後思前。則又差別矣。**[35.4]** 玄沙云。此事限約不得。心思路絕。不因莊嚴。本來真靜。動用語笑。隨處明了。更

無欠少。今時人不悟箇中道理。妄自涉事涉塵。處處染著。頭頭繫
絆。縱悟則塵境紛紜。名相不實。便擬疑[40]心歛念。攝事歸空。閉目
藏睛。隨有念起。旋旋破除。細想纔生。即便過捺。如此見解。即是
落空亡底外道。魂不散底死人。溟溟漠漠。無覺無知。塞耳偷鈴。徒
自欺誑。左右來書云云。盡是玄沙所訶底病。默照邪師。埋人底坑
子。不可不知也。[35.5] 舉話時。都不用作許多伎倆。但行住坐臥處。
勿令間斷。喜怒哀樂處。莫生分別。舉來舉去。看來看去。覺得沒理
路。沒滋味。心頭熱悶時。便是當人放身命處也。記取記取。莫見如
此境界便退心。如此境界。正是成佛作祖底消息也。[35.6] 而今默照
邪師輩。只以無言無說爲極則。喚作威音那畔事。亦喚作空劫已前
事。不信有悟門。以悟爲誑。以悟爲第二頭。以悟爲方便語。以悟爲
接引之詞[41]。如此之徒。謾人自謾。誤人自誤。亦不可不知。[35.7] 日
用四威儀中。涉差別境界。覺得省力時。便是得力處也。得力處。極
省力。若用一毫毛氣力支撐。定是邪法。非佛法也。但辦取長遠心。
與狗子無佛性話厮崖。崖來崖去。心無所之。忽然如睡夢覺。如蓮花
開。如披雲見日。到恁麼時。自然成一片矣。[35.8] 但日用七顛八倒
處。只看箇無字。莫管悟不悟。徹不徹。三世諸佛。只是箇無事
人。諸代祖師。亦只是箇無事人。古德云。但於事上。通無事。見色
聞聲。不用聾。又古德云。愚人除境。不忘心。智者忘心。不除境。
於一切處無心。則種種差別境界自無矣。[35.9] 而今士大夫。多是急性
便要會禪。於經教上及祖師言句中傳[42]量。要說得分曉。殊不知。分曉
處却是不分曉底事。若透得箇無字。分曉不分曉不著問人矣。老漢教
士大夫放教鈍。便是遮箇道理也。作鈍榜狀元亦不惡。只怕挖白耳。
一笑。

答李參政 (泰發)

[36.1] 示諭。華嚴重重法界。斷非虛語。既非虛語。必有分付處。必有
自肯處。讀至此。嗟歎久之。[36.2] 士大夫平昔所學。臨死生禍福之
際。手足俱露者。十常八九。考其行事。不如三家村裏省事漢。富貴
貧賤不能汩其心。以是較之。智不如愚。貴不如賤者多矣。何以故。
生死禍福現前那時。不容偽故也。[36.3] 大參相公。平昔所學。已見
於行事。臨禍福之際。如精金入火愈見明耀。又決定知華嚴重重法
界。斷非虛語。則定不作佗物想矣。其餘七顛八倒。或逆或順。或正

---

40. Translation follows T and Araki = 凝.

41. T = 辭.

42. Translation follows T = 摶.

或邪。亦非佗物。願公常作此觀。妙喜亦在其中。[36.4] 異日相從於
寂寞之濱。結當當來世香火因緣。成就重重法界。以實其事。豈小補
哉。[36.5] 更須下箇注⁴³脚。即今遮一絡索。切忌作寓言指物會。一
笑。

答曾宗丞 (天隱)

[37.1] 左右天資近道。身心清淨。無佗緣作障。只遮一段。誰人能及。
又能行住坐臥。以老僧所示省要處。時時提撕。休說一念相應。千
了百當。便是此生打未徹。只恁麼崖到臘月三十日。闔家老子。也
須倒退三千里始得。何以故。爲念念在般若中。無異念。無間斷
故。[37.2] 只如道家流。以妄心存想。日久月深。尚能成功。不爲地水
火風所使。況全念住在般若中。臘月三十日。豈不能轉業耶。[37.3] 而
今人多是將有所得心學道。此是無妄想中真妄想也。但放教自在。然
不得太緊。不得太緩。只恁麼做工夫。省無限心力。[37.4] 左右生處已
熟。熟處已生。十二時中自然。不著枯心忘懷。將心管帶矣。雖未透
脫諸魔外道。已不能伺其便。亦自能與諸魔外道。共一手同一眼。成
就彼事。而不墮其數矣。除公一人。可以語此。餘人非但不能如公行
履。亦未必信得及也。[37.5] 但於話頭上看。看來看去。覺得沒巴鼻。
沒滋味。心頭悶時。正好著力。切忌隨佗去。只遮悶處。便是成佛作
祖。坐斷天下人舌頭處也。不可忽。不可忽。

答王教授 (大授⁴⁴)

[38.1] 不識。左右別後。日用如何做工夫。若是曾於理性上得滋味。
經教中得滋味。祖師言句上得滋味。眼見耳聞處得滋味。舉足動步處
得滋味。心思意想處得滋味。都不濟事。若要直下休歇。應是從前得
滋味處。都莫管佗。却去沒撈摸處。沒滋味處。試著意看。若著意不
得。撈摸不得。轉覺得沒欄柄可把捉⁴⁵。理路義路。心意識。都不行。
如土木瓦石相似時。莫怕落空。此是當人放身命處。不可忽。不可
忽。[38.2] 聰明靈利人。多被聰明所障。以故道眼不開。觸塗⁴⁶成滯。
眾生無始時來。爲心意識所使。流浪生死。不得自在。果欲出生死。
作快活漢。須是一刀兩段。絕却心意識路頭。方有少分相應。故永嘉

---

43. T = 註.

44. T = 受.

45. T = 没欄柄捉把.

46. T = 途.

云。損法財滅功德。莫不由茲心意識。豈欺人哉。[38.3] 頃蒙惠教。其中種種趣向。皆某平昔所訶底病。知是般事。颺在腦後。且向没巴鼻處。没撈摸處。没滋味處。試做工夫看。如僧問趙州。狗子還有佛性也無。州云。無。尋常聰明人。纔聞舉起。便以心意識領會。博⁴⁷量引證。要說得有分付處。殊不知。不容引證。不容博⁴⁸量。不容以心意識領會。縱引證得。博⁴⁹量得。領會得。盡是髑髏前情識邊事。生死岸頭。定不得力。[38.4] 而今普天之下。喚作禪師長老者。會得分曉底。不出左右書中寫來底消息耳。其餘種種邪解。不在言也。密首座。某與渠同在平普融會中相聚。盡得普融要領。渠自以爲安樂。然所造者。亦不出左右書中消息。今始知非。別得箇安樂處。方知某無秋毫相欺。今特令去相見。無事時試令渠吐露看。還契得左右意否。[38.5] 八十翁翁入場屋。眞誠不是小兒戲。若生死到來。不得力。縱說得分曉。和會得有下落。引證得無差別。盡是鬼家活計。都不干我一星事。[38.6] 禪門種種差別異解。唯識法者懼。大法不明者。往往多以病爲藥。不可不知。

答劉侍郎 (季高)

[39.1] 示諭。臘月三十日已到。要之日用當如是觀察。則世間塵勞之心。自然銷殞⁵⁰矣。塵勞之心既銷殞⁵¹。則來日依前孟春猶寒矣。[39.2] 古德云。欲識佛性義。當觀時節因緣。此箇時節。乃是黃面老子。出世成佛。坐金剛座。降伏魔軍。轉法輪。度衆生。入涅槃底時節。與解空所謂臘月三十日時節。無異無別。到遮裏。只如是觀。以此觀者。名爲正觀。異此觀者。名爲邪觀。[39.3] 邪正未分。未免隨佗時節遷變。要得不隨時節。但一時放下著。放到無可放處。此語亦不受。依前只是解空居士。更不是別人。

又。

[40.1] 吾佛大聖人。能空一切相。成萬法智。而不能即滅定業。況博地凡夫耶。居士既是箇中人。想亦常入是三昧。[40.2] 昔有僧。問

---

47. Translation follows T = 搏.

48. Translation follows T = 搏.

49. Translation follows T = 搏.

50. Substituting T and Araki = 殞 for the Gozan rare variant [歹+負].

51. Substituting T and Araki = 殞 for the Gozan rare variant [歹+負].

一老宿。世界恁麼熱。未審向甚麼處回避。老宿曰。向鑊湯鑪炭裏回避。曰。只如鑊湯鑪炭裏。作麼生回避。曰。眾苦不能到。願居士。日用四威儀中。只如此做工夫。老宿之言。不可忽。此是妙喜得效底藥方。非與居士此道相契。此心相知。亦不肯容易傳授。只用一念相應草湯下。更不用別湯。使若用別湯。使令人發狂。不可不知也。[40.3] 一念相應草。不用佗求。亦只在居士四威儀中。明處明如日。黑處黑如漆。若信手拈來。以本地風光一照。無有錯者。亦能殺人。亦能活人。故佛祖常以此藥。向鑊湯鑪炭裏。醫苦惱眾生生死大病。號大醫王。不識。居士還信得及否。[40.4] 若言我自有父子不傳之祕方。不用向鑊湯鑪炭裏回避底妙術。卻望居士布施也。

答李郎中 (似表)

[41.1] 士大夫學此道。不患不聰明。患太聰明耳。不患無知見。患知見太多耳。故常行識前一步。昧卻脚跟下快活自在底消息。邪見之上者。和會見聞覺知。爲自己。以現量境界。爲心地法門。下者。弄業識。認門頭戶口。簸兩片皮。談玄說妙。甚者。至於發狂不勒字數。胡言漢語。指東畫西。下下者。以默照無言空空寂寂。在鬼窟裏著到。求究竟安樂。其餘種種邪解。不在言而可知也。[41.2] 沖密等歸。領所賜教。讀之喜慰不可言。更不復敘世諦。相酬酢。只以左右向道勇猛之志。便入葛藤。[41.3] 禪無德山臨濟之殊。法眼曹洞之異。但學者無廣大決定志。而師家亦無廣大融通法門。故所入差別。究竟歸宿處。並無如許差別也。[41.4] 示諭。欲妙喜因書指示徑要處。只遮求指示徑要底一念。早是刺頭入膠盆了也。不可更向雪上加霜。雖然有問。不可無答。請左右。都將平昔或自看經教話頭。或因人舉覺指示。得滋味歡喜處。一時放下。依前百不知百不會。如三歲孩兒相似。有性識而未行。卻向未起求徑要底一念子前頭看。看來看去。覺得轉沒巴鼻。方寸轉不寧怗時。不得放緩。遮裏是坐斷千聖頂顠處。往往學道人。多向遮裏打退了。[41.5] 左右若信得及。只向未起求徑要指示一念前看。看來看去。忽然睡夢覺。不是差事。此是妙喜平昔做底得力工夫。知公有決定志故。挖泥帶水。納遮一場敗闕。此外別無可指示。若有可指示。則不徑要矣。

答李寶文 (茂嘉)

[42.1] 向承示諭。性根昏鈍。而黽勉修持。終未得超悟之方。某頃在雙徑。答富季申所問。正與此問同。能知昏鈍者。決定不昏鈍。更欲向甚處求超悟。士大夫學此道。卻須借昏鈍而入。若執昏鈍。自謂我無分。則爲昏鈍魔所攝矣。[42.2] 蓋平昔知見。多以求證悟之心。在

前作障故。自己正知見。不能現前。此障亦非外來。亦非別事。只是箇能知昏鈍底主人公耳。故瑞巖和尚。居常在丈室中。自喚云。主人公。又自應云。諾52。惺惺著。又自應云。諾53。佗時後日莫受人謾。又自應云。諾諾54。古來幸有恁麼牓樣。謾向遮裏提撕看。是箇甚麼。只遮提撕底。亦不是別人。只是遮能知昏鈍者耳。能知昏鈍者。亦不是別人。便是李寶文本命元辰也。[42.3] 此是妙喜應病與藥。不得已略爲居士。指箇歸家穩坐底路頭而已。若便認定死語。真箇喚作本命元辰。則是認識神爲自己。轉沒交涉矣。故長沙和尚云。學道之人不識真。只爲從前認識神。無量劫來生死本。癡人喚作本來人。[42.4] 前所云。借昏鈍而入。是也。但只看能知得如是昏鈍底。畢竟是箇甚麼。只向遮裏看。不用求超悟。看來看去。忽地大笑去矣。此外無可言者。

答向侍郎 (伯恭)

[43.1] 示諭。悟與未悟。夢與覺一。一段因緣。黃面老子云。汝以緣心聽法。此法亦緣。謂至人無夢。非有無之無。謂夢與非夢一而已。以是觀之。則佛夢金鼓。高宗夢得55說。孔子夢奠兩楹。亦不可作夢與非夢解。[43.2] 却來觀世間。猶如夢中事。教中自有明文。唯夢乃全妄想也。而眾生顛倒。以日用目前境界爲實。殊不知。全體是夢。而於其中復生虛妄分別。以想心繫念神識紛飛。爲實夢。殊不知。正是夢中說夢。顛倒中又顛倒。[43.3] 故佛大慈悲老婆心切。悉能徧入一切法界諸安立海。所有微塵。於一一塵中。以夢自在法門。開悟世界海微塵數眾生。住邪定者。入正定聚。此亦普示顛倒眾生。以目前實有底境界。爲安立海。令悟夢與非夢。悉皆是幻。則全夢是實。全實是夢。不可取。不可捨。至人無夢之義。如是而已。[43.4] 來書見問。乃是某三十六歲時所疑。讀之不覺抓著痒處。亦嘗以此問圜悟先師。但以手指曰。住住。休妄想。休妄想。某復曰。如某未睡著時。佛所讚者。依而行之。佛所訶者。不敢違犯。從前依師。及自做工夫。零碎所得者。惺惺時。都得受用。及乎上牀。半惺半覺時。已作主宰不得。夢見得金寶。則夢中歡喜無限。夢見被人以刀杖相逼。及諸惡境界。則夢中怕怖惶恐。自念此身尚存。只是睡著。已作主宰不得。況地水火風分散。眾苦熾然。如何得不被回換。到遮裏。方始

---

52. T = 喏.

53. T = 喏.

54. T = 喏喏.

55. Translation follows T and Araki = 傅.

著忙。先師又曰。待汝說底許多妄想絕時。汝自到寤寐恒一處也。初
聞亦未之信。每日我自顧。寤與寐分明作兩段。如何敢開大口說禪。
除非佛說寤寐恒一是妄悟。則我此病。不須除。佛語果不欺人。乃是
我自末了。後因聞先師舉諸佛出身處。熏風自南來。忽然去却礙膺之
物。方知黃面老子所說。是真語實語如語不誑語不妄語。不欺人。真
大慈悲。粉身沒命。不可報。礙膺之物既除。方知夢時便是寤時底。
寤時便是夢時底。佛言寤寐恒一。方始自知遮般道理。拈出呈似人不
得。說與人不得。如夢中境界。取不得。捨不得。承問妙喜於未悟已
前已悟之後。有異無異。不覺依實供通。子細讀來教。字字至誠。不
是問禪。亦非見詰。故不免以昔時所疑處吐露。[43.5] 願居士試將老
龐語謾提撕。但願空諸所有。切勿實諸所無。先以目前日用境界。
作夢會了。然後却將夢中底。移來目前。則佛金鼓。高宗得[56]說。孔
子莫兩楹。決不是夢矣。

答陳教授 (阜卿)

[44.1] 此道寂寥。無出今日。邪師說法。如惡叉聚。各各自謂得無上
道。咸唱邪說。幻惑凡愚。[44.2] 故某每每切齒於此。不惜身命。欲
扶持之。使光明種子。知有吾家本分事。不墮邪見網中。萬一得眾生
界中。佛種不斷。亦不虛受黃面老子覆蔭。所謂將此深心奉塵刹。是
則名為報佛恩。然亦是不知時。不量力之一事也。[44.3] 左右既是箇中
人。不得不說箇中事。因筆不覺及此耳。

答林判院 (少瞻)

[45.1] 示諭。求一語與信道人做工夫。既看圓覺經。經中豈止一語而
已哉。諸大菩薩。各隨自所疑處發問。世尊據所疑。一一分明剖析。
大段分曉。前所給話頭。亦在其中矣。經云。居一切時。不起妄念。
於諸妄心。亦不息滅。住妄想境。不加了知(此語最親切)。於無了知。
不辨[57]真實。老漢昔居雲門菴時。嘗頌之曰。荷葉團團團似鏡。菱角尖
尖尖似錐。風吹柳絮毛毬走。雨打梨花蛺蝶飛。但將此頌放在上面。
却將經文移來下面。頌却是經。經却是頌。[45.2] 試如此做工夫看。
莫管悟不悟。心頭休熱忙。亦不可放緩。如調絃之法。緊緩得其所。
則曲調自成矣。[45.3] 歸去。但與沖輩相親。遞相琢磨。道業無有不辦
者。祝祝。

---

56. Translation follows T = 傳. Araki also = 得.

57. T = 辯.

答黃知縣 (子餘)

[46.1] 收書。知爲此一大事因緣甚力。大丈夫漢。所作所爲。當如是耳。無常迅速。生死事大。過了一日。則銷了一日好事。可畏可畏。[46.2] 左右春秋鼎盛。正是作業不識好惡時。能回此心。學無上菩提。此是世界上第一等難容靈利漢。五濁界中。有甚麼奇特事。過如此段因緣。趂色力強健。早回頭。以臨老回頭。其力量勝百千萬億倍。老漢私爲左右喜。[46.3] 前此寫去法語。曾時時覷看否。第一記取。不得起心動念。肚裏熱忙。急要悟。纔作此念。則被此念塞斷路頭。永不能得悟矣。祖師云。執之失度。必入邪路。放之自然。體無去住。此乃祖師吐心吐膽爲人處也。但日用費力處。莫要做。此箇門中。不容費力。老漢常爲人說此話。得力處乃是省力處。省力處乃是得力處。若起一念希望心。求悟入處。大似人在自家堂屋裏坐。卻問佗人覓住處無異。[46.4] 但把生死兩字。貼左鼻尖兒上。不要忘了。時時提撕話頭。提來提去。生處自熟。熟處自生矣。此語已寫在空相道人書中。請同此書互換一看。便了得也。

答嚴教授 (子卿)

[47.1] 真實到不疑之地者。如渾鋼打就。生鐵鑄成。直饒千聖出頭來。現無量殊勝境界。見之亦如不見。況於此作奇特殊勝道理耶。[47.2] 昔藥山坐禪次。石頭問。子在遮裏作甚麼。藥山云。一物不爲。石頭云。恁麼則閑坐也。藥山云。閑坐則爲也。石頭然之。看佗古人。一箇閑坐也奈何佗不得。[47.3] 今時學道之士。多在閑坐處打住。近日叢林。無鼻孔輩。謂之默照者。是也。又有一種腳跟元不曾點地。認得箇門頭戶口光影。一向狂發。與說平常話不得。盡作禪會了。似遮般底。喚業識作本命元辰。更是不可與語本分事也。[47.4] 不見。雲門大師有言。光不透脫。有兩般病。一切處不明。面前有物。是一。又透得一切法空。隱隱地似有箇物相似。亦是光不透脫。又法身亦有兩般病。得到法身。爲法執不忘。己見猶存。坐在法身邊。是一。直饒透得法身去。放過即不可。子細檢點來。有甚麼氣息。亦是病。而今學實法者。以透過法身爲極致。而雲門返以爲病。不知透過法身了。合作麼生。到遮裏。如人飲水冷煖自知。不著問別人。問別人則禍事也。所以云。真實到不疑之地者。如渾鋼打就。生鐵鑄成。是也。[47.5] 如人喫飯飽時。不可更問人我飽未飽。昔黃檗問百丈。從上古人。以何法示人。百丈只據坐。黃檗云。後代兒孫。將何傳授。百丈拂衣便起云。我將謂汝是箇人。遮箇便是爲人底樣子也。但向自信處看。還得自信底消息絕也未。若自信底消息絕。則自然不取

佗人口頭辨矣。臨濟云。汝若歇得念念馳求心。與釋迦老子不別。不是欺人。第七地菩薩。求佛智心。未滿足。故謂之煩惱。直是無你安排處。著一星兒外料不得。**[47.6]** 數年前。有箇許居士。認得箇門頭戶口。將書來呈見解云。日用中。空豁豁地。無一物作對待。方知三界萬法。一切元無。直是安樂快活放得下。因示之以偈曰。莫戀淨潔處。淨處使人困。莫戀快活處。快活使人狂。如水之任器。隨方圓短長。放下不放下。更請細思量。三界與萬法。匪歸何有鄉。若只便恁麼。此事大乖張。爲報許居士。家親作禍殃。豁開千聖眼。不須頻禱禳。**[47.7]** 偶晨起稍涼。驀然記得。子卿道友。初得箇入頭時。尚疑恐是光影。遂將從來所疑公案挮照。方見趙州老漢敗闕處。不覺信筆葛藤如許。

答張侍郎 (子韶)

[48.1] 左右以自所得瞥脫處。爲極則。纔見涉理路。入泥入水爲人底。便欲掃除。使滅蹤跡。見某所集正法眼藏。便云。臨濟下有數箇菴主好機鋒。何不收入。如忠國師說義理禪。教壞人家男女。決定可刪。左右見道如此諦當。而不喜忠國師說老婆禪。坐在淨淨潔潔處。只愛擊石火閃電光一著子。此外不容一星兒別道理。真可惜耳。故某盡力主張。若法性不寬。波瀾不闊。佛法知見不亡。生死命根不斷。則不敢如此四楞著地。入泥入水爲人。**[48.2]** 蓋衆生根器不同。故從上諸祖。各立門戶施設。備衆生機。隨機攝化。故長沙岑大蟲有言。我若一向舉揚宗教。法堂前須草深一丈。倩人看院始得。既落在遮行戶裏。被人喚作宗師。須備衆生機說法。如擊石火閃電光一著子。是遮般根器。方承當得。根器不是處用之。則揠苗矣。**[48.3]** 某豈不曉瞥脫一椎。便七穿八穴是性燥。所以集正法眼藏。不分門類。不問雲門臨濟曹洞溈仰法眼宗。但有正知正見。可以令人悟入者。皆收之。見忠國師大珠二老宿。禪備衆體。故收以救此一類根器者。左右書來云。決定可刪。觀公之意。正法眼藏。盡去除諸家門戶。只收似公見解者方是。若爾。則公自集一書。化大根器者。有何不可。不必須教妙喜隨公意去之。**[48.4]** 若謂忠國師說挮泥帶水老婆禪便絕後。則如巖頭睦州烏臼汾陽無業鎮州普化定上座雲峯悅法昌遇諸大老。合兒孫滿地。今亦寂然無主化者。諸公豈是佗[58]泥帶水說老婆禪乎。**[48.5]** 然妙喜主張國師。無垢破除。初不相妨也。

---

58. Translation follows T and Araki = 挮.

答徐顯謨 (稚山)

[49.1] 左右頻寄聲妙喜。想只是要調伏水牯牛。揑殺遮獼猻子耳。[49.2] 此事不在久歷叢林。飽參知識。只貴於一言一句下。直截承當。不打之遶尒。據實而論。間不容髮。不得已。說箇直截。已是紆曲了也。說箇承當。已是蹉過了也。況復牽枝引蔓。舉經舉教。說理說事。欲究竟耶。古德云。但有纖毫即是塵。水牯牛未調伏。獼猻子未死。縱說得恒沙道理。並不干我一星兒事。[49.3] 然說得說不得。亦非外邊事。不見。江西老宿有言。說得亦是汝心。說不得亦是汝心。決欲直截擔荷。見佛見祖。如生冤家。方有少分相應。如此做工夫。日久月深。不著起心求悟。水牯牛自調伏。獼猻子自死矣。記取記取。[49.4] 但向平昔心意識湊泊不得處。取不得處。捨不得處。看箇話頭。僧問雲門。如何是佛。門云。乾屎橛。看時不用將平昔聰明靈利。思量卜度。擬心思量。十萬八千。未是遠。莫是不思量。不計較。不擬心便是麼。咄更是箇甚麼。且置是事。

答楊教授 (彥侯)

[50.1] 左右強項中。却有不可思議底柔和。致一言之下。千了百當。此事殊勝。若不聞於強項中。打發得幾人。佛法豈到今日。非有般若根性。則不能如是。盛事盛事。[50.2] 示諭。欲來年春夏間。棹無底船。吹無孔笛。施無盡供。說無生話。要了無窮無始。不有不無巴鼻。但請來與遮無面目漢商量。定不錯了遮話。[50.3] 又承需道號。政欲相塗糊。可稱快然居士。故真淨老人云。快然大道。只在目前。縱橫十字。擬而留連。便是此義也。[50.4] 某只在長沙。作久住計。左右佗日果從此來。則林下不寂寞也。

答樓樞密

[51.1] 不識別後日用應緣處。不被外境所奪否。視堆案之文。能撥置否。與物相遇時。能動轉否。住寂靜處。不妄想否。體究箇事。無雜念否。[51.2] 故黃面老子有言。心不妄取過去法。亦不貪著未來事。不於現在有所住。了達三世悉空寂。過去事。或善或惡。不須思量。思量則障道矣。未來事。不須計較。計較則狂亂矣。現在事到面前。或逆或順。亦不須著意。著意則擾方寸矣。但一切臨時隨緣酬酢。自然合著遮箇道理。[51.3] 逆境界易打。順境界難打。逆我意者。只消一箇忍字。定省少時。便過了。順境界。直是無你回避處。如磁石與鐵相偶。彼此不覺。合作一處。無情之物尚尒。況現行無明。全身

在裏許。作活計者。當此境界。若無智慧。不覺不知。被佗引入羅
網。卻向裏許。要求出路。不亦難乎。所以先聖云。入得世間。出世
無餘。便是遮箇道理也。[51.4] 近世有一種修行失方便者。往往認現
行無明。爲入世間。便將出世間法。強差排。作出世無餘之事。可不
悲乎。除夙有誓願。即時識得破。作得主。不被佗牽引。[51.5] 故淨名
有言。佛爲增上慢人。說離婬怒癡爲解脫耳。若無增上慢者。佛說婬
怒癡性即是解脫。若免得此過。於逆順境界中。無起滅相。始離得增
上慢名字。恁麼方可作入得世間。謂之有力量漢。[51.6] 已上所說。都
是妙喜平昔經歷過底。即今日用。亦只如此修行。願公趁色力強健。
亦入是三昧。此外時時以趙州無字提撕。久久純熟。驀然無心。撞破
漆桶。便是徹頭處也。

又。

[52.1] 日用工夫。前書已葛藤不少。但只依舊不變不動。物來則與
之酬酢。自然物我一如矣。[52.2] 古德云。放曠任其去住。靜鑑
覺其源流。語證則不可示人。說理則非證不了。自證自得處。拈
出呈似人不得。唯親證親得者。略露目前些子。彼此便默默相契
矣。[52.3] 示諭。自此不被人謾。不錯用工夫矣。大概已正。欛柄
已得。如善牧牛者。索頭常在手中。爭得犯人苗稼。驀地放卻索頭。
鼻孔無撈摸處。平田淺草。一任縱橫。慈明老人所謂。四方放去休
攔過。八面無拘任意游。要收只在索頭撥。未能如是。當緊把索頭。
且與順摩挲淹浸。工夫既熟。自然不著用意隄防矣。[52.4] 工夫不可
急。急則躁動。又不可緩。緩則昏怛矣。忘懷著意。俱蹉過。譬如擲
劍揮空。莫論及之不及。[52.5] 昔嚴陽尊者問趙州。一物不將來時如
何。州云。放下著。嚴陽云。一物既不將來。放下箇甚麼。州云。
放不下擔取去。嚴陽於言下大悟。又有僧問古德。學人奈何不得時如
何。古德云。老僧亦奈何不得。僧云。學人在學地。故是奈何不得。
和尚是大善知識。爲甚麼亦奈何不得。古德云。我若奈何得。則便拈
卻你遮不奈何。僧於言下大悟。二僧悟處。即是樓樞密迷處。樓樞密
疑處。即是二僧問處。法從分別生。還從分別滅。滅諸分別法。是法
無生滅。[52.6] 細觀來書。病已去盡。別證候亦不生矣。大段相近。
亦漸省力矣。請只就省力處。放教蕩蕩地。忽然啐地破。嚗地斷。便
了。千萬勉之。

答曹太尉 (功顯)

[53.1] 某雖年運而往矣。不敢不勉強力。以此事與衲子輩激揚。一日粥
後。撥牌子。輪一百人入室。間有負命者上鈎來。亦有咬人師子。以

此法喜禪悅爲樂。殊不覺倦。亦造物見憐耳。[53.2] 左右福慧兩全。
日在至尊之側。而留意此段大事因緣。真不可思議事。釋迦老子曰。
有勢不臨難。豪貴學道難。非百劫千生。曾承事善知識。種得般若種
子深。焉能如是信得及。只遮信得及處。便是成佛作祖底基本也。
願公只向信得及處覷捕。久久自透脫矣。[53.3] 然第一不得著意安排。
覓透脫處。若著意。則蹉過也。釋迦老子又曰。佛道不思議。誰能
思議佛。又佛問文殊師利曰。汝入不思議三昧耶。文殊曰。弗也。世
尊。我即不思議。不見有心能思議者。云何而言入不思議三昧。我初
發心。欲入是定。如今思惟。實無心想而入三昧。如人學射。久習則
巧。後雖無心。以久習故。箭發皆中。我亦如是。初學不思議三昧。
繫心一緣。若久習成就。更無心想。常與定俱。佛與祖師。所受用
處。無二無別。[53.4] 近年叢林。有一種邪禪。以閉目藏睛。觜盧都
地。作妄想。謂之不思議事。亦謂之威音那畔空劫已前事。纔開口便
喚作落今時。亦謂之根本上事。亦謂之淨極光通達。以悟爲落在第二
頭。以悟爲枝葉邊事。蓋渠初發步時便錯了。亦不知是錯。以悟爲建
立。既自無悟門。亦不信有悟者。遮般底。謂之謗大般若。斷佛慧
命。千佛出世。不通懺悔。左右具驗人眼久矣。似此等輩。披却師子
皮。作野干鳴。不可不知。[53.5] 某與左右。雖未承顏接論。此心已
默默相契多年矣。前此答字。極不如禮。今專遣法空禪人代往致敬。
故不暇入善思惟三昧。只恁麼信手信意。不覺葛藤如許。聊謝不敏而
已。

答榮侍郎 (茂實)

[54.1] 承留心欲究竟此一段大事因緣。既辦此心。第一不要急。急則
轉遲矣。又不得緩。緩則怠惰矣。如調琴之法。緊緩要得中。方成
曲調。但向日用應緣處。時時覷捕。我遮[59]能與人決斷是非曲直底。
承誰恩力。畢竟從甚麼處流出。覷捕來覷捕去。平昔生處路頭。自
熟。生處既熟。則熟處却生矣。[54.2] 那箇是熟處。五陰。六入十
二處。十八界。二十五有。無明業識。思量計較心識。晝夜熠熠。
如野馬無暫停息底是。遮一絡索。使得人流浪生死。使得人做不好
事。[54.3] 遮一絡索既生。則菩提涅槃真如佛性。便現前矣。當現前
時。亦無現前之量。故古德契證得[60]了。便解道。應眼時。若千日。
萬象不能逃影質。應耳時。若幽谷。大小音聲。無不足。如此等事。
不假佗求。不借佗力。自然向應緣處。活鱍鱍地。[54.4] 未得如此。

---

59. T = +箇.

60. T = −得.

且將遮思量世間塵勞底心。回在思量不及處。試思量看。那箇是思量不及處。僧問趙州。狗子還有佛性也無。州云。無。只遮一字。儘你有甚麼伎倆。請安排看。請計較看。思量計較安排。無處可以頓放。只覺得肚裏悶。心頭煩惱時。正是好底時節。第八識相次不行矣。覺得如此時。莫要放却。只就遮無字上提撕。提撕來。提撕去。生處自熱。熱處自生矣。[54.5] 近年以來。叢林中有一種唱邪說爲宗師者。謂學者曰。但只管守靜。不知守者是何物。靜者是何人。却言靜底是基本。却不信有悟底。謂悟底是枝葉。更引僧問仰山曰。今時人。還假悟也無。仰山曰。悟則不無。爭奈落在第二頭。癡人面前。不得說夢。便作實法會。謂悟是落第二頭。殊不知。潙山自有警覺學者之言。直是痛切。曰。研窮至理。以悟爲則。此語又向甚處著。不可潙山疑誤後人。要教落在第二頭也。[54.6] 曹閣使亦留心此事。恐其被邪師輩所誤。比亦如此書。忉忉怛怛。寫與。此公聰明識見。皆[61]有大過人處。決不到錯認方便語。作實法會。但某未得與之目擊。私憂過計耳。聞老居士亦與之是道友。因筆不覺葛藤。無事相見時。試問渠取書一看。方知妙喜相期。不在眼底。彼此氣義相投。又非勢利之交。寫了一紙。紙盡又添一紙。不暇更事形迹。此書亦如是。[54.7] 前書託是箇中人。故曰。切不可道。老老大大。著甚來由。若如此。則好事在面前。定放過矣。寫時雖似率易。然亦機感相投。亦不覺書在紙上。荷公信得妙喜及。便把做事。[54.8] 日用應緣處。便恢張此箇法門。以報聖主求賢安天下之意。真不負其所知也。願種種堪忍。始終只如今日做將去。佛法世法。打作一片。且耕且戰。久久純熟。一舉而兩得之。豈非腰纏十萬貫。騎鶴上揚州乎。

又。

[55.1] 示諭。鐘鳴漏盡之譏。爲君上盡誠。而下安百姓。自有聞絃賞音者。願公凡事堅忍。當逆順境。政好著力。所謂將此深心。奉塵刹。是則名爲報國[62]恩。[55.2] 平昔學道。只要於逆順界中受用。逆順現前。而生苦惱。大似平昔不曾向箇中用心。祖師曰。境緣無好醜。好醜起於心。心若不強名。妄情從何起。妄情既不起。真心任徧知。請於逆順境中。常作是觀。則久久自不生苦惱。苦惱既不生。則可以驅魔王。作護法善神矣。[55.3] 前此老老大大。著甚來由之說。言猶在耳。豈忘之耶。欲識佛性義。當觀時節因緣。以居士前十餘載。閑自有閑時時節。今日仕權在手。便有忙底時節。當念閑

---

61. T = -皆.

62. T = 佛.

時是誰閑。忙時是誰忙。須信忙時却有閑時道理。閑時却有忙時
道理。[55.4] 政63在忙中。當體主上起公之意。頃刻不可暫忘。自警
自察。何以報之。若常作是念。則鑊湯鑪炭。刀山劍樹上。亦須著向
前。況目前些小逆順境界耶。與公以此道相契。故不留情。盡淨吐
露。

答黃門司 (節夫)

[56.1] 收書并許多葛藤。不意便解如此拈弄。直是弄得來活鱍鱍地。真
是自證自得者。可喜可喜。[56.2] 但只如此。從教人道遮官人。不依
本分。乱說乱道。佗家自有通人愛。[56.3] 除是曾證曾悟者方知。若是
聽響之流。一任佗錯龜打瓦。[56.4] 更批判得如來禪祖師禪好。儘喫得
妙喜拄64杖也。且道是賞伊罰伊。一任諸方更疑三十年。

答孫知縣

[57.1] 蒙以所修金剛經相示。幸得隨喜一徧。近世士大夫。肯如左右。
留心內典者。實爲希有。不得意趣。則不能如是信得及。不具看經
眼。則不能窺測經中深妙之義。真火中蓮也。詳味久之。不能無疑
耳。[57.2] 左右詆諸聖師翻譯失真。而汨乱本真。文句增減。違背佛
意。又云。自始持誦。即悟其非。欲求定本。是正舛差。而習僞已
久。雷同一律。暨得京師藏本。始有據依。復考繹天親無著論頌。其
義脗合。遂泮然無疑。又以長水孤山二師。皆依句而違義。不識。左
右敢如是批判。則定甞見六朝所譯梵本。盡得諸師翻譯錯謬。方始泮
然無疑。既無梵本。便以臆見刊削聖意。則且未論招因帶果。毀謗聖
教。墮無間獄。恐有識者見之。却如左右檢點諸師之過。還著於本人
矣。[57.3] 古人有言。交淺而言深者65。招尤之道也。某與左右。素昧
平生。左右以此經求印證。欲流布萬世。於衆生界中。種佛種子。此
是第一等好事。而又以某爲箇中人。以箇中消息。相期於形器之外。
故不敢不上稟。[57.4] 昔清涼國師。造華嚴疏。欲正譯師訛舛。而不得
梵本。但書之于經尾而已。如佛不思議法品中。所謂一切佛。有無邊
際身。色相清淨。普入諸趣。而無染著。清涼但云。佛不思議法品上
卷第三葉第十行。一切諸佛。舊脫諸字。其餘經本脫落。皆注66之于

經尾。清涼亦聖師也。非不能添入及減削。止敢書之于經尾者。識法者懼也。又經中有大瑠璃寶。清涼曰。恐是吠瑠璃。舊本錯寫。亦不敢改。亦只如此注[67]之經尾耳。[57.5] 六朝翻譯諸師。非皆[68]淺識之士。翻譯場。有譯語者。有譯義者。有潤文者。有證梵語者。有正義者。有唐梵相校者。而左右尚以爲錯譯聖意。左右既不得梵本。便妄加刊削。却要後人諦信。不亦難乎。[57.6] 如論長水。依句而違義。無梵本證。如何便決定以其爲非。此公雖是講人。與佗講人不同。嘗參琅[69]琊廣照禪師。因請益琅[70]琊。首楞嚴中。富樓那問佛。清淨本然云何忽生山河大地之義。琅[71]琊遂抗聲云。清淨本然。云何忽生山河大地。長水於言下大悟。後方披襟自稱座主。蓋座主多是尋行數墨。左右所謂依句而不依義。長水非無見識。亦非尋行數墨者。[57.7] 不以具足相故。得阿耨菩提。經文大段分明。此文至淺至近。自是左右求奇大[72]過。要立異解。求人從己耳。左右引無著論云。以法身應見如來。非以相具足故。若爾。如來雖不應以相具足見。應相具足爲因。得阿耨菩提。爲離此著故。經言。須菩提。於意云何。如來可以相成就。得阿耨菩提。須菩提。莫作是念等者。此義明相具足體非。菩提亦不以相具足爲因也。以相是色自性故。此論大段分明。自是左右錯見錯解尔。色是相緣起。相是法界緣起。梁昭明太子謂。莫作是念。如來不以具足相故得阿耨菩提。三十二分中。以此分爲無斷無滅分。恐須菩提。不以具足相。則緣起滅矣。蓋須菩提。初在母胎。即知空寂。多不住緣起相。後引功德施菩薩論末後。若相成就。是真實有。此相滅時。即名爲斷。何以故。以生故有斷。又怕人不會。又云。何以故。一切法。是無生性。所以遠離斷常二邊。遠離二邊。是法界相。不說性而言相。謂法界是性之緣起故也。相是法界緣起故。不說性而言相。梁昭明所謂無斷無滅。是也。此段更分明。又是左右求奇太過。強生節目尔。若金剛經可以刊削。則一大[73]藏教。凡有看者。各隨臆解。都可刊削也。[57.8] 如韓退之。指論語中畫[74]字爲畫字。謂舊本差錯。以退之之見識。便可改了。而只如此論在書中。何也。亦是識法者懼尔。圭峯密禪師。造圓覺疏鈔。密於圓覺。

---

67. T = 註.

68. T = 皆非.

69. T = 瑯.

70. T = 瑯.

71. T = 瑯.

72. T = 太.

73. T = 太.

74. T = 晝.

有證悟處。方敢下筆。以圓覺經中一切眾生皆證圓覺。圭峯改證爲
具。謂譯者之訛。而不見梵本。亦只如此論在疏中。不敢便改正經
也。後來泐潭真淨和尚。撰皆證論。論內痛罵圭峯。謂之破凡夫臊臭
漢。若一切眾生。皆具圓覺。而不證者。畜生永作畜生。餓鬼永作餓
鬼。盡十方世界。都盧是箇無孔鐵鎚。更無一人發真歸元。凡夫亦不
須求解脫。何以故。一切眾生皆已具圓覺。亦不須求證故。[57.9] 左
右以京師藏經本爲是。遂以京本爲據。若京師藏本。從外州府納入。
如徑山兩藏經。皆是朝廷全盛時賜到。亦是外州府經生所寫。萬一有
錯。又卻如何改正。[57.10] 左右若無人我。定以妙喜之言爲至誠。不必
泥在古今一大錯上。若執己見爲是。決欲改削要一切人唾罵。一任刊
版印行。妙喜也只得隨喜讚歎而已。公既得得遣人。以經來求印可。
雖不相識。以法爲親。故不覺忉忉怛怛。相觸忤。見公至誠。所以更
不留情。[57.11] 左右決欲窮教乘。造奧義。當尋一名行講師。一心一
意。與之參詳。教徹頭徹尾。一等是留心教網[75]也。若以無常迅速。
生死事大。己事未明。當一心一意。尋一本分作家。能破人生死窠窟
者。與伊著死工夫厮崖。忽然打破柒桶。便是徹頭處也。[57.12] 若只
是要資談柄。道我博極羣書。無不通達。禪我也會。教我也會。又
能檢點得前輩諸譯主講師不到處。逞我能我解。則三教聖人。都可檢
點。亦不必更求人印可。然後放行也。如何如何。

答張舍人狀元 (安國)

[58.1] 左右決欲究竟此事。但常令方寸虛豁豁地。物來即應。如人學
射。久久中的矣。不見。達磨謂二祖曰。汝但外息諸緣。內心無喘。
心如牆壁。可以入道。如今人纔聞此說。便差排向頑然無知處。硬
自遏捺。要得心如牆壁去。祖師所謂。錯認[76]何曾解方便者也。巖頭
云。纔恁麼。便不恁麼。是句亦剗。非句亦剗。遮箇便是外息諸緣。
內心無喘底樣子也。縱未得啐地折。嚗地破。亦不被語言所轉矣。見
月休觀指。歸家罷問程。[58.2] 情識未破。則心火熠熠地。正當恁麼
時。但只以所疑底話頭提撕[77]。如僧問趙州。狗子還有佛性也無。州
云。無。只管提撕舉覺。左來也不是。右來也不是。又不得將心等
悟。又不得向舉起處承當。又不得作玄妙領略。又不得作有無商量。
又不得作真無之無卜度。又不得坐在無事甲裏。又不得向擊石火閃電
光處會。直得無所用心。心無所之時。莫怕落空。遮裏卻是好處。

---

75. Araki = 綱.

76. T = 會.

77. T = 管.

驀然老鼠入牛角。便見倒斷也。[58.3] 此事非難非易。除是夙曾種得般若種智之深。曾於無始曠大劫來。承事真善知識。熏習得正知正見在靈識中。觸境遇緣。於現行處。築著磕著。如在萬人叢裏。認得自家父母相似。當恁麼時。不著問人。自然求覓底心不馳散矣。雲門云。不可說時即有。不說時便無也。不可商量時便有。不商量時便無也。又自提起云。且道不商量時是箇甚麼。又怕人不會。又自云。更是甚麼。[58.4] 近年以來。禪有多途。或以一問一答末後。多一句爲禪者。或以古人入道因緣。聚頭商確[78]。云遮裏是虛。那裏是實。遮語玄。那語妙。或代。或別。爲禪者。或以眼見耳聞。和會在三界唯心萬法唯識上爲禪者。或以無言無說。坐在黑山下鬼窟裏。閉眉合眼。謂之威音王那畔父母未生時消息。亦謂之默而常照。爲禪者。如此等輩。不求妙悟。以悟爲落在第二頭。以悟爲誑諕[79]人。以悟爲建立。自既不曾悟。亦不信有悟底。妙喜常謂衲子輩說。世間工巧技藝。若無悟處。尚不得其妙。況欲脫生死。而只以口頭說靜。便要收殺。大似埋頭向東走。欲取西邊物。轉求轉遠。轉急轉遲。此輩名爲可憐愍者。教中謂之謗大般若。斷佛慧命人。千佛出世。不通懺悔。雖是善因。返招惡果。寧以此身碎如微塵。終不以佛法當人情。決要敵生死。須是打破遮漆桶始得。切忌被邪師順摩捋。將冬瓜印子印定。便謂我千了百當。如此之輩。如稻麻竹葦。[58.5] 左右聰明有識見。必不受遮般惡毒。然亦恐用心之切。要求速效。不覺不知。遭佗染污。故信筆葛藤如許。被明眼人覷見。一場敗闕。[58.6] 千萬相聽。只以趙州一箇無字。日用應緣處提撕。不要間斷。古德有言。研窮至理。以悟爲則。若說得天花乱墜。不悟總是癡狂外邊走耳。勉之。不可忽。

答湯丞相 (進之)

[59.1] 丞相既存心此段大事因緣。缺減界中。虛妄不實。或逆或順。一一皆是發機時節。但常令方寸虛豁豁地。日用合做底事。隨分撥遣。觸境逢緣。時時以話頭提撕。莫求速效。研窮至理。以悟爲則。[59.2] 然第一不得存心等悟。若存心等悟。則被所等之心。障却道眼。轉急轉遲矣。但只提撕話頭。驀然向提撕處生死心絕。則是歸家穩坐之處。[59.3] 得到恁麼處了。自然透得古人種種方便。種種異解自不生矣。教中所謂。絕心生死。伐心椆[80]林。浣心垢濁。解

---

78. Translation follows T and Araki = 搉.

79. T = 謼.

80. Translation follows T and Araki = 稠.

心執著。於執著處。使心動轉。當動轉時。亦無動轉底道理。自然
頭頭上明。物物上顯。日用應緣處。或淨或穢。或喜或怒。或順或
逆。如珠走盤。不撥而自轉矣。得到遮箇時節。拈出呈似人不得。
如人飲水冷煖自知。[59.4] 南陽忠國師有言。說法有所得。是爲野干
鳴。此事如青天白日。一見便見。真實自見得底。邪師走作不得。
前日亦嘗面言。此事無傳授。纔說有奇特玄妙。六耳不同謀之說。
即是相欺。便好拽住劈面便唾。[59.5] 書生做到宰相。是世間法中
最尊最貴者。若不向此事上了却。即是虛來南閻浮提。打一遭。
收因結果時。帶得一身惡業去。教中說。作癡福。是第三生冤。
何謂第三生冤。第一生作癡福不見性。第二生受癡福無慚愧。不做
好事。一向作業。第三生受癡福盡。不做好事。脫却殼漏子時。入
地獄如箭射。人身難得。佛法難逢。此身不向今生度。更向何生度
此身。[59.6] 學此道。須有決定志。若無決定志。則如聽聲卜者。見
人說東。便隨人向東走。說西便隨人向西走。若有決定志。則把得住
作得主宰。嬾[81]融所謂。設有一法過於涅槃。吾說亦如夢幻。況世間
虛幻不實之法。更有甚麼心情與之打交涉也。願公堅此志。以得入
手。爲決定義。則縱使大地有情。盡作魔王。欲來惱亂。無有得其便
處。[59.7] 般若上。無虛棄底工夫。若存心在上面。縱今生未了。亦
種得種子深。臨命終時。亦不被業識所牽。墮諸惡趣。換却殼漏子轉
頭來。亦昧我底不得。察之。

答樊提刑 (茂實)

[60.1] 示諭。能行佛事。而不解禪語。能與不解。無別無同。但知能
行者。即是禪語。會禪語。而不能行佛事。如人在水底坐叫渴。飯籮
裏坐叫飢。何異。當知禪語即佛事。佛事即禪語。能行能解。在人不
在法。若更向箇裏。覓同覓別。則是空拳指上生實解。根境法中虛捏
怪。如却行而求前。轉急轉遲。轉疏轉遠矣。[60.2] 要得徑截心地豁
如。但將能與不能。解與不解。同與不同。別與不別。能如是思量。
如是卜度者。掃向佗方世界。却向不可掃處。看是有是無。是同是
別。驀然心思意想絕。當恁麼時。自不著問人矣。

答聖泉琰和尚

[61.1] 既得外護者。存心相照。自可撥置人事。頻與衲子輩作佛事。久
久自殊勝。[61.2] 更望室中與之子細。不得容人情。不得共伊落草。

---

81. T = 懶.

直似之以本分草料。教伊自悟自得。方是尊宿爲人體裁也。若是見
伊遲疑不薦。便與之下注[82]脚。非但瞎却佗眼。亦乃失却自家本分手
段。[61.3] 不得人。即是吾輩緣法只如此。若得一箇半箇本分底。亦不
負平昔志願也。

答鼓山逮長老

[62.1] 專使來。收書并信香等。知開法出世唱道於石門。不忘所從來。
爲岳長老拈香。續楊岐宗派。[62.2] 既已承當箇事。須卓卓地做教徹
頭徹尾。以平昔實證實悟底一著子。端居丈室。如擔百二十斤擔子。
從獨木橋上過。脚蹉手跌則和自家性命不可保。況復與人抽釘拔楔。
救濟佗人耶。[62.3] 古德云。此事如八十翁翁入場屋。豈是兒戲。又
古德云。我若一向舉揚宗教。法堂前草深一丈。須倩人看院始得。
巖頭每云。向未屙已前一覷。便眼卓朔地。晏國師不跨石門句。睦州
現成公案放你三十棒。汾陽無業莫妄想。魯祖凡見僧入門。便轉身
面壁而坐。爲人時。當不昧遮般體裁。方不失從上宗旨耳。[62.4] 昔
潙山謂仰山曰。建法幢立宗旨於一方。五種緣備。始得成就。五種
緣。謂外護緣。檀越緣。衲子緣。土地緣。道緣。聞霜臺趙公。是
汝請主。致政司業鄭公。送汝入院。二公天下士。以此觀之。汝於五
種緣稍備。每有衲子自閩中來者。無不稱歎法席之盛。檀越歸向。士
大夫外護。住持無魔障。衲子雲集。可以趁色力未衰時。頻與衲子激
揚箇事。垂手之際。須著精彩。不得莽鹵。[62.5] 蓋近年以來。有一
種禪販之輩。到處學得一堆一擔相似禪。往往宗師造次放過。遂至承
虛接響。遞相印授。誤賺後人。致使正宗淡薄。單傳直指之風。幾掃
地矣。不可不子細。[62.6] 五祖師翁住白雲時。嘗答靈源和尚書云。
今夏諸莊顆粒不收。不以爲憂。其可憂者。一堂數百衲子。一夏無一
人透得箇狗子無佛性話。恐佛法將滅耳。汝看。主法底宗師用心。又
何曾以產錢多少。山門大小。爲重輕。米鹽細務。爲急切來。[62.7] 汝
既出頭。承當箇善知識名字。當一味以本分事。接待方來。所有庫
司財穀。分付知因識果知事。分司列局。令掌之。時時提舉大綱。
安僧不必多。日用齋粥。常教後手有餘。自然不費力。[62.8] 衲子到
室中。下刃要緊。不得拖泥帶水。如雪峯空禪師。頃在雲居雲門相
聚。老漢知渠不自欺是箇佛法中人。故一味以本分鉗鎚似之。後來
自在別處打發。大法既明。向所受遮底鉗鎚。一時得受用。方知妙喜
不以佛法當人情。去年送得一冊語錄來。造次顛沛。不失臨濟宗旨。
今送在衆寮中。與衲子輩看。老漢因掇筆書其後。特爲發揚。使本分

---

82. T = 註.

衲子爲將來說法之式。若使老漢。初爲渠扡泥帶水。說老婆禪。眼開後。定罵我無疑。[62.9] 所以古人云。我不重先師道德。只重先師不爲我說破。若爲我說破。豈有今日。便是遮箇道理也。趙州云。若教老僧隨伊根機接人。自有三乘十二分教接佗了也。老僧遮裏。只以本分事接人。若接不得。自是學者根性遲鈍。不干老僧事。思之思之。

大慧普覺禪師書

[63. *(Postface)*] 大慧禪師。說法四十餘年。言句滿天下。平時不許參徒編錄。而衲子私自傳寫。遂成卷帙。晚年因衆力請。乃許流通。然在會有先後。見聞有詳略。又賢士大夫所得法語。各自寶藏。無緣盡覩。今之所收。殊爲未盡。俟更採集。別爲後錄。　文昌 謹白

Bibliography

Ahn, Juhn Young. "Malady of Meditation: A Prolegomenon to the Study of Illness and Zen." PhD diss., University of California, Berkeley, 2007.

App, Urs. "Chan/Zen's Greatest Encyclopaedist: Mujaku Dōchū (無著道忠) (1653–1744)." *Cahiers d'Extrême-Asie* 3 (1987): 155–174.

Araki Kengo 荒木見悟, trans. *Daie sho* 大慧書, Zen no goroku 17. Tokyo: Chikuma shobō, 1969.

Baroni, Helen. *Ōbaku Zen: The Emergence of the Third Sect of Zen in Tokugawa Japan.* Honolulu: University of Hawai'i Press, 2000.

Broughton, Jeffrey Lyle. *Zongmi on Chan.* New York: Columbia University Press, 2009.

Broughton, Jeffrey L., and Elise Yoko Watanabe, trans. *The Chan Whip Anthology: A Companion to Zen Practice.* Oxford: Oxford University Press, 2015.

Buswell, Robert E., Jr. *The Korean Approach to Zen: The Collected Works of Chinul.* Honolulu: University of Hawaii Press, 1983.

Buswell, Robert E., Jr., trans. *Numinous Awareness Is Never Dark: The Korean Buddhist Master Chinul's* Excerpts *on Zen Practice*, Korean Classics Library: Philosophy and Religion. Honolulu: University of Hawai'i Press, 2016.

Buswell, Robert E., Jr., and Donald S. Lopez Jr. *The Princeton Dictionary of Buddhism.* Princeton: Princeton University Press, 2014.

Byrne, Christopher. "Poetics of Silence: Hongzhi Zhengjue (1091–1157) and the Practice of Poetry in Song Dynasty Chan Yulu." PhD diss., McGill University, 2015.

CBETA Chinese Buddhist Electronic Text Association. http://www.cbeta.org.

Chang Bide 昌彼得, Wang Deyi 王德毅, Cheng Yuanmin 程元敏, and Hou Junde 侯俊德, eds. *Songren zhuanji ziliao suoyin* 宋人傳記資料索引. Vol. 4. Taipei: Dingwen shuju, 1980.

Chinese Text Project. http://ctext.org.

Cleary, J. C. *Swampland Flowers: The Letters and Lectures of Zen Master Ta Hui.* Boston: Shambhala, 1977.

Ershisi shi 二十四史. 20 vols. Vols. 14–16, *Song shi* 宋史, edited by Tuo Tuo 脫脫 et al. Beijing: Zhonghua shuju, 1997.

Fong, Wen C. *Beyond Representation: Chinese Painting and Calligraphy 8th–14th Century*. New York: Metropolitan Museum of Art and Yale University Press, 1992.

Foulk, T. Griffith. "The Form and Function of Koan Literature: A Historical Overview." In *The Kōan: Texts and Contexts in Zen Buddhism*, edited by Steven Heine and Dale S. Wright, 15–45. New York: Oxford University Press, 2000.

Fujimoto Osamu 藤本治. *Mu no michi: Daie zenji no hōgo* 無の道大慧禅師の法語. Tokyo: Shunjūsha, 1991.

Hakuin oshō zenshū hensan kai 白隱和尚全集編纂會, ed. *Hakuin oshō zenshū* 白隱和尚全集. Vol. 2. Tokyo: Ryūginsha, 1967.

Han'guk pulgyo chŏnsŏ p'yŏnch'an wiwŏnhoe 韓國佛教全書編纂委員會, ed. *Han'guk pulgyo chŏnsŏ* 韓國佛教全書. Vol. 5. Seoul: Tongguk taehakkyo ch'ulp'ansa, 1987.

Heine, Steven. *Like Cats and Dogs: Contesting the Mu Kōan in Zen Buddhism*. Oxford: Oxford University Press, 2014.

Henricks, Robert G. *The Poetry of Han-shan*. Albany: State University of New York Press, 1990.

Huang Zongxi 黃宗羲 and Quan Zuwang 全祖望, eds. *Song Yuan xue'an* 宋元學案. 4 vols. Beijing: Zhonghua shuju, 1989.

Hucker, Charles O. *A Dictionary of Official Titles in Imperial China*. Stanford, CA: Stanford University Press, 1985.

Iida Rigyō 飯田利行. *Gakushō Mujaku Dōchū* 学聖無著道忠. Kyoto: Zen bunka kenkyūjo, 1986.

Iriya Yoshitaka 入矢義高 and Koga Hidehiko 古賀英彦. *Zengo jiten* 禅語辞典. Kyoto: Shibunkaku shuppan, 1991.

Ishii Shūdō 石井修道. "Daiei Fukaku zenji nenpu *no kenkyū (jō)* 大慧普覺禪師年譜の研究(上)." *Komazawa daigaku bukkyō gakubu kenkyū kiyō* 37 (1979): 110–143.

Ishii Shūdō 石井修道. "Daiei Fukaku zenji nenpu *no kenkyū (chū)* 大慧普覺禪師年譜の研究 (中)." *Komazawa daigaku bukkyō gakubu kenkyū kiyō* 38 (1980): 97–133.

Ishii Shūdō 石井修道. "Daiei Fukaku zenji nenpu *no kenkyū (ge)* 大慧普覺禪師年譜の研究 (下)." *Komazawa daigaku bukkyō gakubu kenkyū kiyō* 40 (1982): 129–175.

Ishii Shūdō 石井修道. "*Daie goroku no kiso teki kenkyū (ge): Daie den kenkyū no saikentō* 大慧語錄の基礎的研究 (下): 大慧伝研究の再検討." *Komazawa daigaku bukkyō gakubu kenkyū kiyō* 33 (1975): 151–171.

Ishii Shūdō 石井修道. "*Daie Sōkō to sono deshitachi (roku)* 大慧宗杲とその弟子たち (六)." *Indogaku bukkyōgaku kenkyū* 23, no. 1 (1974): 336–339.

Ishii Shūdō 石井修道. "*Daie Sōkō to sono deshitachi (hachi)* 大慧宗杲とその弟子たち (八)." *Indogaku bukkyōgaku kenkyū* 25, no. 1 (1977): 257–261.

Ishii Shūdō 石井修道, trans. *Zen goroku* 禅語録. Daijō butten Chūgoku Nihon hen 大乘仏典中国日本篇12. Tokyo: Chūō kōron sha, 1992.

Jorgensen, John, trans. *Hyujeong: Selected Works*. Collected Works of Korean Buddhism 3. Seoul: Jogye Order of Korean Buddhism, 2012.

Jorgensen, John. "Mujaku Dōchū (1653–1744) and Seventeenth-Century Chinese Buddhist Scholarship." *East Asian History* 32/33 (2008): 25–56.

Jorgensen, John, trans. *Seon Dialogues*. Collected Works of Korean Buddhism 8. Seoul: Jogye Order of Korean Buddhism, 2012.

Jorgensen, John. "Zen Scholarship: Mujaku Dōchū and His Contemporaries." *Zen bunka kenkyūjo kiyō* 27 (2006): 1–60.

Kageki Hideo 蔭木英雄, trans. *Kunchū Kūge nichiyō kufū ryakushū: Chūsei zensō no seikatsu to bungaku* 訓注空華日用工夫略集–中世禅僧の生活と文学. Kyoto: Shibunkaku, 1982.

Kamata Shigeo 鎌田茂雄, trans. *Zengen shosenshū tojo* 禅源諸詮集都序. Zen no goroku 9. Tokyo: Chikuma shobō, 1971.

Kawase Kazuma 川瀬一馬. *Gozanban no kenkyū* 五山版の研究. 2 vols. Tokyo: Nihon koshosekishō kyōkai, 1970.

Keyworth, George Albert, III. "Transmitting the Lamp of Learning in Classical Chan Buddhism: Juefan Huihong (1071–1128) and Literary Chan." PhD diss., University of California, Los Angeles, 2001.

Komazawa daigaku nai zengaku daijiten hensanjo 駒澤大學内禪學大辭典編纂所, ed. *Shinban Zengaku daijiten* 新版禅学大辞典. Tokyo: Taishūkan shoten, 1985.

Komazawa daigaku toshokan 駒沢大学図書館, ed. *Shinsan zenseki mokuroku* 新纂禅籍目録. Tokyo: Komazawa daigaku toshokan, 1962.

Levering, Miriam L. "Ch'an Enlightenment for Laymen: Ta-hui and the New Religious Culture of the Sung." PhD diss., Harvard University, 1978.

Levering, Miriam. "Dahui Zonggao and Zhang Shangying: The Importance of a Scholar in the Education of a Song Chan Master." *Journal of Song-Yuan Studies* 30 (2000): 115–139.

Levering, Miriam L. "Dahui Zonggao (1089–1163): The Image Created by His Stories about Himself and by His Teaching Style." In *Zen Masters*, edited by Steven Heine and Dale S. Wright, 91–116. Oxford: Oxford University Press, 2010.

Levering, Miriam L. "The *Huatou* Revolution, Pure Land Practices, and Dahui's Chan Discourse on the Moment of Death." *Frontiers of History in China*, 8.3 (2013): 342–365.

Levine, Gregory, and Yukio Lippit. *Awakenings: Zen Figure Painting in Medieval Japan*. New York: Japan Society, 2007.

Liu Xu 劉昫, et al., comps. *Jiu Tangshu* 舊唐書. 8 vols. Beijing: Zhonghua shuju, 1975.

Lü Youxiang 呂有祥 and Wu Longsheng 吳隆升, eds. *Dahui shu* 大慧书. Zhongguo chanzong dianji congkan 中国禅宗典籍丛刊. Zhengzhou: Zhongzhou guji chubanshe, 2008.

Mujaku Dōchū 無著道忠. *Daie Fukaku zenji sho kōrōju* 大慧普覺禪師書栲栳珠. Kyoto: Zenbunka kenkyūjo, 1997.

Mujaku Dōchū 無著道忠. *Kidōroku rikō* 虚堂録犂耕. Kyoto: Zen bunka kenkyūjo, 1990.

Ogawa Takashi 小川隆. *Zen no goroku dōdoku* 禅の語録導読, Zen no goroku 20. Tokyo: Chikuma shobō, 2016.

Pojo sasang yŏn'guwon 普照思想研究院, ed. *Pojo chŏnsŏ* 普照全書. Seoul: Puril ch'ulp'ansa, 1989.

Quan Tangshi 全唐詩. 25 vols. Beijing: Zhonghua shuju, 1979.

Richter, Antje, ed. *A History of Chinese Letters and Epistolary Culture*. Leiden: Brill, 2015.

Schlütter, Morten. *How Zen Became Zen: The Dispute over Enlightenment and the Formation of Chan Buddhism in Song Dynasty China*. Honolulu: University of Hawaiʻi Press, 2008.

Schmidt, J. D. *Yang Wan-li*. Boston: Twayne Publishers, 1976.

Shiina Kōyū 椎名宏雄, ed. *Gozanban Chūgoku zenseki sōkan* 五山版中国禅籍叢刊 10: *Shibun sekitoku* 詩文尺牘. Kyoto: Rinsen shoten, 2013.

Shiina Kōyū 椎名宏雄. "*Zenmon nenju shū no shiryō kachi* 禅門拈頌集の資料価値." *Indogaku bukkyōgaku kenkyū* 101 (2002): 51–55.

Shinohara, Koichi. "Ta-huiʼs Instructions to Tseng Kʼai: Buddhist 'Freedom' in the Neo-Confucian Context." In *Meeting of Minds*, edited by Irene Bloom and Joshua A. Fogel, 175–201. New York: Columbia University Press, 1997.

Sturman, Peter C. "The Donkey Rider as Icon: Li Cheng and Early Chinese Landscape Painting." *Artibus Asiae* 55, no. 1/2 (1995): 43–97.

Taehan pulgyo Chogye chong kyoyukwŏn pulhak yŏnguso kyojae pʼyŏnchʼan wiwŏnhoe 大漢佛教曹溪宗教育院佛學研究所教材編纂委員會, ed. *Sajip sagi* 四集私記. Seoul: Chogye chong chʼulpʼansa, 2008.

Takagi Ryūen 高木龍淵, ed. *Zōkan bōchū* Daie Fukaku zenji sho 增冠傍注大慧普覺禪師書. Kyoto: Baiyō shoin, Meiji 36/1903.

Takakusu Junjirō 高楠順次郎 and Watanabe Kaigyoku 渡邊海旭, eds. *Taishō shinshū daizōkyō* 大正新脩大藏經. 100 vols. Tokyo: Taishō issaikyō kankōkai, 1924–1934.

Tanaka Ryōshō 田中良昭, ed. *Zengaku kenkyū nyūmon* 禅学研究入門. 2d ed. Tokyo: Daitō shuppansha, 2006.

Tokyo National Museum TB-1173 and TB-1172. http://www.emuseum.jp/result?s_lang=en&mode=simple&itemCount=8&d_lang=en&word=dahui.

Waddell, Norman. *The Essential Teachings of Zen Master Hakuin*. Boston: Shambhala, 1994.

Waddell, Norman. *Poison Blossoms from a Thicket of Thorn*. Berkeley, CA: Counterpoint, 2014.

Welter, Albert. *Yongming Yanshou's Conception of Chan in the* Zongjing lu: *A Special Transmission within the Scriptures*. Oxford: Oxford University Press, 2011.

Yanagida Seizan 柳田聖山. "*Denbōhōki to sono sakusha* 伝法宝紀とその作者." *Zengaku kenkyū* 53 (July 1963): 45–71.

Yanagida Seizan 柳田聖山. "*Mujaku Dōchū no gakumon* 無著道忠の学問." *Zengaku kenkyū* 55 (February 1966): 14–55.

Yanagida Seizan 柳田聖山. *Shoki zenshū shisho no kenkyū* 初期禅宗史書の研究. Kyoto: Hōzōkan, 1967.

Yanagida Seizan 柳田聖山, ed. *Zenrin shōki sen Kattōgo sen Zenrin kushū benbyō* 禪林象器箋葛藤語箋禪林句集辨苗. 2 vols. Zengaku sōsho 禪學叢書 9. Kyoto: Chūbun shuppansha, 1979.

Yang Wanli 楊萬里. *Chengzhai ji* 誠齋集. Chinese Text Project. http://ctext.org/wiki.pl?if=gb&res=176604.

Yifa. *The Origin of Buddhist Monastic Codes in China*. Honolulu: University of Hawaiʻi Press, 2002.

Yoshizawa Katsuhiro 芳澤勝弘, ed. *Shoroku zokugo kai* 諸録俗語解. Kyoto: Zen bunka kenkyūjo, 1999.

Zen no goroku 禅の語録. 17 vols. Tokyo: Chikuma shobō, 1969–1976.

Zen no goroku 禅の語録. 20 vols. Tokyo: Chikuma shobō, 2016.

Index

Note: All *huatous* appear in **bold italics**. Letter numbers, where appropriate, have been provided in parentheses, e.g., (#34).

illness(es) (*bing* 病) (*cont.*)
  sitting as medicine for specific, 26, 73
  of sudden arising of phantasmal
    thought, 177
  of taking all-at-once awakening as
    "Chan," 127n406
  ten, of the *hwadu* **mu** 無, 40, 40n75,
    109n314
  Yunmen's two types of, 261–262
illness, *gongfu* in the midst of (#40),
  239–242
illusion (*huan* 幻), 55, 56, 57, 57n34,
  105, 121, 151n531, 182, 183, 200,
  200n67, 201, 251, 251n348, 314,
  314n696

Jurchen (Jin), 4, 5, 159

kanna Zen, 10, 12n23, 41n76.
  See also huatou practice
"keep pressing hard," in *huatou*
  practice, 15, 29, 30, 33, 33n61, 44,
  57, 57n36, 83, 124, 132, 133, 137, 178,
  189, 196, 218, 223, 231
"Korean Anonymous," *Notes on Plucking
  out Difficulties from the* Letters,
  xiii, 39, 40
kudzu-verbiage (*geteng* 葛藤), 18, 66, 67,
  95, 103, 118, 119, 201, 243, 265, 271,
  279, 285, 289, 294, 295, 310

laugh, the single/the great, 69n107,
  87, 87n188, 89, 92, 93, 97, 116,
  130, 248
leaping about, Dahui happy to the point
  of, 80, 89, 110
Letters of Dahui (*Letters of Chan Master
  Dahui Pujue*)
  compilation and editing of, 6–7, 9–10
  dating of, 12
  description of, 2, 12
  as dharma talks, 2–3

  editor Huang Wenchang's possible
    rationale for letter selection, 9–10
  influence of, in East Asia, 1, 1n2
    in China, 40–41
    in Japan, 45–48
    in Korea, 41–45
  postwar Rinzai-oriented scholarship
    and, 48, 48n95
  primarily addressed to laypeople,
    2, 9, 51
  range of correspondents' social
    status, 9
  sharing of individual letters beyond
    recipient, 2, 119, 172–173, 197, 210,
    259–260, 289
  tone of, personalized, 3
light-and-shadow, unreal, 260, 261,
  261n405, 263n417, 264, 265,
  308n669, 308n670
Limpid (#18), 137–139, 138n460,
  139n462, 139n463

Man-in-charge, Mr. (*zhuren gong*
  主人公), 179, 180, 180n668,
  180n669, 181n678, 182, 203,
  203n76, 219n174, 245, 246,
  248n327, 251, 252, 271, 295
medicine (*yao* 藥)
  in accordance with illness, 247
  of Dahui, for Vice Minister Liu's
    illness (#40), 240–241
  for the eyes, 101n269
  illusionary, for illusionary illness,
    57, 57n34
  misconstruing illnesses as, 237
  not continuing phantasmal thoughts
    as, 177
  of perfection of stillness, as cure for
    crazed distraction, 154, 173
  realizing one's mistake as, 57n33
  sitting as, for individual
    illnesses, 26, 73

state of being (*xiaoxi* 消息), 235
  before the appearance of the very first
    buddha, 27, 106n297, 308
  of becoming a buddha or patriarch,
    32, 222
  cheerful self-existent, right
    underfoot, 242
  of the common-person realm, 97,
    97n240, 111
  of confidence-in-something, severed,
    263, 263n417
  deployed by Bodhidharma, 146
  of the final day of the twelfth
    month, 191
  good, 32, 202, 204, 204–205n87
  in-this, 297
  of stillness-time, 78, 78n148
  this, 319n723
"stillness" (*jing* 靜) versus "noisiness
  (*nao* 鬧)," 14, 25, 77, 77n140, 78,
  78n148, 79, 79n152, 108, 110,
  111n325, 113, 115, 115n345, 115n347,
  115n348, 123, 124, 124n393, 128,
  145–146n504, 151, 152n537, 154, 155,
  156, 157, 311n682
stillness-sitting (*jingzuo* 靜坐), 19, 20,
  25, 26n53, 84, 113, 115, 115n348, 116,
  118, 123, 124n393, 126, 130, 130n419,
  138, 153
  See also Chan/Zen sitting, sitting
stillness *über alles* (*jingsheng* 靜勝), 57–
  58, 77, 106n295, 111, 113, 115n345, 155,
  156, 157
stopping-to-rest (*xiuxie* 休歇), 26, 53, 61,
  62, 66, 67, 70, 72, 72n119, 73, 74,
  75n129, 89, 123, 126, 126n400, 128,
  147, 233
stringed instrument, tuning, 257, 286
Sudhana, 58–61
Śūraṃgama Sūtra, 46, 71n114, 81n159,
  87n192, 91, 91n208, 94, 96,
  96n237, 97n241, 113n335, 130n418,

  138n456, 168n612, 214n146,
  217n164, 219n175, 247n324,
  249n332, 250, 250n340, 254n360,
  255n365, 284n541, 286n551,
  292n580, 297n610, 299,
  299n624, 301n632, 303n643
sword
  brandishing at the sky, 280–281
  hilt of, 29, 81, 86, 124, 234, 280
  precious, of the Vajra King, 66, 83
  single stroke of, 57, 62, 122, 170, 174,
    182, 221, 234
  for smashing the uncertainty-mind of
    samsara, 124

T'aego Pou, 43–44
Takagi Genseki (Ryūen), xiv, 39n72
"take awakening as the standard"
  (*yi wu wei ze* 以悟爲則), 19, 179,
  179n666, 210, 210n115, 288,
  288n561, 288n562, 310, 310n676,
  311, 311n684, 313n694
taste, 32, 33n60, 43–44, 77, 108n311,
  109n312, 111n322, 127n404, 152n537,
  194n47, 211
tasteless/no taste (*mei ziwei* 沒滋味), 32,
  33, 43–44, 108n310, 204, 222, 233,
  234–235, 315, 315n704
"tense" ("be in a rush")/"slack,"
  avoidance of, in *huatou* practice,
  31, 31n56, 131–132, 132n428, 232,
  280, 286
this matter (*ci shi* 此事), 15, 33n60, 53,
  54, 56, 65, 66, 67, 73, 89, 90, 91,
  94n225, 97n242, 98, 102, 110,
  115n348, 118, 118n363, 120, 123n387,
  130, 135, 136, 141, 145, 145n502, 155,
  163, 178, 178n658, 191, 191n36, 197,
  203, 205, 221, 229, 234, 264, 271,
  272, 273, 275, 279n511, 282, 289,
  305, 307, 312, 314, 318, 320
three-year-old-child, 244